THE
LETTERS AND
PAPERS OF
CHAIM
WEIZMANN

The Letters and
Papers of
Chaim Weizmann

GENERAL EDITOR
MEYER W. WEISGAL

═══

VOLUME II · SERIES A
November 1902–August 1903

═══

Editorial Direction
GEDALIA YOGEV

───

Editor: ENGLISH EDITION
BARNET LITVINOFF

LONDON
OXFORD UNIVERSITY PRESS
1971

Oxford University Press, Ely House, London W. 1

GLASGOW NEW YORK TORONTO MELBOURNE WELLINGTON
CAPE TOWN SALISBURY IBADAN NAIROBI DAR ES SALAAM LUSAKA ADDIS ABABA
BOMBAY CALCUTTA MADRAS KARACHI LAHORE DACCA
KUALA LUMPUR SINGAPORE HONG KONG TOKYO

SBN 19 711219 6

© *1971 by Yad Chaim Weizmann*

PRINTED IN GREAT BRITAIN

CONTENTS

FOREWORD

THE appearance of Volume II of the Weizmann Letters, Series A, following as it does some two years after the publication of Volume I, marks a new phase in the history of the project launched with the establishment of the Weizmann Archives at Rehovoth during the lifetime of the first President of the State of Israel.

As I pointed out in the General Foreword in the first volume, bringing that work before the public involved immense protracted effort, and its consummation constituted something of a triumph over numerous difficult obstacles.

Let me recall, briefly, the chronology of the undertaking.

On 20 February 1949 Dr. Weizmann had written me a letter asking me to undertake the task of collecting his letters and documents and preparing them for 'proper editing and publication'. I took Dr. Weizmann's request to heart, and began acting on it at once.

In the spring of 1957, some four and a half years after Dr. Weizmann's death, the late Mrs. Weizmann formally transferred the custody of her husband's Letters and Papers to Yad Chaim Weizmann, the national memorial set up by the Government of Israel and the Jewish Agency. In 1952 a Board of Trustees was appointed to supervise the policy governing acquisition of the archival material and the rules and regulations for its use, both for our own purposes and for outside scholars engaged on other historical projects. Shortly afterwards I invited a group of eminent scholars and historians to join an Editorial Board; its first formal gathering took place in Rehovoth on 31 March 1958. Subsequently, a smaller Editorial Committee (comprising Prof. Jacob Katz, Prof. Joshua Prawer, Prof. Nathan Rotenstreich, Prof. Jacob Talmon, and Mr. Leonard Stein) was set up to succeed the original Implementation Committee (Sir Isaiah Berlin, Mr. Leonard Stein, the late Sir Lewis B. Namier, and the late Sir Charles K. Webster, with Prof. Jacob Talmon co-opted for part of the time in an advisory capacity) that had assisted me during the preliminary stages. This body met for the first time in October 1961.

Volume I of the English edition, under the meticulous guidance of Mr. Leonard Stein, appeared eleven and a half years after the

Archives were formally incorporated by Yad Chaim Weizmann. With the standards of scholarship firmly set, as evidenced by the wide critical acclaim that greeted the first fruits of our labours, I felt that the distinctive model now available made it opportune to plan an acceleration of the research and editing processes. The intention was to ensure that the Papers in their entirety would be ready in manuscript form, if not fully published, in time to coincide with the hundredth anniversary of Weizmann's birth in 1874.

Rarely has a man's life and career so completely and dramatically paralleled the great developments of his people's history as has Weizmann's with the profound transformation of Jewry in modern times. Here was not only a Zionist leader at the centre of events, guiding the changes in the Jewish situation that created an independent nation out of an oppressed, dispersed people; but also a Russian Jew directly and immediately affected, because of the fate of his family and closest friends, by the resettlement of a great part of East European Jewry in America, by the impact of the Russian Revolution, the apocalyptic dimensions of the European holocaust, the international reverberations of the two World Wars, and the final triumph of Israeli statehood.

For Chaim Weizmann these events were identifiable in his daily progress as an individual as well as in his thoughts and actions as a world leader. They gave his life a special anguish as the tragedies unfolded that could never be assuaged even in its splendid culmination when the new young state, risen from the ashes of Jewry's greatest disaster, chose him as its first President. And as a grace-note, as it were, to his life as one of Jewry's great modern statesmen, there was his equally intense preoccupation with chemistry. Just as his public career reflected the profound political changes wrought in his generation and ours, so his activities as a scientist reflected the remarkable advance of human knowledge during our own era.

The conjunction of Weizmann's interests and activities with the broad-gauge developments of the wider world lend the circumstances of his life a singular importance for his immediate successors and, indeed, for posterity in general. His evolution represents a graph, so to speak, of a demographic process that primarily concerns the Jewish people but to a substantial degree also embraces the flow of European politics and, most recently, the specific history of the Middle East.

The publication of Weizmann's Letters and Papers should therefore be seen as a memoir, in the fullest sense of the term, of the most turbulent period of Jewish history since the inception of the Diaspora almost 2,000 years ago. Yet the whole simultaneously constitutes an absorbing human revelation: the reader senses the organic interconnection of events that, starting apparently from the frailest of roots, evolve into growths of powerful, continuous vitality.

The technical problems confronting the Editorial Board responsible for this enterprise have been formidable. Some 22,000 letters, of a doubtless far larger correspondence, have survived. Mostly they are in Russian, Yiddish, German, French, English, or Hebrew. The translations are being undertaken with a rigorous regard to accuracy and style that to an outsider might seem to border on the fanatical—no small task when it is recalled that many letters were committed to paper nearly three-quarters of a century ago, in a barely legible hand, and frequently refer to persons and events of which there is little or no corroborative record.

At what point in this accumulation of correspondence does one draw the line for publication ? This major problem had already been debated at length both by the Implementation Committee and by the Editorial Board. This was whether to publish all the letters housed in the Archives at Rehovoth (excluding trivial communications and a few likely to wound the feelings of living persons), or to present a selection. Those who advocated their publication in full contended that our dual purpose—historical research and character delineation—would manifestly be better served in this way. In short, this school of thought took the view that elimination would reduce illumination.

The issue came sharply to the fore again after the appearance of the first volume in the English edition. A variety of reactions were evoked among members of the Editorial Board outside Israel as well as in the judgement of reviewers. At a meeting held at the end of December 1968 the Editorial Board, considering the matter once again, debated the arguments for a possible principle of selectivity. The consensus of the meeting was that a more powerful case existed in favour of non-selection than against it, and confirmed the decision. The motivation behind the discussion, and the theme of some of the remarks made by those taking part, may be summed up as follows:

1. Over the years Dr. Weizmann has been misrepresented, sometimes wilfully; his whole leadership regarding important issues
   has been brought into question, often on unsubstantiated
   grounds. Only his own original written communications over
   a period of sixty-seven years can give a proper portrayal of his
   personality.

2. The process of selection applied to correspondence militates
   against genuine scholarship. It must be avoided even though
   the writer of the letters may seem injured by a given document.

3. It would manifestly be wrong to pursue a policy of eliminating
   material which, though seemingly irrelevant, does in fact bear
   an important relationship to the subject which might escape
   the editor at the time.

I think it is a wise decision. It will serve to enhance the value of
the Letters immeasurably as source-material of history no less than
as a subject of interest for that general public desirous of learning
more about the background and inner workings of the contemporary
Zionist movement. Only through the presentation of an unexpur-
gated collection, rather than a selection, of Weizmann's letters can
it be possible, in my view, to achieve an adequate portrayal of his
personality and role in each successive phase of his activities. An
invitation to 'prune' his correspondence might conceivably tempt
the editors into depicting him, say, in a more favourable light at the
expense of historical accuracy.

It is clearly a matter of simple justice, as well as of historical
authenticity, for the role played by Dr. Weizmann to be placed on
record in his own idiom and therefore through the prism of his own
personality. We are thus safeguarded as far as may be possible
against the potency of myth-making on the one hand and of biased
judgement on the other. It is surely essential to recall in their immediate situation the interplay of events and personalities to which
Dr. Weizmann was reacting, and since history is, after all, no more
than the sum total of immediate situations in so far as we can re-
capture them, the literal and ample reproduction of Dr. Weizmann's
own words would seem to be an incomparable instrument in our
duty to conserve the past.

Because the Jewish people may truly be said to owe their survival
to their sense of history, the publication of the Weizmann Letters
and Papers is in a way the first comprehensive *statement* about their
modern incarnation. By good fortune, or perhaps an act of destiny,

that statement is being made by means of the living words of an outstanding son of his people—one who, though no *littérateur*, has bequeathed an account of his day-to-day activities, thoughts, and relationships to us that represents a historical record of priceless worth.

In order to effect the acceleration of the publication programme as described above, we have fortunately been able to recruit additional scholars for our research and editorial team. Mr. Joel Carmichael has been appointed Deputy General Editor, and beginning with 1971 we hope to produce a number of volumes each year. The translations in the present volume were by Dr. Georgette Donchin, Mrs. Barbara Grossman, Arie Luv, Julian Meltzer and Louis Simonson. The research was undertaken by Dr. Evyatar Friesel, Yaakov Rau and Dr. Joseph Schatzmiller, while the Biographical Index was compiled under the direction of Mrs. Hagit Lavsky. I would further express my appreciation to Mrs. Louisa Calef and Mrs. Shoshana Gal of the Weizmann Archives staff, and to Joseph Eligouloff who was indispensable for the preparation of the complex typescript.

We are making preparations, together with the Oxford University Press and Mossad Bialik, Jerusalem, to offer the complete set of both Letters and Papers in the English and Hebrew editions to the public at a subscription price. It is in this mood of confident hopefulness that I now commend this volume to the attention of the public.

MEYER W. WEISGAL

Rehovoth

ABBREVIATIONS

C.Z.A.	Central Zionist Archives, Jerusalem
H.W.	Handwritten
N.L.	Jewish National and University Library, Jerusalem
Or. Copy	Original Copy
Pcd.	Postcard
T.	Telegram
T.W.	Typewritten
Vcd.	Visiting-card
W.A.	Weizmann Archives, Rehovoth
Yivo	Yivo Institute of Jewish Research, New York
Z.C.	Zionist Congress
Z.C. Prot.	Protocol (Stenographic Report) of Zionist Congress, e.g., 5 Z.C. Prot.—Protocol of the Fifth Zionist Congress

LIST OF LETTERS

LIST OF LETTERS

ILLUSTRATIONS

Chaim Weizmann at 60, by Oswald Birley *Frontispiece*

Facing page 144
A greetings-card to Theodor Herzl
Weizmann's place of residence in Geneva
Conference of Russian Zionists, Minsk, 1902

Facing page 145
Reproductions from the University Bureau's copy-book

Facing pages 160, 161, 400.
Some contemporaries of Weizmann

Facing page 401
The Casino in Basle, scene of earliest Congresses
Members of the El-Arish expedition

Facing page 416
Feiwel, Trietsch, Lilien and Buber
Weizmann with Kharkov Zionist group

Facing page 417
A letter to Theodor Herzl

INTRODUCTION

THE second volume of the Weizmann Letters contains 423 letters written over a period of ten months, between November 1902 and August 1903. This compares with 320 letters in the first volume, which covers seventeen years, although the majority of them were written within a span of about two years. Most of the letters that Chaim Weizmann wrote during the 1902–3 period, when he was 28, came about mainly from the expansion of his public activity. These intensified efforts comprised the setting-up of a 'Jewish University Bureau' at Geneva, a more extensive exchange of correspondence with many people in all parts of the world, and the inception of an orderly office routine that embraced the copying of all outgoing letters and a meticulous filing system. After moving to Manchester in 1904, Weizmann transferred the archives of the Jewish University Bureau to that city, together with correspondence dealing with the affairs of the 'Democratic Fraction'. Consequently, these documents were preserved and, together with the rest of his archives, were ultimately deposited in the Weizmann Archives in Rehovoth.

The character of the letters varies considerably during this period. Most were office communications, although these often struck a distinctly personal note. Towards the end of November 1902 the Bureau acquired a typewriter and thereafter most of the letters, including those sent to Russia, were written in German. Only a few original letters have been found and a large part of the correspondence consists of unsigned copies that were kept in the files of the Bureau. Though these copies remained unsigned there is no doubt that the greater part of the original letters bore Weizmann's signature. Those outgoing communications of the Bureau that Weizmann was known not to have signed are not reproduced here. This refers principally to letters dated March and April 1903, when Weizmann was absent from Geneva during his visit to Russia. In addition to the carbon copies there is also extant a letter-book with about 60 'pressed' copies, mostly written in Russian, a few in German.

With the exception of three, all of these letters were written during the period covered by the present volume.[1]

[1] The majority of these copies are in Weizmann's handwriting. But there are also

The number of persons to whom letters were addressed is much
larger in Volume II than in Volume I. The overwhelming majority
of those in Volume I were addressed to three people—Vera Khatzman, Leo Motzkin, and Catherine Dorfman. In Volume II, on the
other hand, there are dozens of addressees. To a large extent this
reflects the wider scope of Weizmann's communications as a result
of his activity in the Jewish University Bureau. But there is also
a certain element of chance involved, as no copies were kept of the
letters Weizmann wrote in his capacity as head of the Zionist Youth
Conference Bureau in 1901 and as head of the Information Bureau
of the Democratic Fraction in 1902. Only a small part of this correspondence has survived, in a number of private archives.

Personal letters, which occupy an important place in the first
volume, are much fewer in the present one. Compared with the 145
letters Weizmann wrote Vera Khatzman, contained in Volume I,
we now have only twenty-three to her, most of them written while
he was in Russia in March–April 1903 or in transit to and from that
country. For much of the period covered by the present volume
Weizmann and Vera Khatzman were together in Geneva.

The plan for the establishment of a Jewish University or institution of Higher Learning is the central theme of Volume II. There
were immediate, pressing reasons for its creation in the exclusion of
large numbers of Jews from existing Universities. But a greater aim
was never far from Weizmann's thoughts: to challenge the apathetic
and even defeatist attitude widespread among the Jewish intelligentsia by establishing an institution in which general studies
could be infused with a positive Jewish content. 'The University',
he said, 'would head the Exilarchate'.

No. 161
(4 Jan.
1903)

We had already perceived the early crystallization of this plan in
Volume I. In the summer of 1902 Weizmann and Berthold Feiwel,
his close personal friend, published a brochure (which also bore
Martin Buber's signature), *Eine Jüdische Hochschule*, in which they
explained the impelling factor in proposing such an institution as
principally the plight of Jewish student youth in Eastern Europe.
When Weizmann returned to Geneva at the beginning of November
1902 he immediately began the organization of the 'Bureau der

a number of them that were typed during the first few days after the Bureau acquired
its typewriter. Later on the Bureau adopted the practice of making carbon copies.
As to problems of deciphering these copies and the effect on translations, see explana-
tory note on p. xliii.

Jüdischen Hochschule' there, thus launching practical and systematic action to implement the proposal. The prior condition for the
orderly conduct of the Bureau—the availability of funds to finance
current activity—had been assured during Weizmann's visit to
Baku and Rostov in the autumn of 1902, when he succeeded in
obtaining pledges for about 4,500 roubles, of which actually about
3,000 roubles had been paid in by the summer of 1903.

In addition to Weizmann, his friend Samuel Levinson, a chemist,
was employed in the Jewish University Bureau as Secretary. Upon
his emigration to the United States in the spring of 1903, Levinson
was succeeded by Saul Stupnitzky. Vera Khatzman and Catherine
Dorfman also helped in the work from time to time. The Bureau
operated in close collaboration with other members of the Democratic Fraction: Feiwel in Zurich, Buber in Vienna, and Davis
Trietsch and Moses Glikin in Berlin. The last-named moved in
January 1903 to Zurich in order to help Feiwel, in a clerical
capacity, in all matters pertaining to the *Hochschule* and the Democratic Fraction, and remained there until his return to Russia in the
spring of the same year. Feiwel went to live in Geneva in May 1903
and took a direct share in administering the Bureau until the Sixth
Zionist Congress (Basle, August 1903), after which he settled in
Berlin. Beginning with March 1903 Alfred Nossig became one of the
Bureau's permanent aides in Berlin. In July 1903 Ben-Zion Mossinson, then studying in Berne, also became a member of the Bureau.

With his return to Geneva at the beginning of November 1902,
Weizmann brought back a plan of action for the preliminary stage
of setting up the Jewish University. It may be assumed that the
principal guide-lines of this plan had been formulated by Weizmann
and Feiwel during their stay at the Swiss vacation resort of Leysin
in the summer of 1902; in all probability Weizmann also discussed
it with Buber when they met in Vienna in October, at the time of
the Annual Zionist Conference.

The most important objective that Weizmann set for himself at
this phase was the creation of an organization, to be headed by
eminent academics, which would undertake the responsibility for
implementing further stages of the scheme, viz., conducting large-
scale propaganda and setting up the institution itself. Within this
framework it was intended to establish Committees for a Jewish
University in a number of large cities, but chiefly in Berlin and
Vienna, as well as a Central Committee under the auspices of which

it was proposed to undertake the preparatory work of the Bureau in Geneva.

A second aim, towards whose attainment the Bureau directed its main efforts in the initial months, was the holding of a series of surveys among Jewish students in Western Europe and Russia as well as among Jewish professors and scholars. The terms of reference of these surveys were defined by Feiwel in the provisional summing up of the results of the only one that actually took place and that was published in the summer of 1903. The terms read: 'To undertake a thorough examination of the material and scientific basis required for the creation of a Jewish University such as the constitution of a Faculty of Jewish Studies, the attitude of Jewish professors and scholars towards Jewish and general studies, the situation and composition of the Jewish student public, and the scope and nature of learning by Jews in Europe.'[1] The statistics which it had been hoped to gather in these surveys were meant to serve as propaganda material in explaining the need for a Jewish University as well as providing basic information.

A great deal of attention is devoted in these letters to a plan for publishing a periodical intended to serve as the organ of the Jewish University Bureau and the Democratic Fraction. At the outset Weizmann adumbrated the importance of the proposed periodical as essentially to establish independence from the official Zionist press, which displayed a lack of sympathy. But after a while, as the prospects grew of the plan being fulfilled, he described its purpose in bolder terms. In a letter to Joseph Pokrassa of Kharkov, written at the beginning of February 1903, he dwelt on the need and possibility of injecting new forces into the Zionist movement and the prospect of 'penetrating areas hitherto barred to Zionism'. He went on: 'To realise these aims the small group of active people whose energies are now divided will have to unite' through the medium of an organ that must be 'directed towards the Jewish élite, towards the authentic Jewish intelligentsia of Western and Eastern Europe. Not to the masses, nor to the family, but to the isolated circles which are lost to us because of their dispersal. The essential pre-condition for such a journal is absolute sincerity, avoidance of and rebellion against the commonplace, faultless make-up throughout.' We find him two weeks later writing to Abraham

No. 247
(4 Feb.
1903)

---

[1] See B. Feiwel, 'Enquete unter den Westeuropäischen Jüdischen Studierenden', *Jüdische Statistik*, Berlin, 1903, pp. 245 ff.

Idelson and Michael Kroll, the heads of the Moscow Centre of the No. 272
(17 Feb.
1903) Democratic Fraction set up after the Conference of Russian Zionists in Minsk in September 1902, in the following vein: 'Our aims lie more in the achievement of a synthesis between East and West: bringing the ghetto to Europe and Europe to the ghetto. . . . Hence the character of the paper we contemplate, a golden bridge as it were on which the intellectuals of Europe will meet with our Jews.'

During the first two months in which the University Bureau operated practical steps were taken to set up a committee only in Vienna. Buber endeavoured to enlist members among Jewish academics there. At various times he seemed on the verge of success, but his efforts were always thwarted by the withdrawal, at the last moment, of potential members. Weizmann had undertaken the initial overtures in Berlin as early as the summer of 1902, and at the beginning of 1903 he asked Trietsch to launch the necessary measures to set up a Berlin Committee. But when Weizmann set out for Russia in the middle of March 1903 no committee at all had been established, save for the one he had set up in Kharkov in October 1902.

By March 1903 the survey of Jewish students from Eastern Europe was all but completed. The Bureau had approached a number of adherents in various university cities, inviting them to supervise the survey in their respective areas. After their consent was obtained, the distribution of the questionnaires began at the end of December 1902. Of about 2,500 circulated, some 1,200 were returned duly filled in. The data were then collated by Feiwel who, as noted above, published the provisional results in the periodical *Jüdische Statistik*, which appeared in the summer of 1903. The survey involved a great deal of administrative work for the Geneva Bureau under Weizmann's aegis: the formulation and preparation of the questionnaires, compilation of lists of volunteer supervisors (*'Vertrauensmänner'*), correspondence with them and the dispatch of circulars and reminders. This intensive activity is reflected in the proliferation of office communications, especially in January 1903, when the survey was at its height. In the nature of things there was a good deal of repetitive routine in these missives, but in their sum total they represent the first group of documents that were the outcome of Weizmann's assiduous administrative activity and demonstrated the executive capacity and practical initiative which were among his outstanding traits.

It was not all smooth going, however; many obstacles had to be surmounted. More often than not Weizmann became furious at the dilatory pace of the work, the absence of replies from those with whom he corresponded and the indifference of friends whose assist-

No. 75
(10 Dec.
1902)

ance he expected. 'Each morning brings me new frustrations', he wrote Feiwel on 10 December 1902, complaining that Buber and

No. 123
(26 Dec.
1902)

Glikin had not answered his letters. 'I am conscious all the time of how the work drags, how time flies, and we have not taken even one step forward. If it is like this at the beginning, what will happen later?' On 26 December 1902 he bitterly addressed Ze'ev Gluskin in Warsaw: 'Everyone is regrettably more involved with his own affairs than with any Jewish ideal, however lofty. Everyone madly pursues his own interests.' But, he promised Gluskin, 'you may rest assured that I am not one of these people who gets easily disheartened by the indolence of our "co-workers". I know them too well for that.' After he described what the Bureau had already achieved 'with our limited resources and even smaller working team', he asserted that 'we would be prepared to work even harder if our friends would only support us properly'. In a similar strain Weizmann wrote Pokrassa towards the end of January 1903 regarding the inaction

No. 235
(24 Jan.
1903)

of the Kharkov Committee and the silence of his friends: 'You do not really know me if you believe that I would allow myself to become disappointed by such things . . . I realise that we are alone, just a small band of workers bearing a gigantic task on our shoulders, waging a desperate struggle lest we get crushed by the weight of the burden. A long time will still have to elapse before better, stronger creative forces rise in Judaism. Until then we are the ones who are called upon to keep watch.' And in the same letter: 'Therefore I don't allow myself to be disappointed by trifles such as these, but keep right on the road.'

In March 1903 Weizmann left for Russia. As on previous occasions he combined his Zionist propaganda mission with a visit to his parents. But he devoted much more time and effort to recruiting active support for his Jewish University plan than to other Zionist matters, and sought to establish committees and mobilize funds, especially for financing the publication of the proposed journal *Der Jude.* Fortune favoured him. Whilst *en route* to Russia he met Buber and Feiwel in Berlin, and together with them and Nossig, was able to set up a committee comprising noted Jewish scholars. From Berlin he travelled to Warsaw and Lodz and succeeded, with the help of Nahum Sokolow, in forming committees in these cities as well. Moreover, large amounts were pledged there—a total of about 7,000 roubles—which he earmarked from the outset for *Der Jude*. He closed his trip to Poland on a note of triumph: 'Our University project is progressing beautifully', he stated in a letter to Catherine Dorfman after returning to Geneva. 'True, I had to fight everywhere, at every level of society: with Poles of the Mosaic persuasion, with the Bund, with Jews generally, with the *Mizrahi*, with Fraction members; but the idea itself charged ahead triumphantly. I found money . . . I found a few people who were prepared to work devotedly. . . . If future developments progress at this rate, then in about a year's time we can start thinking of the beginning of the end.' No. 314 (4 May 1903)

But before Weizmann got back to Geneva his hopes were dashed. On 19 and 20 April 1903, Easter Week, a pogrom was instigated against the Jewish community of Kishinev. It had been fired by an allegation of ritual murder against the local Jews in an anti-semitic Bessarabian newspaper, and with the connivance of the police a mob rushed the Jewish quarter of the city, bent on murder and rampage. During two whole days it spread terror undisturbed, with the result that some fifty Jews were killed and several hundreds injured, many of them seriously. Rape and arson took place on a horrible scale. For months thereafter world Jewry reeled under the impact of that ghastly event and its consequences. Weizmann himself was plunged into profound despondency. 'I have been very depressed lately', he wrote to Catherine Dorfman and Anne Koenigsberg on 10 May that year. 'The news from *Golus* affects me like poison, and is slowly but surely undermining my health. I want to scream and slash out, but haven't the strength.' A few days later he reverted to the same theme in a letter to Nossig: 'I too have been depressed by all these happenings to a point where all desire to work is paralysed.' No. 332 (10 May 1903) No. 335 (14 May 1903)

This feeling of helplessness, however, did not discourage Weizmann from becoming active on behalf of the world-wide movement launched at the time to raise funds for the victims of the pogrom. He worked from the University Bureau and spurred its leading adherents among the student groups in various university cities to lend a hand in the effort. Together with Feiwel, he went to Munich at the end of May to take part in public protest meetings there. He was among the speakers at one of these assemblies and

left the hall in a mood of high exaltation after having been witness,
No. 337
(24 May
1903)
as he wrote Vera Khatzman, to a demonstration of Jewish solidarity: 'There was such an exalted mood, and the various Parties,
including the Bund, responded so nobly—the like of which I never
expected.' It was a rare experience for one accustomed to taking
part in endless debates with the opponents of Zionism.

Weizmann found cause for grave anxiety not only in the general
repercussions of the Kishinev events; that very spontaneous reaction
of Jewish solidarity which he noted at the meeting in Munich was
a source of worry in that it dislocated his plans. The funds promised
him in Warsaw and Lodz were not forthcoming. They were diverted
to the aid of the Kishinev Jewish community. Those who had made
pledges to the University Bureau deferred the anticipated payment.
The periodical *Der Jude* did not appear, although its first issue was
practically ready for the press. Much against his will, Weizmann
was compelled to draw on the funds he had received in Baku and
Rostov in order to finance the current activities of the Bureau. He
approached a large number of friends urging them to find the much-
needed funds, even in the form of loans. Writing to Selig Weicman
No. 345
(30 May
1903)
in Warsaw, he commented: 'We . . . must not lose our heads just
now, but mobilise all our energies and keep striving to build upon
the ruins. . . . Give the people no rest and don't let them hide behind
facile talk. We can in no circumstances permit a standstill to
develop now, lest an enterprise begun with so much effort be
made to suffer . . . the pogrom must not be allowed to extend to the
University! . . .'

He was unable, of course, to alter the course of events. In spite
of several heartening developments during the interim until the
Sixth Zionist Congress, such as the inception of consistent activity
by the Berlin Committee and Ben-Zion Mossinson's joining the
staff of the University Bureau, financial difficulties brought the
entire undertaking to a dead end. Though the Bureau continued to
operate until the spring of 1904, Weizmann was forced, after the
Congress ended, to diverge considerably from the plan of action
drawn up when it was established in November 1902.

Mossinson's enlistment on the staff involved a change in the
original plan, at least from the tactical standpoint. One of the problems that exercised Weizmann and his associates was the determination of the location of the University. Many people in the Zionist
fold, including such outstanding figures as Menahem Ussishkin

and Yehiel Tschlenow, were prepared to support the creation of a Jewish institution of Higher Learning, but on condition that it be located in Palestine. A resolution to this effect was adopted at the Annual Zionist Conference (October 1902) at which Weizmann had delivered an exposition of the plan. It was clear that he, too, would have wished the institution to be situated in Palestine. But it is evident from his correspondence that he did not believe in the immediate practicability of such a move, and to his way of thinking the project was far too important and urgent for a concrete start to be put off until the University could be built in Palestine. Simultaneously, he was hesitant to dismiss this possibility arbitrarily, despite a statement he made in one of his letters to Catherine Dorfman which probably refers to this issue: 'I don't take the opinion of the Zionist Party in general very seriously.' Some months earlier he had already written to Gregory Lurie that, notwithstanding his opinion on the impossibility of erecting a University in Palestine forthwith, 'it is nevertheless necessary, for a whole range of reasons, some of them tactical, some of principle, to refrain at this stage from categorical declarations. If we start by throwing Palestine overboard every time a serious problem arises, there will soon be an end to all our yearnings'. [No. 333 (13 May 1903)] [No. 149 (1 Jan. 1903)]

Six months later Weizmann took a number of additional steps towards a compromise with those who advocated putting up the institution in Palestine. It may be assumed that, in view of the difficulties he encountered, he realized the need to have their support. He was especially concerned with Ussishkin and his group. It was decided to send Isidore Eliashev to Palestine 'in connection with the ultimate choice of a location for the University'. And in a letter to Mossinson dated 4 July 1903, which formed part of the exchange of correspondence within the framework of the agreement reached upon Mossinson's engagement with the Bureau, it was stated: 'Our desire is to establish—if at all possible—a Jewish University in Palestine.' The Bureau undertook to exert a special effort to open initially a department of Philology–Pedagogy. 'We shall do all in our power to establish the other departments in Palestine, but if this proves impossible we shall begin by opening them elsewhere. However, we shall erect no buildings, and make no attempt to remain abroad permanently, in order to be able to transfer the institutions to Palestine at an appropriate moment.' Mossinson, for his part, promised to try and obtain the support of [No. 363 (9 June 1903)] [No. 398 (4 July 1903)]

No. 423
(ca.
20 Aug.
1903)

Ussishkin, with whom he was intimate; and the present volume ends with a telegram that Weizmann sent to Ussishkin, who was then visiting Palestine, reading as follows: 'In principle favour establishing University [in] Palestine. Coming if necessary.' Nevertheless, it would appear that Weizmann's scepticism regarding the practical prospects remains intact, to which testimony is given by the letter he sent Nossig during the very time his negotiations with Mossinson culminated in the exchange of correspondence noted above.

No. 393
(30 June
1903)

Weizmann and his friends recognized Theodor Herzl as the unquestioned leader of the movement, and indeed regarded him with something approaching veneration. But, as described in Volume I, they could not accept his policy of intercession in high places and direct negotiations with the Porte and other governments as being the only or indeed the best course for the movement to adopt under the conditions then current. Weizmann considered that their leader was being badly advised by his immediate lieutenants: while Herzl was engaged in activities that of necessity had to remain confidential, debate was being stifled and those with a different point of view, some of them even members of the Greater Actions Committee, were being denied their rightful say in the formulation of Zionist policy.

Herzl remained largely unmoved by these clamours. As this volume opens he had just received the encouragement of the British Colonial Secretary, Joseph Chamberlain, to go forward with a plan for the possible settlement of the El-Arish region; in January 1903 a group of experts were on their way to the Sinai Peninsula to investigate the area. The project remained under consideration for several months, and necessitated a visit to Cairo by the leader himself. As the year progressed the El-Arish scheme faded, until we arrive at 23 August and the Sixth Congress in Basle. There, a project for a Jewish autonomous region in Africa, the so-called Uganda plan, was to open a new epoch for Zionism and for Weizmann's career.

Meanwhile, Weizmann's preoccupation with the University project meant that the affairs of the Democratic Fraction had to be set aside for a time. The Fraction had been formed on a note of high hope at the end of 1901 to serve as a framework for activity among the 'Youth' groups, which were disillusioned with the policy of the Zionist leadership, and among the supporters of cultural and economic activity (*Gegenwartsarbeit*) in Zionism. But it did not live up to expectations. At about the time of its formation the Fraction was shaken to its foundations by a controversy that undermined the relationship between two of its ranking leaders, Weizmann and Motzkin, whilst from the outset Jacob Bernstein-Kohan, the Russian Zionist leader, who was allied with the 'Youth' elements, had held off from it. Weizmann's enthusiastic efforts as Head of the Information Bureau of the Fraction were adversely affected by these inauspicious beginnings; after several months the Information Bureau virtually ceased to function, and Weizmann began to devote more and more of his attention to the great project of a Jewish University.

But the Fraction was not forgotten. Feiwel urged that a new office of the Fraction be opened in Geneva under Weizmann's direction. The latter agreed in principle on condition that he should have the active assistance of others. Nevertheless, practically nothing was done for several months, and at the beginning of 1903 Weizmann explained this inaction as due to the need to concentrate on the main purpose—the University project—and his unwillingness to spread his efforts over too wide an area. But the imminent Sixth Zionist Congress constituted an impelling factor in the renewal of his activity. He took the initiative in reorganizing the Democratic Fraction and ensuring that it be given proper representation at the Congress. He was, however, somewhat dubious about the demand made in January 1903 by the group of Fraction supporters in Berne that the Information Bureau should resume functioning. He pointed out to the people in Berne that 'all duties . . . were in the main neglected or left totally undone even by those who had assumed the role of leadership'. None the less he promised to 'begin active work' together with Feiwel and the leaders of the Moscow Centre of the Fraction, adding, 'I can assure you it will not be our fault if things are dragged out again.' In mid February he was already planning a circular letter 'calling upon the disunited members of the Fraction to unite and prepare themselves for the Congress'. He wrote optimistically of the pro-Fraction mood rife in Germany and Austria and of the anticipated number of Fraction delegates at the Sixth Congress, and noted that a caucus of the group might possibly be held prior to the Congress. The opening phases of all this revived activity were marked by a consultation with Fraction members in Warsaw, a decision to establish a Fraction Bureau in Berne, and, above all, Weizmann's attempt to explain the character and aims of the Fraction to Herzl.

No. 161
(4 Jan.
1903)

No. 192
(9 Jan.
1903)

No. 272
(17 Feb.
1903)

No. 316
(6 May
1903)

The long letter to Herzl which, after Weizmann's return from a visit to Russia in the spring of 1903, he composed together with Feiwel, occupies an important place not only in the present volume but also in the whole array of Weizmann Letters. It voiced a *cri de cœur* transcending all considerations of political manœuvring and factional interest, coupling this with a warning as to the dire plight and perilous situation of Russian Jewry, and the weakness of the Zionist movement. He asserted that the movement had failed to rally to its banner the flower of Jewish youth in Russia, now immolating itself on the altar of the revolutionary movement in alienation from its own people, and had similarly failed to strike deep roots among Western Jewry.

In this letter he made an unprecedented attempt to persuade Herzl that the constant dependence of the Zionist leadership on the *Mizrahi* faction was harmful to the movement because it estranged Jewish youth in Eastern Europe, while the Executive adopted a disdainful attitude towards the 'young Zionists' and drove them into the arms of the Opposition. This at a time when the Fraction 'forms the connecting link between the older and the younger generation' and was the only group capable of combating the revolutionists, which in fact it was actively engaged in doing. In dwelling on conditions in Russia, he claimed that the Fraction 'alone is freedom-loving and socially-enlightened. It extracts the Jewish essence from among the masses and pours it into a European mould'.

Weizmann endeavoured to explain to Herzl the character and significance of the cultural work that the 'young Zionists' and the Democratic Fraction were sponsoring: '. . . The totality of Jewish national achievement is intended—particularly that literature, art, scientific research, should all be synthesised with Europeanism, translated into modern creativity, and expressed in institutions bearing their own individual character . . . This Jewish culture, being the most vital form of the people's self-expression, is more than a mere part of the national renaissance; next to the larger Palestine ideal of Zionism it represents its only remaining attribute, and can at least offer the modern Jew . . . an approach to a loftier view of life, with scope for enthusiastic action.' But, Weizmann contended, 'it is precisely in this that we are once again under vigorous attack and repression by both sides of the Zionist camp'. Despite all this resistance, he went on, 'the Fraction members have dedicated themselves, to the best of their abilities, to these cultural ends—through periodicals and by means of such institutions as the [*Jüdischer*] *Verlag*, the University Bureau, etc.'. In concluding his report Weizmann promised Herzl 'that it is precisely this youth, rejected by you, who belong among your most faithful and most eager supporters. They are everywhere on the alert . . .' and that 'just a small amount of good-will could convert [them] into the finest working element.' And: 'We are keenly looking forward to the possibility of a united effort, and believe we have offered a way towards it.'

The attempt to inaugurate a new chapter in the relations between the 'young' element that were federated within the Democratic Fraction and the leader of the movement was not very successful. In his reply Herzl ignored the issues which Weizmann had dwelt upon in relation to the position and prospects of the Zionist movement in Russia. He only remarked that the news from Russia was indeed very gloomy and that 'our greatest preoccupation here can only be to despatch aid as speedily as possible'. But, he immediately went on to say, he did not believe that 'the divisiveness which the conduct of the Fraction reveals can serve this common purpose'. Herzl wrote that he had always been sympathetic towards the Fraction and was by no means sensitive about a wise Opposition, but he expressed astonishment at the form of its polemics and that of its friends. He promised to note Weizmann's proposals 'with considerable attention', but added that most could be dealt with only after the Congress. Finally, he described Weizmann as 'a person who has been misled, but nevertheless a useful force who will once more find his way back and proceed along the right road together with all of us'. *No. 336, n. 4 (quoted from Herzl's letter of 14 May 1903).*

For Weizmann this came as a bitter disappointment. Some time after receiving Herzl's reply he wrote Pokrassa: 'We have put our position clearly to Herzl too; he is not, however, receptive to our arguments in certain of its aspects. He has greater trust in his ignorant surroundings than in the words we have written with our life-blood.' He threw himself into the election campaign obsessed by the feeling that there was a widespread move afoot to destroy the Fraction, standing as it were alone against a confederation of enemies within the Zionist fold. He believed that it would never be forgiven the iniquity of its leaders in having supported Ahad Ha'am, champion of 'spiritual' as opposed to 'political' Zionism, in his quarrel with Max Nordau over Herzl's latest book *Altneuland*. Published in October 1902, this fictional treatment of a utopian *No. 364 (10 June 1903)*

Jewish Palestine had been sharply attacked by Ahad Ha'am for its lack of an authentic Jewish spirit, and Nordau had been deputed by Herzl to reply to the criticism. Nordau performed the task with such bitterness as to start a raging controversy throughout the Zionist world. And the Fraction members became swept up in its reverberations. Writing to Nahum Sokolow at the beginning of June 1903, Weizmann declared: 'Woe unto him who bears the mark of Cain in opposition to Nordau.... All have got together to become the hangmen of the young, freedom-loving elements of the movement.'

No. 358
(7 Jan.
1903)

These fears were probably exaggerated, as was pointed out by Victor Jacobson and Simon Rosenbaum, both of them Russian Zionist leaders sympathetic to the Democratic Fraction. Even Weizmann admitted, in the letter to Sokolow quoted above: 'Perhaps I see problems in a darker light than they really are. Would that I were wrong!' But the pessimism that then seized him must also be seen against the background of the march of events in Russia. During his visit there, in April 1903, Weizmann learned of an internal memorandum on Zionism prepared by the Russian Ministry of Interior, which described the Democratic Fraction as a body linked with Social Democracy, whilst there were also reports on the hostile attitude towards the Democratic Fraction adopted by Lopukhin, head of the Police Department in the Ministry. Weizmann feared not only direct action by the Tzarist authorities against the Fraction and its sympathizers, but also that its opponents within the Zionist fold might exploit this situation by seeking to liquidate the group on the grounds that its existence actually endangered the entire Russian Zionist movement.

These obstacles, real or imaginary, did not, however, deter Weizmann from launching a new initiative designed to infuse new life into the Fraction and ensure as large a representation as possible at the forthcoming Congress. Lists of candidates were drawn up, and leading personalities in the Fraction, particularly in Russia, were urged to enlist votes for them at the elections. It was decided to hold, as a preliminary to the Congress, a caucus of the Fraction that would deal *inter alia* with a plan to transform its character from a political faction active only during Congresses into a 'working group' or 'action group' that would undertake certain missions within the movement for national renaissance. Weizmann and Buber also proposed that the preliminary conference should reexamine the Fraction's programme, which had been framed in the summer of 1902. 'Everything we engage upon here', Weizmann wrote to Pokrassa on 10 June, 'is directed towards giving the Fraction a definitive shape and keeping it free from the necessity for improvisation.' No. 364
(10 June
1903)

A month after having written about these matters Weizmann decided to cancel the conference. The reasons for his doing so are not very clear, but at least partly stemmed from the differences of opinion that arose between him and the leaders of the Moscow Centre of the Fraction, Idelson and Kroll, concerning the agenda of the conference in particular and 'the nature and meaning of the Fraction' generally, as well as a desire not to engage in sterile discussions at a conference 'where we tell one another that nothing has been done . . .'. An additional point concerned 'the police and political factors' arising from the situation in Russia. No. 413
(25 July
1903)
No. 403
(7 July
1903)

It became apparent on the eve of the Sixth Zionist Congress that the efforts to rouse the Democratic Fraction out of its lethargy were fruitless. This failure was destined to be reflected in the faltering and indifferent performance put on by the Fraction at the Congress itself, when the Zionist movement was suddenly confronted by the risk of a rupture owing to the East Africa proposal. But the plans formulated by Weizmann and his associates for a resumption of activity by the Fraction and its reshaping as a 'working group' were not shelved, and in the course of time these were included among the central themes of Weizmann's activities, in totally different circumstances, during the post-Congress period.

We have seen how Weizmann was completely absorbed by the University project and to a lesser extent by the affairs and problems of the Democratic Fraction. Nevertheless, his letters also mirror the larger issues which were agitating the Zionist world during these months and the initial symptoms of the crisis that was to reach its apogee with the controversy over the East Africa question. At the Annual Zionist Conference in October 1902, which Weizmann attended, Herzl had admitted that his attempts to reach an agreement with the Ottoman Government concerning a concession for Jewish colonization in Palestine had been abortive. Weizmann had returned to Geneva with the feeling that the Zionist leadership had entered a dead end. 'Vienna was not particularly interesting', he wrote Isaac Rothstein immediately after his return. 'The prevailing mood is below zero.' And on the same day he remarked in a letter to Lurie, 'We are confronted with a serious crisis No. 6
(6 Nov.
1902)
No. 5
(6 Nov
1902)

in all fields of Zionism.' Weizmann returned to that painful subject
two months later, in another letter to Lurie: 'Now . . . straining
every [effort], after all the ringing speeches, after five Congresses
and hundreds of different kinds of meetings and conferences, we
have arrived at the point that for the time being there can be no
more talk of a Charter . . . Faith that has endured five years cannot
do so any longer . . . Palestine is [undoubtedly] a romantic concept:
as a concrete proposition it does not so much as come within our
comprehension. This sickness has paralysed the entire cause, and
must be given a radical cure; at the forthcoming Congress we must
demand, with all our vigour, that some clarification be established
in the question of a Charter, and if it becomes impossible to achieve
this—then we shall have to seek out new paths.'

No. 149
(1 Jan.
1903)

Weizmann did not specifically define, either here or in any other
place, what he meant by 'new paths'. But from the statements he
made in various letters written during this period, there emerged
three objectives to which he ascribed decisive importance: cultural
work, the channelling of Jewish emigration from Eastern Europe,
and, above all, an investigation of settlement possibilities in
Palestine.

There is no need to elaborate here on the subject of cultural activity. Its significance had always been emphasized by the 'young
Zionists', and, as we have seen, Weizmann gave it an honoured
place in his long letter to Herzl of May 1903. The University plan
was projected as a centrifugal element in the cultural programme;
and in his letter to Rothstein cited above he contended that the
importance of the University 'is becoming even more so with the
background of the Zionist situation being what it is today'.

No. 6
(6 Nov.
1902)

At the turn of the century Jews were leaving the Russian Empire
and Rumania at the rate of over 100,000 each year, and after
Kishinev the flow westward became a flood. The demand to channel
and regulate this emigration, so as to give it a national character,
was a strong preoccupation of the Zionist camp. Many of those
making their physical escape to the West were simultaneously dis-
carding the traditional patterns of Jewish life. A special Jewish
congress was in fact summoned by the Zionist Organization in 1904
to 'nationalise the emigration stream'—Weizmann's phrase—and
halt the further dispersal of the Jewish people. But in the absence
of any possibility of diverting a substantial number of the emigrants
to Palestine, these ideas were to a large extent divorced from reality.

Weizmann, too, did not go into detail as to the practical purpose of this objective or the methods of attaining it, and it may be assumed that he himself had no very clear notion of what was required.

The programme of the Democratic Fraction prescribed that a thoroughgoing inquiry into Palestine had to be 'the first step in negotiations with Sublime Porte quarters', for the realization was growing that it would be impolitic for the Zionist Organization to defer all settlement activity until the hoped-for Charter was obtained. The talks concerning Jewish colonization in the El-Arish region did indeed arouse a faint hope that it might be possible to do something in this vital sphere, if not in Palestine then at least in its immediate neighbourhood. But it already became evident prior to the Sixth Congress that these contacts would fail to yield any tangible results; and this fresh setback even reinforced the view held by Weizmann and others, not all of them his close adherents, that a practical and purposeful debate of the whole subject would have to be held at the Congress. Weizmann renewed communication once more with Daniel Pasmanik, his past and future adversary, and David Farbstein, with whom he did not always see eye to eye either, concerning the creation of a group 'whose primary intention would be to "seek clarity on the territorial question" and to ensure that a clear colonization policy would be laid down at this Congress'. Writing to his brother-in-law Abraham Lichtenstein in Pinsk, he stated that the battle-cry of the Fraction during the election campaign must above all be 'a demand for clarity on the question of territory and a scientific investigation of Palestine and the neighbouring countries'. And in a letter to Nahum Sokolow he expressed his opinion that this (territorial) question must serve 'as the vital sinew of our movement'. At the same time it appeared that even in this sphere, too, Weizmann had not yet evolved a clear and methodical view of the path to be taken in order to break out of the vicious circle in which the Palestine policy of the Zionist Organization found itself confined. But he did join with others in a demand for the establishment of a Colonization Commission that would, in contrast to previous commissions of this kind, undertake to launch some positive action.

No. 413
(25 July 1903)

No. 396
(2 July 1903)

No. 415
(31 July 1903)

In fine, the line of thought revealed in his statements was destined to be crystallized in the years to come. Following upon the Sixth Zionist Congress the insistence upon systematic work in Palestine became a primary article in the programme of the

Zionei-Zion—the opponents of those supporting the East Africa settlement proposal. Four years after that, at the Eighth Congress, Weizmann emerged as the outstanding spokesman of the 'Practical Zionists' whose demand for planned Zionist action in Palestine was adopted as the official policy of the movement and ultimately evolved as the concept of 'Synthetic Zionism' that was to be Weizmann's major contribution to the philosophy of the movement.

G. Y.

COPY-BOOK OF THE
JEWISH UNIVERSITY BUREAU

Explanatory Note

THE copy-book mentioned in the Introduction confronted the editors with not a few problems of deciphering. These copies were made by the pressure letter-book method which preceded the carbon-copy system. They were blurred in many places, with some words and even full sentences quite illegible. In the translation of these letters indication is given of the words which were partly smudged, and the deciphering of which required a certain amount of guesswork (although in most of the cases there is no doubt as to the accuracy of the construction), by the use of square brackets (e.g.: 'I do not regard [myself] as competent . . .'). In those cases where the writing was so indistinct as to render entire words unreadable the estimated number of missing words is indicated by dashes within the brackets (e.g.: 'I wrote him at length [----] about this').

The letters taken from the copy-book are: 1–9, 11, 13–24, 26, 28–30, 33, 35, 43, 44, 79, 96, 130, 132, 133, 140, 143–9, 157, 161–4, 167, 169, 188, 272, 340, 350, 409.

ACKNOWLEDGEMENTS

The co-operation of the following institutions and individuals is gratefully acknowledged:

Abe Abramson, 'New York Times', New York
Elyahu Amikam, Tel-Aviv
*B. B. Appelby, Los Angeles
Michael Assaf, Tel-Aviv
*Mrs. Sonia Aviad (Wolfsberg), Jerusalem

O. T. Barker, London
Beaverbrook Library, London
*Benjamin Beck, New York
Miss Myra Becker, Geneva
Mrs. Zehava Beilin, Tel-Aviv
B. B. Benas, Liverpool
Baron O.F. Bentinck, Jerusalem
Dr. Baruch Ben-Yehuda, Tel-Aviv
Nathan Berlin, Salt Lake City
I. Bernstein, London
Menachem Bier, Tel-Aviv
Joseph Brainin, New York
*Mrs. Rivka Bruenn, Hadera

Commercial Solvents Corporation, Terre Haute, Indiana
Prof. Marc Cramer, Musée d'Histoire des Sciences, Geneva
Michael Cylan, Tel-Aviv

Mrs. Trude Deak, London
*Ben Dunkelman, Toronto

Dr. Nathan Eck, Jerusalem
*Baroness Elliot of Harwood, London
Itzhak Eylon, Tel-Aviv

*Moss Fairmont, Ramat-Hasharon
*Prof. Arie Feigenbaum, Jerusalem
*Sir James Fergusson of Kilkerran, Bt., Maybole, Ayrshire
*Bruno Foa, New York
*Dr. O. L. Friedman, Holbrook, N.Y.
Prof. Alexander Fuks, Jerusalem

Miss Irene Gaster, Jerusalem
Vivian Gaster, Cambridge

Mrs. Rosa Ginossar, Jerusalem
†Shlomo Ginossar, Jerusalem
Itzhak Goldin, Tel-Aviv
E. Goldstein, Polish-Jewish Ex-Servicemen's Association, London
*Joseph Goodman, London
*Harry Greenstein, Baltimore, Maryland

*Mrs. Leah Harpaz-Aberson, New York
*Max Hazan, Paris
*Leon Hertz, London

'Jewish Chronicle' Library, London
*Mrs. A. Joffe, Manchester

Dr. Meir Mark Kahan, Tel-Aviv
Dr. Alfred Kalmanowicz, Rishon-Lezion
Dr. G. Katkov, Oxford
Ouri Kessary, Tel-Aviv
Joseph Klarman, Tel-Aviv
Meir Korzen, Tel-Aviv
Raphael Kozenicki, Tel-Aviv

*Prof. N. Lebow, New York
Joseph Leftwich, London
Mrs. Asia Lieber, Haifa
Miss Martha Loewenstein, New York

*Dr. Judd Marmor, Los Angeles
*M. Martins, Manchester
Elyahu Mazur, Tel-Aviv
Mrs. Emma Melitz, Tel-Aviv
Dr. Mattityahu Minc, Ramat-Gan
Dr. Eugène Minkowski, Paris
Prof. M. Minkowski, Zurich
*Z. Morgenstern, London

Dr. Umberto Nahon, Jerusalem
*Emanuel Neumann, New York

*Prof. Chanan Oppenheimer, Rehovoth
Miss Susanna Opper, New York

*Charles B. Parker, Kensington, Maryland

* denotes a contributor of documentary material.
† denotes a person deceased before the compilation of this list (December 1969).

ACKNOWLEDGEMENTS

J. Pictet, Paris
*H. E. Post, Terre Haute, Indiana
Public Record Office, London

Anselm Reiss, Tel-Aviv
M. C. de Rohden, Paris
W. Rosenstock, Association of Jewish
  Refugees in Great Britain, London
*Mrs. Dorothy de Rothschild, London
Abraham Rutenberg, Haifa

*Raphael A. Salaman, Harpenden, Herts.
Edgar Samuel, London
Baruch Sapir, Holon
*Scottish Record Office, Edinburgh
Ludwik Seidenman, New York
Mrs. Leah Shapira, Haifa
Mrs. Miriam Shimrony, Benyamina
Joseph Shofman, Tel-Aviv
*The Silbermann (Caspi) family, Tel-
  Aviv
Dr. Celina Sokolow, London

Mrs. Flora Solomon, London
*C. H. Spiers, London
Leonard Stein, London

L. Ch. Tchorz, Jerusalem
Benjamin Tomkiewicz, Tel-Aviv

*U.S. National Archives and Record
  Office, Washington D.C.
*Mrs. Bertha Urdang, Jerusalem

*Sol W. Weltman, Boston
*Sir Isaac Wolfson, Bt., London

*Yale University Library, New Haven,
  Connecticut

Miss Maisie Zacks, Polish-Jewish Refu-
  gee Fund, London
W. Zirbuchen, Archives d'État, Geneva
Lesser Zussman, Jewish Publication
  Society of America, Philadelphia

THE LETTERS

Russian: Or. Copy. H.W.: W.A.

Geneva, 5/Nov. 02.
Rue Lombard 4.

Dear Samuel Moiseevitch,

I arrived in Geneva yesterday after all kinds of difficulties and hardships, and would now like to tell you, briefly, of the outcome of my talks with Herzl.[2] He received my report enthusiastically, joined the committee[3] and promised his unqualified support. In Dr. Herzl's opinion there is no point in thinking about a University in Palestine at this moment, since the prospects of realising such a project in Zion are slender.

The Small Congress voted in favour of Palestine[4] by a majority of only two (nine against seven).

Abroad,[5] the project has had a favourable reception everywhere, and I hope to organise a European committee for the creation of the Jewish University by the new year. As a matter of fact, I can only now really begin working on it.

I am impatiently waiting for you to send me all the news. I am sorry this is so brief. I have not yet had time to get myself organised. Warmest greetings to your brother,[6] Mme. Zu[sman][7] and yourself. When will you be visiting us?

Very sincerely,

Your
Ch. Weizmann

1. [1] Re Shriro's support of the University project, see Vol. I, n. 11 to No. 276 and bridge-note following No. 317.

[2] W. met Herzl at the end of Oct. 1902 and discussed the plan for a Jewish University with him (see Vol. I, No. 320). For additional details on this discussion, see No. 207 below.

[3] The committee referred to is the Central Committee for a Jewish University. W. intended that this, together with local committees in Berlin, Vienna, and several other places, as well as a special committee for Russia, should help in the preparations for the University.

[4] The Annual Zionist Conference (the 'Small Congress') in fact entrusted the Smaller Actions Committee with the task of furthering the University project, conditional on its being established only in Palestine—see Vol. I, n. 4 to No. 320, where the voting is erroneously given as 7–5.

[5] I.e., outside Russia.

[6] Ilya Shriro.

[7] Partly illegible in the original, but the reference is apparently to Mathilda Zusman, Shriro's sister.

2. To Alexander Nemirovsky,[1] Kharkov. *Geneva,*
6 November 1902

Russian: Or. Copy. H.W.: W.A.

Geneva, 6/Nov. 02.
Rue Lombard 4.

Dear Alexander Yakovlevitch,

I returned from Vienna[2] three days ago. The Small Congress has now ended—it was rather dull. The mood that prevailed was unfortunately far from elevated. Herzl was not very successful and as a result our leader is not in the best of spirits.[3] The need for a greater, more profound effort becomes clearer with every passing minute.

I read my report on the University[4] and the Conference responded most sympathetically. By a majority of two it voted in favour of a University in Palestine.[5] Herzl was for Western Europe.[6] We shall now [----] with all energy to organise a committee, which I hope will be formed in Berlin.[7]

Do remember me most warmly to Dr. Breslav.[8] I don't know his address and so am enclosing a short note for him.[9]

Buber and Feiwel are writing articles for the Encyclopaedia.[10] I saw Birnbaum[11] and he told me that he has finished part of the work and is sending it off to you; so is Farbstein. They are all very concerned about the future of the Encyclopaedia.

Please let me have all your news from Kharkov, dear friend. What is happening about the University?

My warmest regards to Henrietta L'vovna[12] and Maria L'vovna.[13]

---

2. [1] Alexander Nemirovsky was a member of the Kharkov Committee for a Jewish University. In the letters he is addressed in the intimate form.

[2] In No. 1, W. wrote that he returned to Geneva 'yesterday', viz. 4 Nov.

[3] See Vol. I, n. 3 to No. 320.   [4] See Vol. I, n. 5 to No. 320.

[5] This information is not fully accurate—see n. 4 to No. 1.

[6] W. himself believed at this time that it would be impossible to found the University in Palestine immediately. See Nos. 4 and 149, cf. also n. 13 to No. 83.

[7] Probably refers to the Central Committee for a Jewish University—see n. 3 to No. 1.

[8] Member of the *Kadimah* Student Zionist Society in Kharkov. He later became an army doctor and gave up his Jewish interests.

[9] See No. 4.

[10] At the end of 1900 the Kharkov Zionist Society decided to publish an anthology ('Encyclopaedia') which would both expound the theories of Zionism and refute the claims of its opponents. As early as Nov. 1901 Nemirovsky asked W. to enlist contributors for the volume, but apparently received no reply. The book was never published. (See Nemirovsky to W. 14 (27) Nov. 1901, W.A., and No. 215. For the outline of the book see C.Z.A. Z1/314).

[11] W. probably met Birnbaum on his visit to Vienna at the end of October.

[12] Henrietta L'vovna Nemirovsky, wife of Alexander Nemirovsky.

[13] Probably a sister of Henrietta Nemirovsky.

I shall long remember those days in Kharkov,[14] and would like nothing better than to drop in on you this Easter, if it is at all possible.

Keep well, dear friend. Affectionately,

Your Chaim

3. To Michael Aleinikov,[1] Kharkov. *Geneva, 6 November 1902*

Russian: Or. Copy. H.W.: W.A.

Geneva, 6/Nov. 02.

Mr. Aleinikov.

Dear Friend,

My preparations are over and I am now getting down to some real work. For a start, I want to begin a proper correspondence with all my friends. Here, for the moment, are just a few lines. You will learn about everything that transpired in Vienna from my letter to A.Y.[2] Please let me know at once what is new with you. How are things going? Have Futran,[3] Breslav and Greidenberg[4] turned out to be workers, or not? Do write about all these things, my friend. I have not settled in yet since I only returned three days ago. I shall be waiting impatiently for your news. How are our comrades? Warmest regards to Volodia[5] and [----]. My very best wishes to Ramendik[6] and Soskin.[7]

Have you worked out the questionnaire as yet for gathering information on the living conditions of Jewish students?[8] Write immediately.[9]

Affectionately,

Your Chaim

---

[14] Reference to W.'s visit to Kharkov in Oct. 1902—see Vol. I, Nos. 318, 391.

3. [1] Aleinikov was secretary of the Kharkov Committee for a Jewish University. In the letters he is addressed in the intimate form.

[2] Alexander Yakovlevitch Nemirovsky—see No. 2.

[3] Michael Futran, active in Kharkov Jewish affairs, especially Hebrew education.

[4] Boris Greidenberg was director of the district hospital in Kharkov and lecturer in medicine at Kharkov University. He was chairman of the Kharkov Committee for a Jewish University, whose members also included Nemirovsky, Futran and Breslav.

[5] Vladimir Idelson.

[6] Boris Ramendik, member of the *Kadimah* Society in Kiev.

[7] Apparently Vladimir Soskin.

[8] The Jewish University Bureau in Geneva planned a series of inquiries and surveys among Jewish students in Western Europe and Russia. They were to comprise:

[*Footnote 8 continued on p. 6*

4. To Israel Breslav,[1] Kharkov. *Geneva, 6 November 1902*

Russian: Or. Copy. H.W.: W.A.

Geneva, 6/Nov. 02.
Rue Lombard 4.

Dr. Breslav.

Dear Comrade,

As I do not know your address, I am writing to you care of A.Y.[2] He will tell you what happened at the A.C.[3] We shall have to give up the idea of establishing a University in Palestine even though this will lose us the goodwill of a number of Zionists.[4] Herzl is not in favour of Palestine; he joined the committee, in his private

(1) a survey among individual foreign students in Western European universities; (2) a group survey of foreign students in Western European universities; (3) a group survey of Russian students; (4) a survey of Western European students; (5) an inquiry into conditions of study for Jews in Southern Europe. In the event only nos. 1 and 3 were carried out. During W.'s visit to Kharkov in Oct. 1902 it was apparently agreed that the local University committee draw up the questionnaires for Russian students, but this task was later entrusted to Michael Kroll and Abraham Idelson in Moscow, and they distributed the questionnaires at the beginning of 1903. The Russian survey was a failure, only a few places returning replies. The Geneva Bureau prepared questionnaires for Eastern European students in Western Universities, and at the end of Dec. 1902 and in Jan. 1903 some 2,500 questionnaires were distributed in 38 University towns in Germany, Switzerland, Belgium and France. Unlike the questionnaire drawn up in May 1902, which was directed to people of special trust only (see Vol. I, n. 6 to No. 204), the new questionnaire was to individual students. The questions covered: personal data on studies, reasons for studying at a Western University, difficulties over admission to Western Universities, material and social conditions, the student's attitude on the Jewish question, languages at his command, level of pre-University studies and post-graduation intentions. The second part of the questionnaire dealt with Jewish students in general. The student was asked for information about further study among his fellows and for his opinion on the following matters: (*a*) Whether further limitations on the admission of foreign Jewish students to Western Universities were to be envisaged. (*b*) The effect of these limitations on the Jewish people. (*c*) Methods of eliminating or alleviating the hardships affecting Jewish students in the West and the student's opinion of the plan for a Jewish University. The replies received were partially processed, and some provisional, general conclusions were published in 1903 by Berthold Feiwel together with the results of the survey held in Munich. (See *Jüdische Statistik*, ed. A. Nossig, Berlin, 1903, pp. 245–55.) This volume also includes a sample questionnaire and a description of how the survey was organized, as well as its aims. A copy of the questionnaire (W.A., 29/0, 22) and preliminary review of the results of the survey are on file in the W.A. (See box Dec. 1902.) W. sent the completed questionnaires to Feiwel in Feb. 1904 (see W. to Buber and Feiwel, 2 Feb. 1904, W.A.) but they have not been found.

⁹ In his reply of 20 Nov./3 Dec. 1902 (W.A.), Aleinikov complained about the inactivity of the members of the Kharkov University Committee and promised that he would try to stir them up.

4. ¹ W. addresses Breslav in the intimate form.
   ² Alexander Nemirovsky.
   ³ Actions Committee. See letter to Nemirovsky of the same date (No. 2).
   ⁴ Cf. n. 4 to No. 1.

capacity, of course, for the establishment of the University. What have you succeeded in doing in the meantime? Has the committee met yet? What decisions were reached? What activities undertaken?

Please, dear friend, write immediately! It is imperative that we keep up a lively correspondence. For heaven's sake, don't let our work stagnate! Give my sincerest regards to Dr. Futran.[5] I shall write to him too, very soon.[6] Let me just recover a little. I hope to get a prompt reply from you. We are beginning a survey on the life of the student body.[7] Have you done anything yet about this?

Please write at once[8] about all these things to your devoted

Chaim

Heartfelt greetings to comrades.

5. To Gregory Lurie, Pinsk. *Geneva, 6 November 1902*

German: Or. Copy. H.W.: W.A.

Geneva, 6/Nov. 02.
Rue Lombard 4.

Dear Mr. Lurie,

Unfortunately it was impossible for me to reply from Vienna to your kind note.[1] So pathetically little happened in Vienna that it can really be disposed of in two words. The communiqué[2] in *Die Welt* pretty well sums the whole thing up. They [---- ---- ---- further inquiries]. We have put the question that particularly interests you [to] the periodical *Palästina*.[3] Dr. Herzl thought there had been an inaccurate translation from the French. The phrase appeared in *Die Welt* through an error. Of course, no-one thinks about Asia Minor.[4] As you see, it is as vague as it possibly can be; but the mood

[5] Michael Futran.

[6] See letter to Futran of 27 Nov. 1902 (No. 29). This appears to be W.'s first letter to Futran after his return from Russia.

[7] See n. 9 to No. 3.

[8] Breslav replied to this letter, but only on 10 (23) Jan. 1903 (W.A.).

5. [1] Lurie's letter has not been found.

[2] Reference to the report on the Annual Zionist Conference in *Die Welt*, 31 Oct. 1902. For the discussions see Vol. I, ns. 3, 4 to No. 320.

[3] *Palästina*, a German bi-monthly, first appeared in Berlin in Jan. 1902 as the organ of the 'Committee for Economic Research of Palestine' (see n. 6 to No. 125). At the end of the year it was taken over by the *Jüdischer Verlag*, and Davis Trietsch replaced Alfred Nossig as editor.

[4] Reference to a report in *Die Welt*, 8 Aug. 1902, on negotiations by Herzl in Constantinople at the end of July 1902 (see Vol. I, n. 6 to No. 260 and n. 12 to No. 302). The report mentions two memoranda in French prepared by Herzl for the Sultan, in which he formulated 'the conditions for Jewish settlement in a contiguous part of Palestine and in other parts of Asia Minor on the basis of a "charter"'. An article by Trietsch in *Palästina* criticized the report in *Die Welt* and the policy of the Zionist leaders in general. According to Trietsch, there were various possible areas for

was so much below zero that any further steps seemed superfluous. Confidentially, *we are confronted with a serious crisis in all fields of Zionism.* All the more, therefore, does an act such as the establishment of a Jewish University [now] seem absolutely necessary to me. We must create new generations that are less corroded by *Golus*.[5]

Do write to me, Mr. Lurie, as to whether you and Alexander Lurie[6] might be inclined to join a committee contemplated for Russia.

I look forward with great anticipation to your observations on this matter.

[---- ---- ----] well.

Devotedly yours,
Ch. Weizmann

Encl.: List.[7]

6. To Isaac Rothstein,[1] Rostov. *Geneva, 6 November 1902*

Russian: Or. Copy. H.W.: W.A.

Geneva, 6/Nov. 02.
Rue Lombard 4.

Dear Friend,

You made it known to me, through Vera Issayevna,[2] that you would write to me in Vienna. So I waited there impatiently for news from you, but of course heard nothing. As you see, my wanderings are at an end[3] and I have already started to work systematically. Vienna was not particularly interesting. The prevailing mood— below zero.[4] As for the University, the Conference declared itself for Palestine by a majority of two votes.[5]

Herzl thinks the University *is not feasible* in Palestine *at present.* He is in favour of Western Europe. He *joined* the committee.

Let me know at once what is happening with you. Is there any

Jewish settlement in and around Palestine, all of them preferable to Asia Minor. He claimed further that the wording of the report indicated that Palestine was part of Asia Minor (see *Palästina* I (1902), 3–4, pp. 154–9). Apparently Lurie asked W. to clear this matter up at his meeting with Herzl.

    [5] Yidd. 'Exile'.

    [6] Alexander Lurie (1861–1924). Uncle of Gregory Lurie. A Pinsk plywood manufacturer, he was active in Jewish affairs though not a Zionist.

    [7] The list has not been found and its contents are unknown.

6. [1] Rothstein is addressed in the intimate form.

    [2] i.e. Vera Khatzman.

    [3] W. returned to Geneva from Russia at the beginning of November.

    [4] See Vol. I, n. 3 to No. 320.

    [5] See n. 4 to No. 1.

response? Have you collected any money, and how much?[6] What do you propose doing? Please write and keep us [informed] on everything. I, for my part, will not take a single step without informing you. Listen, old friend, this University business is most important, and is becoming even more so with the background of the Zionist situation being what it is today. This is my profound conviction. So far, it is the only concrete and large-scale undertaking to help rouse and uplift Jewry as a whole.

Kindest regards to Maria Grigorievna.[7]

Affectionately,
Greetings to the children,
Your Chaim

Mr. M. I. Rothstein,[8]
Rostov-on-Don.

7. To Abraham Idelson and Michael Kroll,[1] Moscow.
Geneva, 8 November 1902

Russian: Or. Copy. H.W.: W.A.

8/Nov. 02.

Hochschule
Mr. Idelson and Dr. Kroll

I have already written you,[2] dear [----], that my preliminary explorations in a few [----] have succeeded beyond all expectations. The University idea [---- ----] the most diverse strata of society. I must say that the financial side of the undertaking seems to me to present fewer difficulties than does its organisation [----] I hope that by the new year we shall have a committee made up of prominent Jewish names here in the West. By Easter, we should be able to publish a book[3] containing:

---

[6] When he was in Rostov in Sept.–Oct. 1902 W. had received pledges amounting to 400 roubles for the Jewish University Bureau—see Vol. I, bridge-note following No. 317.   [7] Apparently Rothstein's wife.

[8] *Sic.* Actually I. M. (Isaac Michalovitsch).

7. [1] At the Minsk conference of Russian Zionists in Sept. 1902 the leaders of the Democratic Fraction decided to create a Russian centre of the Fraction in Moscow, headed by Abraham Idelson, Michael Kroll and Pesah Marek—see circular of the Russian centre dated 27 Sept. (10 Oct.) 1902, Schwarz Collection, Workers' Archives, Tel Aviv; Kroll to Moses Glikin, 21 Sept. (4 Oct.) 1902, C.Z.A. A179/3. It appears that Idelson and Kroll also promised W. their co-operation on the Jewish University.

[2] W.'s previous letter has not been found.

[3] The book was to have been written by Berthold Feiwel, but in the event he published only provisional conclusions on the results of the survey (see n. 8 to No. 3). For an outline see also Feiwel to Buber, 12 Nov. 1902, Buber Archives, N.L.

a) The University project
b) A statistical survey of Jewish students
c) A statistical survey of monies expended on Higher Education (stipends, etc.)
d) A propaganda section

We are inaugurating a survey of living conditions among Jewish students, mainly at University level.[4] If you agree in principle to work on this, get in touch with Kharkov (Student M. Aleinikov, c/o A. Y. Nemirovsky, 28, Rimarskaya), and with Kiev (M. Weizmann, 3 or 11, Zhilanskaya), [----]. The survey will be conducted through leaflets containing a questionnaire to be prepared by the Berlin Statistical Bureau.[5] I shall let you have all the material.

Another important thing is *Stimmung machen.*[6] What about Minor and Poliakov?[7] It would be as well to have a talk with Berkenheim.[8] Make out a list of *Vertrauensmänner,*[9] talk to them and let me know how they feel. [----] their addresses and put them in touch with me. I intend to be in Moscow in March.[10] The University brochure is being translated into Russian and will be published in Kharkov.[11]

Please keep me informed of whatever steps you intend to take in this matter.

I shall be waiting impatiently to hear from you.

All the best,

Ch. W.

[4] Cf. n. 8 to No. 3.

[5] In point of fact the questionnaire was not yet ready. The next day W. asked Abraham Kasteliansky, secretary of the Jewish Statistical Association in Berlin, to draw up the questionnaire together with Alfred Nossig, chairman of the Association. Kasteliansky was then a member of the committee organized by the Jewish Statistical Bureau, forerunner of the Association, to conduct an inquiry into the position of Jewish students—cf. Vol. I, n. 7 to No. 204. The next day W. also sent Feiwel a copy of the old questionnaire, drawn up in May 1902 but not distributed (see Vol. I, n. 6 to No. 204), for redrafting, and in the middle of November Feiwel sent W. and Kasteliansky his draft of a new questionnaire—see Feiwel to W., without date (*ca.* 15 Nov. 1902), W.A. No. 30/0, 36.   [6] 'Creating a (favourable) atmosphere.'

[7] Lazar Minor (1855–1942), neuropathologist, was a lecturer and subsequently a professor at Moscow University. Lazar Poliakov (1842–1913), banker and philanthropist, chairman of the Moscow Jewish Community.

[8] W. is possibly referring to A. M. Berkenheim, who in 1896 published a series of articles in *Voskhod* about Jewish settlement in Palestine and Argentina. In his reply of 4 (17) Nov. 1902 (W.A.), Kroll wrote: 'No sense in talking to Berkenheim, we all know him. We shall find more suitable people.'

[9] Volunteer supervisors. Lit. 'confidants'.

[10] W. did go to Russia in March 1903, but did not visit Moscow.

[11] The pamphlet *Eine Jüdische Hochschule* was translated into Russian by Dr. Goldberg (first name not known) in Pinsk. W. agreed with Nemirovsky that the Kharkov Committee of the Jewish University should handle publication of the translation (see No. 215). The manuscript was in fact sent to Nemirovsky (see n. 5 to No. 23), but it never appeared in print.

8. To Berthold Feiwel,[1] Zurich. *Geneva, 9 November 1902*

German: Or. Copy. H.W.: W.A.

Geneva, 9/Nov. 02.
Rue Lombard 4.

[My] dear, good Toldy,

Many thanks for your detailed letter.[2] I, too, never thought otherwise than to send you the document.[3] With this in mind I had Pinkus trans[late] and copy it so that it could be sent to you, Kasteliansky and perhaps Nossig.[4] I regard myself as being without great competence in this matter, and anyway you may be sure that I would *never* undertake a thing without your explicit consent, without keeping you informed. I failed to do so this week because I had [----] to do and put off the report until today.

The [Farbstein][5] *business* [---- ---- ---- ---- ---- ---- ---- ----] by no means out of moral considerations, but in view of his [---- ---- nature which is] totally unpredictable. I [---- ---- ---- ---- ---- ----] he [wanted] to write about the Fraction. [I considered it unnecessary] to inform you because I thought that [you] would eventually reach an understanding with him on this point.

Pinkus wrote to me about an essay (The Foundations of Z.), which

---

8. [1] W. addresses Feiwel in the intimate form.

[2] Feiwel to W., 8 Nov. 1902, W.A. Feiwel was replying to a postcard from W. (not found) regarding an attack by Rudolf Schauer on the Democratic Fraction (see n. 1 to No. 10). Feiwel said he wished to publish a rebuttal to Schauer's article in *Die Welt*, and promised to contact David Farbstein on the matter (W. had apparently suggested that Farbstein be asked to reply to Schauer's article), but expressed the fear that Farbstein's reply would also attack the Fraction. Feiwel stated that he had also discussed the Jewish University project with Farbstein, but that Farbstein's views on the subject were 'neither very original nor very serious'. He added that Farbstein combined a certain political and personal opportunism with rigid socialist party slogans, 'resulting in a Zionist subjectivity that is not always of great value'. Feiwel asked W. to keep him informed about the Bureau's correspondence and to consult him before printing the student questionnaires. He warned W. to be wary in his contacts with Pinkus, especially where confidential Zionist matters or questions of great responsibility were concerned, and suggested that, for the time being, he be entrusted only with technical tasks under close supervision. He declared himself willing to carry out the survey in Switzerland to prevent it from being handed to Pinkus. Feiwel suggested that a statement about the activities in connection with the Jewish University project be published in *Die Welt*.

[3] In the original: 'Bogen'. Later in the letter it becomes clear that the reference is to the questionnaire ('Fragebogen') drawn up in May 1902 (cf. n. 5 to No. 7). The W.A. has a stencilled copy of the Russian questionnaire and two manuscript copies of the German translation written by Pinkus and Feiwel.

[4] See n. 5 to No. 7.

[5] Many words in this part of the letter are undecipherable and it is not absolutely certain that the name written here is 'Farbstein'. However, in view of Feiwel's remarks about Farbstein in his letter of 8 Nov. 1902 (see n. 2 above), this is a fair assumption.

apparently he showed you[6] and by which you are said to have been favourably impressed. He wants me to recommend acceptance of the work by *O.u.W.*, or its publication by the *J.V.* What kind of a work is this? Is there anything to it?

Pinkus gets nothing but technical things from me. But what is going to happen to the 'Berne Section for Jewish Statistics' now in his hands?[7] Ever since the Bioux business[8] I have made up my mind about this likeable, frivolous fellow. He really [----] too big, and he must be [finally] made to grow up. He harms [himself] and us [----].

Not a word from Buber. I wrote him in detail [----] about the form his work for the University project ought to take.[9]

The [content] of the letters I [sent off] last week [deals] with [----] affairs. I wrote to the people in Kharkov, Baku, Rostov, Kiev, Moscow, Petersburg, Lurie of Pinsk,[10] individuals whom I had already met during my tour. I informed them all of what took place in Vienna and requested them to let me know about the development of [our] cause in their cities. I did not communicate with *new* people. That I would not do without you or your letter. As soon as replies are received to all this correspondence we shall know what can be further undertaken in Russia.

a) *I want to start preparing for my Easter trip now,*[11] *through correspondence with those reliable individuals whom I have already come [to know].*

b) A communiqué should appear in the Russian-Jewish newspapers similar to one that is going into *Die Welt.*[12]

c) Survey.

---

[6] Pinkus's letter has not been found, but see Pinkus to W., 15 Nov. 1902, 19 Nov. 1902 (W.A.). The work referred to is an essay by Pinkus: 'The Modern Jewish Question: on the fundamentals of Jewish economic history and Zionism' (see L. F. Pinkus, *Die moderne Judenfrage: von den Grundlagen der Jüdischen Wirtschaftsgeschichte und des Zionismus*, Breslau, 1903). Pinkus also asked for W.'s criticism of the essay.

[7] Pinkus was director of the Berne branch of the Jewish Statistical Association, founded in Oct. 1902 for the purpose of compiling statistical data in Switzerland, especially regarding Jews studying there (see circular of the section in C.Z.A. A102/10/2/2).

[8] See Vol. I, n. 8 to No. 293.

[9] The letter to Buber has not been found.

[10] See Nos. 1–7. Letters that W. wrote at that time to Kiev and St. Petersburg have not been found (according to Feiwel's letter of 8 Nov. 1902, W. wrote twenty-five letters on the previous day, but the W.A. has copies of only five dated 6 Nov. and none dated 7 Nov.).

[11] A reference to W.'s planned trip to Russia in the spring of 1903.

[12] The statement about activities connected with the University project—see n. 2 above.

I am sending you the old questionnaire;[3] add your views to it and send it on to Kasteliansky and Nossig if you think this necessary. It must be printed without delay. I would propose the following heading: Jewish Academ. Statistics (Survey initiated by the Bureau for the Jewish University). A few more questions relating to Jewish professors will be added to those already on the paper.[13]

In addition to the questionnaire, smaller papers will have to be drafted, and I see the thing work out in practice as follows: Each reliable individual or census committee receives questionnaire I; the smaller sheet 2 is distributed among the students. (I am sending you a very rough sample. It was prepared in Munich).[14] The large one[15] is to be [filled] out on the basis of the small one. Should it be worded in German only? Everything has to be got ready by the end of this month. We must also draft an accompanying letter which we shall attach to each one.

d) We have to get into touch with Zangwill and Gaster, and with Evans-Gordon, and prepare for the visit to London, perhaps as early as Christmas, in order to look over the ground.[16] Herzl could help us if he, on his part, were to write to these gentlemen.

That, for the time being, is all that I have in mind for the immediate future. Perhaps we could add the things we discussed in Zurich.[17] I am making an effort [to come] to you [soon] even if only for a few hours, perhaps as soon as next Sunday. I am hoping to receive various replies already this week (I shall send you all the letters). We shall require notepaper.[18] I have still not finished setting up the office; I am having difficulties about the typewriter.[19] Could you place an advertisement in [Zurich] perhaps? I have done so here.

Fraction: a change must be effected in this; we have already become a fiction.[20] I cannot take it all on myself alone here. Aberson, Grinblatt, etc., will do nothing, and I have practically no contact

---

[13] In fact, no questions about professors were added.

[14] Apparently a questionnaire drawn up by a group of Jewish students in Munich, who undertook at the beginning of 1902 to compile statistics. Details unknown.

[15] Only one questionnaire has been found, directed to students themselves. Apparently the conclusive questionnaires mentioned here were never drawn up (see n. 8 to No. 3).

[16] For W.'s plan to visit Brussels, London, and Paris during the Christmas holiday see No. 20 and n. 5 there.

[17] W. met Feiwel in Zurich on his return to Switzerland at the beginning of Nov. 1902.

[18] W. had ordered notepaper in Berlin for the Jewish University Bureau in Geneva.

[19] W. intended to buy a typewriter for the Jewish University Bureau.

[20] In his letter of 8 Nov. 1902, Feiwel wrote that an office of the Democratic Fraction directed by W. was needed in Geneva, 'if the Fraction in Western Europe is not to become a fiction'.

with these people. The only ones are Koenigsb[erg], Dorfman; I shall speak to them today and if they agree to work *hard* I shall do so too. (The editor of the *Prager Tageblatt* who applied for entry into the F. is called Julius Loewy.[21] Do you know him, by any chance?) But [what song] is Motzkin [going] to sing?[22]

Dear, good Toldy, this briefly is everything. I want to work hard and diligently, without resting until we get the full machine going. I consider the University the only right and important thing just now. We shall still talk about it. Should I write to Herzl about Zangwill and Gaster? Vera sends regards and kisses as always. She is working hard at the Ecole de Médecine; she is doing quite well.

My warmest regards and kisses to you and Esther.[23] Told, Told, don't neglect your health. [Many warm] regards [to] Manya Sokolow.[24]

Your Chaim

9. To Abraham Kasteliansky, Berlin. *Geneva, 9 November 1902*

Russian: Or. Copy. H.W.: W.A.

Geneva, Rue Lombard 4.
9. Nov. 02.

Dear Comrade,

Our correspondence was interrupted by the holidays.[1] Since then, the matter of the University has advanced considerably, but probably you already know all about this from conversations with our Berlin friends.

Now the most vital question concerns the Jewish academic statistics. Our *Hochschulcomité*[2] has decided to set this in motion

[21] See Julius Loewy to W., 28 Sept. 1902, W.A.

[22] Probably meaning: How would Motzkin react to the creation of a Democratic Fraction office headed by W.? The Programme Committee of the Fraction, of which Motzkin was a prominent member, had decided in June 1902 that until the Fraction's conference its affairs would be managed by the committee; but the committee held no further meetings. On differences between W. and Motzkin at the beginning of 1902, see Vol. I, Nos. 150, 152, 178.

[23] Esther Shneerson, who had studied in Berlin during 1901–2, moved to Zurich in the autumn of 1902.

[24] Nahum Sokolow's daughter, then living in Zurich.

9. [1] Previous correspondence between W. and Kasteliansky has not been found. Presumably they exchanged letters before the 1902 summer vacation about the survey of Jewish students (see n. 5 to No. 7) and the preparation of a bibliography on Universities in connection with the Jewish University project—see Vol. I, No. 238.

[2] 'University Committee.' Officially, there was no such body, and the reference is to the group responsible for setting up the Jewish University Bureau: W., Buber, and Feiwel.

together with the *V[erein] f[ür] J[üdische] St[atistik]*.[3] Feiwel or Pinkus will certainly have written to you about it by now and sent you the projected *Fragebogen*.[4] Would you, dear friend, kindly edit the *Fragebogen* together with Nossig and put it into final shape, and then we shall have it printed at our expense.

You may recall that you promised to get the rest of the bibliographical material about the University. If you would only do this you would be rendering us a great service.

Write how you are, and where you plan spending the winter.

I have only just returned from a trip round the world,[5] and have not yet got myself settled.

Keep well,

Yours,
Ch. Weizmann.

Mr. A. Kasteliansky,
Berlin.

10. To Moses Glikin, Charlottenburg. *Geneva, 12 November 1902*

Russian: Pcd. H.W.: C.Z.A. A179/3.

Geneva, 12/xi. 02.

Dear Glikin,

You probably know about Schauer's outrageous article.[1] We have got to answer it at once. If you could get a few German Zionists to

---

[3] 'Jewish Statistical Association.'   [4] 'questionnaire'—cf. n. 5 to No. 7.
[5] Reference to W.'s visit to Russia.

10. [1] Article by Rudolf Schauer in the Orthodox, anti-Zionist paper *Der Israelit*, 3 Nov. 1902. The article was a reply to another by Joseph Seliger in the same issue, which had been shown to Schauer in advance of publication. Seliger criticized a group of Zionist students in Berne, who, by a vote at a special meeting, had meals served in their refectory on *Yom Kippur* (a letter from Chaim Khissin to W. of 7 Dec. 1902, W.A., indicates that the decision was taken at a meeting of the Academic Zionist Society, most of whose members belonged to the Democratic Fraction). Seliger admitted that most Zionists would probably not condone such behaviour, but alleged that it suited the programme of the Democratic Fraction, 'which has set the elimination of religion as its goal'. In his reply Schauer also condemned the behaviour of the Berne students, but claimed that this had nothing to do with Zionism, and that Zionists had nothing in common with people like 'the Fractionists from Berne' who offended the sensitivities of their brothers. Schauer described the Fraction as a negligible minority in the Zionist camp: Russian assimilationists tainted with nihilistic ideas which, allied to the typical Jewish tendency to criticize and the Diaspora's lack of discipline, produced the breeding-ground for such groups. Schauer added that the Fraction's programme showed its members to be far removed from everyday life—because they lacked contact beyond their own limited circle—and were therefore unlikely to find converts to 'their immature ideas'.

associate themselves with our protest, so much the better. I have no addresses in Leipzig or in Koethen, and this is why I am sending you three circulars.[2] Please send one each to Leipzig and Koethen.

Awaiting your immediate reply,

Yours,
Chaim

11. To Martin Buber,[1] Vienna. *Geneva, 14 November 1902*

German: Or. Copy. H.W.: W.A.

Geneva, Rue Lombard 4
14. XI. 02.

My dear Martin,

Were I now standing beside you I would be singing *Mikita*[2] so long until [----] so annoyed am I by your silence. If you are still alive [----] do give a sign, and incidentally you could also answer the very important questions touched upon in my letter.[3] Listen you, we have got to be conscientious in our communications to each other, or the work will suffer badly. Write immediately to

Your Chaim.

12. To Max Bodenheimer,[1] Cologne. *Geneva, 15 November 1902*

German.: H.W.: C.Z.A. A15/VII/12

Geneva, 15 Nov. 1902
Rue Lombard 4.

Dr. Bodenheimer,
Cologne.

Dear Fellow-Zionist,[2]

In an article which appeared in issue number 87 of *Israelit* Dr.

---

[2] On the basis of Feiwel's proposal in his letter of 9 Nov. 1902 (W.A.), W. sent out a circular letter in the name of the Democratic Fraction's Information Bureau, asking Fraction members to authorize him and Feiwel to sign a joint reply to Schauer's article (see n. 1 above), to be published in *Die Welt* and in the *Jüdische Rundschau*. Copy of the circular, dated 12 Nov. 1902, in W.A.

11. [1] W. uses the intimate form to Buber.

[2] A humorous Jewish folksong in Ukrainian interspersed with Hebrew (see M. Kipnis, *60 Volkslieder*, second edition, Warsaw, p. 140).

[3] Reference to W.'s letter to Buber, mentioned in No. 8. This has not been found.

12. [1] Max Bodenheimer was chairman of the German Zionist Federation at this time.

[2] In the original: 'Gesinnungsgenosse', similarly translated elsewhere.

Schauer of Mainz indulged in an attack upon the Fraction, and in particular Russian-Jewish student youth, in a manner which I consider beneath my dignity to describe.[3]

Apart from the fact that the incident in Berne referred to in the article cannot be blamed on the Fraction, Dr. Schauer surely had no right to elaborate on facts and circumstances which he learned about only from an anti-Zionist article appearing in an anti-Zionist paper.

I merely wish to draw your attention to what may well be a serious consequence of such an article; identifying the objectives of the Fraction with Nihilism, ridiculous as it seems to me, may bring us, and Russian Zionism, to the notice of certain government quarters in Russia in a most unpleasant way, especially when such views are spread by 'party comrades' in Jewish papers. The Fraction, it should be pointed out, achieved recognition at the conference in Minsk.[4] Anyone acquainted with the situation in Russia, even superficially, will be bound to understand Dr. Schauer's article as a deliberate denunciation.

You know well enough how difficult life is made for Russian-Jewish students when abroad; they have to fight against every kind of innuendo,[5] mostly of a nature similar to that uttered by Dr. Schauer. The only difference is that these innuendos always appear in antisemitic publications. How could a Zionist dare to come out with so bitter an indictment at such a critical time?

My East European *Goluskopf*[6] cannot comprehend such 'European' manners!

In the name of many friends I hereby lodge a strong protest against the behaviour of 'party comrade' Dr. Schauer, and in appealing to your Zionist conscience and loyalty I request you, with respect, to take an energetic stand in this affair.

I intend to summon the gentleman before a court of arbitration, but will refrain from doing so if the German National Committee[7] wishes to settle the matter itself.

Most respectfully and with Zion's greetings,
Dr. Ch. Weizmann[8]

Copy.

---

[3] See n. 1 to No. 10.

[4] At the Russian Zionist conference in Minsk (Sept. 1902), the first to be officially permitted by the Russian authorities, the Fraction appeared as an organized group, with its leaders taking part as delegates—cf. Vol. I, bridge-note following No. 308.

[5] In the original: 'Insinuationen'.

[6] Ironical Yidd. term for 'Diaspora mentality' (a reference to Schauer's article, in which he ascribes to the Russian students 'the Diaspora trait of lack of discipline').

[7] The Central Committee of the German Zionist Organization.

[8] In the original the signature is accompanied by the stamp of the Democratic Fraction's Information Bureau.

13. To Berthold Feiwel, Zurich. *Geneva, 15 November 1902*

German: Or. Copy. H.W.: W.A.

Geneva, 15/xi/02.

My dear Toldy,

Your kind letter arrived today,[1] giving me much joy. I was already becoming uneasy because I had not received news from you for such a long time. Thank you very much for all the news. I am particularly delighted also to hear something indirectly by way of Zurich from Buber, who has adopted a complete silence towards me.

I shall not now be coming next Sunday, because there is still a lack of material. On the other hand I expect to come a week on Sunday.

University. There is news from Lilien; he is working on the emblem,[2] so the notepaper will not be ready for some time. Today I wrote again, but what's the good? Trietsch telegraphs that he is coming to Switzerland on Wednesday. Probably he will be bringing brochures along; it would be as well. Should I write to Herzl about Zangwill?[3]

Professor Stein[4] must be worked on,[5] similarly [Oncken].[6] What do you think?

Survey. Still no news from Kasteliansky. Anyway, I would like to see the pages before they go to press.

Circular[7] has been sent out. There are no replies as yet, but they are sure to come. Do you know any German gentlemen to whom they should be sent? Pinkus has advised against writing to Schachtel.[8]

---

13. [1] Feiwel to W., 13 Nov. 1902, W.A. Feiwel wrote, *inter alia*, that Buber was about to draw up a list of Central European authors and professors (likely to support the Jewish University project—see also n. 9 below). With regard to the survey, Feiwel said he had reached agreement with Kasteliansky and the questionnaires could be printed that same month. Feiwel also revealed that the periodical *Palästina* had been taken over by the *Jüdischer Verlag*. He suggested getting in touch with the London weekly, the *Jewish Chronicle*, which had published a favourable article on the Fraction (see n. 11 below).

[2] See Davis Trietsch, 12 Nov. 1902, W.A. The reference is to a design that Lilien had promised to prepare for the Jewish University Bureau's stationery and for the second edition of the brochure *Eine Jüdische Hochschule*. Trietsch also wrote about a forthcoming propaganda trip to Switzerland.

[3] See No. 8.   [4] Ludwig Stein.

[5] In the original: 'in Bearbeitung genommen werden.'

[6] August Oncken (1844–1911), Professor of Economics at Berne University, 1878–1910 (Rector, 1902), a non-Jew.

[7] The circular letter on Schauer's article (see n. 2 to No. 10).

[8] In his letter of 9 Nov. 1902 (W.A.) Feiwel proposed that Pinkus ask Hugo Schachtel, Chairman of the Breslau Zionist Association, to collect signatures to a protest against Schauer's article (see n. 2 to No. 10).

Letters to the professors must go out as soon as possible.[9] I am pleased that 'Palästina' belongs to you.[10] When will Palestine without quotation marks be *ours*?

I shall probably receive the *Jewish Chronicle*[11] from the press-cutting agency. I shall try and establish contact with the *J.C.* through Fuchs.[12]

(no ending or signature)

14. To Michael Altschul, Berlin. *Geneva, 17 November 1902*

German: Or. Copy. H.W.: W.A.

Geneva, 17 / Nov. 02.
Rue Lombard 4.

Dear Dr. [Altschul],

About a week ago I wrote both to you and Mme. Professor Pictet[1]

[9] The Jewish University Bureau was to conduct an inquiry among Jewish professors on the University project. Feiwel appears to have promised to draw up the letter to the professors (see also No. 153), and he may have sent a draft to W. at the beginning of January. On 7 Jan. 1903 W. told Feiwel that 'tomorrow we shall finish the professors' letter . . .' (see No. 178) and on 12 Jan. he informed Simon Guinzburg about the inquiry and told him that 200 Jewish professors were to be approached (see No. 203). The next day W. sent Buber a draft of the letter (see No. 208), but on 21 Jan. he wrote (see No. 228) telling him that it was pointless to send it out unless it was signed by the members of the Viennese Committee for a Jewish University, which Buber was trying at that time to set up (unsuccessfully). No text of such a circular letter has been found, and the available letters do not provide any proof that one was actually sent. However, according to *Hatzefirah* of 10/23 March 1903, W. told the newspaper's reporter that the Jewish University Bureau had contacted 'all the well-known scholars and professors in order to get their views' and that many of them had expressed support of the project. This is not corroborated by any other source. When the Berlin University Committee agreed to handle the academic aspects of the preparatory work (March 1903), the University Bureau undertook to help by holding an 'enquiry among professors and experts in university studies' (see the Bureau's report of May 1903, W.A. No. 30/5/0). In June the Berlin Committee asked the Bureau's representatives to send the addresses of Jewish professors and lecturers required for the inquiry (see circular of 2 June 1903, W.A.), but in the end nothing came of the project.   [10] See n. 1 above.

[11] See n. 1 above. Reference to an article in the *Jewish Chronicle* of 7 Nov. 1902. This summed up the results of the Annual Zionist Conference in Vienna and praised the cultural activities of the Democratic Fraction, of which it gave the details as reported by W. and Buber.

[12] Jacob Samuel Fuchs (1867–1938), editor of the Hebrew weekly *Hamagid* (Cracow), who was then in charge of the paper's London Office. Fuchs was a known supporter of the Democratic Fraction.

14. [1] Hélène, wife of Prof. Raoul Pictet. The letters referred to have not been found. W. spoke with Altschul, then Raoul Pictet's assistant, when he was in Berlin in August (see Vol. I, No. 293) and it appears that he asked Altschul to enlist the support of Berlin professors, especially Pictet, for the University project (cf. No. 41 below).

con[cerning ---- ---- ---- ---- ---- ---- ---- ----]. So far I have not had an answer. I would be most grateful if you would kindly write me a few words on whether you have spoken to Mme. the Professor, and what the outcome of the conversation was.

May I at the same time ask you to be so good as to let me know whether you have achieved anything in the University project. I implore you not to keep me waiting for an answer, dear Doctor. Try and overcome whatever writing inertia may possess you. You can dictate the letter to your typist.

I shall not write again to Mme. the Professor until I receive a reply from you.

With kindest regards,
Ch. Weizmann

15. To Hirsch Hiller,[1] Pinsk. *Geneva, 17 November 1902*

Russian: Or. Copy. H.W.: W.A.

Geneva, Rue Lombard 4,
17 Nov. 02.

My dear Friend,

You must have read in *Die Welt* about all that happened in Vienna.[2] By the way, Herzl joined the University committee. Now there are real prospects for getting some important people in London to join.[3]

What about the brochure? Has it been translated yet?[4] If not, please get Dr. Goldberg to hurry up with it and let me know when it is sent to Kharkov.

What is new in Pinsk? How are you and all your family?

I [----] am overloaded with work, for we are now starting on the statistical research.[5] I shall soon write in detail and let you know how everything is developing.

Kind regards to Liza,[6] Aaron.[7]

Affectionately,
Your Chaim

15. [1] Hiller is addressed in the intimate form.

[2] Reference to the discussions of the Annual Zionist Conference (see Vol. I, ns. 1, 3, and 4 to No. 320; ns. 2 and 3 to No. 1; n. 1 to No. 5).

[3] Cf. No. 8.

[4] Reference to the translation of the Jewish University brochure into Russian—see n. 11 to No. 7.   [5] The student survey—see n. 8 to No. 3.

[6] Liza Hiller, wife of Hirsch H.

[7] Aaron Hiller, son of Hirsch H., was a teacher and prepared W.'s sisters for school. He was active in the Bund and was later exiled to Siberia. He remained in the Soviet Union.

16. To Isidore (Israel) Yasinovsky, Warsaw. *Geneva, 17 November 1902*

Russian: Or. Copy. H.W.: W.A.

Geneva, Rue Lombard 4.
17 XI. 02.

Dear Comrade,

We agreed in Vienna that we would correspond on the project for a Jewish University.[1] This letter is intended to serve as the beginning of such a correspondence. Warsaw, of course, could do a great deal to help but I have no idea at all how to proceed.

May I ask you, dear comrade, to inform me whether you have succeeded in interesting anyone in the matter, and if so whom. Naturally, we are keen on attracting people from academic and financial circles. Furthermore, it is important to obtain money for the preparatory work because our requirements will be many.

I shall be in Warsaw around Easter and we can then discuss all these things more concretely.

I look forward to your letter with much interest.

All the best,

Yours,
Ch. Weizmann

Mr. I. Yasinovsky,
Warsaw.

17. To Joseph Lurie, Warsaw. *Geneva, 17 November 1902*

Russian: Or. Copy. H.W.: W.A.

Geneva, Rue Lombard 4.
17 Nov. 02.

Dr. J. Lurie,
Warsaw.

Dear Comrade,

You must more or less know from the Press how things are progressing. In a few days, after I meet Feiwel, I shall write to you in

16. [1] Yasinovsky took part in the Annual Zionist Conference in Vienna at the end of October.

detail. What has happened to the Hebrew brochure?[1] Please do what you can to hasten its publication. How is יוד?[2]

Reply at once to

Your Ch. W.

18. To Berthold Feiwel, Zurich. *Geneva, 17 November 1902*

German: Or. Copy. H.W.: W.A.

Geneva, Rue Lombard 4.
17 Nov. 02.

My dear Berthold,

For the past two days I have not been feeling very well and was therefore unable to work or write. Many thanks for your letters and the other things you sent me.[1]

Survey. I have studied the questionnaire and will send you my [comments] tomorrow. In my opinion it would be preferable to separate the subjective questions from those of an objective nature. [-] the [attitude towards the Jewish University], and towards anti-semitism, etc., to [be printed] on a separate sheet for distribution only after the simplest questions have been answered. In addition, I would also like to [make] the following suggestion: that we con-duct a survey of *all* students from Russia and compile the data relating to Jewish students from the returns: we shall then be able to draw various parallels and make comparisons.[2] We shall thus have an additional [opportunity] for publishing the [entire] material in one of the foremost Russian periodicals and thereby [gain] its sympathy for our cause.

I have not had answers either from [Buber or] Kasteliansky, and in Berlin everything gets dragged out beyond belief.[3] I already

17. [1] Reference to the Hebrew translation of *Eine Jüdische Hochschule*—see Vol. I, n. 4 to No. 269.

[2] Yidd.: *Yud* (Jew). In Dec. 1902 the 'Ahiasaf' company sold the Yiddish weekly *Der Yud* to its editor Joseph Lurie, who resold it immediately to the proprietors of the new daily *Der Fraind*, which was launched in St. Petersburg in Jan. 1903 and whose editorial board Lurie himself joined.

18. [1] Feiwel to W., undated (W.A. No. 30/0, 36). Feiwel enclosed a draft of the questionnaire for the student survey. No further letter from Feiwel around this time has been found.

[2] See n. 8 to No. 3. In fact, the questionnaire distributed was meant for Jewish students only.

[3] W. had ordered notepaper for the Jewish University Bureau in Berlin, as well as a

regret asking Lilien to do the emblem.[4] After all, one can get along without it just as well, and we would have the notepaper by now: now a few more weeks will pass before salvation comes.

So *Trietsch* will be speaking in Zurich on Saturday, and here on Sunday. The spirit prevailing among the Zionists of Berne is such that I doubt very much whether he will be able to have a meeting there.[5] News will reach us tomorrow morning from Biel and Basle, and this I will pass on to you by telegram.[6] My own visit to Zurich on Sunday is off—I have to be here. It would be marvellous if you could come here. I have absolutely no money at the moment; not until next week. Maybe God can help: perhaps he is helping you?[7] You [can imagine ---- ----] and Vera will be happy. I shall send you *Altneuland*[8] tomorrow.

Prof. Wertheimer[9] here wrote about the University project to Claude Montefiore of London and Senator Levi Montefiore [---- -------] these people very well, and hopes to [win] them over to the cause.

Affaire Schauer: answers to my circulated letter[10] have arrived [from ---- ----] Berlin,[11] the others are still to come.

Tomorrow I hope finally to get a typewriter and will [then] attend to various things.

1) Should I write to Herzl about Zangwill?[12] Should I approach him [----] regarding contact with London? Do please answer this question.

---

second edition of the brochure *Eine Jüdische Hochschule*. Davis Trietsch agreed to look after these matters. W. had also asked Kasteliansky to draw up the questionnaire for the student survey (see No. 9).

[4] See n. 2 to No. 13.

[5] Probably a reference to the tension prevailing in Berne Zionist circles as a result of the *Yom Kippur* incident (see n. 1 to No. 10).

[6] On 12 Nov. 1902 W. wrote to Julius Meyer in Basle about Davis Trietsch's propaganda trip to Switzerland and about the Schauer affair (the letter has not been found, but see J. Meyer to W., 16 Nov. 1902, W.A.). No correspondence has been found between W. and anyone in Biel.

[7] In the letter mentioned in n. 1 above, Feiwel said that if necessary he would come to Geneva with Esther Shneerson and Trietsch.

[8] Reference to Herzl's recently published novel *Altneuland* describing Palestine in 1923, after its settlement by the Jews (see Theodor Herzl, *Altneuland*, first published in Leipzig, 1902).

[9] Joseph Wertheimer, Chief Rabbi of Geneva.

[10] Circular dated 12 Nov. 1902 (see n. 2 to No. 10).

[11] The original probably read: 'were received from Basle and Berlin'. See Glikin to W., 15 Nov. 1902, W.A.; Wortsman to W., 12 Nov. 1902 (No. 29/11/12), W.A. Glikin in Berlin gave the names of six Fraction members who were prepared to sign the reply to Schauer's article. Wortsman in Basle gave permission for his signature to be added.

[12] See No. 8. Feiwel replied on 18 Nov. 1902 (W.A.) that he was on good terms with Zangwill and did not require Herzl's intervention.

2) When should the letters to the professors, etc.,[13] go out ? It is a pity that Buber doesn't write.

Mandels[14] wrote to me about Glikin; he would like to come here very much. You might well make use of him; if Shriro would come soon, then [---- ----] a combination; but without Shriro nothing can be done, and he will not be here before December.[15] Perhaps you can advise.

Pinkus sent me his essay on Foundations.[16] At first, that is the first ten pages, I rather liked it, but later it turned out to be much too much. First Sombart (poor chap), and secondly this ultra-materialistic point of view and colossal ignorance or ignoring[17] of Jewish history. He plagues me to do something about getting the *Jüdischer Verlag* to publish the essay.[18] This is asking too much. What do you think ? He says that you expressed yourself favourably on the article. Please do not forget to write me your honest opinion, although I can guess![19]

Warmest regards to Esther
And embraces[20] from

Your devoted
Chaim

Cheirus[21] is planning another conference.[22] What is the meaning of all these goings on ?

[13] See n. 9 to No. 13.

[14] Abraham Mandels, a student at the Berlin Polytechnic, was a member of the *Kadimah* Society and of the Democratic Fraction. The letter mentioned here has not been found.

[15] In the letter mentioned in n. 1 above Feiwel wrote that in view of his burden of work in connection with the University project, they might consider employing a secretary in Zurich. W. proposes Glikin for the position, but it implied that this would involve additional financial help from Samuel Shriro.

[16] This is a reference to Pinkus's essay 'The Modern Jewish Question: on the fundamentals of Jewish economic history and Zionism' (see n. 6 to No. 8). Pinkus's essay includes many quotations and definitions from Werner Sombart's *Der Moderne Kapitalismus*, first published in Leipzig, 1902. Sombart (1863–1941) regarded the Jews as the founders of modern capitalism.

[17] In the original: 'Ignorierung(anz)'.

[18] See Pinkus to W., 15 Nov. 1902, W.A. Pinkus's first letter on this subject, in which he probably mentioned the matter of the *Jüdischer Verlag*, has not been found (see No. 8).

[19] This matter is not mentioned in Feiwel's reply of 20 Nov. 1902 (W.A.).

[20] In original: 'Nun sei vielmals geküsst'.

[21] Or *Herut*. Hebrew script in the original, meaning 'Freedom'.

[22] The *Cheirus* (*Herut*) association was founded at the time of the Fifth Zionist Congress (Dec. 1901). The immediate purpose of the founders, one of whom was W., was to organize the Jewish masses in London for a campaign to compel the Jewish Colonization Association (I.C.A.) to set aside funds for the achievement of Zionist goals (see Vol. I, n. 4 to No. 152). The initiators of the association, socialist-Zionists grouped around Nahman Syrkin, envisaged a broader programme that would stimulate Zionism among the Jewish masses in various countries and organize their struggle

19. To Martin Buber, Vienna. *Geneva, 20 November 1902*

German: Or. Copy. H.W.: W.A.

Geneva, Rue Lombard 4.
20/Nov. 02.

My dear Martin,[1]

Naturally I want to join the committee. From here I can hardly say whether anything can be done in Russia. Motzkin is there at this very moment and should be able to do something. It is best that *you* write to him. His address is: Number 28, Mariisko-Blagoveshahanskaya, Kiev.[2] He pays very little attention to me now. I would, in addition, send letters signed by the committee to Tschlenow, Kohan-Bernstein, Idelson. I am writing immediately to Nemirovsky in Kharkov and to another person in Russia.[3]

University: When writing to Motzkin you can also ask him what he has done, or intends to do, for the University project. I am waiting impatiently for Trietsch, who should be here any day now, in order to get new brochures and 'the notepaper'.[4] We are now preparing the survey and are working on the questionnaire. We hope that by next week we shall have reached the stage of being able to send it to the printers.[5] Unfortunately, nothing has been done so

against the Jewish bourgeoisie. The group's thesis was that Zionism could succeed only through the medium of the Jewish masses and only if its aims ensured the satisfaction of the social and economic needs of these masses. Others, including Isidore Eliashev and Feiwel, wanted the association to be limited to the struggle against I.C.A. No principles, constitution, or platform had been formulated at the foundation of *Cheirus*, and in Nov. 1902 Syrkin's group sponsored a conference to remedy these shortcomings and work out a programme of action. Perelman wrote W. on 15 Nov. 1902 (W.A.) asking him to take part in the conference; according to him W. had promised to send Syrkin 100 francs for *Cheirus* after his return from Russia. See pamphlets of *Herut* in Hebrew translation in *The Writings of Nahman Syrkin*, ed. B. Katzenelson and Y. Kaufman, Tel Aviv, 1938/9, pp. 77–93, and the article 'The *Herut* Federation', ibid., pp. 191–7; see also circular of *Herut* of Nov. 1902 (W.A., No. 29/0, 12) and letter from Eliashev to W. of 7 Dec. 1902 (W.A.). For the *Herut* Conference see n. 1 to No. 137.

19. [1] Buber wrote to W. on 16 Nov. 1902 and 18 Nov. 1902 (W.A.). In the first letter Buber explained that he had not written because of illness, but that he had already taken steps (to enlist the support of university people in Vienna for the Jewish University project). He reported that 'the university lecturer Pineles will do his all for the cause' and promised to send W. a list of professors soon (see n. 1 to No. 13). In his letter of 18 Nov. 1902 Buber asked if W. would agree to join a committee set up in Vienna to help Nathan Birnbaum pay his debts, and whether he would sign a public appeal on the subject.

[2] In the original the address is also given in Russian.

[3] See No. 20. No further letter from W. about help for Birnbaum has been found.

[4] See n. 3 to No. 18.

[5] Feiwel had sent W. his own draft of the questionnaire—see Feiwel to W., undated (W.A. 30/0, 36).

far to draw in professorial circles. What does Dr. Pineles want to do now ?[6] Please write in detail for once. We must see to it that by Easter we have committees in Vienna, Berlin, Paris, London and Brussels, all consisting of prominent people, so that we can then come out with a really imposing list. Apart from the survey this is the most important question. Otherwise we shan't move. You and you alone must solve this problem. You are capable of it, dear Martin, if you work energetically.

I am happy to be of service in every other respect, such as correspondence,[7] fund-raising, propaganda, etc. Martin, I beg of you, get some work done! Never did the University undertaking seem to me of such tremendous importance as now, when we are going through such a crisis.[8] Surely you share this view. How are things going with Prof. Warburg of Berlin ?

We must make sure we find an illustrious name for Vienna. Kellner might[9] [----] do. What would you think of Notnagel ?[10]

Dear Martin, I urge you to write me at once concerning all your proposals in this regard. I shall begin making arrangements for your trip, and will duly notify you about it[11] as soon as the Trietsch business is settled.[12] He is now in Switzerland.

Kindest regards from

Your Chaim

Vera sends warm greetings.

20. To Alexander Nemirovsky, Kharkov. *Geneva, 20 November 1902*

Russian: Or. Copy. H.W.: W.A.

Geneva, Rue Lombard 4.
20. XI. 02.

Mr. A. Y. Nemirovsky,
Kharkov.

Dear Alexander Yakovlevitch,

Not a word from you now, but I dare not complain in case you

[6] See n. 1 above. Friedrich Pineles (1868–1936) was a lecturer in medicine at Vienna University.   [7] In the original: 'Schreiberei'.

[8] W. probably meant the crisis caused by the breakdown of Herzl's negotiations with the Turkish authorities over a concession for Jewish settlement in Palestine— see Vol. I, n. 3 to No. 320.

[9] Leon Kellner was a lecturer in English at Vienna University.

[10] Herman Notnagel (1841–1905), Professor of Medicine at Vienna University. He was head of an association against antisemitism, but was opposed to Zionism.

[11] In his letter of 16 Nov. 1902 Buber had asked, 'What about the lectures ?'— an allusion to his offer to undertake a propaganda tour in Switzerland—cf. his letter of 12 Nov. 1902, W.A.

[12] Reference to arrangements for Trietsch's propaganda trip to Switzerland.

bring up my old sins,[1] and then I shall really come out of it very badly. But it is most annoying not hearing anything from anybody. Misha,[2] Dr. Breslav, everybody, they all maintain an eloquent silence.

Dr. Birnbaum has written that he sent two pages of manuscript and would very much like you to send him an advance payment so that he can continue his work.[3] He picked me as go-between because I am acquainted with you personally. Let me add that I know for certain that Dr. B. *needs money very badly* at this moment. However, the attached copy of Buber's letter to me, received today, will best clarify [----] this situation for you.[4] Is it possible to do something for Birnbaum in Kharkov?

I shall remain here for another month and will then be going to Brussels–London–Paris for the Christmas holidays. Some promising developments may occur in these cities with regard to the University, and I am going to sound out the position.[5] What is new with you? Let me have Dr. Breslav's address, for heaven's sake, and please give Mishka a good scolding for me. My warmest regards to him nevertheless.

Heartfelt greetings to Henrietta L'vovna and Maria L'vovna.

All the very best to you,

Your Chaim

21. To Abraham Kasteliansky, Berlin. *Geneva, 20 November 1902*

Russian: Or. Copy. H.W.: W.A.

Geneva, Rue Lombard 4.
20. xi. 02.

Mr. A. Kasteliansky,
Berlin.

Dear Comrade,

Why this silence?[1] In point of fact the survey business should be

---

20. [1] Reference to W.'s failure to reply to Nemirovsky's request of 1901 to obtain contributors for his proposed 'Encyclopaedia' on Zionism (see n. 10 to No. 2; No. 215).

[2] Michael Aleinikov.

[3] Birnbaum wrote an article for Nemirovsky's book. His letter to W. has not been found.

[4] See n. 1 to No. 19. Buber's letter referred to here is the one of 18 Nov. 1902 (W.A.).

[5] The journey did not take place then. For W.'s intention to set up Jewish University Committees in the cities mentioned here, see No. 19.

21. [1] See No. 9.

of no less interest to you than to me. Have you received the *Frage-bogen*[2] yet? Did you get in touch with Nossig? I await your answer,

Best wishes,

Yours,

Ch. Weizmann

Stiff read a paper in Kiev which caused quite a sensation.[3] Bulgakov[4] and Ratner are very [enthusiastic] about it.

22. To William Evans-Gordon, London. *Geneva, 24 November 1902*

German: Or. Copy. T.W.: W.A.

Geneva, 4 rue Lombard, 24. XI. 02.

Dear Major,

You will recall that while you were in Pinsk[1] we [spoke] about a project for a Jewish University. I had the honour also to present you with a memorandum on the [subject].[2]

As you are also aware, dear Major, I am about to undertake a journey [---- ---- ---- ---- ----][3] so as to raise the funds required for [the] preparatory work.

[---- ---- ---- ---- ---- ---- ---- ----] of the Jewish University has met with warm approval in almost all sections of the Jewish population.

At present we are intensively engaged in the detailed working out of the project, in order to attract the interest of influential Jewish circles in Western Europe on behalf of this highly important undertaking. If given the opportunity, I would also like to approach the Board of Education in London so as to inform myself on the possibility of implementing our plan in England.[4]

You were kind enough at that time to indicate that I might call upon your valued support; and so, with respect, I am approaching

---

[2] Feiwel sent Kasteliansky his draft questionnaire—see n. 5 to No. 7.

[3] Probably a reference to Nahum Stiff's reply to Bickerman's anti-Zionist article (see Vol. I, n. 3 to No. 301). Stiff failed to get his article published and read it at public lectures in Kiev and Warsaw at the end of 1902. See Memoirs of Stiff in *Yivo Bletter*, vol. 5 (New York, 1933), 3–5, p. 197.

[4] Sergei Bulgakov (1871–1944) was Professor of Economics and Statistics at the Kiev Polytechnic. A non-Jew, he was a Socialist at that time.

22. [1] See Vol. I, No. 317 and n. 3 there.

[2] Probably the brochure *Eine Jüdische Hochschule*.

[3] Not legible in the original. Apparently a reference to W.'s plan to visit London (see No. 20 and n. 5 there).

[4] I.e. establishing the Jewish University there.

you with a request for advice on whether my visit to London would in your judgment be useful at Christmas-time.

I would also inform you that we are now seeking to win Sir[5] Claude Montefiore[6] over to our plan.

Most respectfully yours,

and with kind regards,

Dr. Ch. Weizmann

23. To Boris Greidenberg, Kharkov. *Geneva,* *24 (?) November 1902*

German: Or. Copy. T.W.: W.A.

[24 Nov. 1902][1]

Dear Dr. [Greidenberg],

Since leaving Kharkov I have written to Dr. Breslav among [others][2] concerning the Jewish University, but alas, I have so far received no news whatever [regarding] the progress of this matter in Kharkov. You will, therefore, forgive me for [imposing] on your valuable time to ask for information about activities in Kharkov.[3] May I also take this opportunity to inform you that we [---- ---- ---- ---- ---- ---- ----] and can already report some real success. Thus [---- ---- ---- ---- ----] to attract from [among] influential [academic] circles in Vienna and Berlin. The survey has already begun [and we are now] preparing for a journey to London. We have prospects of interesting Claude Montefiore in the cause.[4]

We will shortly be taking the liberty of sending you, for background information, the questionnaire intended for foreign students.

The Russian translation of our brochure has been sent to Mr. Nemirovsky,[5] and I would respectfully suggest that the Kharkov Committee [undertake] its publication.

Would you kindly inform me how the Committee has been constituted, whether meetings have taken place and with what success,

---

[5] In fact Claude Montefiore did not have a title.

[6] See No. 18.

23. [1] Address and date are unclear in the original. The date has been presumed from the letter's position in the letter-book.

[2] See Nos. 2, 3, 4, 20.

[3] Greidenberg was chairman of the Kharkov Committee for a Jewish University.

[4] See No. 18.

[5] See n. 11 to No. 7. In his letter of 7/20 Nov. 1902 (W.A.) Hirsch Hiller of Pinsk told W. that the Russian translation of the brochure *Eine Jüdische Hochschule* had been completed and sent to Alexander Nemirovsky in Kharkov.

and whether my journey to Kharkov during the [Easter] vacation will be necessary.

Most respectfully and with kind regards, I am,

Yours truly,
Dr. Ch. Weizmann

[6]Dr. S. Greidenberg,
Kharkov.

24. To Isaac Rothstein, Rostov. *Geneva, 24 November 1902*

Russian: Or. Copy. H.W.: W.A.

Geneva, 24 Nov. 02.
Rue Lombard 4.

Dear Friend,

Everything is done so haphazardly in Vienna that I have [----] still had no information about the receipt of money, nor have I been sent your letter.[1] [---- ----] all corresponding steps. I and [---- ----] Resolution as a failure;[2] I am convinced that the Zionist Organisation regards [---- ---- ----] when [----].

Here we do everything possible to [---- ----] the ground [---- ----] obey and then terribly [---- ----].

I receive no [news], either from Baku or from Kharkov. All my enquiries[3] remain unanswered; even to me [---- ----] from all sides [---- ---- ----]. In the meantime, the work is being hindered in a most incredible fashion and time is being lost.

At Christmas I shall be going to London,[4] really just to reconnoitre, and after London I shall put out a circular.

[6] The address is in W.'s handwriting. Several of the letters to Greidenberg are erroneously addressed to 'S. Greidenberg'. His real name was Boris Saulevitch Greidenberg.

24. [1] In his letter of 31 Oct. (13 Nov.) 1902 (W.A.) Rothstein told W. that he had written to him some time before, care of the editorial office of *Die Welt* in Vienna, and that at about the same time he had sent Herzl a cheque for 256 roubles to be deposited with the Jewish Colonial Trust and credited to the Jewish University Bureau. This was the balance of 356 roubles donated for the Bureau in Rostov; the remainder had been sent direct to W.

[2] In his letter of 31 Oct. (13 Nov.) 1902 Rothstein described the resolution on the Jewish University adopted at the Annual Zionist Conference as a 'failure' (the Conference did not approve the resolution proposed by W. and Buber, and made its support of the project conditional on the university's being located in Palestine—see Vol. I, n. 4 to No. 320).

[3] See Nos. 1, 2, 3, 4.   [4] See No. 20 and n. 5 there.

1) Committees in Vienna and Berlin may well be organised as early as the new year.

2) Statistical research on the Jewish student body will be started with a survey soon after the Christmas holidays. We are already [printing] the leaflets.

3) We have succeeded in finding a way to Claude Montefiore in London (he is president of I.C.A.).[5] I don't know yet what will come of it.

4) The Russian text of the brochure has already gone through the censor. It is being published in Kharkov.[6]

I shall let you have some questionnaires as soon as they are printed. This is all I can tell you so far. You were thinking of organising monthly contributions for the *Bureau Hochschule*. Is this feasible? Please let me know. Don't give people a chance to cool off. As for me, I shall share all my news with you. You must do the same.

Keep well, dear friend.

With affection,
Chaim.

Greetings from Vera to you and Maria Grigorievna, to whom my own best wishes.

Mr. Rothstein,
  Rostov-on-Don.

25. To the Editorial Department, *Die Welt*, Vienna.

25 November 1902

German: H.W.: C.Z.A. Z1/340

Geneva, Rue Lombard 4.
25/XI. 02.

The Editorial Department, *Die Welt*,
Vienna.

May I take the liberty of requesting publication of the enclosed declaration.[1]

Most respectfully and with Zion's greetings.

Dr. Ch. Weizmann

[5] Wertheimer had written to Claude Montefiore—see No. 18. Montefiore was at this time a member of the I.C.A. (Jewish Colonization Association) executive, but not its president.

[6] See n. 5 to No. 23.

25. [1] This is a declaration by the Democratic Fraction against Schauer's article

[*Footnote 1 continued on p. 32*

26. To Michael Altschul, Berlin. *Geneva, 26 November 1902*

German: Or. Copy. T.W.: W.A.

Geneva, 26. 11. 02.

Dr. M. Altschul,
Berlin.

Dear Friend,

I know you are very busy, but your persistent silence might also be attributed to writing inertia.

At one time it was still possible to obtain an answer from you, though with difficulty. Now, however, things seem to have become worse. I am hoping that you will respond to my third letter.[1] You know very well how your reply interests me.

[Have] you spoken to Mme. Professor Pictet? Ought I to write to her again?

I am going to London for Christmas on University[2] business and would like to be in possession of your letter by then. Therefore do pull yourself together, dear Doctor, and write to one who greets you most warmly.

Dr. Ch. Weizmann

27. To Theodor Herzl, Vienna. *Geneva, 26 November 1902*

German: T.W.: C.Z.A. Z1/339

Geneva, 4 rue Lombard,
26. 11. 02.

Dear Dr. [Herzl],

May I take the liberty of enquiring whether monies sent to your address from Rostov and Baku for the University Bureau have already been received.[1]

(see n. 1 to No. 10). Written by Feiwel (see his letter of 13 Nov. 1902, W.A.), it comprises a sharp protest against the article itself, a refutation of Schauer's claims and a personal attack on him. It is signed by Abraham Idelson, Michael Kroll, Pesah Marek (in the original erroneously 'A. Marek') representing the Fraction's bureau in Moscow, and Zvi Aberson, Berthold Feiwel and W. for the Fraction's Geneva Bureau. In addition there are forty signatories (mostly students), who had agreed in advance to put their names to the protest. The original (including signatures) in W.'s hand is in C.Z.A. Z1/340. The declaration was not published in *Die Welt* (see n. 6 to No. 83).

26. [1] See No. 14 and n. 1 there.   [2] See n. 5 to No. 20.

27. [1] For the contribution from Rostov, see n. 1 to No. 24. The sum collected in Baku for the University was not transferred until December—see No. 86 and n. 2 there.

According to our agreement these sums were to be deposited in the Jewish Colonial Trust.[2] Would you kindly let me know what formalities are required to have the Colonial Trust release part of the money.[3]

We shall shortly be taking the liberty of sending you a detailed report on the progress of our activities in the University Bureau.[4]

Most respectfully and with Zion's greetings,

Yours,
Dr. Ch. Weizmann

[5]Dr. Th. Herzl,
Vienna.

28. To Michael Aleinikov, Kharkov. *Geneva, 27 November 1902*

Russian: Or. Copy. H.W.: W.A.

Geneva, 27th. Nov. 02.
Rue Lombard 4.

Dear Misha,

This letter should really begin with some classic oaths addressed to your honoured self, but I shall be gracious for once and let it go. Nevertheless I find it disgraceful [----] why all of you should keep your silence. I have not heard a sound from Kharkov. Is it possible that everything has gone dead? I wrote to you, Dr. Greidenberg, Breslav, Al. Yak.[1] Not a word from anyone.

This is of course an ominous sign, and I have no doubt at all that literally nothing has been done in Kharkov to this day. I had at the very least expected that the students, who should be the most concerned in a matter so very close to them, would be more responsive than they have proved.[2]

---

[2] This was probably agreed upon during W.'s visit to Vienna at the end of October. Herzl undertook to act as trustee of donations to the University Bureau (see Herzl to W., 20 Dec. 1903, W.A.).

[3] In reply to this letter Arieh Reich, treasurer of the Vienna Zionist Society, advised that Isaac Rothstein had sent 646 Austrian crowns for the University Bureau to Herzl, who had transferred the money to the Jewish Colonial Trust, to the account of 'Dr. Herzl, Jewish University', but had not yet given instructions about drawing from this account (see Reich to W., 2 Dec. 1902, W.A.).

[4] The report was in fact sent early in Jan. 1903 (see No. 173).

[5] In W.'s handwriting.

28. [1] See Nos. 2, 4, 20, 23.

[2] Aleinikov was himself a student at the time.

I won't shower you with questions. You know perfectly well exactly what interests me, and to what degree.

I hear from Pinsk that [---- ----] Al. Yak.[3] has been sent the manuscript of the Russian translation of the *Hochschule* [brochure].

How do you intend to use it ? Has the money, which will be very, very badly needed, been subscribed ?

In a month's time I shall be leaving for England. I shall stop in Brussels and Paris[4] on the way. I think we may net a few aces of the highest order.

In Vienna and Berlin we have succeeded in clearing some paths into equally exalted places.

For God's sake, Misha, don't let our project die! I consider the University to be an undertaking of the utmost importance. Especially now, when Zionism is going through a crisis[5] [---- ---- ----] in Israel.

[Your] Chaim

Greetings [to all].

29. To Michael Futran, Kharkov. *Geneva, 27 November 1902*

Russian: Or. Copy. H.W.: W.A.

Geneva, Rue Lombard 4.
27. XI. 02.

Dr. M. I. Futran,
Kharkov.

Dear Michael Ignatievitch,

[----] I have been waiting to hear from you as to how things were going. Soon after my return here I wrote to our comrades in Kharkov,[1] but unfortunately received no[2] reply. I am writing to you now in the hope that I shall be more fortunate [----] learn something of what has been done in Kharkov until now. I [---- ----] you, dear Doctor, put [----] question. You will understand that whatever concerns our enterprise [----] in your city is of great interest to me.

On our part we are keeping strictly to the programme as outlined. Statistical research has already begun and by the new year the questionnaires (about 3,500 in all) will have been sent out. We are

---

[3] Nemirovsky. See n. 5 to No. 23.
[4] See n. 5 to No. 20.   [5] See n. 9 to No. 19.

29. [1] See Nos. 2, 3, 4.
[2] The negative is missing in the original, but the context indicates that this was accidental.

still looking for people to join our large committee,[3] and in Vienna as well as Berlin two major organisations will be founded: *Jüdische Hochschule* [---- ---- ---- ----] of very influential people.[4] In another month I shall be leaving for London, Brussels and Paris[5] [---- ---- ---- ---- ---- ----] Claude and Levi Montefiore (the latter is the founder of the Electro-Technical Institute in Liège) in our project.[6] Dr. Herzl has agreed to join the *Hochschulcomité*.[7]

I would very much like to put a few questions to you but am refraining from doing so. For God's sake, Michael Ignatievitch, don't let our project die! You could do so much in Kharkov if only you were inclined; and our work is of sacred importance! I shall not wax lyrical since I am well aware that the University idea is as attractive to you as it is to me.

Warmest greetings,

Yours,

Chaim Weizmann

30. To Abraham Idelson and Michael Kroll, Moscow.

Geneva, 27 November 1902

German: Or. Copy. T.W.: W.A.

Geneva, rue Lombard 4, 27 11. 02.

Dr. M. Kroll and Mr. A. Idelson,
Moscow.

Dear Friends,

To begin, deepest thanks for your kind reply[1] to my letter.[2] I will first of all deal only with that part of it [relating] to the University.

---

[3] I.e. the Central Committee for a Jewish University (see n. 3 to No. 1).
[4] I.e. the local committees planned for these cities—cf. No. 30.
[5] See n. 5 to No. 20.   [6] See No. 18.
[7] 'University Committee.' For Herzl's promise, see n. 2 to No. 1.

30. [1] Kroll to W., 4 (17) Nov. 1902, W.A. Kroll wrote on behalf also of Idelson and Marek, his associates in the Moscow centre of the Democratic Fraction. His letter is devoted mainly to the problem of Zionist propaganda in Russia. Kroll said that the Moscow group was willing to help draw up the questionnaire for Russian students. He told W. that he had sent Poliakov the brochure *Eine Jüdische Hochschule*, and asked him whether he could tell Poliakov about the possibility of a large donation for the University from the industrialist Brodsky (see Vol. I, No. 319 and n. 6 there). He also wanted to know if money should be raised for the Geneva Bureau, advised that the platform of the Democratic Fraction had been translated into Russian (cf. Vol. I, No. 304 and n. 1 there), and asked W. to send him a list of Democratic Fraction members as well as the text of his speeches on his Russian tour (Aug.–Oct. 1902).   [2] See No. 7.

Since I wrote you last, affairs have not [progressed] very much. You are well aware that the [---- ---- ---- ---- ---- ---- ---- ---- ---- ---- ----] I am as yet without any report [concerning] the activities of the gentlemen in Kharkov. The money raised in Baku[3] has still not come in, you can imagine how [----] this is hindering our activities. On my part everything was done for the commencement of work in each locality.

1) *Survey.* The proposed questionnaire is now finished and will be sent to the printers this week. It will be ready in 14 days probably, and then we shall mail it to you. Of course, you will have to adapt the questionnaire to the situation in Russia. Please [alert] all your correspondents [in] the University cities at once to the fact that [you too will shortly] be sending [---- ---- ---- ---- ---- ---- ---- ---- ---- ---- ---- ----]. I believe you will be better able to judge which questions are of importance when you receive the form. I have already notified you about Aleinikov being entrusted[4] with University matters in Kharkov. My brother's address in Kiev is: Weizmann, care of Jek. Dascovskaya, Vladimirskaya 79.[5]

Please let me know whether you need some [money] to conduct the survey. Although our Centre has heavy expenses which we hope our friends will take into account, I may be able to place some resources at your disposal.

2) *Fund-raising.* [---- ---- ---- ---- ---- ----] collect a great deal of money for the preparatory work. We are faced with several long [journeys] to England, and possibly [to America]. You can imagine to what degree we are in need of funds here. Start a subscription campaign and deposit the monies in the Colonial Trust. I believe that Moscow can support us with a considerable sum. This matter must be dealt with as urgently as possible.

3) *Enrolment of co-workers.* Unfortunately, you make no mention in your last letter of the results of negotiations with Minor; did you speak to Poliakov? What other people are [possible prospects]? Do write something, please, about [Dr. Tschlenow's attitude].[6] Over here [we] have reached the point where by Easter we should have committees of prominent personalities in Berlin and Vienna. I am

---

[3] In Baku W. had received pledges of more than 4,000 roubles for the University Bureau—see Vol. I, bridge-note following No. 317.

[4] In the original: 'Vertrauensmann'.

[5] In the letter mentioned in n. 1 above, Kroll had wondered why W. had given him Aleinikov's Kharkov address (see No. 7), and asked for the address of W.'s brother Moses in Kiev.

[6] In his reply of 21 Dec. 1902 (3 Jan. 1903) W.A., Kroll did not write about Tschlenow's attitude on the University project, but several months later he advised W. that Tschlenow and his circle were absolutely opposed to a Jewish University anywhere but in Palestine—see Kroll to W., 20 Apr. (3 May) 1903, W.A.

going [to] London, Brussels and Paris for Christmas[7] and, to judge by all that we now know about them, I hope to be able to form groups of co-workers in these cities also. Naturally, I shall keep you informed of developments.

4) A separate reply will be sent to the other questions raised in your letter.[8]

With the request that you complete the tasks noted above [--------] and heartfelt greetings,

Yours ever,

31. To Max Bodenheimer, Cologne. *Geneva, 28 November 1902*

German: Or. Copy. T.W.: W.A.

Geneva, 4 rue Lombard, 28 11. 02.

Dr. Bodenheimer, Attorney,
Cologne.

Dear Fellow-Zionist,

In reply to your esteemed letter,[1] permit me to inform you that my friends and I cannot, in any circumstances, be satisfied with a correction on the part of Dr. Schauer. We consider it necessary to reply to the gentleman in our 'non-partisan' organ.[2] Enclosed is a copy of our article, which will bear many more signatures, intended for *Die Welt*.[3]

Even after this the Schauer matter will not be considered by us as closed, because we feel compelled to put an end, once and for all, to such enormities.

[7] See n. 5 to No. 20.

[8] See n. 1 above. W. wrote to Kroll again on 28 Nov. 1902 (see No. 35) and to Kroll and Idelson on 2 Dec. 1902 (see No. 50), but these letters do not supply any further answers to Kroll's letter of 4 (17) Nov. 1902.

31. [1] Bodenheimer to W., 19 Nov. 1902, W.A. Bodenheimer was replying to W.'s letter of 15 Nov. 1902 (see No. 12), about Schauer's article (see n. 1 to No. 10). Bodenheimer said he had asked Schauer to publish a statement in *Der Israelit* that would satisfy W. He expressed reservations about Schauer's attack on the Democratic Fraction, but emphasized that the responsibility should not be placed on the German Zionist Organization. He added that he was willing, if W. desired, to ensure that the Organization issue a public disclaimer, but hoped it would be enough if Schauer put things in their true light.

[2] Reference to *Die Welt*.

[3] See n. 1 to No. 25.

From this moment on the position that the German national organization will take on this subject is of complete indifference to us.

Most respectfully,
With Zion's greetings,

32. To Davis Trietsch, Berlin. *Geneva, 28 November 1902*

German: Or. Copy. T.W.: W.A.

Geneva, 4 rue Lombard, 28 11. 02.

Mr. D. Trietsch,
Berlin.

Dear Friend,

Today I received news from Pinsk that 125 roubles have been sent to Lilien's address.[1]

I should think that this money must already be in your possession, and ask you to pay 100 marks to the printers and 60 marks to the news agency. By the way, the Bureau never sends out cuttings from Jewish newspapers. Dr. Goldschmidt[2] should therefore receive an appropriate kick.

No notepaper has arrived from Frankfurt,[3] and this leads me to believe that Lilien has once again made a solemn promise to finish the emblem immediately.[4] Please notify me by telegram whether the notepaper and brochures have been posted. If I receive no reply by Monday, I shall order the notepaper here. I can assure you that this has caused me enough annoyance already. Our work here is being held up and impeded. Please write, dear Trietsch, how things went in Mannheim and Frankfurt.[5]

Warmest greetings,
Your

32. [1] Apparently a reference to funds collected in Pinsk for the University Bureau and sent to Lilien in accordance with W.'s instructions. W. promised to send Trietsch enough money to cover printing costs (for the Bureau's stationery and the second edition of *Eine Jüdische Hochschule*) and for the subscription to a press-cutting agency (see n. 2 below). Trietsch asked W. to send the money to him or to Lilien (see Trietsch to W., 12 Nov. 1902, W.A.). The sum mentioned here does not appear in the University Bureau's balance sheet of 15 July 1903 (W.A.). It is not known who sent the money to Lilien and who notified W. of this.

[2] Max Goldschmidt—owner of the press-cutting agency used by the University. The annual subscription was 60 marks (see Feiwel to W., 9 Nov. 1902, W.A.).

[3] This must be an error, and should read 'from Berlin'.

[4] See n. 2 to No. 13. Lilien never delivered the awaited design.

[5] Reference to Trietsch's propaganda speeches in these cities. See his letter to W. of 28 Nov. 1902, W.A.

33. To Isidore (Israel) Yasinovsky, Warsaw. *Geneva, 28 November 1902*

Russian: Or. Copy. H.W.: W.A.

Geneva, 28. XI. 02.
Rue Lombard 4.

Mr. Isidore Vladimirovich Yasinovsky,
Warsaw.

Dear Comrade,

Your much appreciated letter came today[1] and I hasten to reply. I shall send you the brochure in a few days. The first edition has already been distributed and we are getting the second [ready]. It should be finished in a few days. You will receive it at once.

We shall also be writing to the people whose addresses you sent us and will inform you of the result without delay.[2] You know best whether you will succeed in interesting any of these people. But there can be no doubt that with your help something can be done in Warsaw. Please explore the territory carefully, dear comrade, and keep us fully informed in the meantime.

Keep well. All the best.

Yours,
Ch. Weizmann

34. To Heinrich Loewe, Berlin. *Geneva, 28 November 1902*

German: Or. Copy. T.W.: W.A.

Geneva, 4 rue Lombard, 28 11. 02.

Dr. H. Loewe,
Berlin.

Dear Friend,

Enclosed is a declaration by the Fraction regarding the article

33. [1] Yasinovsky to W., '12/24 Nov. 1902' (*sic* in original, but should be 12/25 Nov. 1902 or 11/24 Nov. 1902), W.A. Yasinovsky suggested that W. contact a number of persons in Warsaw about the University (Samuel Goldflamm, Maximilian Goldbaum, Samuel Poznansky, Ignaz Bernstein, Samuel Lurie, and Julian Kohn), and that W. send them *Eine Jüdische Hochschule*, with a copy to himself. He felt that the initiative should not come from him, since he was regarded as the Warsaw Zionist leader—'I do not think it necessary for me to introduce every matter coming under the Zionist banner'. He himself would do his best to organise a circle in support of the University.

[2] W. asked Trietsch to send the pamphlet to all those mentioned by Yasinovsky (see n. 1 above) and he himself notified them of its dispatch (see No. 54). Neither originals nor copies of these notifications have been found, but see letter to Goldbaum of 9 Dec. 1902 (No. 71).

appearing in issue number 87 of *Israelit.*[1] May I ask you, dear friend, kindly to publish our declaration in your esteemed paper[2] as soon as possible.

With kind regards,

Your

35. To Michael Kroll, Moscow. *Geneva, 28 November 1902*

Russian: Or. Copy. H.W.: W.A.

Geneva, 28. xi. 02
4 Rue Lombard.

Dr. M. Kroll,
Moscow.

Dear Friend,

Today I am sending you the questionnaires, in two separate envelopes[1] and suggest that you get in touch with our comrades and start collecting the statistical data as soon as possible. It is of supreme importance that in each city you find reliable people who will not only commit themselves to the task but will also carry it out conscientiously. If you think that our Bureau should address an appeal to these people, this can of course be arranged.

Once again, dear comrade, let me call your attention to the contents of my last letter about the *Hochschule.*[2] We shall need money and people. Both can be found in Moscow.

With affection. Regards to Idelson and Marek. I am beginning to think that Id. must have forgotten how to write.

Your Chaim

34. [1] The protest against Schauer's article in *Der Israelit*, which was sent to the editorial office of *Die Welt* on 25 Nov. 1902 (see No. 25 and n. 1 there). For Schauer's article see n. 1 to No. 10.

[2] Loewe was editor of the *Jüdische Rundschau*, the organ of the German Zionist Organization.

35. [1] The student questionnaire was not printed until Dec. 1902, and it seems that W. sent Kroll handwritten copies to enable him to draft the questionnaire for Russia —see No. 30 and also No. 98, where W. writes that he sent Idelson 'an outline of the questionnaire'.

[2] See No. 30.

36. To William Evans-Gordon, London. *Geneva, 29 November 1902*

German: Or. Copy. T.W.: W.A.

Geneva, 29. 11. 02.
4 rue Lombard.

Dear Major,

Deepest thanks for your cordial letter of the 27th.[1] You can well imagine how pleased I am to learn that you are taking so great an interest in our cause.

I do not think it necessary to stress the importance of the matter any further. Having yourself been to Russia[2] you are familiar with the situation there and realise how necessary it is to create an institution of Higher Learning for our youth. I always felt that freedom-loving England would support an objective of this kind.

A letter, together with my brochure, is going simultaneously to Sir[3] Claude Montefiore.[4] As Mr. Montefiore is being approached on the University project[5] from other quarters as well, it would be most appropriate, dear Major, if you would take the opportunity to speak to him about it. I would be delighted to learn the outcome of the conversation from you. What do you think about Lord Rothschild[6] and Lord Mayor Samueli?[7]

I shall write to you shortly about my trip to London.[8]

With warm regards and many thanks,

Yours truly,

Major Evans-Gordon,
London.

---

36. [1] Evans-Gordon's letter has not been found. It would appear he expressed his willingness to support the University project, but advised W. not to come to London during the vacation (see Nos. 38, 66).

[2] See Vol. I, No. 317 and n. 3 there.

[3] See n. 5 to No. 22.

[4] The letter to Claude Montefiore has not been found. For his reply see n. 3 to No. 55.

[5] Reference to a letter from Joseph Wertheimer, Chief Rabbi of Geneva—see No. 18.

[6] Nathaniel Mayer, 1st Lord Rothschild, head of the English branch of the family.

[7] W. is referring to Sir Marcus Samuel, later Lord Bearsted (1853–1927). He was Lord Mayor of London in the year 1902/3.

[8] See No. 66.

37. To Georges Levi Montefiore, Brussels. *Geneva, 29 November 1902*

German: Or. Copy. T.W.: W.A.

Geneva, 29 11. 02, 4 rue Lombard[1]

Dear Sir,[2]

Following upon the letter from Prof. Dr. Wertheimer,[3] the Chief Rabbi here, we take the liberty of sending you our Memorandum concerning the project for a Jewish University. It is accompanied with the respectful request that the pamphlet receive your generous attention.

Since this pamphlet's appearance the Jewish University cause has made considerable progress. The Bureau referred to in the pamphlet, and which is brought to your kind notice,[4] has already begun to function.

In assurance of our esteem,[5] dear Sir,[2]

38. To Martin Buber, Vienna. *Geneva, 1 December 1902*

German: Or. Copy. T.W.: W.A.

Geneva, 1. 12. 02, 4 rue Lombard.

Mr. Martin Buber,
Vienna.

Dear Martin,

Many thanks for your letter of 28 November.[1] I am delighted that you have succeeded in organising a committee in Vienna. It would be highly desirable that you establish direct contact between the gentlemen and the Bureau. It is about time that a fund-raising campaign was started in Vienna, because our needs are going to be

37. [1] The original copy also bears the date 4 Nov. 1902, but there is no doubt that the correct date is as given—see Montefiore's reply of 6 Dec. 1902, W.A.

[2] In the original copy the title 'Senator' appears here in Samuel Levinson's handwriting. Montefiore was a member of the Belgian Senate until 1902.

[3] See No. 18.

[4] Montefiore replied on 6 Dec. 1902 (W.A.), that his many duties precluded him from devoting time to the University project.

[5] In the original copy the name 'Montefiore' has been added at the bottom of the letter in an unidentifiable hand.

38. [1] Buber to W., 28 Nov. 1902, W.A. Buber wrote, *inter alia*, that he had set up a provisional, unofficial committee for the University, which he would convene shortly; Herzl had told him that he would have to consult the S.A.C. about joining this committee (see also n. 1 to No. 92).

considerable. Write again briefly regarding Herzl's attitude. I will, naturally, hold him to his word.[2]

Last week we wrote to Major Gordon.[3] In a most cordial letter he has already declared his support for us at all times in London.[4] Letters have also gone out to Claude and Levi Montefiore.[5] I shall report to you on whatever success ensues.

Nothing new has occurred in the Birnbaum matter.[6]

I shall let you know about the propaganda tour by the 15th.[7]

Good wishes from yours ever,

39. To Julius Blau, Frankfurt-on-Main.[1] *Geneva, 1 December 1902*

German: Or. Copy. T.W.: W.A.

Geneva, 4 rue Lombard, 1. 12. 02.

Dr. Blau, Attorney,
Frankfurt-on-Main.

Dear Dr. [Blau],

According to Mr. Trietsch you are in a position to make some valuable material available to our 'Jewish University' Bureau, and have no objection to our using it.[2]

We would be extremely grateful if you would be so kind as to support our aims in this matter.

Most respectfully,

40. To David Wolffsohn, Cologne. *Geneva, 1 December 1902*

German: T.W.: C.Z.A. W55.

Geneva, 1. 12. 02, 4 rue Lombard.

Mr. D. Wolffsohn,[1]
Cologne.

Dear Fellow-Zionist,

Monies for the 'Jewish University' have gone to the Jewish

[2] Herzl had told W. in October that he agreed to join the University committee—see No. 1. [3] See Nos. 22, 36. [4] See No. 36 and n. 1 there.

[5] See letter to Levi Montefiore of 29 Nov. 1902 (No. 37). For letter to Claude Montefiore see No. 36 and n. 4 there. [6] See n. 1 to No. 19.

[7] Buber's planned Swiss propaganda tour.

39. [1] This letter was drafted by Trietsch after a visit to Frankfurt, and he asked W. to send it in his name to Blau—see Trietsch to W., 28 Nov. 1902, W.A.

[2] It is not known what material is meant. No reply from Blau has been found.

40. [1] Chairman of the Board of the J.C.T.

Colonial Bank.[2] According to our agreement, these sums are to be paid out against a receipt signed by Feiwel and myself.[3] We are sending such a receipt to the Jewish Colonial Trust and respectfully request you to give the necessary instructions for the money to be promptly paid.[4]

May I at the same time inform you that a deposit of 3,000 roubles[5] is being made during the next few days. Would you be so kind as to let me know what interest the money will bear.[6]

With kind regards,

Yours,

Dr. Ch. Weizmann

41. To Davis Trietsch, Berlin. *Geneva, 1 December 1902*

German: Or. Copy. T.W.: W.A.

Geneva, 1. 12. 02.

Mr. D. Trietsch,
Berlin.

Dear Friend,

My sincere thanks for your kind letter.[1] Lilien's behaviour is, frankly, shocking. The time may yet come when **Mr.** Lilien will need

[2] This is the money sent from Rostov (see n. 1 to No. 24).

[3] In fact W. had not yet received a reply from Herzl to his letter of 26 Nov. 1902, in which he asked how to withdraw money deposited with the J.C.T. to the credit of the Bureau (see No. 27 and n. 3 there). At a later date the J.C.T. advised him that Herzl's signature was also required—see No. 65.

[4] Neither the accompanying letter to the J.C.T. nor the J.C.T.'s reply, which W. sent to Feiwel (see No. 65), has been found. The receipt mentioned here is evidently for the sum of 600 francs which W. wanted to draw from the Bureau's account with the J.C.T. (*ibid.*).

[5] Reference to contributions from Baku for the University Bureau. In Baku W. received pledges of over 4,000 roubles (see Vol. I, bridge-note following No. 317). On 13 Dec. W. notified the J.C.T. that he was expecting 2,283 roubles from Baku for the University Bureau (see No. 86). This sum was eventually increased to 2,508 roubles (see the University Bureau's balance-sheet of 15 July 1903, W.A.). Nos. 42, 43 show that when he received no reply from Shriro, W. telegraphed Moses Zeitlin about the money promised, and Zeitlin replied by telegram that it would be sent immediately.

[6] No reply from Wolffsohn has been found.

41. [1] Trietsch to W., 28 Nov. 1902, W.A. Trietsch reported that Lilien had not yet designed the emblem for use on the University Bureau's notepaper and the second edition of *Eine Jüdische Hochschule*. He also enclosed the text of a letter that he wished W. to send to Blau in Frankfurt (see No. 39). He said that he was going to visit Switzerland at the end of January or the beginning of February to lecture on Zionist topics, and that Daniel Pasmanik had suggested that he contact him in this connection since he was in touch with the Swiss Zionist Federation (Pasmanik was then a member of the Federation's executive). Trietsch said that subject to W.'s agreement he proposed to accept Pasmanik's offer.

something from our Bureau, and we shall then recollect his kindness. May I ask you, dear Trietsch, to ensure that the brochures are finished immediately; we shall of course do without the emblem.

A letter has gone off to Dr. Blau. I would be happy if you were to come to an understanding with Pasmanik about your journey, but would request you to keep me informed of the arrangements.

Another difficult request. Please find out why Dr. Altschul, of 109 Brunnenstrasse, has not reacted to my three letters.[2] I fear he may be ill. Glikin is now our employee[3] and can look after this matter. Altschul was to have negotiated with some professors, but my chief interest in him concerns Pictet. Please find out from him without delay. I am striving to raise some money in all directions, and expect to achieve results soon.

With warmest greetings,

Your

42. To Berthold Feiwel, Zurich. *Geneva, 1 December 1902*

German: Or. Copy. T.W.: W.A.

Geneva, 1. 12. 02.

Mr. B. Feiwel,
Zurich.

Dear Berthold,

A telegram has at last come from Baku saying that the money is being sent off today.[1] I am enclosing a letter from Major Gordon,[2] which please return. It has already been suitably answered.[3] Letters have already gone to the Montefiores.[4]

I am at the same time returning the letter from Dr. Sarah Rabino-vich[5] to you; my comment is that her proposal lies completely

---

[2] See Nos. 14, 26. The first of the three letters, written about 10 Nov. 1902 (see No. 14), has not been found.
[3] W. and Feiwel had decided to invite Glikin to come to Zurich and work with Feiwel on a salary basis for the University project and the Democratic Fraction (see Feiwel to Glikin, 26 Nov. 1902, C.Z.A. A179/3).

42. [1] See No. 40 and n. 5 there.
[2] Probable reference to letter from Evans-Gordon of 27 Nov. 1902, not found (see No. 36 and n. 1 there; No. 38).   [3] See No. 36.
[4] Letter to Levi Montefiore of 29 Nov. 1902 (No. 37). For letter to Claude Montefiore see No. 36 and n. 4 there.
[5] Sarah Rabinovich (subsequently Margolin). She later became an economist and contributor to the Press. She was due to go to Galicia as representative of the Jewish branch of the 'Committee against the Traffic in Women and Girls', in order to investigate Jewish social and economic conditions in the region. In a letter

outside the range of our affairs and in my opinion is not worth discussing. The whole question is indeed a very interesting one, but what has it to do with our University?

Lilien's emblem is absolutely out; we must give up hope of getting anything from Lilien in which he has no personal interest. I ordered the printing of the brochure without the emblem today, otherwise it never will be ready.[6] I shall also write to Lilien and give him a piece of my mind.[7]

We exchanged the typewriter today.

Pinkus keeps on bothering me with letters and telegrams. I don't know how to extricate myself from this business.[8]

Heartfelt greetings to you and Esther,

Your

43. To Moses Zeitlin, Baku. *Geneva, 1 December 1902*

Russian: Or. Copy. H.W.: W.A.

Geneva, Rue Lombard 4.
1. XII. 02.

Dear Moissey L'vovitch,

I have been meaning to write to you for a long time, but there has been so much fuss and bother that I could never get into the proper mood. On my return here I found an enormous amount of all kinds of work awaiting immediate attention. Now everything is beginning to quieten down, but not for long as I have to leave again soon.[1] I have a million questions to ask you.

You can probably guess, Moissey L'vovitch, what they are concerned with, but I shan't touch on them in my very first letter to you. When I recall the hours we spent together in Baku[2] I feel very

to Herzl she proposed setting up an 'Academy of Social Work for Jewish Women and Girls', and apparently wrote to Feiwel on the same subject—Feiwel sent her letter to W., but it has not been found. See Rabinovich to Herzl, 26 Oct. 1902, C.Z.A. Z1/339; Feiwel to W., 29 Nov. 1902, W.A.

[6] See No. 41 and n. 1 there.

[7] No such letter to Lilien has been found.

[8] Pinkus had asked for W.'s criticism of his essay 'The Modern Jewish Question' and his help in getting it published. (See n. 6 to No. 8; and Pinkus to W., 15 Nov. 1902, 19 Nov. 1902, W.A.). Telegrams from Pinkus have not been found.

43. [1] Reference to W.'s contemplated journey to London, Paris, and Brussels, which however did not take place at that time.

[2] At the time of W.'s visit to Baku in the autumn of 1902 (see Vol. I, bridge-note following No. 317).

happy and I am sure we shall meet again often throughout our lives and find common ground and will not be [---- ----] view-point. Now, a little business: [---- ---- ----] [*Bureau*] '*Jüdische Hochschule*' and during this time we have succeeded in the following:

1) Gaining the interest of fairly wide circles (of the academic world) in Berlin, Vienna, Prague and London.[3] Due to a very influential Englishman (*ein echter*)[4] we managed to gain access to Sir[5] Claude Montefiore; he seems to be interested in our project[6] so I may soon have to go to London for discussions. Committees have been organised in these cities and will soon begin to function.[7] 2) We have worked out the questionnaire and sent it to all institutions of Higher Learning in Western Europe with Jewish students, and we feel that the survey is bound to give us ample statistical material of the utmost importance for our project. Altogether, close on 3,000 questionnaires[8] have been sent out. 3) We intend publishing a book, now being written, on the *Hochschule* and in it we shall try to give the idea a firm basis and announce a detailed plan for the project itself.[9] 4) We are preparing for a visit to America.[10] So far, quite a lot has been done in this short period of just one month. Various activities have been *inaugurated* [---- ---- ---- ---- ----].

I would dearly like to know what your attitude is towards the University project. As it happens, we have barely spoken about it.

What is new in Baku? Please forgive me for bothering you with the telegram.[11] Shriro persisted in not replying and I had to know.

---

[3] In August 1902 W. discussed the University project with Jewish professors in Berlin and also with a Jewish banker—possibly Heinrich Meyer-Cohen (see Vol. I, No. 293). At this time Buber was trying to enlist the support of Viennese academic circles. With regard to London, all that is known is the attempt to interest Claude Montefiore and William Evans-Gordon in the project (see Nos. 18, 36). As for Prague, it is known that W. contacted Julius Loewy and sent him *Eine Jüdische Hochschule*. Loewy replied on 18 Nov. 1902 (W.A.) that, in his opinion, the project was not yet ripe for discussion but that nevertheless he would bring the matter up with 'Bar-Kochba', the Prague Student Zionist Society. He promised to let W. know the outcome, but no further letter from Loewy on the subject has been found.

[4] 'An authentic one' (meaning a non-Jew. In this case Evans-Gordon).

[5] See n. 6 to No. 22.

[6] W. asked Evans-Gordon to talk to Claude Montefiore about the University project (see No. 36), but W.'s letter to Evans-Gordon of 8 Dec. 1902 shows that the latter had not till then replied. In the meantime a negative reply had arrived from Montefiore himself (see No. 55 and n. 3 there).

[7] In fact, preparations for setting up a committee were taking place only in Vienna, and even this committee never materialized.

[8] In fact, distribution of the questionnaire started only at the end of December (see No. 138).

[9] See No. 7 and n. 3 there.

[10] The possibility of a visit to the United States on a mission for the University Bureau had already been mentioned in No. 30.

[11] See n. 5 to No. 40.

This time I shall be brief. I hope you will write; I shall be waiting impatiently for your letter.

Warmest regards to Berta Isaakovna.[12]

Keep well. All the very best.

Your Ch. Weizmann

Warmest greetings to the Itzkovitzes.[13]

44. To Isaac Rothstein, Rostov. *Geneva, 1 December 1902.*

Russian: Or. Copy. H.W.: W.A.

1/XII. 02, Geneva.

Dear Friend,

There is absolute chaos in Vienna. In a day or two I shall write to the Actions Committee again and then everything will get published.[1]

They have not written to me from the office at all, even [though I] asked them a long time ago to publish all the news about the University, as well as about money[2] [---- ---- ---- ---- ---- ---- ---- ---- ----] long letter. There will probably be interesting news.

With affection.

Warm regards to Maria Grig[orievna].

Your Chaim

Vera sends her best wishes.

Mr. Rothstein,
    Rostov-on-Don.

---

[12] Probably Zeitlin's wife.
[13] A family in Baku.

44. [1] Rothstein told W. that he had wanted the names of the Rostov contributors to the Geneva University Bureau published in *Die Welt* but Vienna had replied that they could only announce the 256 roubles that Rothstein had sent to Herzl and not the 100 roubles W. himself had received. (See n. 1 to No. 24.) Rothstein requested W. to ask the Zionist office in Vienna to announce the additional 100 roubles as well. (See Rothstein to W., 8 (21) Nov. 1902, W.A.)

[2] *Die Welt* of 21 Nov. 1902 published an item about the receipt of 646 Austrian crowns from Rothstein in Rostov for the Geneva University Bureau. No further announcement appeared, and no letter from W. to Vienna on the subject has been found. See also No. 161 and n. 20 there.

45. To Israel **Breslav**, Kharkov. *Geneva, 2 December 1902*

German: Or. Copy. T.W.: W.A.

Geneva, 4 rue Lombard, 2. 11. 02.[1]

Dr. Breslav,
Kharkov.

My dear Friend,

You deserve to receive a letter from me giving you a thorough dressing down! You have shrouded yourself in a lofty silence; I do not like you at all in this attitude. I hope that you will now break the ice and reply to the thousand and one questions that I should not even be putting to you. You know how eagerly I await your news, for it is bound to be of interest. You are kind, and so will not let your patient friend write six letters in vain. It would appear that the post no longer functions from Geneva to Kharkov. I wrote to Nemirovsky three times, to you once, to Aleinikov twice, and once each to Greidenberg and Futran[2]—all to no purpose. You must admit that I really do have cause for irritation. But there are no limits to my goodwill—especially when it is *I* who need people. Well, joking aside, let us get to the point.

From my many letters, which must surely have been brought to your attention, you will have been informed about the state of our affairs. We have made every possible effort not to waste a moment in initiating all the tasks set out in the programme. We have established contact with various important personalities and soon hope to form a circle of effective co-workers and fellow-combatants in our good cause. We have begun the statistical enquiry and are now preparing for several important journeys.[3] If all our friends would support the cause with enthusiasm we would soon be able to advance considerably.

I am placing great hope in Kharkov, where we certainly have dedicated co-workers. You must ensure that an effective group of *selected* people is formed. I must inform you that the problem of material support for the Bureau is of prime importance. The significant measures we are planning demand commensurate means. I do not wish to elaborate, we have already discussed every aspect in

---

45. [1] *Sic* in original, but it is clear from the content that the correct date is 2 Dec.

[2] See Nos. 2, 20 (the W.A. has copies of only two letters to Nemirovsky), and Nos. 3, 4, 23, 28, 29.

[3] W. was contemplating visits to London, Paris and Brussels at Christmas, and was also considering a visit to the United States (see Nos. 20, 43).

great detail[4] as the occasion arose. You are wholly familiar with the situation and appreciate it just as much as I do.

Nimm alle Kraft zusammen die Lust und auch den Schmerz . . . ![5]
I had better conclude in case I become more surly or perhaps wax lyrical. But this time you are going to reply!

With devotion and friendship,

Your

46. To Heinrich Loewe, Berlin. *Geneva, 2 December 1902*

German: Or. Copy. T.W.: W.A.

Geneva, 2. 12. 02, 4 rue Lombard

Dr. Heinrich Loewe,
Berlin.

Dear Friend,

Many thanks for writing.[1] I have sent your kind letter, together with the manuscript, to our friend Feiwel in Zurich. As soon as a reply comes from him I shall return to the subject.

Our 'Jewish University' Bureau would ask the following of you, dear Doctor: Your editorial office[2] must surely be in possession of addresses of the student societies in most German universities. We would be most grateful to you if you would kindly make these addresses available to us. We need them for the purpose of conducting a survey among Russian and Rumanian Jewish student youth. We would also be very grateful if you would give us the addresses of reliable people to whom we might send our questionnaire, and who might take over the conduct of the survey in particular cities. Naturally, Russian or Rumanian Jews would be preferable. We are mainly concerned with the following cities, with which we have no connection at all: Aachen, Breslau, Koenigsberg, Kiel, Stuttgart,

---

[4] During W.'s visit to Kharkov in Oct. 1902.

[5] 'Gather all your strength, the pleasure and the pain.' A quotation from the poem 'Des Sängers Fluch', by Uhland.

46. [1] Loewe's letter has not been found, but one he wrote to Glikin shows that he refused to publish in the *Jüdische Rundschau* the Democratic Fraction's protest against Schauer's article for fear of legal action. Loewe suggested a revised version to W.—the 'manuscript' mentioned here, but which has also not been found. (See Loewe to Glikin, 30 Nov. 1902, C.Z.A. A179/3; and Nos. 34, 94. For the reply see n. 1 to No. 25).

[2] The editorial office of the *Jüdische Rundschau*.

Wuerzburg, Erlangen, Jena, Halle, Rostock, Tuebingen, Giessen, Hanover, Dresden, etc.[3]

With many thanks in anticipation, and with kind regards,

Yours sincerely,

47. To Moses Glikin, Charlottenburg. *Geneva, 2 December 1902*

German/Russian: T.W./H.W.: C.Z.A. A179/3

Geneva, 4 rue Lombard, 2. 12. 02.

Mr. Moses Glikin,
Charlottenburg.

My dear Friend,

Please forgive me for only now replying to your letter and to the one received from Mandels.[1] This was not due to negligence or inattention, but a few things required clarification before we could reach a decision. Well, our friend Feiwel has already written to you that we have decided that you should come to Switzerland.[2] You must, dear Glikin, be a little patient until we manage to get the money we are at present in need of, a matter that will take until the new year by the latest. You will then be able to go to Zurich without delay. I trust that everything will turn out for the best for you and for us.

And now for matters of business:

1) Please see that all our printed material, such as notepaper bearing the heading 'Jewish University', envelopes, the second printing of the University brochure, questionnaires, etc., is speedily taken care of. You must remind our friend Trietsch about it and help him to settle these things, as he has so much

---

[3] Glikin told W. on 10 Dec. 1902 (W.A.) that he had spoken to Loewe, but that the latter could not supply many addresses. No reply by Loewe to this letter has been found.

47. [1] Glikin's letters and the one from Mandels have not been found. In the middle of November Mandels wrote to W. about Glikin's employment by the University Bureau (see No. 18) and it can be assumed that Glikin also wrote about this.

[2] See No. 41 and n. 3 there.

to do. We need everything urgently. I request you, therefore, to proceed as quickly as possible.

2. I have already written three times to Dr. Altschul, at No. 109 Brunnenstrasse,[3] but till now am still without a reply. Please visit him and enquire the reason for his silence. I fear he may be ill. Dr. Altschul was to have negotiated with various people on University affairs. Ask him whether he has achieved anything. Above all, however, induce him to reply to my various letters.

3. A letter is going out by this same post to Dr. Heinrich Loewe[4] in which I have asked him to send me the addresses of Russian–Jewish students in all German University cities. We need these addresses for our forthcoming survey and we think that Dr. Loewe can provide a consolidated list from his editorial office. Perhaps you can procure such a list elsewhere too. But it must be a complete list for all German Universities. Furthermore, the addresses must be of reliable individuals. Please get in touch with Dr. Loewe and help to arrange the compilation of such a list. Regarding Altschul, you must consult with Mr. Trietsch, to whom I wrote yesterday about it.[5]

May I once again implore you to deal most urgently and precisely with all matters. Where is Motzkin hiding?[6] Is Kunin already in Berlin?

Warmest regards to you and to all our friends,

Yours ever,
Chaim

[7]Forgive my writing to you in German. Our typewriter can only write this way, and as a matter of fact I must now conduct all my correspondence in a language everyone understands.

20 m. to Mandels,[8] to whom warm regards, should have been sent [by] Buber. If this has not yet been done I will send it at once.

I embrace you,

Your
Chaim

---

[3] See n. 2 to No. 41.
[4] See No. 46.
[5] See No. 41.
[6] Motzkin was then staying in Kiev.
[7] Added in Russian in W.'s handwriting.
[8] Nothing is known about this payment.

48. To Berthold Feiwel, Zurich. *Geneva, 2 December 1902*

German: Or. Copy. T.W.: W.A.

Geneva, 2. 12. 02.

Mr. Berthold Feiwel,
Zurich.

Dear Toldy,

A letter came from Heinrich Loewe[1] today, and I am sending it on to you with the request that you let me have your comments by return. There is, for the time being, nothing new at the Bureau; we are working diligently and putting out feelers in every direction. I believe that some things suffer through the work not being centralised. I [know] nothing, for instance, about Buber's negotiations on our behalf. Everything should be arranged in such a way that the various individuals and circles are brought into direct contact with the Bureau.

How do we stand regarding the list of professors?[2] What did Werner write?[3] Have you kept copies of all the letters you have sent out? I shall send you mine at the end of the week—we are now writing almost everything in German—please send me your letters too. How is the survey proceeding? What can Moses of Mannheim do for the cause?[4]

I consider that now is the most appropriate time for the formation of Committees and small groups for the 'Jewish University'.[5] Please let me know what you think.

The Fraction notices have just gone out in Russian; in German tomorrow.[6]

Kindest regards from your

---

48. [1] See No. 46 and n. 1 there.

[2] Reference to a list of professors and lecturers likely to support the University project. In his letter of 28 Nov. 1902 (W.A.), Buber promised to send such a list.

[3] Werner proposed setting up a 'Jewish University' group in Vienna—see No. 60; n. 1 to No. 92.

[4] In a letter to W. of 29 Nov. 1902 (W.A.), Feiwel wrote: 'Dr. Moses of Mannheim made a number of recommendations to me in connection with the University.'

[5] For this programme see also Nos. 50, 51. In No. 160 W. writes that the programme had been suggested to him by Rothstein when they met in Rostov in the autumn of 1902.

[6] No copy of the 'notice' has been found. Kroll wrote to W. on 2/15 Dec. 1902 (W.A.): 'We gladly accept your proposal to continue the Information Bureau [of the Democratic Fraction in Geneva] and are pleased to appoint you resident delegate abroad'. This possibly refers to the notice mentioned here.

49. To David Pinski, New York. *Geneva, 2 December 1902*

German/Russian: T.W./H.W.: Yivo Archives, New York.

Geneva, 2. 11. 02,[1] 4 rue Lombard

Mr. D. Pinski,[2]
New York.

Dear Sir,

We are taking the liberty of sending you the enclosed statement relating to the project for a 'Jewish University', which is submitted for your kind attention. We would add that the 'Jewish University Bureau' mentioned in the pamphlet is already functioning and commends itself to your favourable notice.

May we request you to notify us whether you are in the position, and are willing, to support our aims in any way.

In anticipation of your reply, which would be most appreciated,[3] we have the honour to remain,

Most respectfully,
Dr. Ch. Weizmann

Warmest greetings,[4]
Ch. Weizmann.

50. To Abraham Idelson and Michael Kroll, Moscow.
Geneva, 2 December 1902

German: Or. Copy. T.W.: W.A.

Geneva, 4 rue Lombard, 2. 12. 02.

Dr. M. B. Kroll and Mr. A. Idelson,
Moscow.

Dear Friends,

Further to our previous letters,[1] we now take the liberty of making a proposal with an earnest request for its favourable consideration. From what we can now estimate, the running expenses of the Bureau

49. [1] *Sic* in original, but the letter cannot have been written on 2 Nov. since W. only returned to Geneva on the 4th (see No. 1). The correct date must be 2 Dec. 1902.

[2] W. knew the writer David Pinski from their student days in Berlin.

[3] Pinski replied on 26 Feb. 1903 (W.A.), that he could not do anything for the University Bureau since he had stopped writing for the press; but he contacted Morris Rosenfeld, who published an article in *Die Yiddishe Welt* (see also No. 409 and n. 1 there).   [4] Words added in W.'s handwriting in Russian.

50. [1] See Nos. 7, 30, 35.

for the 'Jewish University' will be in the neighbourhood of 250–300 francs (monthly). By running expenses we mean postage, salaries, and such minor expenditure as a small amount of printing. You will be aware, however, that we are faced with greater expense, mostly in the financing of large-scale propaganda. Now, we already have a fund; and although this is not substantial and is open to expansion, we would prefer to retain it as a reserve for major expenses to come, or perhaps for a special activity. We believe that the enthusiastic support of our friends will enable our running expenses to be covered by means of their respective contributions.

Our proposal, therefore, is that you in Moscow, and people in other large centres with your help, form 'Jewish University' groups. These would maintain the most active contact with us and would support both the Bureau and the entire University enterprise in all aspects. Our respective responsibilities can, of course, be formally established. We neither desire nor are able to specify the method by which you constitute these groups. We merely wish to stimulate them and set out principles for their organisation.

If they co-operate with us wholeheartedly, we conceive the groups as the basis for a large University organization in the future. The groups must, therefore, be constituted with the greatest care and with consideration for their homogeneous composition in attitudes towards the University question.

We entreat you, dear friends, carefully to consider this proposal which, we are strongly convinced, can be most productive if properly executed. We are appealing to Moscow in the first instance because we are persuaded that you will set a fine example and convert words into deeds.

With kind regards,

As ever yours,

51. To Jacob Bernstein-Kohan, Kishinev. *Geneva, 3 December 1902*

German: Or. Copy. T.W.: W.A.

3. 12. 02.

Dr. Bernstein-Kohan,[1]
Kishinev.

My dear, good Friend,

For some time now I have been on the point of writing you[2] a long

---

51. [1] Also referred to frequently as 'Kohan-Bernstein'.
[2] Bernstein-Kohan is addressed in the intimate form.

letter, dear Yasha. However, I knew that you have had many
personal affairs to arrange[3] and attend to just lately, and so did not
wish to distract you with our problems. Frankly, I have been quietly
hoping throughout for a sign of life from you, but to my regret it
never came. Within the difficult atmosphere that prevailed in Vienna
we did not succeed in having a full discussion or in clearing up
various matters[4] and so I left with a heavy heart—but with the
firm resolve to devote all my energies to working for the University
idea. I did not express all my thoughts on the matter to you, but
my stand is briefly as follows: I regard the University as the only
concrete venture with great cultural significance capable of stimu-
lating new forces and liberating new impulses within the cultural
movement. With it an opportunity is being created for every Jew
who values Jewishness[5] and the European-Jewish synthesis, and
who considers it to have promise, to invest his energies in a
direction that will lead to important results.

In Vienna you promised us your cooperation. I now wish briefly
to describe the work we have already begun and what still remains
to be initiated. In accordance with the plan outlined in the brochure,
our endeavours are now being directed towards the formation of
committees or groups of selected influential and educated persons
in the larger centres.

We can already note some successes in this field.

1) Groups such as these are already being formed in Berlin and
Vienna. We are now seeking to establish contact in other large
cities with circles as described above. 2) In another week the statistical survey of Russian-Jewish youth studying abroad is to begin.
We have prepared questionnaires and will be sending them to all
Jewish students. A survey is likewise to be carried out in Russia
itself. We have sent the questionnaire scheme to Idelson with the
request that he come to an agreement with all our friends regarding
the means of conducting the survey.[6] You, I hope, will help us with
the entire project. I need not tell you how important your co-
operation is. 3) We deem the time to be appropriate for small 'Jewish
University' groups to be formed in the cultural centres of Russia
so as to disseminate and reinforce the idea. As already noted, the

---

[3] He was at the time a candidate for the post of 'official rabbi' in Kharkov, but
when elected he was not recognized by the authorities.

[4] W. and Bernstein-Kohan met in Vienna in Oct. 1902 at the Annual Zionist
Conference, where Herzl reported on the failure of his negotiations in Constantinople
—see Vol. 1, n. 3 to No. 320.

[5] In the original: 'das Jüdische'.

[6] W. advised Kroll about despatch of the questionnaire on 28 Nov. 1902 (No. 35),
and he may have sent the questionnaire to Idelson's address.

groups should be of closed, intimate circles of selected intellectuals which will support the Bureau in every respect. The respective obligations (of the Bureau and of these groups) are to be formally established. The groups should later develop into one large organisation for the 'Jewish University'. Do please let me have your views immediately on this, dear friend. You above all could do the chief part of our work in this sphere. It is a large and rewarding field.

In closing, let me ask you again to look at all this with your utmost goodwill, and to reply in detail.[7] Is the Kharkov business finally settled?[8]

With kindest regards and all good wishes for your health,

Affectionately,

Ever yours,

52. To Simon Guinzburg, Saratov. *Geneva, 3 December 1902*

German: Or. Copy. T.W.: W.A.

3. 12. 02.

Engineer S. Guinzburg,
Saratov.

Dear Friend and Fellow-Zionist,

As doubtless you have already learned from newspaper reports, our Bureau has been put into operation. Our Moscow friends will inform you in detail of the activities already begun. We are working at pressure here in bending every effort to drive forward, and can happily point to a number of successes. Our main efforts are now being directed towards establishing close contact with all our friends, to stimulate them to activity and, on the other hand, to gain inspiration from them. Before initiating a large-scale propaganda campaign we would like unity to prevail within our inner circle of co-workers. I assume that you are familiar with our programme and therefore request you to work for our cause in your own circle, and in co-operation with the centre in Moscow which is in lively correspondence with us.

We earnestly recommend that a favourable atmosphere be created so that it might spread from man to man in your city and in those other places within your sphere of action. I would, at the same time, like you to bear in mind something that you already know, that

---

[7] W. received no reply to this letter—see No. 126 and n. 5 there.
[8] See n. 3 above.

our Bureau has embarked upon important tasks and is confronted by still greater ones. In order to carry them out properly, there is a need, in addition to the intellectual forces we are now endeavouring to enlist, for material resources also. Although a certain amount is already at our disposal we wish, however [---- ---- ----] to be reserved for a larger undertaking. The running expenses of the Bureau (250–300 francs monthly) ought to be covered by the circles of friends who are more close to us. We entreat you to support us in this direction.

Kindest regards to you, as well as to Mr. Berligne.[1]

Yours faithfully,

53. To George Halpern, Munich. *Geneva, 3 December 1902*

German: Or. Copy. T.W.: W.A.

Geneva, Rue Lombard 4.
3. 12. 02.

Mr. George Halpern,
Munich.

Dear Sir,

You must have been very surprised at my silence, but as you know I have been travelling constantly and could only recently resume my regular activities. My propaganda campaign in Russia on behalf of the University was fairly successful, and I consider the continuation of our programme as set out in our brochure to be absolutely essential. Part of the material requirements for the preparatory effort is already available to us, but the rest has still to be found. If you are interested, I can supply you at an early date with a detailed report on the work already begun.

Following our conversation in Pinsk[1] I would now ask whether you are prepared to cooperate on the project and to what degree. Can you do anything in Munich, by cultivating Prof. Graetz[2] for example? Will you be going to England soon?[3]

52. [1] Eliahu Berligne, then living in Tzaritzyn.

53. [1] Halpern came from Pinsk and probably met W. when they spent their summer holiday there.

  [2] Leo Graetz (1856–1941), physicist, son of the historian Heinrich G. From 1893–1908 lecturer and from 1908–26 professor of physics at Munich University.

  [3] At the time Halpern was engaged in a research project on Jewish workers in London (see G. Halpern, *Die Jüdischen Arbeiter in London*, Stuttgart and Berlin, 1903).

I do not wish to put too many questions to you now, I merely
wanted to show signs of life and offer my excuses. You may be
assured that I will now make every effort to be prompt in correspondence with you. I am looking forward with pleasure to your
letter, and greet you warmly.[4]

Yours faithfully,

54. To Davis Trietsch, Berlin. *Geneva, 3 December 1902*

German: Or. Copy. T.W.: W.A.

Geneva, 3. 12. 02.

Mr. D. Trietsch,
Berlin.

Dear Friend,

I confirm my telegram[1] of today's date saying: Where are notepaper, brochures, greatest difficulties? At the same time I acknowledge with thanks the receipt of some very attractive notepaper[2] on
which, however, I still fail to observe a Hebrew inscription.[3]

Has Lilien reached a decision,[4] by any chance? I prefer not to write
to him any more. Glikin has been informed that he is to assist you
in carrying out University business[5] at all times. Believe me, dear
Trietsch, I always find it difficult to burden you with duties. I know
how involved you are on all sides. Please forgive me once and for all.

Please see that better-quality brochures[6] are sent to the following:

1. Dr. Samuel Goldflamm, Granicza 10, Warsaw.
2. Attorney Maximilian Goldbaum, Orla 8, Warsaw.
3. Dr. Samuel Poznansky, Tlomacka, Synagogue Building,
   Warsaw.
4. Ignaz Bernstein, Granicza 12, Warsaw.
5. Samuel Lurie, Zelna 46, Warsaw.
6. Attorney Julian Kohn, Schkolna 5, Warsaw.

---

[4] No reply to this letter has been found.

54. [1] Not found.

[2] Reference to a sample of the notepaper that Trietsch had sent (see No. 55).

[3] In the original, as well as in subsequent letters: 'Jüdische Inschrift', i.e., Hebrew
words on the letterhead of the University Bureau.

[4] Regarding the emblem Lilien had promised to design for the Bureau (see n. 1
to No. 41).

[5] See No. 47.

[6] In the original: 'Edelbrochüre'. A quantity of *Jüdische Hochschule* pamphlets
was printed on special paper.

All these people have been advised that brochures are being sent.[7]
Kind regards from

Yours ever,

P.S. How do you like our typewriter?

55. To Berthold Feiwel, Zurich. *Geneva, 3 December 1902*

German: Or. Copy. T.W.: W.A.

3. 12. 02.

Mr. Berthold Feiwel,
Zurich.

Dear Toldy,

Here is the notepaper,[1] of which I have only received a sample.
Many thanks for sending the 65 francs.[2] Enclosed is a letter from
Claude Montefiore[3] whom we may regard as our first failure. More
like this will follow, but it should not discourage us in the least.

For the past three days we have been doing nothing but despatching letters to all points of the compass to stimulate our friends
everywhere to work. Some[4] fund-raising activities have also been
initiated. I would be pleased if you would draft the letters for our
representatives[5] and the financiers for me. I have to send out a
large number of them and the matter is urgent.

We are conducting all our correspondence in German now, so that
you will have the opportunity to look through the outgoing letters.

I cannot write about my visit to England before a reply is
received from Major Gordon.[6] Have you written to Zangwill? This
is most important.[7]

My regards, dear Toldy, and warm greetings to Esther too.

Your

[7] No letters or copies of letters to these persons have been found. See also n. 2 to
No. 63.

55. [1] The University Bureau's new writing-paper. Apparently the original of the
letter, as distinct from the copy that has been preserved, was written on the new
notepaper.   [2] Nothing is known about this sum.
   [3] See Claude Montefiore to W., 1 Dec. 1902, W.A. Montefiore replied to W. (see
No. 36) that he did not support the University project, and that he could see no
prospects of raising funds for such a venture in England.

[4] In the original W. wrote 'eine' instead of 'einige'.

[5] Probably a reference to the 'Vertrauensmänner', i.e., those who were to conduct
the student survey in the various cities.

[6] See letter to Evans-Gordon of 29 Nov. 1902 (No. 36).

[7] See No. 18 and n. 12 there. Feiwel notified W. on 8 Dec. 1902 (W.A.) that he
had written to Zangwill.

56. To L'Écho Sioniste, Paris. *Geneva, 4 December 1902*

German: Or. Copy. T.W.: W.A.

4. 12. 02.

The Editors, *Écho Sioniste*,[1]
Paris.

Dear Fellow-Zionists,

May I take the liberty of requesting that you make available to our Bureau any addresses you might possess of Russian Jewish students or organisations in French-speaking countries. We intend shortly to embark upon a survey among Jewish students. Unfortunately, we still have no contacts in such places as Brussels, Liège, Ghent, Antwerp, or in many French cities either. We would be most obliged to you if you would put us into touch with some persons of reliability.

With sincere thanks in anticipation,

I remain,

Most respectfully and with Zion's greetings,

57. To Hirsch Hiller, Pinsk. *Geneva, 4 December 1902*[1]

German: Or. Copy. T.W.: W.A.

4. 12. [02].

Mr. Hirsch Hiller,
Pinsk.

My dear Friend,

I must first ask for your kind forgiveness for not replying to your friendly letter[2] till now. We here are somewhat over-loaded with work and can no longer use our time as we would wish. I want to reply briefly to your inquiries. You will understand that we can as yet say nothing with certainty, as everything is still in its beginnings. We have endeavoured to create a circle of co-workers from among people of significance in Berlin and Vienna. We have inaugurated a statistical survey of Jewish students abroad; we have established

56. [1] French Zionist monthly edited in Paris by A. Raskine. W.'s letter was published in the December issue, p. 255.

57. [1] The notepaper is damaged where the year should appear.
[2] Hiller to W., 7/20 Nov. 1902, W.A. Hiller had advised W. that the Russian translation of the Democratic Fraction's platform was ready (see n. 5 to No. 23), and had inquired about the Annual Zionist Conference's decision on the University and about developments in this field.

contact with eminent representatives of the Press and in the academic world, and we firmly believe that we shall succeed in organising large committees by Easter. Upon the completion of the statistical study, the work of the committees will be made public, and by then we shall certainly have a European Press apparatus at our disposal.

Wherever possible in Russia too, we are trying to form quite small, closed groups of interested people. This is both to effect co-operation with the Bureau and to raise necessary running expenses. We wish to keep the sums already raised as a reserve fund for a more substantial undertaking ahead. I believe that with a little effort you will not find it difficult to form a small group in Pinsk, in the way indicated above. The reports in *Die Welt* regarding Vienna are fairly accurate.[3]

By a majority of two votes the Small Congress decided that the only place where the University should be established was Palestine. Herzl joined our committee, nevertheless.[4]

As you can judge from reports, something has already been achieved during this brief period, and we are confident that our work will become still wider and more intensive. Long live life![5]

In conclusion, our Bureau takes this opportunity to express its warmest gratitude to you for your efforts.

At your service as always, should you require any information, and with kindest regards,

I am

Your

58. To Joseph Lurie, Warsaw. *Geneva, 4 December 1902*

German: Or. Copy. T.W.: W.A.

Dr. J. Lurie,[1]
Warsaw.

Dear Friend,

I really must express my amazement at receiving nothing from you in reply to my numerous enquiries.[2] Meanwhile a great deal of

[3] *Die Welt* of 7 Nov. 1902 carried a report on the discussions of the Annual Zionist Conference in Vienna concerning the University project and on the Resolution passed (see Vol. I, n. 4 to No. 320).

[4] I.e., Herzl agreed to join the committee for a University, although he did not believe the institution could be set up in Palestine immediately—cf. No. 1.

[5] In the original: 'Es Lebe das Lebendige!'

58. [1] In the original: Lury.

[2] Only one previous letter from W. to Lurie, of 17 Nov. 1902 (see No. 17), has been found.

time has passed and I have no idea of the fate of the Hebrew translation of the brochure.[3] Would you please be so kind as to write me
about this without further delay.

I really was expecting to receive news from you, or perhaps some
suggestions, concerning activities in Warsaw. You can imagine what
a depressing effect the silence of our closest friends has on us.

Anticipating your early letter,

I am your

[A post-script by Samuel Levinson]

59. To Abraham Kasteliansky, Berlin. *Geneva, 4 December 1902*

German: Or. Copy. T.W.: W.A.

4. 12. 02.

Mr. A. Kasteliansky,
Berlin.

Dear Friend,

Regarding University business we would like to make the following request to you: Would you perhaps be so good as to ask Mr.
Eduard Bernstein for his opinion of our programme ?[1] Naturally we
are prepared, should you think it necessary, to despatch an official
letter to Bernstein, but we think it appropriate for you to discuss
it with him first. Our brochure is available to you at the *Jüdischer
Verlag*. Would perhaps Kautsky,[2] Leo Arons,[3] etc., also come into
consideration ?[4]

Looking forward to your esteemed reply, and with kindest
regards,

I am
Your

[3] Lurie had promised to look after the translation of the brochure *Eine Jüdische
Hochschule* from German into Hebrew, and this was apparently discussed when W.
visited Warsaw in August 1902—see Vol. I, n. 11 to No. 297.

59. [1] For W.'s meeting with Bernstein in Aug. 1902, see Vol. I, No. 302.

[2] Karl Kautsky (1854–1938), Marxist theoretician and exponent of German
Social Democracy, opposed to Zionism.

[3] Leo Arons (1860–1919), physicist, active in the Social-Democratic party in
Germany, especially in the fields of education and culture.

[4] In his reply of 21 Dec. 1902 (W.A.), Kasteliansky expressed the opinion that an
appeal to Bernstein, Kautsky, and Arons would be pointless. 'All these gentlemen,
as far as I know them, have neither interest in nor understanding for anything
Jewish, and certainly not for a purely cultural Jewish project.'

60. To Martin Buber, Vienna. *Geneva, 5 December 1902*

German: Or. Copy. T.W.: W.A.

5. 12. 02.

Mr. Martin Buber,
Vienna.

Dear Martin,

Following my previous letter[1] I wish to remind you once again that:

1) I need to be absolutely clear regarding Herzl.[2] What was his answer to you? Has he already spoken to the Actions Committee? The moment I am definitely informed about this I shall write to him.

2) I am still without the list of professors[3] or the names of those people who have definitely identified themselves with a committee.[4] On what basis has the committee been constituted? Is it in the form of independent groups, or do they wish to co-operate with the Bureau?

3) Dr. Werner wanted to form a 'Jewish University' group.[5] Feiwel has also written to him about it. What came of this?

4) I am all in favour of having the running expenses of the Bureau covered by the groups in formation and thus get them to lose their platonic character, as is essential. We ought to keep the money I have raised[6] as a reserve.

Please, dear Martin, for the sake of the cause do answer these questions by return, and also let me know whether you agree to point four and whether you will take the appropriate steps forthwith. With Vienna to the fore it will be easy for us to put over similar ideas in other cities.

Kindest regards,

60. [1] See No. 38.
 [2] On the subject of Herzl joining the University committee, see No. 38 and ns. 1, 2 there.
 [3] See n. 2 to No. 48.
 [4] The Vienna University Committee—see n. 1 to No. 38.
 [5] See also n. 1 to No. 92.
 [6] Reference to the funds W. collected in Rostov and Baku—see Vol. I, bridge-note following No. 317.

61. To Chaim Lubzhinsky, Warsaw. *Geneva, 5 December 1902*

German: Or. Copy. T.W.: W.A.

5. 12. 02.

Mr. Ch. Lubzhinsky,
Warsaw.

Dear Sir,[1]

We have the honour to inform you that our Bureau for the 'Jewish University' has already begun to function. All the activities referred to in the brochure have already been initiated. We are now endeavouring to organise committees in the larger European centres and to prepare a major propaganda effort. We are also seeking to establish contact with friends of our cause everywhere.

We aim to form smaller groups of interested people in Russia too, to be in constant communication with the Bureau and to support every facet of our undertaking. The financial situation of the Bureau is such that we are now in possession of a fund that potentially could be much greater; we wish to keep this as a reserve for the wider activities before us. The running expenses of our Bureau are not insignificant, and we hope to cover them by monthly contributions from our closed circle of co-workers. We would be most obliged if you would assume the task of creating a favourable atmosphere for our cause in your own business and financial circles.[2] Kindly remit whatever funds as may come in to Wolffsohn, Bankers, at Karolingerring, Cologne. Our brochures are at your disposal in any desired quantity, and we will happily supply you with any other information.[3]

Respectfully,

62. To Vladimir (Zeev) Tyomkin, Elizavetgrad. *Geneva, 6 December 1902*

German/Russian: T.W./H.W.: C.Z.A. A157/2.

Geneva, Rue Lombard 4.
6. 12. 02.

Mr. W. Tyomkin,
Elizavetgrad.

Dear Fellow-Zionist,

We had the honour to send you our brochure some time ago. We

61. [1] Chaim Lubzhinsky was W.'s brother-in-law. The impersonal style of the letter is probably due to its formal nature, but presumably the original contained a handwritten postscript that does not appear in this copy.

[2] Lubzhinsky was a businessman.

[3] No reply from Lubzhinsky has been found.

assume there is little need to add anything to the particulars contained therein.

At present our Bureau is engaged in forming a committee of co-workers so as to further the undertaking. Our intention is to enlist the assistance of specially suitable people for the purpose, initially, of completing preliminary investigations relating to the project, and then to prepare for the propaganda effort that is due to begin towards the end of 1903. The co-operation of the committee now in formation should in the first instance cover the distribution of information, possibly assistance on the survey, and the attraction of eminent Jewish personalities—especially professors, scholars, authors, artists. It should also help to start smaller 'Jewish University' groups.

Should you regard the project for a 'Jewish University' sympathetically, we extend to you, Sir, this most cordial and respectful invitation to join our committee of co-workers, and we assure you forthwith that our Bureau will readily and at all times be glad to support any activities that your efforts might stimulate. Please regard us as being completely at your service in this matter.

We would be delighted to have your co-operation in the ideal we are seeking to further. We feel confident that such co-operation will in no circumstance be in vain, while given favourable circumstances it will have far-reaching significance.

Your immediate reply—which we trust will be in the affirmative —will enable us to make our plans accordingly.

We remain,

Most respectfully and with regards,
Dr. Ch. Weizmann

[1]Dear Friend,

In sending you my heartfelt greetings, do please let me know how you are, how things stand with you, and do let me have your circulars.[2]

Affectionately,[3]
Your Chaim

Regards to your family, although I have never met them.[4]

---

62. [1] What follows is in W.'s handwriting in Russian. Unlike the German part of the letter, Tyomkin is addressed here in the intimate form.

[2] Reference to the circulars sent by Tyomkin as Zionist regional representative for the Elizavetgrad area.

[3] In the original: 'I kiss you'.

[4] No reply from Tyomkin has been found.

63. To Isidore (Israel) Yasinovsky, Warsaw. *Geneva, 6 December 1902*

German: Or. Copy. T.W.: W.A.

6. 12. 02.

Mr. I. Yasinovsky, Attorney,
Warsaw.

Dear Fellow-Zionist,

Further to the matters referred to in your much appreciated letter,[1] we have today sent letters and brochures to these gentlemen: Kohan-Bernstein, Dr. Poznansky, Dr. Goldflamm.[2]

May we ask you, dear friend, to communicate with the gentlemen mentioned and report to us on your negotiations.

Would you kindly let us know whether anything can be done in Lodz, Plotzk, etc.

We hope that you are now restored in health, and will be delighted to hear from you again soon.

Kind regards,

Your

64. To Saul Lurie,[1] Darmstadt. *Geneva, 6 December 1902*

German: Or. Copy. T.W.: W.A.

6. 12. 02.

Mr. Saul Lurie,
Darmstadt.

Dear Friend,

You are doubtless familiar with the position regarding the University project through reports in the newspapers. At the time of their

---

63. [1] See No. 33 and n. 1 there.

[2] On 3 Dec. W. asked Trietsch to send the brochure *Eine Jüdische Hochschule* to the persons mentioned here, as well as to Maximilian Goldbaum and Samuel Lurie, and pointed out that he had already notified them that they would be receiving it (see No. 54). The letter to Glikin of 12 Dec. (No. 84) indicates that up to that date W. had not heard from Trietsch and was not sure if the brochures had indeed been sent. Apparently the present letter was written on the assumption that they had; cf. No. 71, which shows that W. assumed that Goldbaum had also received a copy. Trietsch notified W. on 17 Dec. 1902 (W.A.) that they had been sent to Warsaw 'long ago', but on 11/24 Dec. 1902 Yasinovsky wrote to W. (W.A.) that he alone had received a copy, and he presumed the others had been held up by the Russian censor.

64. [1] The letters to Saul Lurie are written in the intimate form.

appearance I sent you a number of brochures without, however, receiving any reply from you. I would now ask whether you may be inclined to do something for our cause in Darmstadt, or are willing to be active on its behalf in any other way. You might attempt to interest a few professors in Darmstadt in forming a small group to support us intellectually and materially. Naturally we are prepared to supply further information, and we would be happy to establish communication with you and our Darmstadt friends.

With all good wishes and greetings to you and the newly formed Society.[2]

As ever yours,

65. To Berthold Feiwel, Zurich. *Geneva, 6 December 1902*

German: Or. Copy. T.W.: W.A.

Geneva, 6. 12. 02.

Mr. Berthold Feiwel,
Zurich.

Dear Toldy,

I have just received your letter,[1] in which I found that not a single question had been answered. I am urgently compelled to request you once again to look up all my letters and to reply to everything, albeit briefly.

Enclosed is a letter from the Jewish Colonial Trust and a blank sheet of paper containing my signature. Do please write at once to Herzl. You must add your signature to the letter.[2] At the same time copies of out-going correspondence are going off to you, which please return to me with comments as required. Not a word from Buber, naturally. One can write till one's fingers drop off before achieving the sight of a two-line missive.

Kind regards,

Your

[2] The Student Zionist Society *Maccabea* in Darmstadt, founded by Saul Lurie and others in the autumn of 1902 (see Weinreb to Nordau, 20 June 1903, C.Z.A. A119/33/19/4).

65. [1] Feiwel to W., 5 Dec. 1902, W.A.

[2] The letter from the J.C.T. has not been found, but its contents can be adduced from Feiwel's letter to Herzl, written over W.'s signature with his own added. Feiwel said that the J.C.T. had informed them that since the University Bureau's account was also in Herzl's name, his signature was necessary for withdrawals (see n. 3 to No. 27). He asked Herzl to give instructions for the transfer of 600 francs to the Geneva Bureau and suggested changing the name of the account to avoid troubling him in the future (this letter, undated, in C.Z.A. Z1/340). See also No. 40 and n. 4 there.

66. To William Evans-Gordon, London. *Geneva, 8 December 1902*

German: Or. Copy. T.W.: W.A.

8. 12. 02.

Major W. Evans-Gordon,
London.

Dear Major,

Further to our previous letter[1] I have the honour to inform you that, in consequence of your much appreciated advice, I have provisionally given up the journey I intended to make to London[2] in the hope instead of going there in February.[3] Meanwhile a letter has been received from Sir[4] Claude Montefiore with a completely negative reply.[5] Mr. Montefiore believes nothing can be done for our cause in England. I am definitely of another opinion, and I trust, dear Major, that you too are not that pessimistic.

We would be most obliged if you would kindly inform us whether you have spoken to Montefiore and others.[6]

Do please forgive us for presuming to encroach upon your time. Your were so kind and so willing to help us, it would be criminal if we did not avail ourselves of a force such as you represent.

Our kindest regards,

Most respectfully,

67. To David Brailovsky,[1] Kharkov. *Geneva, 8 December 1902*

German: Or. Copy. T.W.: W.A.

8. 12. 02.

Mr. D. Brailovsky,
Kharkov.

Dear Friend,

From what I have heard you have close associations with our friends in Kharkov. I would, therefore, like to ask you to render us a service. You are familiar with the University project[2] in its

---

66. [1] See No. 36.   [2] See No. 36 and n. 1 there.
   [3] W. did not in fact visit London until the autumn of 1903.
   [4] See n. 5 to No. 22.   [5] See n. 3 to No. 55.
   [6] No reply by Evans-Gordon to this letter has been found.

67. [1] David Brailovsky, brother of Zina Brailovsky of Rostov—a friend of V.K.— was then studying in Kharkov.
   [2] Brailovsky received the brochure *Eine Jüdische Hochschule* from V.K. (see V.K. to W., 18 (31) Aug. 1902, W.A.), and it can be assumed that W. talked to him when he visited Rostov in the autumn of 1902.

entirety, and are aware of what I was doing in Kharkov[3] some time ago. Now, I am very surprised that since my departure I have not received a single word from any of the people in Kharkov. I have written in every direction,[4] but no-one reveals any sign of life. Could it be that our cause there is completely sunk ? It simply doesn't seem possible after the great success the University idea had there. I cannot possibly conceive of any reason for this passivity. For heaven's sake, dear friend, do please write to me about the state of our affairs there, if indeed any state exists. I have sent about six registered letters to the various members of the committee, including two to Aleinikov, but all in vain.

You can imagine what fun there is in writing your fingers away without being honoured by these gentlemen to the extent of a single syllable.

I do not wish to complain any more. This is, alas, the fate of even the best causes among the Jews. I now very much hope that my present attempt will succeed and that you will write to me forthwith about everything concerning our enterprise in Kharkov.

Please speak to Dr. Breslav, Messrs. Futran, Aleinikov, etc. Ask them whether they are accustomed ever to reply to letters. If they have no such habitude I shall naturally not be annoyed at all.

At all events, we would be happy to establish closer contact with you, dear friend. We know that you can work energetically and we hope that you will stimulate the gentlemen in Kharkov into activity. Kindly be discreet in dealing with the content of my letter.

Looking forward to your immediate reply,[5] I remain with warm regards,

Yours,

68. To Victor Jacobson, Simferopol. *Geneva, 8 December 1902*

German: Or. Copy. T.W.: W.A.

8. 12. 02.

Dr. Victor Jacobson,
Simferopol.

Dear Friend,

As you will have learned from our exchange of correspondence,[1]

---

[3] W. visited Kharkov in Oct. 1902 and spread the idea of a Jewish University. On his initiative a University committee was set up (see Vol. I, No. 319 and n. 3 there).   [4] See Nos. 2, 3, 4, 20, 23, 28, 29, 45.

[5] Brailovsky only replied on 10 (23) Jan. 1903 (W.A.), when he told W. that the University committee had not yet done anything.

68. [1] The subject had apparently been mentioned in correspondence between

and from subsequent newspaper reports, we have lately been seeking
to convert the idea of establishing a Jewish University into a reality.
With this intention we have published a brochure, despatched to
you under separate cover, in which we outline the reasoning
behind the project as well as the project itself. During the holidays,
furthermore, I undertook a propaganda tour which, in addition to
its purely Zionist purpose, served the University idea as well. We
succeeded in raising a considerable portion of the amount required
for preparatory work, and in arousing warm interest in the undertaking among many different circles of the Jewish population: intellectuals and financiers, Zionists and non-Zionists.[2]

We are now in a position, therefore, to initiate more systematic
activities. These have already begun, in part, and may be divided
as follows:

1) The formation of committees, preferably composed of academic people, in the large European centres so as to develop
the project on a regular basis and deepen awareness of it as an
idea. We can already report distinct success towards this. We
have managed to win over some noted personalities in Berlin
and Vienna, so that the constitution of committees[3] in these
cities seems to be assured.

2) The initiation of surveys into the condition of Jewish students
in Western Europe and Russia. In this direction, too, something has been achieved. We expect to complete a part of the
statistical study during the second half of the current semester.
As soon as the questionnaires now in process of being printed
are ready, we shall have the honour of sending you some copies
for your information.

3) In Russia we aim to create a favourable atmosphere for the
project within the sphere of influence of our friends, and with

W. and Jacobson in the summer of 1902 (see Vol. I, n. 24 to No. 238; No. 278).
These letters have not been found.

   [2] W. propagated the Jewish University idea in Rostov, Baku, and Kharkov—
see Vol. I, bridge-note following No. 317 and Nos. 318, 319.

   [3] The extant correspondence shows that the campaign to enlist support for the
University in Berlin academic circles had so far not gone beyond putting out feelers.
W. wrote on 20 Aug. 1902 that he had established contact with Professors Senator,
Levin, and Landau, adding that he did not yet know 'what will come out of all this'
(see Vol. I, No. 293). In November W. contacted Altschul and asked him to talk to a
number of Berlin professors, especially Pictet, but by the time the present letter was
written he had not received a reply (see No. 41 and cf. No. 84). With regard to Vienna,
Buber wrote on 28 Nov. 1902 (W.A.) that a University committee was about to be
set up there and mentioned Professor Politzer and the lecturer Pineles as possible
members, but see letter to Feiwel of 10 Dec. 1902 (No. 75): 'If I were certain that
by now there were people for the committee in Vienna, I would go there, and to
Berlin.'

their help to create small, closed groups of selected people for the 'Jewish University'. Their purpose will be to establish close communication with us and prepare the forthcoming propaganda effort together with the plan of organisation, as well as supply the finance for current activities.

4) Arranging visits to England, America, etc.

Having taken it upon ourselves to give you this brief description of our plan, we request your goodwill in examining it. At the same time, should you regard our undertaking with sympathy, we have the honour to invite your co-operation.

In anticipation of your reply,[4] which will be much appreciated, we remain,

Most respectfully and with regards,

69. To Ben-Zion Friedland and Moses Weizmann, Kiev. *Geneva, 8 December 1902*

German: Or. Copy. T.W.: W.A.

8. 12. 02.

Messrs. B. Friedland and M. Weizmann,[1]
Kiev.

Dear Friends,

We have, as you see, begun activities at our Bureau. The first and most important task will, of course, be the statistical study. The outline of a questionnaire, intended for use in Russia, has gone off to Moscow.[2] In the event of your not having a report as yet from Idelson and Kroll, kindly write to them immediately so that you will be in contact with regard to the statistical study.

At the same time we would ask you to supply our Bureau with the necessary information on Kiev. It would be very good if you or other of our friends would speak with a few gentlemen, i.e. Ratner, Prof. Bulgakov, Private-Lecturer Frankfurt,[3] etc. Please find out also whether there is a Mr. Rostovtsev,[4] a chemist, at the Poly-technic, enrolled as professor or lecturer.

---

[4] Jacobson's reply has not been found.

69. [1] Friedland and Weizmann (brother of Chaim W.) were members of *Kadimah* in Kiev.

[2] See No. 35.   [3] Not identified.

[4] Probably a reference to Sergei Rostovtsev, Russian translator of the book by Karl Graebe (Professor of Chemistry at Geneva University, whom W. assisted): *Guide pratique pour l'analyse quantitative*, Geneva, 1893. The Russian translation appeared in 1901. It is not known whether Rostovtsev was at the time a lecturer at the Kiev Polytechnic or at any other Russian institution.

As a general principle, please make it your energetic endeavour to interest persons from the world of scholarship and the better writers in our common cause, thus creating a small Kiev group which will be in permanent, close contact with us.

Try and induce Dr. Mandelstamm to active participation in the undertaking.[5] Being on the spot you can assess the situation much better than we can from here. We therefore consider it superfluous to make any definite proposals to you; on the contrary, we expect suggestions on your part.

As a general rule, we would like you to win some of the better elements among Jewish students over to our idea. We have as yet few resources and meagre strength at our disposal. The more we have of these, the swifter will be our progress.

We are, of course, at your service. We shall readily assist you to the utmost in your efforts.[6]

With best regards to you and all our friends,

Your

70. To Isidore (Israel) Eliashev, Zurich. *Geneva, 9 December 1902*

German: Or. Copy. T.W.: W.A.

Geneva, 4 rue Lombard, 9. 12. 02.

Dr. I. Eliashev,[1]
Zurich.

Dear Friend,

The mere knowledge that you are in the vicinity made me happy today, but why do you plan to remain in Zurich for such a short time? Or is it that you intend visiting another Swiss city? I shall come to Zurich on the 25th, though I expect nothing from the gathering.[2] We have too few useful people in the *Cheirus*[3] to be able to initiate any kind of endeavour.[4]

With warmest regards,

Your

---

[5] For Mandelstamm's previous activity on behalf of the University project see Vol. I, No. 319.   [6] No reply to this letter has been found.

70. [1] The letter is written in the intimate form.

[2] Eliashev had written to W. from Zurich on 7 Dec. 1902 (W.A.). He asked W. to participate in the *Cheirus* conference to be held in Zurich on 25 Dec., explained the differences among the members about the aims of the organization (see n. 22 to No. 18), and wrote about the agenda of the conference. Eliashev added that he did not have much faith in the conference, but felt, like Feiwel, that the way must be paved for future action.   [3] In the original: 'Cheirusorganisation'.

[4] W. did not take part in the *Cheirus* conference.

71. To Maximilian Goldbaum, Warsaw. *Geneva, 9 December 1902*

German: Or. Copy. T.W.: W.A.

9. 12. 02.

Maximilian Goldbaum,
Warsaw.[1]

Dear Sir,

We have had the honour to send you, through the *Jüdischer Verlag* in Berlin, our brochure entitled 'A Jewish University'.[2] If you would be good enough to read this publication with care all further explanation would be superfluous.

At present our Bureau is engaged in creating a committee of co-workers so as to further the undertaking. We are concerned first of all in arranging, with the co-operation of suitable personalities, the preliminary research for the project; and secondly, to prepare for the propaganda effort which is to begin soon. The activities of our co-workers in the committee now being formed in Warsaw[3] should extend initially to distributing information, possibly assisting in the surveys, attracting eminent Jewish personalities—particularly professors, scholars, writers, artists; and later to form smaller 'Jewish University' groups, etc.

Should you regard the project for a Jewish University sympathetically, we extend to you, Sir, a most cordial and respectful invitation to join this committee of co-workers. We can give you our immediate assurance that our Bureau will be happy to support you at all times and in every way in the work that your initiatives may engender. Please regard us as being completely at your service in this matter.

(End of letter missing)[4]

72. To Moses Glikin, Charlottenburg. *Geneva, 9 December 1902*

Russian: Pcd. H.W.: C.Z.A. A179/3

Geneva, Rue Lombard 4.
9/XII. 02.

Dear Glikin,

I cannot understand why you have not replied to my letter.[1] I am

71. [1] W.'s handwriting in the original copy. Marginal corrections in an unidentified handwriting are not given here.
   [2] See No. 54, but cf. n. 2 to No. 63.   [3] Cf. n. 1 to No. 33.
   [4] No reply from Goldbaum has been found.

72. [1] See No. 47.

impatiently waiting for news. What about our *Drucksachen*?[2] It is impossible to get a reply from Berlin. For God's sake, write!

Your Ch. Weizmann.

73. To Gregory Lurie, Pinsk. *Geneva, 9 December 1902*

German: Or. Copy. T.W.: W.A.

9. 12. 02.

Mr. Gregory Lurie,
Pinsk.

Dear Friend,

Subsequent to our many discussions in Pinsk,[1] we are permitting ourselves this brief description of the activities we have already initiated, in the hope that our aims will be of interest to you.

In accordance with the programme outlined in the brochure we have attempted the following:

1) First of all, to win a circle of eminent personalities, mostly from the academic world, over to our plan. We have in fact succeeded in forming several groups of such people.[2] The function of these groups is both to undertake the further elaboration of the project and to create the foundations of a future organisation, besides a propaganda effort.

2) Statistical studies, through surveys among Jewish students in Western Europe as well as in Russia. The appropriate questionnaires are now being printed and will be sent for your kind examination as soon as they are ready.

3) To create smaller, closed 'Jewish University' groups consisting of selected persons whose purpose will be to support the work of the Bureau intellectually and materially, in permanent co-operation with us. We have sought to bring about the formation of such groups through our friends.[3]

We would be most happy, dear Mr. Lurie, if you would support us in the work we have inaugurated. We believe you can render our cause great service both personally and through your connections.

In warmly inviting you to co-operate with us, we remain, most respectfully and with kind regards,

[2] 'Printed material'—see No. 47.

73. [1] W. stayed in Pinsk, with two interruptions, from August until the end of October 1902 (see Vol. I).

[2] Reference to Jewish University committees. In fact, up to this time steps towards the formation of a committee had been taken only in Vienna (see n. 1 to No. 38).

[3] See Nos. 50, 51, 52, 57, 61, 62, 68, 69, 71.

74. To Berthold Feiwel, Zurich. *Geneva, 9 December 1902*

German: Or. Copy. T.W.: W.A.

Geneva, 9. 12. 02.

Mr. Berthold Feiwel,
Zurich.

Dear Berthold,

Thank you very much for writing.[1] I am not in the least annoyed by your remarks, which were well intentioned. I must merely make the point that all the errors contained in the copies were corrected in the originals. The example of 'Senator' is a pure misunderstanding. We are not talking about Professor Senator, whom we would have accorded a more respectful title, but about Senator Levi Montefiore. I am in full agreement with you regarding the style, but these things will improve.

Where are the questionnaires? It is high time that we sent them out. Have you received proofs from the printers? Please don't forget to reply immediately.

No news from *Die Welt*.[2]

All good wishes,

Your

75. To Berthold Feiwel, Zurich. *Geneva, 10 December 1902*

German: Or. Copy. T.W.: W.A.

10. 12. 02.

Mr. Berthold Feiwel,
Zurich.

Dear Berthold,

Today I again have to start my letter with a complaint. You must have noticed from the copies how I implored Buber and Glikin for

74. [1] Feiwel to W., undated (? 8 Dec. 1902), W.A. In his letter Feiwel criticized the style of some Geneva Bureau letters, which W. had sent him for perusal (see No. 65). As an example he cited the salutation 'Dear Mr. Senator' in the letter to Georges Levi Montefiore (see No. 37 and n. 2 there), which he mistakenly took to be intended for Professor Herman Senator in Berlin.

[2] About the Democratic Fraction's protest against Schauer's article, which had been sent to the editors of *Die Welt* for publication (see No. 25 and n. 1 there).

information on the matters touched on in my various letters.[1] I am sitting here without a reply. If things go on like this the situation will become downright impossible. We simply cannot waste our time here in futile letter-writing. If Martin is now involved in other affairs to the extent that he hasn't the time to take care of small things, then there is no prospects of his being useful to the cause in any way later, when the tasks will become greater and more complicated. It makes matters all the worse when, having relied upon someone in the belief that he can be useful, one is sorely disappointed afterwards.

If Glikin was in no hurry to carry out my urgent instructions at a time when he knew he was to be employed by us,[2] then I am all for cancelling the engagement. It is quite unheard of to be delayed in one's work for so long, and by one's closest friends at that. Each morning brings me new frustrations. I am conscious all the time of how the work drags, how time flies, and we have not taken even one step forward. If it is like this at the beginning, what will happen later? I could ask a whole lot of questions, but I shall leave it. A change has absolutely got to take place. This way our activities cannot meet with the slightest success.

We want to utilise the coming holidays to set everything on the right track. Please write forcefully to Buber.[3] I shall do the same.[4] If I were certain that by now there were people for the committee in Vienna I would go there, and to Berlin. Otherwise we shall never emerge from the talking stage, which I can no longer abide.

Levinson[5] and I are prepared to work much harder even than hitherto, but we are making no headway because we are short of everything we need. I am writing to Trietsch as well today, and will ask him what he thinks about my coming to Berlin.[6] I would also like your opinion on the views expressed here.

Forgive me for being so agitated. I feel it deeply that we are, after all, unable to achieve what we had set out to do.

Your very devoted

---

75. [1] See Nos. 38, 47, 60. Apparently copies of these letters were among those W. sent to Feiwel on 6 Dec. (see No. 65).

[2] See n. 3 to No. 41.

[3] Feiwel had written to Buber on the previous day about setting up a committee for the University in Vienna; it appears that he did not write again after receiving W.'s letter (see Feiwel to Buber, 9 Dec. 1902, Buber Archives N.L.; Feiwel to W., 12 Dec. 1902, W.A.).

[4] See No. 76.

[5] Samuel Levinson, W.'s assistant at the University Bureau.

[6] See No. 77.

76. To Martin Buber, Vienna. *Geneva, 10 December 1902*

German: Or. Copy. T.W.: W.A.

10. 12. 02.

Mr. Martin Buber,
Vienna.

Dear Martin,

You know that I am a kind and patient man, but now my patience seems to be at an end. This is the fourth letter in which I could go on repeating a host of questions,[1] but I really must give up because I receive no replies. If you believe that I can do anything for our cause when I am treated by my closest and dearest friends in this fashion you are definitely mistaken. Frankly, we have not as yet taken our undertaking a single step forward. We have great responsibilities to the cause and to public opinion. Absolute strangers have placed their confidence in us and pinned their hopes on our ability and capacity for work. We have not yet proved that we can justify these hopes. We on this side are prepared to place all our energies at the service of the cause but we are prevented from doing anything when our friends deny us every kind of assistance and display no interest.

I still do not know what arrangements you have made with Herzl,[2] Werner,[3] the contemplated University committee, the various professors. We are still without the list[4] that was announced 14 days ago, etc.

I now ask you quite detachedly: is systematic work possible under such conditions? I am aware that you have a great deal to do, but I too have other matters beside the University project to attend to, and I also have to worry about my personal future.

Until now I have had nothing but frustration from the whole business.

I would go to Vienna if I were convinced that matters had reached a point where a committee could be constituted there. In that case I would leave here on the 21st and remain in Vienna until the 25th so as to return to Geneva by way of Berlin and Frankfurt.

This is the last time I shall ask you to reply in detail to all the questions put in my previous letters.

I am deeply sorry to have to write such letters, but things are

---

76. [1] See previous letters to Buber (Nos. 11, 19, 38, 60). Buber wrote to W. on 16 Nov., 18 Nov., and 28 Nov. (W.A.) but did not reply to all the questions put by W.
[2] Regarding Herzl's joining the Jewish University committee see n. 1 to No. 38.
[3] See No. 60.
[4] Buber had promised on 16 Nov. to send this list—see n. 1 to No. 19.

getting beyond me. If, therefore, you attach any value to all that
has been said here you will answer by return.

Your

77. **To Davis Trietsch, Berlin.** *Geneva, 10 December 1902*
German: Or. Copy. T.W.: W.A.

Geneva, 10. 12. 02.

Mr. D. Trietsch,
Berlin.

Dear Friend,

I have already sent off lamenting notes to Feiwel and Buber[1] that
would have done honour to a Jeremiah. You are the third in the
alliance, although towards you I have the least justification for complaint. You may, at an appropriate opportunity, deliver a friendly
poke in the ribs to our friend Glikin and tell him that the mail goes
just as well from Berlin to Geneva and not only from Geneva to
Berlin. One might be casual as a Fraction member, but never as an
employed official.[2]

I have no idea what is happening to the brochure, for it cannot be
at the printers so long.[3] Furthermore, I do not know what is happening to the questionnaire. In brief, I am as wise as I was three weeks
ago.

My visit to London during this holiday must, it seems, be called
off. According to Gordon the season is too unfavourable, because of
the holidays.[4] What do you think of a visit to Berlin? I want to
try and create a solid 'Jewish University' group there at long last.
However, I would like first of all to have your opinion on Warburg.
Would he join a committee if one is formed?

Dear Trietsch, I entreat you most strongly to reply to this letter.
I am miserably affected by the poor way in which the Bureau functions. For my part I do everything to promote our affairs, but even
the best intentions suffer from the lack of interest evinced by such
'friends'.

Warmest regards from

Your

P.S. Dr. Blau is silent as a fish.[5] Have you the power to make him
talk? Should he be written to once more?[6]

77. [1] See Nos. 75, 76.   [2] See n. 3 to No. 41.
  [3] Reference to the second edition of *Eine Jüdische Hochschule.*
  [4] See n. 1 to No. 36.   [5] See No. 39 and n. 1 there.
  [6] Trietsch replied on 17 Dec. 1902 (W.A.). He welcomed W.'s proposal to visit
Berlin. He thought it ought to be possible to persuade Warburg to join the Berlin
University committee and probably also Professors Philippson, Landau, Levin,
'and a whole flock'. Trietsch also asked W. to write Blau again.

78. To Arieh Reich, Vienna. *Geneva, 10 December 1902*

German: Or. Copy. T.W.: W.A.

10. 12. 02.

Mr. A. H. Reich,
Vienna.

Dear Friend,

You will be rendering our Bureau a great service if you would be so kind as to let us have a few addresses from the administrative office.[1] Since we wish to conduct a survey of Jewish youth studying in Western Europe, we would like to have addresses of reliable persons or groups in the University cities.

We are concerned in the first instance with people from Russia in the following cities: Koenigsberg, Breslau, Dresden, Stuttgart, Aachen, Strasbourg, Kiel, Greifswald, Rostock, Giessen, Erlangen, Jena, Halle, Hanover, Marburg, Wuerzburg, Freiberg (Saxony), Freiburg (Breisgau), Brunswick, etc.

Should you have no addresses of Russians, please send me the addresses of non-Russian friends whom I might contact.[2]

Thanking you in anticipation, and with kindest regards,

I am

Your

79. To Joseph Lurie, Warsaw. *Geneva, 11 December 1902*

Russian: Or. Copy. H.W.: W.A.

Geneva, Rue Lombard 4.
11/XII. 02.

I really cannot understand, dear Lurie, why I have still received no replies to any of my letters.[1] If you are so busy that you cannot scribble a couple of lines, at least let me know whom else I can get in touch with about the Hebrew [----] brochure.[2]

You will then be rid of my letters. It is a painful realisation when one's closest friends evince the least inclination to help in an endeavour as arduous as our undertaking is, and then to find them shrugging their shoulders because it doesn't move faster.

Your Ch. Weizmann.

78. [1] Reich was an official in the Central Office of the Zionist Organization in Vienna.
[2] No reply from Reich has been found.

79. [1] See Nos. 17, 58.
[2] The Hebrew translation of *Eine Jüdische Hochschule.*

8o. To Aaron Eliasberg, Paris. *Geneva, 12 December 1902*

German: Or. Copy. T.W.: W.A.

Geneva, 4 rue Lombard, 12. 12. 02.

Mr. Aaron Eliasberg,
Paris.

Dear Aaron,[1]

In reply to your letter I wish to inform you that we are expecting with pleasure your report on the French universities.[2] Feiwel is planning the publication of a wider study regarding the scheme for a Jewish University.[3] You might communicate with him about it.

I cannot help your not understanding which public the brochure was intended for. I can only observe that the first edition of one thousand copies has been exhausted, so that a second edition has become necessary. There still seem to be people who read, after all. May I ask you to make it a rule, if you wish to raise an objection, not to get lost in phraseology and clichés, but to state clearly and precisely what you mean. The brochure is being read in all kinds of circles. We do not pretend that its significance approaches that of a scientific work, but it is intended to be more than a mere proclamation and is meant as a clear presentation of our objectives. We on our part know that we have fulfilled this purpose. A second, longer statement by more competent people is in preparation and will follow.

Now a small request: some time ago we applied to the editorial office of the *Écho Sioniste* to send us addresses of Russian-Jewish students in the French-speaking countries[4] for our survey. We have had no answer as yet. You probably meet the people of the editorial office. You will be doing us a service if you can get addresses from them relating to Brussels, Liège, Ghent, Bordeaux, Lyon, etc.

Buber's address is 38 Porzellangasse, Vienna.

Kindest regards from

Your

8o. [1] Eliasberg is addressed in the intimate form.

[2] The letter has not been found, but according to No. 83, Eliasberg, who had recently moved from Heidelberg to Paris, proposed making a report on French universities as a contribution to the University Bureau's preparatory work. It is not known whether he himself took the initiative in this, or whether W. asked him to prepare such a report (for previous correspondence with Eliasberg on the University project, see Vol. I, No. 230; No. 250 and n. 1 there). Eliasberg's report has not been found.

[3] See No. 7 and n. 3 there.   [4] See No. 56.

81. To the President, Student Zionist Society, Antwerp.

Geneva, 12 December 1902

German: Or. Copy. T.W.: W.A.

The President, Student Zionist Society,
Antwerp.

12. 12. 02.

Dear Fellow-Zionist,

Miss Koenigsberg has forwarded your kind letter[1] on to us and we are very pleased to be able to establish contact with you. You will already be familiar with our aims from the Jewish Press. A brochure, sent to you under separate cover, will enlighten you on our programme of activities.

We are prepared to provide you with additional information as required concerning activities already initiated, and would be most grateful if you would let us know whether and in what manner you, or your society, could help to further our cause. Are you able, perhaps, to interest some professors or other significant personalities in the project?

Among other things, we are about to conduct a survey on the situation of Jewish students in Western Europe. You would be facilitating our task, and would thereby earn our gratitude, if you could provide us with the addresses of reliable people in Belgian and Dutch Universities. The addresses which we would appreciate receiving from you should relate to Russian-Jewish students.

At the same time we would respectfully ask whether you would be inclined to undertake the survey in Antwerp. In that case we shall place our questionnaire and other printed material[2] at your disposal.

Our local friends will write to you about the other Zionist matters.[3]

With every good wish and our thanks in anticipation.

I am,
With Zion's greetings,

81. [1] Apparently a letter not found, to Anne Koenigsberg offering the society's help to the University Bureau.

[2] The society's secretary replied that it would conduct the survey in Belgium but it had no contacts in Holland (G. Katzman to W., 22 Dec. 1902, W.A.).

[3] Probably a reference to matters raised in the letter to Anne Koenigsberg (see n. 1 above). It is not known who was to have written to the society about these matters; in his letter of 22 Dec. 1902 the society's secretary confirmed receipt of 'your letters of 12 Dec. and 15 Dec.'.

82. To the Administration, Wuerzburg University.[1]
Geneva, 12 December 1902

German: Or. Copy. T.W.: W.A.

The University Administration,
Wuerzburg.

Geneva, 4 rue Lombard, 12. 12. 02.

The undersigned requests that you kindly send him some addresses of students from Russia.

Thanking you in anticipation, I remain,

Your obedient servant,

83. To Berthold Feiwel, Zurich. *Geneva, 12 December 1902*

German: Or. Copy. T.W.: W.A.

Geneva, 12. 12. 02.

Express Post.

Mr. Berthold Feiwel,
Zurich.

Dear Toldy,

I gratefully acknowledge receipt of the copies.[1] At the same time I confirm my telegram of today saying: 'Request immediate telegraphic reply whether questionnaires being printed, whether proofs arrived. Most disturbed at your not writing.'[2]

A letter has indeed come from Glikin, and in it he informs me that they know nothing about the questionnaire in Berlin. Is it really possible that they have not yet been printed?[3]

I shall try to put this question for the last time, and also remind you that in your last letter you wrote: 'You will hear again[4] tomorrow.'[5] Well, three tomorrows have already passed and I still have no news. I do not wish to labour the point with you on the effect this

82. [1] Identical letters were sent to the administrative offices of the Aachen and Stuttgart Polytechnics (original copies in W.A.). No reply to any of the three letters has been found; see also No. 145 and n. 4 there.

83. [1] I.e., of Geneva Bureau letters sent to Feiwel for perusal (see No. 65).

[2] The telegram itself has not been found.

[3] Glikin wrote to W. on 19 Dec. 1902 (W.A.) that Trietsch had not yet received the text of the questionnaire for the student survey. No. 84 shows that Feiwel sent the questionnaire to the Berlin printer direct, and not through Trietsch, as W. thought.

[4] In orig: 'auf Wiederlesen'.

[5] See Feiwel to W., undated (? 8 Dec. 1902), W.A.

has upon me. In reply to my frequent, detailed letters I invariably receive a few hastily written lines, apparently merely to be rid of it.

I repeat, this is the last time I shall return to the subject. I shall stop writing if I am to be treated in this way. I cannot be held responsible if this were to bring about grave consequences for the cause. You know very well that I want to devote all my energies to it; you know that I am prepared to neglect everything outside of it. I cannot, however, reconcile myself to the thought that I am to be the only one who gets worked up over every detail and who feels totally forsaken by his friends.

Enclosed is a letter from *Die Welt* which arrived yesterday.[6] I also received news that the money from Baku[7] was sent off six days ago, so it should be in Vienna by now. I am sending you a blank sheet of paper with my signature. We can now write to Herzl that in addition to the 600 francs,[8] another 1,400 should be paid out for the following: typewriter 540 francs, which I must pay without fail within a week, printing, salaries, office equipment, and possibly for a journey.[9] I would suggest that all this be specified to Herzl.[10] I intend to request his collaboration once more in writing,[11] to contact him confidentially about the possibility of establishing a University in Palestine.[12] Ussishkin writes that the Odessa committee has decided to create a 'Pinsker' fund for a University in Palestine.[13] It would appear that these people propose embarking upon a detailed investigation of the possibilities of founding a school in Palestine.

[6] Reference to a letter of 9 Dec. 1902 from Kokesch and Marmorek to W., on behalf of the S.A.C. (W.A.), stating their inability to publish the protest against Schauer's article in *Die Welt*, 'inasmuch as we cannot allow the use of such a tone against fellow Zionists in the party's organ', and asking for the strongly personal note to be removed (for the protest, see n. 1 to No. 25).

[7] Presumably this news was sent by Zeitlin—cf. n. 5 to No. 40, and see also No. 86.

[8] See n. 2 to No. 65.

[9] A probable reference to W.'s trip to Vienna and Berlin—cf. Nos. 75, 76, 77.

[10] The letter was written and dispatched to Herzl on 13 Dec. 1902 (C.Z.A. Z1/340). Feiwel wrote about money matters, as instructed by W., and expressed his certainty that the Actions Committee would agree to Herzl's joining the University committee (see n. 1 to No. 38).

[11] No such letter to Herzl has been found (see n. 1 to No. 92).

[12] Both W. and Herzl felt at this time that the University should be located in Western Europe (see Nos. 2, 4, 149). It appears that W. nevertheless wished to discuss with Herzl the possibility of establishing it in Palestine. Feiwel, too, told Herzl in the letter mentioned in n. 5 above: 'The main aim we have set ourselves in our present work is to establish the University in Palestine.'

[13] A circular from Ussishkin (in his capacity as Regional Leader for Ekaterinoslav) of 15 (28) Nov. 1902 reports the opposition of the Annual Zionist Conference to locating the University in Europe and support for its establishment in Palestine (see Vol. I, n. 4 to No. 320). The circular also announces that the *Hovevei Zion* Conference in Odessa (Nov. 1902) decided to create a fund in the name of Leo Pinsker, half to be earmarked for the establishment of a University in Palestine. The circular was sent to W. by Ussishkin (copies in W.A. and C.Z.A. Z1/383). See also No. 129.

We on our part must in no circumstances be by-passed, and must build up contacts with the forces that matter.[14]

We here are certainly of the opinion that we would be in a far better position if we could already point to a few committees in Vienna and Berlin. Then they would have to reckon with us. Unfortunately, nothing definite exists as yet,[15] except for Buber's two-line reports.

At all events, it is most necessary to get a written document once and for all from Herzl stating his position on a University in Palestine. You could, therefore, compose the letter in this vein.

News has arrived from Aaron Eliasberg—he is prepared to make a study of the French universities and supply the Bureau with a detailed report.[16]

Glikin wrote comprehensively today.[17] He could not reply sooner because Dr. Altschul was away. He protests his readiness to take prompt care of all matters. It seems that in my irritation I have done him an injustice.[18]

With many kind regards,

Yours ever,

84. To Moses Glikin, Charlottenburg. *Geneva, 12 December 1902*

German/Russian: T.W./H.W. C.Z.A. A126/24/7/2/2

Geneva, 12. 12. 02.

Mr. M. Glikin,
Berlin.[1]

Dear Friend,

Many thanks for your letter.[2] I have already written to you about your coming here by January 1st.[3]

---

[14] No further letter from W. on this matter has been found; he wrote to Ussishkin on 28 Dec. 1902 and 13 Jan. 1903 (see Nos. 129, 205), but the University question is not mentioned in either letter.

[15] In the original: 'nichts Definitives'. [16] See also No. 80 and n. 1 there.

[17] See n. 2 to No. 84. [18] See No. 75.

84. [1] Glikin lived in Charlottenburg, now a part of Berlin.

[2] Glikin to W., 10 Dec. 1902, W.A. Glikin wrote about current Bureau matters. His letter indicates that the reason for Altschul's failure to reply to W. (see Nos. 14, 26) was his absence from Berlin; nevertheless he (Altschul) had spoken to Pictet and had promised to write to W. Glikin said he had discussed publishing the protest against Schauer's article with Loewe, and he described Loewe's proposed text as 'apologetica' (see No. 34; No. 46 and n. 1 there). Glikin announced his intention of coming to Zurich at the end of December to begin working for the Bureau, and gave the addresses of several students at German Universities who could be contacted in connection with the survey. [3] See No. 47.

I do not see any report in your letter regarding the second edition of the brochure. What about it?

On the 3rd of this month I wrote to Trietsch and asked him to send six brochures to Warsaw.[4] He was given the exact addresses. Kindly enquire if and when these brochures went off, as it is most important. In addition, send a brochure to Mr. I. Yasinovsky, Medowa 15, Warsaw.

Dr. Altschul has still not written, one can almost lose all one's patience. Press Trietsch for an answer. Ask him how matters stand with Dr. Blau of Frankfurt and Prof. Warburg.[5] What does Trietsch think about my coming to Berlin?[6] I must have answers from Altschul, Trietsch and yourself within a week at the latest, and you must all be specific. Never delay anything, dear Glikin, treat everything with the greatest urgency. I need not impress you with their importance.

Regarding addresses, try and make your contacts with Dresden and Koenigsberg through the Berlin colony;[7] dig them out from under the earth.

Hoping to see you soon,

Yours ever,
Chaim

[8]I have just received a reply to my telegram[9] to Feiwel,[10] saying that the *Fragebogen* are being printed in Berlin. It would be a good idea to find out from Pass and Garleb[11] whether they are ready. Apparently Feiwel got in touch with the printers himself, not through Trietsch.

Thanks for the invitation.[12]

Your Ch. W.

Regards to comrades.

---

[4] See No. 54.

[5] In his letter of 10 Dec. 1902 (No. 77) W. asked Trietsch if he would try and obtain a reply from Blau to his letter of 1 Dec. 1902 (No. 39), and asked Trietsch to ascertain whether Warburg would be willing to join the University committee.

[6] See No. 77.

[7] The foreign student colony in Berlin.

[8] What follows was added in Russian in W.'s handwriting.

[9] The telegram has not been found, but for text see No. 83.

[10] It appears that Feiwel replied by telegram (not found).

[11] A Berlin printing press.

[12] In the letter mentioned in n. 2 above, Glikin invited W. to the *Chanuka* party (on the Feast of Lights, and commemorating the Maccabean revolt) of the Berlin *Kadimah*.

85. To Hugo Schachtel, Breslau. *Geneva, 12 December 1902*

German: T.W.: C.Z.A. A102/10/2/2

Geneva, 12. 12. 02.
Rue Lombard 4

Mr. Hugo Schachtel,
Breslau.

Dear Fellow-Zionist,

May we take the liberty of requesting you kindly to let us have some addresses of students from Russia with a sense of responsibility who may be residing in Breslau. We need them for the survey which is about to start among Jewish students in Western Europe.

It would give us great pleasure, in any case, to establish closer relations with you on everything to do with the University. I presume that you are acquainted with the progress of this matter through our friend Feiwel.[1] I feel that something might be achieved for our venture in Breslau.

We look forward with great interest to hearing from you regarding the above, and remain,

Most respectfully and with regards,

Dr. Ch. Weizmann

86. To the Jewish Colonial Trust, London. *Geneva, 13 December 1902*

German: Or. Copy. T.W.: W.A.

13. 12. 02.

The Jewish Colonial Trust,
For the attention of Mr. D. Levontin[1]
London.

Dear Friend,

You will doubtless be aware that the Bank has money on deposit for the Jewish University Bureau. In addition to the sums already there, you should have received, or will be receiving any day, another 2,283 roubles from Baku.[2]

---

85. [1] On 15 Dec. 1902 Schachtel replied that Feiwel had not written for a long time.

86. [1] Zalman David Levontin was Manager of the J.C.T. at the time.

[2] The money sent from Rostov was deposited in the Bureau's account at the J.C.T. (see n. 3 to No. 27). As for Baku see n. 5 to No. 40 and cf. No. 83 and n. 7 there.

Some time ago we requested a small payment,[3] and we now require another[4] 2,000 francs. The matter is being held up, however, because the signature of Mr. Herzl is required and, as you know, he is ill.[5] Nevertheless we have a few payments to meet next week and ask you therefore to expedite the matter. Would you be so kind as to contact Mr. Herzl about this so that disbursements might be made more promptly in the future?[6] I would ask, most respectfully, that you telegraph Mr. Herzl since, as already stated, we are being pressed. Or could I not draw a cheque on the Bank payable in a fortnight?

I do hope, dear friend, that you will expedite this matter, and so do me a great service.

With my sincerest thanks in anticipation, and with cordial regards,

I am,

Yours faithfully,

87. To Gregory (Zvi) Bruck, Vitebsk. *Geneva, 13 December 1902*

German: Or. Copy. T.W.: W.A.

13. 12. 02.

Registered.

Dr. G. Bruck,
Vitebsk.

Dear Friend,[1]

You will recall that in Vienna[2] we agreed to keep in touch with each other regarding the University project. You were kind enough to promise your valued co-operation. You will be familiar, up to a point, with our plan of work, divided as follows:

1) The formation of committees in the larger European countries. Some success in this direction has been registered in Vienna and Berlin.[3]

---

[3] See n. 2 to No. 65.

[4] An error in the original. On the previous day W. wrote Feiwel (see No. 83) to ask Herzl to give instructions to the J.C.T. to pay 1,400 francs to the University Bureau, in addition to the 600 francs requested previously (see No. 65). Thus the total amount was 2,000 francs, and not 'another 2,000 francs'.

[5] Cf. n. 3 to No. 89.

[6] Feiwel suggested to Herzl that the name of the account with the J.C.T. ('Dr. Herzl, Jewish University Bureau') be changed so that in future his signature would not be required for withdrawals—see n. 2 to No. 65.

87. [1] The letter is written in the intimate form.

[2] At the Annual Zionist Conference (Oct. 1902).

[3] But cf. No. 83; n. 3 to No. 68.

2) A statistical study of living conditions among Jewish students in Western Europe. This rather difficult task has also been started.

3) The formation of smaller 'Jewish University' groups in the larger Russian cities which, together with us, will further the cause both as an idea and in material terms. We are neither able, nor do we wish, to direct such groups from here. We can only recommend that these small societies, which we hope will develop into a basis for the future organisation of the 'Jewish University', be composed of carefully selected persons.

We wish to make our Bureau as financially independent of influence as possible. We have in mind the launching of a large fund to extend the forthcoming propaganda effort (in America, England, etc.). You can give us substantial support in this direction.

4) Arranging visits to America, England, Palestine.

Naturally, we would gladly supply you with all information most promptly. We are also allowing ourselves the hope that you will place at least some of your proven energy at the service of our ideal.

In looking forward with keen interest and appreciation to your reply,[4] which I trust will be in the affirmative, I send you my warmest regards.

Cordially and ever faithfully,
Your

88. To the Committee, *Hashahar*[1] Circle, Geneva.
Geneva, 13 December 1902

Russian: Vcd. H.W.: W.A.

Geneva, 13. XII. 02.

This is now the second time that the regular session of the Circle has been put off for no valid reason. And this despite the fact, as I well know, that problems both of theoretical and practical significance need to be examined.

I consider the Circle's inactivity to be disgraceful, and that its existence is pointless, serving only to mislead people.

---

[4] Bruck replied that in view of his vote against a European location for the University at the Annual Zionist Conference (see Vol. I, n. 4 to No. 320), he doubted his right to take any action on this matter. He promised to raise the question at the forthcoming meeting (of Regional Leaders), after which he would write to W. See Bruck to W., 7 (20) Jan. 1903 (pmk.), W.A. No further letter from Bruck has been found.

88. [1] For the founding of *Hashahar*, see Vol. I, No. 152 and n. 15 there.

I hereby request that my protest be brought to the attention of the meeting.[2]

Ch. Weizmann.

89. To Davis Trietsch, Berlin. *Geneva, 13 December 1902*

German: Or. Copy. T.W.: W.A.

Geneva, 4 rue Lombard, 13. 12. 02.

Mr. D. Trietsch,
Berlin.

Dear Friend,

Many thanks for your letter, which arrived today.[1] I am indeed happy to learn that the brochures will soon be ready.

In the meantime you will have received my letter to which I am anxiously awaiting your reply.[2]

And now a request. Our friend S. Lurie, of Darmstadt, who at this moment happens to be here, has arranged to loan our Bureau 300 marks. We urgently need to have this in our possession by Tuesday, or Wednesday at the latest. Lurie has issued an order for this purpose to the banking house of Meyer and Co., Berlin W, behind the Catholic Church (the exact number is in the directory, I think it is No. 2) payable in your favour. You can thus receive this money on Monday afternoon, or by the latest on Tuesday morning, whereupon please send it to us by telegraph. The Colonial Trust has held up remittance of our money for a few days because of Herzl's illness,[3] but as we have a debit-note to cover on Wednesday we have been compelled to make this arrangement. Please, friend Trietsch,

[2] The draft of the reply to this letter by Catherine Dorfman—a member of the *Hashahar* executive—dated 13 Dec. 1902, has been found among her papers (now in W.A.). Dorfman protested vehemently against W.'s letter. She explained the reason for postponing the *Hashahar* meeting and took exception to his criticism. He himself, she said, had defended the need for the Circle's existence 'when people used to tell you that there is no room for a healthy organism under such abnormal conditions, in the light of its diverse and incompatible components'.

89. [1] Trietsch to W., 3 Dec. 1902, with postscript of 11 Dec. 1902, W.A. In the postscript Trietsch reported that he had given the second edition of *Eine Jüdische Hochschule* to the printers and that Lilien would be producing the design of the emblem for the University Bureau within the next few days. He said that Altschul had spoken to Pictet (see No. 14) and would be reporting either to W. direct or through Trietsch himself.   [2] See No. 77 and n. 6 there.

[3] Reich had advised W. on 2 Dec. (W.A.) that Herzl was unwell, but no letter has been found giving this as the reason for delaying the transfer of the sum requested by W. and Feiwel (see No. 65 and n. 2 there). As it happened, Herzl had written to W. on the previous day saying that he had instructed the J.C.T. to send 600 francs to the University Bureau, but apparently his letter had not yet reached W. (see Herzl to W., 12 Dec. 1902, W.A.).

help us out of the predicament. You may charge the transfer cost to our Bureau account.[4]

Is Lilien really doing the emblem or is it merely a mirage ? What's happened about your propaganda tour ?[5]

Meanwhile we have received some signs of life from our Russian correspondents at last.[6] Putting pressure on people does help, after all.

Kindest regards from

Your devoted

90. To David Farbstein,[1] Zurich. *Geneva, 13 December 1902*

German: Or. Copy. T.W.: W.A.

Geneva, 13. 12. 02.

Confidential!

Dr. D. Farbstein,
Zurich.

Dear Friend,

I shall try and come to Biel.[2] You know the reasons why I have withdrawn from all activities in Switzerland. Thanks to some unpleasant elements a certain spirit has infiltrated the organisation,[3] a sort of frightening, unrestrained opportunism, and I have finally to ask myself whether we are still in any way comrades to all these people decked out in the cloak of Zionism.[4] If this continues I shall

[4] Trietsch advised W. on 17 Dec. 1902 (W.A.) that he had carried out the request regarding the money.

[5] Trietsch's planned propaganda trip to Switzerland. Trietsch replied on 17 Dec. 1902 (W.A.) that he would probably set out at the end of January or the beginning of February.

[6] Only a letter from Futran of 24 Nov. (7 Dec.) 1902 has been found (see n. 1 to No. 91). There is also a letter from Aleinikov dated 20 Nov. (3 Dec.) 1902 (W.A.), but it is clear from No. 100 that this letter had not yet reached W.

90. [1] Written in reply to a letter from Farbstein that has not been found.

[2] For the conference of Swiss Zionists there, 21 Dec. 1902. See also No. 118.

[3] Reference to the Swiss Zionist Federation.

[4] On W.'s activity in the Swiss Zionist Federation, as distinct from his activity among foreign students in Switzerland, there is only fragmentary information (see, e.g., Vol. I, Nos. 29, 32, 33, 35, 49). It appears that after 1900 W. ceased all activity in the Swiss Zionist Federation until his participation in the Biel conference in Dec. 1902. In a report in *Hamelitz* of 3/16 July 1902, W. is described as 'a man who has no affinity with the Swiss organisation'. It seems that W.'s main objection to the Swiss Zionists was that their Zionism was of a philanthropic kind, i.e. Swiss Jews were to help their oppressed brethren in the East and not attempt to instil in them a true Zionist consciousness—see report on W.'s speeches at the Swiss Zionist Conference in Biel in *Die Welt* of 23 Jan. 1903, and the report on his address at the Swiss Zionist Conference in Fribourg (28 June 1903) in *Hamelitz* of 11/24 July 1903.

consider it my duty in the future to pursue 'laissez-faire' tactics also. Struggling against these elements, which unfortunately put on a great show, would be a waste of energy and a form of parish politics.[5]

If in your opinion the possibilities of forming a true Zionist group exist,[6] or if you wish to direct Swiss Zionism, so-called, into proper channels, then I shall be with you with all my heart.

I share the view that the Fraction can and should become more socially-conscious.[7] Are you the man to present a positive programme? I give you a guarantee of support by all Fraction comrades.

We shall certainly be able to have a discussion in Biel, but I would like you to drop me a line before then.

All good wishes,

Your

P.S. Von-Diller's[8] address is: Mme A. Ivanschine, 5 rue Gassendi, Paris.

91. To Michael Futran, Kharkov. *Geneva, 13 December 1902*

German: Or. Copy. T.W.: W.A.

13. 12. 02.

Dr. M. Futran,
Kharkov.

Dear Friend,

Many thanks for your letter.[1] So you finally have shown a sign of life. You will certainly be aware, from numerous letters to our friends in Kharkov,[2] of the progress of the activities engaged upon by our Bureau. We trust that you will now embark upon the work on a

[5] In the original: 'Kirchturm Politik'.

[6] Possible reference to a group formed by Farbstein and Pasmanik (see No. 176 and n. 2 there).

[7] This sentence was apparently written in reply to a passage in Farbstein's letter to W. Farbstein, who advocated socialist views, was a member of the Democratic Fraction, albeit a critical one—cf. n. 2 to No. 8.

[8] Not identified.

91. [1] Futran to W., 24 Nov. (7 Dec.) 1902, W.A. Futran told W. that the Kharkov University committee had convened once and had decided to call a public meeting to explain the project. He expected some progress after this meeting.

[2] See Nos. 2, 3, 4, 20, 23, 28, 45, 67. W. also wrote one letter to Futran direct—see No. 29.

systematic basis in accordance with the comprehensive talk we had
some time ago in Kharkov.[3]

We eagerly await further detailed reports from you, since a substantial part of the task, particularly the survey, has to be rounded
off before the end of this winter. We shall continue, as before, to
keep you informed on our activities.

Looking forward to a full report at your earliest, and with kind
regards,

I am

Your

92. To Martin Buber, Vienna.[1] *Geneva, 14 December 1902*

German: Or. Copy. T.W.: W.A.

Geneva, 4 rue Lombard, 14. 12. 02

Mr. Martin Buber,
Vienna.

Dear Martin,

Nothing was further from my mind than to cause you

---

[3] During W.'s visit to Kharkov in Oct. 1902—see Vol. I, Nos. 318, 319.

92. [1] This is in reply to Buber's letter to W. of 12 Dec. 1902 (W.A.). Buber wrote
that he could not complete all the work he had undertaken because of illness. Several
lecturers, editors, and financiers had agreed to join the University committee as a
result of his appeal, but he had postponed the inaugural meeting because he wanted
everyone to be present and because he expected to enlist additional members.
In Buber's opinion the Vienna committee could not be expected to find the funds
necessary for the running expenses of the University Bureau, and he proposed the
creation of local groups in Russia for this purpose. The main function of the Vienna
committee, as of the one to be formed in Berlin, should be to pave the way for a
European central committee and to present proposals for accomplishing the project,
particularly with regard to finance, for which purpose it should contact financiers.
Buber emphasized that there should not be excessive haste and that care should be
taken in choosing the provisional committee in Vienna, most of whose members
would probably wish to join the central committee when this came into existence.
He said that he would shortly give instructions for the setting up of a committee
in Berlin, and suggested that W. take part in the inaugural meetings of both committees. He reported that Werner wished to organise a 'Jewish University' society to
look after fund-raising, but Feiwel and he (Buber) felt that the time was not ripe for
this. Summing up, Buber proposed establishing four different kinds of bodies: (A)
central committee, to be set up in the spring of 1903, which would elect an executive
committee. (B) Local committees in Berlin and Vienna, and possibly also in Munich
and elsewhere. (C) Local groups in Russia, which would raise funds for the Bureau
and function along the lines of the Western committees. (D) Societies to enable a
wider selection of people an opportunity to support the project. Buber also expanded

[*Footnote 1 continued on p. 94*

unhappiness.[2] You can imagine, however, how anxious I was getting about your activities. If I had received your letter a week earlier it would not have occurred to me to bring pressure upon you in any way. Now everything is all right, so don't take it amiss if occasionally I let a stronger expression escape me. There are worries great and small which can exhaust a man more than even the most difficult, if positive, activity.

Well, I am in complete accord with your chief proposals, and I also share the view that nothing should be rushed. Only we must make energetic plans with the aim of having the committee completely organised by Easter. We have, in various ways, already stimulated the formation of small groups in Russia which we fervently hope will produce some money for us.[3]

My visit to Vienna, therefore, will not have much point since you are well on the way to completing arrangements with the people. I cannot say anything about Berlin as yet, because I am waiting for news. Toldy is also opposed to a visit to Vienna.[4]

We will see to it from here that you get your Swiss tour arranged for the middle of January. It would moreover be most satisfactory if you could arrange to stay here for a longer period (I hereby cordially invite you to stay with me). For your health's sake it is essential that you take a rest for once, far from the bustle of the big city. I urge you, dear Martin, to think about it.

I have settled everything regarding Birnbaum. Nemirovsky has written nothing as yet, and another letter is going off to him today.[5]

Many kind regards from yours ever,

on his meeting with Herzl in November (see n. 1 to No. 38): Herzl had said that he would join the central committee, but would have to consult the Executive about joining the local committee. Buber felt that the matter was not important, for even if Herzl could not join the local Vienna committee, they would still be able to use his name, and anyway he would not be able to do any work. For the time being there was no need for W. to write to Herzl (cf. No. 60). Buber asked W. to arrange his propaganda trip to Switzerland. He also told W. that he was sending him copies of the appeal concerning Birnbaum for him to sign and forward to Bernstein-Kohan, Idelson and others (see n. 1 to No. 19).

[2] Reference to W.'s letter to Buber of 10 Dec. 1902 (see No. 76).

[3] See Nos. 50, 51, 52, 57, 61, 62, 68, 69, 71, 73.

[4] In his letters to Feiwel and Buber of 10 Dec. 1902, W. said that he might come to Vienna and Berlin to help set up the committees. Feiwel replied on 12 Dec. 1902 (W.A.) that he felt this was unnecessary at the present stage, while Buber suggested that W. take part in the inaugural meetings of the committees once they were set up (see n. 1 on p. 93).

[5] W. had approached Nemirovsky on the Birnbaum matter on 20 Nov. 1902 (see No. 20), but no further letter mentioning the subject has come to light except the one dated 31 Dec. 1902 (No. 148).

93. To the Smaller Zionist Actions Committee, Vienna.
Geneva, 14 December 1902

German: T.W.: C.Z.A. Z1/337

Geneva, 4 rue Lombard, 14. 12. 02.

The Zionist Actions Committee,
Vienna.

Dear Fellow-Zionists,

We cannot see how else to react to Schauer's outrageous behaviour than as indicated in our earlier article.[1] Since you refuse to accept this, and thereby deny us the opportunity of answering Mr. Schauer in a manner appropriate, we find ourselves compelled to obtain justice through a different course. I allow myself only this one observation: we shall leave no honourable means unexplored in order to put 'fellow-Zionists' of the Schauer type in their proper place.

May I request, in all courtesy, that you find it possible to publish the enclosed brief announcement.[2]

Most respectfully and with Zion's greetings,

Dr. Ch. Weizmann

94. To Heinrich Loewe, Berlin. *Geneva, 14 December 1902*

German: Or. Copy. T.W.: W.A.

Geneva, 14. 12. 02.

Dr. Heinrich Loewe,
Berlin.

Dear Friend,

Unfortunately we see no possibility of expressing our attitude towards Schauer in words other than those employed in our article earlier. However, since you refuse to print this[1] we would ask only

93. [1] For the refusal of the Smaller Actions Committee to publish in *Die Welt* the Democratic Fraction's protest of 25 Nov. 1902 against Schauer's article in *Der Israelit*, see n. 6 to No. 83. For the protest itself see n. 1 to No. 25.

[2] A 'declaration' in the form of a letter to the editor of *Die Welt*, dated 15 Dec. 1902, W.A. The declaration was written by Feiwel—see his undated letter (? 13 Dec. 1902), W.A. It mentions the protest (see n. 1 above) that had been sent to *Die Welt* but not published 'on the pretext that its tone and personal vein made it unacceptable' (cf. n. 6 to No. 83). The signatories point out that they are 'presenting a strong protest', and announce that they have 'taken steps to bring the matter before another Zionist forum' (cf. n. 1 to No. 101, concerning Feiwel's proposal to have the affair submitted to the Court of the Zionist Congress). The declaration, signed by Marek, Kroll, Idelson, Aberson, W., and Feiwel, was published in *Die Welt*, 19 Dec. 1902.

94. [1] The Democratic Fraction's protest against Schauer's article, rejected by Loewe for publication in the *Jüdische Rundschau* (see No. 34; No. 46 and n. 1 there).

that you accept the enclosed announcement.[2] We shall find another way of getting at Mr. Schauer.

With kind regards,

Your

95. To Berthold Feiwel, Zurich. *Geneva, 14 December 1902*

German: Or. Copy. T.W.: W.A.

Geneva, 14. 12. 02.

Mr. Berthold Feiwel,
Zurich.

Dear Toldy,

Many thanks for both your letters.[1] I was never of the opinion that great things for our cause could be expected from the other gentlemen, within the Zionist movement or outside it. I also knew that for a long time to come we would be able to depend only upon ourselves and upon the few who stood by us. It was for this very reason that I was pained to note a perceptible cooling off even in our own circles. I am now glad it was not a cooling off on the part of others, but possibly a rise in temperature on my part.

SURVEY: We are already in possession here of a few addresses to which questionnaires may be sent without further ado. It is not easy to obtain all the addresses, but we shall get to that too, shortly.

BROCHURES: Have not arrived yet, but Trietsch writes that they will be ready next week.[2] Lilien is even working on the emblem, but I think the University will be finished first.

---

[2] This is a declaration similar to the one sent the same day to the S.A.C. for publication in *Die Welt*—see No. 93 and n. 2 there. The declaration was not published in the *Jüdische Rundschau*.

95. [1] Feiwel to W., 12 Dec. 1902, and undated letter (? 13 Dec. 1902), W.A. The letter of 12 Dec. was in part a reply to W.'s of 10 Dec. 1902 (No. 75). Feiwel reminded W. of what he had told him in the summer: 'If someone wants to do something in Zionism nowadays, he can rely only on himself', but promised that he would fulfil his duty towards the University in spite of personal difficulties. The rest of this letter, as well as the undated one, deals with current matters. The letter of 12 Dec. 1902 also includes a list of *Vertrauensmänner*, the volunteer supervisors helping the University Bureau in various countries.

[2] See Trietsch to W., 3 Dec. 1902, W.A.

CIRCULARS:[3] Going out tomorrow. We shall also prepare letters for the people supervising the work.[4]

BUBER has written in detail.[5] I am enclosing his letter, together with the one from Trietsch. Tomorrow I shall send you some money,[6] as well as copies of outgoing mail.

DECLARATION[7] goes out today.

SHRIRO has written a cordial letter[8] with the information that approximately another 800 roubles will be found in Baku.

More tomorrow.[9]

Yours ever,

96. To Samuel Shriro, Baku. *Geneva, 15 December 1902*

Russian: Or. Copy. H.W.: W.A.

15 December 02.

Mr. S. M. Shriro,[1]
Baku.

Dear Samuel Moiseevitch,

I must frankly confess that I was quite worried by your silence and unable to account for it. It even occurred to me that for some reason you might be angry with me, and I am delighted that everything is all right. I am very sorry to hear about your brother's[2] illness. May I offer both to yourself and to him my sincerest wishes for his speedy recovery.

Our work here is progressing *most successfully*. More important, we have managed to interest a great many people, both distinguished professors and prominent financiers among them, in Berlin, Vienna, Munich, Brussels and London.[3]

[3] Reference to a University Bureau circular dated 15 Dec. 1902 regarding the survey among Jewish students, W.A. The circular appeals to the recipient to conduct the survey in his own city and to set up committees for the purpose, if possible including some non-Zionist members so as to give the survey as wide a scope as possible. W.'s signature is printed on the circular.

[4] Apparently a reference to the covering letters to be sent with the questionnaires.

[5] See n. 1 to No. 92.

[6] In his letter of 12 Dec. 1902 (W.A.) Feiwel asked W. to send him money, because he could not pay his rent. See also No. 101 and n. 2 there.

[7] Declaration regarding Schauer's article, sent to *Die Welt* for publication.

[8] Not found.

[9] The next letter to Feiwel to come to light is dated 17 Dec. 1902 (see No. 101).

96. [1] Written in reply to a letter from Shriro that has not been found (see No. 95).

[2] Ilya Shriro.

[3] On the subject of Berlin, Vienna, and London—cf. n. 3 to No. 43; n. 3 to No. 68. In the meantime W. had received a negative reply from Claude Montefiore in London

We do not want publicity as yet, but towards Easter time a propaganda campaign is to be launched under the banner of these committees. I shall be going to London in February (they told me that nothing can be done at present because of the holidays),[4] and from there to Russia—St. Petersburg and Moscow.[5]

We have begun the statistical research into the Jewish student body with the distribution of 6,000 questionnaires.[6] Through this we shall be able to gather an enormous amount of material for propaganda.

Next week I am going to Berlin.[7] Negotiations are in train with a number of people there, requiring my presence from time to time. So far I am very pleased with our rate of progress.[8] We are meeting with a most encouraging response in all areas. Moscow and Kharkov, too, have notified us that things are proceeding very satisfactorily.[9] A group of people interested in the University, and prepared to do everything they can for it, has already been organised. Do remember, Samuel [Moiseevitch],[10] . . . .
. . . .

I should be very grateful to you, S.M., if you would write to me from time to time. Don't begrudge me words. Write about your brother's health, and about your coming here; and do come soon.

One more request: You telegraphed that you were sending the oil.[11] I should like to give this matter my serious attention so if you have not sent it yet please make the necessary arrangements to do so. Or have you changed your mind? I would very much like to know, and would be pleased if you could write to me about this.

(see n. 3 to No. 55), but Buber had written about progress in enlisting support in Vienna (see n. 1 to No. 92). Regarding Munich, all that is known is that W. asked Halpern on 3 Dec. to work for the University project (see No. 53), but Halpern's reply has not been found. As for Brussels, see No. 37 and n. 4 there regarding W.'s appeal to Georges Levi Montefiore and the latter's negative response. Nothing is known concerning any further activity on behalf of the University project in Brussels at this time.   [4] See n. 1 to No. 36.

[5] W. visited London only in the autumn of 1903. He went to Russia in the spring of 1903, but did not visit either St. Petersburg or Moscow.

[6] Distribution of the questionnaires started only at the end of December (see No. 138).

[7] W. did not visit Berlin at this time after all.

[8] This was probably written to reassure Shriro—cf. Nos. 75, 76.

[9] Cf. letters W. had received lately from Moscow and Kharkov (see n. 1 to No. 30 and n. 1 to No. 91).

[10] Followed in the original by an illegible paragraph.

[11] The telegram has not been found. It appears that W. accepted a proposal by Shriro, who had an oil business in Baku, to conduct research into the production of a colourless and odourless soap from oil waste. Shriro wrote to W. on 11/24 May 1903 (W.A.): 'My brother Ilya will bring you a sample of oil soap that should be improved. Please deal with this if you can'. But W. and Shriro did not reach a definite agreement on the matter until Sept. 1904 (see W. to Gaster, 2 Oct. 1904, W.A.).

I have investigated the matter and the chances of great success are very good. Now that the holidays are approaching I shall be able to concentrate on it, that is, if I knew that you were still as interested as when we talked. Do please let me know.[12]

Keep well.

All the best [----]

Your Ch. Weizmann.

97. To Gregory Lurie, Pinsk. *Geneva, 16 December 1902*

German: Or. Copy. T.W.: W.A.

16. 12. 02.

Mr. Gregory Lurie,
Pinsk.

Dear Friend,

Although we have as yet received no reply to our earlier letter,[1] we nevertheless believe this is not due to lack of interest on your part. Other reasons must have prevented you from writing.

May we ask that you kindly advise us whether you consider it important for our Bureau to contact Mr. Kann at The Hague.[2] If this is so, we would rather that you wrote to him first, and inform us accordingly. Upon being recommended to Mr. Kann by you we would write him in detail from here and send him all the necessary printed material as well.

We await with interest your views concerning the above, together with your other reports.[3]

Most respectfully and with regards.

---

[12] No reply to this letter has been found.

97. [1] See No. 5.

[2] W. had written: 'Kahn-Haag'. Jacobus Kann and Lurie were both active in the J.C.T. It appears that W. wanted to interest Kann in the University project.

[3] Lurie answered W. in the second half of December, but the letter has not been found (see No. 149). It is not known if Kann is mentioned in that letter, and no letter from W. to Kann has been found.

98. To Abraham Idelson and Michael Kroll, Moscow.
Geneva, 16 December 1902

German: Or. Copy. T.W.: W.A.

16. 12. 02.

Registered.

Dr. M. Kroll and Mr. A. Idelson,
Moscow.

Dear Friends,

We had the honour to reply to your last communication in three successive letters.[1] We also sent you the outline of the questionnaire. We cannot believe that you have not received our various letters since they were nearly all sent by registered post. At all events, it would be most desirable that you confirm receipt to us, if only by postcard, so that we may have the assurance that you are in possession of them and we are not perhaps waiting in vain. Despite our many requests that you reply to our letters as promptly as possible we are, alas, continually ignored by you in this respect. You will understand how anxious we are here to receive your answer, your views on our proposals, and the results of your endeavours.

When you who are closest to us, dear friends, treat us like this, what can we expect from outside people?

We do not wish to repeat every question or to raise new ones; this we shall do only upon receipt of your news. We trust that you will not compel us to write again in this way, but will let us have a full report by return.

With kind regards,

Your

99. To the Jewish Colonial Trust, London. *Geneva, 17 December 1902*

German: Or. Copy. T.W.: W.A.

17. 12. 02.

The Jewish Colonial Trust,
For the attention of the Manager, Mr. D. Levontin.

We have received your esteemed letter of the 15th, and thank you for your kind remittance of 600 francs.[1] At the same time, may we

98. [1] See No. 30 and n. 1 there; Nos. 35, 50.

99. [1] Herzl to W. and Feiwel, 12 Dec. 1902, W.A., relates to this transfer. Herzl agreed therein to W.'s and Feiwel's request about making his signature unnecessary in the future (see n. 2 to No. 65, and cf. also No. 86). Nevertheless they continued withdrawals from the Bureau's account through Herzl (see No. 251 and n. 7 there; No. 300 and n. 7 there; No. 390).

express our appreciation of your friendly co-operation. We have in the meantime also received a letter from Dr. Herzl, in which he informs us that he has already attended to the matter.

Most respectfully and with regards,

Your

100. To Michael Aleinikov, Kharkov. *Geneva,*
17 December 1902

German: Or. Copy. T.W.: W.A.

17. 12. 1902.
Registered.

Mr. M. Aleinikov,
Kharkov.

Dear Friend,

A man could burst a blood-vessel having to deal with correspondents, or rather 'non-correspondents' such as you![1] If I thought this was normal Kharkov behaviour I would remain calm, but it doesn't appear so. Enough for the present. You won't drive me into exceeding the limits of 'European' courtesy.

I do not wish to enumerate the long list of letters I have sent. You are perfectly aware that the present one is your third.[2] We are still ignorant here of the fate of the Russian translation of our brochure.[3] If you have no intention of publishing it in Kharkov I shall have to dispose of the manuscript elsewhere, with the bitter regret that such a simple business has been dragging on. I shall have to thank our Kharkov friends for that. At the very least [do drop] me a line: Yes or No. Should it be in the negative, I request that the manuscript be sent to Dr. M. B. Kroll, Moscow Rasgulai, Dobroslobodsky Pereulok, Dom Kirilova.

For the moment, and as long as this indolence reigns among you all, it is absolutely pointless to touch on any other questions.

Yours ever,

---

100. [1] The W.A. have on file a letter from Aleinikov dated 20 Nov./3 Dec. 1902, in which he writes that he has just returned to Kharkov and that all activity there on behalf of the University stopped after the first meeting of the local committee (see also n. 1 to No. 91). It is clear from what W. says here that he had not yet received Aleinikov's letter.

[2] See Nos. 3, 28.

[3] See n. 10 to No. 7; n. 5 to No. 23.

101. To Berthold Feiwel, Zurich. *Geneva, 17 December 1902*

German: Or. Copy. T.W.: W.A.

Geneva, 17. 12. 02.

Mr. Berthold Feiwel,
Zurich.

Dear Toldy,

Thank you very much indeed for your welcome letter and the printed matter.[1] I am returning the *Jüdische Rundschau* to you today, together with the copies and the bibliography. I am also sending you 50 francs[2] by this post.

In the circumstances I shall not be travelling to Berlin,[3] but will probably go to Biel[4] on Saturday evening, and will be in Zurich on Monday.

In my opinion Schauer should not be summoned before the Congress Court while Nordau is president,[5] but before an ordinary court of arbitration. Anyway, we shall discuss this when we meet.

Rosenfeld was here and told me about the shocking business regarding Lurie-Eliashev;[6] really, one no longer knows whom to trust. Everyone is just blatantly pursuing his own interests. Nevertheless, dear Toldy, do not get discouraged. There are other people too.

---

101. [1] Feiwel to W., 16 Dec. 1902, W.A. Feiwel reiterated that there was no need for W. to visit Vienna (cf. No. 75; No. 92 and n. 4 there)—he would be going there himself once matters had progressed sufficiently. He said he would write and ask Buber and Werner to organize a local University group in Vienna with a regular correspondence service, even if it had only a few members, and that he would ask Buber, who was about to go to Berlin, to set up a similar group there. Feiwel returned to W. the bibliography dealing with universities, and asked for copies to send to Berlin and Vienna so that it might be completed. He enclosed a copy of the *Jüdische Rundschau* (see n. 7 below) and also suggested that the Schauer affair be brought before the Congress Court (see n. 1 to No. 10; n. 6 to No. 83; n. 2 to No. 93).

[2] In his letter of 16 Dec. 1902 Feiwel confirmed receipt of 50 francs from W. (cf. No. 95 and n. 6 there), and it appears that W. sent him another 50 francs.

[3] On 10 Dec. W. had written to Feiwel about his possible visit to Vienna and Berlin to assist in the setting up of the committees (see No. 75); but by 14 Dec. he had abandoned the plan to visit the former city (see No. 92), and in the event he also decided not to go to Berlin in view of Buber's imminent visit there (see n. 1 above and cf. No. 102).   [4] For the conference of Swiss Zionists.

[5] Nordau was an extreme opponent of the Democratic Fraction (see also No. 316 and n. 23 there).

[6] A reference to Lurie's sale of the Yiddish weekly *Der Yud* to the owners of *Der Fraind* (see n. 2 to No. 17). It was originally intended that *Der Yud* should continue to appear under the joint ownership of Lurie, Eliashev, and Feiwel (cf. Vol. I, n. 29 to No. 238), and it emerges from Feiwel's letter to W. of 16 Dec. 1902 that Feiwel had borrowed money to finance his part of the transaction. Since Lurie sold the paper at a loss, however, this money was not returned at once, but Feiwel was promised that he would get it back by 1905.

Loewe also sent me the *Rundschau* in which he praises the Fraction's activities.[7]

Some brochures should arrive tomorrow. I am sending notepaper tomorrow. I think another item will have to be added to the questionnaire: 'What are your views on a University in Palestine?' or perhaps this wording: 'Where, in your opinion, should the University be established, in Palestine or Western Europe?' (England? Switzerland? Belgium? Holland?)[8]

Kindest regards to you and all our friends,

Your

P.S. We are now writing to Glikin asking him to have the questionnaires printed at once.[9] It would be good if the proof-reading could be done in Berlin. You can arrange everything necessary. On Trietsch's advice we wrote to Dr. Blau of Frankfurt[10] but have had no reply. Trietsch thinks we ought to write again.[11] What do you think? Please return the Trietsch letter.[12]

102. To Moses Glikin, Charlottenburg.[1] *Geneva, 17 December 1902*

German: T.W.: C.Z.A. A179/3.

Geneva, 4 rue Lombard, 17. 12. 02.

Mr. M. Glikin,
Berlin.[1]

Dear Friend,

Many thanks for dealing so promptly with our affairs.[2] The text of the questionnaire got lost at the printers. Feiwel sent in a new

---

[7] A reference to Loewe's review of the *Jüdischer Almanach*—the first book published by the *Jüdischer Verlag* (see Vol. I, n. 14 to No. 238). Loewe described the *Almanach* as 'the first project of the Zionist Democratic Fraction', and pointed out that 'in this field of positive productive deeds and compilation, [the Fraction] is ahead of other Zionists in courage and success'. The review appeared in the *Jüdische Rundschau* of 12 Dec. 1902.

[8] In fact such an item was not included in the questionnaire. For the location of the University, cf. No. 83 and n. 13 there.

[9] In his letter of 16 Dec. 1902 Feiwel informed W. that he had received a telegram from Berlin, reporting that the manuscript of the questionnaire had disappeared at the printers. He was therefore sending them a copy.

[10] See No. 39 and n. 1 there.

[11] See Trietsch to W., 17 Dec. 1902, W.A. It appears that Trietsch erred in the date (perhaps it was 16 Dec.), since a letter sent from Berlin could not have reached W. on the day it was written.

[12] A reference to Trietsch's letter of 3 Dec. 1902, which W. sent to Feiwel on 14 Dec. 1902 (see No. 95).

102. [1] See n. 1 to No. 84.

[2] This is apparently a reply to an undated letter from Glikin (? 15 Dec. 1902), W.A. No. 30/0, 34, in which he writes about University Bureau matters.

manuscript yesterday.[3] You must make absolutely sure that the things are printed at once. Not a single day must be lost, because we consider it most important that the forms[4] are still distributed during Christmas. We already have quite a large list of addresses here, and furthermore, have notified many quarters about the distribution of the forms;[5] so we must not drag the thing out in any circumstances. Our friend Trietsch will most certainly give you his kind support.

We shall receive the money in a few days.[6] I shall then send you your own and Mandels's.[7] Get ready for the journey. But you won't be admitted to Switzerland unless you fulfil our requirements as follows:

1) Notepaper and envelopes: 500 double sheets and 500 single. But we would very much like to have the Jewish imprint as well.[8] It would of course be ideal if the emblem were also shown on the paper. Speak to Lilien. Beg him in the name of all of us. Perhaps this will help.[9]

2) Brochures.

3) Questionnaires.

I do hope, dear Glikin, that you will take note of all this. Dig up some addresses from Jena and Halle.

Warm regards to you and Trietsch.

Your
Chaim.

P.S. As Buber is going to Berlin there would be no point in my visit for the time being.[10]

103. To Bernard Chapira, Paris. *Geneva, 17 December 1902*

German: Or. Copy. T.W.: W.A.

17. 12. 02.

Mr. Bernard Chapira,
Paris.

Dear Fellow-Zionist,

At the suggestion of our friend A. Eliasberg[1] we are taking the

---

[3] See n. 9 to No. 101.   [4] In original: 'Bogen'.

[5] A reference to the circular sent to the people supervising the survey, dated 15 Dec. 1902 (see n. 3 to No. 95).   [6] See No. 99 and n. 1 there.

[7] The payment to Glikin was intended to cover his travel expenses to Switzerland, where he was to start work as an official in the University Bureau. The reason for the payment to Mandels is not known—W. asked Glikin on 26 Dec. to pay him 20 francs (see No. 121).   [8] See n. 3 to No. 54.

[9] Cf. n. 1 to No. 89.   [10] See ns. 1, 3 to No. 101.

103. [1] No letter from Eliasberg containing such a suggestion has been found. Cf. n. 1 to No. 114.

liberty of approaching you with the request that you print the following brief announcement in your periodical:[2]

'The "Jewish University" Bureau is, among other activities, conducting a survey relating to the position of Russian and Rumanian Jewish students in West European Universities. We request all our friends in those Universities with French and Italian as the languages of instruction to send us their addresses as soon as possible, so that we might send them all information necessary as well as printed material. In view of the importance of this task, we hope that all our friends will grant us their active support.'

We have compiled a questionnaire which we shall shortly send on to you for your information. As soon as we have the addresses, we shall begin to distribute the forms.

We would be most happy if you would support us in our activities.

Most respectfully and with Zion's greetings.

104. To Esther Kleinman,[1] Montpellier. *Geneva, 18 December 1902*

German: Or. Copy. T.W.: W.A.

18. 12. 02.

Miss E. Kleinman,
Montpellier.

Dear Madam,

We hasten to reply to your esteemed letter[2] and would inform you of the following:

1. You will, of course, have to explain the purpose of the statistical study when distributing the questionnaire. Actually, everything is there to be read in the questionnaire. The forms are now being printed, and you will receive them all prepared. You will therefore be spared the trouble of having to offer people lengthy explanations.

[2] Reference to *L'Echo Sioniste*, Paris.

104. [1] Esther Kleinman, born in Romny, Ukraine. In 1902–3 she studied in Heidelberg and Montpellier, and later in Berlin. From 1908 she lived in Kiev.

[2] Kleinman to W., 17 Dec. 1902, W.A. Kleinman confirmed receipt of the circular of 15 Dec. 1902 (see n. 3 to No. 95), and undertook to conduct the survey in Montpellier. She asked several questions about procedures, to which this is the reply. Kleinman also criticized a statement in the circular that 'a survey of this type is naturally worthless if conducted only among like-minded persons', claiming that its value would be in no way impaired if it were restricted to one party (i.e. the Zionists).

2. On each questionnaire there is a note to the effect that one may choose to sign or not. The choice, therefore, is left to those being questioned should they wish to remain anonymous. Thus there is no obligation.

3. Unfortunately, we do not yet have the Russian translations of our brochure. It is being published in Kharkov.[3] We shall send you a copy as soon as they arrive.

I do not understand your objection to the self-explanatory note that, if possible, all students should participate in the survey. We wish to have statistics on students (Jewish), and not statistics on Zionist students, who form but a small part of the entire Jewish student body. This was the meaning of my statement that a limited survey would have no value for our purposes.

We thank you for your friendly, ready co-operation, and send our good wishes to you and to our friends.

105. **To Samuel Ginis, Baku.** *Geneva, 19 December 1902*

German: Or. Copy. T.W.: W.A.

19. 12. 02.

Engineer Ginis,
Baku.

Dear Friend,

Believe me, it was neither out of negligence nor forgetfulness that I have not written to you all this time; so you need not be resentful, dear friend. Ever since leaving you I have been so over-loaded with work that until now I have somehow had no time even to revive after the long journey,[1] not to mention recover from it. I am yearning for the approaching holidays to get some time to arrange various things and bring order into my own affairs. Furthermore, I did not want to present you with empty phrases, and so I postponed writing from day to day in the hope that I would soon be able to report something of interest.

These simple reasons, honestly stated, should serve to excuse me in your eyes. You must believe me when I assure you that when I reflect on my stay in Baku even now, and I very often do, I am still impressed by your personality and our discussions.

Now, to the point. If I were to describe the state of the University project briefly, it could be expressed in one sentence: everything is

---

[3] See n. 11 to No. 7.

105. [1] A reference to W.'s trip to Russia in the summer and autumn of 1902, during which he also visited Baku—see Vol. I, bridge-note following No. 317.

in flux, everything is in motion. One is so dependent in one's activities upon other people, and during our initial steps we are in such need of the goodwill of these 'co-workers' who tire very easily, that substantial success in a brief period of time becomes impossible.

Yet it would not be immodest to declare that, despite the meagre force at our disposal, something noteworthy has already been achieved. We have established very valuable connections in every leading city, we have aroused the interest of important personalities in our programme; as regards Berlin and Vienna, we have enlisted professors, men of European reputation, in the University committee.[2] This was not easily accomplished. You know these high-class Jews[3] of Western Europe, how these heroes of Israel twist and turn when it comes to participating publicly in a Jewish cause. Here too, however, it has been our experience that a concrete undertaking such as the University project can gain warm approval even among hitherto inactive circles. It is to be hoped that by Easter we shall have launched the committees and thereby created the basis for a wide-scale propaganda effort.

As for the scientific planning of the project itself, this is in the hands of competent people under the leadership of our friend Feiwel, as well as Professor Kellner and Pineles of Vienna.[4]

The statistical study of the position of Jewish students has now begun. For this purpose we have contacted almost all Universities in Western Europe. We have everywhere endeavoured[5] . . .

106. To Theodor Herzl, Vienna. *Geneva, 19 December 1902*

German: T.W.: C.Z.A. Z1/340.

Geneva, 4 rue Lombard, 19. 12. 02.

Personal.

Dear Dr. [Herzl],

Permit me to reply to the letter from the Actions Committee[1] privately.

[2] Cf. n. 3 to No. 68. In the meantime Buber had written that several more personalities were willing to join the Vienna committee (see n. 1 to No. 92), and Trietsch had written from Berlin that he believed that Professors Warburg, Philippson, Landau, and Levin 'and a whole flock' were willing to join the committee (see Trietsch to W., 17 Dec. 1902, W.A.).   [3] In the original: 'Grossjuden'.

[4] For Feiwel, see n. 3 to No. 7. Nothing is known about the activity of Kellner and Pineles in connection with the scientific aspects of the University project. Cf. No. 294 and n. 8 there.   [5] The end of the letter is missing.

106. [1] Herzl and Kokesch (on behalf of the Smaller Actions Committee) to W., 16 Dec. 1902, W.A. They stated that the Fraction's declaration of 15 Dec. 1902 on the

We are far indeed from any desire to make a public scandal out of the Schauer matter,[2] bearing in mind the damage this might cause the Zionist movement. We shall attempt to bring the case before the Congress Court.[3]

Nevertheless, I would like to emphasise why this entire affair makes us so indignant. You are aware how Jewish students, unable to gain admission in their homeland,[4] have to struggle here in Western Europe. Our student youth are being chased from one country to another, persecuted everywhere, welcome nowhere. Particularly now, when we are about to launch a great project in the establishment of a Jewish University; particularly now, when we are striving for the sympathy of intellectual circles; particularly now, when we are endeavouring to bring the plight of our youth to the attention of West European society, Dr. Schauer's innuendos seem like a crime.

Decidedly, what we wish to contest here is not a Fraction matter. Many people have already maligned us without knowing us, and we are consoled by the fact that we share the fate that Zionism had to bear in its beginnings.

This, however, is a different case. A Zionist has, quite disgracefully, attacked Jewish youth as a whole. We all know what lies behind accusations such as Nihilism, etc. The division existing between Western and Eastern Jews, which we are constantly trying to bridge, is surely not being narrowed by the kind of outbursts which Dr. Schauer—a gentleman who seems to be very proud of his Europeanism—has permitted himself. Moreover, to attack struggling and practically defenceless people who are unfortunately permanently dependent upon the goodwill and hospitality of others—I do not know how one is to describe such behaviour.

It wounds me grievously to observe *Die Welt* actually praise Schauer's attack.[5] In the final analysis, one may overlook the act of

Schauer affair would be printed in *Die Welt* (see No. 93 and n. 2 there), but requested that no further steps be taken in public and that the matter be brought before the Congress Court.

[2] For Schauer's article see n. 1 to No. 10.

[3] But cf. No. 101, in which W. expressed his opposition to bringing the matter before the Congress Court.

[4] For the limitations imposed on the admission of Jews to Russian Universities see Vol. I, n. 3 to No. 113.

[5] *Die Welt* of 14 Nov. 1902 published a letter of protest from several Berne Zionist societies against the Academic Zionist Society because it had served meals in its refectory on *Yom Kippur* (see n. 1 to No. 10). An introduction to the letter of protest by the editors describes the incident and censures the desecrators of the fast. The introduction points out that Dr. Schauer had been given the opportunity 'to reject . . . Zionist complicity in the tactlessness of individuals, and to make clear that even freethinking Zionists strongly condemn the provocation of Orthodox circles'.

an individual, but the matter takes on a very different aspect when it is endorsed by a body so esteemed by us as the Actions Committee.

I cannot conceive how this unfortunate notice ever reached *Die Welt.*

I wanted, dear Doctor, to express all this to you frankly, in the manner in which I am accustomed with you, and I am convinced that you will understand me.[6]

Most respectfully and with kind regards,

Yours very sincerely,

Ch. Weizmann

107. To Charles (Yeheskel) Wortsman, Basle. *Geneva, 19 December 1902*

German: Or. Copy. T.W.: W.A.

19. 12. 02.

Mr. Ch. Wortsman, Chemist,
Basle.

Dear Friend,

In reply to your various letters[1] we must inform you that it is unfortunately not possible from our side to obtain a delegate's mandate for you in respect of Biel, because everything has now been allocated.

The questionnaires are now being printed and will be sent to you very shortly. You will observe from the questions that on collation of the replies, we shall be able to ascertain how many Universities still admit Russian Jews, and which they are. In view of the fact that we are going to publish the results of the statistical study, the problem you raise is indirectly answered. For the time being we cannot say any more.

---

[6] No reply to the above letter has been found.

107. [1] See Wortsman to W., 16 Dec. 1902, 18 Dec. 1902 (pmk.), W.A. In the earlier letter Wortsman asked W. to send him questionnaires for the student survey, even though there were only three or four Russian Jewish students in Basle. Wortsman added that Basle University could take some 200 more Russian students and that there were other Universities prepared to accept students of Russian origin. He suggested that the University Bureau look into the matter and publish its findings immediately. In his postcard dated 18 Dec. 1902 Wortsman asked W. to have him appointed a delegate to the Swiss Zionist Conference at Biel.

May we remind you of your promise to speak with some of your lecturers[2] about the programme. We would be obliged if you would inform us of the outcome of such discussions. Our friend Julius Meyer made us a similar promise; his reply is likewise yet to be received.[3]

It is still not decided whether I shall be going to Biel,[4] but I shall be in Zurich on Tuesday at the latest.

Kind regards,

Your

108. To the Editorial Department, *Die Welt*, Vienna.

Geneva, 19 December 1902

German: Or. Copy. T.W.: W.A.

19. 12. 02.

The Editorial Department, *Die Welt*,
Vienna.

We would be most grateful if you would make space available in your esteemed journal for the following announcement:[1]

'The "Jewish University" Bureau is now engaged, among other activities, in conducting a survey on the situation of Russian and Rumanian Jewish students in Western Europe. We request all friends of our cause in Universities where the language of instruction is German [to support][2] us in this undertaking by sending us the addresses of persons who may be prepared to supervise the survey in individual cities. As soon as we receive these addresses we shall make our questionnaire and other printed material available.'

(Signed) 'Jewish University Bureau'

By Order: Dr. Ch. Weizmann,[3] 4 rue Lombard, Geneva.

Most respectfully, with Zion's greetings.

---

[2] Lecturers at the University of Basle.

[3] It is not known when these undertakings were given. See also No. 147.

[4] In the event W. did take part in the Biel conference. Cf. No. 90 and n. 4 there; No. 110.

108. [1] The announcement was not published in *Die Welt*. See also No. 224.

[2] The words 'to support' are missing in the body of the letter, but 'support us' has been added in the margin of the original.

[3] The signature is typed.

109. To Heinrich Loewe, Berlin. *Geneva, 19 December 1902*

German: Or. Copy. T.W.: W.A.

19. 12. 02.

Dr. Heinrich Loewe,
Berlin.

Dear Friend,

Very many thanks for your kind letter of the 14th.[1] We are delighted at your readiness to support our undertaking and we will of course avail ourselves of your help. We would be most grateful to you if you would allocate space in your esteemed journal for the following announcement:

'The "Jewish University" Bureau is now engaged, among other activities, in conducting a survey on the situation of Russian and Rumanian Jewish students in Western Europe. We request all friends of our cause in Universities where the language of instruction is German [to support][2] us in this undertaking by sending us the addresses of persons who may be prepared to supervise the survey in individual cities. As soon as we receive these addresses we shall make our questionnaire and other printed material available.'

(Signed) 'Jewish University Bureau' (name and address)[3]

With kindest regards,

Yours sincerely,

110. To Berthold Feiwel, Zurich. *Geneva, 19 December 1902*

German: Or. Copy. T.W.: W.A.

Geneva, 19. 12. 02.

Mr. Berthold Feiwel,
Zurich.

Dear Toldy,

By now you must have received the money together with

109. [1] Not found.

[2] The words 'to support' are missing in the original copy; cf. No. 108 and n. 2 there.

[3] *Sic* in the original copy. The printed version published in the *Jüdische Rundschau* of 2 Jan. 1903 was altered as follows: 'Signed: Dr. Ch. Weizmann, Privat Dozent, Geneva, (Switzerland), 4 Rue Lombard'.

everything else sent to you.[1] We have received the 600 francs here,[2] and have discharged some of our debts.

Letters have been sent out to all our people[3] and replies have come in from some of them.[4] If the questionnaires were here, we could even have started on their distribution. My visit to Biel is still not settled;[5] even if I were to go there I would consider it superfluous in those surroundings to speak about the University, let alone propose a resolution.[6] A conference in which Pasmanik, Salkind,[7] etc., do all the talking is not for us. I shall try and be in Zurich as early as possible. We shall then discuss and work things out thoroughly. Incidentally, I still haven't had your reply with respect to Dr. Blau,[8] so please write immediately if anything can still be done from this side and I can take care of it before my departure.

The replies from Russia are again coming in in dribs and drabs, with the gentlemen taking their time. I have discovered that Motzkin is still in Kiev.[9] Evidently nothing will come from his propaganda tour.[10] It is therefore all the more necessary to prepare for a journey to Russia. We have got to raise funds, and must also find people who will work actively in their localities.

Warm regards,

Yours ever,

111. To Ch. Ozhinsky, Munich. *Geneva, 20 December 1902*

German: Or. Copy. T.W.: W.A.

20. 12. 02.

Mr. Ch. Ozhinsky,
Munich.

Dear Sir,

Many thanks for your much appreciated letter of the 19th,[1] and for your kind readiness to support our aims.

---

110. [1] See No. 101.   [2] See No. 99 and n. 1 there.

[3] A reference to the circular of 15 Dec. 1902 (see n. 3 to No. 95).

[4] See letters from Wortsman (16 Dec. 1902), Eliasberg (17 Dec. 1902), Khissin (17 Dec. 1902), and Kleinman (17 Dec. 1902), W.A.

[5] W. did eventually take part in the Swiss Zionist Conference at Biel. Cf. No. 90 and n. 4 there.

[6] Feiwel had suggested (letter of 17 Dec. 1902 W.A.) that W. move a resolution at the Biel Conference supporting the establishment of a Jewish University if he felt this might be successfully carried.

[7] Pasmanik and Salkind were opponents of the Democratic Fraction.

[8] See No. 101.   [9] See Glikin to W., 10 Dec. 1902, W.A.

[10] In the summer of 1902 it was agreed that Motzkin should undertake propaganda for the University project in Moscow and St. Petersburg—see Vol. I, No. 316.

111. [1] Not found.

Our people in Berlin will be sending you, at our request, a proof of the questionnaire together with a number of our brochures. You may sell the brochures at 50 pfg. a copy.

Some circulars dealing with the survey[2] are being despatched to you under separate cover. These circulars are intended for non-Zionists too.

Awaiting your early reply, we remain,

Most respectfully and with Zion's Greetings,

112. To Moses Glikin, Charlottenburg. *Geneva,*
20 December 1902

German/Russian: T.W./H.W.: C.Z.A. A126/24/7/2/2.

Geneva, 4 rue Lombard, 20. 12. 02.

Mr. M. Glikin,
Berlin.[1]

Dear Friend,

Would you please send a proof of our questionnaire, together with our brochure, to each of the following:

1. Mr. A. Eliasberg, 8, Bd. Arago, Paris. 25 brochures
2. Mr. Ch. Ozhinsky, Blütnerstrasse[2] 2/3 Left, Munich. 10 copies
3. Mr. I. Raskin, Zionist Public Reading Room, Grimmaische-strasse 17.1, Leipzig. 6 copies

Also kindly send some proofs of the questionnaire on to me immediately.

With kind regards,

Your
Ch. Weizmann

[3]Please send a few brochures to the 'Herzl' Academic Society, University of Koenigsberg, Prussia.

[4]My very best wishes for the holiday to our comrades. Instead of a telegram, I have cancelled 2 francs worth of J.N.F. stamps.[5]

---

[2] The circular of 15 Dec. 1902 (see n. 3 to No. 95).

112. [1] See n. 1 to No. 84.

  [2] *Sic* in original. Should be Blütenstrasse.

  [3] This sentence, in German, is handwritten by W.

  [4] What follows is in W.'s handwriting (in Russian).

  [5] The holiday greeting was for *Chanuka*, see n. 12 to No. 84. The stamp was a fund-raising device of the Jewish National Fund.

113. To Bernard Chapira, Paris. *Geneva, 20 December 1902*

German: Or. Copy. T.W.: W.A.

20. 12. 02.

Mr. Bernard Chapira,
Paris.

Dear Sir,

In immediate reply to your kind letter of the 19th,[1] we would respectfully inform you that we intend to conduct several surveys. We have begun with Russian and Rumanian students because they are the most numerous, and in Germany are subject to the same rules of admission. Also, the conditions in which German and Austrian or Galician students live are different. We shall therefore include them in a separate survey. After that will come the students from the South and the East. Moreover, a survey is being initiated within Russia itself.[2]

Once collated and classified, this statistical material as a whole will be of enormous propaganda value. It will most certainly have to be taken into consideration when the programme for a University is being prepared.

We are delighted at your readiness to support our cause. Certainly you may act in the name of the Bureau together with Mr. Eliasberg, to whom we are writing separately.[3] We would, however, like you to keep us constantly informed on the steps you take. The greatest caution, and the most meticulous selection of people, are most earnestly recommended. We are very anxious to gain eminent personalities in Paris from the world of scholarship and finance for our cause. Can you do anything in this direction? I shall definitely be passing through Paris on my way to England at the end of February.[4] I hope that by then you will have grown more familiar with the situation in Paris.

With kind regards and sincerest thanks,

113. [1] Chapira to W., 19 Dec. 1902, W.A. Chapira promised to publish the announcement W. had sent him in *L'Echo Sioniste* (see No. 103). He suggested that the survey cover all Jewish students studying in French Universities and not only those of Russian and Rumanian origin. Chapira said he had spoken with Eliasberg, who intended to set up a committee to take charge of the survey in Paris, and passed on Eliasberg's request for details and for authorization to act in the name of the University Bureau (cf. No. 114 and n. 1 there). Chapira declared his willingness to help with 'anything concerning the future University in Palestine'.

[2] For outline of the survey—see n. 8 to No. 3.

[3] See No. 114.

[4] W. did not in fact visit Paris until July 1903.

114. To Aaron Eliasberg, Paris. *Geneva, 20 December 1902*

German: Or. Copy. T.W.: W.A.

20. 12. 02.

Mr. Aaron Eliasberg,
Paris.

Dear Friend,

Many thanks for all your letters.[1] We were not able to deal with them before today because of an accumulation of work. At this moment the questionnaires are being printed, and they will be sent on to you immediately they are ready. I wrote to Berlin today asking that they send you a proof, at least.[2] You will also be receiving brochures for sale or free distribution, at your discretion.

Mr. Chapira has written us a most friendly letter, and today we replied to the effect that he contact you regarding the survey and other possible moves. Naturally, you may act in the Bureau's name. Today I am leaving for a few days in Zurich, so please write to me there care of Feiwel, Zürichbergstrasse,[3] 19.

With kind regards,

Yours ever,

P.S. Three copies of the circular are enclosed.[4] They are also being sent to non-Zionists.

115. To the President, 'Theodor Herzl' Society, Koenigsberg. *Geneva, 20 December 1902*

German: Or. Copy. T.W.: W.A.

20. 12. 02.

The President[1], 'Herzl' Academic Society,
Koenigsberg, Prussia.

Dear Mr. President,

We were delighted to learn from your kind letter[2] that your Society

114. [1] See Eliasberg to W., 15 Dec. 1902, 17 Dec. 1902, W.A. Eliasberg sought elucidation on the distribution of the brochure and volunteered to conduct the survey in Paris. He apparently wrote another letter, not found (see No. 103; No. 113 and n. 1 there). [2] See No. 112.

[3] W. was about to leave for Biel to take part in the Swiss Zionist Conference. From Biel he was due to go on to Zurich.

[4] Circular of 15 Dec. 1902 (see n. 3 to No. 95).

115. [1] The president of the society was a student named Friedman.

[2] Shereshevsky, in the name of the 'Th. Herzl' Society, to the Jewish University

has signified its readiness to supervise the conduct of the survey in Koenigsberg.

You will be receiving the questionnaires, at our request, from our *Jüdischer Verlag* in Berlin. You will also find brief instructions on how they are to be utilised.

Some copies of our circular,[3] which is also intended for non-Zionist circles, are enclosed. We would mention that we are concerned, in the first place, with a survey among Russian and Rumanian Jewish students. The other surveys will follow.[4]

Most respectfully,

with Zion's greetings,

116. To I. Raskin, Leipzig.[1] *Geneva, 20 December 1902*

German: Or. Copy. T.W.: W.A.

Geneva, 4 rue Lombard, 20. 12. 02.

Dear Fellow-Zionist,

Many thanks for your kind letter.[2] We would inform you that students at the Business College are indeed eligible for inclusion in the survey. At our request, you will be receiving samples of our questionnaires from Berlin.

We would be most grateful if you would kindly let us have addresses for Halle and Jena. Separately, we are sending you some circulars,[3] also intended for non-Zionists, as well as a few brochures.

With Zion's greetings,

Mr. I. Raskin,
Leipzig.

Bureau, 18 Dec. 1902, W.A. Shereshevsky stated that the society would willingly undertake any task entrusted to it in connection with the University, and asked for instructions as to how the survey should be conducted.

[3] Circular of 15 Dec. 1902 (see n. 3 to No. 95).

[4] See n. 8 to No. 3.

116. [1] Raskin was at the time working in a shop in Leipzig. His first name is not known.

[2] Raskin to W., 18 Dec. 1902, W.A. Raskin reported that the *Ziona* Society in Leipzig would be meeting to discuss implementation of the survey. He asked whether people enrolled at the Leipzig School of Commerce should be included, or if the survey should be restricted to students of the University.

[3] Circular of 15 Dec. 1902 (see n. 3 to No. 95).

117. To Hugo Schachtel, Breslau. *Geneva, 20 December*
1902

German: T.W.: C.Z.A. A102/10/2/2.

Geneva, Rue Lombard 4
20. 12. 02.

Mr. Hugo Schachtel,
Breslau.

Dear Friend,

We are deeply appreciative of your kind letter.[1] We have already
written to the gentlemen whose addresses you were good enough to
send us.[2]

Our Bureau has begun its activities in all fields, in accordance
with the plan outlined in our brochure. May we take the liberty of
mentioning some of them: besides conducting surveys (the one concerned with Russian and Rumanian students in Western Europe is
not the only one we contemplate carrying out),[3] we are seeking to
create the contacts through which a wide-scale propaganda effort
might be possible. We can already point to some success in this
regard. In Berlin and Vienna, for example, committees of outstanding personalities are about to be formed. Our intention is to establish
links with people belonging to the world of scholarship and finance
in all the larger centres. The committees mentioned above, and
those still to be formed, will serve this purpose in addition to their
other functions.

It is our view that Breslau can likewise support us in these objectives. We therefore ask most sincerely, dear friend, whether you
could do anything in this respect. Should you feel that the presence
of one of our colleagues would be useful, you need only send us a
line.

Awaiting an early reply with your views on the above, we remain,
Most respectfully,

and with regards,[4]

Dr. Ch. Weizmann

117. [1] Schachtel to W., 15 Dec. 1902, W.A. As requested by W. (see No. 85), Schachtel
had provided the names and addresses of eight Russian students studying in Breslau,
noting that some of them had joined Zionist societies, but 'apparently they are more
interested in Russian or socialist matters rather than Jewish affairs'. Schachtel asked
what they could do in Breslau for the University project—Feiwel had not written to
him for some time and he wanted information.

[2] Apart from the letter to the student Friedman of 4 Jan. 1903 (No. 159) no letters
from W. to the persons listed by Schachtel have been found (see n. 1 above), but
No. 139 indicates that he also wrote to the student Tatarsky.

[3] See n. 8 to No. 3.

[4] 'And with regards' added in W.'s handwriting.

118. To Vera Khatzman,[1] Geneva. *Biel, 21 December 1902*

Russian: H.W.: W.A.

Biel, 21/XII. 02.
Hotel Bielerhof,[2] 12 noon.

Dear Verochka,

Unspeakable boredom. We got together but so far nothing has been done. Pasmanik is conference chairman, myself vice-chairman. A disgusting group of people has assembled here. Very few interesting Zionists. Farbstein is still not here. The conference is being conducted abominably. The people gathered within these four walls have absolutely nothing in common. They are not united by a single idea.[3] Pasmanik's talk on propaganda was most pathetic and trivial.[4]

The discussions were fairly interesting in themselves, but just a voice in the wilderness. I feel tired. Hope to leave this evening.

I kiss you many times, Verochka.

Your Chaim

119. To Vera Khatzman, Geneva.[1] *Zurich, 22 December 1902*

Russian: H.W.: W.A.

Dear Verochka,

Forgive me, my sweet, the letter I wrote yesterday[2] will not reach you before tomorrow. I was so preoccupied, so excited and outraged, that I forgot to post it in time. The conference terminated in a disgusting way. The black gang got their just deserts. A resolution was carried against Schauer censuring his conduct and branding what he did as the act of an informer. We have won. No resolution was moved against the Berne group. The gang's proposal to censure

118. [1] For W.'s relationship with V.K. at this time, see Vol. I, p. 15. They married in 1906.

[2] Address in German script in the original.

[3] For W.'s opinions on Swiss Zionism, see No. 90 and n. 4 there.

[4] For an outline of Pasmanik's speech, see *Israelitisches Wochenblatt für die Schweiz* of 26 Dec. 1902.

119. [1] The content of the letter indicates that it was written in Zurich the morning after the Biel Conference, i.e. 22 Dec. 1902.

[2] See No. 118.

the Berne group came up towards the end of the conference, but we broke up the meeting and dispersed.[3] I left Biel yesterday at 8.30 in the evening, a wreck, and very tired.

We have already discussed[4] a great many things here. Please, little one, open the letter from the *Verlag*[5] and take out a questionnaire for yourself. I won't need it since they have them here. I am very, very pleased that you are not going to Paris.[6] The mere thought of it made me feel lonely, darling. I shall be back on Wednesday; of course I shall telegraph you, and you, dear girl, will meet me.

Here everything is as it was. Esther[7] is in Geneva at the moment. You will certainly be seeing her. Remember me to Saul.[8] Ask him not to leave before I come. Surely he is not in such a great hurry!

Verochka, my darling, I hug and kiss you again and again.

Your Chaim.

Warmest greetings, dear Vera. Do come to Zurich for a few days. Toldy.[9]

---

[3] It appears that a considerable part of the Biel Conference was devoted to the *Yom Kippur* meals incident at the Berne students' refectory and to Schauer's article on the subject (see n. 1 to No. 10). The debate reflected the struggle between the Democratic Fraction and the Academic Zionist Society on the one hand and their opponents among the Berne Zionist students—'the black gang' as W. calls them here—on the other (cf. Vol. I, No. 219 and n. 4 there). The *Israelitisches Wochenblatt für die Schweiz* of 26 Dec. 1902 writes that Berne student circles were strongly represented at the conference 'and had the upper hand in the debate'. The student Israel Auerbach condemned the serving of meals on *Yom Kippur*, while W. said that he 'favours education towards tolerance, since Zionism will not attain its goals tomorrow'; he opposed a debate on religious questions and described it as a 'rubber question' (*Kautschukfrage*). 'Religion is a private matter and is not for debate here.' The report says that several students proposed draft resolutions on the matter, but these were voted down. It says nothing about a resolution on Schauer's article, but it appears that towards the end of the conference—after the correspondent of the *Israelitisches Wochenblatt* had left the hall—two condemnatory resolutions were adopted, one against Schauer's article and the other against the Academic Zionist Society. The latter was presumably adopted after W. and his friends had left the hall (see report in *Zionistische Korrespondenz* of 3 July 1903, according to which the Swiss Zionist Conference at Fribourg of 28 June 1903 repealed both the Biel resolutions, claiming that the conference was no longer authorized to pass resolutions when these were voted upon).

[4] W. went to Zurich to meet Feiwel. From No. 122 it is seen that during their talks they crystallized a plan to found the periodical which was to become the focus of the activities of W., Feiwel, and Buber in 1903.

[5] I.e. the *Jüdischer Verlag* in Berlin.

[6] It seems that V.K. had contemplated visiting Paris in the Christmas vacation.

[7] Esther Shneerson, who was then living in Zurich.

[8] Saul Lurie, then visiting Geneva.

[9] Added in German by Feiwel.

120. To the Jewish Colonial Trust, London. *Geneva, 26 December 1902*

German: Or. Copy. T.W.: W.A.

26. 12. 02.

The Jewish Colonial Trust,
For the attention of Mr. D. Levontin,
London.

Dear Friend,

Receipt of the cheque for 1,400 francs[1] is hereby gratefully acknowledged.

Naturally, we shall seek your permission in advance, as well as Dr. Herzl's,[2] whenever we intend to issue cheques payable by the Bank.

Warm regards,

Yours,

121. To Moses Glikin, Charlottenburg. *Geneva, 26 December 1902*

German/Russian: T.W./H.W.: C.Z.A. A126/16/2.

Geneva, 4 rue Lombard, 26. 12. 02.

Mr. M. Glikin,
Berlin.[1]

Dear Friend,

Under separate cover I am sending you a money order for 250 francs,[2] and would ask you to pay Trietsch 100 marks for Pass and Garleb and 20 marks to Mandels. The rest is for yourself.[3]

---

120. [1] This amount was transferred from the University Bureau's account with the Jewish Colonial Trust in accordance with Feiwel's request in his letter to Herzl of 13 Dec. 1902 (see No. 83 and n. 10 there).

[2] Apparently W. was acting on the Jewish Colonial Trust's request in the letter in which they advised the transfer (not found). Herzl had earlier cancelled the requirement for his signature on withdrawals from the Bureau's account with the J.C.T. (see n. 1 to No. 99).

121. [1] See n. 1 to No. 84.

[2] The Motzkin Archives, which include, *inter alia*, papers of Glikin of the same period (C.Z.A. A126/4), have the counterfoil of the postal order sent by W. on 26 Dec. 1902. W. first wrote '201 marks' (then approximately equivalent to 250 Swiss francs), but altered it to '220 marks'. On the back he wrote, 'I am sending you 220 marks, i.e. 19 more than mentioned in the letter'.

[3] See n. 7 to No. 102.

You may therefore set out on your journey at once. I again repeat the requests I have so often made:

1. Notepaper and envelopes: 500 double sheets and 500 single. The Jewish inscription is not necessary for the envelopes.

2. Brochures.

3. Questionnaires—2,000 copies. Ask the printers to wrap them in packages of 100. If the emblem is not ready[4] do not wait a single moment longer but take everything with you. If you are unable to leave immediately, I would prefer that you send everything by express post. I need to have it all here by Tuesday without fail. We have so much work with the distribution, etc., that we would like to utilise the holidays for this purpose.[5] As soon as you receive this letter please inform me by telegram whether everything is ready and when you are coming.

Naturally you will be going to Zurich.[6] At the same time I am reminding you of the fact that there has still been no reply from Altschul.[7] Please talk to the gentleman now, before your departure.

We are keenly anticipating your arrival here and hope that you have arranged everything properly and that you will arrive safely.

With warm regards, (till we meet again!)[8]

Yours ever,
Chaim

[9] Write to Feiwel about your arrival. Regards to comrades.

122. To Davis Trietsch, Berlin. *Geneva, 26 December 1902*

German: Or. Copy. T.W.: W.A.

Geneva, 4 rue Lombard, 26. 12. 02.

Mr. D. Trietsch,
Berlin.

Dear Friend,

Because of my visit to Zurich I was unfortunately unable to reply promptly to you, and am only now getting round to it.[1] The questionnaires have arrived, for which many thanks, and I am pleased

---

[4] Cf. n. 1 to No. 89.   [5] The University's Christmas vacation.
[6] See n. 3 to No. 41.   [7] See No. 14; n. 1 to No. 89.
[8] 'Till we meet again!' added in Russian in W.'s handwriting.
[9] What follows is added in Russian in W.'s handwriting.

122. [1] See Trietsch to W., undated (18 Dec. 1902 ?),W.A. No. 30/0, 54.

that all the printed material is now ready. A Jewish inscription on
the envelopes is superfluous. One hundred marks have been sent to
you, via Glikin, for Pass and Garleb.[2] At this moment I am also in
a position to make 250 francs from our funds available to the
Jüdischer Verlag.[3] The money is going off today.

I have given Glikin detailed instructions on what he is to bring
with him.

We analysed the situation thoroughly in Zurich together with
Berthold,[4] and have come to the conclusion that we must all strive
together to have a publication of our own, for all our purposes. We
can rely neither on the official nor the semi-official Zionist papers.
The case of *Der Yud* is proof enough how one is betrayed in the end
even by the most trustworthy of people.[5] Since we no longer have
Ost und West either,[6] we are dependent upon the goodwill of the
markedly ill-intentioned official [papers].[7] My first and immediate
objective now is to strengthen the *Verlag* so that it can publish one
of its own. I shall write today in fact to all our real friends[8] in the
hope that something of this sort can be achieved. I shall leave
nothing to chance in order to help extricate the *Verlag*,[9] and thereby all of us, from the crisis. All I would ask of you is that you write
and tell me how much is required for the continued operation of the

---

[2] See No. 121.

[3] W. had promised Trietsch at their meeting in Vienna in Oct. 1902, that he would
send him money for the *Jüdischer Verlag* (see Trietsch to W., 12 Nov. 1902, W.A.).
At a Board meeting of the *Verlag* in May 1903 Trietsch said that W. had undertaken
to give the *Verlag* 1,600 marks (the date of the promise was not mentioned), and
Feiwel explained that the intention was to give the *Verlag* ten per cent of the receipts
of the Jewish University Bureau. (See minutes of the meeting of 15 May 1903,
W.A.).

[4] In the original: 'Wir haben in Zürich mit Berthold . . .', which might imply that
another person or other persons were present, but this phrasing may be due to the
influence of Russian idiom.

[5] A reference to the failure to acquire the periodical *Der Yud* (see Vol. I, n. 29
to No. 238; n. 6 to No. 101 above).

[6] At the end of 1902 Trietsch and Lilien resigned from the editorial staff of the
monthly *Ost und West* because of a dispute with the publisher (see Lilien to Herzl
12 May 1903, C.Z.A. HVIII/551a, and Trietsch's letters to Schachtel from the beginning of 1903, C.Z.A. A102/10/2/2).

[7] This is inspired by the refusal of *Die Welt*, organ of the Zionist Organization, and
of the *Jüdische Rundschau*, organ of the German Zionists, to publish the protest of
the Democratic Fraction against Schauer's article (see n. 6 to No. 83; n. 1 to No. 46).

[8] The matter is mentioned in the letter to Gluskin of 26 Dec. 1902 (No. 123) and
in letters to Kroll and Idelson of 26 Dec. 1902 and to Guinzburg of 27 Dec. 1902 (Nos.
125, 127).

[9] The financial position of the *Jüdischer Verlag* was precarious; it was operating
almost without capital of its own, and its directors owed it money. Moreover, its
publication programme was behind schedule (see Feiwel to Buber and Lilien, 22
Jan. 1903, Buber Papers, N.L.; Trietsch to W., 4 Jan. 1903, W.A.; Schimmer to W.,
11 March 1903, W.A.).

V. together with a publication (I am thinking of a weekly). I am also writing to Russia so as to obtain the 500 roubles for the *V.*[10]

I must say that for a long time now I have been worried about the future of the *V.*, but the situation has never been clear to me. Also, I had no wish to interfere where I was not asked. But there has got to be a change.

I shall be leaving on a journey in two month's time. As you know, I can always achieve something in Russia and I hope this time it can be done for the *Verlag*. On consultation with Feiwel we concluded that a trip to Berlin was not necessary for the time being. In another two months I shall be there.

With all good wishes,

Your

P.S. The list of addresses[11] is going out the day after tomorrow.

123. To Wolf[1] (Ze'ev) Gluskin, Warsaw. *Geneva, 26 December 1902*

German: Or. Copy. T.W.: W.A.

26. 12. 02.

Mr. W. Gluskin,
Warsaw.

Dear Friend,

Thank you for your brief note of the 22nd.[2] You are mistaken, friend Gluskin, if you regard our silence towards you as signifying a standstill in our work. At Mr. Yasinovsky's request our Bureau in fact wrote on the 3rd to the following gentlemen in Warsaw:[3] Dr.

---

[10] When he met W. in Zurich a few days earlier, Feiwel may have asked him to obtain 500 roubles for the *Jüdischer Verlag*. The sum is not mentioned in any of W.'s letters to Russia, but he told Trietsch on 7 Jan. (No. 175) that he was trying to procure 500 roubles and that he expected a reply 'any day'.

[11] Addresses of persons of reliability in University towns in Germany, Austria, and France, to whom Trietsch was to send questionnaire forms for the student survey (see No. 131).

123. [1] Wolf is the equivalent of the Hebrew Ze'ev.

[2] See Gluskin to W., 9/22 Dec. 1902, W.A. Gluskin mentions letters he had received from W. and from W.'s brother-in-law (apparently Chaim Lubzhinsky) and goes on: 'I did not reply since this matter will only come up at the general meeting in March or April, and until then I cannot say anything'. W.'s previous letter to Gluskin has not been found, and it is not clear what 'this matter' refers to. Gluskin also wrote that he had heard nothing from the University Bureau or the *Jüdischer Verlag*.

[3] See No. 54 and n. 7 there; No. 63 and n. 2 there.

Goldflamm, Attorney Goldbaum, Dr. Poznansky, Ignaz Bernstein, Samuel Lurie, Attorney Kohn. Unfortunately we are still without a reply either from Yasinovsky or from the other people. Dr. Lurie, who is also on our list of correspondents, is totally silent.[4] Everyone is regrettably more involved with his own affairs than with any Jewish ideal, however lofty; everyone madly pursues his own interests.

You may rest assured that I am not one of those people who get easily disheartened by the indolence of our 'co-workers'. I know them too well for that. Not a single day passes without our doing something for the University cause. Despite our limited resources and even smaller working team a certain amount has nevertheless been achieved. We have interested and won over well-known personalities, we have made valuable contacts, we have begun a great statistical study of Jewish students in Europe. For this last purpose we have compiled a questionnaire (which I shall shortly be sending you), and we have created links with students in all Universities. As you can imagine, all this requires great effort and stamina. We would be prepared to work even harder if our friends would only support us properly. The *Jüdischer Verlag* is also struggling valiantly and overcoming all its obstacles.[5] My conviction is that we shall prosper only when we have a newspaper to serve all our undertakings: one that is our own, completely independent, and free from all empty official Zionist rhetoric; a newspaper to rally all the creative forces within Zionism. What do you think about it? Can you, who are capable of so much, help us? Are you in a position to do anything material in Warsaw?

May we ask you, in the name of our Bureau, in the name of our publishing house, to look into the matter and work with us. Can you perhaps talk about these undertakings to Yasinovsky, to whom we are writing today,[6] as well as to the gentlemen mentioned above? We know you 'can' if you 'will'.[7]

With most sincere regards,

Yours ever,

[4] Joseph Lurie replied to W.'s letters (Nos. 17, 58, 79) on 11 (24) Dec. 1902 (W.A.), but his letter had not yet reached W.

[5] Cf. n. 9 to No. 122.

[6] No letter of the same date to Yasinovsky has been found. W. wrote to him on 29 Dec. 1902 (see No. 134), but did not mention his appeal to Gluskin, or the plan to found a periodical.

[7] In his reply of 25 Jan. 1903 (W.A.) Gluskin wrote that he did not know how he could be of any help, since he was neither learned nor rich; he recognized the importance of a periodical, 'but this, too, requires money'. Moreover, he was busy, and could not do anything.

124. To Berthold Feiwel, Zurich. *Geneva, 26 December 1902*

German: Or. Copy. T.W.: W.A.

Geneva, 26. 12. 02.

Mr. Berthold Feiwel,
Zurich.

Dear Berthold,

The enclosed letters are from Moscow and from Mr. Schachtel of Breslau,[1] which please return at once together with your remarks. We need these letters and so I am asking you to send them back immediately, together with the others belonging to the Bureau that are still in your possession.[2]

The remittance has now arrived from London,[3] and today I sent money to Trietsch, and to Glikin[4] who can soon be expected.

Also enclosed is an Appeal[5] which is going off today to be printed in Russian and German.

We are absolutely ready for the survey.

Yours ever,

125. To Abraham Idelson and Michael Kroll, Moscow. *Geneva, 26 December 1902*

German: Or. Copy. T.W.: W.A.

26. 12. 02.
Registered.

Dr. M. B. Kroll and A. Idelson,
Moscow.

Dear Friends,

Many thanks indeed for your most interesting letter of the 15th.[1]

124. [1] A letter from Kroll of 2/15 Dec. 1902 (see n. 2 to No. 125) and one from Schachtel of 22 Dec. 1902 (see n. 1 to No. 139).

[2] W. told Feiwel on 14 Dec. that he had sent them (see No. 95).

[3] See No. 120.

[4] See Nos. 121, 122.

[5] A reference to a printed leaflet headed 'Geneva, January 1903'. The leaflet was distributed with the student questionnaires and gave a short explanation of the project for a Jewish University and the purpose of the survey (copy in C.Z.A. Z1/340).

125. [1] Kroll to W., 2/15 Dec. 1902, W.A. In reply to W.'s letter of 2 Dec. 1902 (see No. 50) Kroll wrote that the Russian survey was in preparation, and that the questionnaires would be distributed at the beginning of the next University term. Kroll thought there was no sense in starting a fund-raising drive in Moscow to finance the preparatory work of the University Bureau, since this would only 'break

We on our side are in agreement with all it contains and would only add that we would like you too to implement the plan, as you approve it, for raising funds for the preparatory work by means of concerts, etc. Will you please enlighten us also on the activities of the Union of High School Students? We have not sent you any brochures because we thought this might create difficulties with the censor. Now that this point has been surmounted[2] we shall send copies to you and Idelson respectively today and every subsequent alternate day. Please confirm their receipt.

I shall write to you another time on Fraction business.[3]

After earnestly considering the situation with Feiwel,[4] we have come to the conclusion that it is imperative for us to combine our efforts and obtain a newspaper to serve all our aims. We are merely tolerated by the official and semi-official Zionist Press, we have to exert the utmost pressure to secure space for every couple of lines we submit. The really creative forces are now in the opposition; the Press, unfortunately, is in hands that are hostile to us.[5] While the Statistical Bureau, the Palestine Commission,[6] your Bureau,[7] our organisation,[8] and the *Jüdischer Verlag* have all to labour under the greatest difficulties as with meagre strength they swim against the tide, the official [Press] indulges in phrase-mongering without ever producing a useful thought.

this great project up into mere trifles'; once an international committee was set up, it would be possible to raise large sums of money. He suggested other ways of obtaining money immediately: by organizing concerts and personal appeals. Kroll also reported that the (Jewish) all-Russian Union of High School Students had decided to set aside one per cent of its budget for the University project. He said that Minor could not for the time being be relied upon, but that once a committee of prominent personalities was formed, he too would join it. Poliakov was taking a rest, but would certainly be active later. The absence of the brochure *Eine Jüdische Hochschule* was hindering their implementation of W.'s proposal to set up University groups in other cities (see No. 50). Kroll suggested forming a committee in Moscow, which would in due course look after the setting up of groups in other places. In his opinion, things should not be rushed but should be prepared on the broadest possible base before they started to collect money. The rest of Kroll's letter is devoted to Democratic Fraction matters—he is in favour of maintaining the Information Bureau and planning the publication of Zionist literature.

[2] There was Russian censorship on both outgoing and incoming mail. It is not clear why W. writes that 'this point has been surmounted'—possibly he assumed that Kroll's request for copies of the brochure (see n. 1 above) meant that he and Idelson did not foresee difficulties with the censor, but cf. n. 1 to No. 134; No. 254.

[3] No letter dealing with Democratic Fraction matters has been found.

[4] The construction is similar to that used by W. in his letter to Trietsch of 26 Dec. 1902 (see No. 122 and n. 4 there).   [5] Cf. No. 122 and n. 7 there.

[6] The Committee for Economic Research in Palestine (Komité zur wirtschaftlichen Erforschung Palästinas) was founded in Berlin in 1901. Among its members were Feiwel, Motzkin, and Nossig. The periodical *Palästina* served as the committee's organ (see n. 3 to No. 5).   [7] The Democratic Fraction's office in Moscow.

[8] The University Bureau in Geneva.

Clearly, we shall continue working in isolated units so long as no rallying-point is created to unite all constructive elements, and this can only be achieved by a free, independent, well-edited publication. The *Jüdischer Verlag* must be so strengthened as to be able to produce one. The *J.V.* must also establish a branch in Russia. Since under proper management the undertaking could also be financially profitable, I believe we could get a small syndicate[9] of our friends together to take the matter in hand. Then we would really have a Party. If not we are condemned, in Heine's words, 'to contend with dogs in petty journals'.

I believe that Guinzburg of Saratov and Berligne of Tzaritzyn could do something for this.

The Aberson lecture has (according to Aberson) already grown into a volume.[10] Bukhmil's address is No. 6, rue du Faubourg St. Jaumes, Montpellier.

With my kindest regards,

As ever yours,

Confidential.

126. To Jacob Bernstein-Kohan, Kishinev. *Geneva, 27 December 1902*

German: Or. Copy. T.W.: W.A.

Geneva, 4 rue Lombard, 27. 12. 02.

Registered.

Dr. J. Bernstein-Kohan,
Kishinev.

Dear Friend,

On the 3rd of this month we sent you a long letter in which we outlined the situation regarding the University project as well as our plan of activity.[1] I assume you received the letter, and I do not wish to repeat the points detailed there. If you take an interest in our affairs, you will surely write and ask for a report on all these things. I would gladly fulfil such a request and merely await an indication from you that you want it. Otherwise all this writing is

---

[9] In the original: Konsortium.

[10] A lecture by Aberson at the conference of Young Zionists (Dec. 1901) on 'Zionism's Attitude to Trends in Judaism', which was to be edited and expanded for publication, but was never actually printed (cf. Vol. I, No. 225 and n. 1 there; see also No. 129 below). Kroll wished to publish the lecture in the framework of publications of the Democratic Fraction's Moscow centre (see Kroll to W., 29 Sept. (12 Oct.) 1902, W.A.).

126. [1] See No. 51.

obviously quite superfluous. We have so much to do that we feel
entitled to expect our closest friends to relieve us of fruitless correspondence.

I do not propose to remind you of our brief discussions in Vienna.[2]
I would simply like you to write honestly whether you intend to
support our aims and co-operate in the cause.

You justifiably complained during the year about the unsystematic, negligent way our friends work.[3] Well, something concrete was
initiated here, a project which, properly managed and conducted
with enthusiasm, could develop into a major undertaking. Why do
well-qualified people like you, who are also good workers and trail-
blazers, stand so coldly to one side ? Why do you allow yourselves
to be riddled with petty doubts, lacking the courage to take up
something great, or the self-confidence to meet a challenge ?

I wanted to have this said, and I realise that you will perhaps be
displeased with me over it. Unhappily, I see only too clearly how
weakness and despondency have invaded our leading ranks, and you
would be the last from whom I would withhold feelings such as these.

In the hope at least of receiving a sign of life,[4] I remain,

Yours ever,

127. To Simon Guinzburg, Saratov. *Geneva, 27 December 1902*

German: Or. Copy. T.W.: W.A.

Geneva, 4 rue Lombard, 27. 12. 02.

Registered.

Engineer S. Guinzburg,
Saratov.

Dear Friend,

On the 3rd of this month we wrote you in considerable detail
about the University project.[1] We also asked for your kind support.
I assume you received the letter and I do not wish to repeat the
points detailed there. If you take an interest [in the subject], you will
doubtless write for information on all matters relating to it. I would
gladly fulfil such a request and only await an indication from you
that you want it. Otherwise all this writing is obviously quite super-

---

[2] During the Annual Zionist Conference, Oct. 1902—see No. 51.

[3] For Bernstein-Kohan's criticism about the shortcomings of Democratic Fraction
members, see also n. 8 to No. 377; No. 413.

[4] W. received no reply to his letters to Bernstein-Kohan, which later he came to
believe had been seized by the Russian authorities (see No. 377).

127. [1] See No. 52.

fluous. We have so much to do that we feel entitled to expect our closest friends to relieve us of fruitless correspondence.

You are always complaining, justifiably, about the unsystematic, negligent way our friends work. Well, something concrete was initiated here, a project which, properly managed and conducted with enthusiasm, could develop into a major undertaking. Why do well-qualified people like you, who are also good workers and trail-blazers, stand so coldly to one side ? Why do you allow yourselves to be riddled with petty doubts, lacking the courage to take up something great, or the self-confidence to meet a challenge ?

I hope this time you will at least be impelled to reply to these few words.

Yesterday I sent a very full letter to Moscow about the plan to establish a journal that would serve all our aims.[2] Of the many papers which it is now our misfortune to have and which continue to sprout like mushrooms, none is entirely at our disposal. We are powerless, and will remain so unless we have our own free organ. If we are really serious about our affairs—the Fraction, the Statistical Bureau, the Palestine study and, last but not least,[3] the University—then we have to use all our energies in strengthening the *Jüdischer Verlag* in Berlin and in establishing another in Russia.[4] In this way we would be able to bring out a periodical with a minimum of delay. You, who have so much to contribute, ought to neglect nothing. I have no desire to specify once again the requests made in my previous letter. All repetition tends to have a diminishing effect. I would only note that I am prepared to visit your part of the world at some date in the future to conduct propaganda for our ideas. It is up to you, however, to make a beginning now.

Anticipating your immediate reply, I am

Yours very sincerely,

128. To the President, 'Theodor Herzl' Society, Koenigsberg. *Geneva, 27 December 1902*

German: Or. Copy. T.W.: W.A.

27. 12. 02.

The President,[1] 'Theodor Herzl' Academic Society,
Koenigsberg, Prussia.

Dear Sir and Fellow-Zionist,

In immediate reply to your esteemed letter of the 24th,[2] here are

---

[2] See No. 125.   [3] English in original, 'last not least' (*sic*).
[4] See No. 125.

128. [1] See n. 1 to No. 115.
[2] Shereshevsky in the name of the 'Th. Herzl' Society to the University Bureau,

the addresses now in our possession. We hope to send you the others later.

1. Raskin, Zionist Reading Room, 17, Grimmaischestrasse, Leipzig
2. Miss Bass, c/o Mezger, 6, Ladenbergerstrasse, Heidelberg
3. Moses Lokatczer, student engineer,[3] 77, Leipzigerstrasse, Koethen in An[halt]
4. [J.] Rosenbaum, 12, Tschirnerstrasse, Mittweida
5. A. Kroll, Friedberg (Hesse)
6. Jeremias Schick, 8, Georg-Friedrichstrasse, Karlsruhe
7. S. Lurie, 73, Viktoriastrasse, Darmstadt
8. A. Mandels, 2, Stuttgarter Platz, Charlottenburg, Berlin
9. Epstein, student, Marburg
10. Ch. Ozhinsky, The University, Munich
11. Tatarsky, Maccabea Academic Society, 16, Gertrudenstrasse, Breslau
12. Markov, student, Freiberg in S[axony]
13. Ch. Khissin, 24, Freiestrasse, Berne
15. Ch. Wortsman, 26, Feldbergstrasse, Basle
16. B. Feiwel, 19, Zürichbergstrasse, Zurich
17. 'Bar-Kochba' Academic Society, Prague

Most respectfully,
and with Zion's greetings,

129. To Menahem Ussishkin, Ekaterinoslav. *Geneva, 28 December 1902*

Russian: H.W.: C.Z.A. A24/125/ל.

Geneva, 28. XII. 02.
Rue Lombard 4.

Dear Michael[1] Moiseevitch,

In a few days you will receive a detailed letter from me concerning some of the Zionist problems in which you are interested.[2] At the same time I shall reply to both your circulars, for which I was very grateful.[3]

24 Dec. 1902, W.A. Shereshevsky had asked for addresses of Zionist societies in Germany, Austria, and Switzerland 'which we need in order to organise Zionists'.

[3] 'cand. ing'—an engineering student in the final stage of his studies.

129. [1] Ussishkin's Russian name.

[2] See No. 205.

[3] Apparently a reference to circulars from Ussishkin (in his capacity as Zionist representative for the Ekaterinoslav region), of 30 Sept. (13 Oct.) 1902 and 15 (28) Nov. 1902, C.Z.A. Z1/383. The first circular deals with Jewish Colonial Trust matters and with questions regarding the organization of Russian Zionists. For the second circular, see n. 13 to No. 83.

I am writing to you now on a purely private matter. It is about our friend Aberson. As you know, he is a man of outstanding ability, and his contribution to our cause is bound to be of real importance. This is my profound conviction. A.'s financial position is critical. I am sure you understand how impossible it is to work, study and write when one has to struggle for one's daily bread, living in constant want with no hope of things improving. The dissertation on which A. has been working so hard[4] has not as yet been finished solely because his energies are being sapped through his having to slave for the barest necessities of life. We can do very little for A. here. It is for this reason that I make this plea to you that you arrange some sort of stipend for him. He is a competent man, and a force of great importance to us.

It is clearly and unequivocally in our own interest to give a chance to a man who has so completely proved his ability to make his way, and to help ease the struggle which he has had to wage over the past three or four years, all with little success. I feel sure that you will respond to my appeal and act 'כאדם העושה בתוך שלו'.[5]

Please, my friend, answer at once. Perhaps something can be arranged with a publishing house. In the meantime, A.'s paper, which I have seen for myself, has grown into a sizeable pamphlet, even a small book. I am absolutely sure there is nothing like it yet in our literature. I am convinced that if only you would 'wish it', you could 'do it'.[6]

Keep well,

Your Ch. Weizmann.

130. To A. Bass, Liège. *Geneva, 28 December 1902*

Russian: Or. Copy. H.W.: W.A.

28/Dec. 02.

Dear Mr. Bass,[1]

I attach herewith some of our circulars in German.[2] I am sending you our brochure under separate cover.

This deals with a project for the establishment of a Jewish

---

[4] See n. 10 to No. 125.

[5] Heb.: 'as a man attending to his own affairs'.

[6] Ussishkin replied to this letter (see No. 205), but his reply has not been found.

130. [1] First name not known.

[2] Apparently a reference to a circular of 15 Dec. 1902 (see n. 3 to No. 95) and to the leaflet concerning the survey (see n. 5 to No. 124).

Institute of Higher Learning. You will find therein the details for its implementation which we are now working on.

First among the necessary preliminary tasks will be a statistical survey of Jewish students in Europe, through questionnaires, etc.

As we have your address in Liège we are taking the liberty of asking you not to decline responsibility for [distributing] these questionnaires in your city. (What we request of you is explained in greater detail in the German circular.)

Whatever your attitude towards the Jewish University project, the statistical survey of the student body in itself [---- ----] that I trust you will not refuse to participate in this useful cultural undertaking.

With kind regards,

Dr. Ch. Weizmann.

131. To Davis Trietsch, Berlin. *Geneva, 28 December 1902*

German: Or. Copy. T.W.: W.A.

Geneva, 4 rue Lombard, 28. 12. 02.

Mr. D. Trietsch,
Berlin.

Dear Friend,

You have doubtless received both my last letter and the money by now, and I hope that all the printing has in the meantime been completed.[1]

The list of addresses is, unfortunately, not yet ready as we are still waiting for replies from many cities. Nevertheless, I am sending you a list of what we now have.[2] But I would like you to wait a little longer before mailing, as we have decided to enclose both the Russian translation and an Appeal in German and Russian.[3] This printed matter will leave here on Wednesday and should, therefore, be in Berlin by Friday. You can then send everything off next Saturday. In the meantime more addresses are likely to be added. The mailing for Germany, Austria and France should be done from Berlin. We shall look after Switzerland, and save postage. We already have reliable people to whom all questionnaires destined for each city will go in one package. Please enclose the envelopes.

I am awaiting your reply to my last letter, and remain,

With kind regards,

Yours,

131. [1] See No. 122.   [2] The list has not been found.
[3] See n. 5 to No. 124.

132. To Julius Loewy, Prague. *Geneva, 28 December 1902*
German: Or. Copy. H.W.: W.A.

28. XII. 02.

Mr. Julius Loewy,
Prague.

Dear Sir,

I shall reply fully to your much appreciated letter of the 26th. in two days time.[1]

I am enclosing some circulars from our Bureau[2] with the request that you send them out to students of the 'Bar-Kochba' Society.[3] I am eagerly awaiting an answer from these gentlemen.[4]

I would be most grateful if you would kindly send [me] the addresses of Russian or Rumanian Jewish students that you may know of at other Austrian Universities.

Kind regards,

Respectfully,

Dr. Ch. Weizmann

133. To M. Schmidt, Vienna. *Geneva, 28 December 1902*
Russian: Or. Copy. H.W.: W.A.

28. XII. 02.

Mr. M. Schmidt,
Vienna.

Dear Friend,

I enclose two circulars intended for the Jewish students in Vienna.[1] I do not possess a single address of any Russian student in Vienna, and would be most grateful if you would kindly pass the circulars on to the proper people.

From the contents of the circulars you will see what this is all about. I must have an immediate answer, so please be kind enough,

---

132. [1] Neither Loewy's letter nor a further one from W. to him has been found.
[2] See n. 2 to No. 130.
[3] The Prague Student Zionist Society.
[4] No reply from Loewy or from members of 'Bar-Kochba' has been found.

133. [1] See n. 2 to No. 130.

for old time's sake,[2] to put me in touch with members of the Vienna student circle.[3]

Kindest regards,

Yours,

Ch. Weizmann.

134. To Isidore (Israel) Yasinovsky, Warsaw. *Geneva, 29 December 1902*

German: Or. Copy. T.W.: W.A.

29. 12. 02.

Mr. I. Yasinovsky,
Warsaw.

Dear Friend,

We gratefully acknowledge receipt of your esteemed communication of the 24th.[1] Following your advice we shall write today to the gentlemen you mention.[2]

Dr. Yelsky of Lodz, you will recall, was in Vienna with us.[3] He evinced so little interest that it can be justifiably assumed that he will do hardly anything for this cause. Perhaps his interest could be aroused if he were spoken to personally; we shall do this sometime in the early future.

We are delighted with the good fortune you have had with the gentlemen in Warsaw, and hope you will continue on the same lines and with equal success.

At present we are completely absorbed here by the statistical enquiry into Jewish students. This work will be reaching the final

---

[2] W. and Schmidt corresponded in 1901 in connection with preparations for the conference of young Zionists. W.'s letters to Schmidt have not been found, but a number of Schmidt's letters are in the W.A.

[3] No reply to this letter has been found, but see n. 2 to No. 182.

134. [1] Yasinovsky to the University Bureau, 11/24 Dec. 1902, W.A. Yasinovsky wrote that apart from himself, no one had received the brochure *Eine Jüdische Hochschule* and he assumed that the other copies had been held up by the Russian censor (for despatch of the brochure to Warsaw, see No. 54; No. 63 and n. 2 there). He reported having spoken with Goldflamm, who had expressed his unqualified support for the University project, and suggested that W. write to him and to the Warsaw notary, Landau, whose support Yasinovsky hoped to enlist. He also suggested writing to a number of persons in the Polish provinces, among them Yelsky, the Zionist representative for the Lodz region.

[2] No letters to the persons mentioned by Yasinovsky in his letter have been found, neither have their replies, with the exception of a letter from Golde of 5 Feb. 1903 (see n. 1 to No. 254).

[3] On the occasion of the Annual Zionist Conference in Oct. 1902.

stage of its preparation this week, and we shall be able shortly to send you a progress report.

With kind regards,

Yours respectfully,

135. To Ben-Zion Friedland and Moses Weizmann, Kiev.
Geneva, 29 December 1902

German: Or. Copy. T.W.: W.A.

Geneva, 4 rue Lombard, 29. 12. 02.

Messrs. B. Friedland and M. Weizmann,
Kiev.   Registered.

Dear Friends,

On the 8th of this month, that is, at least three weeks ago, we wrote to you in great detail about our activities here.[1] We also made a plea, in all sincerity, that you support us in our task. Additionally, we requested information on the situation in Kiev. We on our part are accustomed always to receive a reply to a courteous letter, even if only a negative one. Naturally, we have neither the power nor the desire to compel you to work. We wrote, however, on the basis of your declared wish to co-operate,[2] and now you are letting us down.

Consequently, we are obliged to repeat once again all the requests we expressed in our previous letter:

1. What is happening to the statistical study?
2. Have you tried to enlist the interest of Mr. Ratner, Prof. Bulgakov, Private-Lecturer Frankfurt, etc?
3. Have you spoken to Mandelstamm?
4. Have you investigated the existence at the Polytechnic of a certain Mr. Rostovtsev, a chemist?

We really do not consider these tasks to be so arduous, and we do not intend to theorise on the reasons why you never answer. We now anticipate a definite reply, but should you not do so, we shall disturb you no more.[3]

Kind regards,

Your

---

135. [1] See No. 69.

[2] No previous letters from Friedland and Moses Weizmann have been found, and it would appear that the promise was made verbally. W. met his brother when visiting Russia in Aug.–Oct. 1902, and he may also have met Friedland during his visit to Kiev in the middle of Oct. 1902 (see Vol. I, No. 319).

[3] No reply to this letter has been found.

136. To Sh. Margolin, Liège. *Geneva, 30 December 1902*[1]

Russian: Or. Copy. H.W.: W.A.

30. XII. 02.

Mr. Sh. Margolin,[2]
Liège.

Dear Comrade,

I am very grateful for your cordial letter, received today,[3] and I hasten to reply. We accept your offer with great pleasure. We suggest, in order to deal more conveniently and efficiently with the matter, that you organise a special statistical committee to conduct the survey. It is essential to enlist the co-operation of students representing all the trends in the Jewish student body of your city.

Whatever their attitude towards Zionism or the question of a Jewish University, all Jewish students irrespective of their opinions must surely regard the survey sympathetically.

I have the address of Mr. A. Bass[4] in Liège (rue St. Remy, 35). Be good enough to get in touch with him. I am sending you two circulars in German which deal with this matter.[5]

As soon as I hear from you, I shall send you the questionnaires as well as the brochure. We have contacts in Antwerp[6] but not so far in Brussels, and it would be greatly appreciated if you could find us a contact there.

Let me know if you think there is any point in our approaching the colony[7] directly. I should imagine that you would have no difficulty in getting a committee together and making all arrangements necessary.

Are there any Jewish students in Amsterdam, Leyden, Ghent, etc.?

Awaiting your prompt reply, *mit Gruss*![8]

Dr. Ch. Weizmann.

---

136. [1] On the original copy, '30. XII. 02' has been added in Levinson's handwriting.

[2] First name not known.

[3] Margolin to W., 28 Dec. 1902, W.A. Margolin offered his help in conducting the survey in Liège, and said he could also obtain addresses in Brussels and Antwerp. He pointed out that there were 100 foreign students in Liège, but that only two of them were Zionists.

[4] See No. 130.

[5] See n. 2 to No. 130.

[6] See No. 81.

[7] The foreign student colony in Liège.

[8] 'with greetings'.

137. To Berthold Feiwel, Zurich. *Geneva, 30 December 1902*

German: Or. Copy. T.W.: W.A.

Geneva, 4 rue Lombard, 30. 12. 02.

Mr. Berthold Feiwel,
Zurich.

Dear Berthold,

Thank you very much for your detailed letter.[1] It was certainly wise of me not to yield to your entreaties, and I have extricated myself from *Cheirus* in time.[2] Thus I was spared three days of talk.

A letter is going off to Schachtel today.[3]

A telegram arrived from Glikin the day before yesterday, to the effect that all printed material will go off on Monday.[4] It should therefore be here as early as tomorrow. We shall begin despatch right away.[5] I presume Lilien never got the emblem done.[6] I have sent 400 francs to Berlin.[7]

137. [1] Feiwel to W., 29 Dec. 1902, W.A. Feiwel wrote about the *Cheirus* conference, which had taken place in Zurich from 25 Dec. 1902 to 28 Dec. 1902 (cf. n. 22 to No. 18 ; No. 70 and n. 2 there). Feiwel reported that Syrkin, Mirkin, Perelman, and Abramovich had put *Cheirus* forward as a 'fraction'. The decision was carried by a vote of 7 to 6, and after the vote Eliashev, Wortsman, Pinkus, Radutsky, Shneerson, and Feiwel left the conference (for the debate at the conference and resolutions, see *The Writings of Nahman Syrkin*, pp. 193–7, and see also Wortsman to W., 7 Jan. 1903, W.A.). Feiwel also dealt with Democratic Fraction matters, expressing his opinion that they should at least open an office that would make a list of the Fraction's members and set up a 'correspondence service'. Feiwel received a letter from Werner, who explained that because of the pressure of his work in the Jewish Statistical Bureau in Vienna he was unable to set up a University committee there (cf. n. 1 to No. 92), but suggested various people for membership of such a committee (see n. 9 below). Feiwel promised to send W. a (draft) letter for professors the following day—see n. 9 to No. 13.

[2] For W.'s participation in *Cheirus*, see n. 22 to No. 18.

[3] See No. 139 and n. 2 there.   [4] See Glikin to W., 28 Dec. 1902, W.A.

[5] Despatch of questionnaires for the survey.

[6] The emblem for the University Bureau—cf. n. 1 to No. 89.

[7] In his letter of 29 Dec. 1902 Feiwel asked how much money W. had sent to the *Jüdischer Verlag*. On 26 Dec. W. sent Glikin in Berlin 220 marks (about 270 Swiss francs). This was not intended for the *Jüdischer Verlag* (see No. 121 and n. 2 there), but on the same day W. notified Trietsch that he was sending him 250 francs for the *Verlag* (see No. 122 and n. 3 there). Accordingly, on 26 Dec. W. sent 520 francs to Berlin, and not 400, as stated here. There may be two explanations for the discrepancy: W. may in fact have sent Trietsch only 120 francs and not 250, or he may have been referring here only to the money he sent for the *Verlag*. If the latter is the case, it can be assumed that he also took into account the money remaining to Trietsch out of the sum of 125 roubles sent from Pinsk to Berlin and addressed to Lilien (see No. 32 and n. 1 there): after deducting payments W. asked him to make from this money, Trietsch would have about 105 marks left, roughly equivalent to 130 francs. Thus, together with the 250 francs advised by W. on 26 Dec. Trietsch must have had from W. the equivalent of about 380 francs. W. may have rounded this off to '400 francs'.

It is most essential that the letter for the professors is here by tomorrow, when it will be immediately typed and reproduced.[8]

The names supplied by Dr. Werner are fairly good ones.[9] But we must obtain a few better-sounding names, known in Russia. I shall be writing to Buber[10] today about this.

Regarding Fraction business, separately.[11]

Warmest greetings to you,

Ever your

138. To Martin Buber, Vienna. *Geneva, 30 December 1902*

German: Or. Copy. T.W.: W.A.

30. 12. 02.

Mr. Martin Buber,
Vienna.

Dear Martin,

Dr. Werner has written concerning the Vienna committee for the University. He mentioned a few names and, of course, no objection can be raised against them.[1] But may I point out that it is most essential for us to win over some famous personalities. Regrettable as it may be, this has great value, particularly among moneyed Jews. Please notify me how far you have progressed in this direction. As soon as you have a few definite people, do let us know whether we may communicate with them from this end, and how. This last point is most important.

We also need the list of professors. Please send whatever you have ready at once. It is high time that we brought ourselves to the notice of these people.[2] We hope to utilise the holidays for completing the mass of correspondence involved. I implore you, dear Martin, to get down to finishing this task immediately.

We have now prepared everything for the survey. Distribution of the questionnaire should begin tomorrow. I am glad that this at least is nearing completion, as we must now devote all our energies

[8] The letter to the professors was never sent—see n. 9 to No. 13.

[9] See n. 1 above. Werner suggested Leon Kellner, Adolf Schwarz, Dr. Kernberger, Adolf Gelber, Richard Rappoport, and Bernard Fuchs.

[10] See No. 138.

[11] No letter to Feiwel dealing with the Fraction has been found, but on 7 Jan. 1903 W. instructed Feiwel that all activity concerning the Fraction should be postponed until Glikin arrived in Switzerland (see No. 178).

138. [1] See n. 1 and n. 9 to No. 137.
[2] See n. 9 to No. 13.

to the formation of committees. There are only three brief months left before my visit to Russia. Absolutely necessary as this journey is, it will nevertheless lose half its usefulness if we cannot by then demonstrate the existence of a strong committee.

I await news from you with the keenest interest.

Always yours ever,

139. To Hugo Schachtel, Breslau. *Geneva, 30 December 1902*

German: T.W./H.W.: C.Z.A. A102/10/2/2.

Geneva, 30. 12. 02.

Mr. Hugo Schachtel,
Breslau.

Dear Fellow-Zionist,

Please excuse this somewhat tardy reply to your communication of the 22nd,[1] which was very much appreciated. I had to discuss it with our friend Feiwel.[2]

We should be most obliged if you would provide us with the addresses you have in mind. We shall try and write to these people. You are perhaps aware that *Ost und West* has passed into new hands.[3] I think we may still be able to plant an article in it. Incidentally, Buber wrote an article about the University in this periodical some time ago.[4]

Many thanks for letting us have this information.
Greetings.

Most respectfully,
Dr. Ch. Weizmann

[5]No reaction from Mr. Tatarsky[6] to my letter about the survey.

139. [1] Schachtel to W., 22 Dec. 1902, W.A. Schachtel described the anti-Zionist atmosphere among educated and wealthy Jewish circles in Breslau. As a result, it would only be possible to win support for the University if the Zionist aspect were not stressed and if the task were undertaken through people not identified with Zionism. He suggested writing to a number of persons and then, if they were willing, speaking to them personally. Schachtel proposed publishing an article on the University project in the monthly *Ost und West*, to which many leading Jewish personalities in Breslau subscribed.

[2] See No. 124. In his letter of 29 Dec. 1902 (W.A.) Feiwel suggested that W. ask Schachtel for the addresses of likely people in Breslau.

[3] In fact *Ost und West* did not change hands. W. is evidently referring to the resignation of Trietsch and Lilien from its editorial staff. See n. 6 to No. 122.

[4] Buber's article 'A Spiritual Centre' ('Ein geistiges Centrum'), *Ost und West*, Oct. 1902.   [5] What follows has been added in W.'s handwriting.

[6] Tatarsky (first name not known), medical student and member of the Breslau Student Zionist Society *Maccabea*. W. approached him about conducting the survey in Breslau (the letter has not been found).

140. To Aaron Eliasberg, Paris. *Geneva, 31 December 1902*

Russian: Or. Copy. H.W.: W.A.

31. XII. 02.

Dear Aaron,

Owing to the accumulation of work at the printers in connection with the new year, our *Fragebogen* were delayed for a few days. They are now ready, and I have received a parcel for Geneva. On Sunday, or Monday at the latest, everything will be sent on to you from Berlin and you can then get to work.

All the best,

Your Chaim.

141. To Moses Glikin, Charlottenburg. *Geneva, 31 December 1902*[1]

German: T. C.Z.A. A179/3.

WIRE WHETHER EVERYTHING DESPATCHED[2] URGENTLY REQUIRED

WEIZMANN

142. To Moses Glikin, Charlottenburg. *Geneva, 31 December 1902*

Russian: Pcd. H.W.: C.Z.A. A179/3.

Geneva, 31. XII. 02.

Dear Glikin,

Why are you so mean with your postcards? I telegraphed you today[1] about the despatch of the *Drucksachen* which, according to Trietsch's letter, were *not* sent on Monday. This is *most* unpleasant.[2] It impedes our work here. We must have the brochures.

When are you coming? Addresses?[3]

Your Chaim

Who will be responsible for the *Enquête* in Berlin?

141. [1] Date according to the telegram and its postmark.

[2] A reference to the second edition of *Eine Jüdische Hochschule* and the notepaper of the University Bureau, printed in Berlin—see n. 2 to No. 142.

142. [1] See No. 141.

[2] Trietsch to W., 29 Dec. 1902, W.A. Trietsch wrote that the brochure *Eine Jüdische Hochschule* and the Bureau's notepaper would be sent in the next few days.

[3] In an undated letter (about 18 Dec. 1902; W.A. No. 30/0, 54) Glikin told W. that he hoped shortly to send more addresses (of people who might be entrusted with the conduct of the survey of students in the German provinces).

143. To Isaac Gruenbaum, Warsaw. *Geneva, 31 December 1902*

Russian: Or. Copy. H.W.: W.A.

31. XII. 02.

Mr. S. Gruenbaum,[1]
Warsaw.

Dear Comrade,

Dr. Lurie informs me that he has given you the Hebrew translation of the brochure *Eine Jüdische Hochschule*.[2] I would be grateful
to you if you could let me know at once what is happening to the
brochure, and how soon you will be handing it in to the censor. It
has been lying around at Lurie's for an eternity.

I would very much like [---- ----] about the University project in
general.

Warmest regards,

Your Ch. Weizmann.

144. To Charles (Yeheskel) Wortsman, Basle. *Geneva, 31 December 1902*[1]

German: Or. Copy. H.W.: W.A.

Mr. Ch. Wortsman,
Basle.

Dear Friend,

A parcel of 10 questionnaires was despatched to you today, together with the Appeal announcement.[2] Would you kindly distribute them [among] the Russian and Rumanian Jews in your city
and also ensure that they are filled in.

Ever your

Ch. W.

---

143. [1] The letter was addressed to Stanislaus Gruenbaum, but was intended for his
brother Isaac. The mistake probably occurred because Gruenbaum asked for his
letters to be sent care of his brother (see Gruenbaum to W., 19 Jan. 1902, W.A.).

[2] Lurie to W., 11 (24) Dec. 1902, W.A. Lurie wrote that the translation he had
given to Gruenbaum still needed editing.

144. [1] The date has been determined by the letter's position in the University
Bureau's letter-book.

[2] See n. 5 to No. 124.

145. To Davis Trietsch, Berlin. *Geneva, 31 December 1902*

German: Or. Copy. H.W.: W.A.

31. XII. 02.

Dear friend Trietsch,

I shall reply to your letter[1] tomorrow.[2] For the moment two small requests (quite small!): 1. Send me three marks' worth of German postage stamps (20 pfg. each). 2. Please write at once to the administrative departments of the Technical Colleges in Dresden and Hanover asking for their enrolment lists.[3] Please enclose 50 pfg. in postage stamps with each letter. They refused to send me the lists because I had no German stamps.[4] I have no addresses for these two cities. Kindly do this *at once*; I need the printed matter[5] urgently. And the 'emblem' ?[6] The questionnaire has arrived.

Warmest greetings.

Your
Ch. W.

Happy New Year!

146. To Davis Trietsch, Berlin. *Geneva, 31 December 1902*[1]

German: Or. Copy. H.W.: W.A.

Dear Trietsch,

Today there were despatched to the *Jüdischer Verlag*: a) Appeal announcements [in German]: b) Forms [---- survey ---- ---- ---- ----].[2] Now the following has to be done.

1) For *France, Belgium* and *Holland*, duplicate copies (German with Russian translation) in respect of each student. Please enclose

---

145. [1] Trietsch to W., 29 Dec. 1902, W.A. Trietsch reported that Altschul had spoken to Pictet several times (see No. 14 and n. 1 there); it had become clear that Pictet was not likely to be of any real use for the University project at that time, but he was interested and might be useful later on.

[2] In fact W. wrote only on 2 Jan. 1903 (see No. 152).

[3] Probable reference to lists of Russian students—cf. No. 82.

[4] No letters from W. to the Dresden and Hanover Technical Colleges have been found, but he may have been referring to his application to Wuerzburg University and to polytechnics in Aachen and Stuttgart—see No. 82 and n. 1 there.

[5] See n. 2 to No. 142.   [6] Cf. n. 1 to No. 89.

146. [1] In the University Bureau's letter-book this letter appears between one dated 31 Dec. 1902 and another dated 1 Jan. 1903. It was evidently written on 31 Dec.: the additional addresses that W. promises to send 'the day after tomorrow' are included in the letter to Trietsch of 2 Jan. 1903 (see No. 152).

[2] Part of the sentence in the original copy is smudged and illegible. No. 152 indicates that W. sent Trietsch, in addition to the leaflet on the student survey (see n. 5 to No. 124), the Russian translation of the questionnaire.

a few Appeal announcements in German with every package. They are for those Rumanians who do not understand Russian.

2) For the German Universities: everyone to receive a questionnaire and Appeal in German. In all cases some [Russian copies] to be enclosed with each package.

The day after tomorrow further addresses are going to you. Would you kindly send off the package for [Paris] (urgently!).

Your
Ch. W.

147. To Julius Meyer, Basle. *Geneva, 31 December 1902*

German: Or. Copy. H.W.: W.A.

31. XII. 02.

Mr. Julius Meyer,
Basle.

Dear Friend,

Have you spok[en] with the professors?[1] What is happening in Basle regarding the University project?

Happy New Year.

Yours ever,
Ch. Weizmann

[Would] you perhaps [.............................][2]

148. To Alexander Nemirovsky, Kharkov. *Geneva, 31 December 1902*

Russian: Or. Copy. H.W.: W.A.

31. XII. 02.

Dear Alexander Yakovlevitch,

Don't you consider it necessary to answer any of my letters?[1]

Did you reply to Birnbaum?[2] At least send me a postcard with one word on it: 'Yes' or 'No'.

What about the brochure?[3] Warmest regards to all yours.

Your Chaim

147. [1] See also No. 107.   [2] The end of the sentence is illegible.

148. [1] See Nos. 2, 20.   [2] See No. 20.
   [3] A reference to the Russian translation of *Eine Jüdische Hochschule*—see n. 11 to No. 7; n. 5 to No. 23.

149. To Gregory Lurie, Pinsk. *Geneva, 1 January 1903*

Russian: Or. Copy. H.W.: W.A.

Vertraulich.   Geneva, Rue Lombard 4.
                                                            1. I. 03.

Dear Gregory Aronovitch,

Truthfully, your last letter quite astonished me. Surely you do not take the view that it is impossible even to discuss the question of Palestine ?[1] Just imagine our succeeding in creating a Jewish University in Palestine under English protection ; the subject would promptly take a completely new turn.

My opinion is as follows: although it is *impossible* to establish a *Hochschule* in Palestine it is nevertheless necessary, for a whole [range] of reasons, some of them tactical, some of principle, to refrain at this stage from categorical declarations.

If we start by throwing Palestine overboard every time a serious [problem] arises, there will soon be an end to all our yearnings. *You must [help] us find a way* through all these questions. Well, so much for the *Hochschule*.

And now general Zionist matters. I have been on the point of writing to you for some time, but my work has been keeping me very busy. Since my arrival from [----] my thoughts have dwelt constantly on this basic question: 'Can our cause make any progress this way, or not ?' What we [heard] in Vienna of 'success', of 'diplomacy', etc., gave so little comfort that one must be either a fantast or an idiot to believe for one moment that the movement can continue developing on such a basis.[2]

Ideology, romanticism, etc., keep . . . .
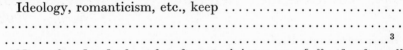
. . . .
. . . .[3]

Now after [----] of work, after straining every [effort], after all the ringing speeches, after five Congresses and [hundreds] of different kinds of meetings and conferences, we have arrived at the point

---

149. [1] Presumably this letter was in reply to one from Lurie in which he expressed his opposition to the decision of the Zionist Annual Conference to support the establishment of a Jewish University conditional on its being located in Palestine (see Vol. I, n. 4 to No. 320). Lurie's letter has not been found.

[2] At the Zionist Annual Conference, which took place in Oct. 1902 in Vienna, Herzl reported on the failure of political negotiations in Constantinople (see Vol. I, n. 3 to No. 320). W. alludes here to the hopes pinned by many upon the diplomatic activities of the Zionist leadership and to the speeches regarding so-called successes achieved in this field.

[3] In the original copy, two and a half lines are blurred and undecipherable.

that *for the time being there can be no more talk of a charter*.[4] We are told nothing definite, of course, and everything is covered with a blanket of strange secrecy; every word from Mr. Marmorek[5] is a *Staatsaktion*,[6] and clearly Vienna can and will say nothing! But to any thinking person, *der es mit dem Zionismus ernst meint*,[7] it is obvious that things cannot go on as they are.

We have to bring the game out into the open. Not only does no-one know how the negotiations for a charter were conducted, no-one even saw the charter[8] as it was conceived. Faith that has endured five years cannot do so any longer, and the decline of Zionist strength is probably caused wholly by this attitude [----] towards the central question of Zionism.

Even now, Palestine is [undoubtedly] a romantic concept: as a concrete proposition it does not so much as come within our comprehension.

This sickness has paralysed the entire cause, and must be given a radical cure; at the forthcoming Congress we must demand,[9] with all our vigour, that some clarification be established in the question of a charter, and if it becomes impossible to achieve this—then we shall have to seek out new paths.[10]

Even if the situation, and our views on Palestine, are both so hopeless, Zionism will not die as a result.

I know many people who are prepared to give up Palestine. I most certainly do not subscribe to their views but on the other hand I do not share the opinion of people who stand by the seashore in the expectancy of fair weather.

Live initiative is stifled under such conditions.

There are immense tasks which the Zionists ought to tackle, if only they were realistic politicians and not dreamers: the centralisation[11] and regulation of the whole emigration movement[12] are necessities for us. But we are eternally [caught up] in waiting and hoping, and

---

[4] Since 1898 Herzl had been seeking a 'charter' from the Turkish government in order to secure a legal basis for Jewish colonization in Palestine.

[5] Apparently Oskar Marmorek of Vienna, a member of the Zionist Smaller Actions Committee who deputized for Herzl whenever he was away from Vienna.

[6] 'Act of State.'   [7] 'Who takes Zionism seriously.'

[8] During Herzl's time various plans for a charter were formulated, but they were not published (see Böhm's *Die Zionistische Bewegung*, Tel-Aviv, 1935, Vol. I, pp. 272 ff.).

[9] The Sixth Zionist Congress, which had been scheduled to convene in the summer of 1903.   [10] Cf. n. 2 to No. 176.   [11] In orig.: 'Localizatzie'.

[12] An allusion to the mass migration of Jews from Eastern Europe, mainly to the United States, which began in 1881 and continued up to the First World War. At that time the demand was heard in Zionist circles that measures be taken to channel Jewish migration so as to prevent the further dispersal of the Jewish people. (See, e.g., Trietsch's article 'The Jewish Emigration Question' published in *Die Welt* of 2 Jan. 1903, and the article 'The Land Question' in *Der Fraind* of 4/17 Sept. 1903)

so have no time for this problem. ....
....
.............................[13] It would be futile just now to enumerate, as I could, the many other concrete problems of this kind.

I feel it is necessary, in the light of all these matters, to gather people 'dedicated to Zionism' together into one serious group with a serious periodical. We do not have a single publication in which to express independent viewpoints.

I have brought all these questions to your notice in the knowledge that you will always adopt a balanced attitude towards our party activities, and I would very much like to have your opinion on them.

[The cause] is important and the field of possible activities extensive, [----] to apply one's efforts.

I trust I shall be receiving a detailed answer from you.[14]

With kind regards,

Yours,

Ch. Weizmann.

150. To Moses Glikin, Charlottenburg. *Geneva, 2 January 1903*

Russian: Pcd. H.W.: C.Z.A. A179/3.

Geneva, 2. i. 03.

Rue Lombard, 4.

Dear Glikin,

I am surprised not to have heard from you.[1] Did you receive the money? Where is the notepaper? Where are the new brochures? This failure to keep to an arrangement makes me feel as if I am up against a blank wall. Who is going to supervise the *Enquête* in Berlin?

Yours,

Ch. W.

[13] In the original copy two and a half lines are undecipherable.
[14] No reply to this letter has been found.

150. [1] W. had not yet received a reply to his letter to Glikin of 26 Dec. 1902 (see No. 121).

151. To Chaim Khissin, Berne. *Geneva, 2 January 1903*

German: Or. Copy. T.W.: W.A.

2. 1. 03.

Mr. Ch. Khissin,
Berne.

Dear Friend,

A package containing 300 questionnaires, Russian translations of the questions (approx. 200) and also some Appeals in German,[1] is on its way to you under separate cover.

Further to my previous letter,[2] I repeat my request that you begin the survey at once. I am drawing your attention once more to the need to organise a census committee composed of the various elements within the student body. Naturally, those invited to participate in the work will do so as private persons and not as representing some tendency or other.

I hope that you will now do everything necessary to enable the survey in Berne to be concluded as speedily as possible.

Kind regards,

Yours,

152. To Davis Trietsch, Berlin. *Geneva, 2 January 1903*

German: Or. Copy. T.W.: W.A.

Geneva, 4 rue Lombard, 2. 1. 03.

Mr. D. Trietsch,
Berlin.

Dear Friend,

You should by now have received the Russian translation of the questionnaire together with an Appeal notice in German,[1] despatched to you the day before yesterday. But there is still no sign of the printed material due from you.[2] The degree to which this obstructs our work must surely be clear to you. We had been prepared to devote our holidays[3] to some major tasks, but the holidays are

151. [1] See n. 5 to No. 124.
  [2] Apparently W. had sent Khissin the circular of 15 Dec. 1902 (see n. 3 to No. 95). On 17 Dec. 1902 Khissin informed W. that he was prepared to conduct the survey in Berne (W.A.).

152. [1] See No. 146. As to the notice, see n. 5 to No. 124.
  [2] See No. 121.   [3] I.e. University vacation at Christmas.

nearly over now and we have hardly been able to accomplish anything—so short are we of material. We are in especial need of brochures, which are being asked for on all sides; as a consequence we had to discontinue much of our work.

Now that everything relating to the survey is in Berlin, we hope that you will work with more speed so that we shall at least have one thing finished.

In addition to the addresses already sent to you,[4] would you please send questionnaires to the following:

1. Mr. A. Bass, 35, rue St. Remy, Liège—100 copies both of the German questionnaires and the Russian translation.
2. Mr. L. Bielsky, 40, Seidenstrasse, Stuttgart—100 copies of the Russian translation.
3. Mr. Ch. Ozhinsky, 2/3 L[eft], Blüthenstrasse, Munich—75 Russian translations in addition to the quantity of questionnaires already specified.
4. Mr. Boris Rabinovitch, 4, Eilfschorsteinstrasse, Aachen—2 German questionnaires.
   Kind regards,

Yours,

153. To Berthold Feiwel, Zurich. *Geneva, 2 January 1903*

German: Or. Copy. T.W.: W.A.

Geneva, 2. 1. 03.

Mr. Berthold Feiwel,
Zurich.

Dear Berthold,

I am very worried at your silence. In your last letter you wrote that you were not well.[1] Is your present silence and this news in any way connected? I very much hope not. I am disturbed all the more because the letter for the professors, of which you advised us, has not yet arrived.[2] Please let me know at once how your health is.

Today at long last the questionnaires arrived from Berlin, together with some old brochures. Apparently the second edition has not yet been printed. I believe the people there are making fools of

---

[4] Sent to Trietsch on 28 Dec. 1902 (see n. 2 to No. 131).

153. [1] See Feiwel to W. 29 Dec. 1902, W.A.
[2] See n. 9 to No. 13. In a letter of 29 Dec. 1902 (W.A.) Feiwel promised that the letters to the professors would be sent out the next day.

us, it is inconceivable that things should take so long. Not a sound out of Glikin. In brief, everything is at a standstill again. The holidays are over without our having had an opportunity to utilise them.

Today a package will be on its way to you containing 100 questionnaires, their Russian translations, and Appeals in German.[3] So you can deal with distribution in Zurich.

There is no other news. Buber is silent. Anticipating your reply by return, and with best wishes,

Your

154. To Moses Glikin, Charlottenburg. *Geneva, 3 January 1903*

German: T.W.: C.Z.A. A126/24/7/2/2.

Geneva, 3. 1. 1903.

Mr. M. Glikin,   Express Post
Berlin.[1]

Dear Friend,

In answer to your very full letter of 31 Dec.,[2] we would inform you of the following:

1) The questionnaires have been duly received. As you are by now aware, we on our side have been working much faster than is the custom in Berlin, so that we have long had the Russian translation of the questionnaires finished, printed, and sent off to Berlin. Our mailing list, sent to Mr. Trietsch,[3] also specified the exact number of copies for each city. We have of course arranged for the actual despatch from Berlin in order to save on postage.

2) We have supplemented the mailing list with the addition of the following names: a) Mr. J. Rosenbaum, 12, Tschirnerstrasse,

---

[3] See n. 5 to No. 124.

154. [1] See n. 1 to No. 84.

[2] Glikin to W. 31 Dec. 1902, W.A. Glikin wrote, *inter alia*, that he had sent part of the material that W. had ordered in Berlin (see No. 121) and that he would send the rest after he received the emblem that Lilien promised to design. Glikin added that he was postponing his coming to Switzerland because he needed to finish arranging the affairs of *Kadimah*, the Student Zionist Society, of which he was chairman. He also wished to supervise the survey in Berlin as difficulties were expected there and because of a lack of co-operation on the part of the students, who tended to oppose every activity initiated by the Zionists. According to him, there were then no people in Berlin prepared to devote themselves to Zionist matters. He asked for directives on how to form the survey committee and proposed that Buber, when he got to Berlin, should address a gathering of Russian and Rumanian students about the University project and on the importance of the survey. Glikin asked why he had to come to Zurich rather than Geneva (see n. 3 to No. 41).

[3] See n. 2 to No. 131; No. 152.

Mittweida, Saxony. We have just learned that this gentleman's new address is 16, Bahnhofstrasse—100 German questionnaires with 50 Russian translations. b) Jeremias Schick, 8, Georg-Friedrichstrasse, Karlsruhe—140 German questionnaires and 40 Russian translations.

Will you please attend to this at once, and also ensure that the addresses previously notified are dealt with immediately. I have already despatched a circular[4] from this address in which I informed our correspondents that the questionnaires have gone out. Therefore you must not delay for a single moment. We on our part are endeavouring to complete the business speedily and punctually, and it will not be our fault if it drags on. You may guess whose it will be.

3) Although your last telegram[5] stated that all printed material would be sent on Monday, it is now Saturday, and except for the questionnaires and some old unwanted brochures nothing has arrived. I have already pleaded most earnestly with you to stop worrying about the emblem.[6] Lilien will keep us on a string for months and still do nothing. But we do need notepaper and brochures. Really, I cannot repeat the same thing ten times over in letters and telegrams.

4) For the present, it will be more practical for you to go to Zurich. Feiwel has a great deal of writing to do and he is without assistance. Your having no passport is a nuisance.[7] Can't you bring a document with you from the Berlin police to the effect that you have had one? Otherwise you are going to find yourself with problems.

5) From our end it is difficult to do anything for the survey in Berlin. But nevertheless we think a meeting of the colony would be a mistake. It will only result in long speeches and fruitless discussion. Please try, unofficially, to attract people of various shades of opinion in the colony. Don't act as a Party man; and interest the others in their private capacities rather than as official Party representatives. Get a large committee together, compile a list of students and then divide it up among the members of the committee. This done, you need not, in my opinion, remain in Berlin any longer. The others will then be able to carry on just as well. I believe we shall have fewer

---

[4] Circular dated 1 Jan. 1903, W.A. Signed by W., this began with a note to the supervisors (*vertrauensmänner*) that the questionnaires were being sent to them together with the Russian translation. The recipients were again requested to appoint survey committees (cf. n. 3 to No. 95) and to endeavour to make the survey as extensive as possible.

[5] Glikin to W. 28 Dec. 1902, W.A.   [6] See No. 121.

[7] In the letter of 31 Dec. 1902 Glikin wrote that his passport was with his father in Russia.

problems with the survey in other German towns. In Berlin one must naturally proceed with care and tact.

I would like an immediate answer as to whether all the packages have been despatched, what has been done in Berlin for the survey in the meantime, and whether Trietsch has ordered the lists from Hanover and Dresden.[8] Show him this letter. Also, let me know when you will be coming.

Where are all the other Berlin Zionists hiding? Are you absolutely alone? I am most curious to know Motzkin's whereabouts. He was to have undertaken a propaganda tour.[9] Did it take place? How is *Kadimah*?

Kind regards,

Yours,
Ch. Weizmann.

155. To Theodor Herzl, Vienna.[1] *Geneva, 3 January 1903*[2]

German: Pcd. H.W.: C.Z.A. Z1/340.

Heartfelt greetings[3] to our מאור הגולה[4]

Dr. Ch. Weizmann
Dr. D. Pasmanik
M. Kisseleva[5]
Weinstein[6]
V. Khatzman
E. Dorfman
?Hetira[7]
Grinblatt[8]
M. Berman[9]

---

[8] See No. 145.   [9] See n. 10 to No. 110.

155. [1] The greeting is written on an illustrated postcard (*Meor Hagolah*, designed by Lilien). On the margin of the card the Hebrew word *Hashahar*, the name of the Student Zionist Society in Geneva, is printed. The signatures appear partly below and partly on the margins. The occasion that prompted the special greeting is not known.
[2] Date of the Geneva postmark.
[3] In orig.: 'Herzengruss'.
[4] Heb.: 'Light of the Exile'. A title classically given to Rabbi Gershom ben Judah (960–1040).
[5] Miriam Kisseleva, later Smilansky (1885–1969). She was then a student and active Zionist in Geneva. Subsequently she became a doctor prominent in public affairs in Palestine.   [6] Sonia Weinstein.
[7] Deciphering of signature uncertain.   [8] Rosa Grinblatt.
[9] Moses Jacob Berman, a Berlin student and later an agronomist in Palestine.

N. Berestovisky
Bernard Mochenson[10]
Rafalkes[11]
BR[12]
Syrkin
Agnes Brailovsky
M. Tarle

156. To M. Tarle, Geneva. *Geneva, 3 January 1903*

German: Or. Copy. T.W.: W.A.

3. 1. 03.

Dear Miss Tarle,

Kindly let us know whether you have already formed the census committee for Geneva, and if so, the names of [its] members.

Yours sincerely,

157. To Abraham Kasteliansky, Heidelberg. *Geneva, 3 January 1º*

Russian: Or. Copy. H.W.: W.A.

3. ɪ. 03.

Mr. A. Kasteliansky,[1]
Heidelberg.

Dear Comrade,

Our *Fragebogen* are now printed and the survey has begun in a number of cities. Would you be so good as to undertake supervision of the operation in Heidelberg? If you are unable to do this yourself, can you get a friend to assume responsibility for the work? Better still, organise a committee made up of people of various points of view who would distribute the questionnaires among their friends and collect them afterwards.

---

[10] Bernard Dov Mochenson (1882–1956), then a student in Geneva and secretary of the local Zionist Society. Later he was among the founders of the Herzlia High School in Palestine and taught there.

[11] Miriam Rafalkes, later Cohen (1879–1967). She was then a student and member of the Democratic Fraction in Geneva. From 1904 she was a teacher in Palestine.

[12] Perhaps should read: B.K.

157. [1] See Kasteliansky to W. 21 Dec. 1902, W.A., in which K. refers to his temporary stay in Heidelberg.

Would you know anyone in Freiburg-in-Breisgau? How is the statistical bureau getting along?[2]

Awaiting your reply,

Yours,

Ch. Weizmann.

158. To Saul Lurie, Darmstadt. *Geneva, 4 January 1903*

German: Or. Copy. T.W.: W.A.

4. 1. 03.

Dear Saul,

Thank you very much for sending us the press-cutting, as well as for the other news.[1] You will in the meantime have received the questionnaires, for we have ensured that everything necessary in this regard has been done.

A more detailed reply will follow in a few days.[2]

Ever yours,

159. To Friedman,[1] Breslau. *Geneva, 4 January 1903*

German: Or. Copy. T.W.: W.A.

4. 1. 03.

Dear Sir,

Many thanks for your kind communication of the 2nd.[2] We have, in the meantime, arranged for the questionnaires to be sent to Mr. Tatarsky.[3] Please take delivery of them there.

---

[2] Refers to the Jewish Statistical Association (originally the Jewish Statistical Bureau) of which Kasteliansky was the secretary.

158. [1] Lurie wrote to W. on 3 Jan. 1903 (W.A.) attaching to his letter a review by S. Rundstein of *Eine Jüdische Hochschule* published in the weekly *Allgemeine Zeitung des Judentums* of 2 Jan. 1903. Lurie also reported details concerning preparations for conducting the student survey in Darmstadt.
[2] W. wrote again to Lurie on 5 Jan. 1903 and on 9 Jan. 1903 (see Nos. 166, 193), but in these letters there is no specific reply to Lurie's letter of 3 Jan. 1903.

159. [1] Friedman was a medical student in Breslau, of Russian origin, whose first name is not known. On the original copy W. wrote: 'Friedman, Breslau'.
[2] Has not been found.
[3] See n. 6 to No. 139.

We have approached you on the recommendation of our friend Schachtel,[4] and we trust the matter rests in good hands.

> Yours respectfully,

160. To Isaac Rothstein, Rostov. *Geneva, 4 January 1903*

German: Or. Copy. T.W.: W.A.[1]

4. 1. [03].[2]

Engineer I. M. Rothstein,
Rostov.

Dear Friend,

Many thanks for your letter,[3] which arrived today. We sent you our questionnaire a few days ago and you will have received this in the meantime. You must not interpret our silence as indicating a lull in our work. We are honestly trying to do everything possible to further this difficult venture. Our energies were until now completely absorbed in the preparation of the statistical inquiry. As you can imagine, persuading practically all the University students in Central Europe to co-operate is hardly the easiest of tasks. Now that we have taken care of a major portion of that operation we can start on the formation of the committees. Buber has meanwhile been taking a number of steps to this end,[4] so we shall soon be in a position to announce the list of committee members. I would put it to you that it is in no way our fault if some things do not proceed

---

[4] Friedman's name is included in the Breslau student list which Schachtel sent to W. on 15 Dec. 1902 (see n. 2 to No. 117). On 3 Jan. 1903 Schachtel wrote to W. (W.A.) that he had heard from Tatarsky that Friedman had already replied to W.'s letter.

160. [1] 'Recommandé' stamped on orig.

[2] From the content of the letter this may be assumed to be the correct date, though the original stated 1902.

[3] Rothstein to W. undated (*ca.* 31 Dec. 1902), W.A. Rothstein wrote that in Rostov activity for the University might be possible but only after he received from W. copies of the *Jüdische Hochschule* pamphlet and the Bureau reports. Rothstein questioned the accuracy of a report appearing in the Russian periodical *Russkiye Vedomosti*, according to which Jewish philanthropists in England intended to establish a Jewish University in that country, and he asked if there was any connection between this and W.'s plan to visit England. In his opinion it would be preferable to have the University in Switzerland, for language reasons, because it was closer to Russia, and in view of the low cost of living there. Rothstein complained that the list of Rostov people who contributed money to the University had not been published in *Die Welt* (see n. 1 to No. 44) and he enclosed a new list to be published in the reports of the Bureau.

[4] See n. 1 to No. 92.

as fast as we would wish. We do not let a day pass without sending our letters to all parts of the world; and even in those places where we suspect that not more than one person capable of doing some work exists, we try and involve him. But we are against rushing our moves; we want everything to be carried out with due calm and caution.

Our tasks are divided up as follows:

1) A statistical survey, already under way and conducted by census committees constituted in every University city.

2) On the basis of this statistical data, together with other precise information, we shall proceed with the planning of the University project itself. In this regard we are in touch with a number of scholars[5] and will study the problem together with them.

These two aspects represent that part of our work of which the completion is totally within our responsibility, and you may rest assured that it will be carried through with energy and thoroughness.

3) Formation of the committees. As I have already noted, this too is under way, although it is a matter in which we depend upon the goodwill of others.

4) It has always been my view that we need to form small groups in every city where we have people interested in the project. Their function will be to spread the word within closed circles, and to support our Bureau both materially and morally. As you know, our Bureau has some finance to tide us over for the time being, but we must not lose sight of the fact that our expenses will grow as the project develops. Your idea, which you outlined to me in Rostov,[6] to constitute small 'Jewish University' societies everywhere, would of course be the practical answer to this problem.[7] I hope we can succeed in carrying it out. But in that case we should . . . .[8]

161. To Isaac Rothstein, Rostov. *Geneva, 4 January 1903*

Russian: Or. Copy. H.W.: W.A.

Geneva, 4. i. 03.

Dear Friend,

In my official letter[1] to you I described everything connected with

---

[5] Concerning W.'s efforts to interest academics in Berlin see Vol. I, No. 293, also n. 1 to No. 14 above. Regarding Buber's efforts in this direction see n. 1 to No. 92.

[6] W. met Rothstein in Rostov during his visit there in Sept.–Oct. 1902.

[7] See also Nos. 50, 51.   [8] The end of the letter is missing.

161. [1] See No. 160.

the University in considerable detail. There is not much more to be added. You ask about Fraction activities. There is not much doing now, but I keep thinking that you will find yourself *mitten im Schaffen*[2] there.

I give little time to Fraction activities because I devote myself to one subject only, and absolutely refuse to do more than one thing at a time. In my opinion the Zionist movement is going through a difficult and critical period in general. We tend to gloss over everything, and patch up a fabric so tattered that nothing can hold it together any more. Ever since my return from Vienna[3] I feel restless. I see no prospect for any further Zionist work if we go on as before. For six years we have waited for the charter[4] with folded arms. This period of utter faith in romantic phraseology [must] come to an end [---- ---- ---- ----].

It is sinful [---- ---- to go on with it]. I am up to my eyes in work and worry, and remember, my friend, that I am all alone here. I have a secretary[5] but he is only [---- ----].

And so, after carefully thinking the current situation over, I feel that it is most unlikely that the Zionist Party will be able to go on like this. Our political workers rose to the fore [----] no accession of new forces. One can complain as much as one likes about our [assi]-milated intelligentsia, but there is no more to it than that.

All the creative, effective forces in Zionism have dispersed in different [----] because the centre of gravity is constantly changing, and everything is *im Flusse*.[6] As a result it is without a base, and whatever happens seems to come by chance.

Those of us who are young appear to be unable to close our [ranks]; the older generation should [have been] sent packing ages ago. Why? We suffer both from a paucity of numbers and a lack of unity. In principle, a Fraction is a good thing. But as an organisation, as a source of power, we are like the figure nought standing alone. We all tuck ourselves away in our private lairs, busy with 'our own affairs', so that there is no-one and nothing! . . . . But enough of this Jeremiad! I could say a great deal more about the 'friends' of our movement. They are worse, much worse, than our enemies.

But what is to be done? In [----] Russia we have to assume that it is only possible to work at random, in the way now being done. Any proper economic activity[7] can only lead to Bundism,[8] to

---

[2] 'in the hub of activity'.

[3] I.e. the meeting of the Zionist Annual Conference in Oct. 1902. See Vol. I, No. 320.   [4] See also n. 4 to No. 149.

[5] Samuel Levinson.   [6] 'in a state of flux.'

[7] Probably meaning trade union activity among Jewish workers. At the Zionist

[*Footnotes 7 and 8 continued on p. 157*]

a degenerate, vicious assimilation. *Conditio sine qua non* for Zionism in Russia is total neutrality towards Russian politics. Nothing [----] and whatever there is [---- ----] of economics in Zionism—is merely phrase-mongering. [Artels][9] again, and so on and so forth, but they are half-measures, nothing more than *Seifenblasen*.[10] The Jewish position will not change through this. It will not advance our movement one step, for, let me repeat, everything is being erected on a volcano. Even cultural activities are conducted ineffectually and are left to chance. We have not created a single cultural institution in Russia, nor shall we create one—only *Flickarbeit*.[11]

Serious work on a sound basis can be carried out, but only in those places abroad where there are real Jewish masses: America, Galicia, England.

Nationalisation[12] *of the emigration stream.* Our work must become international, or rather, intra-national. In America, where there are over a million Jews, there is no Zionism. What *Die Welt* writes about American Zionism isn't worth the paper it is printed on.[13] Such thieves and swindlers have gathered round the movement that it is shameful, shameful, shameful. *The same holds true for England.* I know it only too well. All sorts of de Haases, Gottheils,[14] and other bright and lesser stars—they have monopolised our movement in England and America and are a gang of scoundrels. We must put an end to this clique, and Russian [----] Zionist youth to work there. Only then will it become possible to display our strength and create a moral and practical Zionist force.

The University will, I am sure, play an important role in these activities. I do not ascribe to this view out of romanticism, and I do not devote all my time to it because I am a peddlar of culture. [My God], how debased this word has become! *The University* is the

Youth Conference (Dec. 1901) the Zionist attitude to the Labour movement was discussed. W. argued there, in a debate with Motzkin, that a decision in principle had to be taken on whether the Zionist movement should participate in local political life, or whether it should maintain neutrality. In the event of the latter course being adopted, W. argued, Zionism would not be able to participate in the Labour movement, this being political. (See Report of the Youth Conference, W.A.)

[8] Concerning the Bund see Vol. I, n. 3 to No. 55.

[9] Concerning the artels of the artisans and the Zionist participation in their establishment see Vol. I, n. 13 to No. 135.

[10] 'soap-bubbles'.   [11] 'patch-work'.

[12] See n. 12 to No. 149.

[13] Frequent reports appeared in *Die Welt* about Zionist activities in the United States.

[14] Jacob de Haas, one of the founders of the English Zionist Federation. In 1902 he went to the United States where he became Secretary of the Federation of American Zionists (subsequently Zionist Organization of America). Richard Gottheil was the President of the F.A.Z. De Haas and Gottheil were known as faithful followers of Herzl and his policy.

key to the work. It must provide us with a generation that will rise on our ashes, a Jewish generation that will create a synthesis between Europe and the Jewish people. This is why I should like to have the University in England, for that country is the most important focal point for us.[15]

The University will head the Exilarchate. But what of Russian Jewry? To this there can be only one answer; and unpleasant though it is, it had better be made clear—better than any kind of utopian fantasy. In Russia there will always exist a tendency towards Zionism and casual Zionist activities. An organisation, suspended in the air[16] withal, there always will be [----], and badly prepared. But our real forces and our real organisational structures will always be located abroad.

I have already written to you about the University.[17] Now a word about the periodical. This is absolutely necessary, and we must implement the proposal I made in my last letter.[18]

The Rostov money appears in the report.[19] For some reason *Die Welt* does not publish my Bureau communiqués. I sent them to Herzl.[20] There will be a meeting of the University committee[21] in Vienna on the 17th of this month and we shall then turn over a new leaf. The *Russkiye Vedomosti*[22] story is a success.

There is nothing new with me personally. Am up to my neck in work and don't feel too well either. Why? Only the devil knows.

Do write in detail, dear friend, and [don't] be angry with me. Many thanks to you, and particularly to Maria Grigorievna for having remembered me. I was delighted by the [postcards].

With affection,

Your Chaim.

Warmest regards to the children.

[15] On this subject W. disagreed with Rothstein (see n. 3 to No. 160).
[16] In Russia a national Zionist Organization was not permitted (see Vol. I, p. xxxiv).
[17] See No. 160.
[18] Probably meaning the other letter to Rothstein of this same date (No. 160), of which the last part has not been found; perhaps the plan to issue a periodical was mentioned in the missing part of the letter.
[19] See n. 3 to No. 160. The funds contributed in Rostov for the University are mentioned in the report of the University Bureau of the end of Jan. 1903 (W.A. No. 30/0, 25), the earliest Bureau report found.
[20] No Press announcement by the University Bureau containing the contributions made in Rostov has been found. In his letter to Herzl of 20 Jan. 1903 (No. 224) W. complained that the notice concerning the student survey, whose publication he requested in *Die Welt*, did not appear (see No. 108), but he mentioned no other notice.
[21] Buber apparently notified W. about this in a telegram which has not been found, but which is mentioned in No. 170. See also n. 2 to No. 189.
[22] *Russian Newspaper*, paper of liberal tendencies which had a large circulation in Russia before the Revolution. Concerning the communiqué see n. 3 to No. 160.

162. To R. Galante, Brussels. *Geneva, 5 January 1903*

Russian: Or. Copy. H.W.: W.A.

5. I. 03.

Dear Miss Galante,

On the advice of friends in Liège,[1] we sent you a brochure today, together with our circulars and questionnaire. This will give you some idea of the nature of the survey. I would be grateful if you would let me know at once whether you are willing to undertake the task of conducting the survey and of organising a census committee.

If, for some reason, you are unable to take this work upon yourself, we would be most obliged to you if you would let us have names and addresses of a few people whom we might approach instead.

Most respectfully,

Dr. Ch. Weizmann.

163. To Charles (Yeheskel) Wortsman, Basle. *Geneva, 5 January 1903*

Yiddish: Or. Copy. H.W.: W.A.

5. I. 03.

Dear Friend,

Our comrade Buber would like to come to Switzerland to conduct a short propaganda campaign.[1] Obviously, he needs money for expenses. What do you think, Reb[2] Yeheskel, will the people in Basle join us in this matter? Let me know at once. Doubtless you have received the questionnaires. Do write if you have need of additional copies. How are things in general? What has happened to *Cheirus*?[3] I've heard that you did not join the Society!

Yours ever,
Chaim

Mr. Ch. Wortsman,
Basle.

162. [1] See Margolin to W. 3 Jan. 1903, W.A.

163. [1] Cf. n. 1 to No. 92.
[2] A deferential form of address—see Vol. I, n. 1 to No. 1.
[3] See n. 1 to No. 137.

164. To Chaim Khissin, Berne. *Geneva, 5 January 1903*

Russian: Or. Copy. H.W.: W.A.

5. I. 03.

Dear Khissin,

Buber is contemplating a propaganda [tour] through Switzerland. Would our circles in Berne be willing to contribute part of the expenses, and how many meetings would have to be held in Berne ?[1]

You have already received the circulars. I should be very glad if you would scribble a few lines about the progress of our work.

Best wishes,

Yours,
Ch. Weizmann.

165. To Moses Lubzhinsky, New York. *Geneva, 5 January 1903*

German: Or. Copy. T.W.: W.A.

5. 1. 03.

Mr. M. Lubzhinsky,[1]
New York.

Dear Friend,

I am sending you our brochure under separate cover and would ask you to study it with care.

You will be able to visualise the entire plan from this publication. I would draw your attention to the fact that we have already put in a great deal of work here, and are doing everything possible to bring this enterprise into effect. We intend to launch a major propaganda campaign shortly and are consequently bearing America in mind as well. It is most likely that I will go over there this summer. But before we decide on such a difficult step we would like to establish at least a few connections through correspondence, and hope you will be of use to us in this regard.

The question is, what are the possibilities of interesting significant Jewish people from the world of learning and of finance in the project ?

164. [1] Khissin wrote on 8 Jan. 1903 (W.A.) that he requested David Jochelman, chairman of the Academic Zionist Society in Berne, to reply to W., but no letter from Jochelman concerning the matter has been found.

165. [1] Moses Lubzhinsky was the brother of Chaim L., W.'s brother-in-law. The letter is in the intimate form.

You would earn our gratitude if you would send us the addresses of such people.[2] We should also be delighted if you would personally interest yourself in the project and do something for it.

Sincerest good wishes,

Your

166. To Saul Lurie, Darmstadt. *Geneva, 5 January 1903*

German: Or. Copy. T.W.: W.A.

Geneva, 5. I. 03.

Mr. S. Lurie,
Darmstadt.

Dear Saul,

We are in urgent need of addresses in Marburg, Strasbourg, Goettingen, Bonn, Jena and Freiburg (in Breisgau). We shall ourselves write to the Universities concerned, but German postage stamps must be sent to them (50 pfg. for each University). Do please arrange this on our behalf from Darmstadt. The postage will be gratefully refunded.[1]

You will meanwhile have received the questionnaires. We shall be very happy to have word at your earliest regarding the survey in your area.

Other than this, no news.

With kind regards,

Your

167. To Julius Meyer, Basle. *Geneva, 5 January 1903*

German: Or. Copy. H.W.: W.A.

5. I. 03.

Dear Friend,

Martin Buber would not be averse to doing a tour of Switzerland.[1] He could then give two lectures in Basle. Would the Basle Zionist Association defray part of the travel expenses, and if so, how much?

---

[2] Lubzhinsky's reply has not been found.

166. [1] In his reply of 7 Jan. 1903 Lurie wrote that he would fulfil W.'s request.

167. [1] Cf. n. 1 to No. 92.

Please drop me a line about this. How are things going other-wise? When will you be [in] Geneva? Please let me know about it in good time.

Ever yours,
Ch. Weizmann

Mr. J. Meyer,
    Basle.

168. To Berthold Monash, Mulhouse. *Geneva, 5 January 1903*

German: Or. Copy. T.W.: W.A.

5. 1. 03.

Dear friend Monash,

Would you please send me the addresses of a few Russian-Jewish students in the School of Chemistry at Mulhouse.[1]

With regards,

Your

169. To Berthold Feiwel, Zurich. *Geneva, 5 January 1903*

German: Or. Copy. H.W.: W.A.

5. 1. 03.

Dear Toldy,

A letter arrived today from Schachtel with a list of the 'mighty ones' of Breslau.[1] I don't think there is any purpose in writing to these people just now. It would be more effective if we communi-cate with them only when letters can be signed by some good-sounding names. Frankly, we are not famous *as yet*.

I am yearning for a really detailed letter from you.

Warmest regards to Esther and yourself.

Your
Chaim

All good wishes to Miss Sokolow.[2]

---

168. [1] Monash replied on 17 Jan. 1903 (W.A.) that there were no Russian-Jewish students at the School of Chemistry in Mulhouse.

169. [1] Schachtel to W. 3 Jan. 1903, W.A. Attached to the letter was a list of Jewish notables in Breslau. Schachtel wrote: 'I am sending you the requested addresses herewith. I hope that you will use them to greater advantage than my pessimism predicts.' (Cf. n. 2 to No. 139).

[2] Maria Sokolow.

thanks. I am glad to have your rough costing for a periodical. I have already written as the occasion arose to all our friends on this subject,[2] and will now forward these particulars also.

Thank you for sending on all the printed matter, which I expect will arrive here tomorrow. You are evidently an incorrigible optimist in that you still believe in the possibility of an emblem.[3]

I shall speak to Dr. Pasmanik about your propaganda tour. Incidentally, he only recently told me that he would arrange for you to come without fail. I am sending you the Schauer article as requested.[4]

All steps have been taken to ensure the immediate receipt of 500 roubles,[5] and I am expecting a reply any day now. My dear Trietsch, don't worry, it will soon be here.

University Committee:

Information telegraphed (naturally!) by Buber[6] leads me to assume that he is earnestly engaged in forming a committee in Vienna. Berlin must follow immediately. It is absolutely vital that the committees be formed soon. In a little while we shall no longer be able to do anything on our own, and we have to consider coming a little more before the public. Of course, the survey will make a name for us and give us a certain authority, but only in circles of secondary importance to us. I have already mentioned to you that the formation of the committees must be achieved by the end of February at the latest. I shall, furthermore, be undertaking my tour[7] then. Please send Buber 150 copies of the questionnaire with an equal number of Russian translations.

Kindest regards,

Your

was designing the emblem for the Bureau. He supplied details about the situation of the *Jüdischer Verlag*, sent an estimate of costs for a periodical which W. and Feiwel proposed launching (see No. 122), and asked whether it would be advisable to write to Pasmanik again concerning his propaganda tour to Switzerland in view of the latter's failure to reply (see n. 1 to No. 41). Trietsch assured W. that he could be relied upon to set up a committee for the University in Berlin.

[2] See Nos. 123, 125, 127, 149, 161.

[3] See n. 1 above. Trietsch had already written on 12 Nov. 1902 (W.A.) that Lilien was preparing the emblem.

[4] See n. 1 to No. 10.

[5] W. had promised that he would endeavour to obtain 500 roubles for the *Jüdischer Verlag*—see n. 10 to No. 122.

[6] See n. 21 to No. 161.

[7] W.'s contemplated trip to Russia.

176. To David Farbstein, Zurich. *Geneva, 7 January 1903*

German: Or. Copy. T.W.: W.A.

Geneva, 4 rue Lombard, 7. 1. 03.

Dr. D. Farbstein,
Zurich.

Dear Dr. [Farbstein],

Enclosed is the power of attorney as requested.[1] I hope you will initiate proceedings and carry them through at your earliest. It is not Schauer alone, but rather the whole mass of assimilated Philistines of whom he is the prototype, that we are seeking to challenge.

My conversation with Dr. Pasmanik centred on the question of creating a group according to the spirit in which we were then talking.[2] I, too, am of the opinion that this affords us a modus vivendi for working amicably together. Your position on the cultural question[3] and the University,[4] as described by Pasmanik, most

---

176. [1] After the Zionist Smaller Actions Committee refused publication in *Die Welt* of the protest by the Democratic Fraction against the Schauer article, it was decided to take other steps against the author (see n. 1 to No. 10; n. 1 to No. 25; n. 6 to No. 83; n. 2 to No. 93). Feiwel proposed bringing the matter before the Zionist Congress Court, but W. was against this, and proposed arbitration instead (see n. 1 to No. 101). It may be assumed that it was decided to request Farbstein to represent the Fraction when W. and Feiwel met in Zurich during the second half of Dec. (see No. 119), and in his letter of 3 Jan. 1903 (W.A.) Farbstein accepted, while expressing doubt as to the advisability of litigation against such a person as Schauer. With his letter Farbstein enclosed a form giving him power of attorney (see No. 177). In the ~ent arbitration did not take place.

[2] It appears from Farbstein's letter of 3 Jan. 1903 that Pasmanik wrote to him abou, this discussion and Farbstein asked that W. also write to him about it. The discussion apparently concerned the organization of a Zionist group which would give priority to a solution of the settlement problem in Palestine. Pasmanik notified Herzl of the formation of this group on 20 Jan. 1903 (C.Z.A. Z1/340). He explained that if there was no hope of obtaining a 'charter' from the Sultan and international guarantees for its fulfilment (cf. Vol. I, n. 3 to No. 320), a minimum programme should be drawn up. According to this programme the Zionists would seek concessions from the Turkish government that would ensure the success of the settlement effort even in the absence of substantial autonomy with international guarantees. Should these requirements be fulfilled, 'we shall all undertake cultural work to organize the masses'. Pasmanik informed Herzl that he and some of his friends desired to propagate this idea, and that it had found support among the *Mizrahi*, the Centre, and the Democratic Fraction. The group would sustain this activity until its proposals were adopted. (See also n. 3 below as well as n. 7 to No. 90; n. 27 to No. 413.)

[3] Regarding Farbstein's views on the cultural question, see his letter to the editor of *Hamelitz* of the 3rd day of Passover 5663 (14 April 1903) published in the issue of 11/24 April 1903. Farbstein wrote there that 'all arguments and disputes about culture . . . are mere theorising. While our people lack bread they are in no need of culture either . . .' In Farbstein's opinion, culture was a problem for the future when the Jews would have a land of their own: 'And I see this to be my principal task,

[*Footnotes 3 and 4 continued on p. 169*]

certainly meets with my entire approval.[5] I think it can all be synthesised into our programme. Pasmanik further intimated that the programme is now in preparation. I would be grateful, dear Dr. Farbstein, if you would send it to me in outline.

Kindest regards,

Your

177. To David Farbstein, Zurich. *Geneva, 7 January 1903*

German: Or. Copy. T.W.: W.A.

Geneva, 4 rue Lombard, 7. 1. 03.

Dr. D. Farbstein,[1]
Zurich.

Esteemed Fellow-Zionist,

The Zionist Democratic Fraction desires to summon Dr. Schauer before a Court of Arbitration for his articles in *Israelit*. The intention is that we on our side and Dr. Schauer on his choose one arbitrator each. The Chairman of the Court shall be nominated by the two arbitrators. Should they fail to agree on a Chairman, then let him be nominated by the Congress Court.[2]

The Zionist Democratic Fraction hereby appoints you its arbitrator with the request that you take the matter in hand.

With Zion's greetings,

In the name of the Zionist Democratic Fraction,

that the land problem should be solved first.' He proposed 'that all Zionists who consider the land problem as the principal question should unite, because the land problem and the problem of bread outweigh all the others'. See also Farbstein's article in *Die Welt* of 20 Dec. 1901 in which he maintained that cultural activities in the diaspora were without point.

[4] Farbstein was among the initiators of the decision taken at the Zionist Annual Conference of 1902 which made the support of the Zionist Organization for the University project conditional upon its being established in Palestine (see Vol. I, n. 4 to No. 320). According to a report in *Die Welt* of 23 Jan. 1903, Farbstein said at the Swiss Zionist Conference in Dec. 1902 that 'while bread cannot be assured to the Jewish masses, the Zionist Organization should not engage in establishing a rich man's cultural institution that will be without purpose for the Jewish people, at least for the present'.

[5] Nothing else is known about the explanation that Pasmanik offered to W. regarding Farbstein's attitude to these questions, but it would seem that he sought to moderate it.

177. [1] This power of attorney was formulated by Farbstein (see n. 1 to No. 176). W. added the salutation and 'with Zion's greetings'.

[2] The Zionist Congress Court.

178. To Berthold Feiwel, Zurich. *Geneva, 7 January 1903*

German: Or. Copy. T.W.: W.A.

Geneva, 7. 1. 03.

Mr. Berthold Feiwel,
Zurich.

Dear Toldy,

Enclosed is a letter from Trietsch.[1] You will see that the printed material is on its way and should arrive here tomorrow. Part of it will of course be sent on to you immediately. Tomorrow we shall have the professors' letter ready, and this will be forwarded to you for your signature as requested.[2] Please return the Trietsch letter at once.

Levinson is unusually happy (?)[3] about a so-called resolution by which the CK[4] has been got out of the way. Do you know anything about it ?

We shall leave Fraction activities until Glikin's arrival.[5] He can then take care of the entire correspondence.

Warmest greetings from

Your

P.S. I wrote to Farbstein about Schauer yesterday.[6] Man, send me a book to read!

179. To Michael Kroll, Moscow. *Geneva, 7 January 1903*

German: Or. Copy. T.W.: W.A.

7. 1. 03.

Dr. M. B. Kroll,
Moscow.

Dear Friend,

We are sending you by separate registered post the bibliographical

178. [1] The letter of 4 Jan. 1903—see n. 1 to No. 175.

[2] Refers perhaps to the final formulation of the letter to the Jewish professors, a draft of which was prepared by Feiwel—see n. 9 to No. 13 and No. 137.

[3] Question mark in original.

[4] Thus in orig. No reply has been found in the Feiwel letters to the question posed here and the matter remains unexplained.

[5] Glikin was due in Zurich to assist Feiwel in Jewish University matters and in the affairs of the Democratic Fraction.

[6] Doubtless refers to No. 176, which, however, has the same date as this letter.

material we have compiled on University education.[1] We would be very grateful if you would kindly let us know what material of this type is available in Russian.

At the same time I confirm with thanks receipt of your circular,[2] to which I shall make a detailed reply in two days' time.[3] The survey here is in full swing. It is possible that we may complete the statistical study by the time I leave for Russia.[4]

Will you, dear friend, let us know soon how the matters you have undertaken for the Bureau[5] are proceeding.

Kindest regards to you and all Moscow friends.

Ever yours,

180. To Bernard Chapira, Paris. *Geneva, 7 January 1903*

German: Or. Copy. T.W.: W.A.

7. 1. 03.

Mr. Bernard Chapira,
Paris.

Dear Friend,

Thank you very much for the information you were so good as to send us on the 3rd of this month.[1]

We agree with all your proposals. However, please do not send any questionnaires to Montpellier or Nancy, as we have already communicated with the local people concerned and the printed material has already gone off to them.[2]

Under separate cover we are sending you an additional 300 questionnaires (you should have already received from Berlin the 400 for Paris). Enclosed with them are the questions in Russian translation and Appeal announcements in Russian (added to the Russian translation), besides copies of the Appeal in German.[3] We would

---

179. [1] This bibliography exists in the W.A. (No. 29/0, 9).

[2] Circular No. 3 of the Democratic Fraction Centre in Moscow. Kroll had notified W. that he had sent it on (3 Jan. 1903) 21 Dec. 1902 (W.A.), but the letter itself did not reach W. until 8 Jan. (see n. 1 to No. 187).

[3] W. wrote an additional letter to Kroll on the following day (see No. 187), but the circular is not mentioned there.

[4] In March 1903.

[5] See n. 1 to No. 125.

180. [1] Chapira to W. 3 Jan. 1903, W.A. Chapira described how he intended to conduct the survey in France and gave his assurance that he would attempt to interest intellectuals and financiers in the University project.

[2] See Nos. 104, 171.

[3] See n. 5 to No. 124.

also like you to take over the conduct of the survey in the provinces.[4]

Waiting to hear from you as early as possible,

We remain with kind regards,

Most respectfully,

181. To Maria Bass, Heidelberg. *Geneva, 8 January 1903*

German: Or. Copy. T.W.: W.A.

Geneva, 4 rue Lombard, 8. 1. 03.

Miss M. Bass,
Heidelberg.

Dear Madam and Fellow-Zionist,

Our grateful thanks for your much appreciated letter of the 7th.[1] The questionnaires were despatched today to Mr. Kasteliansky's address.

I cannot understand why the other people are resisting a statistical survey of the Jewish student body. Whatever one's attitude to the question of creating a Jewish University, the survey is nevertheless a very desirable exercise in which every Jew should take part irrespective of his views.

But I am quite sure you have yourself employed arguments similar to this, and in all likelihood you will also accomplish whatever is necessary.

With Zion's greetings,

182. To Martin Buber, Vienna. *Geneva, 8 January 1903*

German: Or. Copy. T.W.: W.A.

Geneva, 4 rue Lombard, 8. 1. 03.

Mr. Martin Buber,
Vienna.

Dear Martin,

Yesterday I wrote to let you know that you would be receiving

---

[4] In fact it appears from Chapira letter mentioned in n. 1 above that he intended to send the questionnaire to University cities in the French provinces as well.

181. [1] Bass to W. 7 Jan. 1903, W.A. Bass stated that she would conduct the survey in Heidelberg together with Kasteliansky. She had asked three more people, identified with various political tendencies, to participate in conducting the survey. These did not give a positive reply, wishing first to be acquainted with details of the University project.

150 questionnaires from Berlin.[1] I received a letter today from the 'Leo Pinsker' Russian Student Zionist Society. They want to take over supervision of the survey in Vienna.[2] Will you please pass the questionnaires over to this society at Nos. 20 and 19, Hahngasse, Vienna, IX.

Kind regards,

Your

183. To Charles (Yeheskel) Wortsman, Basle. *Geneva, 8 January 1903*

German: Or. Copy. T.W.: W.A.

8. 1. 03.

Dear Mr. Wortsman,

You are mistaken in your views regarding the survey.[1] From the information we have received a good start has been made in every city. Ensure that you get back the few questionnaires that are nevertheless completed. You have got to talk to the people concerned.

Warmest greetings from

Your

184. To the Executive, 'Leo Pinsker' Society,[1] Vienna. *Geneva, 8 January 1903*

German: Or. Copy. T.W.: W.A.

8. 1. 03.

The Executive, 'Leo Pinsker' Society,
Vienna.

Esteemed Fellow-Zionists,

You will be receiving the questionnaires you requested, together with Russian translations and Appeal announcements in both

182. [1] See No. 170.
  [2] The letter of the 'Leo Pinsker' Society has not been found. It is to be assumed that it was written in reply to W.'s letter to M. Schmidt of 28 Dec. 1902 (No. 133). Schmidt was a Russian Zionist student leader in Vienna.

183. [1] In the letter of 7 Jan. 1903 (W.A.) Wortsman wrote, *inter alia*, that in addition to himself there were only four other Russian Jewish students in Basle and that none had as yet returned the questionnaire. In view of this he doubted the success of the survey in other cities. Furthermore, he thought the questionnaire contained too many items.

184. [1] See n. 2 to No. 182.

languages, from Mr. Buber, 38 Porzellangasse. I am enclosing herewith copies of each printed item, as well as a brochure.

When you examine these documents you will see at once how to fill them in.

In order to make the survey as thorough and comprehensive as possible, we suggest that you create a census committee composed of students of diverse viewpoints.[2] This committee can then be responsible for the distribution of the documents as well as for their collection on completion. If it is to succeed, the operation should not be undertaken as a partisan venture.

We would be very glad to hear at your earliest how everything is progressing.

Do you by any chance have addresses of Russian-Jewish students at other Austrian Universities?

With kind regards and many thanks,

Yours faithfully,

185. To Michael Futran, Kharkov. *Geneva, 8 January 1903*

German: Or. Copy. T.W.: W.A.

8. 1. 03.

Dr. M. Futran,
Kharkov.

Dear Dr. [Futran],

You must surely share the view that from time to time letters require to be answered. Having written in vain to all our friends in Kharkov[1] on several occasions, we have nevertheless to bother you once again with the request that you inform us how our cause is actually faring over there. Can it really be that everything has gone down the drain again! That would be most regrettable.

We recently sent our questionnaire for your kind attention. Should you so wish, and on receipt of your letter, we shall send you a detailed report of our work here.

Most respectfully, I am,

Yours truly,

---

[2] This proposal is mentioned in the circular distributed together with the questionnaires (see n. 4 to No. 154).

185. [1] See Nos. 2, 3, 4, 20, 23, 28, 45, 67, 100, 148. W. also wrote to Futran himself twice, and had received a reply to his first letter (see No. 29 and n. 1 to No. 91).

186. To Abraham Kasteliansky, Heidelberg. *Geneva, 8 January 1903*

German: Or. Copy. T.W.: W.A.

8. 1. 03.

Dear Mr. Kasteliansky,

The questionnaires you requested for Heidelberg and Freiburg[1] were despatched to your address today.

Would you kindly begin the survey immediately.

Feiwel's address is: 19, Zürichbergstrasse, Pension Phoenix, Zurich.

With kind regards,

Yours,

187. To Michael Kroll, Moscow. *Geneva, 8 January 1903*

German: Or. Copy. T.W.: W.A.

8. 1. 03.

Dr. M. B. Kroll,
Moscow.   Registered.

Dear Friend,

You can well imagine the pleasure given me by your letter, which I received today.[1]

Whatever gave you the strange idea that I must be treating you gently? Ever since I came to know you in Minsk[2] I have had no

---

186. [1] In his letter to W. of 5 Jan. 1903 (W.A.), Kasteliansky expressed his readiness to conduct the survey in Heidelberg and also in Freiburg, if necessary. See also n. 1 to No. 181.

187. [1] Kroll to W. (3 Jan. 1903) 21 Dec. 1902, W.A. Kroll wrote that he was enthusiastic about the University idea; he promised W. that he would do everything necessary in Moscow, and he asked W. to believe in the Moscow people's readiness to do their utmost. He reported on a plan to raise funds for the University Bureau; he stated that the questionnaire was being prepared afresh for the student survey in Russia; that the proposal to issue a periodical (see No. 125) was received positively in Moscow and that he would write about it to S. Guinzburg in Saratov. As to W.'s request to mobilize support in Russia for the *Jüdischer Verlag* (ibid.), Kroll felt this would encounter difficulties, as the *Verlag* published in German only, and not in Russian. Motzkin had informed Kroll that his health had improved and that he would be prepared to begin to work (cf. n. 10 to No. 110). Kroll also related that the members of the *Kadimah* Society in Moscow had joined the Democratic Fraction.

[2] At the Russian Zionist Conference (Sept. 1902).

doubt that our affairs would be well looked after in your hands. If there are times when things are not promptly done, I know from my many years of experience that the fault frequently lies with those people who do not take matters as seriously as one would like. I realise that you are overwhelmed with work and have [to get through all your tasks] in extremely difficult circumstances. Therefore it is not a question of my being gentle with you. Rather, I ought to apologise for bombarding you so often with my letters, requests and entreaties.

You must ascribe the reason for my persistence, however, to my concentration exclusively upon one activity, and in this I am convinced that I have done the right thing. Once the University project passes into other, and I hope better, hands, I shall melt into the party ranks. At present, however, I believe I know exactly what is still required to consolidate our Bureau. I shall therefore carry on urging into action all those of our friends with the capacity and willingness to work. Moreover, my dear friend, you have to bear in mind that our project is now in full swing. There are many who scoff and many who are enthusiastic. We must not invite the gloating of the former or inflict disappointment on the latter. Should our cause founder through our failure to make the greatest effort to see it through, we shall have compromised ourselves for many years to come. On the other hand, if we manage to bring an enterprise of European proportions before the public, to attract new people to activity and to greater responsibility, it will be a triumph whose significance we cannot as yet fully comprehend.

Certainly, beginnings are not easy by any means. Sometimes we are compelled to take a leap in the dark, but experimentation is always necessary before moving on to a course of systematic action. We are being as careful as possible at present. Everything continues to be done at our own risk. Moreover, it is not beyond the bounds of possibility that we shall later share in the fate of all those within the Jewish fold who try something creative—of having no room left on our behinds to receive all those delightful kicks (including myself, the typewriter!)—but all risks have to be taken.

From all the above you may understand why I appeal to you, as one of our closest collaborators, so frequently. You may also gather that I shall give you no rest for a long time to come.

You will recognise why I am also concerned with the financial independence of our Bureau as well. Both by aspiration and necessity we have to work in freedom. Woe to us if we have to turn to the treasury of some Party, for then we shall be sold! Therefore we must leave nothing undone that may strengthen us.

A brochure is on its way to you; others, of the second edition, will follow tomorrow.

I am happy that Motzkin has been revived from the dead. Does he contemplate being in Moscow?

I have already written you about my travel plans.[3] Do try, dear friend, and complete what you want to do for the Bureau by the beginning of February, because I intend to be in Russia as early as the beginning of March. Just thinking of those Moscow days to come makes me happy.

Warmest greetings, from yours very sincerely,

188. To Aaron Ginzburg (Hermoni), Nancy. *Geneva,*
9 January 1903

Hebrew: Or. Copy. H.W.: W.A.

9. I. 03.

Dear Friend,

Thank you for your letter.[1] I am sending you [40] copies today, together with the Russian translation.[2] Please make sure, my friend, that you do your utmost to arrange matters. Perhaps you will succeed in enlisting a few more anti-Zionists, that will surely make things right—don't you agree? And you have to know how to talk to the ignorant. Kasteliansky is at present living in Heidelberg. His address is:

Heidelberg, Anlage 48^{II}.

You will receive the rules of *Hashahar* within a few days. You surely have not forgotten Aberson's temperament[3] when he has something to do, or to d[eli]ver. [---- ---- ----] him daily so that he should not forget to bring me the rules.

With best wishes and Zion's greetings,

Chaim Weizmann.

Mr. A. Ginzburg,
Nancy.[4]

[3] W. had already informed Kroll and Idelson on 8 Nov. 1902 (see No. 7) that he proposed visiting Moscow in March.

188. [1] Ginzburg to W. 8 Jan. 1903, W.A. Ginzburg consented to conduct the survey in Nancy, but he expected difficulties: '. . . the thirty Russian-Jewish students are absolute asses and listen to no one who is not as red as themselves. I am certain that if I put statistical questions to them they will suspect that Russian government agents are setting a trap for them. . .' Ginzburg added that he would try and enlist the help of Social Democratic friends. He again requested the rules of *Hashahar*—see No. 171 and n. 2 there.

[2] Of the questionnaire.

[3] Aberson was one of the leaders of the society in Geneva. See W.'s description of his personality in *Trial and Error*, Eng. edition, London, 1949, pp. 87–90.

[4] Name and address in German in orig.

189. To Berthold Feiwel, Zurich. *Geneva, 9 January 1903*

German: Or. Copy. T.W.: W.A.

Geneva, 9. 1. 03.

Dear Toldy,

Silence on your part again. The printed material has not arrived from Berlin, naturally. But to top it all I received a telegram four days ago saying: 'Everything on its way.'[1] Meanwhile demands for brochures arrive and I find it extremely painful not to be able to send anything. A letter came from Buber together with an incomplete list of professors.[2] A meeting to constitute the University committee is taking place in Vienna on the 17th. of this month. Then Buber will go to Munich.[3] I still think it would be a good idea to arrange for him to tour Switzerland. Can you do something about this in Zurich?

After making preparations in advance with reliable individuals, we have so far distributed questionnaires in the following places: Leipzig, Koethen, Friedberg, Montpellier, Darmstadt, Antwerp, Koenigsberg, Paris, Munich, Breslau, Stuttgart, Freiberg (Saxony), Berlin, Aachen, Liège, Mittweida, Karlsruhe, Heidelberg, Halle, Berne, Zurich, Nancy, Vienna, Freiburg (Breisgau), Basle.

We are still corresponding with the following: Prague, Brussels, Strasbourg, Brunswick, Giessen, Dresden, Winterthur, Hanover, Goettingen, Wuerzburg, Lyon, Greifswald, Lausanne.

We have no addresses for these: Jena, Rostock, Erlangen, Tuebingen, Kiel, Bonn, Marburg, Fribourg (Switzerland).

According to our information there are no Jews (Russian of course) in the following cities: Glons-Liège, Amsterdam, Ghent, Leyden, Neuchâtel.

Our Paris friends have undertaken the survey for the French provinces.[4] We still have no addresses for the Austrian provinces.

From what we've heard the survey is proceeding fairly well. I do

---

189. [1] Apparently referring to a telegram from Glikin which has not been found—cf. No. 190.

[2] Buber to W. 6 Jan. 1903, W.A. Buber enclosed with his letter a list of Jewish professors and lecturers likely to be interested in the University project and he promised to send a supplementary list also, together with a list of non-Jewish professors and Jewish writers. Buber reported that the inaugural meeting of the Vienna committee for the University would certainly take place on 17 Jan. 1903. He also requested W. to inform him of the preparations being made for his propaganda tour in Switzerland.

[3] Buber was invited to lecture in Munich. See also n. 3 to No. 260.

[4] See n. 4 to No. 180.

not know Marek's address, but you can write him care of Dr. M. B. Kroll, whose address I have added in Russian below.[5]

Please let me hear something from you soon.

Warmest greetings,

Yours ever,

190. To Moses Glikin, Charlottenburg. *Geneva, 9 January 1903*

German: T.W.: C.Z.A. A126/24/7/2/2.

Geneva, 4 rue Lombard, 9. 1. 03.

Mr. M. Glikin,
Berlin.[1]

Dear Friend,

What do you really think about when you send your telegrams ?[2] We know exactly how long it takes for a parcel to arrive from Berlin to Geneva. First you send a message and then you take at least another week. Please take note of how often I have to send you letters and telegrams. I most decidedly hold you responsible for these delays. Our work suffers to such an extent that we shall be compelled never to turn to Berlin again. I telegraphed the *Jüdischer Verlag* to send Buber 50 brochures.[3] According to information reaching us today, he received *thirteen* copies after ten letters.[4] *Buber needs the brochures urgently.* Make a rule for yourself: always answer me precisely as to the time and manner in which things are done. Reject all theorising on probabilities. I rely on what you tell me to plan my day's work ahead, but you constantly let me down.

Enclosed is a copy of a letter to Feiwel[5] from which you will learn the state of our survey.

Kind regards,

Your
Dr. Ch. Weizmann

---

[5] In all likelihood W. added the address by hand. It does not appear in the copy of this letter that has been preserved.

190. [1] See n. 1 to No. 84.

[2] Glikin telegraphed W. on 28 Dec. 1902 (W.A.). that he would send all the printed material the next day and apparently at the beginning of January he sent an additional telegram, not found, in which he reported that the material had been despatched (see n. 1 to No. 189).

[3] The telegram has not been found.

[4] See Buber to W. 6 Jan. 1903, W.A.

[5] See No. 189.

191. To Chaim Khissin, Berne. *Geneva, 9 January 1903*

German: Or. Copy. T.W.: W.A.

9. 1. 03.

Mr. Ch. Khissin,
Berne.

Dear Friend,

The questionnaires you requested are being posted to you today.[1] We on our part are almost done with the distribution of the forms among all the Universities of Central Europe. We have found people everywhere to take over the conduct of the survey. Enclosed is a newspaper cutting which should interest you.[2] Please return it.

We would be most grateful if you would inform us, however briefly, of the mood prevailing among the Berne students and their attitude towards our project.

Regarding the Fraction,[3] separately.

Kind regards,

Your

192. To the Democratic Fraction, Berne. *Geneva, 9 January 1903*

German: Or. Copy. T.W.: W.A.

Geneva, 9. 1. 03.

Dear Fraction Comrades,

I have taken note of your decisions[1] and shall communicate them to Mr. Feiwel.

I find it very painful at this juncture to revert to the affairs of the Fraction. If ever a conference of our comrades were to take place, I know full well who would be made the scapegoat and have to patiently endure all abuse.

191. [1] In a letter of 8 Jan. 1903 Khissin informed W. that the Democratic Fraction group in Berne undertook to conduct the student survey there.

[2] The content of the newspaper cutting is unknown. Perhaps the reference is to the cutting that W. sent to Feiwel on 11 Jan. 1903 (see n. 5 to No. 202).

[3] See No. 192.

192. [1] Khissin sent W. on 8 Jan. 1903 the text of resolutions adopted at the meeting of the Fraction group in Berne on 5 Jan. 1903 (W.A.). The group wanted the Fraction Information Bureau to resume its functions and a Fraction Conference to be called early in the year. It also expressed concern that in the absence of a closely knit organization the Fraction might be incapable of participating in the elections for the Sixth Zionist Congress and might be in danger of disintegration.

If however, you would examine the wretched circulars[2] of the Information Bureau you would see how often our colleagues were called upon to do some work. Sad to state, 20 letters elicited on the average but one response.

All duties, both of an active and passive nature, were in the main neglected or left totally undone even by those Fraction members who had assumed the role of leadership.

Work is impossible under such conditions.

If the Fraction wishes to accomplish anything there will have to be a radical change. I would remind you that the I.B. is only a post-office box, though indeed one in which nothing has ever been deposited. I have been breaking my head over these matters for a long time. Together with Feiwel and our Moscow friends[3] we shall in a little while begin active work. I can assure you it will not be our fault if things are dragged out again.

With Zion's greetings,

193. To Saul Lurie, Darmstadt. *Geneva, 9 January 1903*

German: Or. Copy. T.W.: W.A.

Geneva, 9. 1. 03.

Mr. Saul Lurie,
Darmstadt.

Dear Saul,

Heartfelt thanks for your frequent letters.[1] The printed material you requested will be despatched to your address today. It will not be our fault, really, if it is delayed. We make honest efforts here to reply by return, often despite a pile-up of work. Unfortunately, everything gets dragged out in Berlin so that we are most unpleasantly inconvenienced.

From the copy enclosed of a letter to Feiwel[2] you will gather how we stand with the survey.

We have done everything possible to ensure the success of the survey. But now the matter is out of our hands, though I persevere in the hope that we may yet reach our objective.

[2] I.e., the four newsletters published by the Information Bureau of the Democratic Fraction between Jan.–April 1902 (W.A.).

[3] I.e., the members of the Democratic Fraction Centre in Moscow.

193. [1] Lurie to W. 3 Jan. 1903; 7 Jan. 1903; 9 Jan. 1903; W.A. Lurie reported on his progress with the survey in Darmstadt; in another letter, 8 Jan. 1903, he wrote that he had received the questionnaires but not the leaflets for distribution to the participants in the survey (see n. 5 to No. 124).

[2] See No. 189.

I would be very happy to learn of the progress of your efforts with Prof. Gundelfinger.[3] We would also be grateful if you would send us a list of those persons who, in your opinion and perhaps with your assistance, may become interested in the project. At one time you spoke of Khissin in Moscow.[4] You wanted, I believe, to write to him.

Anticipating your very welcome news, I am,

Yours ever,

194. To D. Berkovitch, Berlin. *Geneva, 10 January 1903*

German: Or. Copy. T.W.: W.A.

10. 1. 03.

Dear Mr. Berkovitch,

We are most grateful to you for writing and for your cordial proposal.[1] The Berlin survey is in the hands of Mr. M. Glikin, 98, Kantstrasse, Charlottenburg. We shall be very happy if you will contact our friends there. We have written to Mr. Glikin accordingly.[2]

Yours respectfully,

195. To ---- Gotz, ----.[1] *Geneva, 10 January 1903*

German: Or. Copy. T.W.: W.A.

10. 1. 03.

Dear Mr. Gotz,

Thank you very much for your kind letter.[2] We are sending off the printed material to your address today, as requested. Our brochure will follow in a few days.

[3] Sigmund Gundelfinger (1846–1910). During 1879–1907 he was a Professor of Mathematics at the Polytechnic in Darmstadt. Apparently Lurie promised to speak to him about the plan for a Jewish University.

[4] Apparently meaning Joseph Khishin, one of the first members of the *Hovevei Zion* in Moscow. In 1890 Khishin was active in the committee to establish a Jewish University to be called College of Torah, Science, Languages and Jewish Studies.

194. [1] Berkovitch to W. 'January 1903', W.A. No. 30/0, 69. Berkovitch, an engineering student from Rumania, wrote that he was prepared to help in gathering statistics about students from Rumania, and perhaps other countries, who were studying in Berlin.

[2] See No. 197. From the wording of this letter it would appear that the letter to Glikin was written earlier. Cf., however, there: 'We replied to [Berkovitch] today.'

195. [1] First name and place of residence unknown.
[2] Not found.

When you have collected the completed questionnaires please send then back to us.

With regards,

196. To I. Glikin, Brunswick. *Geneva, 10 January 1903*

German: Or. Copy. T.W.: W.A.

10. 1. 03.

Mr. Glikin,
Brunswick.

Dear Sir,

We have the honour to inform you, in reply to your kind letter,[1] that we are posting the questionnaires as requested to your address today, and we ask most respectfully that you distribute them among your colleagues, and whenever possible involve their participation in the survey.

We are happy to make our brochure, *Eine Jüdische Hochschule*, available to you. Would you kindly clarify what you mean by 'programme.' We shall gladly provide you with any other information.

Would you please collect the completed questionnaires and send them on to us.

We thank you for your efforts, and respectfully send our good wishes.

197. To Moses Glikin, Charlottenburg. *Geneva, 10 January 1903*

German: T.W.: C.Z.A. A126/24/7/2/2.

Geneva, 10. 1. 03.

Mr. M. Glikin,
Berlin.[1]

Dear Friend,

The printed material[2] is still not here, and I am completely baffled.

196. [1] I. Glikin (first name not known) to W. 9 Jan. 1903 (in orig. a slip of the pen: 9/1/93), W.A. Glikin wrote that he would undertake to conduct the survey in Brunswick, and although the majority of students were not Zionist sympathizers, he expected a positive response. He intended to call the students to a meeting to discuss the matter and for this reason 'it would be most desirable to receive the major features of your programme'.

197. [1] See n. 1 to No. 84.   [2] See n. 2 to No. 154, n. 2 to No. 190.

I am delighted that you will soon be coming to us,[3] only it's going to be bad for you when we meet! Please let me know whom I am to correspond with in Berlin regarding the survey, but don't exactly look out for the least reliable of people.

A Rumanian Jew, an engineering student D. Berkovitch, No. 56, Brandenburgstrasse, Berlin, had offered his help with the survey among Rumanians in Berlin. We replied to him today.[4] Please get in touch with him at once.

You can bring me Lilien's head[5] and some good cigars—not coachmen's cheroots (and for me too, says the typewriter), as well as addresses for Jena, Kiel, Tuebingen, Rostock, Erlangen.

We are sending you a list of those cities to which we have already forwarded questionnaires.[6] Look how fast we work—unlike certain other people.

Till we meet again,

Your
Ch. W.

198. To S. Perlmutter, Goettingen. *Geneva, 10 January 1903*

German: Or. Copy. T.W.: W.A.

10. 1. 03.

Mr. S. Perlmutter,
Goettingen.

Dear Sir,

In immediate reply to your esteemed letter of the 8th,[1] we beg to inform you of the following:

You may, without difficulty, be allowed to sit for the Doctoral examination at the University in Berne as indeed in Lausanne where, however, the language of instruction is French. In Zurich, and possibly also Geneva, you would have to take an examination

---

[3] See n. 5 to No. 178.   [4] See n. 1 to No. 194.

[5] W. was angry at Lilien for not keeping his promise to design an emblem for the University Bureau—see n. 3 to No. 175.

[6] The list that was sent to Glikin has not been found, but on the previous day W. sent him a copy of a letter to Feiwel which contained, *inter alia*, the list of cities to which questionnaires had been sent (see Nos. 189, 190).

198. [1] Perlmutter (first name not known) to W., 8 Jan. 1903, W.A. Perlmutter wrote that he supported the plan to establish a Jewish University. His uncertain status as a medical student at Goettingen University prevented him, temporarily, from participating in the project as he would desire, but he was prepared to submit details about himself. Perlmutter asked W.'s advice about the possibilities of continuing his studies in Switzerland.

in Latin. At any rate, we recommend that before making your decision you communicate in writing with the appropriate Rector's office, because regulations are subject to constant change.

By holding a Doctorate from a foreign University, you will be permitted to take the State examination in Russia on presentation of a Matriculation certificate.[2] People usually arrange this so that they take their finals in a Russian *Gymnasium* first and then sit for the State examination.

Under separate cover we are sending a few questionnaires, together with Russian translations, to your address. We would earnestly request you to pass these on to any Russian and Rumanian Jewish colleagues in Goettingen, and have them filled in. Kindly collect the questionnaires when completed and post them to our address.

We trust you will be able to perform this small service, which will not take up too much of your time and will earn our gratitude.

Most respectfully, and with regards,

We remain,

199. To Hugo Schapiro, Dresden. *Geneva, 10 January 1903*

German: Or. Copy. T.W.: W.A.

10. 1. 03.

Mr. Hugo Schapiro,
Dresden.

Dear Sir,

In immediate reply to your kind letter of the 8th,[1] we are today sending the printed material to your address as requested.

We are most grateful for your readiness to take over the survey in Dresden, and trust that you will succeed in bringing the rest of your colleagues into the effort, and in this way carry out the survey as thoroughly as possible.

When you have collected the completed questionnaires, kindly forward them on to us.

Many thanks for sending us the address in Freiburg. We shall make use of it.

Most respectfully,

[2] Perlmutter had completed his studies at the Business School in Kiev (see his letter of 8 Jan. 1903).

199. [1] Schapiro to W., 8 Jan. 1903, W.A. Schapiro asked that questionnaires be sent to him for the survey in Dresden. He proposed that a student named Singer, at Freiberg where many Russian Jews were studying, should also be contacted. Schapiro was a student at Dresden, but no further information about him has come to light.

200. To Leonid Bielsky, Stuttgart. *Geneva, 11 January 1903*

German: Or. Copy. T.W.: W.A.

11. 1. 03.

Mr. L. Bielsky,[1]
Jewish Students Union,
Stuttgart.

Dear Sir,

In reply to your kind letter of the 9th,[2] we hereby wish to inform you that surveys of type 2 and 4 will be conducted only after the first has been completed. You can imagine how much work the present survey has already given us, and will continue to give us. There may be only ten people in Stuttgart,[3] but there are other cities with over three and four hundred. The distribution, collection and classification of the documents will keep our Bureau engaged for a considerable time yet. After due deliberation, we decided that it was preferable, in the interest of the enterprise, to conduct the surveys in stages.

It was with great pleasure that we learned from your letter of the formation of a committee, and we ask most sincerely that you bring the first and most important part of the effort to a successful conclusion.

Most respectfully,

201. To Jacob Labendz, Brunswick. *Geneva, 11 January 1903*

German: Or. Copy. T.W.: W.A.

11. 1. 03.

Mr. Jacob Labendz,
Brunswick.

Dear Sir,

In reply to your esteemed letter of the 8th,[1] we would respectfully

---

200. [1] Bielsky was a student of architecture in Stuttgart and a Zionist member of the Jewish students committee there.

[2] Bielsky to W., 9 Jan. 1903, W.A. Bielsky reported that a committee had been organized to conduct the survey in Stuttgart and he asked for questionnaires of types 2 and 4—that is, group-questionnaires intended for foreign students studying in Western Europe and questionnaires for Western European students. In fact, such questionnaires had not been formulated (see n. 8 to No. 3).

[3] Bielsky asked for ten copies of the questionnaires intended for the West Europeans.

201. [1] Labendz to W., 8 Jan. 1903, W.A. Labendz reported that he was prepared to inform you that yesterday we sent 20 questionnaires to a student named Mr. Glikin.[2] Your letter, however, only arrived today, and we are grateful for your readiness to take charge of the matter. We are today despatching an additional 20 copies to your address, with the sincere request that you get in touch with Mr. Glikin or any other gentlemen concerned.

The brochure will follow in a day or two.

In the expectation of hearing from you, we beg to remain, with kind regards,

Yours faithfully,

202. To Berthold Feiwel, Zurich. *Geneva, 11 January 1903*

German: Or. Copy. T.W.: W.A.

Geneva, 11. 1. 03.

Mr. Berthold Feiwel,
Zurich.

Dear Berthold,

Thank you for writing so warmly[1] and for sending the letters.

I have read Trietsch's letter, now returned to you, with great interest. I consider it superfluous for me to visit Vienna now, because our interests there will be very ably represented by Trietsch and Buber. But if you think my presence is necessary, naturally I shall go. Please telegraph your reply so that I can still communicate with Buber and Trietsch and make preparations.[2] You must bear in mind that at the end of February I shall be starting on my journey for England and Russia.[3]

conduct the survey in Brunswick where, according to him, there were about forty Jewish students, and he asked for a corresponding number of questionnaires. He wrote that he would call a meeting of the students to deal with the survey. No information about him has come to light except that he himself was a student in Brunswick.

² See No. 196.

202. ¹ Feiwel to W., 9 Jan. 1903, W.A. Feiwel returned a number of letters belonging to the Bureau in Geneva and he also sent W. a letter he received from Trietsch. The content of the letter is unknown, but apparently Trietsch asked Feiwel to come to Vienna to discuss the affairs of the *Jüdischer Verlag* and the Jewish University with Buber, Lilien, and himself (see No. 207 as well as Feiwel to W., 17 Jan. 1903, 22 Jan. 1903, W.A.). Feiwel wrote that he could not go to Vienna but proposed that W. go there in order to further the affairs of the University, the *Jüdischer Verlag*, and the proposed periodical.

² Feiwel replied on 12 Jan. 1903 (W.A.) that he now considered a journey by W. to Vienna to be unnecessary.

³ In March W. went to Russia, but he did not visit England until the autumn of 1903.

We are sending you the list of people we can depend on in the University cities.[4] This list keeps growing because new addresses are constantly being added. We hope that by the end of this week we shall be both completely done with the distribution and in receipt of replies from some of the cities.

The enclosed newspaper cutting should be of great interest to you. Please return it.[5]

How is the survey going in Zurich? We still have no addresses for Austria.[6] I do not know whether *Die Welt* has published an Appeal announcement.[7] There ought to have been a reaction from somebody. You are an avid reader of *Die Welt*. What about it? Can you by any chance get us a few addresses for Austria?

The printed matter is still not here.[8] It seems to be going up the chimney.[9] The moment the things get here I shall send everything on to you, paper and clips included.

Warmest regards to you and all our friends,

Your

203. To Simon Guinzburg, Saratov. *Geneva, 12 January 1903*

German: Or. Copy. T.W.: W.A.

12. 1. 03.

Engineer S. Guinzburg,
Saratov.

Dear Friend,

Many thanks for your friendly letter[1] and for your readiness to work for our cause. The following information will acquaint you, in brief, with the state of our affairs:

[4] I.e., who had undertaken to conduct the survey. The list itself was not found.

[5] The content of the cutting is unknown. On 12 Jan. 1903, Feiwel wrote to W. (W.A.): 'I made use of the Berne cutting'.

[6] The 'Leo Pinsker' Society undertook to conduct the survey in Vienna (see No. 182) but W. lacked names and addresses of reliable people at other Austrian Universities (see No. 189).

[7] Meaning the notice sent to the editors of *Die Welt* in Dec. (No. 108) relating to individuals to be entrusted with the survey. The notice was not published (see No. 224).

[8] See n. 2 to No. 154; n. 2 to No. 190.

[9] Orig. a play on words: 'sie scheinen mit dem Feuerzug zu gehen.'

203. [1] The letter from Guinzburg, not found, was in reply to W.'s of 27 Dec. 1902 (No. 127). From No. 210 it appears that Guinzburg promised to work on behalf of the University.

1) We have endeavoured, both by correspondence and personal approach, to interest people in our undertaking whenever and wherever possible. These efforts have been crowned with success to the extent that on the 17th of this month we are proceeding with the formation of a significant 'Jewish University' committee in Vienna. Then it will be Berlin's turn, and in this way we shall have created a nucleus composed of important people to enable us to conduct propaganda on a substantial scale. Unfortunately, I cannot as yet announce the names of committee members, but shall do so the moment publication becomes possible.

2) Similarly, we shall soon be taking steps to set up groups in other West European cities, for example, Paris, London, Munich. We have had to proceed with the greatest caution in this regard and in no circumstances must precipitate matters. We aim at the creation of an international 'Jewish University Society' which will take the entire project in hand.

3) The links we have sought to establish in Russia have for the time being been restricted to our own circle of friends, and we have looked to them for the manpower required and for material resources for the preparatory work. As you are aware, we have found a little money[2] in Baku, Rostov, and possibly Kharkov, and as a result were able to hazard the first steps. At the same time I am able to inform you that our tentative approaches to the 'mighty ones' in Russia have yielded solid assurances,[3] and we feel quite justified in our hope of commanding ample financial means for our project —that is, if our preparations are adequate and our propaganda campaign is properly handled.

4) By preparations we mean: a) A thorough investigation into Jewish student conditions. In accordance with a predetermined plan, we have initiated a survey for this purpose. We have got into touch with Jewish students in almost all Central European Universities. Until now, we have sent over two thousand copies of our questionnaire to thirty different locations. A sample of the questionnaire is going off to you under separate cover. You can imagine to what degree this task makes demands upon us, and will continue to do so. When this material has been gathered together and classified, that is by the end of the winter semester, we shall take steps to issue a special publication.[4] b) Another survey, among professors,

[2] Regarding the pledges for funds given in Baku and Rostov see Vol. I bridge-note following No. 317; see also n. 1 to No. 24 above, and n. 5 to No. 40. The University Bureau received 200 roubles from Kharkov in March 1903 (see n. 9 to No. 294).

[3] Only the prospect of receiving a large sum from one of the Brodsky brothers in Kiev is known—see Vol. I, n. 6 to No. 319.

[4] Apparently meaning the book that Feiwel was to write—see n. 3 to No. 7.

has already been initiated. We shall be sending for your kind attention a copy of the letter being distributed to some two hundred Jewish professors.[5] c) The detailed elaboration of the project itself, requiring a comprehensive examination of the requirements of a University. This task will be assigned to a special committee of leading experts. d) Determination on the location of the University, a matter that will necessitate some journeys and cultivating the authorities concerned. I shall be travelling to England in February so as to gather information from appropriate sources regarding the situation there.[6]

5) On completion of the work broadly described here, we shall have created, in our view, the basis for a real propaganda campaign. This can then get under way with the entire European apparatus engaged.

You will see, my dear friend, that we have brought a movement into existence in the briefest of time and despite limited means. We can cite a great deal of favourable publicity in the newspapers, although our Bureau has made it a firm principle not to be forced into the open until we have quietly completed our tasks as planned.

We must be on our guard against our friends as well as our enemies. So many projects are launched nowadays, but they run aground through being shouted from the housetops and because of amateurish management. We have no intention of being lost in the morass of such half-baked projects. We are therefore endeavouring to work independently, in freedom and obscurity, until we have gathered our strength and have solidly established our Bureau. This brings me to answer one point in your kind letter. You will readily understand that all these efforts, if they are to be efficiently and thoroughly carried out—as they must—will naturally require funds. Here again we did not wish to appeal to the public at large. If we exploit the public now for trifles we shall lose some part of it later when we shall need to go for bigger stakes. At present the Bureau needs about 300 francs per month. We are trying to obtain this money from our more intimate fellow-workers. But in our view it would be inappropriate to go about collecting small amounts for the Bureau, for the prestige of the entire enterprise would certainly become tarnished as a consequence. We would therefore prefer, through a medium fully in keeping with the dignity of the cause, such as special activities, that you raise more substantial sums all at once for this purpose. Our intimate associates, being more

---

[5] In fact, the survey of professors did not take place—see n. 9 to No. 13.

[6] In the event W. visited England only in the autumn of 1903. Regarding W.'s wish that the University be established in England, see also No. 161.

conversant with the situation, may of course make monthly contributions. In this connection may I state that we have written neither to Tzaritzyn nor to any of the other cities you mention.

Kindly forward such sums as you may raise for the preliminary work to the Jewish Colonial Bank, endorsed to the *Jüdische Hochschule.*

This letter has grown too long and I am anxious to send it off. I shall be writing shortly regarding the other questions.[7]

I conclude, dear friend, with my earnest plea for your active support. Our beginnings are marked by difficult but rewarding tasks. Those of us conscious of the need for the establishment of a Jewish centre are now being called upon to render a service which is simultaneously the most difficult and the most important. It is a monumental undertaking, in fact, but the work is well begun and must be seen through to its consummation.

With kind regards,

Yours ever,

204. To S. Drabkin, Winterthur. *Geneva, 12 January 1903*

German: Or. Copy. T.W.: W.A.

12. 1. 03.

Mr. S. A. Drabkin,
Winterthur.

Dear Sir,

Thank you very much for your kind letter of the 10th.[1]

We have also written to Mr. Stein of Winterthur on the same subject, and we would respectfully suggest that you get into touch with this gentleman; most likely this would lighten your work considerably.[2]

Would you please inform us of the quantity of questionnaires you require, in German and in Russian [translation]? They will be promptly sent on to you.

In anticipation of your early reply, we have the honour to remain,

Most respectfully,

[7] No further letter to Guinzburg has been found.

204. [1] Not found. Drabkin (first name not known) apparently proposed to conduct the survey in Winterthur.

[2] In a reply to W.'s postcard of the 16 Jan. 1903 (not found), Stein (first name not known) wrote on 18 Jan. 1903 (W.A.) that he was unable to conduct the survey in Winterthur.

205. To Menahem Ussishkin, Ekaterinoslav. *Geneva,*
13 January 1903

Russian: H.W.: C.Z.A. A24/125.

Geneva, Rue Lombard 4.

Confidential! 13. I. 03.

Dear Mr. Ussishkin,

Thank you for your prompt reply concerning Aberson.[1] When I spoke about a scholarship I meant that it might be possible to find five or six people in Ekaterinoslav, each of whom would contribute five or six roubles a month for one year. Aberson would then be saved. One cannot watch a man being destroyed and do nothing. But given a chance to work for a year, or a year and a half, he would no longer be in such acute need. I managed with great difficulty to ensure his tuition fees, otherwise he would have been expelled from the University, but now באו מים עד נפש.[2] I approached a number of our 'great' men, such as Dr. Marmorek[3] and others, but nothing came of it. For heaven's sake, help! As to the dissertation, I shall do all I can to send you the text as soon as possible.[4] Aberson is existing *de facto* on a semi-starvation diet; it is hard to work under such conditions.

And now to business. You promised to write to me about the 'guard'.[5] Since I arrived here from Vienna there has not been a moment when I haven't been thinking about the fate of our movement. I am convinced that there must be a complete change, for it seems to me that further navigation along this 'parliamentary' river-bed is out of the question. This is why I attribute no importance to 'organization',[6] be it of one kind or another. What use is it? To this

---

205. [1] Ussishkin's letter has not been found. It was in reply to W.'s of 28 Dec. 1902 (No. 129) asking for financial assistance for Aberson.

[2] Heb.: 'He has reached the end of his tether.' Lit. 'The waters have entered (my) soul'. From Psalms, lxix, 1.

[3] Apparently Alexander Marmorek of Paris; W.'s letter to him has not been found and it is not known who else was approached.

[4] I.e., the expanded text of the lecture given by Aberson at the Zionist Youth Conference—see n. 10 to No. 125.

[5] At the Conference of Russian Zionists in Minsk (Sept. 1902) Ussishkin proposed organizing a Zionist 'guard' to be called *Bnei Akiva*. Membership would consist of young, unmarried men, volunteers serving the movement for a given period and with specially assigned tasks. It may be assumed that when they met in Vienna at the Zionist Annual Conference in Oct. 1902 Ussishkin promised W. to write to him about the plan.

[6] At the Conference of Russian Zionists in Minsk Ussishkin proposed a number of changes in the Russian Zionist organizational structure.

day, the entire system has not provided us with a single new man—
all the work is done by the old workers, the old [יון]צ [בבי]חו.[7] Will
changing the system bring in new people? A handful of active
workers would dissolve in the limitless waters of the *Golus*.[8] The
conditions under which we are forced to work in Russia allow us no
possibility of creating a Zionist force, and as a result all our work has
the quality of impermanence; for everything is built on a volcano.[9]

Now is the time to create a cadre, call it a 'guard' if you like,
which would take all activity into its hands. This cadre must
definitely not be exclusively 'Russian', but inter-territorial rather.
One group of people, an *avant-garde*, should now go to Turkey and
Palestine, and enter Turkish political life, etc., etc.; another group
should remain and work where they now live; groups must go to
England, America and Galicia. In America, England and Galicia
there are great masses of Jews, but no Jewish national work of any
kind is being done. American Zionism is worth nothing, it would be
better if it did not exist.[10] There, and in those countries where conditions are so different, we could create a large Jewish organisation
all the quicker. The rallying theme must be nationalisation of
emigration[11] and the unification of the *Golus* in its entirety through
Zionism and under the hegemony of Russian Jewry, which is the
most 'Jewish'. The guard must therefore be divided into brigades or,
if you prefer, into groups ruled from a single centre, and working
as a united will throughout the globe. It doesn't matter that there
would be too few people to start with, but this order of missionaries
must encompass a maximum purpose from the outset.

French missionaries are far more effective bearers of French
policy throughout the world than are their embassies, etc. We, too,
must create such missionaries.

I could provide you with a number of such people, prepared to do
this work and, I think, suitable for it.

Our initial requirements need to be all-embracing: 1) *Organic
Zionism*, a term that I think needs no elucidation. 2) Political
training. 3) Education, preferably comprehensive. 4) Knowledge of
the Hebrew language and literature. I should be most interested if
it were possible for you to inform me of your plans and the thoughts
that guide you.

I shall probably begin my tour around the world as early as this
summer. I want to see Jews wherever they are: America, Palestine,

[7] Heb.: *Hovevei Zion* ('Lovers of Zion'). See Vol. I, p. 16.

[8] Yidd.: Diaspora.

[9] See also No. 316 where a detailed description is given regarding the Zionist
situation in Russia.

[10] Cf. No. 161.   [11] See n. 12 to No. 149.

Transvaal, etc. I want to give up the work I have been doing, and for the next five years or so work on the international scene. Whether I shall succeed in doing this is another question. At all events it is my hope.

I shall write you about the *Hochschule* another time. I wish to wait until your notes appear in the Press.[12]

Please write soon.

Keep well.

Mit Zionsgruss,[13]

Ch. W.

206. To A. Bass, Liège. *Geneva, 13 January 1903*

German: Or. Copy. T.W.: W.A.

13. 1. 03.

Mr. A. Bass,
Liège.

Dear Sir,

Thank you very much for your kind letter.[1] We look forward with interest to hearing from you in the future.

We should be most obliged if you would please let us have an address in Brussels. Mr. Margolin has already given us the address of a Miss Galante.[2] We have written to this lady twice[3] without, however, receiving any reply.

Thanking you in anticipation, we remain,

Yours respectfully,

207. To Davis Trietsch, Vienna. *Geneva, 13 January 1903*

German: Or. Copy. T.W.: W.A.

Geneva, 4 rue Lombard, 13. 1. 03.

Mr. D. Trietsch,
Vienna.[1]   Registered.

Dear Friend,

Berthold has sent me your letter,[2] from which I gather that on the 15th you will all be in Vienna. I would very much like to join you

---

[12] Perhaps W. was hoping that the newspapers would publish further information on Ussishkin's plan for a 'guard' (see n. 5).   [13] 'With Zion's greetings.'

206. [1] Not found.   [2] See Margolin to W., 3 Jan. 1903, W.A.
   [3] Only one of these letters has been found—see No. 162.

207. [1] The letter is addressed to Trietsch 'temporarily in Vienna'.
   [2] See n. 1 to No. 202.

there, but I consider the expensive journey to be unnecessary. I am fully convinced that you can represent me in the University project. Buber has written that the inaugural meeting of the University committee will definitely take place on the 17th.[3] You can imagine how eagerly I am anticipating the result of this meeting. It is, after all, the first and most important step. I have been asking myself about the relationship between this committee and our Bureau. It is beyond question that arrangements will have to be made for executive authority to continue in our hands, although responsibility will no longer be borne on the shoulders of just three or four people.

All my efforts are directed towards keeping our Bureau independent of Party influence. I would refer you to one other very important detail: do what you can to speak to Herzl about the University. Here are some facts for your information:

1) When I took leave of him in Vienna[4] he gave me a formal undertaking that he would join the University committee, adding these words: 'Call upon me when you need me, leave me alone when you don't. I shall be able to help you sooner than you think.'

2) In Buber's presence, Herzl stated that he had to consult with the Actions Committee as to whether he might join a committee.[5] There has as yet been no reply either to an enquiry from Feiwel[6] on this subject or to my letter posted on the 7th of this month.[7] I presume that Herzl was seeking to cover his retreat through the remark he made in Buber's presence.

3) A month ago we sent an innocuous announcement concerning the survey to the Editorial Board of *Die Welt*.[8] It was a request to student societies to make their mailing lists available for us. *That* was not printed!

I do not wish to write to *Die Welt* any more. We shall nevertheless try and place a further announcement in this journal. Perhaps the Editorial Board members themselves suppressed it. Uprimny,[9] the so-called 'editor', is not on the best of terms with us.

[3] See Buber to W. 6 Jan. 1903, W.A.
[4] After the Zionist Annual Conference (Oct. 1902).   [5] See n. 1 to No. 92.
[6] Feiwel wrote to Herzl on 13 Dec. 1902. W.'s signature appears on the letter to which Feiwel added his own (C.Z.A. Z1/340). It expressed conviction that the Zionist Actions Committee (the 'A.C.') would permit Herzl to join the University committee, and asked that Herzl notify them whether the Actions Committee had already consented.   [7] See n. 3 to No. 173.   [8] See No. 108.
[9] Julius Uprimny (?–1935) was at the time the editor of *Die Welt*. (He continued formally in office until 1905, though in fact editorial control was transferred to Siegmund Werner at the beginning of Feb. 1903.) In a conversation with Buber Uprimny maintained that the announcement did not reach him (see Buber to W. 23–24 Jan. 1903, W.A.).

From the above you will see that a clarification as to where Herzl stands in relation to our undertaking is most urgent.

I entreat you to inform me in detail and as meticulously as possible about all that transpires. If our Bureau is materially secure, and if we have our publication, and if a good committee comes into existence in Vienna, then we shall be independent. Otherwise we shall be placed in a situation difficult to maintain, there will be friction, and this will be attributed in Vienna to the spirit of Fractionalism.

Therefore try and inform yourself fully, friend Trietsch. Spare no effort in shaping the committee into a really strong and cohesive group.

All this is, naturally, intended for Buber too.

Kindest regards and best wishes,

Your

208. To Martin Buber, Vienna. *Geneva, 13 January 1903*

German: Or. Copy. T.W.: W.A.

Geneva, 4 rue Lombard, 13. 1. 03.

Mr. Martin Buber,
Vienna.

Dear Martin,

Regarding your travel plans, I am still waiting for replies from some societies.[1] They are bound to come, and so your trip will materialise.

Within five days at the latest you will be receiving a telegram in which I shall set out your exact itinerary. Today I wrote to Trietsch at your address.[2] Should he not be in Vienna, please open the letter and read it.

So now I am waiting the result of the meeting on the 17th.[3] You must ensure that the committee establishes a close relationship with the Bureau. Another essential would be the formation, from among the committee's ranks, of a sub-committee with the special responsibility of working out a programme for the project in association with us here. We have compiled a large bibliography[4] in which

---

208. [1] W. approached Wortsman, Khissin, and Meyer regarding the propaganda tour to Switzerland planned for Buber (see Nos. 163, 164, 167) and he asked Feiwel whether he could do something for Buber in Zurich (see No. 189).

[2] See No. 207.

[3] The inaugural meeting of the committee for the Jewish University in Vienna due on 17 Jan.

[4] See n. 1 to No. 179.

specialists will easily find their way, and proposals for the contemplated Jewish University must be left to them. Other members of
the committee should concern themselves particularly with the
propaganda campaign and the attraction of important personalities.
I am sending you a draft letter intended for the professors.[5] It is
very important for this letter to carry the signatures of the committee. I think you ought to obtain the permission of the gentlemen
at your meeting to use their names. Perhaps you can have the words
'The Management Committee consists of . . . . .' printed on the
letterhead. Executive authority must, in the meantime, remain in
our hands.

I have already written to Trietsch in detail about Herzl,[2] and
would ask you too to get the exact position clear. If possible please
telegraph a report on the outcome of the deliberations.

With best wishes for a total success.

Hoping to see you soon,

As ever yours,

209. To Isaac Gruenbaum, Warsaw. *Geneva, 13 January 1903*

German: Or. Copy. T.W.: W.A.

13. 1. 03.

Dear friend Gruenbaum,

Some time ago we asked you about the fate of the Hebrew translation of the brochure,[1] but have so far received no answer. Since
we need to be clear and without equivocation on this, will you kindly
let us have your reply without delay.[2]

Kind regards,

210. To Michael Kroll, Moscow. *Geneva, 13 January 1903*

German: Or. Copy. T.W.: W.A.

13. 1. 03.

Dr. M. B. Kroll,
Moscow.

Dear Friend,

Further to our recent communication,[1] we now wish to suggest

[5] See n. 9 to No. 13.

209. [1] See No. 143.

[2] From No. 279 it would appear that this postcard to Gruenbaum was returned
by the Post Office to the University Bureau (the card itself has not been found and
only the copy has been preserved).

210. [1] See No. 187.

possible modalities for a periodical to you.[2] A newspaper such as *Ost und West*,[3] but resembling the *Almanach*[4] in format and appearance, would cost 12,000–15,000 marks in the first year without taking income into account. It may be assumed, however, that income during the first year would be sizeable enough to enable us to achieve our ends if we had 5,000 marks available. We could then rely on the co-operation of our Berlin printers,[5] which would be guaranteed. The first publicity issue could appear in March, and the second in October when all periodicals begin their year, and after we have had the summer for preparation.

The second possibility is a non-illustrated newspaper, more or less in the format of *Palästina*,[6] 32 pages if a weekly, 48 if a fortnightly, and 80 if a monthly. The paper is intended as an organ for the Fraction, Statistics, University, etc. First year's costs discounting income: if a weekly, about 13,000 marks; fortnightly, about 9,000; monthly, about 7,000, all on the basis of 2,000 copies plus publicity issues. These proposals are more easy to make than to carry out. If we had 2,000 roubles in our possession we could start a good number of things. I am placing the proposals before you for your guidance, and I trust they will be of use to you.

Guinzburg of Saratov wrote a letter full of contrition yesterday[7]; he wants to work for the University with all his energy. I strongly urge you to encourage him from your side too. We have done everything possible from here. I ought to discuss various other plans with you, but for the present I shall let them rest. As I have said, my intention now is to establish the Bureau as firmly as possible. Once this is done, we shall try and bring up the other questions.

With many kind regards,

Yours ever,

211. To Bernard Chapira, Paris. *Geneva, 13 January 1903*

German: Or. Copy. T.W.: W.A.

13. 1. 03.

Dear friend Chapira,

Your message concerning the state of health of our friend

---

[2] The proposals mentioned here were sent to W. by Trietsch on 4 Jan. 1903 (W.A.).

[3] Concerning the monthly *Ost und West* see Vol. I, n. 8 to No. 302.

[4] The *Jüdischer Almanach*—see Vol. I, n. 14 to No. 238.

[5] The firm of Pass und Garleb.

[6] The bi-monthly *Palästina*—see n. 3 to No. 5.

[7] The letter mentioned in No. 203. Obviously it was not written, but probably received, 'yesterday'.

Elia[s]berg saddened me very much.[1] We trust, however, that henceforth you will take the work over yourself[2] and bring it to a successful conclusion.

Looking forward with great interest to your news, which we receive with appreciation, I have the honour to remain,

Yours respectfully,

212. To Isidore (Isaac) Mamlock, Strasbourg. *Geneva,* *14 January 1903*

German: Or. Copy. T.W.: W.A.

14. 1. 03.

Mr. I. Mamlock, Chemist,
Strasbourg, Alsace.

Dear Sir,

Thank you for your most friendly letter of the 13th,[1] and for your kind readiness to support our endeavour.

We are at present occupied, among other matters, with a survey of Jewish students from Russia and Rumania in Western Europe. Would you be agreeable, together with other people, to supervise this survey in Strasbourg? As soon as we receive your kind reply we shall send you whatever quantity of questionnaires, etc., you may require. For your information we are enclosing our brochure, *Eine Jüdische Hochschule*, as well as a sample of our questionnaire with its Russian translation and our circular regarding the survey.[2]

We would also be obliged if you could inform us whether one may find influential people from the world of scholarship and finance in Strasbourg who might be won over to our cause.

Thanking you in anticipation, we have the honour to remain,

Most respectfully,

---

211. [1] Chapira's letter has not been found. In a letter to W. of 9 Jan. 1903 (W.A.) Rachel, mother of Aaron Eliasberg, reported that her son was ill and would not be able to work for a considerable period.

[2] I.e., activities connected with the student survey in France.

212. [1] Mamlock to W. 13 Jan. 1903, W.A. Mamlock wrote that he was prepared to concern himself with the affairs of the University in Strasbourg.

[2] Apparently the circular of 1 Jan. 1903—see n. 4 to No. 154.

213. To Alexander Nemirovsky, Kharkov. *Geneva,* *14 January 1903*

German: Or. Copy. T.W.: W.A.

14. 1. 03.

Dear Mr. Nemirovsky,

On frequent occasions we have requested information from you on the situation regarding the brochure,[1] but so far have been left without a reply of any kind.

We are now seeking an answer from you for the last time. If we still hear nothing, we shall have to look on the matter as being entirely lost.[2]

Yours faithfully,

214. To K. Pomerantz, Freiberg. *Geneva,* *14 January 1903*

German: Or. Copy. T.W.: W.A.

14. 1. 03.

Mr. K. Pomerantz,
Freiberg, Saxony.

Dear Sir,

Our sincere thanks for your kind letter[1] and for your generous offer to support our project. Unfortunately, the Russian translation of the brochure is not yet in our possession, and we would therefore like you to make whatever use you can of the German edition for your lecture. We are sending you a copy of the second edition of our brochure today.

213. [1] I.e., publication of the Russian version of *Eine Jüdische Hochschule* (see n. 11 to No. 7). The subject was raised in No. 148, and possibly in letters to Nemirovsky that have not been found. Cf. No. 215, in which W. writes that he sent 6–7 letters to Nemirovsky. W. also inquired about the translation in a letter to Greidenberg (see No. 23) and in two others to Aleinikov (see Nos. 28, 100). W.'s additional approach to Nemirovsky was apparently connected with the request by Pomerantz of 13 Jan. that W. send him a Russian translation of the brochure (see n. 1 to No. 214).
[2] No reply to this letter has been found, but see n. 1 to No. 235.

214. [1] Pomerantz (first name not known) to W., 13 Jan. 1903, W.A. Pomerantz reported that he intended calling together Russian and Rumanian Jewish students at the Mining Academy in Freiberg so as to read the brochure *Eine Jüdische Hochschule* to them, and he therefore asked for a Russian translation. Pomerantz added that following the meeting he would distribute the questionnaires.

Regarding the survey, we were at one time in contact with a student, Mr. Markov,[2] to whom furthermore we sent a number of questionnaires. We are posting another 20 copies to you today, and would ask you to get in touch with Mr. Markov, or perhaps some other gentlemen, for the distribution of the questionnaires and to ensure that they are filled in. Please collect them on completion and send them back to us.[3]

With many thanks in advance,

We remain,

Most respectfully,

215. To Joseph Pokrassa, Kharkov. *Geneva, 14 January 1903*

German: Or. Copy. T.W.: W.A.

14. 1. 03.

Mr. J. Pokrassa,[1]
Kharkov.   Registered.

Dear Friend,

We have written to Kharkov more than ten times already, and to various addresses at that.[2] So far no one has deemed us worthy of a reply.[3] Those gentlemen who became enthusiastic for our cause so promptly seem to have cooled off just as quickly. The reason for this silence is completely beyond me. I had also agreed with Mr. Nemirovsky that our Kharkov people take over publication of the Russian version of the brochure. The text has lain in Kharkov for many months, and we have no idea whether it was ever sent to the printers.[4] Our manifold enquiries never received an answer. We tried through letters to all these gentlemen: Greidenberg, Breslav, Aleinikov, Nemirovsky, Futran, Brailovsky—to some of them two and three times.

I had no wish to harass you with University matters and always

---

[2] See Markov to W., 25 Dec. 1902, W.A. W.'s letter to Markov has not been found.

[3] No additional letter from Pomerantz has been found, but Markov notified W. on 5 Feb. 1903 (W.A.) that he was sending him 15 questionnaires completed by Freiberg students.

215. [1] The letters to Pokrassa were written in the familiar form.

[2] For the list of letters sent to Kharkov see n. 1 to No. 185.

[3] The W.A. holds two letters from Kharkov written in Dec. 1902: from Aleinikov of 20 Nov./3 Dec. 1902 and from Futran of 24 Nov. (7 Dec.) 1902. The letter from Aleinikov was received by W. after considerable delay—date of receipt is not known (see n. 1 to No. 100) but W. confirmed receipt of Futran's on 13 Dec. (see No. 91).

[4] See n. 11 to No. 7; n. 5 to No. 23.

turned to members of the committee elected while I was over there.[5] I now see, however, that the entire committee was apparently not serious about the business and I must, alas, stop writing to these people. I recall very well how angry Mr. Nemirovsky became at the time when we omitted to answer him about the Encyclopaedia.[6] I readily admitted that it was unfair to drag things out, but I could always cite in defence the fact that there was not a moment when I was not preoccupied with another, equally important, Jewish matter. Even if I was wrong, and I felt guilty myself, there really is no reason why Mr. Nemirovsky should allow himself to ignore six or seven letters[7] containing nothing more than requests for a little information. I don't even want to talk about the others.

I am convinced that you are interested in the progress of our work. At this moment I find it impossible to give you a report on the state of our enterprise. Much that has been started is already nearing completion. As soon as there is a sign of life from you, and nothing would make me happier, I shall write to you with all details. I don't want to put the thousand and one questions to you about how our cause looks in Kharkov. My conjectures are on the pessimistic side. But I would like to have it clear whether anything might be expected of you, or whether it was all just rhetoric. The Kharkov people generally take pride in their 'work'. I am now compelled, however, to form a somewhat different opinion. I trust that you will not follow the shining example of others and will reply, be it ever so briefly, even by postcard, to the main points of this letter.

I am, with kindest regards,

Ever yours,

216. To R. Galante, Brussels. *Geneva, 16 January 1903*

German: Or. Copy. T.W.: W.A.

Geneva, 4 rue Lombard, 16. 1. 03.

Miss R. Galante,
Brussels.

Dear Miss Galante,

Sincere thanks for your kind letter and for your efforts.[1] We shall

---

[5] See Vol. I, n. 3 to No. 319.   [6] See n. 10 to No. 2.
[7] Only three letters to Nemirovsky have been found—see Nos. 2, 20, 148. An additional letter was sent that day (see No. 213).

216. [1] Galante to W., 14 Jan. 1903, W.A. Galante informed W. of her inability to conduct the survey in Brussels, but Yoffe, a non-Zionist student, was prepared to assume the responsibility.

write to Mr. Yoffe today and despatch 100 questionnaires to his address,[2] on the assumption that there are that many students in Brussels.

Most respectfully,

217. To Isidore (Israel) Yasinovsky, Warsaw. *Geneva,* *16 January 1903*

German: Or. Copy. T.W.: W.A.

16. 1. 03.

Mr. I. Yasinovsky,
Warsaw.

Dear Friend,

Subsequent to your kind letter we wrote at once to the gentlemen both in Warsaw and the provinces, but unfortunately remain till now without an answer.[1]

We believe it preferable for initial contact to be made with such people locally, from Warsaw; and only afterwards, once we are convinced of an individual's favourable attitude, should links be established with the Bureau.

We are therefore allowing ourselves the liberty of reverting to our original suggestion, by asking you to try and form a small 'Jewish University' group in Warsaw. If you believe you may harm the cause by taking the initiative upon yourself,[2] you may entrust the task to someone else.

We should be very pleased to have your valued opinion on this matter. Try and make a start, good friend. Although such a beginning may only constitute a tiny cell, we believe our enterprise will evoke such sympathy that even the smallest cells can be relied upon to demonstrate a capacity for development.[3]

With sincerest regards, we remain,

Most respectfully,

[2] See No. 218.

217. [1] See n. 1 to No. 33, n. 2 to No. 63, and n. 1 to No. 134.
[2] See n. 1 to No. 33.
[3] Concerning Yasinovsky's reply see n. 7 to No. 245.

218. To B. Yoffe, Brussels. *Geneva, 16 January 1903*

German: Or. Copy. T.W.: W.A.

16. 1. 03.

Mr. Yoffe,[1]
Brussels.

Dear Sir,

Miss Galante informs us that you were kind enough to give her an undertaking that you would take charge of the survey in Brussels.[2] We assume that you have already read the printed material sent to the young lady, and that you are informed on the purpose and nature[3] of the survey.

At all events we are posting our brochure to your address, and are enclosing our circular regarding the survey with this letter.[4]

Simultaneously, we are sending you a package containing 100 questionnaires, together with an equal number of Russian translations.

We would greatly appreciate your sending us the prospectus of Brussels University; we are also interested in University income and expenditure for the last few years. Such figures are probably to be found in the official University reports, or in the Brussels University report for the World Exhibition in Paris.[5] If these documents have to be purchased, please be so kind as to send them to us C.O.D.

Thanking you very much in advance, we remain,

Yours faithfully,

219. To B. Lurie, Wuerzburg. *Geneva, 16 January 1903*

German: Or. Copy. T.W.: W.A.

16. 1. 03.

Mr. B. Lurie,[1]
Wuerzberg.

Dear Sir,

Thank you for your kind letter of the 14th.[2] Under separate cover, we are sending five questionnaires [to] your address.

218. [1] Yoffe's first name is not known.
    [2] See n. 1 to No. 216.
    [3] Orig.: 'Art', probably referring to the manner of carrying out.
    [4] Apparently the circular of 1 Jan. 1903—see n. 4 to No. 154.
    [5] The Exhibition took place in Paris in 1900.

219. [1] First name not known.
    [2] Not found.

May we ask you to distribute these and have them filled in, then to collect the completed forms and send them back to us.

Should there be any Russian women students at your University, please have them participate in the survey also. We shall then send you the appropriate number of forms required.

Most respectfully,

220. To Joseph Lurie, St. Petersburg. *Geneva, 16 January 1903*

German: Or. Copy. T.W.: W.A.

16. 1. 03.

Dr. Joseph Lurie,
St. Petersburg.

Dear Friend,

I thought I would give you time to become acclimatized in your new environment.[1] It may be assumed that you are by now a citizen of the royal capital,[2] and I am now taking you up on your recent promise to me to become active in Petersburg on behalf of our Bureau.[3]

Until now we were reluctant to form any ties there, because in the case of such a large number of people it was most difficult from our end to assess the situation. You would indeed be rendering us a great service by providing us with a list of persons who, in your view, might be considered suitable for our cause.

You may perhaps be aware that I intend to visit Petersburg in March.[4] It is vital, therefore, that some advance preparation be made through correspondence. Petersburg is an important place, and I am convinced much can be done there.

In our opinion the best way to begin would be to interest a small circle of intellectuals in the problem, and they could be regarded as the basis for a larger organisation later. Can you do something for us in this direction, friend Lurie?

You probably have connections in the journalistic world already, and these could very well be utilised.

---

220. [1] After the weekly *Der Yud* ceased publication at the end of 1902 (see n. 2 to No. 17), Lurie transferred from Warsaw to St. Petersburg, where he joined the editorial staff of the new Yiddish daily *Der Fraind*.

[2] Orig.: 'Haupt und Residenzstadt'.

[3] See Lurie to W., 11 (24) Dec. 1902, W.A.

[4] In the event W. did not visit St. Petersburg.

I earnestly hope, in view of the little time left before my departure, that you will reply promptly.

With kind regards and best wishes,

Yours,

221. To Berthold Feiwel, Zurich. *Geneva, 16 January*
1903

German: Or. Copy. T.W.: W.A.

Geneva, 16. 1. 03.

Mr. Berthold Feiwel,
Zurich.

Dear Berthold,

How curious that in Berlin and Vienna plans change from day to
day! I was absolutely convinced that Buber would be in Vienna on
Saturday to attend the inaugural meeting of the University committee, and therefore not a little surprised when your telegram arrived.[1]
Trietsch was also to have been in Vienna.[2] Now it appears that
neither Buber's visit to Munich nor Trietsch's to Vienna material-
ised. I am glad about the first, but the second is regrettable. Yesterday I telegraphed Buber whether the committee was being formed
today. As yet there is no reply, and this makes me feel it is doubtful.
Has everything fallen through again?

I am holding back the posting of the professors' letter,[3] because I
feel it would be more purposeful if it already carried the signatures
of the Vienna committee. If there is no committee, however, our
calculations have gone awry. Time flies with such enormous speed,
the committee problem must be solved soon.

Today I received a telegram from Shriro.[4] He is already in
Lausanne; I shall visit him on Sunday. The notice prepared for
Die Welt did not appear.[5] I am furious that they did not print our

---

221. [1] Feiwel thought Buber was due to lecture in Munich on Saturday 17 Jan.
1903—the day projected for the inaugural meeting of the Vienna committee for the
University (see n. 2 to No. 189). On 14 Jan. 1903 he sent telegrams to W., Trietsch,
and Lilien proposing that they all meet in Munich on that date, but two or three days
later he telegraphed again withdrawing his proposal (the telegrams have not been
found—see Feiwel to W., 17 Jan. 1903, W.A.).

[2] See n. 1 to No. 202.

[3] See n. 9 to No. 13.

[4] The telegram has not been found. Regarding Shriro's support for the University
project see Vol. I, n. 11 to No. 276 and the bridge-note following No. 317.

[5] In the letter of 12 Jan. 1903 (W.A.) Feiwel undertook to send W. a notice for
publication in *Die Welt* to replace the previous notice from the University Bureau
which was not printed (see No. 108).

innocuous appeal. I still have no addresses for Austria.[6] Do you have anybody to whom one may write ? Please don't forget. I shall send you the account you requested tomorrow.[7]

Kind regards,

Yours ever,

P.S. The first completed questionnaires arrived from Basle today. How is it going in Zurich ? Did Glikin turn up ?[8] He seems to travel at the same speed as the printed matter.[9] Incidentally, the Berlin notepaper[10] is practically useless. Such wonderful reciprocity between Berlin and Geneva!

222. To B. Epstein, Marburg. *Geneva, 20 January 1903*

German: Or. Copy. T.W.: W.A.

20. 1. 03.

Mr. B. Epstein,[1]
Marburg.

Dear Sir,

We are today sending off to your address the 15 questionnaires requested in your kind letter of the 17th,[2] just received.

The function of the census committee is to distribute the forms and ensure that they are filled in, also perhaps to approach people individually so as to talk it over with them. Naturally, this is not so important in the case of Marburg, where there are so few students. But it would do some good if you would try and draw in some people from the other camp for this work.

We respectfully ask you to act promptly in collecting the completed questionnaires and sending them on to us.

With all good wishes,

[6] See n. 6 to No. 202.

[7] In the letter of 12 Jan. 1903 Feiwel asked W. to notify him how much money he had given to the *Jüdischer Verlag*, and what additional sums he might be able to allocate in the near future (cf. n. 7 to No. 137). The account mentioned here has not been found.

[8] See n. 5 to No. 178.

[9] The printed material ordered by W. in Berlin in November (see listing in No. 102) and not sent until the end of December and the beginning of January.

[10] The headed notepaper of the Bureau of the Jewish University that was printed in Berlin.

222. [1] First name not known.

[2] Not found. Apparently Epstein requested enlightenment on the functions of the survey committees whose establishment the circular of the University Bureau had recommended (see n. 3 to No. 95; n. 4 to No. 154).

223. To Aaron Ginzburg (Hermoni), Nancy. *Geneva,*
20 January 1903

German: Or. Copy. T.W.: W.A.

20. 1. 03.

Dear Mr. Ginzburg,

Would you kindly return the completed questionnaires to us
with the wrapping marked 'Commercial'.

By the end of this week you will receive the material you
requested.[1]

Regards,

Your

224. To Theodor Herzl, Vienna. *Geneva, 20 January 1903*

German: Or. Copy. T.W.: W.A.

20. 1. 03.

Dr. Theodor Herzl,
Vienna.

Dear Dr. [Herzl],

On December 19th last year we sent *Die Welt* a brief announcement in which we requested student societies to send us their
addresses.[1] We needed them for the survey. Unfortunately, this
announcement has not as yet been printed.

We are taking the liberty of enquiring most respectfully of you
whether we may rely on *Die Welt* to publish our communication.

We enclose herewith the copy of an announcement which is going
to the editorial office by today's post.[2] We would be most grateful
if you would kindly let us know whether these few lines will get
printed.

Most respectfully and with Zion's greetings,

223. [1] See Ginzburg to W., 17 Jan. 1903, W.A. Ginzburg reported that the survey in
Nancy was being conducted with the help of Social Democratic students. He asked
if he was to send the questionnaires as 'Printed Matter'. Ginzburg added that he was
waiting for the rules he had requested of the *Hashahar* Society (see n. 2 to No. 188).
He also asked W. for information on the Democratic Fraction and its programme.

224. [1] See No. 108, and n. 9 to No. 207.

[2] This notice was printed in *Die Welt* of 30 Jan. 1903. It contained a brief report on
the Jewish University and the student survey, and concluded with a request that
students prepared to conduct the survey in cities where the Bureau still had no one
for this purpose (particularly in Austria) should notify the Bureau.

225. To Isidore (Isaac) Mamlock, Strasbourg. *Geneva, 20 January 1903*

German: Or. Copy. T.W.: W.A.

20. 1. 03.

Mr. I. Mamlock,
Strasbourg.

Dear Sir,

Sincere thanks for your kind letter[1] and for your willingness to take our project in hand.

In accordance with your request we are sending you 30 questionnaires which please distribute and have filled in. Kindly send the completed questionnaires back to us.

We are in the process of forming a larger committee in Vienna. As soon as this has been constituted, we shall take the opportunity to establish closer contacts among Jewish professorial circles.[2]

Thanking you once again for your kindness in writing,

We remain,

Most respectfully and with
Zion's greetings,

226. To Berthold Feiwel, Zurich. *Geneva, 20 January 1903*

German: Or. Copy. T.W.: W.A.

Geneva, 20. 1. 03.

Mr. Berthold Feiwel,
Zurich.

Dear Toldy,

Forgive me for not writing until today. I was away for two days[1] and found your express letter only last night.[2] I also received a lengthy letter from Buber[3] which, I must say, caused me a great

225. [1] Mamlock to W., 19 Jan. 1903, W.A. Mamlock reported that he would supervise the survey in Strasbourg and try and bring the plan for a University to the attention of the students; but in his opinion it was premature to approach Jewish academics and men of wealth in view of their indifference to Jewish problems.

[2] Cf. No. 208.

226. [1] W. had been to visit Samuel Shriro in Lausanne (see No. 221).

[2] Feiwel to W., 17 Jan. 1903, W.A. Feiwel wrote, *inter alia*, about his efforts to arrange a meeting in Munich (see n. 1 to No. 221).

[3] Buber to W., 15 Jan. 1903, W.A. Buber reported that he was compelled to postpone the inaugural meeting of the Vienna Committee from the 17th to the 25th

deal of distress. The meeting was postponed to the 25th for reasons that are not quite clear to me. Is it possible that we are being obstructed by the Actions Committee? Herzl may show indifference, but he never adopts the tactics of the opposition.

It seems more necessary than ever to me that you go to Vienna regarding all this. Neither Buber nor I can substitute for you in such a situation. I must emphasise, and repeatedly, that whatever happens we must succeed in forming the committee in Vienna and Berlin in the near future. Otherwise the value of my Russian journey will be utterly wasted, with great harm being done to our cause. Although Trietsch has the best of intentions, nothing much is going to result from them.[4] He is too busy, and if anything is to be accomplished for us in Berlin someone has to devote himself exclusively to our concerns for a while. This will never happen with Trietsch, and I am afraid it will be a long time before we achieve anything in Berlin.

I would be glad to have your views on the matter. Enclosed is a copy of the announcement that has gone to *Die Welt*.[5]

With kind regards,

Yours ever,

227. **To Abraham Kasteliansky, Heidelberg.** *Geneva, 20 January 1903*

German: Or. Copy. T.W.: W.A.

20. 1. 03.

Dear friend Kasteliansky,

In immediate reply to your letter[1] we are sending you, by this same post, the 25 questionnaires you have requested. Would you kindly let us know how the survey is coming along in your area.

Regards,

Your

of the month, as Adolf Schwartz (Rector of the Jewish Institute for Religious Studies in Vienna) and Leon Kellner (a Herzl intimate) refused to participate. 'And so it looks as if they are agitating against us', Buber wrote. 'Who? I do not know as yet.' He would be writing to Herzl, from whom he expected to learn the position. In the meantime he had asked a few younger people to join together for consultation purposes—these would not be members of the committee, but would probably participate in its activities.

[4] Trietsch promised to try and organise a committee for the University in Berlin (see Trietsch to W., 4 Jan. 1903, W.A.).

[5] See n. 2 to No. 224.

227. [1] Not found.

228. To Martin Buber, Vienna. *Geneva, 21 January 1903*

German: Or. Copy. T.W.: W.A.

Geneva, 21. 1. 03.

Mr. Martin Buber,
Vienna.

Dear Martin,

Your latest[1] letter has caused me much distress. I don't know what to think. It doesn't seem possible that the Actions Committee would in some way do our cause any injury. One can expect an attitude of indifference, but never hostility. At all events, your information on this point is so scanty that I cannot form a clear picture of the situation.

A thousand reasons compel me to insist yet again with all my strength that the committee be formed. Should such a group not come into existence this very month we shall have damaged our endeavour substantially, and be condemned anew to conducting small-scale activities only, with our contacts confined to our closest friends. There would be no point whatsoever in approaching professors, etc. Our letters would never get replies from such people. But things would be different if a committee signed this circular.[2] As yet nothing has happened in Berlin either. In the event of no committees being formed I shall not go to Russia, and this too will weaken us because we are so short of money. So you see, dear Martin, the work must go forward now with full energy. I don't know whether you quite realise what the situation is. Failure to form a committee would be a grievous blow to me.

As regards your trip, the situation is as follows: the societies in Berne, Geneva, Basle, Zurich, all agree to your coming to address them. But their contribution towards the expenses may reach 120 francs at the maximum. The societies are very poor indeed. It is immaterial when you come; this depends on you alone. So let me know at once whether you are set on making the trip and when. The moment I have exact details from you, I shall attend to the rest.

Kind regards,

As ever yours,

228. [1] See n. 3 to No. 226.
[2] See n. 9 to No. 13.

229. To the Editorial Department, *Voskhod*, St. Petersburg. *Geneva, 21 January 1903*

German: Or. Copy. T.W.: W.A.

21. 1. 03.

The Editorial Department,
Voskhod,
St. Petersburg.

We should be greatly obliged if you would print the enclosed announcement from our Bureau in your worthy newspaper.[1]
Kindly publish it in Russian if you consider this necessary.
Thanking you in anticipation, I have the honour to remain,

Most respectfully,

230. To Charles (Yeheskel) Wortsman, Basle. *Geneva, 21 January 1903*

German: Or. Copy. T.W.: W.A.

Geneva, 4 rue Lombard, 21. 1. 03.

Mr. Ch. Wortsman,
Basle.

Dear Friend,

Many thanks indeed for your conscientious and prompt attention to the survey. Forgive me for only replying[1] today to you. I have been out of town for two days. We have taken note of all your information and shall be taking it into account when compiling the statistics.

229. [1] The announcement appeared in *Voskhod* ('Sunrise') of 16 (29) Jan. 1903. It stated that the Jewish University Bureau in Geneva invited plans and proposals for the establishment of a University, and that any funds raised for this purpose should be sent to the Jewish Colonial Trust. The brochure *Eine Jüdische Hochschule* was obtainable from the *Jüdischer Verlag* in Berlin. The notice also referred to the student survey being conducted by the Bureau in Western Europe. The notice was also sent to the weekly *Budushchnost'* ('The Future') but was not published. (Copy of the letter to *Budushchnost'* of 21 Jan. 1903 in W.A.) However, a Munich report on Bureau activities was published in *Budushchnost'* of 31 Jan. (13 Feb.) 1903 (see n. 2 to No. 281).

230. [1] Wortsman to W., 15 Jan. 1903, W.A. Wortsman reported that most of the questionnaires he had distributed were already completed and returned to him, and he described the opportunities for admission of foreign students at the University of Basle. Wortsman asked W. to help him obtain a position as a chemist at the oil refineries in Baku or at the Brodsky brothers' sugar refinery in Kiev.

As to your personal enquiry, I shall be happy to do everything in in my power. You may depend on that.

I do not wish to write to the gentlemen about Buber, it would be better for you to speak to them when the moment is appropriate.[2]

Kind regards,

Yours,

231. To Berthold Monash, Mulhouse. *Geneva, 21 January 1903*

German: Or. Copy. T.W.: W.A.

21. 1. 03.

Mr. Berthold Monash,
Mulhouse, Alsace.

Dear Monash,

Warmest thanks for your detailed letter.[1] It is a pity that you have discovered no Russian Jews in Mulhouse. So there is one school, then, without this element.

I am not yet able to give a definite reply to the proposal of Dr. Elias. My holiday plans are not yet made. I still have a great deal to get through and only by February will everything be cleared up. Moreover, I don't know whether I am the right speaker for this kind of Jew. These people have heard Nordau and are going to hear Marmorek[2]—they are therefore used to oceans of rhetoric. The money-bags will not understand my way of talking Zionism at all. I would find it extremely difficult to adjust to the environment. And as for describing the situation in Russia to them, they have no

---

[2] Replying to W.'s letter of 5 Jan. 1903 (No. 163), Wortsman advised him to contact Joel Weil, president of the Basle Zionist Society, and the Zionist Federation in Switzerland in connection with finance for Buber's propaganda tour in Switzerland (see Wortsman to W., 7 Jan. 1903, W.A.).

231. [1] Monash to W., 17 Jan. 1903, W.A. Monash's point about there being no Russian Jewish students in Mulhouse related to the survey. He proposed, on behalf of the physician Dr. Alfred Elias, that W. give a lecture in Mulhouse on Zionism, adding that it would be advisable for him to begin by describing conditions in Russia and not to deviate from the socio-political theme 'because the people here have a wide understanding of financial matters'. Monash wrote that in his opinion there would be no point in discussing the University project before a large audience in Mulhouse as the people did not set great store on academic studies and intellectual aspirations. On the other hand a lecture to an intimate group of the Jewish intelligentsia might, perhaps, be useful.

[2] Monash wrote that Alexander Marmorek would be lecturing in Mulhouse.

appreciation for the positive aspects of our life, while the negative strikes them as a lament uttered for the extraction of a sigh, and perhaps a penny.

You will see that I visualise the physiology of these Jews to be quite otherwise than how you describe it.

The case of Dr. Bienstock still does not seem fully clear to me.[3] Is this gentleman definitely in search of an assistant now, or merely contemplating having one? What are the conditions? The man I have in mind seems to me to be very suitable. But he will only agree to a firm arrangement. Lilien has not yet sent anything.[4]

Kind regards,

Yours,

232. To Michael Kroll, Moscow. *Geneva, 21 January 1903*

German: Or. Copy. T.W.: W.A.

21. 1. 03.

Dr. M. B. Kroll,
Moscow.

Dear Friend,

Once again a long period has passed without any news from you. My journey is only a month and a half away[1] and I shall obviously have to depend on your reports for my preparations. Has anything been done for the Bureau in the meantime? Please let me know about this without fail.

The meeting of the Vienna committee has been postponed, apparently on account of opposition within official Zionist circles.[2] It will take place on the 25th of this month.

Hoping to hear from you, if possible immediately.

Yours,

[3] Dr. Berthold Bienstock of Mulhouse had asked W., through Monash, to write to him about the physician recommended by W. as his assistant (Isidore Eliashev—see No. 239).

[4] Monash wanted to know whether W. had received his photograph from Lilien and he asked that it be sent to him.

232. [1] His visit to Russia.
[2] See p. 3 to No. 226.

233. To A. Bass, Liège. *Geneva, 22 January 1903*

German: Or. Copy. T.W.: W.A.

22. 1. 03.

Mr. A. Bass,
Liège.

Dear Sir,

In reply to your kind letter of the 20th,[1] may we respectfully inform you that we suggested the appointment[2] of census committees only because we thought we would then be able to carry out the task more easily. But if you feel you can do better without a committee, by all means proceed alone. To us all that matters is that we quickly receive *many* replies. Whether you can achieve this result by yourself or in co-operation with others, we leave entirely to your own judgment; and we have every confidence that you will devote the utmost energy to this good cause.

Our heartfelt thanks for your efforts relating to Brussels.[3] We have already despatched questionnaires there, at the request of Miss Galante.[4]

We are enclosing herewith our announcement for the Jewish Press,[5] from which you may gauge the current position of the survey.

Respectfully, and with kind regards,

234. To Berthold Feiwel, Zurich. *Geneva, 22 January 1903*

German: Or. Copy. T.W.: W.A.

Geneva, 22. 1. 03.

Dear Berthold,

Many thanks for writing so warmly,[1] but I shall not reply at length just now because I have a good suggestion: I have to be in Berne on Saturday night[2] on Party business.[3] By a happy coincidence

233. [1] Not found.   [2] See n. 3 to No. 95.
   [3] Cf. No. 206.   [4] See No. 218.
   [5] It is not clear whether the reference is to the notice sent to Herzl for publication in *Die Welt* (see n. 2 to No. 224) or to the one for *Voskhod* and *Budushchnost'* (see n. 1 to No. 229).

234. [1] Feiwel to W., 21 Jan. 1903, W.A. Feiwel wrote, *inter alia*, of Buber's difficulties in his attempts to organize a committee for the University in Vienna (see n. 3 to No. 226): 'It is possible that the Actions Committee is acting against the University, not directly, but through certain individuals.' Feiwel advised that he would not be able to go to Vienna before the end of February.
   [2] 24 Jan. 1903.
   [3] The nature of the 'Party business' is not known. It may be that W. was to give a lecture in Berne (cf. n. 5 to No. 272).

we have no laboratory work on Saturday afternoon. I shall in that case be in Berne by two o'clock and I beg you also to be there at the same time. We shall have the entire afternoon at our disposal to thrash out a host of matters. This is most essential. It is, I think, superfluous to repeat this request, we shall use the opportunity to discuss serious business. Do, please, do this without fail, Toldy.[4] I would have come to you in Zurich, but I must be in Lausanne at noon on Sunday,[5] so I shall already be leaving Berne early on Sunday morning.

With my kind regards,

Your

235. To Joseph Pokrassa, Kharkov. *Geneva, 24 January 1903*

German: Or. Copy. T.W.: W.A.

24. 1. 0[3].

Mr. J. Pokrassa,
Kharkov.

Dear Friend,

Many, many thanks for your kind and comprehensive letter[1] received today, and to which, as [you] see, I am replying immediately.[2] Your malice and vindictiveness are partly, but not completely, justified. It never [occurred to me] that such tremendous disparity between word and deed could be possible in Kharkov. I usually see people in Kharkov for a few days only, and always in

---

[4] The meeting did not take place until 1 Feb. because Feiwel was travelling at the time to Frankfurt and Mannheim (see Feiwel to W. 22 Jan. 1903, W.A.).

[5] Shriro was then in Lausanne—cf. No. 246.

235. [1] Pokrassa to W., 6/19 Jan. 1903, W.A. Pokrassa notified W. that the committee for the University in Kharkov had, as was to be expected, done nothing. 'Surely you remember that all our friends, and I myself, were utterly opposed to organizing a committee of heavy-weights such as the imposing group which you brought together and formed into a committee?' (Concerning its composition, see Vol. I, n. 3 to No. 319.) It had done nothing regarding the Russian translation of *Eine Jüdische Hochschule* (see n. 11 to No. 7) until he, Pokrassa, discovered it untouched at Nemirovsky's and got Aleinikov to prepare it for the Censor. Pokrassa asked W. for news regarding the project, adding that much could be achieved in Kharkov if the work were undertaken by reliable people, and he promised his active support.

[2] Many words near the margins of the original copy are incomplete or missing, similarly in No. 236. Generally, deciphering the correct meaning presented little difficulty, except where indicated by brackets.

a dedicated spirit, so I had reached a false conclusion when I assumed that they were capable of sustained enthusiasm for anything more than a single hour. I had the best of intentions. Had I known the position earlier—believe me—I would not have written a line or wasted a moment. You do not really [know] me if you believe that I would allow myself to become disappointed by such things. If you were to see the letters I send in all directions from here you would know my opinion exactly about working within the Jewish fold. I realise that we are alone, just a small band of workers [bearing] a gigantic task on our shoulders, waging a desperate struggle lest we get crushed by the weight of the burden. A long time will still have to elapse before better, stronger creative forces rise in Judaism. Until then we are the ones who are called upon to keep watch. Whether we do so well or badly is for the future to judge.

Therefore I do not allow myself to be disappointed by trifles such as these, but keep right on the road. And now to business!

You ask for a report on our activities and objectives. Enclosed with this letter is an attempt to do so, in a condensed version.[3] I think you will get all you need from this.

Please, dear friend, forget any feelings of revenge and keep your eyes fixed on our good cause. Remember, whatever support comes from a friend will now be more than doubly appreciated. We are now at the beginning of a difficult but glorious endeavour. I persist in my unshakeable conviction that our aspiration will match our ability[4] provided all creative forces work harmoniously together. Do all [you] can—even more, shake the people out of their slumber, heap scorn on them, tell them the truth, the whole truth, and they will [---- ---- ----]. Regarding the brochure, I strongly urge you to bring it out soon. It has lain long enough in Mr. Nemirovsky's wastepaper basket, it has completed its *Gilgel*[5] and may now see the light of day. If you think it useful you may get in touch with Mr. I. Rothstein, 65, Pushkinskaya, Rostov-on-Don.[6] He is fully informed.

Again, many thanks and kind regards to you and yours and all 'our friends'.

Ever yours,

[3] See the interim report of the Bureau of the Jewish University, end Jan. 1903, W.A. No. 30/0, 25.

[4] Thus in orig.

[5] From the Hebr.: *Gilgel nefesh*, 'transfiguration of the soul'.

[6] Cf. n. 1 to No. 237.

236. To Michael Aleinikov, Kharkov. *Geneva, 24 January 1903*

German: Or. Copy. T.W.: W.A.

24. 1. 03.

Mr. M. Aleinikov,
Kharkov.

Dear Friend,

Your postcard came today,[1] but there also arrived with it a letter from Pokrassa,[2] and from this I learned what I had long suspected: so far not one finger has been lifted on behalf of our cause in Kharkov. I am not putting the blame upon any one reason or any specific person. But I have been enriched by one more experience. However, there is one thing I do not understand. How did the Russian version of the brochure fade so completely into the limbo of the forgotten, although we unwearyingly reminded you of it five or six [times]?[3] You have still not given me a clear answer about the fate of the brochure, but I have patiently accommodated myself to everything. It was always my belief that the students among our co-workers would be precisely the ones to stimulate work among the old, the stale, the serene, the overfed, the people who have no doubts about anything but who rest at ease on their cheap Zionist laurels. You may stand out as torch-bearers in other movements, but you [remain] inert when Judaism takes its turn. I [----] am becoming reproachful, even bitter, and feel it best to close. If you wish to, you can ascertain the [----] of our cause from the letter to Pokrassa.[4]

With best wishes and kind regards,

Your

237. To Isaac Rothstein, Rostov. *Geneva, 24 January 1903*

German: Or. Copy. T.W.: W.A.

24. 1. 03.

Mr. I. Rothstein,
Rostov-on-Don.

My good friend,

I regret I am unable to take up every point made in your kind

---

236. [1] Aleinikov to W., 7/20 Jan. 1903, W.A. Aleinikov excused himself for not writing and promised that within a few days steps would be taken on behalf of the University and the Russian translation of the brochure, after which he would be writing at greater length.   [2] See n. 1 to No. 235.

[3] Only two previous letters to Aleinikov containing references to the Russian translation of the brochure have been found (see Nos. 28, 100).   [4] See No. 235.

letter.[1] Let me assure you that we are striving here to do everything to complete the preliminary work as quickly and as thoroughly as possible. You know perfectly well that many things fail to move as fast as one would have thought.

I am not of your view, either, about immediate approaches to the mighty ones. Should we encounter a rebuff at this juncture, we shall in consequence block our path for the future. Only after the committees are certain to be formed and the groundwork is done shall we have something concrete in our hands, and I am convinced we shall then achieve much more.

I believe it to be tactically right that we confine ourselves at present to our own circle of close friends and address ourselves to a limited audience. Let me assure you, I too would like to see our great enterprise develop. But I am deliberately restraining myself, for we must not act in haste.

Naturally, we welcome your idea to give prompt support to our Bureau. I don't wish to labour the point, I know you will do all you can.

I would advise you to get in touch with our friend J. Pokrassa, at the office of Hoffman and Deuel[2] in Kharkov, regarding the brochure and other University matters. Funds earmarked for the University are sent to us promptly by the Bank.[3]

Most sincere regards to you and yours.

Yours,

238. To Regina Schimmer, Berlin. *Geneva, 24 January 1903*

German: Or. Copy. T.W.: W.A.

24. 1. 03.

Dear Miss Schimmer,

Forgive me this small imposition. But I know that Mr. Trietsch

---

237. [1] Rothstein to W., 3/16 Jan. 1903 (in the orig. 1902 appears in error), W.A. Rothstein disagreed with W. about the Zionist situation in the United States and about the possibilities for Zionist activity in Russia (see No. 161). He also dealt with the weakness of the Democratic Fraction and with the shortage of good people in the Zionist camp. Rothstein proposed immediate contact with Jewish men of wealth and the I.C.A. so as to solicit their support for the University, because without their assistance the institution would not be established. He stressed his own readiness to work for the undertaking in Rostov and to handle the publication of the Russian translation of *Eine Jüdische Hochschule.*

[2] Cf. n. 1 to No. 235.

[3] I.e.' money raised in Baku and Rostov and deposited with the Jewish Colonial Trust.

is not in Berlin at the moment[1] and so I am turning to you.[2] Be so good as to send 200 questionnaires with an equal number of Russian translations, to Ch. Ozhinsky, at No. 2, Blüthenstrasse, Munich.[3]

Thanking you in anticipation, and with kindest regards,

239. To Berthold Bienstock, Mulhouse. *Geneva,* *28 January 1903*

German: Or. Copy. T.W.: W.A.

Geneva, 4 rue Lombard, 28. 1. 0[3].

Dear Dr. [Bienstock],

Forgive me for replying only today to your kind letter of the 24th. I was unwell for a few days. I have been in touch with Dr. Eliashev, who is the gentleman I would like to recommend to you.[1] He should be replying definitely within the next few days, when I shall let you have his answer.

I consider the gentleman to be most suitable in respect of character, social attributes, etc. I am not in a position to judge his medical knowledge. He studied in Berlin and took his examination there.

Most respectfully, and with Zion's greetings,

Yours faithfully,

240. To Berthold Feiwel, Zurich. *Geneva, 28 January* *1903*

German: Or. Copy. T.W.: W.A.

Geneva, 28. 1. 03.

Dear Berthold,

I presume you have returned from your journey[1] and that you will soon let us hear from you. There is nothing new here. Our work has come to a standstill again. This could have been foreseen, and I emphasised all along that without a committee we could go no further. Unfortunately I can accomplish nothing in this respect and I really do not know how to extricate myself from the situation now.

There has been another postponement in Vienna.[2] Buber does not

---

238. [1] Trietsch was in Vienna at that time.

[2] Schimmer was the secretary to the *Jüdischer Verlag* in Berlin.

[3] They were asked for by Ozhinsky in his letter to W. of 21 Jan. 1903 (W.A.).

239. [1] See n. 3 to No. 231. The letter from Bienstock has not been found.

240. [1] Feiwel had been in Frankfurt and Mannheim (see his letter of 22 Jan. 1903, W.A.).

[2] See Buber to W., 23–24 Jan. 1903, W.A. Buber said he would endeavour to organize the Vienna committee for the Jewish University despite the refusal of Schwartz and Kellner to join it (see n. 3 to No. 226). He intended to call 40 academics

appear to be in a very optimistic mood. If nothing happens on the
1st, the game will be half-lost for a considerable time to come. In
my opinion it is pointless creating fresh links from here. Matters
have reached a point where a more authoritative body must assume
the leadership, but of course without our withdrawal.

I have written to Trietsch a number of times,[3] but personally I
do not consider his work in Berlin to be of great value for the
University. He can give only his spare time, which he never has, to
do anything, and obviously little can come out of that. Meanwhile
worries accumulate, responsibilities constantly expand, and I simply
do not know what can be undertaken now.

I have approached a few comrades in Russia, like Kohan-Bernstein,
Bruck, etc.[4] No one has reacted. So the conclusion is once more
inescapable that one is absolutely alone; if at least this little group
could be held together—but it too is splintered into a thousand
fragments.

I am sending you Buber's letter[2] together with a letter from Dr.
Bienstock concerning Eliashev.[5] Please tell Eliashev to write to me
at once. He can also write to Bienstock direct.

The questionnaires are coming in slowly. From some places, such
as Berne, Darmstadt, Munich, we have news that the survey is going
well, with a fair quantity of forms completed and already collected.
At all events I have already circularised a request to our key people
to expedite the survey.[6]

A very clear answer from Kharkov at last, to the effect that
nothing has so far been done there.[7] Some hope still exists that the
gentlemen may yet convert their grandiloquence into actions, but
I really have no confidence in high-sounding rhetoric any more.

Glikin is now in Zurich, so please write to me as to how you wish
to arrange the Fraction's work with him.[8] I have some plans, but
I am hardly in the mood to go into them in detail at this moment.

Kindest regards, from your

P.S. What has Farbstein done so far about the Schauer business?[9]

to a meeting on 1 Feb. in order to select a committee. The invitation would be signed
by Buber, Friedrich Pineles, and Adolf Gelber. 'This, in my opinion, is the only way
still open that promises success', Buber wrote.

[3] See Nos. 175, 207.   [4] See Nos. 51, 87, 126.

[5] The letter of 24 Jan. 1903 which has not been found—see No. 239 ; n. 3 to No. 231.

[6] A circular of 28 Jan. 1903, W.A. It requested acceleration of the student survey
so that a beginning might be made to process the data by the middle of February
in readiness for publication in early summer.

[7] See n. 1 to No. 235.

[8] Glikin began employment with the University Bureau in Zurich, and it was decided
that he was to handle Democratic Fraction matters as well.

[9] See n. 1 to No. 176.

241. To Joseph Dubosarsky, Berlin. *Geneva, 30 January 1903*

German: Or. Copy. T.W.: W.A.

30. 1. 03.

Dear Dubosarsky,

Glikin writes that you have taken over the supervision of the survey in Berlin.[1] Would you please let us know at once what the position is. Was a special committee formed ? Are the questionnaires distributed yet ? Have some already been completed ?

We would appreciate your expediting the matter, because we wish to have the survey accomplished by mid-February without fail.

In anticipation of your immediate, detailed report,

We are, with regards,

Yours,

242. To Berthold Feiwel, Zurich. *Geneva, 30 January 1903*

German: Or. Copy. T.W.: W.A.

Geneva, 30. 1. 03.

Dear Berthold,

A postcard has just arrived from Buber[1] with the news that Gelber[2] and Pineles have refused to sign the invitation, meaning that nothing is going to happen on Saturday. Buber nevertheless expects to achieve something by the 8th. I don't really know now what to do about the visit to England. If such a journey is decided upon, a letter will have to go to Gordon[3] within a matter of days. I cannot possibly go to Russia without being able to refer to a committee. It has therefore become essential for me to organise something, at least here in Switzerland. I consider it most desirable for us to meet for a talk, in Berne or elsewhere. For my part this can be arranged for

241. [1] Dubosarsky took the survey over from Glikin when the latter went to Zurich to work for the University Bureau. The letter from Glikin in which he notifies W. about this has not been found.

242. [1] Buber to W., 28 Jan. 1903 (pmk.), W.A. It was the invitation to the meeting projected for 1 Feb. to form a University committee (see n. 2 to No. 240). Buber wrote that he was seeking alternative signatories and had postponed the meeting to 8 Feb.

[2] Adolf Aaron Gelber (1856–1923), publicist, writer, and Shakespearean scholar, and on editorial staff of *Neues Wiener Tageblatt*.

[3] William Evans-Gordon—cf. Nos. 22, 66.

this coming Sunday,[4] so let me have your answer by telegram. I am in any case writing today to Trietsch;[5] perhaps he can concentrate on this task and achieve something in Berlin. I could then leave at the end of February and do a number of things for our project, as well as attend to other matters.[6]

Regarding the other points raised in your letter, I shall report separately.[7] As soon as a more substantial number of questionnaires has been accumulated, I shall send them on to you.[8]

Kindest regards,

Your

243. To Davis Trietsch, Berlin. *Geneva, 30 January 1903*

German: Or. Copy. T.W.: W.A.

Geneva, 4 rue Lombard, 30. 1. 03.

Mr. D. Trietsch,
Berlin.

Dear Friend,

I received news from Buber today that the University meeting arranged in Vienna for this Saturday and so eagerly awaited will not be taking place.[1] This is now the second time that the people on whom Buber had relied have at the last moment left him in the lurch.[2] It is already February and the formation of the committee is receding even further into the distance. As I have already explained in my letter to Vienna,[3] the creation of committees is an absolute pre-requisite without which my trip will not be possible. You will understand that I cannot undertake a tedious, difficult journey to Russian cities, where I would be exposed to all kinds of unpleasantness on account of legal discrimination,[4] if I cannot refer to any committee. Making the journey now is going to be much more difficult for me than during the summer holidays. Therefore, unless I have an assurance that it will be useful, I dare not embark upon it. The same holds true for England.

---

[4] 1 Feb. 1903. [5] See No. 243. [6] Cf. n. 4 to No. 243.

[7] The letter from Feiwel and an additional reply from W. have not been found.

[8] Feiwel had undertaken to process the results of the student survey—see n. 3 to No. 7.

243. [1] See n. 1 to No. 242. [2] See n. 3 to No. 226.

[3] Apparently the letter to Buber of 21 Jan. 1903 (see No. 228), written when Trietsch was in Vienna (see Buber to W. 23 Jan. 1903, W.A.).

[4] In Russia public meetings were forbidden, and Zionist gatherings took place in the synagogues. See also Vol. I, n. 1 to No. 119–20 concerning W.'s arrest while making a Zionist speech in Nikolayev, Aug. 1901, and the letter to V.K. of 29 March 1903 (No. 299 below): 'I had some unpleasantness with the police in Lodz.'

If I am to travel, I must leave not later than the end of February, so that I have at least a month at my disposal. Is it possible to do something in Berlin within the time still left ? I know you are going through a trying period, but you must be well aware that my journey would be useful in other respects[5] as well. I shall try to work over there for a newspaper, etc.

See if you can't get a good group together in Berlin, Trietsch. I want to draw your attention to the stagnation which has set in here, because all our planning was so organised that we ought by now to be coming before the public with a committee. Furthermore, all our correspondents have been prepared for a public campaign, conducted in the name of a University committee, by this Easter. Therefore I cannot show my face to these people if the assurance I gave them remains unfulfilled. You and Buber, the only ones capable of concerning yourselves with this matter, were always of the opinion that it would not be too difficult to form the groups. Now that these serious difficulties have arisen in Vienna we must hope things will proceed more easily in Berlin. This I must stress, however: I know from experience, and I think you will agree with me, that to achieve anything one must of necessity utterly dedicate oneself for a period. I do not know how Buber worked, but it does not appear to me that he was thorough.

I think I have described the situation clearly to you, and request that you send me an immediate, unequivocal answer. If nothing now happens in Berlin either, we shall have to adopt other measures, and in any event reconcile ourselves to a very sad situation. Do remember that the people we have in mind will certainly not be available in the summer. I am sure you realise how this matter is interconnected with all the other things in which we are interested and that you will now leave nothing undone about organising, at the very least, one small committee in Berlin.

I would be extremely happy to learn of the outcome of your visit to Vienna. Probably you were unable to see Herzl.[6] He did not react to our two letters anyway.[7]

Awaiting your reply, I remain,

With kindest regards,
Your

Express Post.

[5] A reference to the *Jüdischer Verlag* of which Trietsch was director. On 26 Feb. W. promised Trietsch to work for the strengthening of the *Verlag*, 'so that it can publish (a newspaper) of its own' (see No. 122).

[6] W. asked Trietsch to discuss the University project with Herzl when in Vienna, (see No. 207), but from Buber's letter of 23 Jan. 1903 (W.A.) W. learned that Herzl was not himself in Vienna at that time.   [7] See n. 3 to No. 173; No. 224.

244. To Bernard Chapira, Paris. *Geneva, 30 January 1903*

German: Or. Copy. T.W.: W.A.

30. 1. 03.

Mr. Bernard Chapira,
Paris.

Dear Friend,

May we enquire about the survey in Paris and the provinces, and ask for more information about its progress? We are most anxious to complete the survey by the middle of next month. We are enclosing a circular which we have sent to our responsible people, and from this you will note our reasons for seeking to expedite the survey.[1]

We should also be very happy to learn about any other steps you may have taken on behalf of our cause, and with what results.

Looking forward to your kind communication, I remain,

With kindest regards,

Yours faithfully,

245. To Martin Buber, Vienna. *Geneva, 4 February 1903*

German: Or. Copy. T.W.: W.A.

Geneva, 4 rue Lombard, 4. 2. 03.

Dear Martin,

I was pleased to learn from your postcard[1] that you have succeeded in enlisting Prof. Ehrmann's interest.[2] The important thing now of course is that his interest should not remain platonic, but that he commit himself in deeds. I shall be waiting impatiently for news of what went on at the meeting on Monday.[3] On talking

---

244. [1] See n. 6 to No. 240.

245. [1] Buber to W. [31?] Jan. 1903, No. 30/2/8, 1 (W.A.). Buber reported that Prof. Salomon Ehrmann (see n. 2 below) evinced great interest in the plan for a University and that he had invited the professor to a meeting on 4 Feb. He also promised to send 'some good news' to W. before long. Buber also wrote of his inability at that time to embark on a propaganda tour in Switzerland because of lack of funds (cf. No. 228).

[2] Salomon Ehrmann (1854–1926), dermatologist and lecturer (subsequently professor) at Vienna University. He was incumbent chairman of the Vienna Jewish community.

[3] The meeting called by Buber for Sunday (not Monday), 8 Feb. 1903 to organize a committee for the University (see n. 1 to No. 242).

matters over with Berthold[4] we have come to the conclusion that my visit to Russia must not be postponed,[5] lest considerable delay in our work should again ensue. We now have every prospect of attracting additional funds for the Bureau. We have received another thousand roubles for a newspaper,[6] and this should serve to advance the University cause. I hope to find the rest of the money in Russia, and so bring our much-desired newspaper into realisation. A great deal would thereby be achieved. The news I have lately received from Moscow and Warsaw is quite favourable and points to the success of my trip.[7]

Please, Martin, do telegraph or write urgently on Monday. I am thinking of leaving by the end of this month, in order to give myself plenty of time.

Awaiting a full report from you,

Affectionately,

Your

P.S. I find it absolutely impossible to come to Vienna and do not believe my journey there could be of any value.[8] It would take me at least a week to become acquainted with the situation.

246. To Davis Trietsch, Berlin. *Geneva, 4 February 1903*

German: Or. Copy. T.W.: W.A.

Geneva, 4 rue Lombard, 4. 2. 03.

Mr. D. Trietsch,
Berlin.

Dear Friend,

We have still had no reply to our last letter.[1] I take it that you are so busy with University business that you haven't the time even to write to us.

---

[4] W. met with Feiwel on 1 Feb. 1903 (see No. 246).

[5] Earlier W. had informed Buber that he would not go to Russia unless committees were established in Vienna and Berlin (see No. 228).

[6] It was promised W. by Samuel Shriro—see n. 5 to No. 246.

[7] Kroll and Idelson wrote to W. about their plan to raise funds in Moscow for the University (see n. 1 to No. 249). Yasinovsky wrote to W. on 13/26 Jan. 1903 (W.A.) that Samuel Goldflamm was about to call together all those people in Warsaw whom W. had approached, but that he—Yasinovsky—was endeavouring to have the meeting postponed until such time as W. would visit Warsaw.

[8] In the postcard mentioned in n. 1 above Buber asked W. whether he could come to Vienna for the meeting on 8 Feb. (see n. 3 above).

246. [1] See No. 243.

Last Sunday I had a meeting with Berthold[2] and we have come to the conclusion that a visit to Russia is necessary. We also gave careful consideration to the plan for a periodical[3] and did something for this too. We travelled over to Lausanne, where Mr. Shriro lives,[4] and received a thousand roubles towards the periodical.[5] So you see, a beginning has been made. News lately received leads to the expectation that my journey will meet with success. But it stands to reason that this will occur only if the conditions as described in my previous letter[6] are fulfilled.

I wanted to let you have this news simply because I have been hoping to write you in a cheerful vein at least once. I also had a selfish motive, to stimulate you through this news to a more intensive effort.

Yours ever,

247. To Joseph Pokrassa, Kharkov. *Geneva, 4 February 1903*

German: Or. Copy. T.W.: W.A.

4. 2. 03.

Mr. J. Pokrassa,
Kharkov.   Registered.

Dear Friend,

We have not yet had a reply to our detailed letter of the 24th of last month.[1] However, we are hoping that one will soon reach us, and that this time it may be more cheerful than the letters we have hitherto received from Kharkov.

I have had letters from both Aleinikov and Brailovsky.[2] The two gentlemen are full of complaints and excuses. This of course does not help our cause very much. I share your view completely that a

---

[2] W. and Feiwel met on Sunday, 1 Feb. 1903.

[3] It is to be assumed that the ideas and proposals relating to the projected periodical as mentioned in No. 247 emerged from the discussion that W. and Feiwel had on this matter.

[4] Shriro's permanent home was in Baku, but his wife and children were then living in Lausanne.

[5] It would appear from No. 251 that the sum was promised but not paid. In the balance sheet of the University Bureau of 15 July 1903 (W.A.), however, an income item of 900 roubles from Lausanne is listed. Presumably this was the sum actually paid by Shriro.   [6] See No. 243.

247. [1] See No. 235.

[2] See Aleinikov to W., 7/20 Jan. 1903 and Brailovsky to W., 10 (23) Jan. 1903, W.A. From the two letters it would appear that until then nothing had been done in Kharkov to advance the University project.

great deal can be done in Kharkov,[3] and it is regrettable that even the students betray indifference to a cause which they should be the first to be interested in promoting.

But I do not wish to complain. There will be many more disappointments of this kind, both great and small, and I am prepared for them. We have been most occupied[4] of late with the problem of how best to launch the propaganda campaign for our enterprise. Through experience gained from our *Jüdischer Verlag* in Berlin we have been able to verify that an interest in Judaism exists in the intellectual circles of Western Europe, deeper than we had thought. Notwithstanding the limited means of the *Verlag* we have succeeded in organising a circle of people who till now kept themselves remote from Jewish affairs. The more that is done in this direction the larger will the circle become; as more new forces flow towards us we may succeed[5] in penetrating areas hitherto barred to Zionism.

To realise these aims the small group of active people whose energies are now divided will have to unite, and for this we need some stimulus to drive us forward. I am thinking of a periodical.[6]

In these times Jewish newspapers are being born every day, particularly in Russia.[7] To my knowlege they cannot by their very nature achieve the aims that we on our side pursue. The periodical I have in mind has to be directed towards the Jewish élite, towards the authentic Jewish intelligentsia of Western and Eastern Europe. Not to the masses, not to the family, but to the isolated circles that are lost to us because of their dispersal. The essential pre-condition for such a journal is absolute sincerity, avoidance of and rebellion against the commonplace, faultless make-up throughout. It must be a truly distinguished newspaper of the kind that people want to read.

We are in the happy situation of being able to bring together writers of the highest European reputation for such a paper. The *Jüdischer Verlag*, by which it would be published, already commands such status that people who would never write for other Jewish papers (*Die Welt* or whatever) could happily come to us.[8]

[3] Cf. n. 1 to No. 235.

[4] In the orig. 'beschäftigte ich mich' (I have been occupied) was amended to 'beschäftigten wir uns' (we etc. . . .). This and other corrections on the original copy were entered in W.'s handwriting.

[5] In the orig. the word 'konnte' (could) was crossed out and replaced by 'vermochte' (was capable).

[6] Cf. n. 3 to No. 246.

[7] Early in 1903 the Hebrew newspapers *Hatzofe* (Warsaw) and *Hazman* (St. Petersburg) and the Yiddish *Fraind* (St. Petersburg) began publication.

[8] The orig. 'kommen werden' (will come) had been corrected to 'kommen konnen' (could come).

If we had a paper that Jewish intellectuals would read this would provide us with a good medium for propaganda among those circles at present difficult of access.

We are considering beginning provisionally with a bi-monthly. Such an undertaking would require a sum of approximately 5,000 roubles. We must try to get this amount as soon as possible. A few days ago we managed to obtain a thousand roubles[9] for this purpose. We plan to go ahead with the formation of a Limited Company similar to Ahiasaf.[10] The shares would be priced at 100–150 roubles each.

Chief Editor, Berthold Feiwel; Editorial Committee, Buber, Dr. Ch. Weizmann, and perhaps one other person. Administration would be by the *Jüdischer Verlag* headed by Dr. Trietsch.

We are extremely interested in the creation of such a paper at the earliest possible moment. A start has been made. I am conscious that if our friends demonstrate their goodwill, they will also make practical contributions to the scheme. We do not really need[11] to emphasise the high importance of the matter.

I ask you, dear friend, to give this plan your consideration and see if something can be done for the cause in Kharkov, albeit in the form outlined above.[12]

Awaiting your early reply, I remain,

With kindest regards,

Your

248. To Ch. Ozhinsky, Munich. *Geneva, 6 February 1903*

German: Or. Copy. T.W.: W.A.

Geneva, 4 rue Lombard, 6. 2. 03.

Mr. Ch. Ozhinsky,
Munich.

Dear Friend,

I had already written briefly yesterday to Mr. Lvovitch regarding

[9] The sum promised by Shriro—see n. 5 to No. 246.

[10] This was a publishing house in Warsaw engaged in the promotion of modern Hebrew literature. Ahiasaf was managed by a committee of public figures.

[11] The orig. had 'Ich brauche nicht' corrected to 'Wir brauchen nicht'.

[12] In his reply of 1(14) Feb. 1903 (W.A.), Pokrassa reported on the University committee meeting in Kharkov of 13 Feb. 1903 (see also n. 9 to No. 294). Pokrassa was enthusiastic about the plan to publish a periodical and made suggestions for its accomplishment.

the possibility of my travelling by way of Munich.[1] I think you ought to know that my time is very limited, because I am faced with a difficult trip.[2] I must, therefore, ask you to spare me. While I would very much like to address your banquet in Munich, I would find a visit there in the middle of February impossible. May I therefore recommend that you try our friend Berthold Feiwel, of 19, Zürichbergstrasse, Zurich. I consider him better suited to speak on a literary subject, and he would indeed be glad to accept your invitation, or so I would hope. Then I could be completely at your disposal during the earliest days of March.[3]

The news of the Munich students' attitude towards the University question made me very happy.[4] Would you please let me know whether the resolution about which they wrote us at the time has already been publicised and made known in their circles ? This would be most desirable, especially now that the survey is everywhere in progress.

I would at the same time request you to let us have the questionnaires as soon as possible.

With kindest regards,

Your

249. To Abraham Idelson and Michael Kroll, Moscow.

Geneva, 6 February 1903

German: Or. Copy. T.W.: W.A.

6. 2. 03.

Mr. A. Idelson and Dr. M. B. Kroll,
Moscow.

Dear Friends,

We acknowledge with many thanks receipt of your letters[1] with

248. [1] Lvovitch had asked W. to come to Munich and deliver a propaganda speech to the Jewish student body. Ozhinsky wanted W. to speak on a literary theme at an evening gathering of the Zionist Student Society *Kadimah* (see Lvovitch's letter of 3 Feb. 1903 and Ozhinsky's of 4 Feb. 1903, W.A.). W.'s letter to Lvovitch has not been found.   [2] I.e., W.'s journey to Russia.

[3] W. intended to stop over in Munich on his way to Russia (see No. 255). It seems, however, that he did not do so—on 14 March 1903 Samuel Levinson wrote to Ozhinsky: 'Dr. W. left for Russia two days ago. If he has not yet been in Munich, he is certainly not going there'.

[4] Ozhinsky informed W. on 21 Feb. 1903 (W.A.) that at their general meeting the Russian student body in Munich decided, by a large majority, to express its sympathy for the Jewish University project. A committee was empowered to distribute the text of the resolution to all student groups as well as Jewish newspapers, and to conduct the survey locally (the resolution was published, *inter alia*, in *Hatzefirah*, 20 Jan./2 Feb. 1903).

249. [1] Kroll to W., 13 (26) Jan. 1903, Idelson to W., 15/28 Jan. 1903, W.A. Kroll the questionnaire.[2] Our only objection to the letter is that we consider the query under item 16a to be out of place.

We were very pleased with the news that a number of steps have been taken on behalf of the Bureau, although I do not share Idelson's pessimistic view that it is so hard to raise funds. I am well aware how difficult your position is to maintain and that the forces at your disposal are few. I trust, however, that through a co-operative effort something will be achieved.

The plan for a periodical is coming ever closer to realisation, as you will see from another letter sent under separate cover to you.[3]

The committee problem will be reaching a solution within the present month and during the first days of March (new style) I shall be leaving on my journey. I shall travel by way of Berlin, Warsaw.

With many kind regards.

Ever yours,

250. To Max Bienenstock, Cracow. *Geneva, 6 February 1903*

German: Or. Copy. T.W.: W.A.

6. 2. 03.

Mr. Max Bienenstock,
Cracow.

Dear Sir,

My sincere thanks for your kind letter of the 1st,[1] and for your readiness to take the survey in hand.

We are despatching our printed material to you for your information. At the same time we have arranged for 50 questionnaires to be sent to Cracow. You will be receiving these from our *Jüdischer Verlag* in Berlin.

Most respectfully,

reported on a plan to raise funds in Moscow for the University Bureau, stating as his opinion that the success of the activity would depend on establishing a committee of well-known people. He further reported that questionnaires for the student survey in Russia were being printed. Idelson reported that funds collected in Moscow would cover local expenses only; according to him no fund-raising on a scale to finance the activities of the Bureau should be attempted at that time as interfering with future efforts to raise funds for the University.

[2] Presumably the questionnaire referred to in n. 1 above. No copy of this document has been found and the nature of the item queried is not known.

[3] The letter concerning the periodical has not been found, but from No. 272 it would appear that it had been sent. It may be assumed that it was similar in content to W.'s letter to Pokrassa of 4 Feb. 1903 (No. 247).

250. [1] Not found.

251. To Berthold Feiwel, Zurich. *Geneva, 6 February 1903*

German: Or. Copy. T.W.: W.A.

Geneva, 6. 2. 03.

Dear Berthold,

Many thanks for writing so fully.[1] Of course, I had a great deal more to tell you, but somehow could not bring myself to say all I felt and so I put it off for another time.[2] We shall be seeing each other again soon, and be able to talk to our heart's content. Shriro was here yesterday. Naturally, I got him to repeat his promise, thereby making doubly sure of his pledge of a thousand roubles.[3] Incidentally, this was easy, because he is absolutely delighted with the *Almanach*.[4] Tomorrow I am going to Lausanne again to deliver a lecture there.[5] Naturally I shall also try and settle financial questions.[6] With this letter I am returning the blank form to you countersigned, and together with another form which must be used when writing to the bank and to Herzl.[7] At the appropriate moment you could also ask Herzl where he stands regarding the University.[8]

I posted off some letters concerning the periodical[9] to certain people today, and expect successful results.

Otherwise, nothing new today. I have received addresses from Lemberg and Cracow for the survey.[10] I am sending you the copies in my possession.

Warmest regards,

As ever yours,

251. [1] Not found.

[2] W. and Feiwel had met in Berne on 1 Feb. 1903 (see No. 246).

[3] Promised by Shriro for the projected periodical—see No. 246.

[4] *Jüdischer Almanach* (see Vol. I, n. 14 to No. 238).

[5] Reporting from Lausanne, *Hamelitz* of 16/29 April 1903 stated: 'There is neither a Zionist institution nor society here . . . debates with anti-Zionists were held a few weeks ago . . . this was the first visit of Messrs Weizmann, Aberson, etc. But they did not succeed in forming a Zionist society here.'

[6] Probably W. intended taking up the financial problems of the University Bureau with Shriro, as it had received only part of the sum pledged to W. in Baku (see n. 5 to No. 40).

[7] Feiwel wrote to Herzl over W.'s signature on 7 Feb. 1903, adding his own (C.Z.A. 21/342). He asked Herzl to instruct the Jewish Colonial Trust to transmit to the University Bureau 600 francs from its account to cover the costs of the survey.

[8] Cf. No. 207; n. 3 to No. 226. The subject is not referred to in Feiwel's letter to Herzl (see n. 7 above).

[9] W. wrote on this subject to Idelson and Kroll (see n. 3 to No. 249). See also the letter to Pokrassa of 4 Feb. 1903 (No. 247).

[10] They were the addresses of Krisnapoller and Bienenstock—see Nos. 250, 252.

252. To I. Krisnapoller, Lemberg. *Geneva, 6 February 1903*

German: Or. Copy. T.W.: W.A.

6. 2. 03.

Mr. I. Krisnapoller,[1]
Lemberg.

Dear Sir,

Sincere thanks for your kind letter of the 3rd,[2] and your generous offer to take the survey in hand.

We are posting our printed material to your address for your background information. At the same time we have arranged for the despatch of 50 questionnaires to Lemberg. You will be receiving these from our *Jüdischer Verlag* in Berlin.

Most respectfully,

253. To Leonid Bielsky, Stuttgart. *Geneva, 9 February 1903*

German: Or. Copy. T.W.: W.A.

9. 2. 03.

Dear Mr. Bielsky,

Thank you very much for the questionnaires, duly received.

Most respectfully,

254. To Paul Golde, Wloclawek. *Geneva, 9 February 1903*

German: Or. Copy. T.W.: W.A.

9. 2. 03.

Mr. Paul Golde,
Wloclawek.

Dear Sir,

In reply to your kind letter of the 5th,[1] we would respectfully

252. [1] First name not known.
 [2] Not found.

254. [1] Golde to the University Bureau, 5 Feb. 1903, W.A. He acknowledged receipt of W.'s letter of January (not found) and said he supported the University project and was prepared to help in its achievement.

inform you that failure so far to receive our brochure may well be due to the Post Office or the Censor. We are sending our brochure to your address again, by registered mail, and trust that this time it will arrive.

Enclosed is an extremely condensed report[2] on the state of our affairs which you may wish to study. From our side we cannot, of course, determine exactly the nature of the work, or its planning, that you may wish to undertake for the project. We feel this is best left to your own initiative.

May we bring to your notice, however, that we are making preparations for a propaganda tour in Warsaw and the Polish provinces. It would therefore be most desirable to begin at once by establishing connections with individuals or groups, and so prepare the ground for the propaganda effort, particularly among intellectual circles. This seems to me to indicate an important responsibility which our friends in Poland are best suited to discharge.

In conclusion, we are happy to express our appreciation for your co-operation, and look forward to your kind reply at your earliest.[3]

Most respectfully,

255. To Davis Trietsch, Berlin. *Geneva, 9 February 1903*

German: Or. Copy. T.W.: W.A.

Geneva, 4 rue Lombard, 9. 2. 03.

Mr. D. Trietsch,
Berlin.

Dear Friend,

I very much appreciate your writing.[1] It would be excellent if you could bring together the gentlemen of whom you speak into a single organisation. I think you have enough names. You may omit Dr. Simonsohn,[2] for I do not believe he looks upon our cause with sympathy.

[2] See interim report of the Bureau of the Jewish University, end Jan. 1903, W.A. No. 30/0, 25.   [3] No reply from Golde has been found.

255. [1] Trietsch to W., 5 Feb. 1903, W.A. Trietsch wrote that he intended inviting the following for consultation on the establishment of a Berlin committee for the Jewish University: Otto Warburg, Louis Levin, Martin Philippson, Leopold Landau, Heinrich Meyer-Cohen, Paul Arons, Louis Maretzky, Salinger, Franz Oppenheimer, Alfred Nossig, Walter Munk, Emil Simonsohn, and Michael Altschul. Trietsch also asked why Pasmanik had not replied on the subject of Trietsch's intended propaganda tour in Switzerland (see n. 1 to No. 41).

[2] Emil Simonsohn (1861–1938), Berlin Zionist and member of the Colonization Committee of the Zionist Congress. Simonsohn's name appeared with a query mark in the list given in n. 1 above.

Meanwhile you should have received my second letter.[3] I am now trying desperately to find money for the periodical. Presumably we shall have the thousand roubles by the end of March.[4] I shall have obtained the balance in Russia by then, so it may be safely assumed that a larger sum of money will be transferred to the *Verlag* in April, thereby assuring publication of the paper. Most likely I shall leave here not later than March 5th, travelling by way of Munich to Berlin and Warsaw, and probably returning via Vienna.

I have just spoken to Pasmanik; he took your address and intends writing to you this very day. I believe he will do nothing about your coming here. It would be better, therefore, to communicate with Feiwel, Farbstein and Khissin, at 24, Freistrasse, Berne. I cannot do any more, unfortunately, because I shall not be here at the beginning of March.

In anticipation of an early reply with lots of news,

I remain,

Yours,

P.S. Would you kindly have 10 questionnaires, with Russian translations, despatched to Zurich. I have none left here.

256. To Saul Lurie, Darmstadt. *Geneva, 9 February 1903*

German: Or. Copy. T.W.: W.A.

Geneva, 9. 2. 03.

Dear Saul,

I really must implore your forgiveness for my silence.[1] But I have had many worrying days of late and could not, despite the best of intentions, utter a friendly word. My morale has now improved but I do not feel completely well. And in addition little things keep coming up, like lectures, etc., to wear me out.

Circumstances are my excuse, dear friend, and I trust you will not have hard feelings towards me.

Nothing of importance has occurred in the University project. We have concentrated all our activities on forming committees, and so long as this objective is not happily achieved we can make no

[3] Trietsch replied to W.'s letter of 30 Jan. 1903 (No. 243) on 5 Feb., but in the meantime W. had written him another letter (see No. 264).

[4] The sum promised by Shriro—see n. 5 to No. 246.

256. [1] Lurie to W., 30 Jan. 1903 (W.A.). The letter reveals that W. had asked him by telegram (not found) for the loan of some money and Lurie had sent it.

progress. We have good reason to hope, however, that groups will be formed in Berlin and Vienna during the current month, and immediately after I shall be off on my journey to Russia.

Where will you be staying during the holidays? How is the work going?[2] Do you see Aaron often?[3]

Questionnaires are coming in every day, though in dribs and drabs. We have already begun to sort out the data in certain cities. Probably we shall soon be receiving the forms from you too.

Kindest regards,

Yours ever,

257. To S. Markov, Freiberg. *Geneva, 9 February 1903*
German: Or. Copy. T.W.: W.A.

9. 2. 03.

Dear Mr. Markov,

Thank you very much for sending us the questionnaires.[1] Would you kindly let us have the remainder as soon as possible.

Most respectfully,

258. To Felix Pinkus, Berne. *Geneva, 9 February 1903*
German: Or. Copy. T.W.: W.A.

Geneva, 9. 2. 03.

Dear Felix,

I could not quite get to the point of writing to you until now, because all kinds of things stood in my way. I was surprised by the tone of your letter today and its over-hasty conclusions.[1] Naturally, I shall make no attempt to change your mind, for I don't think I would succeed. I should like, however, to repeat what I have already said. All of you are ready to criticise, but you refuse to face up to the

[2] Apparently referring to Lurie's chemistry studies.

[3] In his letter of 30 Jan. 1903 Lurie wrote that he had visited Aaron Eliasberg, who was recovering at Wiesbaden (cf. n. 1 to No. 211).

257. [1] Markov (first name not known) to the University Bureau, 5 Feb. 1903, W.A.

258. [1] Pinkus to W., 7 Feb. 1903, W.A. Pinkus wrote that he had withdrawn from the Democratic Fraction owing to his disagreement with its programme, and because of his conviction that the Fraction was incapable of representing democratic principles. He was prepared to co-operate in the contemplated periodical and the student survey.

fact that, right until the present, all the work of our group has been done by two, or at the most three, people. And of course they had to do the work of ten. They had simultaneously to make propaganda, organise, play their part in Congresses and conferences, contend with opponents in and out of Zion. Obviously, all this was impossible to sustain. A reaction set in because no intake of new blood was in evidence. I spent the entire summer travelling from city to city, wearing myself out in Minsk and Vienna,[2] trying with all my strength to represent our group in the manner it warranted. Yet the people with limitless free time have been contributing nothing to the organisation of our activities. A situation was created whereby we had to do all the giving while the others never demonstrated the slightest initiative.

In Russia, the Fraction is organised and continues to function.[3] And here we have a large number of individuals who are all of them good critics but poor workers. I know full well that there is fertile ground in Western Europe for the formation of a strong group. But for this we need man-power at this instant, both to convene and to conduct a conference of the Fraction. Neither Toldy nor I can undertake that. He has his hands full with a range of uncompleted tasks, while I have to leave again in three weeks on a long and difficult journey, with my regular activities all in dislocation. Who is there then to do the work? Our younger comrades have neither the required connections nor the experience. Furthermore, many of them lack the goodwill. Motzkin is calmly ensconced in Kiev and doesn't lift a finger.[4] I therefore keep asking myself how it can be possible to engage on any initiative calling for people, time and money. You have it easy, of course; you can withdraw at any moment and wash your hands of the whole business. For Berthold and me, totally committed as we are with our whole beings, it is much more difficult to find a solution to the present crisis that would be both practical and appropriate. Naturally, we shall make an attempt at it, as we agreed in Berne.[5] But in any case this no longer interests you.

As for the periodical, its realisation seems to be assured upon my return in April. I shall be in Berne in a fortnight and we shall discuss

[2] W. is referring here to his propaganda tour in Russia during the summer and autumn of 1902, his participation in the Zionist Annual Conference in Minsk (Sept. 1902), and in the Zionist Annual Conference in Vienna (Oct. 1902). See letters of that period in Vol. I.

[3] Regarding the establishment of a Democratic Fraction Centre in Russia, see n. 1 to No. 7.

[4] Kroll wrote to W. on 13 (26) Jan. 1903 (W.A.): 'After Motzkin came to life, he went back to rest again'. Cf. n. 10 to No. 110; n. 1 to No. 187.

[5] See No. 246 and n. 2 there.

it there in greater detail.[6] For the moment it is a question of money, and a good part of that has already been raised.[7] The rest will be found.

Please be discreet about this letter.

. As ever
Yours,

259. To Jeremias Schick, Karlsruhe. *Geneva, 9 February 1903*

German: Or. Copy. T.W.: W.A.

9. 2. 03.

Mr. J. Schick,
Karlsruhe.

Please allow us to state in reply to your postcard[1] that we wish you to leave nothing undone to bring the survey, which began so well in Karlsruhe, to a successful conclusion. Of course I cannot say which would be the best method. Perhaps it would be advisable for the committee to call a special meeting. This is what was done in Munich and Darmstadt[2] with very good results. The student body in Munich went so far as to adopt a favourable resolution by a vast majority and had it published in the Jewish Press. I am convinced that Karlsruhe will follow the example set by the other cities and will not become the invidious exception in our undertaking.

You can imagine with what effort and difficulty the survey was organised, quite apart from its considerable cost. It would be a great pity if this work, so desirable in itself, were to be wrecked because of minor, petty obstacles. This must not happen.

Taking all this into consideration, we repeat our request and remain convinced that our co-workers in Karlsruhe will spare no effort to see the survey through.

In comradeship,[3]

Yours truly,

[6] W. was due to give a lecture in Berne on 21 Feb.—see No. 262.
[7] Presumably the thousand roubles promised by Shriro—see n. 5 to No. 246.

259. [1] Schick to W., 6 Feb. 1903 (pmk.), W.A. Schick reported that in Karlsruhe a committee had been established to conduct the survey. The questionnaires had been distributed, but there had been difficulty in collecting them. No information on Schick has come to light other than that he was a Karlsruhe student.
[2] For the student gathering in Munich, see n. 4 to No. 248. No report of a gathering in Darmstadt has been found.
[3] Orig.: 'Mit kollegialem Grüss.'

260. To Martin Buber, Munich. *Geneva, 13 February 1903*

German: Or. Copy. T.W.: W.A.

Geneva, 4 rue Lombard, 13. 2. 03.

Mr. Martin Buber,
Munich.

Dear Martin,

I at once passed your information about the committee[1] on to Berthold,[2] so as to have his opinion also regarding the conditions which the gentlemen have made. We can accept the condition declaring the University not to be a Zionist undertaking, but not an anti-Zionist one. That it will not be a religious institution goes without saying. But we cannot agree to a change of name, in any circumstances. Incidentally, I am most curious to know what names were proposed.

As far as I can see, hardly anything can be done in Vienna in the immediate future. I do not believe much will be achieved in Munich either.[3] Meanwhile there remains only one hope: that something may result in Berlin before my departure. When will you be in Vienna again? I shall probably be leaving here on March 5th. Perhaps you can succeed in pushing something through by then.

With warm regards and best wishes for success in Munich.

Your

---

260. [1] Buber to W., 9 Feb. 1903 (pmk.), W.A. Buber reported that in addition to Prof. Ehrmann (see n. 1 to No. 245) several more people had consented to join the Vienna committee for the Jewish University. Among them were Prof. Emil Szanto and Wilhelm Stiassny, as well as Herzl. Ehrmann, Szanto, and Stiassny joined on condition that emphasis would be on the non-Zionist nature of the project and that it should be made clear that the intended University would have no special religious orientation. Ehrmann proposed a name other than 'Jewish University'. These were the reasons causing a postponement of the meeting Buber was due to convene so as to nominate a committee (see n. 1 to No. 242).

[2] The text of Buber's postcard was sent to Feiwel and Trietsch in letters of 11 Feb. 1903, and apparently signed by Levinson (original copies in W.A.). It is stated therein: 'In the opinion of W. these conditions may be acceptable (see n. 1 above), but the original name must remain.'

[3] Buber was due to lecture in Munich on 16 Feb. 1903 on 'Jewish Culture and Cultural Policy' and he undertook to speak on the University project as well (see Buber to W. 9 Feb. 1903, W.A.; Buber to Ehrenpreis 11 Feb. 1903, Ehrenpreis Papers, fol. 20, N.L.). The present letter was addressed to him 'temporarily in Munich'.

261. To Ch. Ozhinsky, Munich. *Geneva, 13 February 1903*

German: Or. Copy. T.W.: W.A.

Geneva, 4 rue Lombard, 13. 2. 03.

Mr. Ch. Ozhinsky,
Munich.

Dear Fellow-Zionist,

May I ask you kindly to hand Mr. Martin Buber the letter enclosed herewith.[1] Buber is due to speak in Munich on the 16th.[2]

I would at the same time urge you to conclude the survey immediately, if possible. I have to complete this work before my departure. I shall be in Munich from 5th–8th March.[3]

Kind regards,

Your

262. To David Jochelman, Berne. *Geneva, 13 February 1903*

German: Or. Copy. T.W.: W.A.

Geneva, 4 rue Lombard, 13. 2. 03.

Mr. Jochelman,
Berne.

Dear Friend,

Kindly let me know whether you can arrange my lecture for Saturday, the 21st.[1] May I at the same time ask you and Khissin, most sincerely, to make sure that the survey will be completed soon. Once the forms are filled in please send them on to us, as we have already begun our work.

In anticipation of your reply by return,

and with kind regards, I remain

Yours,

P.S. You were right about the telegram. I shall pay the fine.[2]

261. [1] See No. 260.
   [2] See n. 3 to No. 260.
   [3] See ns. 1, 3 to No. 248.

262. [1] W. was to lecture in Berne on a Zionist topic (see also No. 268).
   [2] Explanation unknown.

263. To Saul Lurie, Darmstadt. *Geneva, 13 February 1903*

German: Or. Copy. T.W.: W.A.

Geneva, 13. 2. 03.

Dear Saul,

I could not reply by telegram to your postcard received today,[1] as I am unable to give you a definite answer.

It is much too difficult for me to travel to Darmstadt now, and all the more so because I shall be going to Russia in three weeks. If a lecture could usefully be held in Darmstadt at that time, then I am prepared to give one. But I must have your answer within the next few days, because I have also promised to lecture in Munich.[2] I must arrange my itinerary with this in mind also,[3] so I am asking you for an early reply. I really cannot believe that it is absolutely essential to have a speech delivered in Darmstadt at this stage. At the same time, may I ask you to conclude the survey as quickly as possible, because I also wish to complete all the statistical work by the time I leave.

With kind regards,

Your

264. To the Jewish Colonial Trust, London. *Geneva, 14 February 1903*

German: Or. Copy. T.W.: W.A.

14. 2. 03.

The Jewish Colonial Trust,
London.

For the attention of Mr. D. Levontin.

We hereby acknowledge with thanks receipt of your remittance of 600 francs.[1] At the same time I confirm receipt of two shares[2] for Mr. Fainstein.[3] As I am going to Russia shortly I will deliver these to him personally.

Most respectfully and with Zion's greetings,

263. [1] Not found.
[2] See No. 248.
[3] From No. 284 it would appear that in the event W. did not go to Darmstadt.

264. [1] See n. 7 to No. 251.
[2] Eng. in orig. Presumably shares of the Jewish Colonial Trust.
[3] Probably Abraham Asher Fainstein (1870–1944), a Pinsk Zionist.

265. To Davis Trietsch, Berlin. *Geneva, 14 February 1903*

German: Or. Copy. T.W.: W.A.

Geneva, 14. 2. 03.

Mr. D. Trietsch,
Berlin.

Dear Friend,

I shall only be able to send you the money you request on Monday.[1] I would ask you, however, to let me have it back for our own use in three weeks, as our needs will become great by then.

It is a little too late for the 'notepaper', because we have already ordered some here. There is no harm done, though; we shall make some use of it. Why aren't you at all happy about the thousand roubles for the periodical?[2] You don't seem to believe it. You are wrong.

Committee, committee, and nothing but committee! Stamp your feet until the people come out from under the ground. Everything depends on this move. I keep receiving news from Russia that a great deal can be done if . . .[3]

I implore you from my heart to keep me informed of every step you take regarding the committee. It seems that Buber is going to accomplish nothing in Vienna.[4] We must therefore try all the harder to organise something in Berlin—I mean something really good.

With kind regards,

Your

P.S. Dr. Goldstein, the press-cuttings man,[5] does a very poor job. Recently (four days ago) a highly significant article appeared in

---

265. [1] In a letter of 12 Feb. 1903, W.A. Trietsch asked W. to lend the *Jüdischer Verlag* 'a few hundred marks' to enable him to make an advance to Nathan Birnbaum for work he was preparing for the *Verlag* (W. sent only 100 marks—see No. 267). Trietsch stated that he would be sending the Bureau the notepaper printed in Berlin and he reported on progress in forming a committee for the University there.

[2] W. informed Trietsch on 4 Feb. 1903 (see No. 246) about Shriro's promised financial support for the projected periodical, but in his letter of 12 Feb. Trietsch did not mention the subject.

[3] Doubtless the unfinished sentence related to the frequently expressed view that fund-raising success for the Bureau in Russia depended on the existence of a sponsoring committee composed of people of note, as, e.g., stressed in a letter from Kroll of 13 (26) Jan. 1903 (see n. 1 to No. 249). On that date Hirsch Hiller wrote to W. (W.A.) that there would be a purpose in approaching men of substance in Pinsk only after a local committee for the University had been established.

[4] Regarding the repeated postponements in forming the Vienna committee for the Jewish University see n. 3 to No. 226; n. 1 to No. 242; n. 1 to No. 260.

[5] Thus in the orig., but refers to Max Goldschmidt, who had a press-cuttings agency in Berlin.

the *Frankfurter Zeitung* on the subject of Russian and Jewish students abroad.[6] It is an article of the greatest importance to our affairs. I looked for it in vain among the cuttings that arrived yesterday. As we do not correspond directly with the firm would you please write them requesting the article, and also advise them that we never receive cuttings from Jewish newspapers. They take no notice of the Swiss Press either where the problem of Russian students is now being discussed daily.

266. To Berthold Feiwel, Zurich. *Geneva, 14 February 1903*

German: Or. Copy. T.W.: W.A.

Geneva, 14. 2. 03.

Dear Berthold,   Express Post.

Thank you for writing.[1] I still cannot make up my mind about a visit to Zurich.[2] Saturday I have to go to Berne[3] and it won't be long before 'the journey' starts.[4] As for Mr. Dimant, the matter is quite clear.[5] This gentleman applied to the Bureau which, as the questionnaire states, answers all enquiries, and requested replies to these two questions:

[6] The *Frankfurter Zeitung* article appeared on 9 Feb. 1903, and dealt, *inter alia*, with the difficult entrance requirements demanded of Russian students at Prussian Universities and with the regulations limiting the number of Jewish students at Russian universities.

266. [1] Feiwel to W., 13 Feb. 1903, W.A. (see n. 2 below).

[2] Feiwel informed W. on 9 Feb. 1903 (W.A.) that on 11 Feb. a meeting of Russian students would be taking place in Zurich to discuss the Jewish University project. Feiwel feared that those sponsoring the meeting intended to come out against the project and interfere with the student survey, and that anti-Zionist ideas might be expressed during the discussion. He requested W. to participate in the meeting, but from an additional postcard of 10 Feb. (W.A.) it appears that W. replied by telegram that he would not be able to do so. In a letter of 13 Feb. Feiwel reported that the meeting had taken place with most of the participants opposing the University project, but that he had succeeded in preventing the adoption of an unfavourable resolution. A further meeting was due to take place on 16 Feb. and Feiwel asked W. to attend so as to counter any attacks on Zionism and prevent the adoption of a resolution opposing the University project (see Feiwel to W. 13 Feb. 1903, W.A.; orig. has 13 Dec. 1902—an error). For the meeting of 16 Feb. see n. 7 to No. 271.

[3] See No. 262.   [4] W.'s journey to Russia.

[5] Dimant (first name unknown) wrote to W. on 9 Feb. 1903 (W.A.) and posed the questions mentioned later in the letter. He explained that he needed the answers for the student gathering in Zurich (see n. 2 above). W.'s reply has not been found, but its gist is repeated in the present letter. Feiwel's letter of 13 Feb. related that Dimant spoke against the University project at the meeting and argued, *inter alia*, that the University Bureau had received a sum of 40,000 roubles (see n. 7 below). Feiwel was angry that W. had replied to Dimant instead of referring him to Feiwel. Dimant had quoted from W.'s letter at the meeting and Feiwel had hesitated to contradict him lest Dimant used the letter in rebuttal.

1) Are the million francs[6] to come from one person, or from several (whether the Baku monies, etc.,[7] are included)?

2) Do we intend to raise the funds required for the project from individuals or through various organised activities,[8] etc?

You will see that these are the kind of questions I could easily answer in a couple of lines and this is what I did as follows to 1): The million has been pledged by an individual and the Baku sums are not included. To question 2) I replied broadly that we are likely to employ both methods, though as it happens we attach greater importance to the first. I do not see how the man could infer anything else from the letter. The 40,000 francs[9]—would that we had it! —is pure fiction. If he gathered anything from the letter other than what is described above, that is his fault. My letter could give absolutely no cause for misunderstanding.

Please telegraph if it is essential for me to come. I shall do so, although I am not in favour of it.

There will be money on Monday because the cheque for 600 francs has already arrived.[10]

Trietsch replied today: 'Notepaper coming on Monday, this time definitely,[11] and we should telegraph 100 marks to him (i.e. to the *Jüdischer Verlag*).[12] Doubtless you can see the connection.

The report you requested,[13] and the duplicating machine, will be sent off by Tuesday at the latest. I have not been feeling very well and could not work effectively. I conveyed your opinion about the committee to Buber. I wrote him in Munich,[14] where he is due to speak on the 16th.

[6] A possible gift of a million francs for the Jewish University had been discussed by W. and Brodsky, the Kiev industrialist, in Oct. 1902 (see Vol. I, n. 6 to No. 319). Expectation of this sum was mentioned in a University Bureau announcement distributed at the end of Dec. 1902 and in Jan. 1903 (see n. 5 to No. 124).

[7] The funds raised in Baku and Rostov in the autumn of 1902 (see Vol. I, bridge-note following No. 317. Almost 5,000 roubles had been pledged in these cities). In his letter of 9 Feb. 1903 Dimant asked: 'Does this million (see n. 6 above) include the 35,000 roubles and 3,500 roubles contributed in Rostov and in Baku?' It may be that W. did not correct these figures in his reply, thus resulting in Dimant's misconception of 40,000 roubles.   [8] Orig.: 'Veranstaltungen.'

[9] *Sic.* An error that should read roubles (see ns. 5, 7 above).

[10] See No. 264.

[11] Trietsch wrote to W. on 12 Feb. 1903 (W.A.) that he would send him 'good quality notepaper'. W. was dissatisfied with the notepaper previously supplied by Trietsch (see No. 221).

[12] In fact Trietsch asked for a loan of several hundred marks (see n. 1 to No. 265).

[13] In his postcard of 10 Feb. 1903, Feiwel asked W. to send him 'a digest of the Fraction report'. Meaning perhaps circular No. 3 of the Democratic Fraction Centre in Moscow (see n. 2 to No. 179).

[14] See No. 260. Neither this nor any other letter of Feiwel's that has been found contains his views on questions relating to the formation of the Vienna committee for the University.

I would very much like you to arrange your visit to Berne for next Saturday.[15] I have turned down invitations to Mulhouse, Darmstadt and Munich, because I want to sustain my work intensively right until my departure.[16]

All my good wishes,

Your

267. To Davis Trietsch, Berlin. *Geneva, 16 February 1903*

German: Or. Copy. T.W.: W.A.

Geneva, 16. 2. 03.

Mr. D. Trietsch,
Berlin.

Dear Friend,

I confirm my telegram sent today:[1] 'One hundred marks despatched[2] request news concerning committee.'[3] At the same time I acknowledge with thanks receipt of your memorandum,[4] and wish to emphasise at once that I am not in agreement with every point therein.

I do not believe we have to plan our undertaking so as to kill off *O[st] und W[est]*. We shall have adequate resources at our disposal

---

[15] Feiwel was about to go to Berne in connection with his studies (see his postcard of 10 Feb. 1903). Concerning W.'s plan to go to Berne on Saturday 21 Feb. 1903, see No. 262.

[16] W. hesitated to accept an invitation from Monash to speak in Mulhouse—see n. 1 to No. 231, but no direct refusal has been found. Although W. turned down lecture invitations from Munich and Darmstadt, he proposed visiting these two cities in March on his way to Russia (see Nos. 248, 263).

267. [1] The original telegram has not been found.

[2] See n. 1 to No. 265.

[3] The committee for the University that Trietsch was trying to create in Berlin.

[4] An undated memorandum (W.A., No. 30/0, 13) by Trietsch on the launching of a monthly magazine to be published by the *Jüdischer Verlag* and to be called *Juda, Illustrierte Monatschrift für Ost und West* (Judah—Illustrated Monthly for East and West). The memorandum embraced a plan which is described as having been prepared by Trietsch and Lilien with the assistance of Buber (who subsequently denied part-authorship, see n. 1 to No. 282). Proposals were outlined for the publication of the periodical, its lay-out, contents of first issue (see n. 5 below), publicity attracting subscribers and financing. It was suggested that the first issue appear in mid-March 1903, but be dated 1st October. 'The issue will completely smother *Ost und West*' the memorandum said (concerning the monthly *Ost und West* see Vol. I, n. 8 to No. 302). The authors of the memorandum thought that *Ost und West* would succumb to the competition and cease publication by the beginning of 1904, at the latest.

to produce a good quality periodical if we constantly work towards maintaining a high level of content. With our connections we are bound to give *O. u. W.* a knock sooner or later.

If our Bureau desires to participate substantially in the project, it will of course be doing so primarily in its own interests, which happen to coincide with the interests of the *Jüdischer Verlag* in this regard. We visualise the publication as a medium leading us to those East and West European intellectual circles significant for the University. I believe we shall attain this provided ours is a newspaper of distinction and free from narrow partisanship. An organ comprising only the most carefully selected features and around which writers of European reputation are gathered is bound to obtain a readership. I feel we shall be able to cover the financial side of the project very well and here of course we can implement all those proposals to be found in the technical part of the memorandum.

I believe it would be best to begin working towards publication this April, when I shall have returned from Russia.

Incidentally, I am surprised not to find any mention of the University in the proposed make-up of the first issue.[5]

What are your views on the editorial arrangements for the paper?

Now again, the committee. Time is passing swiftly and you will soon have the doubtful pleasure of seeing me in Berlin. You can imagine how things will be if there is no committee . . .

Now a small request: could you send me, through the *J.V.*, Jacob Wasserman's book *Der Moloch*.[6] I am also anxious to have a copy of Rosenfeld.[7]

With kindest regards.

P.S. The notepaper is not yet here. Could it possibly have the emblem this time?[8]

---

[5] In the memorandum from Trietsch (see n. 4 above) the following themes were suggested for the first issue of the periodical: an 'Introduction to Jewish Culture', by Buber; the first of a series of articles on Jewish artists; a review of Herzl's novel *Altneuland* by Feiwel; an article 'A Jewish Home' by Trietsch; a poetry section, short stories, illustrations, more book reviews, news and announcements, aphorisms, possibly a music supplement, possibly extracts from *The Jew* by Gorky, and a Jewish ballad by Münchhausen.

[6] Publ. in Berlin, 1903.

[7] Orig.: 'einen Rosenfeld'; apparently meaning *Ghetto Songs* by Morris Rosenfeld, translated into German by Feiwel (see Vol. I, n. 15 to No. 238).

[8] The emblem for the University Bureau notepaper that Lilien had promised to design in Nov. 1902.

268. To David Jochelman, Berne. *Geneva, 16 February 1903*

German: Or. Copy. T.W.: W.A.

Geneva, 16. 2. 03.

Mr. D. Jochelman,
Berne.

Dear Friend,

Subsequent to your suggestion, I shall speak in Berne on Sunday.[1] Would you kindly take over the arrangements for the meeting. I shall be in Berne by about 9 o'clock on Saturday evening, so that we can agree on the details on Sunday. Our friend Feiwel may possibly be in Berne at the same time.[2]

Theme: Zionism and its Development.

I don't think it is fair for the Berne people to receive the entire admission proceeds.[3] We equally are as poor as church mice here and would also like to get something out of it. Anyway, better to arrange the *'Chaluka'*[4] *post factum*.

With warm regards to you and all our friends in Berne,

Your

269. To Joseph Nussbaum, Neu Sandec. *Geneva, 16 February 1903*

German: Or. Copy. T.W.: W.A.

16. 2. 03.

Mr. Joseph Nussbaum,
Neu Sandec.

Dear Sir,

In reply to your kind letter of the 11th,[1] we have the honour to

268. [1] Jochelman informed W. on 15 Feb. 1903 (W.A.) that on Saturday evening, 21 Feb., a meeting of the Russian student group in Berne would take place and he, therefore, proposed that W. lecture on Sunday, 22 Feb. See also n. 1 to No. 280.

[2] See n. 15 to No. 266.

[3] In his letter of 15 Feb. 1903 Jochelman proposed that the proceeds of the admission charge to W.'s lecture should be devoted to the acquisition of books for the reading room of the Academic Zionist Society in Berne.

[4] Heb.: 'Distribution'. Specifically, the distribution of charity among Jews in the Holy Land. The term is of course used ironically here.

269. [1] Nussbaum to the University Bureau, 11 Feb. 1903, W.A. Nussbaum sought information regarding the University project and asked where funds for the undertaking were to be sent,

send you our brochure herewith. We hope it will enable you to familiarise yourself with the main aspects of our project, as well as with the work that has already been initiated.

Remittances should be sent to the Jewish Colonial Trust, marked for the account of the Jewish University Bureau, or to Dr. Herzl.

We would gladly provide you with any further information and remain,

Yours faithfully and with Zion's greetings,

270. To Joseph Pokrassa, Kharkov. *Geneva, 16 February 1903*

German: Or. Copy. T.W.: W.A.

16. 2. 03.

Mr. J. Pokrassa,
Kharkov.

Dear Friend,

You too have become a Kharkovite! Although there is probably nothing of importance to report, it nevertheless would have been nice if you had written a postcard confirming the receipt of our various letters.[1]

I recently sent you a communication on the subject of the projected magazine.[2] This enterprise is developing well and we can predict being able to make a start on the periodical as early as April. Of course, we do not as yet have the resources necessary, but the idea must be set in motion and so we do not intend waiting until all our friends have expressed their opinions.

I have come to the conclusion that he walks best who walks alone.

Aleinikov has the peculiar habit of being seized by a writing fever. He then produces a convulsive postcard, only to retire into Nirvana again for another spell. If our Bureau had a surfeit of postage stamps we would, of course, make an effort to rouse the man out of his serene contemplation. Since the Swiss postal authorities will render us service only for cash, we must forego this intriguing enterprise.

What interests me more than anything is the metempsychosis of the Russian brochure.[3] I get enquiries time and time again and

---

270. [1] See Nos. 235, 247.   [2] See No. 247.

[3] The Russian translation of *Eine Jüdische Hochschule*, given to Aleinikov to prepare for the Russian Censor's scrutiny (see n. 1 to No. 235). In his reply of 13/26 Feb. 1903 Pokrassa reported that the translation made by Dr. Goldberg of Pinsk was not satisfactory and he proposed that W. request Vladimir Idelson, who had undertaken to edit the Russian version, to prepare a new translation (see also Idelson, to W., 13/26 Feb. 1903, W.A.).

receive complaints without knowing what to reply to people. If the brochure has still not been submitted to the Censor, please tell those concerned that I renounce all further claims upon them. We shall produce a new text and do what is necessary from our side. Probably there is no hope of getting the text back from Kharkov. Poor brochure! As I am leaving here in three weeks at the latest, I am asking you to write at once so that I may know where I stand.

Kind regards to you and yours,

As ever,

271. To Berthold Feiwel, Zurich. *Geneva, 16 February 1903*

German: Or. Copy. T.W.: W.A.

Confidential.   Geneva, 16. 2. 03.

Dear Berthold,

You too have most likely received the memorandum from Trietsch on the periodical.[1] I do not know whether you have already replied at length.

I would, however, like to share my opinion on this project with you. As demonstrated by his plan, Trietsch seems to hold other views of the character and significance of the journal.

1) To me it would seem improper and indecent to aim at the destruction of *Ost und West* from the very outset. I would have no objection if in time our periodical brings about the demise of *O.u.W.*, but it would certainly be an affront to good manners, and damage the prestige of our paper, if we put ourselves on a level with Mr. Wintz,[2] etc., or even came into conflict with him. The idea of publishing an issue in March but dating it October 1st seems to me quite the wrong tactics. Anyway, we could raise our paper to a level so high as to render *Ost und West* invisible. If we can count upon a sum of approximately 5,000 roubles, as we plan to, we shall be able to compete with any Jewish periodical. The chances are such that we shall really be able finally to start working on the paper in the spring.

2) In my opinion the paper ought to cater principally to the better intellectual circles. Therefore it cannot be devoted, even in

---

271. [1] See n. 4 to No. 267.
[2] Leo Wintz, the editor of *Ost und West.*

part, to Trietsch's interests and ideas. All party politics in the narrow sense of the term must be excluded. Only in this way can we be sure that the journal will be read in circles highly important to us.

3) Editorship. I told you in Berne[3] that you are the only person who could edit such a paper. I would work for it solely under this condition. I believe that for the time being you can attend to the editing from Zurich. Later, after the project has grown, a solution will be found.

4) It is immediately evident to me, from the suggested make-up of the first issue,[4] that Trietsch sees the essence of the paper differently from 'ourselves'—I think I can speak for you too. Strange that not a word about the University is to be mentioned in this issue.

5) I can point to further minor objections, but they are superfluous at this moment, when we are faced with greater doubts of principle. For example, I am absolutely opposed to appearing constantly with 'model Gentiles'[5] such as Münchhausen,[6] and now Gorky also. I am in favour of an excellently produced fortnightly. We might keep all the illustrations together, perhaps as a supplement. But those technical details are not my field.

Have you had any news from Buber? I am also very anxious about the result of today's meeting in Zurich.[7] Please, let me know the outcome at once. I am sending you 100 francs and a parcel of questionnaires. Unfortunately, the completed ones are slow in coming in. Tomorrow we are sending out a sharp letter,[8] and perhaps this will help. I also sent Trietsch 100 marks today, with the request that he return the money to us in three weeks.[9]

Please let me know whether you are against the appearance of a publication as early as the middle of March, as set out in the plan.[10]

Awaiting your immediate reply,

Ever yours,

[3] During their meeting on 1 Feb. 1903 (see No. 246).

[4] See n. 5 to No. 267.

[5] Orig.: 'Re[no]mirgoim' (Yiddish).

[6] Börris von Münchhausen (1874–1945), German ballad-writer. In 1900 he published a volume of poems on Biblical themes called *Juda*, with illustrations by Lilien.

[7] On 16 Feb. 1903 a second student meeting dealing with the University project took place in Zurich (cf. n. 2 to No. 266). On 17 Feb. Glikin sent W. a report on the meeting (W.A.). Prominent among the Zionist speakers were Feiwel and Aberson, the latter travelling from Geneva specially to participate. The Zionists succeeded in preventing the adoption of a resolution opposing the University project.

[8] This circular (which has not been found) was apparently sent out on 18 Feb. 1903 (see No. 276).

[9] See n. 1 to No. 265; No. 267.

[10] That is, in accordance with Trietsch's plan—see above, also n. 4 to No. 267.

272. To Abraham Idelson and Michael Kroll, Moscow.
Geneva, 17 February 1903

Russian: Or. Copy. H.W.: W.A.

17. ii. 03.

Dear Friends,

I am choosing this occasion to write to you away from the Bureau because I also want to talk about the Fraction. In a day or two we shall be sending out a circular calling upon the disunited members of the Fraction to unite and prepare themselves for the Congress.[1]

However, let me bring to your attention the fact that certain sections of the German and Austrian Zionist movement, (Frankfurt-on-Main, Mulhouse, Hanover, Mannheim, Prague, Cracow), are in a pro-Fraction frame of mind; and that without doubt a great many more Fraction members will turn up at the Congress than we thought possible. *Er zählt die Häupter seiner Lieben und sieh, es sind statt sechse sieben.*[2] It is precisely [these ----] who are the most valuable material for us, because there is little one can do with those Russian Fraction members who are only temporarily resident abroad; the majority of them are students and have nothing in common with the local people. [Part-timers ---- ---- ----] they [----] here among the Jewish student body, and if there had been any militant Zionists in our student 'colonies'[3] they might have played a key role. Unfortunately [----] none and [----] demand. No young people have as yet come forward.

It is really frightful, you know. From among the Jewish students throughout Switzerland, plus a considerable part of Germany, one can find only two or three Zionist speakers. The following may throw some light on the situation: in the course of the past two months [Aberson] and I have spoken twice in Lausanne and once in Berne,[4] where I shall have to speak again; today Aberson is in Zurich,[5] where I shall be speaking next week, and three weeks later [I shall be] in Karlsruhe, Munich and Darmstadt. I have declined Leipzig, Berlin, Mulhouse.[6] Once we had Motzkin but he is quite inactive

272. [1] The Sixth Zionist Congress, which was scheduled to meet in the summer of 1903. The circular has not been found, but see n. 3 to No. 295.

[2] 'He counted the heads of his loved ones and behold, there are not six but seven.'

[3] The foreign student groups in the University cities of Central and Western Europe.

[4] W. addressed a meeting in Lausanne on 7 Feb., the same day apparently as Aberson spoke there (see n. 5 to No. 251). No reports about the lectures mentioned here by W. and Aberson in Berne have been found. On 22 Jan., however, W. wrote to Feiwel (No. 234) that he was about to visit Berne on 'Party business', so perhaps he lectured there on that day.

[5] W. was due to speak in Berne on 22 Feb. (see No. 268). Aberson participated in the student gathering which took place in Zurich on 16 Feb. (see n. 7 to No. 271).

[6] W. apparently planned to go to Zurich following his visit to Berne but it is

now[7] [----]. Feiwel and Buber work hard and successfully among the Germans, [---- ---- ----] where the work is of an entirely different nature. The only activity possible among them is via publications: Press and literature. This is what will make Jews out of these semi-people. In this respect the *Jüdischer Verlag* has played, and will continue to play [a significant] part. Then there is the periodical, about which I wrote in my last letter[8] [----].

When we add the University idea to all this enterprise—it is of no less importance—the following becomes clear: such projects create a force and are themselves given propulsion by that force. This kind of interaction, of which we all [---- ----]. Of course, [----] is still rudimentary but very [----].

I feel that if I were a free man it might well be possible, during the coming three to four years, to achieve a great deal in the direction I have described.

We may succeed in convening a conference of the Fraction prior to the meeting of the Sixth Congress, which is due to take place, (semi-officially in London),[9] in September. Whatever happens we who reside abroad will start the idea on its way.

Now the periodical. Yesterday I received an *Exposé*,[10] prepared by Lilien, Trietsch and Buber, from Berlin. They think they can publish the first issue, for publicity purposes, as early as March. It will take the form of an *Einladung zum Abonnement*,[11] under the title *Zeitschrift für Ost und West.*[12] By 'West' the very far West, including America, is understood. I doubt whether [----] can come out in March, more likely April.[13]

In my last letter,[8] [---- ----] which was really more of a circular, I summarised the main features of the project to you. You will find in it a reply *implicite* to your demand that the publication be in Russian.[14] Unquestionably it is a requirement that ought to be

not known whether he actually did so. Concerning his projected lectures in Munich and Darmstadt and his refusal to do so in Mulhouse, see n. 16 to No. 266. No details are known of W.'s plans to visit Karlsruhe or his refusal to lecture in Leipzig and in Berlin.

[7] Cf. n. 10 to No. 110.

[8] Refers to the letter mentioned in No. 249 and not found. See also n. 3 there.

[9] In fact the Sixth Zionist Congress met in August in Basle.

[10] See ns. 4, 5 to No. 267.   [11] A subscription form.

[12] 'Periodical for East and West'. For the exact name as proposed in a memorandum see n. 4 to No. 267.

[13] Part of the sentence is blurred and is unreadable. Cf. No. 270: 'This enterprise is developing well and we can predict being able to make a start on the periodical as early as April.'

[14] In his letter of 13 (26) Jan. 1903 (W.A.) Kroll wrote regarding the periodical: 'there is no need to discuss its value. The only matter of importance is the language question. Will it meet with great success in German?'

fulfilled. But a paper in Russia will answer needs which are not relevant to people over here. *We have to* [----] to the Jewish intelligentsia of Western Europe, a tremendous intellectual force.

Friends, in practice our Fraction can put its democratic programme into effect only in stages, and only among the masses. It has become quite clear to me that we ourselves are not a group of democrats, but rather *l'intellectuelle dans le sionisme*,[15] if one may use the term. This does not exclude the democratic process in our activities among the *broad mass of people*, but our aims lie more in the achievement of a synthesis between *Ost und West*[16] bringing the ghetto to Europe and Europe to the ghetto in [----] sense of the word. This is why it is so hard, and why we must not spare ourselves, but must . . .[17] We belong to the era of transition, the beginning [----].

Hence the character of the paper we contemplate, a golden bridge as it were on which the intellectuals of Europe will meet with our Jews. This is why the paper must fulfil the requirements I summarised in my last letter,[18] why it must be an *Elite-Organ*. The irony of fate: that it should be the democratic Fraction which brings aristocratic undertakings into being—an *Elite-Organ, Hochschule, Kunstverlag*, etc.

But there is another side to the coin: work among the masses, in the Jewish ghetto. For this we need a paper in Yiddish, Hebrew, Russian. Here we have to use other methods.

Given these conditions, what can we achieve? In the first place, the initial series of projects; the other, a second series, only in part. And this despite the fact that they are of equal importance.

We need people for the second series. We shall always lament, yourselves and I, our shortage of workers. This will continue until we receive an infusion of fresh blood from somewhere. New, fresh forces! We shall have it only for our first objectives. *Voilà!*

Out of the multiplicity of programmes, recipes, doctrines, we are still reduced to the empirical approach pure and simple, and all the accepted patterns go to the devil as soon as they clash with Jewish reality. How I hate all formulae; how they have entangled and drained us; how useless they are when applied to the Jews!

My personal approach to Zionism changes every six months Sometimes I build a balanced, harmonious theory and then, when half a year goes by, I have to revise it, adjust it, etc., etc.

But I am lapsing into lyricism, which suits me as little as a cross

[15] *Sic.*

[16] W. is here referring of course to geographical regions and not to the periodical of that name.

[17] The dots are in the original.

[18] Refers to the letter mentioned in No. 249 and not found. See also n. 3 there.

to the devil! I long to return to Russia, and shall leave here as soon
as I can. I think a great deal can be done. But I had better not put
the cart before the horse.

Listen, friends. If you have any b--- money, do send it. I don't
want to touch the money in the bank[19] for my journey and I haven't
any to spare. We live from hand to mouth, and that with difficulty.
Write at once. The entire tour will cost about 150-200 roubles.

We shall discuss everything at length when I am in Moscow.
I await your news impatiently,

Affectionately,
Chaim.

The committee is in process of formation. When I am in Moscow I
shall be able to speak of a committee in being.[20] More details in my
next letter.

273. To Martin Buber, Vienna. *Geneva, 18 February 1903*

German: Or. Copy. T.W.: W.A.

18. 2. 03.

Mr. Martin Buber,
Vienna.

Dear Martin,

A few days ago I received a memorandum, prepared by Trietsch,
Lilien, and yourself[1] in part, on the proposed periodical.

I have sent my confidential comments on the memorandum to
Berthold,[2] and am forwarding a copy of this letter to you, for
information. Please keep it confidential. Berthold takes exactly the
same position.

Whatever happens, I hope we shall very soon arrive at some
formula around which we can all unite so as to proceed with the
project. I would like to point out, however, that the time has
already come for us to compile a list of contributors to the periodical,
and set out its programme and objectives in a prospectus. Insofar
as contributors are concerned, it is most important that we invite
the kind of people who are likely to be on the committee.[3] Please

---

[19] That is, the University Bureau account at the Jewish Colonial Trust.

[20] Presumably W. meant the committee for the Jewish University then on the
point of being organized by Buber, although it was never finally established. Trietsch's
attempt to organize a committee in Berlin was only in its early stages.

273. [1] See n. 4 to No. 267.
[2] See No. 271.   [3] The committee for the University.

write to me about this at once. A letter can reach me in Berne on Monday addressed care of Miss H. Krinsky, Villa Frey, Schwarzthorstrasse. I shall be meeting Berthold there and it would be really good if your reply were to be available by then so that we could discuss it together.

Please tell me at the same time what success you had in Munich,[4] and your further steps in Vienna. If you could at least form a group of between three to five people, this would constitute a nucleus for the time being—the rest would follow. Something will be achieved in Berlin too,[5] and so we would have our start.

I am impatiently awaiting your letter, and remain,

Ever yours,

274. To the 'Theodor Herzl' Society, Koenigsberg.
Geneva, 18 February 1903

German: Or. Copy. T.W.: W.A.

18. 2. 03.

The 'Theodor Herzl' Society,
Koenigsberg, Prussia.

Our grateful thanks for your kind letter.[1]

The questionnaires mentioned should arrive within the next few days.

Most respectfully and with Zion's greetings,

275. To Davis Trietsch, Berlin. *Geneva, 18 February 1903*

German: Or. Copy. T.W.: W.A.

18. 2. 03.

Mr. D. Trietsch,
Berlin.

Dear Friend,

I have been fretting with impatience for a progress report on the committee.[1] But it still has not come. I hope you will take my various pleas to heart and write on this matter at once.

[4] Buber addressed a meeting in Munich on 16 Feb. 1903 (see n. 3 to No. 260).

[5] That is, in organizing a local committee for the University.

274. [1] Shereshevsky to the University Bureau 16 Feb. 1903, W.A. Shereshevsky reported that he had sent fifty-three questionnaires, completed by students in Koenigsberg, to the Bureau.

275. [1] The Berlin committee for the University.

As for the periodical, I would add that the compilation of a list of contributors is of immediate, vital importance. This must be preceded by the precise formulation of a programme. With these two things in my possession, my work in Russia will be much easier. If we can cite a fair number of distinguished contributors our problem is half solved. Such names as Professors Warburg, Oppenheimer, etc., would naturally be most desirable. I implore you, dear friend, to write me at once about all this.

On Saturday I am going to Berne, where I shall meet Berthold. Therefore do send your reply by return, special delivery, to Berne care of Miss H. Krinsky, Villa Frey, Schwarzthorstrasse. It is most important that we have your answer by the time we meet. Your letter should reach us on Sunday.[2] We shall write you again in detail from Berne.[3]

The notepaper has still not arrived.

Kind regards,

Your

276. To Berthold Feiwel, Zurich. *Geneva, 18 February 1903*

German: Or. Copy. T.W.: W.A.

Geneva, 18. 2. 03.

Mr. Berthold Feiwel,
Zurich.

Dear Berthold,

I am anxiously awaiting a full reply from you regarding the periodical.[1] Have you written to Trietsch about it?

If we intend publishing an issue in March or April, we have to begin to invite the contributors, define the character and objects of the periodical in a prospectus, and distribute this among people of trust. The very best would be to do this before my trip, for then I would have information about the journal to give to people. We therefore have to reach agreement with Trietsch and Buber

---

[2] In his reply of 20 Feb. 1903 (W.A.) Trietsch wrote that, in his opinion, there was no need to compile a list of contributors in advance of the appearance of the first issue. If the issue were of high calibre, contributors would be found without difficulty.

[3] No such letter has been found.

276. [1] In his letter of 18 Feb. 1903 (W.A.) Feiwel wrote that his opinion of Trietsch's proposals for the periodical was similar to W.'s (cf. n. 4 to No. 267; No. 271).

and make a definite decision on the future editorship. There must be absolute clarity in this respect.

What would Lilien's position be? Frankly I am not sure whether he can be useful to us in this undertaking. Please, Berthold, let me have a note from you at once on this.

The Koenigsberg people have advised us of 53 questionnaires.[2] A second circular[3] regarding the survey is going out today, and we may assume that this time it will not miss the mark. Evidently our key people have to contend with shocking indolence everywhere.

Do let me know whether you are coming to Berne on Saturday. I shall probably be leaving from here on Saturday at five o'clock. Should you get to Berne earlier, I would also come a little earlier. But this time we shall work intensively without allowing ourselves to be disturbed.

Kind regards,

As ever yours,

277. To Israel Breslav, Kharkov. *Geneva, 20 February 1903*

German: Or. Copy. T.W.: W.A.

20. 2. 03.

Dr. Breslav,
Kharkov.

Dear Friend,

I know many casual people, and there are times when my insignificant self is compelled to behave casually, but I have never come across such a breed as in Kharkov. One may be polite or rude towards them, humble or superior, but all in vain. It is impossible to squeeze even one solitary line out of certain persons. As recently as one month ago I was still suffering from the illusion that you would surprise us with stunning news of the great progress of the University project in Kharkov. I have now been thoroughly disabused of this fantastic notion by the receipt of some quite specific reports; I see that everything has run aground.[1]

---

[2] See n. 1 to No. 274.

[3] This is apparently the 'sharp letter' mentioned in No. 271, the purpose of which was to urge those responsible to bring the survey to a close. This circular has not been found.

277. [1] See n. 1 to No. 235; n. 2 to No. 247.

You can imagine how painful all this is without my needing to elaborate. In the one city so capable of assuming an important role in this movement such indolence as is current there is the least excusable. A host of sombre thoughts present themselves as one calmly reviews the conduct of our Kharkov friends. And beyond the strange silence there is the utter neglect of the most elementary, commonly accepted rules of communication. Through a Yes or a No, in a brief answer of about two lines, you would enable those of us already so overloaded with work to spare ourselves this tedious, useless letter-writing. As I look through the Kharkov correspondence, by which I of course mean that going from Geneva to Kharkov,[2] I feel like laughing at myself. So much effort, so much hope and anticipation, and not even a small thing like the brochure accomplished.[3] What is one finally to think ? Is there really no vitality left in the Jewish intelligentsia to convert promises made, and forthrightly made, into deeds ? Of course, other questions could follow, but this will suffice for the moment. Well, let it not be assumed that I shall write again. I shall leave the necessary final airing of our differences to our personal encounter.

I am clinging to one glimmer of hope, that the spell of Olympian tranquillity will be broken and something will yet *be done*, even in Kharkov. I can assure you that I am not of the type that easily lets go. Something must happen, and will.

Kind regards,

Your

278. To Boris Greidenberg, Kharkov. *Geneva, 20 February 1903*

German: Or. Copy. T.W.: W.A.

20. 2. 03.

Dr. S. Greidenberg,[1]   Registered.
University Lecturer,
Kharkov.

Dear Dr. [Greidenberg],

About three months ago we had the honour to address a lengthy letter to you which, among other matters, contained a request that

---

[2] See Nos. 2, 3, 4, 20, 23, 28, 29, 45, 67, 91, 100, 148, 185, 213, 215, 235, 236, 247, 270.

[3] The Russian translation of *Eine Jüdische Hochschule*—see n. 11 to No. 7; n. 1 to No. 235; n. 3 to No. 270.

278. [1] Thus in the orig.—see n. 6 to No. 23.

you inform us of the progress of the University project in Kharkov.[2] Obviously, we were most interested in your reply, but waited in vain, and were obliged to write to the other members of the committee elected at the time.[3] Unfortunately these approaches did not succeed either. Our efforts came to grief, but, dare I say it, not for lack of any goodwill on the part of the Bureau here.

We were always ready to supply information and carry out any task that might have led to activity by the Kharkov committee. It is useless brooding over the unhappy outcome of what began with such promise. The time lost is indeed to be regretted, but one must be prepared for even greater difficulties than these in an undertaking as complicated as ours. Obviously it has never occurred to us to surrender a post like Kharkov lightly. We are furthermore convinced, dear Doctor, that in spite of everything you will take the matter up now and leave nothing undone so as to recover what has, for whatever reason, been neglected.

Finally, we have one more request: please do not ever leave us without an answer. You can well imagine the painful effect this has upon one who writes his fingers away to get a point clarified, but remains as uninformed after ten letters as before he had written one.

As before, we are at your disposal for all information, but in this matter we must obviously await some kind of sign from you.

Most respectfully yours, we are,

With greetings,

279. To Joseph Lurie, St. Petersburg. *Geneva, 20 February 1903*

German: Or. Copy. T.W.: W.A.

20. 2. 03.

Dr. J. Lurie,
St. Petersburg.

Dear Friend,

To our regret we have still not had a reply to our letter of the 16th of last month.[1] We had attached great importance to obtaining the information requested of you, but it is now too late. We

---

[2] See No. 23.

[3] Greidenberg was chairman of the Kharkov committee for the Jewish University. Regarding letters to other members of the committee during the period of Nov. 1902–Jan. 1903 see Nos. 2, 3, 4, 20, 28, 29, 45, 91, 100, 148, 185, 213, 236.

279. [1] See No. 220.

have established no connection with Petersburg and for the time being I shall have to abandon my visit there.

We wrote to Mr. Gruenbaum twice. He was to have attended to the Hebrew edition of the brochure.[2] The first time we had no reply, the second our card came back. Thus we are still without news of how the matter stands. Since we have already spent a considerable sum on the brochure, we would deeply regret losing everything again. We ask you most earnestly, therefore, to let us have Mr. Gruenbaum's correct address at once. Please be so good as to write him about the brochure yourself.

As I am leaving here within three brief weeks, your letter will reach me only if you reply by return of post.[3]

Kind regards,

Your

280. To Vera Khatzman, Geneva. *Berne, 21 February 1903*

Russian: Pcd. H.W.: W.A.

Berne,[1] 21/II. 03.

Dear Verochka,

On the insistence of Shriro, I telegraphed you from Lausanne to ask you to come here [tomorrow] for the day. Then, if you wish, you could go to Berne with Mme. Shriro. Mr. Sh[riro] is leaving [for Berne today] but I advise you not to go there [----] things are easier in Lausanne. Toldy is already here. I have not seen [him]. I was met by Glikin.

Aberson is here, of course. A real battle is brewing. I shall write

---

[2] See Nos. 143, 209.

[3] In his reply of 16 Feb. (1 March) 1903 (W.A.) Lurie told W. that he had not replied because of pressure of work, but he believed that much could be done in St. Petersburg for the University project. He reported that the censor had rejected the Hebrew translation of *Eine Jüdische Hochschule*, and he would attempt to use influence in St. Petersburg in the matter.

280. [1] W. was due to speak in Berne on 'Zionism and its Development' on the evening of 22 Feb. 1903 (see No. 268). Following his visit to Lausanne he arrived in Berne on Saturday, 21 Feb. 1903, and on that evening he participated in a gathering of the Russian student group. Aberson, Glikin, and Feiwel also came to Berne. At this gathering a debate lasting three nights took place between the Zionists and the Bundists. W. addressed the gathering each evening, while Aberson and Feiwel also spoke on behalf of the Zionists (see report in *Hamelitz* of 24 Feb./9 March, 1903, which includes a résumé of W.'s speeches).

tomorrow. In any case, telegraph Mme. Shriro[2] in Lausanne at Riant Site.

My love and kisses,

Your Chaim

281. To Samuel Grusenberg, St. Petersburg. *Geneva,*
26 February 1903

German: Or. Copy. T.W.: W.A.

26. 2. 03.

Dr. S. O. Grusenberg,
St. Petersburg.

Dear Dr. [Grusenberg],

We acknowledge with many thanks receipt of your kind letter of the 20th,[1] as well as the two issues of your esteemed periodical.[2]

We had intended writing to you for a long time, and your letter anticipated us. We had wanted to approach you on the question of the University. So you can imagine how happy your letter made us.

For your information, we are sending a very brief report on the progress of our efforts.[3] We can now add a postscript to the news it contains, for we have in the meantime been successful in forming committees in Vienna and Berlin, small though these at present are.[4] Naturally, they are to be expanded, probably in the early future. Meanwhile responsible, influential circles (professors,

---

[2] Elizabeth (Liza, Elisheva) Shriro (1872–1938), who together with her children was then living in Lausanne.

281. [1] Grusenberg to W., 7/20 Feb. 1903, W.A. Grusenberg, editor of the Russian Jewish weekly *Budushchnost'* ('The Future'), wrote that in St. Petersburg a circle of adherents to the idea of a Jewish University was being organized which he hoped would arouse public interest. He therefore requested W. to send him material on the project and keep him informed on its progress. Grusenberg asked, *inter alia*, where the University would be established and whether the project had to have a connection with the Zionist Organization, there being many non-Zionists who might help the cause. He further stated that they intended to set up committees in various localities in Russia and he asked for W.'s opinion regarding a plan of activities, and whether it was necessary to tie the groups to a centre in St. Petersburg.

[2] Grusenberg enclosed with his letter issue No. 6 of *Budushchnost'*, dated 7 (20) Feb. 1903, and apparently he also sent W. No. 5 of 31 Jan. (13 Feb.) 1903. In issue No. 5 a favourable report spoke of the establishment of the Jewish University Bureau in Geneva, and of the resolution in support of the plan adopted by the student gathering in Munich (see n. 4 to No. 248). Issue No. 6 contained an editorial warmly supporting the University project and explaining the importance of such an institution.

[3] Probably the Bureau report of the end of Jan. 1903 (W.A. No. 30/0, 25).

[4] At the time that the letter was written efforts to set up committees in Vienna and in Berlin continued, but no committee had as yet been finally established.

scholars, etc.) have been won over to our cause in Russia too—Kharkov, Moscow, Kiev.[5] As you rightly point out in the sixth issue of your paper, we have always sought, in our approaches to these groups, to emphasise views that unite us all. We have thus created the conditions for attracting non-Zionists to our activities.

We shall continue to regard our enterprise as being oriented neither to one particular party nor to all of them, but as standing above parties. The results ensuing from this united effort will forever remain the common heritage of all Jewry.

Thus the answer to one of the questions in your kind letter is that we are anxious to interest non-Zionists too in our cause.

As for the location of the University, it has now become clear that only two countries offer possibilities: England and Switzerland. The question will be decided only after a more detailed study has been made.

As the report indicates, we are seeking to create as many committees as possible, wherever we can. Their main task shall be to conduct propaganda on behalf of the University and to raise funds for the preliminary work and for the project itself. Since conditions vary from country to country, indeed from city to city within the same country, we must leave the initiative for local effort to the people on the spot. In due course there will naturally come an opportunity for co-ordinating procedures among all the groups in respect of such basic activities as propaganda and fund-raising. From this point of view the formation of a central organisation in St. Petersburg is to be welcomed.

I had intended to visit St. Petersburg. I shall now wait for your valued advice in this regard. I shall be setting out on my journey to Berlin, Warsaw and Moscow on behalf of the University on March 10th, new style. So if my presence could be of any value in Petersburg I would be prepared to go there. Our friend Feiwel will be travelling at the same time to Austria (Vienna, Prague, Budapest, etc.).

The survey of Russian-Jewish students abroad is now coming to a close. We are already collating the information received and hope, during the summer, to be in a position to publish a more extensive work on the subject. This will at the same time embrace proposals for the project itself, and is being prepared by a commission of experts.[6] In a few days we shall make available to you

---

[5] As to support for the project by Kharkov University professors, see Vol. I, n. 4 to No. 319. No information regarding support from academic circles in Moscow or Kiev has been found.

[6] The orig. has 'Letzteres wird von einer Kommission aus Fachleuten bestehend vorbereitet'. Apparently this sentence must be interpreted as referring to the future

the consolidated bibliographical material (on the essentials of a University). I feel there ought to be people in Petersburg's academic circles who could eventually participate in the implementation of the project. The same applies to Kharkov.

You will see, dear Doctor, that we can only indicate the tasks. Within a brief period, and with what is still a small working force, something considerable has nevertheless been achieved. We anticipate great things from our forthcoming travels. Once we have completed the groundwork here in some degree, and the Bureau's situation is finally established, we shall undertake a journey to England and America, a trip for which we are indeed already making our preparations.

We are sending the second edition of our brochure to your address.

Again with many thanks,

We are,

Most respectfully,

P.S. We are of course entirely at your disposal and look forward with interest to the favour of your esteemed reply.

282. To Martin Buber, Vienna. *Geneva, 27 February 1903*

German: Or. Copy. T.W.: W.A.

27. 2. 03.

Mr. Martin Buber,
Vienna.

Dear Martin,

From your last letter sent to Berne[1] I can surmise that you share the opinion of Berthold and myself and that you are opposed to

programme—in the middle of March the Berlin committee for the Jewish University decided to appoint a programme sub-committee (see n. 8 to No. 294).

282. [1] Buber to W. and Feiwel of 20 Feb. 1903, W.A. Buber denied Trietsch's story that he was part-author of the Trietsch–Lilien plan for the contemplated periodical (see n. 4 to No. 267) and he declared his opposition to their proposals regarding the lay-out and contents of the organ. He went on to express his own view that the organ had to be a militant periodical with defined objectives and well-researched articles, so that it could serve as a platform for a variety of opinions and reflect an editorial emphasis of 'a radical-social view and modern cultural standpoint'. Buber further stated that Feiwel had proposed to him that they jointly edit the periodical and in his reply he expressed his readiness to transfer to Berlin for that purpose, but he agreed with W. that Feiwel should be the sole editor (see W. to Feiwel of 16 Feb. 1903—No. 271—a copy of which was sent to Buber on 18 Feb. 1903). Buber added that he was already compiling a list of contributors to the periodical and was prepared to present a table of contents for the first issue.

the Trietsch–Lilien memorandum. If I know Trietsch, however, he will certainly not move from his position and so we may very likely be forced to take the matter in hand independently. As for the editorship, I must at once point out that it never occurred to me to have Toldy appointed sole editor. If you are going to Berlin, as you state in your letter, then it is obvious both of you will take charge of affairs.

The list of contributors, as well as a prospectus for the journal, is a high requirement, immediately if possible, so that it can still be sent out before I go to Russia. Therefore send me the material at once, please. We shall deal with the printing here. I shall see Halpern in Munich and come to an understanding[2] with him on everything outstanding.

How far have you got in the committee business? Would it now be possible to make reference to the existence of a committee in Vienna? This is of the utmost importance. According to a report received from Petersburg yesterday, great interest has been aroused there for the University.[3] So it is not unlikely that I shall be there too. This makes it all the more necessary for us to have a footing in Western Europe.

Please write and send me everything required at once.

Kind regards,

Your

283. To Moses Lokatczer, Koethen. *Geneva, 27 February 1903*

German: Or. Copy. T.W.: W.A.

27. 2. 03.

Dear Mr. Lokatczer,[1]

We gratefully acknowledge receipt of the questionnaires and would request that those still outstanding be kindly sent to us without delay.

Kind regards,

Yours faithfully,

[2] In his letter of 20 Feb. 1903 Buber wrote that in Munich nothing could be done (for the University project), but that George Halpern (who was then studying in Munich) had good ideas for a programme to publicize the scheme in London and that he also had good connections there. Regarding W.'s plan to visit Munich see n. 3 to No. 248.

[3] See n. 1 to No. 281.

283. [1] Nothing has come to light on Lokatczer other than that he was a student at Koethen.

284. To Saul Lurie, Darmstadt. *Geneva, 27 February 1903*

German: Or. Copy. T.W.: W.A.

27. 2. 03.

Dear Saul,

Thank you very much for sending the forms. Please let us know how many are still outstanding. When will you be going to Russia? I plan to be in Berlin between the 10th and the 14th.

Ever yours,

285. To A. Rosenberger, Pribram. *Geneva, 27 February 1903*

German: Or. Copy. T.W.: W.A.

27. 2. 03.

[Three copies of letters of 5 March 1903 are preserved in the W.A. to Ozhinsky, Rosenfeld, and Pokrassa. In the letter to Pokrassa it is stated that 'Dr. W. was away today' and it would appear that the three letters were sent by Samuel Levinson. No other letters from the University Bureau or from W. have been found for the period between 27 Feb. 1903 to 10 March 1903].

Dear Mr. Rosenberger,

Thank you very much for your kind letter of the 21st.[1]

We have arranged for 25 questionnaires, which we would like you to distribute, to be sent to your address. Please forward the completed forms to the Bureau.

Thanking you in anticipation, we remain,

Yours faithfully,

286. To William Evans-Gordon, London. *Geneva, 10 March 1903*

German: Or. Copy. T.W.: W.A.

Geneva, 4 rue Lombard, 10. 3. 03.

Dear Major,

Permit me to put a small request to you. My friend D. Trietsch

285. [1] Rosenberger to the University Bureau, 21 Feb. 1903, W.A. Rosenberger expressed his readiness to conduct the survey in Pribram (Bohemia).

of Berlin, a newspaper editor,[1] would like to translate your article
'Our Aliens at Home'.[2] Would you kindly authorise him to do so?

I trust you will be agreeable. Should this be so, my friend Trietsch
wonders whether you would kindly place the photographs appearing
in the article at his disposal; or whether you could ask the periodical
to let him have the printing-blocks of the pictures.[3]

With many thanks in anticipation, and kind regards,

I am,

Yours truly,[4]

287. To Martin Buber, Vienna. *Geneva, 10 March 1903*

German: Or. Copy. T.W.: W.A.

10. 3. 03.

Dear Martin,

Thank you for your letter.[1] I am leaving at the latest by the end
of this week. As Berthold is going to Berlin with me,[2] we think
it superfluous to carry on a correspondence with Trietsch over the
periodical. Please, Martin, let me know, care of the *Verlag*, how
you get on with the committee's formation, specifically indicating
names to which I may refer.

Always,

Your

---

286. [1] Trietsch was editor of the monthly *Palästina*.

[2] See Trietsch to W., 5 March 1903, W.A. In the article referred to, 'Whence came
our Immigrants', Evans-Gordon described his impressions and conclusions from a
journey through the Jewish Pale of Settlement in Russia in 1902 (see Vol. I, n. 3
to No. 317). The article was published in the American monthly *The World's Work*
April issue 1903 (*sic*) pp. 3276–81 and was reviewed in the London *Jewish Chronicle*
of 6 March 1903 (*sic*) under the heading 'Our Aliens at Home'. It would therefore
appear that Trietsch saw the review and not the article itself. Although these dates
do not seem to correspond, Trietsch doubtless wrote his letter on the basis of the
Jewish Chronicle review—possibly he put the wrong date on the letter or perhaps he
saw this issue of the *Jewish Chronicle* a day before its official publication. The reviewer
may not have seen the actual magazine, dated April 1903, in which the article appeared. This is also indicated by his reference to the article's being accompanied by
many pictures, for no pictures appear in the issue. Perhaps the reviewer saw the
manuscript of the article, or a proof, before it appeared in print.

[3] Cf. n. 2 above.

[4] On 20 Feb. 1903 Levinson wrote to Trietsch (W.A.) that he was sending him 'a
letter received from Major Evans-Gordon as well as a letter from his publisher'.
(They have not been found.)

287. [1] Not found.

[2] W. was due to visit Berlin on his way to Russia.

288. To I. Glikin, Brunswick. *Geneva, 10 March 1903*

German: Or. Copy. T.W.: W.A.

10. 3. 03.

Mr. I. Glikin,
Brunswick.

Dear Sir,

Our very sincere thanks for your kind letter of the 25th,[1] as well as for the questionnaires duly received.

We trust, however, that you will be able to send us more questionnaires.

Most respectfully,

289. To Davis Trietsch, Berlin. *Geneva, 10 March 1903*

German: Or. Copy. T.W.: W.A.

10. 3. 03.

Dear friend Trietsch,

Berthold and I will definitely be in Berlin towards the end of this week, and will attend to whatever is necessary. I can spend two days with you at the most, because my time-table is tightly worked out. I have written to Evans-Gordon.[1] We are leaving here on Thursday[2] at the latest.

Kind regards,

Your

290. To Berthold Feiwel, Zurich. *Geneva, 10 March 1903*

German: Or. Copy. T.W.: W.A.

10. 3. 03.

Dear Berthold,

I have just received your telegram[1] and am delighted with your decision to come to Berlin. I hope to be in receipt of the money

---

288. [1] Glikin to W., 25 Feb. 1903, W.A. Glikin reported on difficulties encountered in collecting the questionnaires in Brunswick, and he was therefore sending only nineteen in the meantime.

289. [1] See No. 286.
[2] 12 March 1903.

290. [1] Not found.

either today or tomorrow,[2] and will send it on to you immediately. The enclosed letter from Buber should interest you.[3] I do not think it necessary to write to Trietsch about the periodical as you will soon be arranging everything personally. It is not unlikely that I, too, will be leaving on Thursday, in which case we can travel together. But do not tie yourself down, as my travel plans are not yet definite.

With kindest regards to you and all our crowd.

Your

291. To Hillel Katel, Friedberg (Hesse). *Geneva, 10 March 1903*

German: Or. Copy. T.W.: W.A.

10. 3. 03.

Mr. G. Katel,[1]
Friedberg.

Dear Sir,

Our sincere thanks for your kind letter of the 5th.[2] We have duly received the questionnaires. Should any points require elucidation we shall certainly take advantage of your warm offer of cooperation, for which we are very grateful.

Most respectfully,

292. To Vera Khatzman, Rostov. *Berlin, 15 March 1903*

Russian: H.W.: W.A.

Berlin, 15/III. 03.
Hotel Reich

Dear Verochka,

This is my second day in Berlin.[1] There was such a commotion here yesterday that even though I started writing to you several

---

[2] Referring perhaps to the 200 roubles (530 francs) contributed in Kharkov to the University Bureau (see Pokrassa to W., 13/26 Feb. 1903, W.A.). On 4 March 1903 the University Bureau requested Pokrassa to transfer the sum by telegraph (see copy of the letter to Pokrassa of 5 March 1903, W.A.). See also n. 9 to No. 294.

[3] Apparently relates to the letter from Buber mentioned in No. 287.

291. [1] Hillel Katel was a student at the Friedberg Polytechnic and chairman of the *Tseirei Zion* Student Society there. He signed his letters 'G. Katel' in accordance with the Russian pronunciation of the letter 'H'.

[2] Katel to W., 5 March 1903, W.A.

292. [1] W. visited Berlin on his way to Russia for consultations with Buber, Trietsch, Lilien, and Feiwel on the Jewish University Bureau, and to set up a local committee for the University. Buber and Feiwel were in Berlin for the meeting of directors of the *Jüdischer Verlag*, which took place on 15 March 1903 (see Buber to Ehrenpreis, 10 March 1903, in the Ehrenpreis Papers, fol. 20, N.L.).

times I had to stop, as somebody was always interrupting. To add to it all, the guests here kept coming and going with an enormous number of packages and purchases.

And you, darling girl, must have already arrived, exhausted, my sweet. I want you to have a thorough rest at home at once, so that you can get strong. How are things at home? How is everybody? How do you find them? I know I don't have to ask you to give everybody my regards. Kiss them all affectionately for me.

Today Toldy, Buber, Nossig[2] and I divided the tasks up among ourselves, as well as the list of professors to be approached. We shall visit some of them and tomorrow we shall probably all dine together and the committee will actually come into being. I very much hope to be able to leave tomorrow evening.[3]

Everything will be ready in Warsaw.[4] During today and tomorrow Manya Sokolow will be seeing everybody and speaking to them all. I have also written to old Sokolow.

The girls[5] promised to do everything possible for the evening's arrangements in Warsaw. We must hope for success. This evening there is a *Purim* party[6] here, with probably the whole of *Jung-Juda*[7] coming.

As for our periodical,[8] the prospectus is already being printed.

[2] Nossig consented to join the Berlin committee for the University (see n. 3 to No. 293), whereupon he became active in the affairs of the University Bureau until the Sixth Zionist Congress of Aug. 1903.

[3] W. wrote 'afternoon' and then erased it. In fact he remained in Berlin until 17 March.

[4] That is, for the meeting on behalf of the University project (see No. 296).

[5] Maria Sokolow and apparently the sisters Salomea (Lunia) and Helena Krinsky, all of whom Warsaw residents then studying in Switzerland. Cf. No. 303 where W. asked V.K. to write to him care of Salomea Krinsky in Warsaw.

[6] *Purim* commemorates the events recorded in the Book of Esther, and on this occasion was marked by a masked ball given by the Zionist Society in Berlin and the Society of National Jewish Women (see *Jüdische Rundschau*, 27 March 1903).

[7] 'Young Judea.' According to Dr. Elias Auerbach, who was active in the Berlin Zionist student circles in those days, it was customary to use the expression to describe the younger Zionist generation (see letter from Dr. Auerbach of 1 Oct. 1965, W.A.).

[8] In the University Bureau report of May 1903 (W.A. No. 30/5/0) it is stated that the consultations between Buber, Feiwel, and W. in Berlin during March resulted, *inter alia*, in a decision to establish a journal to be called *Der Jude* ('The Jew'), 'intended to be especially effective among Jewish intellectual circles in western Europe by arousing interest in general Jewish cultural problems and the University project in particular, and . . . to establish ties between the Jewish and the non-Jewish public'. It was agreed that the *Jüdischer Verlag* in Berlin would be responsible for the management and circulation of the periodical, 'whereas the content and editorial management of the journal is to remain under the auspices of the Jewish University Bureau'. In the prospectus mentioned in the present letter (see C.Z.A. K2/8/1/1) it is stated that the publication would be named *Der Jude, Revue der Jüdischen Moderne* and that the first issue would appear in May 1903. In fact, the plan was never realized.

Editors: Toldy and Buber. Publisher—myself. It will not be illustrated, but will have an art supplement instead. Lilien and Trietsch wanted something else, and we had to fight this out.[9] I can't say I like Lilien. He is extremely ambitious.

There is an article by Nordau in *Die Welt* answering Ahad Ha'am's review of *Altneuland*.[10] I could never have imagined Nordau descending to slanderous vilification of this type, verging on the behaviour of an informer. We decided to write an article in reply,[11]

[9] See n. 4 to No. 267; n. 1 to No. 282.

[10] In an article in *Die Welt* of 13 March 1903 Max Nordau condemned a critique by Ahad Ha'am of Herzl's novel *Altneuland* (see n. 8 to No. 18). Ahad Ha'am had written ironically about the manner in which Herzl described the settlement of Palestine once a charter had been received from the Turkish government—how everything would be achieved efficiently, smoothly, and within a brief period. But his major criticism was directed at the kind of society, as described in *Altneuland*, that would arise in Palestine. Ahad Ha'am argued that the main characteristics of such a society would imitate other nations and there would be nothing to distinguish it as a Jewish society. Essentially, it would be a society of extreme tolerance with a streak of obsequiousness, and devoid of a true national spirit. 'Apish copying', an absence of original national characteristics, the spirit of 'slavishness amid freedom', all these would be the effect of western Diaspora influence.

Nordau's reply, written at Herzl's behest, described Ahad Ha'am's arguments as 'partly foolish, partly limited and malicious'. In Nordau's view, Herzl was depicting a society with a European-Jewish outlook, and indeed this was the type of society that should be set up in Palestine. Later in his article Nordau takes issue with Ahad Ha'am on the character and aims of political Zionism and its interpretation of the Jewish problem. The article is full of bitter personal attacks: Ahad Ha'am apparently wanted the Jewish people to develop its essential uniqueness 'amid Asian savagery—the enemy of culture'. According to Nordau, Ahad Ha'am was against tolerance. 'Outsiders should perhaps be destroyed or, at least, be driven out as in Sodom and Gomorrah . . . the only European heritage that he might wish to take to *Altneuland* would be the principles of the Inquisition, the manners of the Jew-haters and the anti-Jewish edicts in Russia.' Nordau dismissed Ahad Ha'am's essays as 'nonsense, empty and obscure pretensions'. They were 'a hodge-podge of words in vogue gathered from various European feuilletonists, expressions improperly understood, a chaos of mixed-up terms in which one seeks in vain for an intelligent thought clearly and intelligibly stated'. Further, Nordau argued that Zionism 'created platforms' from which Ahad Ha'am's ideas could be disseminated, while he himself reciprocated with 'vile, treacherous attacks'. Nordau described Ahad Ha'am as 'belonging among the worst enemies of Zionism'. The controversy created a violent storm among the public and in the Jewish press. (See Ahad Ha'am's article in *Hashiloah*, Vol. 10, issue No. 60 (Dec. 1902), pp. 566–78; Nordau's article in *Die Welt* of 13 March 1903. (See also Herzl to Nordau 22 Feb. 1903, C.Z.A. HBIII/41).

[11] A declaration composed in reply to Nordau's article (see n. 10 above) was published in many Jewish newspapers. It was sent out by Buber, W., and Feiwel and in addition was signed by fifteen other Zionist personalities. It stated, *inter alia*: 'There is no need to defend the man who helped to create spiritual Zionism; this fearless man of truth in thought and deed; this man of ethical excellence who is regarded by the best East European Jews with honour, respect and trust. This genuine and perfect Jew who, long before the advent of political Zionism, appeared as the most radical combatant on behalf of the national movement and who issued the call for redemption of the people, the language and the land. It is superfluous to defend Ahad Ha'am against the defamations and degradations contained in Nordau's article. But we consider ourselves honour-bound to protest most vigorously, in the name of

and also, as a token of protest, inscribe Ahad Ha'am's name in the J.N.F. Golden Book.[12]

There are bound to be fierce repercussions at the Congress.[13] The struggle between East and West within Jewry has now worsened, and the editors of *Die Welt* have lightly flung the apple of discord into our camp. I trust that we shall finally succeed in letting the world know where hegemony in Jewry rightfully belongs—in the hands of the author of *Degeneration*[14] or in those of the young, spiritually free Eastern Jews.

Darling, remember me most cordially to the Rostov Zionists— especially to Rothstein.

Warmest regards to Nyusya and Esfir.

Many loving kisses and embraces, my Verochka,

Your Chaim.

[IN GERMAN]

A warm farewell kiss—Toldy

Kindest regards—Buber

293. To Vera, Sophia, Issay, and Theodosia Khatzman,[1]
Rostov. *Berlin, 17 March 1903*

Russian: H.W.: W.A.

Café Monopol, Berlin N.W. 17. III. 03.

My darling girl,

In all the hustle and bustle of Berlin it is almost impossible, with the best will in the world, to find a quiet moment for a real letter. So please forgive me, dearest Verochka, if this is brief.

I am leaving here at seven o'clock today. Berthold is leaving too, for Lausanne.[2] Nevertheless we have managed to get something

many Western European Jewish authors . . .' (see *Hatzefirah* of 23 March/5 April 1903 and also the circular letter signed by Buber, W., and Feiwel of 18 March 1903, Ehrenpreis Papers, fol. 22, N.L.).

[12] Early in the history of the Zionist Organization the Golden Book was devised as a method of honouring individuals and commemorating events. Inscriptions were (and still are) entered against payment of a fee used by the Jewish National Fund (J.N.F.) for the purposes of land reclamation. The various volumes are housed in Jerusalem.

[13] The Sixth Zionist Congress due to meet in the summer of 1903.

[14] Nordau was the author of *Degeneration* (Max Nordau, *Entartung*, Berlin 1892–93).

293. [1] Issay (Isaiah) and Theodosia were V.K.'s parents.

[2] Feiwel was due to visit Shriro in Lausanne (see No. 297).

going here. The University committee has been formed;[3] it is
small as yet, consisting of the following: Prof. Warburg, Prof.
Oppenheimer, Prof. Meyerhoffer,[4] Prof. Landau and Dr. A. Nossig.
There still remain Senator, Lewin and Baginsky[5] to be approached
by the others.

By the way, these gentlemen suggest, and are willing to undertake, a re-examination of the scheme to establish the University
in Germany. They are of the view that all our efforts must be directed
towards realisation of the project, if only in part.

Two professors from the Polytechnic have promised to work out
detailed plans for a Technical department[6] as soon as possible.

As to the periodical, we had long discussions here about it and
finally decided to call it *Der Jude*. Editors: Toldy and Buber;
Publisher, me. The first issue is being prepared now. There will
be splendid articles, among others, by Brandes[7] and Zimmel.[8]
Fiction—Wasserman.[9]

We have also decided to convene a special conference a few days
prior to the Congress to deal with the cultural question.[10] I hope

[3] According to the University Bureau report of May 1903 (No. 30/5/0, W.A.),
the Berlin Committee for the Jewish University was intended to function not only
as a local committee but also as the nucleus of a West European and American
committee. It was named in the report as 'The Berlin Central Committee'. Buber
informed the Zionist Actions Committee on 21 March 1903 that in Berlin 'a temporary central committee' had been set up (see C.Z.A. Z1/343).

[4] Wilhelm Meyerhoffer (1864–1906), lecturer in chemistry at Berlin University.
Later Meyerhoffer maintained that he was not in fact invited to join the committee
(see No. 393 and n. 2 there). However, he participated in the meetings of the committee in the summer of 1903 (see n. 2 to No. 382; n. 1 to No. 393).

[5] Adolf Baginsky (1843–1918), pediatrician and hospital director. Professor at
Berlin University.

[6] Nossig's later letters indicate this to be a reference to Heinrich Rubens (1865–
1922) and Ludwig Grunmach (1851–1923), both professors of physics at the Berlin
Polytechnic (see Nossig to W. 11 May 1903; 30 May 1903, W.A.). In the event Rubens
and Grunmach did not prepare a programme for the Technical department (cf.
n. 1 to No. 367) and in June 1903 W. himself drafted one for the Berlin Committee
(see n. 5 to No. 386). See also n. 8 to No. 294.

[7] Georg Brandes, 1842–1927 (orig. name Morris Cohen), lecturer in the history of
literature at Copenhagen University. Herzl failed in 1896 to gain his support for
Zionism but Brandes was interested in the Jewish problem and following the Balfour
Declaration of 1917 he supported the establishment of a Jewish national home in
Palestine.

[8] George Zimmel (1858–1918), philosopher and sociologist, was at that time a
professor at Berlin University.

[9] Jakob Wasserman the novelist (1873–1934).

[10] Buber informed the Zionist Actions Committee on 21 March 1903 of a plan to
convene 'a conference on Jewish cultural activities' in July 1903. Buber wrote that
the intention was to create a special platform to deal with the subject and thus avoid
a renewed controversy on cultural problems at the Zionist Congress (see C.Z.A.
Z1/343. Regarding the agenda proposed for the conference see Buber to Ehrenpreis
5 April 1903, Ehrenpreis Papers, fol. 22, N.L.).

to form an organisation there which will take the University in hand. So now you have a brief résumé of all that has been achieved. Needless to say we are again burdened with an endless load of work.

And you, my darling? I don't want to interrogate you. You must know that everything about you interests me. Write in the minutest detail. Tomorrow morning a new refrain will begin in Warsaw. We are on fire.

I have now to go with Buber to Prof. Landau. I met a million acquaintances here, of course. I am very happy about leaving today. The patent is applied for.[11]

Verusenka, remember me to Nyunechka, Esfir and the Rothsteins. I kiss you very ardently and embrace you even more tenderly, my Verunka, whom I am already beginning to miss.

Your Chaimchik

Dear Sofochka,

Forgive me for not writing to you separately. Verochka will tell you something of the hectic life I lead, and how hard I have to work. Always burning, never remaining in one place.

My dear, I send you my heartiest congratulations on the occasion of your birthday and sincerest wishes for a calm, full and contented life.

Don't be angry with your harassed but ever-loving and most respectful Chaim, who thinks so highly of you.

I kiss Nyunechka and unkind Rayka.

Regards to Misha

Dear Mama and Papa,

Confess how often you have chided me in your thoughts. As

[11] Relates to the German patent application for a chemical process of W., Samuel Levinson, and Anatole Dengin (cf. No. 294), who were about to make a similar application in the United States. On 17 March 1903 W. requested Levinson to register the patent in the United States 'in our three names' (see No. 294) and in his reply of 19 March (W.A.) Levinson wrote that he and Dengin were about to give a deposition in a sworn affidavit before the American consul in Geneva. Levinson undertook to write to the United States, and if W. did not wish to appear among the patentees because of his connections with the Bayer Works in Elberfeld (see Vol. I, n. 15 to No. 55), his name could be removed. In fact, on 1 March 1904, an American patent was granted in the names of Dengin and Levinson: U.S. Patent Office, Patent No. 753,372, March 1, 1904; Anatole Dengin and Samuel Levinson of Geneva, Switzerland; process of making condensation products from dicarbo acids and bromaded phtalic acids with naphtols. Nothing is known about a patent granted in Germany.

a matter of fact, I have deserved it. But what is one to do when it's necessary זאָף צוא רייסין[12] into tiny pieces! In the summer we shall all meet and be able to spend a few days together in peace and quiet, and talk about everything and everybody.

Regards to Aunt and the children,[13] and דער באַבע זאָל גיזונד זיין.[14]

I kiss you,
Chaim

294. To Samuel Levinson, Geneva. *Berlin, 17 March 1903*

German: H.W.: W.A.

Berlin, 17. III. 03.
Café Monopol

Dear Levinson,

Thank you for your frequent letters.[1] Deichler has failed to respond to my invitation, twice extended, to come to a meeting. I presume he has now left, and so I shall clarify the publication question by correspondence.[2]

Patent Registration will shortly be arranged.[3] As for registration in America, please deal with this immediately in the name of the three of us,[4] for it is completely independent of the German patent. Over here the decision on registration cannot be known before a lapse of six weeks, but we do not need to wait.

Committee: definitely formed, though for the moment small in size and composed of the following:[5] Prof. Warburg, Prof. Fra[nz] Oppenheimer, Prof. Meyerhoffer,[6] Dr. A. Nossig, Prof. Landau. The idea has had a decisive success. Please compose a few short letters on the typewriter, roughly on these lines:

'The Jewish University Bureau has the honour to bring to your attention the information that a provisional committee has been organised in Berlin composed of the following persons. . . . It will

---

[12] Yidd.: 'to be torn'.

[13] Maria Mamurovskaya and her daughters, Lydia and Deborah Chernin.

[14] Yidd.: 'to grandmother, may she keep well'.

294. [1] Only one of these letters, dated 14 March 1903, has been preserved. Levinson sent on to W. letters from Greidenberg and Aleinikov (see n. 9 below) and proposed that W. include Kharkov in his Russian tour.

[2] Apparently refers to the series of articles published by W. and Deichler in 1903 on the results of their chemistry research (see Vol. I, n. 10 to No. 92).

[3] See n. 11 to No. 293.

[4] W., Levinson, and Dengin—see n. 11 to No. 293.

[5] Cf. n. 3 to No. 293.

[6] Cf. n. 4 to No. 293.

be given full publicity only after the project has been elaborated in all its details.[7]

'A small committee of well-known experts has been entrusted with the task of working out the conception.[8] It will, among other matters, give serious consideration to the possibility of establishing the Jewish University in Berlin. The Berlin committee has undertaken to make the necessary approaches to the Government. Both the Berlin committee and the Jewish University Bureau are of the view that a partial realisation of the project is desirable at the *earliest possible* moment. Our efforts will now be concentrated, therefore, on the relief of immediate hardship by seeking to establish a small department of Technology and an Institute of Jewish Studies. Of course, all this is strictly confidential.'

I shall write again in detail from Warsaw; I am off there today at seven. I have replied to Greidenberg and Aleinikov.[9] Please get into touch with me in Warsaw. I shall try and get to Kharkov.

Affectionate greetings to you, and to dear Dengin,

Yours ever,
Ch. Weizmann

295. To Catherine Dorfman, Geneva. *Warsaw, 18 March 1903*

Russian: Pcd. H.W.: W.A.

Warsaw, 18/III. 03.

[----][1] Well! I can't understand why you couldn't find the addresses *in the copy-book in the press*,[2] which must [----] be in the room.

[7] Regarding the distribution of the circular see n. 6 to No. 298.

[8] In the report of the University Bureau of May 1903 (No. 30/5/0 W.A.) it is stated that the Berlin Committee undertook to appoint a professorial subcommittee to prepare the academic aspects of the project. Apparently the allocation to two Polytechnic professors of the programme for the Technical department (see n. 6 to No. 293) constituted the first move in establishing this subcommittee. In the same report it was noted that the University Bureau would supply material required for the programme's preparation by means of a survey among professors and experts in University studies (cf. n. 9 to No. 13).

[9] See Greidenberg to W. 23 Feb. (8 March) 1903; Aleinikov to W. 23 Feb. (8 March) 1903, W.A. Both had written concerning the sessions of the Jewish University Committee in Kharkov and the general meeting which it had organised. The committee decided to publish the Russian translation of *Eine Jüdische Hochschule* (see n. 11 to No. 7) and raise funds for the University Bureau. 200 roubles (530 francs) had already been remitted to the Bureau (cf. n. 2 to No. 290) and Greidenberg wrote that in his opinion it would be possible to obtain 1,000 roubles.

295. [1] A corner of the postcard had been cut away and some words of the first few lines are missing.

[2] Copies of hand-written letters were made by pressing the copy-book.

For heaven's sake, find them and send them out![3] Berlin was successful beyond all expectations. A brilliant committee was organised:[4] Warburg, Oppenheimer, Nossig, Prof. Landau, Prof. Meyerhoffer;[5] among non-Zionists, Philippson.[6]

I only arrived today and am sounding things out. Tomorrow, the Fraction.[7] Am on fire. Full of hope. Our periodical is being made ready for publication. It will be called *Jüdische Revue: Organ für das Moderne Judenthum*.[8] Editors: Buber, Feiwel and myself. Will write soon. Many kisses.

Regards to Anya,[9]

Chaim

296. To Vera Khatzman, Rostov. *Warsaw, 21 March 1903**

Russian: H.W.: W.A.

Warsaw, 8/III. 03.

My dear Verochka,

Your note, which I have been waiting for so impatiently, arrived from Rostov today.[1] Each time I thought of you making this long journey all alone something within me seemed to give way, and I am happy that you are home at last. Now have a good rest, and in the warmth at home among your near and dear, you should be able to work and relax at the same time.

Darling, this is the fourth day since my arrival in Warsaw. I never imagined that I would find it such hard going; mainly because of the special conditions here, and because the Jews are divided into a large number of groups that have nothing in common with each other. There are 'Poles of the Mosaic persuasion', Hassidim,

---

[3] Presumably the reference here is to the distribution of a circular among members of the Democratic Fraction, which has not been found. On 17 Feb. 1903 W. wrote to Kroll and Idelson (No. 272) that 'in a day or two' he would send out a circular calling upon members of the Fraction—'to unite and prepare themselves for the Congress', and it is possible that the distribution was delayed. The fact that W. requested Dorfman to handle the matter further supports the assumption that the reference is to a Fraction circular, University matters being handled by Levinson.

[4] Cf. n. 3 to No. 293.

[5] Cf. n. 4 to No. 293.

[6] In earlier letters the name of Martin Philippson was not included among Berlin committee members (see Nos. 293, 294) and his name is also missing from the list published in the University Bureau report of May 1903 (No. 30/5/0 W.A.).

[7] See n. 3 to No. 296.

[8] For another version of its title cf. n. 8 to No. 292.

[9] Anne Koenigsberg.

296. * The Gregorian date. [1] Not found.

our Litvaks,[2] all of different worlds, and to throw a bridge from one section of this population to another is very laborious work. I have already had meetings devoted to the Fraction,[3] while a meeting to discuss the University is taking place on Monday with all the local aristocracy in attendance.[4] I have been asked to go to Lodz but don't know whether this will come to anything since I must save my strength for Moscow, for which I have high hopes.[5]

Otherwise I found everything in order here. My sister[6] is happy and at home, and everything is all right.

Please, my dear, write to me. After I leave Warsaw things will ease up and I shall reply more promptly. I have never found things as hard as I do in Warsaw.

I kiss you endlessly and send greetings to everybody.

Your ardent and ever-loving Chaimchik

297. To Vera Khatzman, Rostov. *Warsaw, 25(?) March 1903*

Russian: H.W.: W.A.

Warsaw, 2[–]/III. 03.[1]

My good, dear Girl,

Despite my exhaustion I write to tell you, if only very briefly, of my impressions. There was a great deal of work to do in Warsaw; I had to call on people who had long since lost their Jewishness. I went. The sight of these well-fed, unfeeling folk wrung my heart. However, contrary to all expectations, everything went off well.

---

[2] Orig. 'Lithuanians', a term used to describe the Jews of Lithuania and White Russia.

[3] According to Isaac Gruenbaum, the affairs of the Democratic Fraction were discussed at a meeting in the home of Chaim Lubzhinsky, with Gruenbaum acting as chairman. A brief opening address by W. was followed by a discussion. W.'s reply to the debate was 'interesting and at times devastating' (see Gruenbaum letters of 30 March 1965 and 21 April 1965, W.A.).

[4] A detailed description of one meeting concerned with the University project held in Warsaw during W.'s visit there is given in his letter to Dorfman of 4 May 1903 (see No. 314), but it is not clear whether the reference there is to the first meeting which took place on Monday, 23 March 1903 or the second on 29 March 1903 (see No. 300).

[5] W. did not visit Moscow (see n. 3 to No. 302; No. 303).

[6] It is not clear whether the reference is to W.'s elder sister, Miriam Lubzhinsky, who lived in Warsaw, or to his sister Gita studying at the Music Conservatoire there.

297. [1] The second numeral of the date is blurred in the original. The approximate date on which the letter was written has been determined by the words 'I am so terribly tired that I have decided to take a break for two days and then go to Lodz.' And see letter to Levinson of 27 March 1903 (No. 298): 'I am going to Lodz today. ...'

An effective and important committee has been formed.[2] Tomorrow I have a meeting with them and we shall map out the work.

I am so terribly tired that I have decided to take a break for two days and then go to Lodz together with old Sokolow. A great deal can be done there. From Lodz, I shall go home and then on to Moscow.[3] I have heard nothing from Grusenberg in St. P., which is why I shall not go there at all.[4]

Verunka, I already feel terribly depressed. If I live in a whirl-pool now, what will it be like later? I console myself with the thought that I shall not have to do without you for long in Geneva. You must have written to me in Pinsk. Papa is due here tomorrow and will bring me your letters.

Please, my own, my lovely darling, describe everything in the greatest detail, everything that happens around you, what you do, and how your studies are proceeding. In short, everything. I beg of you, write at length and in the minutest detail. Please don't mind my not writing as often as I usually do. I shall make up for it soon and report about everything. Toldy is in Lausanne at Shriro's. There will be a lot to tell, as I have accidentally learned a great many unpleasant things.[5]

By the way, I have told them at home about our relationship.[6] I am waiting impatiently for your letters.

Warm greetings to Sofochka, Nyunya, Misha and Rayka. My regards to your father, mother and grandmother. Kiss everybody for me.

You, darling, I kiss and take to my heart.

Your Chaimchik.

Mirl[7] and the children send kisses.

---

[2] The members of the committee were August Minkovsky and Samuel Goldflamm, who were joined later also by B. Koral and J. Muttermilch—see report of University Bureau of May 1903 (W.A. No. 13/5/0) and the letter of the Warsaw Committee members to W. of 23 June 1903, W.A.

[3] But see No. 302 and n. 3 there.

[4] Grusenberg did not answer W.'s letter of 26 Feb. 1903 (No. 281), in which he wrote that he was awaiting news from Grusenberg in connection with his proposed visit to St. Petersburg, nor did Grusenberg reply to the two further letters W. wrote him from Berlin and Warsaw (cf. No. 356).

[5] The implication of this is obscure.

[6] W. had until then not disclosed to his parents the character of his relationship with V.K., although they had declared their love for each other in the spring of 1901. It should be recalled that W.'s first fiancée, Sophia Getzova, had twice stayed at the home of his parents in Pinsk (see Vol. I, Nos. 28, 40) and cf. letter of 10 Aug. 1902 (Vol. I, No. 276): 'I cannot tell my family yet . . . in view of all that happened in the past.'

[7] Miriam Lubzhinsky.

298. To Samuel Levinson, Geneva. *Warsaw, 27 March 1903*

German: H.W.: W.A.

Warsaw, 27. III. 03.

My dear Friend,

Unfortunately I have had to stay here longer than I thought. Because of some complicated circumstances the situation is difficult in Warsaw.[1] And in addition I have been in bed for two days, unable to move. An influential committee has been organised here,[2] and moreover we have received 2,000 roubles for preparatory work.[3] I am going to Lodz today and shall remain there for two full days. I hope to accomplish something there too.

I no longer plan to visit Petersburg because I have barely sufficient time for Moscow.

I shall write from Pinsk about the patents.[4] I hope to be in Moscow a week from Saturday.[5]

You may send circulars to Kharkov, Rostov, Ginis of Baku, Petersburg, Paris, Warsaw.[6]

Warm regards,

Yours ever,
Chaim

299. To Vera Khatzman, Rostov. *Warsaw, 29 March 1903*[1]

Russian: H.W.: W.A.

My dear, my good, my sweet Darling,

If you could only see me now, you would immediately forgive

298. [1] Cf. No. 296.   [2] See n. 2 to No. 297.

[3] In the University Bureau report of May 1903 (No. 30/5/0 W.A.) it is again stated that in Warsaw about 2,000 roubles were pledged to the Bureau, but ultimately only 200 roubles were received from this source (see financial report of the University Bureau of 15 July 1903, W.A.).

[4] See n. 11 to No. 293. Only one letter written from Russia by W. to Levinson has been found (No. 302) and the patents are not mentioned therein.

[5] See, however, n. 3 to No. 302.

[6] In the letter of 19 March 1903 (W.A.) Levinson asked who were to receive the circular regarding the establishment of the Berlin Committee for the University (see No. 294). Levinson replied to the present letter on 30 March 1903 (W.A.), stating that he had sent the circular only to Isaac Rothstein in Rostov and to Samuel Ginis in Baku, but for various reasons he was delaying its dispatch to other places. He proposed sending the circular, in a revised form, to a larger circle of sympathizers, but it is not known whether additional circulars were in fact distributed.

299. [1] At the top of the letter there is a marking in English by an unknown hand 'Warsaw, 24. IV. 03' but by comparing it with the letter to Levinson of 29 March 1903 (see No. 300) it is evident that it too was written on this date.

me for not writing. I look worse than I did after the Fifth Congress,[2] but have been rewarded by winning all along the line: we were completely victorious. I raised 5,000 roubles in Lodz for our preparatory work.[3] We are holding the final meeting in Warsaw today, and I expect to raise this much again.[4] So the goal has been reached. Tomorrow I shall be going home, remaining there for two days. Then on to Moscow.[5]

I shall find your letters at home. I cannot describe how much I miss you. I am fidgety and restless in my few quiet moments. One look at my darling would make me happy. Here I am at least surrounded by the warmth of friends and relatives, but what the Polish Jews are like I shall tell you when we meet.[6] Not in my wildest dreams did I imagine this kind of moral prostitution. But an idea can conquer, even here.

Once I am home, we shall all be writing to you fully. Mirl and Gita[7] send their kisses. They love you very, very much.

I had some unpleasant business with the police in Lodz,[8] but after two days' bother it all ended well.

At all events success was enormous, and in spite of my desperate physical fatigue I feel cheerful and in good spirits; and you, my own dear Verochka, know that victory is ours.

I kiss everybody. But you I embrace and press to my heart.

Your worn out Chaimchik loves you very much.

Regards to friends.

300. To Samuel Levinson, Geneva.[1] *Warsaw, 29 March 1903*

German: H.W.: W.A.

Warsaw, 29th.

Mr. Levinson,
Geneva.

Dear Friend,

As Dr. Weizmann is exceedingly tired because of his strenuous

[2] The Zionist Congress of Dec. 1901.

[3] In Lodz a committee for the University was set up headed by Stanislav Yarochinsky, Michael Kohn, and Dr. (Moritz) Posnansky—see University Bureau report, May 1903, No. 30/5/0 W.A. The pledges of financial support given to W. in Lodz were not in fact fulfilled.

[4] In the event 2,000 roubles were pledged in Warsaw for the University Bureau—see n. 3 to No. 298.   [5] See, however, n. 3 to No. 302.

[6] See also Nos. 296, 314.   [7] Gita Weizmann (see n. 6 to No. 296).

[8] Nothing more is known about this incident.

300. [1] The letter was written and signed by Saul Stupnitzky, but its style and

[*Footnote 1 continued on p. 281*]

activities during the past few days, I am directed to inform you of the following in his name: First, Dr. Weizmann asks you please to forgive him for having left you so long without any news, due to the exceptionally complicated and difficult circumstances. 'Nothing had been prepared in advance, we had to do everything ourselves and hence the postponement of these reports. Despite many local difficulties[2] in Warsaw, I have succeeded in holding a few meetings here,[3] not to mention one large gathering of which the results will be evident only by tonight. I trust these will be excellent. Notwithstanding, I paid a brief visit to Lodz and there held a meeting which exceeded all expectations. Five thousand roubles were subscribed on the spot, a sum which should be collected during the current month.[4] Warsaw will contribute a similar amount.[5] But I feel very tired now and in need of rest, so I am going to Pinsk for a few days and after that to Moscow,[6] thus concluding this present tour and returning to Geneva.

'As for the money you require, please get in touch with Mr. B. Feiwel, care of Shriro in Lausanne, so that he can get it from London.[7] I am writing to him also.[8] Should you be in urgent need, do write to me in Moscow and I shall send you the money by telegraph.

'Once again, please forgive me. The circumstances were so extraordinarily difficult and I had no possibility of writing to you.'

On behalf of Dr. Weizmann, I remain,

Yours faithfully,
S. J. Stupnitzky

301. To Vera Khatzman, Rostov. *Pinsk (?)31 March 1903*[1]

Russian: H.W.: W.A.

Dear Verochka,

I got home this morning and shall remain here until Saturday

the usage of the first person singular in the lower portion indicates that it was dictated by W., whose direct words are here enclosed by quotation marks not in the original.

[2] See Nos. 296, 314. [3] See n. 3 to No. 296; No. 297.
[4] Cf. n. 3 to No. 299. [5] Cf. n. 3 to No. 298.
[6] See, however, n. 3 to No. 302.

[7] Feiwel wrote to Herzl on 2 April 1903 (the orig. erroneously has it '2 March 1903') requesting that the Jewish Colonial Trust be instructed to send him 1,000 francs (from the University Bureau account). Feiwel noted that the funds were needed for W.'s propaganda tour to Russia and for publishing the results of the student survey. Feiwel's letter was written and signed on a sheet of notepaper previously signed while blank by W. (See C.Z.A. Z1/343).

[8] No letter from W. to Feiwel during the Russian trip has been found.

301. [1] The date of writing has been estimated from the words 'I got home this

[*Footnote 1 continued on p. 282*]

evening,[2] when I leave for Moscow.[3] Things ended brilliantly in Warsaw. We ought to collect close to six or seven thousand roubles in both cities.[4] It was a tremendous success.

I am surprised by the absence of any letters from you. Has anything happened? Verunchik, my dear, you would surely not have just stopped writing without reason. If I don't hear from you tomorrow I shall telegraph. You can understand how wholeheartedly I join the family in their request.[5] Papa is not at home just now but he asked me to send you his warmest invitation[6] and we shall all be very happy to see you in our house. Verochka, darling, why don't you write?

What's new at home? How is father? His health? Mother? The children? The victory we won in Warsaw exceeded all our expectations. I found myself in the very camp of the assimilationists and they were forced to retreat. Their best people were involved in this fight with me but they are all under the table now.[7] You can't conceive how happy we were, how we all thought of you every minute and regretted your not being with us. Now everything is provided for—periodical, Bureau, all our activities.

Verunchik, my dear, I am waiting impatiently for news from you. Write at once. Warmest greetings and kisses to Sofochka, Nyunya, your parents, Rayka, Mishka. Your aunt,[8] the children,[9] grandmother.

I kiss my beloved Verochka again and again.

Chaimchik.

morning.' W. wrote on 29 March 1903 (see No. 299) that he was going to Pinsk the next day, and presumably he arrived there on 31 March 1903.

[2] 4 April 1903.

[3] See, however, n. 3 to No. 302.

[4] In Lodz, 5,000 roubles were pledged for the Jewish University Bureau (see No. 299). Regarding Warsaw, W. wrote to Levinson on 27 March that from there 2,000 roubles would be received (see No. 298) and on 29 March he wrote that Warsaw, like Lodz, would yield 5,000 roubles; but from the University Bureau report of May 1903 (No. 30/5/0 W.A.) it emerges that in Warsaw only approximately 2,000 roubles were pledged.

[5] It would seem that after W. told his parents about his relationship with V.K. (see n. 6 to No. 297) the family wrote and invited her to visit Pinsk. Their letter has not been found.

[6] Apparently when he met W. in Warsaw (see No. 297).

[7] Cf. No. 314.

[8] Maria Mamurovskaya.

[9] Lydia and Deborah Chernin.

302. To Samuel Levinson, Geneva. *Bakhmach, 8 April 1903*[1]

German: Pcd. H.W.: W.A.

Bakhmach, I don't know the date, 3 o'clock[2]

Dear Friend,

It is going to be Kharkov instead of Moscow. The Muscovites wanted me for ten days—impossible because of lack of time, and so I had to forgo the visit.[3] Warsaw, Lodz, Kharkov, are enough for this time. As it is, my friend, I shall already be a few days late coming back. Would you please arrange everything together with Dengin in the laboratory. Dengin, to whom my best regards, can start up the work. I want this very much, dear friend.

I would estimate the material result of the tour to be 8,000 roubles, all for preparatory work—and therefore beyond our expectations.[4] I could collapse with fatigue. Perhaps I shall write you again from Kharkov. One request: when you receive this card, telegraph me in Pinsk 'Presence in Geneva urgent' and similarly the following day again. If not, my family will not in any circumstances let me go but detain me throughout the entire *Easter*[5]—which is impossible. You must extricate me by telegram. God, I'm so tired I am afraid of some illness. We shall arrange further steps in matters of chemistry together.

Affectionately,

Your Chaim.

Don't forget the telegrams, and my affectionate regards to Dengin.

303. To Vera Khatzman, Rostov. *Kharkov, 9 April 1903*[1]

Russian: H.W.: W.A.

27 March 1903

Dear Verochka, my darling.

Both your letter and telegram arrived yesterday.[2] My dear,

302. [1] Date according to Russian postmark.

[2] This sentence alone is written in Russian.

[3] See also No. 303, in which W. gives another, and probably more correct, reason for cancelling his visit to Moscow. Possibly he was unwilling to specify the real reason in a letter sent abroad for fear of censorship; see also Kroll to W., 20 April (3 May) 1903, W.A. Kroll states there that if W. came to Moscow during the Tzar's visit it would be impossible to organize a large meeting.

[4] Cf. n. 4 to No. 301.

[5] The University vacation continued until the end of April.

303. [1] Written on the headed notepaper of A. Y. Nemirovsky, 28, Rimarskaya Street. This is the Gregorian date. [2] Not found.

I knew you wouldn't come,[3] though somehow in my heart I
hoped—perhaps. You are surprised by the change in my itinerary
and all this rapid movement from one place to another. But this
is how the situation has developed, my Verochka. Circumstances
over which we had no control made it impossible for me to visit
Moscow. They are so strict there now that no Zionist meeting of
any kind can be held. All this is related to the Tzar's arrival.[4]
As a visit to Kharkov would also be quite useful, I decided to take
advantage of the few days that suddenly became available to me
and so came here. It was a good thing I did.

The *Hochschule* can only profit by it.[5] I shall return home on
Saturday during the daytime,[6] remain two or three days, and then
I leave for abroad. I am tired beyond all limits and feel incapable
of any kind of work. Moreover, I am not in the best of moods.
I had a meeting with Tyomkin (the representative) here yesterday.
He has come from Petersburg,[7] where unbelievable things are
happening. New restrictions have been introduced against the
Jews which will also affect the privileged classes.[8] Unpleasant
developments concerning Zionism[9] are expected. In short, we are
getting a nice holiday present. I can't see how the Jews can be

[3] V.K. was invited by the W. family to visit Pinsk (see n. 5 to No. 301) but it
appears that she notified them of her inability to come.

[4] For cancellation of W.'s trip to Moscow, see n. 3 to No. 302.

[5] It appears from later letters that, when in Kharkov, W. discussed future activities
with Greidenberg, Chairman of the Kharkov Committee for the Jewish University
(see, e.g., No. 369). It is stated in the University Bureau report of May 1903 (W.A.
No. 30/5/0) that the Kharkov Committee has 'undertaken publicity and propaganda
activities in the large cities of Central Russia'; see also No. 321. See also No. 328
concerning support by the Kharkov group of the plan to publish a journal.

[6] 11 April 1903.

[7] Tyomkin, area leader for the Elizavetgrad Region, visited St. Petersburg,
Moscow, and Kharkov, mainly in connection with the affairs of the 'Geulah' Com-
pany for the purchase of land in Palestine. (See Circular No. 10 of Elizavetgrad Region,
C.Z.A. Z1/195.)

[8] It was already known in February that a regulation was due to be enacted
(officially approved on 10 (23) May 1903) concerning the ban on Jews who were
entitled to live outside the Pale of Settlement ('privileged classes', see n. 6 to No.
316) to acquire and lease immovable property in rural areas outside the Pale. See
Hazman, 10 (23) Feb. 1903, and also *Budushchnost'*, 23 May (5 June) 1903.

[9] The legal status of the Zionist Organization in Russia was unclear. The existence
of a country-wide organization was not permitted but there was no prohibition on
Zionist activities and an official permit was even given for the holding of the Second
Conference of Russian Zionists at Minsk (Sept. 1902). On the other hand, the importa-
tion into Russia of the shares and provisional certificates of the Jewish Colonial
Trust was forbidden in Oct. 1902. W. apparently learned from Tyomkin for the first
time that a memorandum on Zionism had been prepared in the Russian Ministry
of Interior and that it was feared that new restrictions on Zionist activity would be
introduced. (Concerning the memorandum, see n. 3 to No. 305; n. 3 to No. 306;
No. 316 and ns. 11–20 there; also n. 12 to No. 346). For restrictions imposed on
Zionist activity in Russia in 1903, see also n. 5 to No. 414.

restricted any further. And yet deep in my heart I am rather pleased that the privileged groups will now get it. Let them find out for themselves what assimilation means. I am so consumed with rage and vexation that I am afraid to meet people. I feel like shouting abuse in their faces.

You can well imagine, my dear, how all this tells on me, without a sound nerve in my body. I yearn to be back in the laboratory. I implore you, Verochka, to come as soon as you can. You cannot imagine how much I miss you. I cannot remain alone for a moment —it is frightening.

I have written you at less length than usual this time[10]—try and understand, my friend, that there is not one moment in the day that I can call my own. There has not been one reasonably peaceful hour. Yet, as you know full well, I have not been away from you in spirit for a single minute.

Toldy is in Lausanne with the Shriros. I have no idea where Sheychik is. Probably in Pinsk. Nothing of outstanding interest is happening in the Zionist world.

Verussik, write to me, my darling, to Warsaw c/o Lunia,[11] for there will be no-one at Mirl's during the holidays; and then [write] to Geneva.

I cannot write any more, I am absolutely at the end of my tether. I wish you and all our dear ones a happy holiday. I feel that mine will not be so happy. Far from it. Thank all your family for telling me off so nicely.[12] I would love to answer every one of them and repay their chidings in kind, but I can't even hold my pen any longer. I have no strength left, and my mood is below 0. I kiss all of you, dear people. Believe me when I say that I suffer the torments of Tantalus in being just 'a step or two' away from you and still am unable to see you.

I kiss you all and wish you a גוט יו״ט.[13]

> I kiss you, Verusya, my joy, my darling.
> Your, your, your Chaimchik.

---

[10] I.e., in the course of his current visit, in contrast to his previous visits to Russia in the summers of 1901 and 1902.

[11] Salomea (Lunia) Krinsky, who was then at her parents' home in Warsaw.

[12] Members of V.K.'s family apparently 'told him off' for not visiting Rostov.

[13] Yidd.: 'happy holiday'. The first night of Passover fell on 11 April 1903.

304. To Vera Khatzman, Rostov. *Kiev, 10 April 1903*[1]

Russian: Pcd. H.W.: W.A.

Kiev, Friday (not sure of the date)

My dearest Girl,

Tomorrow I shall be home at last.[2] My fatigue beggars description. In Kharkov there were un[----].[3] Volodia Idelson will be calling on you to tell[4] you [----]. I still don't know how many days I shall spend at home. Probably very few. I am sorry that [----] to get together, and I had such grandiose plans. I must get some rest soon, or I shall fall off my feet. My brothers[5] must have already arrived home and I shall see them tomorrow. I wish you all the very best and the happiest of holidays.

You should not have all scolded me so.[6] *Ich habe es gut gemeint.*[7] I kiss you endlessly, my joy.

Regards and kisses to all.

Chaim.

Warm regards to Nyusya and Esfir.

305. To Vera Khatzman, Rostov. *Pinsk, 14 April 1903**

Russian: H.W.: W.A.

Pinsk, 1 April 03.

My dearest Verochka,

You cannot imagine what a disappointment it was for all of us that you didn't come.[1] Well, what can one do? I hope you will be able to meet my family on your way to Geneva, at least. As you

---

304. [1] Dated according to Kiev postmark.

[2] In Pinsk.

[3] The postcard had been damaged where omissions are indicated.

[4] For W.'s visit to Kharkov see n. 5 to No. 303. Nothing else is known of his activities in this city.

[5] Samuel and Moses Weizmann, then studying in Kiev.

[6] The statement apparently relates to the 'telling off' by V.K.'s family; cf. n. 11 to No. 303.

[7] 'I intended it for the best.'

305. * The Gregorian date. [1] See n. 3 to No. 303.

know from Haya's note,[2] I was 'telegraphically' summoned to Minsk.[3] I would rather die than undertake this trip, for it involves a great deal of unpleasantness. It means starting discussions in certain 'circles' over Zionism all over again. This time, apparently, their relations with us will at long last be clarified. I shall do everything in my power in this regard. I shall not write anything about myself now. My state of mind cannot be described. My one wish is to find myself in my flat or even in some hospital—it is all the same to me—just so that I can rest.

You know, Verochka, I am not too pleased with your relatives. They don't write to me at all. The good Lord knows that if I don't write much, it is because I haven't the strength. I am in a state of utter prostration.

Sheychik has just been to see me. He will write to you. You may possibly return together, as he is staying on for some time yet.

I shall come back here in two days and remain until the end of the holidays,[4] and on the night of the last day I shall leave for Berlin via Warsaw.

Volodia Idelson must have told you all about Kharkov.[5] I have a great favour to ask of you and the others: come as soon as possible. You cannot imagine, my own one, what joy it would be for me to be with you, if just for a moment. But it is best not to write about it . . . I shall only get more upset.

I must close. I kiss you and everybody again and again.

Your Chaimchik.

[2] Apparently a note added by Haya Lichtenstein, W.'s sister, to a previous letter to V.K. The note has not been found.

[3] It appears that W. was called to Minsk by Simon Rosenbaum to discuss a memorandum on Zionism which had been prepared by the Russian Ministry of Interior. The memorandum stated *inter alia* that there was a connection between the Democratic Fraction and the Social Democratic movement, and there was a danger that the activities of the Fraction in Russia would be banned. The leaders of Russian Zionism were also apprehensive about further restrictions on general Zionist activity and apparently decided to intercede with St. Petersburg and, *inter alia*, dispel the charges against the Democratic Fraction made in the memorandum. (For the memorandum of the Ministry of Interior and the statements therein concerning the Fraction, see ns. 11–18 to No. 316. As to the connection between W.'s visit to Minsk and the dangers threatening the Fraction, see Glikin to W., 30 June 1903, W.A. Concerning fears of restrictions on Zionist activity, see also n. 9 to No. 303. For W.'s visit to Minsk, see n. 3 to No. 306).

[4] The last days of Passover fell on 18/19 April 1903.

For W.'s visit to Kharkov see n. 5 to No. 303.

306. To Vera Khatzman, Rostov. *Luninets, 17 April 1903*

Russian: H.W.: W.A.

> Luninets Station again, on the way
> home from Minsk. Friday (am not
> sure of the date)[1]

My darling Verochka, my lovely girl,

I am going home at last. I shall spend the last two days of the holidays there and on Sunday night set out again. I can't write to you about the purpose and meaning of this trip. I shall have to tell you all about it when we meet. I sent for Motzkin[2] and he arrived: sour, listless, and probably sick. My mission is completed.[3]

This time I have succeeded in getting to know the Zionist position in Minsk, and I must say we should be pleased with the large number of good comrades.

I am not putting any questions to you in the hope that I shall find your letters waiting for me at home. I long to rest. I shall probably travel up with Sokolova, Lunia,[4] etc. We shall meet in Warsaw. I shall not be stopping off anywhere on the way. Address your letters to Geneva.

My dear! I implore you, again and again, to come as soon as possible. You cannot remotely imagine how I long for you and how I feel.

Are you making any arrangements for the Bureau?[5]

How are Nyusya and Esfir? And Rothstein? Verusya, give them my warmest regards. I don't think I have to apologise for not writing. The good Lord knows that I am at the end of my tether, in a state of utter exhaustion. This trip proved much too strenuous and it will take a long time for me to forget it.

Many kisses to your dear sisters, parents and brothers.

306. [1] The letter was apparently written on Friday, 17 April 1903, when W. was returning from the visit to Minsk about which he had informed V.K. on 14 April 1903 (see No. 305).

[2] Motzkin was presumably staying in St. Petersburg at that time—cf. No. 327.

[3] See n. 3 to No. 305. It would seem that Rosenbaum had shown W. the memorandum on Zionism prepared for the Russian Ministry of Interior, and that whilst in Minsk W. had drafted a memorandum on the Democratic Fraction with the object of explaining its true character to the Russian authorities. It was apparently agreed that Rosenbaum would submit W.'s memorandum to the Ministry of Interior in St. Petersburg (see Glikin to W. 18 (31) May 1903, W.A., and also n. 2 to No. 331) W.'s memorandum has not been found. During his stay in Minsk W. also held consultations on a propaganda campaign for the Jewish University project in White Russia and Lithuania (see University Bureau report of May 1903, W.A. No. 30/5/0). He also delivered an address at a meeting of *Poalei-Zion*—see n. 21 to No. 314.

[4] Manya Sokolow and Salomea (Lunia) Krinsky.

[5] Refers to fund-raising in Rostov for the Jewish University Bureau.

Verussik, write in minutest detail about everything. I shall begin to lead a fairly normal existence and will write every day, but hope to shorten our separation to the absolute minimum. I can't live without you. I kiss my good, my dear Verochka.

Your Chaimchik.

307. To Vera Khatzman, Rostov. *Berlin, 22 April 1903*

Russian: Pcd. H.W.: W.A.[1]

22/iv. 03.

My Darling,

In Berlin at last. Tomorrow I shall be pressing on.
I kiss you again and again, my dear Verochka.

Chaim.

[GREETINGS ADDED, IN GERMAN AND RUSSIAN, BY REGINA SCHIMMER, DAVIS TRIETSCH, FELIX PINKUS, MARIA SOKOLOW AND ONE OF THE KRINSKY SISTERS].

308. To Vera Khatzman, Rostov. *Berlin, 23 April 1903*

Russian: Pcd. H.W.: W.A.

Berlin, 24/iv. 03.[1]

My darling Verochka, my lovely one,

I arrived here yesterday and am now leaving. I am very tired but already feel much better. The first issue of our paper is ready and will soon appear.[2] I hope it will be all right.

Had a long letter from Geneva.[3] They are waiting for you impatiently at home and in Warsaw.[4] Darling, you will go. It will give them the greatest pleasure, indescribable joy. They will receive you as you deserve.

---

307. [1] The message was written across the postcard's illustration of the railway station on Friedrichstrasse.

308. [1] Thus in orig. but the date of the Berlin postmark is 23 April 1903.

[2] Plans for the first issue of the periodical *Der Jude* were being advanced at this time by Buber and Feiwel (see Feiwel to Buber, 16 April 1903, 18 April 1903, W.A.), but the publication never appeared.

[3] Apparently from Levinson, not found.

[4] The reference is to the home of W.'s parents in Pinsk and of his brother-in-law Chaim Lubzhinsky in Warsaw—cf. n. 3 to No. 303; No. 305.

Herzl's journey to Egypt has apparently been very successful and has had positive results in terms of colonisation.[5]

I kiss you again and again, my Verochka.

Chaimchik.

Greetings and a kiss to all.

309. To Vera Khatzman, Rostov. *Karlsruhe, 24 April 1903*

Russian: H.W.: W.A.

Karlsruhe,[1] 24. IV. 1903

My dear Verochka,

On my way to Geneva, I stopped off for a few hours in Karlsruhe to see our friends there. I am writing to you now, my dearest girl, while waiting for the train. I spent only one day in Berlin. Everybody was away. I did a little work in the *Verlag*, where the financial position is now quite critical.[2] Something will have to be done to put an end to all these difficulties. Tomorrow I shall be in Lausanne and there I shall meet Toldy. I have a great deal to discuss with him.

You know, Verochka, I find it more and more difficult to understand Toldy. His relations with Esther[3] are disingenuous. He keeps both Manya Sok[olow] and Esther on a string; first one, then the other. He and the girls are all profoundly unhappy. Berthold is, beyond doubt, a good and honest man but weak as a baby, like a little boy. The situation incapacitates him for work and makes him nervous and ineffectual, etc.

---

[5] Herzl paid a visit to Cairo from 23 March to 4 April 1903 to discuss a plan for Jewish settlement in the Sinai Peninsula, particularly the El-Arish area, with the British Consul-General (Lord Cromer) and the Egyptian Government. Herzl hoped the plan would have the effect of extricating the Zionist movement from the impasse consequent upon the failure of negotiations with Turkey for a charter for Jewish settlement in Palestine. Negotiations had been proceeding since Oct. 1902 with the British Colonial Secretary, Joseph Chamberlain, and the Foreign Secretary, Lord Lansdowne, while a Zionist survey commission visited Sinai in March 1903 and Leopold Greenberg conducted talks in Cairo. The Egyptian Government rejected any proposal to grant autonomy to the settlers, the details of which would be specified in a charter, but showed readiness to discuss settlement plans. None the less, the negotiations broke down, principally because of the refusal of the Egyptian Government to guarantee the requisite water from the Nile (see Bein, *Theodore Herzl*, London 1957 edition, pp. 433 ff.).

309. [1] Written on the headed notepaper of the Hotel Tannhäuser.
    [2] See n. 9 to No. 122.
    [3] Esther Shneerson, later married to Feiwel.

Verusya, in Geneva I expect to find your letter with the happy tidings of your arrival.

I have already asked you several times to be sure and not forget about my family when you plan your journey.[4] Please stop in Pinsk and Warsaw. You will see how well you get along with them, my darling.

A few words, my dear, about your last letter.[5] I truly don't know the reason for this strange fear of our life in Geneva. Is it because this time I wrote less than I did last summer? Verunchik, don't be unjust to your Chaimchik, who loves you dearly, and whose understanding and respect for you grow ever deeper. My dear, forget all that and get here soon; everything will be fine.

My warmest regards to all the dear ones.

Chaimchik kisses you ardently.

Nadinka Rabinovitch[6] asks to be remembered to you. Don't forget her, she adds.

310. To Jacob Bernstein–Kohan, Kishinev. *Geneva, 27 April 1903*

German: Or. Copy. T.W.: W.A.

27. 4. 03.

Dr. J. Kohan-Bernstein,
Kishinev.

Dear Friend,

You can imagine how the first newspaper reports about Kishinev alarmed us,[1] and particularly how great our concern was for you and your family. We surmised, rightly we think, that you were in the thick of the wildest disorders. Your telegram,[2] painful though it was, has fortunately relieved us of the greatest anxiety and we

---

[4] See Nos. 301, 305, 308.

[5] Not found.

[6] Nadia R. was then living in Warsaw—see No. 313. No further details are known about her.

310. [1] A pogrom was waged against the Jews of Kishinev on 19 and 20 April 1903. Forty-nine Jews were killed, hundreds were injured, and considerable damage was done to property. The pogrom had been preceded by a hardening of the anti-Jewish policy of the Russian authorities and anti-semitic agitation in the press. The sources of incitement, no less than the scale of violence, roused the Jewish world to vigorous protest, and in this it was joined by many non-Jews in the West.

[2] The first reports on the disturbances in Kishinev were telegraphed from the Rumanian frontier by Bernstein-Kohan's emissary (see *The Bernstein-Kohan Book*, in Hebrew, Tel-Aviv 1945–6, p. 129), and it is likely that this was one such telegram.

are at your disposal if we can be of any help. Up to this moment we are without detailed information on the excesses. We requested this from you in a telegram[3] today and are awaiting the speediest report possible. As we have already stated in our telegram, we wish to organise a large relief committee for Western Europe from here, so as to participate as much as possible in helping the distressed. We shall seek to attract important personalities and bring the organisation into existence in such a manner as to achieve the best possible results.[4] You may trust us to do everything in our power. But we must await information from you on the extent of the damage and the kind of help you need, and then we shall get everything promptly under way.

Again, you know you have our deepest sympathy. We are convinced your old courage and strength will not completely desert you, even in this painful situation. This reassures us somewhat. You on your part may rest assured that your friends will stand faithfully by you.

With our sincerest and deeply-felt wishes for the well-being of yourself and your family.

Yours ever,

311. To Vera Khatzman, Rostov. *Geneva, 28 April 1903*

Russian: H.W.: W.A.

Geneva, rue Lombard 4.
28/April 03.

Dear Verochka,

I can't understand why I don't hear from you. I would be very happy if the reason for your silence were that you are too busy getting ready to leave. I am miserable here without you, but with you everything would be just right. We have an enormous amount of work both in the laboratory and the Bureau. We are printing a report now on the state of affairs in the Bureau, for distribution

---

[3] Not found.

[4] Considerable fund-raising activity on behalf of the Kishinev victims was conducted in Western Europe and Russia. At the end of April the Jewish University Bureau at Geneva issued a circular (not found) containing an appeal for donations for the victims and asking that contributions be sent to the Bureau. On W.'s initiative fund-raising campaigns were organized in Liège and Karlsruhe (see Mamlock to W., 15 May 1903, W.A.; Jaffe to W., 5 May 1903, 23 June 1903, W.A.; *Der Fraind* 6/19 May 1903); and see also n. 1 to No. 361. As regards W.'s participation in these activities at Munich, see ns. 1, 3 to No. 337. As to activities in Geneva, see No. 311 and also *Hatzofe* for 1/14 May 1903, 8/21 May 1903, and 23 May/5 June 1903.

to all members of the various committees.[1] I am also working on a memorandum for Dr. Herzl on the situation in the Zionist movement.[2] All this is extremely important and must be done at once. The Kishinev happenings have given us added work. We want to organise a collection here in town and then start to collect pledges throughout Western Europe.[3] This morning I collected 300 francs from students.

I still haven't had any time to rest, because work which cannot wait has constantly intervened. It is a good thing that Toldy is here now and we can work together, although he is leaving on the 4th.[4] Nevertheless we can do a great deal until then, and so when you get here, my dearest, we shall be able to be together all the time.

And what's new with you, Verussik? Why are you now begrudging me your letters? Come quickly, darling, quickly, quickly! I so want us to be together. How I shall caress you, press you to my heart, my dearest girl, my love! I await you impatiently. I am on tenterhooks. *Der Jude* will soon come out. We are still short of money; the issue is ready.[5] We have a great many good contributors,[6] and if we overcome the initial financial difficulties the paper will be on its way. I kiss you, my dear Verochka, many times. Come soon to your loving

Chaimchik.

Warm regards to Sofochka and all the dear ones.

---

311. [1] Report of the Jewish University Bureau, May 1903, W.A. No. 30/5/0. The report details preparatory work for the establishment of the Jewish University carried out during the period Sept. 1902 to April 1903: W.'s travels in Russia, collection of funds, action taken to set up committees, propaganda, plan to publish a periodical, preparation of bibliography, and the student survey. The future plans of the Bureau were also given in general outline. The report was intended for limited distribution and only 50 copies were printed (see No. 333).

[2] See No. 316.

[3] See ns. 1, 4 to No. 310.

[4] Feiwel spent some time in Geneva from April to June 1903. In May he went to see his parents in Brno and also visited Vienna, Budapest, Prague, and Berlin (see Feiwel to Mayer, 20 May 1903, Eugen Mayer Papers, Jerusalem, and see also No. 313).

[5] Cf. n. 2 to No. 308.

[6] In the first issue of *Der Jude* the intention had been to publish, *inter alia*, articles by William Evans-Gordon, Martin Buber, Nathan Birnbaum, Eduard Bernstein, Ernst Mueller, Hirsch David Nomberg, Joseph Popper, and Berthold Feiwel, and an article had also been received from Nahum Sokolow (see Feiwel to Buber, 18 April 1903, W.A.). See also No. 328, in which it is stated that a contribution had been received from the editor of the *Neue Deutsche Rundschau* (Oskar Bie) for the first issue.

312. To Catherine Dorfman, Zurich.[1] *Geneva, 30 April 1903*[2]

Russian: Pcd. H.W.: W.A.

Dear Katyusha,

As Lilien is preparing the cards I shall send you my head[3] in a few days. Otherwise I shall send you my copy. I shall write soon.[4] You cannot conceive how loaded I am with all sorts of work. Today I gave the printers my memorandum on the *Hochschule*[5] and I am now writing about the situation in Zionism,[6] [and in] the laboratory. My kisses to you and Anna.

Chaim.

Am awaiting a letter from Kohan-Bernstein. He telegraphed that he was writing.[7]

313. To Vera Khatzman, Rostov. *Geneva, 30 April 1903*

Russian: H.W.: W.A.

Geneva, 30/IV. 03.

My dear Verusya,

Your precious letter arrived today.[1] Darling, and I thought you were already on your way here! Now I am not sure that this letter will find you at home, and I want it to very much. My little bird, the easiest itinerary for you would be Rostov–Kiev and then Kiev–Pinsk–Warsaw. You change only once without difficulty, and there is an inexpensive, excellent connection. Moisseychik[2] will tell you all about it. But, darling girl, don't forget to let my people know in good time when you are due to arrive, in Pinsk and

312. [1] With the conclusion of the winter term 1902/3 Dorfman and Koenigsberg left Geneva to continue their studies in Zurich.
[2] Date of Geneva postmark.
[3] It appears from No. 314 that the reference is to W.'s photograph.
[4] See No. 314.
[5] See n. 1 to No. 311.
[6] Refers to the letter to Herzl of 6 May 1903 (No. 316).
[7] Cf. No. 310. Bernstein-Kohan's telegram has not been found.

313. [1] V.K. to W., 6 (19) Apr. 1903 W.A. She wrote, *inter alia*, that she was considering travelling to Switzerland via Kiev (where she would visit Samuel Weizmann) and Warsaw, but that she did not propose to go to Pinsk as the journey was inconvenient for her. She asked W. to send her addresses of various people (see below).
[2] Moses Weizmann, then studying in Kiev.

in Warsaw. Both papa and my brother-in-law[3] are very anxious to see you, but as you know, they are away from home a good deal.

Now addresses: Nadia Rabinovitch lives in Warsaw, Theatre Square number 11. (Telephone, 1890.) You can phone her from Chaim's office.[3] You should inform her also in good time of your arrival. The Krinskys are in Zurich, Zürichbergstrasse, Plattenhof. Toldy is here. He is leaving on Saturday for a visit to his parents[4] but will return in a fortnight.[5] In fact, you can meet him if you get to Vienna two weeks from now. In any event let Buber know that you will be passing through Vienna. His address: Postlagernd, Thurngasse, Vienna IX. If you take the Berlin–Basle route, be sure to inform Miss Ina Schimmer, Grossbeerenstrasse 75, *Jüdischer Verlag*, Berlin.

I can't understand, dearest, why you want to go to Mulhouse[6] by way of Olten. If you travel via Berlin you will pass through Mulhouse anyway. If you take the Vienna–Zurich route, then in order to get to Mulhouse you have to make a detour that will take five hours more, since Mulhouse is in Alsace and four and a half hours travel from Basle, while Zurich–Basle is two and a half hours.[7] I already find it hard to write to you, feeling as I do that you will be here any minute. It is impossible to describe in a letter all that I have felt and lived through, and I'd rather not write to you about my experiences in a fragmentary way. Do come soon. I find it hard to hold everything back.

Give my heartfelt regards to Esfir and Nyusya. I shall be very, very glad, both for Nyusya and for my family, if she will visit them.[8]

My best wishes to everybody at home. I shall write them a long letter soon.

Verunya, I kiss you lovingly. Kiss everybody for me.

Your ardently loving
Chaim.

Toldy kisses you.

[3] Chaim Lubzhinsky.
[4] Joseph Feiwel (?–1904) of Brno, and his wife Charlotte, née Schnabel.
[5] See No. 311.
[6] V.K. apparently wished to visit Benjamin Herzfeld, who was then living at Mulhouse.
[7] W. sketched the routes of two separate journeys in the margin of the letter.
[8] I.e., W.'s parents in Pinsk. Anna Ratnovskaya (Nyusya) was V.K.'s close friend and they were about to return from Rostov to Geneva together.

314. To Catherine Dorfman, Zurich. *Geneva, 4 May 1903*

Russian: H.W.: W.A.

Geneva, 4/v. 03.
Rue Lombard 4.

Sweet Katia, dear friend,

Believe me, it was not indolence or a lack of desire to share experiences with you[1] that limited my writing to brief little notes. Nothing of the sort. I very much wanted to share everything that took place with you, dear girls, but it was physically impossible for me to say everything in a letter. I saw so much; I heard, experienced and felt so much sorrow and joy that any attempt to describe it in a letter, or in words of any kind, could only be a pallid reflection of the Jewish reality: the Jewish reality that is drenched in blood.

This is why, despite myself, I asked you, my dear friends, to be patient; but please believe me, I suffered from my inability to write no less than you. Inasmuch as I could, I have reported everything in my memorandum to Herzl.[2] I described my impressions and put down my thoughts without any attempt at concealment or exaggeration. I wrote concisely, but the report took up 18 long pages covered by my small handwriting nevertheless. I am rewriting it now, and the day after tomorrow at the latest I shall send you a copy. I hope you will find the answer to a great deal in it, if not to everything.

I have prepared a similar kind of report on the *Hochschule*[3] and am now having it printed. I am getting the proofs today and will send them on to you.

Yes, the *Hochschule* project is progressing beautifully. True, I had to fight everywhere, at every level of society: with 'Poles of the Mosaic persuasion', with the Bund, with Jews generally, with the *Mizrahi*, with Fraction members; but the idea itself charged ahead triumphantly. I found money (about 9,000 roubles),[4] I found a few people who were prepared to work devotedly, while our Jewish bourgeoisie showed all the sympathy of which it is

---

314. [1] Here and elsewhere in the letter it is unclear whether the style of address is singular or plural, i.e. if Dorfman alone or Anne Koenigsberg also was intended. Despite the salutation W. addresses both of them on occasion and the latter part of the letter expressly states that it is also intended for Koenigsberg.

[2] See No. 316.

[3] See n. 1 to No. 311.

[4] The reference is to money promised to W. in Lodz and Warsaw for the Jewish University Bureau; according to the Bureau's report for May 1903 (W.A. No. 30/5/0), a total of about 7,000 roubles was promised in these two cities.

capable. If future developments progress at this rate, then in about *a year's time we can* start thinking of the beginning of the end.

The battle in Warsaw was interesting. It took place in the very heart of the assimilationist circles; the entire Polish intelligentsia had been mobilised against me. So was the Bourse and even the Christian liberal Press. The speakers who came to the meeting[5] are noted in Warsaw as 'silver-tongued' orators; you should have seen how I wiped the floor with them. My address embraced the entire *Zionist* platform and lasted for three hours. The audience seethed, but listened benumbed.[6] Then came Dr. Nussbaum,[7] leader of the assimilationists in Poland. He thundered against me and against my 'miserable' project, which will 'ruin' Jewry and which has so alarmed the inhabitants of Warsaw that they are now in fear of a pogrom. After him, Professor Hertz of Lemberg[8] spoke against the implementation and feasibility of the project. The editor of *Izraelita*[9] (Grossglück),[10] who had made mincemeat of me even before the meeting,[11] then followed.

I listened calmly until the end, with immense patience that required no little effort. I took the floor to reply in defence of my programme at midnight, and finished at four in the morning. The meeting had begun at 7 p.m. Naturally, I cannot possibly relate the entire discussion to you, but I succeeded in demonstrating that Dr. Nussbaum and company were not Jews; and that since 'Poles' had not been invited, I was at a loss *en qualité de quoi* these gentlemen were appearing at the meeting. This fell like a bomb-shell, and exploded with enormous effect. I rejected their arguments and talked about the Jewish Press, the editorial gentlemen and our relations with them. In brief, my resolution was carried by a majority of all against two.[12] From 4 a.m. on, the Warsaw telephone was kept busy informing Jewry of the victory.

The next day I was besieged by reporters. By the way, in an interview[13] which appeared in *Hatzefirah* the term 'apostolic' mission[14] is used, through no fault of mine I assure you. The man

[5] It is not clear whether the reference is to a meeting held on 23 March 1903 (see No. 296) or to another which took place on 29 March 1903 (see No. 299).

[6] The word is not quite clear in the original.

[7] Henrik Nussbaum (1849–1937), physician and philosopher. He was an extreme opponent of Zionism and favoured assimilation. [8] Not identified.

[9] A Jewish weekly in the Polish language with anti-national tendencies.

[10] Israel Leon Grossglueck (1851–1904) was the secretary of the Jewish community in Warsaw from the beginning of the 1870s. Towards the end of his life he was on the editorial staff of *Izraelita*.

[11] W., who did not know Polish, apparently learned of this by hearsay because his name is not mentioned in any article published in *Izraelita* at that time.

[12] The text of the resolution is not known.

[13] Eng. in the original. [14] Thus in original.

(Yatzkan[15] from *Hatzefirah*)[16] who wrote up the interview was the same one who lambasted me two years ago in the highly-regarded *Hamelitz*.[17]

Matters were much simpler in Lodz, Kharkov, and Minsk. In Lodz the meeting represented 7,000,000 roubles (this is how much those present were worth). However they kept their money, but pledged and signed for only a part of it. Nevertheless the sum was fairly impressive.[18]

Moreover, I became better acquainted with both the Bund and the *Poalei-Zion*. In Pinsk,[19] Homel, Bobruisk[20] and Minsk,[21] *Poalei-Zion* is a very gratifying phenomenon, our only fighting force. The Bund is undoubtedly a powerful *destructive* force, but one that will soon destroy itself. Bund propaganda is mostly conducted among adolescents and *déclassés* (dentists, 'externs', *orem bakhurim*,[22] etc.), and is propelled by such slogans as 'Your Ahad

[15] Name in Hebrew script in original. Samuel Jacob Yatzkan (1874–1936), Zionist journalist and writer. He had been on the editorial staff of *Hamelitz* (St. Petersburg) and from 1902 of *Hatzefirah* (Warsaw). In 1906 he was among the founders of the Yiddish daily *Haint* in Warsaw.

[16] See article by Samuel Yatzkan in *Hatzefirah*, 10/23 March 1903. The article begins by praising W., and recalling the powerful impression he made on the Russian Zionist Conference at Minsk (Sept. 1902), his eloquence, the vision of a Jewish University and his unflagging efforts for its attainment. The interview focused mainly on the plan for a Jewish University. W. told Yatzkan that in his opinion six years of preparatory work were required: two years to collect the data, two years for propaganda and publicity, and two years for practical preparations. But his associates were of the opinion that three years would be sufficient. W. also discussed the work already done: the survey among students and the difficulties this had encountered, the approaches to academics and their reactions (see also n. 9 to No. 13), the committee set up in Berlin and the moneys pledged, as well as the attitude of the Zionist Organization towards the plan. Yatzkan's article was published before W.'s first meeting in Warsaw on the evening of 23 March 1903 (see No. 296). Apart from this article, no press reports have been traced concerning W.'s activities in Warsaw.

[17] Yatzkan was a correspondent of *Hamelitz* until 1902, but no article from his pen attacking W. has been found in this periodical.

[18] Concerning W.'s visit to Lodz, Kharkov, and Minsk, see Nos. 299, 300, 303, 304, 306.

[19] Joseph Bregman tells in his memoirs (see *Davar*, 5 Dec. 1944) of a debate between Zionists and members of the Bund held in Pinsk at Passover 1903, at which those taking part included, among others, W., a representative of *Poalei-Zion* (A. Rubenchik), and Kalman Tepper for the Bund.

[20] Nothing is known of W.'s visits to Homel and Bobruisk.

[21] In his memoirs published in *Davar* (22 April 1935) Isaac Berger dwells on a *Poalei-Zion* meeting held in Minsk during the Passover period to hear an address by W. (Berger wrote that this gathering took place during Passover 1902 but W. was not then in Russia and it may be assumed that the date was Passover 1903.) The meeting was dispersed by the police but the organizers managed to hide W. before the police arrived. Berger describes W. as 'the first intellectual visitor who had come on Zionist affairs to the workers'.

[22] Yidd.: 'poor fellows', generally applied to students at Talmud academies. Cyrillic in orig.

Ha'am!' 'Our Gorky!' 'We don't need a Jewish family or Jewish abstinence!' 'We need hard drinking and debauchery, a large, generous Russian nature!' 'We are on the eve of revolution!' 'We declare war on Jewish ideology!' etc. This is how one of the most prominent Bund agitator-organisers preached in my presence.[23] There is a veritable slaughter of the innocents. Syphilis, debauchery and complete demoralisation have appeared in Jewish towns, and with them a most tragic development in the break-up of families. May thunder and lightning strike Gorky, the Bund, the Russian liberals, etc., etc! My instinct was always to sense an enemy in them and I am now convinced of this more than ever before.

My conscience is clear. I fought the Bund to the best of my ability wherever I encountered it. I spoke about the Fraction, the *Mizrahi*, etc., etc...
....[24]

I now live very quietly. There is nobody here. Berthold was here for a while but has left.[25] I do not meet with Aberson and company, and am very grateful for the rest, as I need it so badly. I have three students in the laboratory. They seem to understand the work and it is now going very well.

Of course, I would have loved to have one or two of my 'real' friends here, but you, dear girls, flew away.[26] Hard luck! There is more than enough of work and one of these days I shall send you some. I know nothing as yet of the situation regarding the circulars, nor of the work being done by the Berne people.[27] I shall turn to this in a day or two.

Everything is fine at home. My vagabonds[28] are fine boys, studying hard and rendering their due to the cause. Only one sister is a Bundist (true, she is only 15)[29] but the old folk take it hard.

I am cheerful and in a hopeful mood. Yesterday I vastly enjoyed the sun, fresh air, freedom, and even wanted to go to Salève.[30]

---

[23] Not identified.
[24] Seven lines illegible, and deleted in the original.
[25] See n. 4 to No. 311.   [26] See n. 1 to No. 312.
[27] This apparently refers to a circular by the Democratic Fraction distributed in May or the beginning of June (not found). Wortsman wrote to W. on 13 June 1903 (W.A.): 'In your last circular you wrote that the Fraction Bureau was in Berne and that money was needed.' No further information has been found concerning the establishment of such a bureau in Berne apart from a hint in W.'s letter to Wortsman of 15 June 1903 (No. 378): 'The Berne people have done very little for the Fraction. On my return from my journey I had to get all the machinery going.'
[28] I.e., W.'s brothers.
[29] Apparently Minna Weizmann. (For her membership of the Bund see Haya Weizmann-Lichtenstein, *In the Shadow of our Roof*, in Hebrew, Tel-Aviv 1947/8, p. 135.)
[30] A mountain near Geneva.

What poisons this state of well-being is the thought of Kishinev. The anticipated letter from Y. M.[31] has not yet arrived. I shall wait one more day and telegraph him for the third time.

I shall not put any questions to either you or Anya.[32] You must surely be aware that I want to know everything.

This letter is, of course, also *giltig*[33] for Anya, to whom I send my warmest regards.

I am sending a picture of myself.

Shall I be coming to Z[urich]? I would very much like to. Possibly very soon, for I shall be going to meet Vera who is on her way from Russia.

Well, this ought to be enough. You will get a clear idea of everything, more or less, from the reports.[34]

I kiss you both, dear girls.

Chaim.

315. To Theodor Herzl, Vienna. *Geneva, 6 May 1903*

German: T.W.: C.Z.A. H VIII/915.

Geneva, 4 rue Lombard, 6. 5. 03.

Dr. Theodor Herzl,
Vienna.   Registered.

Dear Dr. [Herzl],

I am taking the liberty of submitting the enclosed memorandum, intended exclusively for yourself.[1]

As you will judge from the contents, its disclosure even within a narrow circle could be most dangerous.

Most respectfully, and with Zion's greetings,

Yours faithfully,
Dr. Ch. Weizmann.

---

[31] Jacob Mitayeriah Bernstein-Kohan; as regards the expected letter, see Nos. 310, 312. W. was unaware that Bernstein-Kohan was not at that time in Kishinev but was visiting St. Petersburg in order to persuade the authorities to take action against those responsible for the Kishinev pogrom (see *The Bernstein-Kohan Book*, in Hebrew, Tel-Aviv 1945–6, pp. 130–5).

[32] Anne Koenigsberg.

[33] 'valid'.

[34] See above and ns. 2, 3.

315. [1] See No. 316.

316. To Theodor Herzl, Vienna. *Geneva, 6 May 1903*

German: T.W.: C.Z.A. H VIII/915.

Geneva, 4 rue Lombard, 6. 5. 03.

Dr. Theodor Herzl,
Vienna.

Dear Dr. [Herzl],

May I take the liberty, in the name of my friend Feiwel as well as myself, of submitting this memorandum for your attention. We feel we have a duty to address it to you because of our conviction that it merits consideration on your part as Zionism's leader precisely at this juncture in our affairs. Our purpose is twofold: to place before you an interpretation of the contemporary Zionist position in Russia and Western Europe, certain features of which may be new to you; and to illustrate a picture particularly of Zionist youth but also of Jewish youth in general.

In our view it is all the more necessary that this be done now both because of the change that has lately come about in many aspects of the situation, and because of the impending Congress.[1] Furthermore, you will not deny the desirability of your becoming more closely acquainted with some specific Zionist facts before the Congress convenes, or of the clarification of misunderstandings. These misunderstandings have led to estrangement between the leadership and a substantial segment of Zionist youth—through no fault of the latter—since the last Congress.[2] We do not know whether we may count upon your attaching much importance to us as individuals or to any communication from us. But as the possibility of an understanding between youth and leadership becomes increasingly more slender, we are all the more anxious to fulfil, on our side at least, what seems to us to be a Zionist duty.

This decision to communicate with you is reinforced by the impressions I received while in Russia. I have been there twice during the past six months, and had occasion to visit the most important Jewish centres in north and south Russia.[3] It is not my wish to detain you with a report on the economic situation of the Jews in Russia, though I am convinced that a realistic Jewish picture cannot be obtained from even the most ideal of theories—not that we have any ideal ones. The events in Kishinev have shed a glaring light upon the fate of *one* city.[4] In my travels I made the alarming

---

316. [1] The Sixth Zionist Congress, due to take place in the summer of 1903.

[2] The Fifth Zionist Congress (Dec. 1901).

[3] W. had visited Russia from Aug. to Oct. 1902 and from March to April 1903.

[4] See n. 1 to No. 310.

discovery that distress has grown to a frightening degree. As a consequence of the present crisis, the destitute in some Lithuanian towns have increased by 30 per cent. This could be verified in various ways, such as in the distribution of מעות חטים[5] before Easter. More terrible still is the all-pervading sense of helplessness and perplexity resulting from legal restrictions that grow more severe daily,[6] and are to be intensified to a point beyond endurance in the near future.[7] These restrictions are said to be an answer to the growing Jewish revolutionary movement.[8] But the Jewish revolution is the product of unlimited political and economic disabilities. This vicious circle, constantly opening and then closing again, can be broken in both senses only by Zionism.

You may be aware that a Commission is at present conducting an investigation into the Jewish question.[9] Through reliable sources

[5] Heb.: 'corn money', which it was customary to distribute among the poor before Passover Eve. The amount of corn money distributed was an accepted means of estimating the poverty rampant among Russian Jewry.

[6] Legal restrictions imposed on the Jews of Russia took three main forms:

(a) *Right of domicile.* Jews were permitted to live only in the Pale of Settlement, which comprised fifteen provinces in the western part of the Empire together with Russian Poland proper. But even in this area residence was forbidden to Jews in certain large cities and villages, nor were they allowed to own immovable property in the rural districts of the Pale. Residence outside the Pale was permitted to various classes of privileged persons (merchants who were members of the First Guild, graduates of higher educational establishments, ex-soldiers who had served 25 years in the Army, and certain categories of artisans).

(b) *Employment.* Some categories of employment were restricted or forbidden altogether (the Law, Civil Services, trade in intoxicating liquors, estate management, railways).

(c) *Education.* A *numerus clausus* was enforced in secondary schools and higher educational establishments. Under this restriction these schools were permitted to accept only a certain percentage of Jewish students (see Vol. I, n. 3 to No. 113).

[7] For the anticipated harsher measures limiting the right of Jews to acquire immovable property, see n. 8 to No. 303.

[8] For the role of the Jewish Bund in the Russian Social Democratic movement, see Vol. I, n. 2 to No. 54. As to the extent of Jewish participation in the revolutionary movement during the early years of the century, see, e.g., Motzkin (ed.) *Die Juden-pogrome in Russland*, Cologne 1909, pp. 243–7; according to the figures published by the Russian Ministry of Justice, almost 30 per cent of those accused of political offences in the years 1901–3 were Jews (ibid., p. 244).

[9] Beginning with the 1870s, the Russian authorities periodically appointed commissions to consider questions relating to Jews and the restrictions imposed on them (see n. 6 above). It is not clear what commission is referred to here, nor has any evidence been found for the details given by W. as to its deliberations. But it is known that the commission headed by Baron von Goldenban, appointed in 1899 to deal with the restrictive regulations, proposed a number of relaxations. In April 1902 the Minister of Interior, Sipyagin, proposed that Jews be permitted to live in 101 additional localities of the Pale which had hitherto been classified as agricultural settlements and forbidden to them. This relaxation was enacted by a regulation dated 10 (23) May 1903—see *Budushchnost'* of 23 May (5 June) 1903. *Die Welt* reported on 24 April 1903 that a commission appointed by the Tzar had recommended that Jews be permanently deprived of the right to acquire or lease immovable

I have learned that the majority of the Commission (which includes the head of the Police Department, Lopukhin, and is in close touch with a number of Zionists),[10] did not assume an unfavourable attitude on the Jewish question. But as from now the Commission's conclusions will be determined by the Tsar's endorsement of several points voted by the anti-semitic minority. Incidentally, it is not unlikely that this Commission will invite a Jewish sub-committee to participate in its deliberations. There is even a motion on the table not to hear assimilationists. A few Zionist names, such as Dr. Bernstein-Kohan, Rosenbaum and others, have been proposed. As always, one may predict that the ever-increasing anti-Jewish current will claim additional victims.

This anti-Jewish current is reflected in the position that the Russian government is now taking up towards Zionism. A memorandum consisting of seven printed sheets is now in the hands of the Minister of the Interior, v. Plehve, in which all the activities of Zionism[11] are discussed in great detail. It contains descriptions of all the leaders of the movement. Regarding yourself, for example, the following phrase appears among others: 'Dr. Theodor Herzl, one of the editors of the *Neue Freie Presse* (a newspaper hostile to Russia).' The report was written by a Pole named Poznansky (a Christian) with a truly astonishing knowledge of the facts. Thus the entire correspondence exchanged between the Viennese A.C. and the Russian A.C. is reproduced.[12] The summing-up is unfortunately inimical to Zionism.[13] The movement is described

property outside urban areas. This recommendation, too, was given legal effect on 10 (23) May 1903—see n. 8 to No. 303. See also Circular Notice of the Police Department in the Russian Ministry of Interior of 11 (24) Aug. 1903 concerning the need for re-examining and unifying the statutes regulating the position of Jews in Russia. A French translation of this circular was published in the *Bulletin Mensuel* of the *Alliance Israélite Universelle*, Aug.–Sept. 1903, pp. 194–6. W. had apparently heard of the deliberations of the commission referred to here from Tyomkin when they met in Kharkov after Tyomkin's visit to St. Petersburg, and from S. Rosenbaum when he visited Minsk in mid-April (see No. 303; and No. 306 and n. 3 there).

[10] It is not clear who these unspecified Zionists were.

[11] The memorandum was called 'Zionism'. Copies are available in the C.Z.A. and the National Library in Jerusalem. The printed circular was signed by Lopukhin, the Director of the Police Department in the Russian Ministry of Interior, but nothing is known of the Poznansky mentioned as its author. This memorandum, which details the history, institutions, and personalities of the Zionist movement, was shown to W. by Rosenbaum on the occasion that he visited Minsk.

[12] The memorandum gives no direct quotations from the exchange of letters between the Zionist Smaller Actions Committee and the Zionist Regional Leaders (the Russian members of the Zionist Greater Actions Committee), but W. apparently deduced from the considerable familiarity shown by the author with the problems of relationship between the S.A.C. and the Regional Leaders that he was aware of this exchange of correspondence—probably from copies made by the Russian censorship or from letters impounded by the authorities.

[13] The memorandum does not include a summing-up, and it would appear that W.'s

as something still not to be taken seriously,[14] the A.C. in particular being charged with an incapacity to carry out the decisions of the Congress.[15] Among the points made one states that despite the Basle Programme's 'in accordance with the public law of the country',[16] the A.C. has never sought to legalise the movement in Russia (this refers to the funds and the organisation).[17]

The Fraction is called a non-Zionist secret revolutionary group, 'a bridge across which one travels to and from Socialism'.[18]

reference here was to the general tendency animating the author, as reflected in the content and style of the memorandum. The author states, e.g., that most Russian administrative officials adopted a negative attitude towards Zionism, 'which is involved in collecting substantial amounts of money and in constant secret meetings where the discussions are not limited to questions pertaining to Zionism alone'. They also looked unfavourably upon the growing unity forged by Zionism among the Jewish masses (p. 126).

[14] Various passages in the memorandum reflect an attitude of contempt towards the Zionist movement in spite of its considerable activities—see, e.g., p. 27, where the author deals with the dissemination of Zionism in Russia in the period between the First and Second Zionist Congresses (1897–8): '. . . but the success of Zionism was not actually so great and significant. . . . The majority of the Jewish masses . . . was of course alien to the true Zionist idea. To be a Zionist it was enough to pay 40 kopeks [the cost of a Zionist shekel].' The author states that 'the upper class [of Russian Jewry] continued to hope for assimilation among the Russian population' and that the intelligentsia feared that it would suffer persecution on account of Zionism (p. 28). Elsewhere the author contends that 'the bearers of culture, who realized better than Herzl the . . . low degree of development of the masses of the people in Russia, understood that it was impossible to establish an independent government with such elements' (p. 58). The memorandum declares that the Zionists 'achieved nothing concrete' (p. 59) and that at the Conference of Russian Zionists at Minsk (Sept. 1902) 'nothing of importance was achieved' (p. 143).

[15] The memorandum dwells on the lack of co-ordination prevailing among the executive bodies of the Zionist movement, stating that the Zionist Greater Actions Committee, as well as the conferences of Zionist Regional Leaders in Russia, often deviated arbitrarily from the decisions of the Congress (p. 65).

[16] The 'Basle Programme' of the Zionist Organization, adopted at the First Zionist Congress (1897), specified the methods for attaining the objectives of the movement and, *inter alia*, dwelt on 'the organization and binding together of the whole of Jewry by means of appropriate institutions, local and international, in accordance with the laws of each country'. The memorandum does not in fact refer to this passage but to Article 9 of the Statutes of the Zionist Organization adopted at the First Congress (the memorandum wrongly states Article 8), in which it sets forth: 'The organization and propaganda of Zionists in their respective countries are conducted in accordance with the needs and laws of that country, and the Actions Committee should be instructed as to their form' (I Z.C. Prot., p. 152). The memorandum affirms that, in spite of what was stated in the statutes, the Russian Zionists concealed the existence of the Organization, and of their own activities, during the period between the First and Second Congress. It was only after they were assured of the tolerant attitude of the Russian Government, and when they were granted frequent permits to hold meetings, that the Zionists decided to give their actions a somewhat more overt character (p. 28).

[17] I.e. the Jewish Colonial Trust, the Jewish National Fund, and the Zionist Organization, all lacking legal status in Russia. Unsuccessful efforts had indeed been made by the Zionists to secure legal status for the Colonial Trust. See also n. 9 in No. 303.

[18] The memorandum devotes considerable space to reviewing the attitude of the

Kohan-Bernstein is portrayed as the revolutionary leader,[19] myself as the agitator.[20]

Although we shall return to this point later, we must also dwell on it here for a moment. Although our hardest struggle everywhere[21] is conducted against the Jewish Social Democrats (the *Jüdischer Arbeiterbund* of Russia and Poland)[22] it seems astonishing that the report seeks to identify us with our most bitter opponents; but only apparently astonishing, because the substance for this conception is drawn from Zionist journals, from Nordau's pronouncements, from denunciations by Schauer and Slousch, and from articles by Kleinman in *Hamelitz*, etc.,[23] where members of the Fraction are labelled Anarchists, Nihilists, etc.

That this report is influenced *solely* by the Zionist side is evidenced

Zionists to the Social Democratic movement (see also n. 19 below). It refers, *inter alia*, to 'the Fraction which operates partly on the basis of the Basle Programme and in its second part blends with the Social Democratic elements of Zionism' (p. 117). Further, however, the memorandum declares that the methods of Zionists and the Jewish Social Democrats differed, and 'even the Democratic Fraction of the Zionists has expressed itself in opposition to the Socialists and refused to co-operate with them' (p. 126). The memorandum also asserts: 'Even the hopes placed by the Socialists on the Zionist youth have been dissipated. They had intended sowing in this fertile soil the first seeds of Zionist Socialism, but the Jewish youth at its sessions at the Basle Conference [the Zionist Youth Conference of Dec. 1901] did not adopt any positive decisions and only decried the Socialist-Revolutionary programme' (p. 116).

[19] The memorandum quotes the chief of the Gendarmerie for the province of Bessarabia in describing Bernstein-Kohan as 'a well-known worker for the Zionist movement in Kishinev, a movement which in many matters goes hand in hand with the revolutionary Social Democratic movement among the Jewish intelligentsia and working youth' (p. 125). It also quotes an alleged statement by Bernstein-Kohan that to defend Zionist ideas 'we must be ready, if the need arises, to fight against the existing regime' (p. 126).

[20] The memorandum describes *in extenso* the propaganda which Weizmann conducted in anticipation of the Zionist Youth Conference (Dec. 1901) and mentions the propaganda tour which he held in south Russia in the summer of that year.

[21] For debates between W. and members of the Bund see Vol. I, No. 60; Vol. I, No. 157 and n. 1 there; also n. 1 to No. 280 *supra*; and No. 314 and n. 19 there.

[22] The Bund—or in its full Yidd. title, *Allgemeiner Jiddischer Arbeiterbund in Lite, Poiln un Russland*—'General Confederation of Jewish Workers in Lithuania, Poland, and Russia'.

[23] For Schauer's attack on the Democratic Fraction, see n. 1 to No. 10. For the articles by Kleinman and Slousch alluded to here, see Vol. I, n. 6 to No. 156. Nordau expressed his opinion on the Zionist Youth Conference (Dec. 1901), at which the Democratic Fraction was established, in an interview with a correspondent of *L'Echo Sioniste* published in the issue of 15 Jan. 1902. Nordau defined the participants in the Conference as 'true products of *Galut*' and said that 'blinded as they are by their sudden transition from the régime of the whip and barbarism to freedom, they have never understood true civilization . . . nor the unique situation in which we find ourselves. They speak to us of a Democratic Left, as though our whole people do not constitute a Left and a Democracy'. In opposing Herzl they forgot that his authority stemmed from the confidence which the movement reposed in him. Nordau said that at the time when every Jew must work for unity, the 'Youth' were working for schism.

in the fact that the Russian Gendarmerie, the best-informed organisation in Russia, has imposed no difficulties on the activities of the Fraction. The report, however, emanates from the political police, which is on bad terms with the Gendarmerie.[24]

Incidentally, it should be noted that steps have been taken by several of our friends, with myself, to place the Fraction in its proper light.[25] It appears, from what has been said above, that future Zionist activities will encounter much greater difficulties in Russia. Following the restrictions placed upon the Jewish Colonial Trust,[26] limitations may well be expected on the work of propaganda and fund-raising[27] as well.

The immediate result, however, will most likely be a proposal by the government to legalise the movement. This is an eventuality that we must prepare for as speedily as possible.[28]

All this would not be so unhappy for Zionism in Russia had the circumstances in which Jewish youth finds itself not been so bad there, and partly, alas, through the fault of the Zionists themselves. In western Europe it is generally believed that the large majority of Jewish youth in Russia is in the Zionist camp. Unfortunately, the opposite is true. The larger part of the contemporary younger generation is anti-Zionist, not from a desire to assimilate as in Western Europe, but through revolutionary conviction.

---

[24] The Gendarmerie and security police (the political police, *Okhrana*) were subordinate to the Police Department of the Russian Ministry of Interior, but the commander of the Gendarmerie had special status as Vice-Minister of Interior. At that time there was a strained relationship between the commander of the Gendarmerie, General von Wahl, and the head of the Police Department, Lopukhin, arising from a duplication of powers and policy divergences, especially respecting Zubatov, chief of the Security Police in Moscow, whose activities von Wahl found objectionable (see V. I. Gurko, *Features and Figures of the Past*, Stanford, Calif. 1939, pp. 191, 639–40). For Lopukhin's negative attitude towards the Democratic Fraction, see also No. 364 and n. 1 there.

[25] See n. 3 to No. 306.   [26] See n. 9 to No. 303.

[27] For the restrictions on Zionist activity imposed by the Russian Ministry of Interior on 24 June (7 July) 1903, see n. 5 to No. 414.

[28] Possibly W. feared that the Russian Government might offer legal status to the Zionist Organization with the proviso that it restrict itself to emigration matters and would not engage in the cultural and economic activities of which the Russian Government disapproved (for the attitude of the Russian Government towards these questions, see Herzl's notes on his conversations with the Minister of Interior, von Plehve, in Aug. 1903, in *The Complete Diaries of Theodor Herzl*, ed. Raphael Patai, New York and London, 1960, vol. iv, pp. 1522–8, and also the circular of the Russian Ministry of Interior of 24 June (7 July) 1903, concerning restrictions on Zionist activity—see n. 5 to No. 414). According to B. Michaelevitsch, von Plehve, in a conversation with Simon Rosenbaum, proposed conferring legal status on the Zionist Organization on condition that there would be a public denial of the charges saddling him with responsibility for the pogrom in Kishinev (see article by M. Mishkinsky in *Zion*, in Hebrew, vol. 25, issue III–IV, p. 249, based on the memoirs of Michaelevitsch).

It is impossible to calculate the number of victims, or describe their character, that are annually, indeed daily, sacrificed because of their identification with Jewish Social Democracy in Russia. Hundreds of thousands of very young boys and girls are held in Russian prisons, or are being spiritually and physically destroyed in Siberia. More than 5,000 are now under police surveillance, which means the deprivation of their freedom. Almost all those now being victimised in the entire Social Democratic movement are Jews,[29] and their number grows every day. They are not necessarily young people of proletarian origin; they also come from well-to-do families, and incidentally not infrequently from Zionist families. Almost all students belong to the revolutionary camp; hardly any of them escape its ultimate fate. We cannot enter here into the many factors, political, social and economic, that continuously nourish the Jewish revolutionary movement; suffice to say that the movement has already captured masses of young people who can only be described as children.

Thus, during my stay in Minsk, they arrested 200 Jewish Social Democrats, not one of whom was more than 17 years old.[30] It is a fearful spectacle, and one that obviously escapes West European Zionists, to observe the major part of our youth—and no-one would describe them as the worst part—offering themselves for sacrifice as though seized by a fever. We refrain from touching on the terrible effect this mass-sacrifice has upon the families and communities concerned, and upon the state of Jewish political affairs in general. Saddest and most lamentable is the fact that although this movement consumes much Jewish energy and heroism, and is located within the Jewish fold, the attitude it evidences towards Jewish nationalism is one of antipathy, swelling at times to fanatical hatred. Children are in open revolt against their parents. The elders are confined within tradition and Orthodox inflexibility, the young make their first step a search for freedom from everything Jewish. In one small town near Pinsk, for example, youngsters tore the Torah Scrolls[31] to shreds. This speaks volumes.

Naturally, the tragic complications of the situation can only be slightly conveyed here. Nevertheless you can form a picture for yourself, dear Doctor, of the kind of environment in which we

[29] Cf. n. 8 above.
[30] According to the periodical of the Bund, *Poslednye Izvestia* (issues of 25 March (7 April) 1903 and 28 March (10 April) 1903), 300 members of the Bund were arrested in Minsk on the charge of taking part in an illegal assembly. This incident took place a short time before W. came to Minsk in mid-April 1903, but it was doubtless still a topic of conversation at the time of his visit there.
[31] No more is known of this incident.

Zionists labour: in part stubbornly Orthodox, in part petty-
bourgeois, and then the assimilating mass, not to mention the
proletariat of *Luftmenschen* that defies organisation.

Now visualise the location within this environment of the few
young Zionists with an adequate armour of independent thinking
and European education to combine with their Jewish knowledge:
on the one side the revolutionaries with their powerful arguments
drawn from tragic day-to-day realities, their ideal of personal
heroism and the magnetism inherent in martyrdom; on the other
side Zionism as it is generally conceived and represented in Russia.
First, there is the great mass of *Mizrahi*, with 10,000 adherents.[32]
You know very well, dear Doctor, that this group enjoys the
special patronage of the A.C. We would be the last to impose difficulties upon the effort to enrol the Orthodox into Zionism, even
though our activities are frequently inhibited or paralysed by them.
We do not deny the need to draw all segments of the population
into the national movement. Indeed, we have often gone to the
length in our propaganda campaigns of defending the *Mizrahi*,
and of identifying ourselves with them in the name of Zionist
solidarity,[33] when our opponents have used them against us. But
in the last analysis something we could not express at Congresses,
and have refrained from ventilating in the Press, has to be said:
blatant promotion of the *Mizrahi* at the Congresses, in the Press
and through administrative acts, not only betokens a profound
lack of understanding but also carries with it incalculable damage
and mischief.

True, in matters concerning the Congress, in questions of organisation and finance, etc., the Orthodox have always sided with the
Congress majority, and ostensibly remain loyal to the A.C. Doubtless this is why they are accorded such preference and respect,
and enjoy greater privileges than other delegates in their freedom
of speech, etc. The leadership, however, seems unable to assess or
determine the kind of ideological sacrifice involved for the Zionist
movement as a whole in wooing the *Mizrahi*—ideological sacrifice
at present, but ultimately to be of a more concrete nature. We have
no desire to stress that, in Western Europe, an exaggerated idea
exists[34] of the influence and following of the rabbis, bearing no

---

[32] There were 11,000 registered members of the *Mizrahi* at the beginning of 1903
(see *Die Welt*, 27 March 1903, p. 13).

[33] See, e.g., article in *Hamelitz* of 24 Feb. (9 March) 1903 on the debates between
the Zionists and members of the Bund held in Berne in Feb. 1903: '. . . and it was
wonderful to hear how Mr. Weizmann defended the *Mizrahi* from the coarse humour
which the Yiddish speaker poured on it.'

[34] In the original this word has been added above the line.

relation to the facts (I established the absence of influence on the part of the rabbis at the London Congress,[35] and such influence as existed then did not increase subsequently).

We wish only to define the ideological sacrifice already referred to, and to touch upon its consequences. The admitted or implicit objective of the *Mizrahi* is to weave religion into Zionism, understandably from their point of view, and to project their orthodoxy as the foundation of Zionism. (This is discernible from their report on the latest conference,[36] as well as from their circulars, announcements, etc.)[37] It would not be so bad in itself but for a failure by West European Zionists to comprehend the spiritual (cultural) aspects of Judaism, which they identify with the formalism of the pietists. As a consequence they not only flirt with Orthodox Jewry, but anachronistically and with intrinsic dishonesty apply the *Mizrahi* point of view first to the West European situation and then to the overall Zionist situation. In the discourse about raising cultural levels, held at the Fifth Congress and subsequently published,[38] religious education is given the highest priority.

Most German Zionists, particularly in Berlin, resort to religion as a bait. Even leaders who are otherwise complete free-thinkers go in for the kind of tactics which they calculate would be tolerated by the Orthodox. In practice this becomes partisanship for religious Zionism and the suppression of spiritual freedom. Western European conditions are such that they produce ugly manifestations like the denunciation of the Sabbath and *Yom Kippur*,[39] together with a Zionism so distorted as to alienate people of modern, honest outlook because they recognise within the movement the hollow Jewish ceremonial and formalism[40] from which they fled; Eastern Europe, on the other hand, sees the cultivation of *Mizrahi* Zionism as *the* Zionism. This will lead straight to catastrophe. If there is anything in Judaism that has become intolerable and incomprehensible

[35] In an address at the Fourth Zionist Congress in London on 16 Aug. 1900 W. declared that the rabbis in Russia lacked communication with the masses of the people outside the synagogue, and denied their assertion that they were supported by millions of Jews (see 4 Z.C. Prot., pp. 222–3).

[36] The second conference of the *Mizrahi*, which took place at Lida from 24–26 Feb. 1903 (Gregorian date). Reports appeared in the Jewish press (see *Die Welt*, 27 March 1903).

[37] See collection of *Mizrahi* leaflets at the Jewish National and University Library in Jerusalem.

[38] The reference is to S. Krenberger's address on 'Enlightenment and Education of the People', published as a supplement to 5 Z.C. Prot., pp. 437–43.

[39] Reference to Schauer's article of Nov. 1902 in which he linked a condemnation of the Zionist students' *mensa* at Berne for serving meals on *Yom Kippur* with an attack upon the Democratic Fraction (see No. 10, n. 1).

[40] Orig.: 'das hohle jüdische Ceremoniell und Formelthum.'

to the best of Jewish youth, it is the pressure to equate its essence with the religious formalism of the Orthodox. *Mizrahi* represents the element that in the natural course of events is dying by degrees. Their fanatically religious viewpoint and way of life has no bridge leading to contemporary youth.

We have already spoken of the youth. In the midst of their boundless misery they are in search of an ideal. We are absolutely convinced that Zionism can provide that ideal, but it grieves me to state with equal conviction that Russian Zionism cannot do so. The younger generation is urged to express the spirit of ancient Jewish heroism in European forms and values, but comes, unhappily, to *Golus* nationalism[41] and to false perspectives regarding a Jewish future linked with the future of the Russian people.

The *Mizrahi* know of only one kind of heroism, that of Orthodox dogmatism and de-humanised passive resistance.

Youth aside, what have we left beside the *Mizrahi*? A petty-bourgeois Zionism exhausting itself in the most superficial propaganda activities, with well-meaning but sterile speeches worn thin by repetition. This is despite its readiness for sacrifice, a strong feeling of Jewishness, and a number of capable leaders. But they are unable to provide a solution to the blood-stained Jewish reality (Dr. Sapir's prize-winning brochure)[42] except in petty social activities and mutual admiration, as even their leader and most gifted organiser Ussishkin[43] was forced to admit. With its disregard of reality and ignorance of modern ideas theirs is a moral as well as a physical surrender to the *Golus* yoke. In the face of resistance by the youth, this brand of Russian Zionism is given an annual endorsement of legality through the Congress. The events which led to the secession[44]

[41] Orig.: 'Golusnationalismus'. The reference is to the ideological trend in Judaism, principally advanced by Simon Dubnow and Chaim Zhitlovsky, which asserted the practicability of a national existence in the Diaspora and aspired to recognized autonomous status for Jews in the countries of their domicile, especially in civilized lands. The programme of the Bund also included a demand for Jewish cultural autonomy (see Vol. I, n. 11 to No. 54).

[42] The reference is to J. Sapir's work, in Russian, *Zionism—a Popular Scientific Account of the Character and History of the Zionist Movement*, Vilna 1903. The book also appeared in German translation and won the S. J. Velikovsky Prize.

[43] In an address on organizational questions at the Russian Zionist Conference at Minsk (Sept. 1902) Ussishkin criticized the Zionist Regional Leaders for lacking in Zionist devotion. He also attacked the heads of the local Zionist societies for being 'much worse' than the Regional Leaders. 'We have many people', said Ussishkin, 'but only for office-bearing, narrow-mindedness, squabbles over honours; for work, there is no one' (see *Hatzefirah*, 2/15 Sept. 1902).

[44] During the final session of the Fifth Zionist Congress on 30 Dec. 1901, the Democratic Fraction members walked out of the hall in protest against the rejection of Buber's motion calling for an immediate vote on draft resolutions formulated by the Cultural Committee (see 5 Z.C. Prot., p. 402).

and formation of the Fraction[45] at the last Congress were, in a minor way, proof of this. The Congress reflected in miniature the larger situation of real life.

When we bring our brand of Zionism to Jewish youth, the first thing that is hurled against us, often derisively, is Zionism as it is seen, heard and approved. But this youth cannot now, and will not ever, share anything with the kind of Zionism which bears the stamp of the *Mizrahi* or the narrow petty-bourgeoisie. And all that remains of Zionism that is neither *Mizrahi* nor petty-bourgeois is denounced as atheistic, anarchist, revolutionary. Therefore a man like Kohan-Bernstein, a man around whom the future of Zionism in Russia was concentrated, had his spirit broken and was forced to retreat,[46] while an Avinovitzky[47] became the hero of the *Mizrahi* and the large Congresses.[48]

As a consequence there has been no increase worth mentioning among active Zionists for years, despite gallant efforts on the part of the youth. Whatever is built gets destroyed by the Zionists themselves, as for example the Kohan-Bernstein bureau.[46]

For years now I have been travelling around Russia for months at a time. I know almost every Zionist who in some degree stands out, and I always meet the same old faces!

It seems incomprehensible that you and Nordau, men who know European political movements, should treat the *Mizrahi* as the picked troops, as if they really represented a political party already half-way to maturity. Their *Zionist aspiration* is purely one of words. Their horizon and political perspective are so limited that they can have no understanding whatsoever of a modern approach.

Precisely because of its political immaturity, and its apparent freedom from political pretension, this group will one day use its growing power in a most unexpected and stubborn manner. It will choose a decisive moment to defy the leadership. In practice, it is already seeking to dominate our propaganda campaign, our funds, our educational activities and our voting system![49]

[45] The creation of the Democratic Fraction was decided upon at the Zionist Youth Conference held a few days prior to the Fifth Congress.

[46] For the opposition aroused by the activities of the Zionist Correspondence Centre (the 'Postal Bureau') at Kishinev headed by Bernstein-Kohan, and its closure in Dec. 1901, see Vol. I, n. 1 to No. 43; Vol. I, n. 12 to No. 144.

[47] Feibush Avinovitzky, an extreme opponent of the inclusion of cultural and economic activities in the programme of the Zionist Organization (cf. Vol. I, No. 134), was at this time close to *Mizrahi*, as were other political Zionists, and he took a prominent part in the *Mizrahi* Conference at Lida (Feb. 1903).

[48] The full Zionist Congresses which after 1901 were held biennially, as opposed to the Annual Conference or 'Small Congress' which met in the intervening years.

[49] In the elections to the Russian Zionist Conference at Minsk (Sept. 1902) the *Mizrahi* alone availed themselves of the emerging party system to gain places for

311

(Thirty-six *Mizrahi* delegate mandates were invalidated in Minsk,[50] not one of the Fraction's.)[51] The process of secularising[52] the Synagogue, a completely wholesome manifestation,[53] is now being forced into decline. The *Mizrahi* regard the Synagogue as their domain, substituting 'sermons'[54] in the place of popular Zionist lectures, so that the awakening national consciousness is being repressed into the *Golus* formalism that is so life-alienating.

In general, Zionism has not so far penetrated to the masses. It commands a following, briefly described here, which the Russian police report—not unjustifiably by any means—refrains as yet to regard with seriousness.[55] Of the more valuable segments of the population, the youth and the workers, only a small proportion is Zionist; the few working-men's associations (the *Poalei-Zion* movement) owe their formation to the initiative of Fraction members.[56]

The spectacle witnessed during the past few years in Poland, a people divided only into assimilationists of the worst type and Chassidism, so that there is practically no Zionism, is being repeated in Lithuania, but with the appropriate variations: *Mizrahi* in the place of Chassidism, and Jewish revolutionaries in the place of Poles of the Mosaic persuasion.

The position of young Zionists is almost tragic. Misunderstood by the leadership, confined, driven into opposition, they have to struggle bitterly, both against foes from without as well as against adherents to Zionism, to make the slightest advance.

There is no defence against the calumnies that the Fraction is forced to endure and that, as indicated above, emanate from within our own ranks. Conditions being what they are in Russia, public justification of oneself would demand the denunciation of others and would bring personal disgrace.

The Fraction forms the connecting link between the older and

---

their own candidates. The *Mizrahi* organized an electioneering campaign throughout the Pale of Settlement.

[50] For doubts as to the validity of the credentials of *Mizrahi* delegates at the Minsk Conference, and the invalidation of a number of them, see *Hatzefirah* 25 Aug. (7 Sept.) 1902.

[51] Delegates of the Democratic Fraction were not elected to represent their group but organized themselves only on the eve of the Conference (see Vol. I, n. 2 to No. 308).   [52] Orig.: 'Die Verweltlichung'.

[53] Owing to the ban on public assemblies in Russia, it was customary to hold Zionist meetings in synagogues.

[54] Orig.: 'Droshes' (Yidd.)   [55] See n. 14 above.

[56] Concerning the association between *Poalei-Zion* and the Zionist youth movement that established the Democratic Fraction in 1901, see Vol. I, n. 6 to No. 140. Isaac Berger, head of the Minsk Centre of the *Poalei-Zion* societies, was a member of the Fraction and in 1902 tried to bring about co-operation between the two groups (see Berger to W. 21 Jan. (3 Feb.) 1902, W.A.).

the younger generation. It alone is capable of assuming the struggle against the revolutionaries, which indeed it does. It alone is freedom-loving and socially enlightened. It extracts the Jewish essence from among the masses and pours it into a European mould. But what that Jewish essence is, the European Zionists refuse to comprehend; even the leadership has still to recognise it. Witness the Ahad Ha'am–Nordau[57] affair, fast becoming so acute as almost to constitute a conflict between East and West European Jewry. What we regard as Jewish culture has till lately been confused with Jewish religious worship,[58] and when culture in the literal sense was discussed, the Zionists of West Europe thought that it referred to the improvement of educational facilities in East Europe. Perhaps it is now understood, because of the specific activities of Fraction members, that the totality of Jewish national achievement is intended—particularly that literature, art, scientific research, should all be synthesised with Europeanism, translated into modern creativity, and expressed in institutions bearing their own individual character.

We believe that this Jewish culture, being the most vital form of the people's self-expression, is more than a mere part of the national renaissance; next to the larger Palestine ideal of Zionism it represents its only remaining attribute, and can at least offer the modern Jew dissatisfied with a Shekel contribution an approach to a loftier view of life, with scope for enthusiastic action. Perhaps it is the only reply that we can make to our opponents, since the economic and political reply must be postponed to the future. Yet it is precisely in this that we are once again under vigorous attack and repression by both sides of the Zionist camp: by the West European Zionists who are utterly remote from Jewish culture, neither regarding it as a significant force nor comprehending its connection with the individuality of the Jews in the East; and by the *Mizrahi*, because they see every development not in the direction of Orthodoxy as apostacy, and treat it accordingly.

The final night of the Fifth Congress[59] gave clear evidence of

[57] See n. 10 to No. 292.

[58] Play on words in the orig.—'Kultur' and 'Kultus'.

[59] During the final session of the Fifth Zionist Congress, held on the evening of 30 Dec. 1901, Buber and W. gave a detailed explanation of the draft resolutions presented by the Cultural Commission, and Rabbis Rabinowitz and Reines spoke against the inclusion of cultural work in the programme of the Zionist Organization. Rabinowitz concluded: 'A cultural, economic and spiritual elevation is of no benefit.' Reines stated, *inter alia*, 'The cultural question is a disaster for us. Culture will destroy everything. Our environment is definitely Orthodox, it will become forfeit because of culture' (see 5 Z.C. Prot., p. 395). For differences over the question of culture, see also Vol. I, n. 9 to No. 86.

this. They were not even capable of understanding that in addition to the national purpose—the advancement of Jewish culture—there was also a major Zionist propagandist and educational purpose: to convey some Jewish content to the Western Jew and some refinement of his Judaism to the Eastern Jew; and thereby to create an opportunity for a bridge between the two. For Congresses and apparent unity notwithstanding, they continue to face each other as strangers today not less than they did seven years ago.[60] Despite all resistance, the Fraction members have dedicated themselves, to the best of their abilities, to these cultural ends—through periodicals and by means of such institutions as the *Verlag*,[61] the University Bureau, etc. Regarding the University and the *Verlag*, a separate report will follow.[62]

If these activities have led to some not inconsiderable success, then we are entitled to declare that, had they been adapted to the needs of the Zionist movement and its officials as a whole, these same instruments could have eliminated much friction to bring immeasurably greater results.

Returning to the Russian situation, we feel compelled to state that we have, to the best of our knowledge, kept our interpretation of it free from a pessimistic or partisan coloration. If conditions within Zionism are such that it cannot fulfil what a large, serious political movement demands, this does not represent the last word to be said about Russia. Political foresight requires Zionism to base its calculations[63] on the possibility that, in addition to its own internal difficulties, it may have to submit to the sudden paralysis of its activities through arbitrary governmental action.[64] The first conclusion to be drawn from this is that the leadership must not depend upon Russia exclusively for the building of Zionist strength. The second requirement to be deduced from the above is this: so long as conditions in Russia prevail roughly as they are now, our leaders must not only cease to restrict the activities of Zionist youth and weaken it through the patronage of other groups, they must also encourage its progress by all available means. Only then will Zionism attract a really significant following of political maturity, prepared for sacrifice.

In these circumstances Zionism must, as a cardinal principle,

[60] I.e. before the First Zionist Congress of 1897.

[61] The *Jüdischer Verlag* publishing house in Berlin. For its establishment see Vol. I, n. 14 to No. 238.

[62] For report of the Jewish University Bureau see n. 1 to No. 311. This report does not deal with the affairs of the *Jüdischer Verlag*.

[63] Orig.: 'kalkul'.

[64] Cf. n. 9 to No. 303; n. 3 to No. 305.

take all measures necessary to strengthen the movement and transfer its centre of gravity outside of Russia. There are further reasons for such a move. It seems a grave injustice that almost three-quarters of Zionist contributions are made by the neediest Jews—and those who furthermore carry a hundred other burdens— while Western Europe, England and America contribute nothing approaching the proportion demanded by their condition and means. This holds true not only for non-Russian Jews, but much more for non-Russian Zionists. The readiness for sacrifice will, there-fore, have to be increased many times over outside Russia, with the enrolment of wider circles than has been attempted hitherto. Russian restrictions make the necessity for this all the greater. Moreover, Western Jewry will have to be enlisted particularly if the investigation and exposure of the problems of our movement are to be undertaken in earnest. Certainly we shall need its assistance in any practical endeavours which may be in the offing. Finally, a movement such as ours must set great store upon political maturity, and this is found in greater abundance beyond the frontiers of Russia.

Although Zionism may have spread territorially, most active workers in the movement outside Russia are of the view that seven years of endeavour have not shown a proportionate growth in intensity. This again is symptomatic of our failure to secure the support of but an insignificant fraction of the youth. For years this mass of human material has yielded only a small number of really useful, dedicated workers, and all because of Zionism's superficial approach. On the contrary, we have even lost many who, on the conclusion of their academic careers, have denied Zionism or turned away from it. It is also characteristic that we have lost a number of serious collaborators of former times without finding replacements for them.

We have an accurate picture of the German, Austrian and Swiss organisations. Regarding the last-named, its true significance will be clearly deduced from this one example: Dr. Farbstein had for a time considered in all seriousness the conversion of the organisation into one of Zionist *philanthropy*,[65] on the grounds that the majority of its members merely contributed the Shekel and otherwise had nothing in common with Zionism as a national movement. We successfully opposed the plan, but the fact remains that we can count only on small sums of money from this source and only a worthless, possibly harmful, following.

[65] No further information about this plan has been found. For W.'s objections to the philanthropic character of Swiss Zionism see also n. 4 to No. 90.

You are yourself familiar with the situation in Austria, with its hundreds of thousands of Jews. The small number of workers has not multiplied. They have practically no propagandists, and the organisation seeks to organise and reorganise itself[66] annually without recognising that the reasons for its stagnation are not to be ascribed to its external forms. Now that an attempt is being made to introduce the movement into Hungary, and this indeed could be transformed in time into fertile Zionist territory, an impossible combination with Magyar nationalism[67] is being striven for on the one hand, while on the other the Austrian local committee recommends the distribution of *Mizrahi*-sponsored journals[68] for propaganda purposes.

In Germany there is activity and propaganda in plenty, but all

[66] See, for example, the new statutes of organization brought before the second Conference of Austrian Zionists in May 1902 and published in full in *Die Welt* of 16 May 1902.

[67] The statutes of the Hungarian Zionist Organization, which had been drawn up by its President, Janos Ronai, and adopted on 22 March 1903 at the Hungarian Zionist Conference at Pressburg, contained the following articles: (1) 'In full support of the Basle Programme, Hungarian Zionists aspire to the establishment of a homeland in Palestine for homeless Jews that would be guaranteed by public law'; (2) 'Hungarian Zionists have no desire to be considered a political-national group nor to conduct a nationalities policy in Hungary' (see *Ungarische Wochenschrift*, journal of Hungarian Zionists, of 27 March 1903). On 24 April 1903, *Ungarische Wochenschrift* reported that Soma Visontai, President of the Zionist Society in Budapest, had proposed amending these two articles, 'out of his desire that our patriotism should be given full expression therein'. As regards clause (1), Visontai suggested adding the word 'only' before 'homeless Jews', whilst he proposed that clause (2) read as follows: 'Hungarian Zionists, as loyal sons of the Hungarian Fatherland, do not desire to be considered a political-national group, and have no other wish than to pursue Hungarian political objectives.' The editor of *Ungarische Wochenschrift*, J. Gabel, asserted that 'most . . . fellow-Zionists welcomed' the proposed amendments, but several Zionists had expressed the view that the new text for article (2), as proposed by Visontai, was contrary to the intent of the leaders of the Zionist movement, and consequently Nordau was asked to give his opinion on the question. In a letter to Gabel dated 18 April 1903, and published in that issue, Nordau wrote that, from a Zionist viewpoint, there could be no objection 'to the plan . . . formulated by . . . Dr. Janos Ronai and Dr. Soma Visontai', adding: 'the nationality question in Hungary is exclusively a question of language . . . In this linguistic sense the Jews of Hungary certainly do not constitute a nationality because they do not speak a language of their own, and consequently you only define an irrefutable basic fact when you declare that you do not form a nationality in Hungary, do not conduct a nationality policy and only wish to work in Hungary towards Hungarian national objectives.' See also Nordau's article 'Zionism and Jewish Nationalism' in *Die Welt* of 27 March 1903, in which he explained his view that there was no contradiction between Jewish national consciousness and loyalty to the Hungarian State. Nordau's letter was strongly criticized in Zionist circles—see, e.g., S. Bernfeld's article in *Hazman* of 15/28 May 1903.

[68] No such recommendation is known, and the allusion is apparently to the decision of the Hungarian Zionist Conference (22 March 1903) to ask the *Mizrahi* Executive in Russia to distribute propaganda material among religious Jews in Hungary (see *Die Welt*, 3 April 1903, p. 3).

of a most superficial kind and, as already noted, by compromising either with clericalism or with exaggerated German patriotism. Despite journeyings to and fro and so-called 'brilliant successes', how effective is this propaganda[69] in fact? It may be assessed in our failure to win support from among the intellectuals and in the existence of a following, totally unreliable and eternally fluctuating, that is the reverse of national-Zionist. Thus the people in Berlin, their organisation consisting of many hundreds of people notwithstanding, were able, after countless meetings and speeches, to muster little more than a hundred votes at the last community council elections. Contrast this with the thousands of votes won by their opponents.[70] This was largely because they wished to be more Orthodox than the Orthodox.

As to the situation in England, if our information is correct, you yourself are reported to be far from happy with it,[71] dear Doctor.

Regarding America, it is best to remain silent.

The limited success achieved by Zionism outside Russia, a fact that brilliantly delivered reports do not always admit and frequently evade, should not by any means lead to the conclusion that Zionism can have no attraction for the Jews concerned. This may of course be so on any current assessment. Russian Zionism towers over the West European variety because of the readiness for sacrifice and its undiluted Jewish consciousness which, taken together, constitute as it were an organic Zionist force. West European Zionism is in many respects simply a passive form of nationalism and, consciously or not, continues in an acceptance of assimilation. Judaism is mostly expressed in religious affiliation and, apart from Zionist organisational forms, not at all in Jewish learning; nor in an absorption in questions relating to the Jewish people; nor in participation in Jewish cultural activities of a vital nature. The Zionist belief leads to the Judaism of the future, but it has neither contact with contemporary Judaism nor even elementary understanding of the Jewish masses and their way of life. There is frequent discussion on this, but only in the sense that one would discuss a wretched, obscure creature for whom 'something must be done'—that is, detachedly and without

---

[69] Alludes to travels by Zionist propagandists.

[70] At the community elections held in Berlin in Dec. 1901 the Zionists obtained only about one per cent of all votes cast. (See *Die Welt*, 27 Dec. 1901.)

[71] See article in *Hatzefirah* of 24 Jan./6 Feb. 1903, which dwelt on the profusion of trivial disputes among English Zionists, and stated that 'many representatives of (Zionist) Societies complained about each other' to Herzl when he visited England in Jan. 1903. See also Vol. I, n. 10 to No. 144.

identifying oneself with him. Our Zionist Press outside Russia reflects this brand of Zionism. Its un-Jewish content can only faintly echo the immensely tragic fate of the masses, supporting its frequently embarrassing ignorance of Judaism with the vacuous repetition of abstract arguments. Little wonder that this Press is no longer being attacked as it was in other days; it is simply skipped as so much *quantité négligeable*.

Perhaps you regard these judgments as pessimistic, or rigid, or unjust; perhaps you will still continue for the present to disbelieve us, or fail to understand us fully. But a movement is already stirring into rebellion against this form of Zionism, for it will not be identified with it. *Our desire* is to take this final opportunity to prevent an inner struggle, possibly a split, within Zionism.

We wish to give you our conception of what Zionism outside Russia, so important for the movement's future, is to become.

In view of the frightening, catastrophic situation that grows daily more acute, the sphere of West European Zionist activity and responsibility must be greatly expanded. With its poverty of means and magnitude of difficulties, our movement requires for its material and moral revitalisation the type of man that all other movements have had, resolved to a complete and undivided dedication to his cause. It would be a demonstrative act of the highest relevance to our youth if, as an example, the A.C. and leading figures would cease to devote only a fraction of their time, energy and interest to the movement, as is now the case with so many of them.[72] Undoubtedly the effort involved would be repaid many times over. Indeed, success would be far greater than the sacrifice demanded. Furthermore, our following must enlarge its scope of obligation. There are Jews in Russia who contribute a third, and sometimes one half of their incomes to Jewish causes; among West European Zionists, and they are really wealthy in comparison, donations are hardly larger than the amounts previously given for other national or Jewish purposes. The youth above all must show greater self-sacrifice, one might say greater fanaticism.

Additionally, an intimate relationship must be sought between Eastern and Western Jews. To this end, as well as for the sake of the national purpose, every effort must be made to inject Western European Zionism with Jewish content. The Jewish form of society created by Zionism is an abstract thing. This content can be found through concrete endeavour and through institutions,

[72] Office-holders in the Zionist Organization, with the exception of the secretaries of the Bureau in Vienna, were unpaid and consequently had to devote a large part of their time to professional employment.

particularly in fields of Jewish culture, literature, art, science and economics.

We must not direct our propaganda effort, as hitherto, exclusively towards the petty bourgeoisie. We must aspire rather to the capture of the intellectuals, and through them of Jewish public opinion as a whole. In this way Jewish capital will be attracted. But this will only become possible if we can show the intellectuals a genuinely modern movement of cultural and scientific responsibility. To do so we must not only eliminate unattractive petty bourgeois, conservative and clerical overtones. More urgently, we must demonstrate cultural achievements in modern Judaism; and most urgently, provide an unequivocal answer to basic Zionist *questions of the utmost gravity*. This is something we cannot do today, not only because diplomatic activity is protected from public discussion, not only because of our wavering tactics as in our relations with welfare organisations,[73] and not even because of those questions which can indeed be answered. The demand, repeatedly made, for an investigation of Palestine and the adjoining countries[74]— surely the primary, most natural concern of serious Zionism— always dies away when, as in the case of Trietsch, it does not lead to the near-excommunication of the individual concerned.[75]

[73] I.e., the large philanthropic foundations, the Jewish Colonization Association and *Alliance Israélite Universelle* (see Vol. I, n. 8 to No. 113; n. 16 to No. 144; head-note to No. 150).

[74] Resolutions on the need to investigate settlement conditions in Palestine were adopted at the preliminary meeting of Zionist Youth at Munich (April 1901) and the Zionist Youth Conference at Basle (Dec. 1901). A similar desideratum was included in the programme of the Democratic Fraction, which was formulated in June 1902.

[75] Davis Trietsch had long favoured a 'Greater Palestine' plan. He argued that the Zionist settlement programme should not be confined to the area of Turkish Palestine and that, as it was impossible to embark upon large-scale settlement there immediately, colonization by Jews should take place in adjacent territories—Cyprus, the El-Arish area and other zones in the Sinai Peninsula, and even in Asia Minor. Trietsch's proposals encountered the strongest opposition by the majority at Zionist Congresses, on the grounds that they deviated from the Basle Programme. Though Herzl himself did not repudiate them in principle, his relations with Trietsch nevertheless became very strained after 1899; and at the Fifth Zionist Congress (Dec. 1901) Herzl condemned statements made by Trietsch there as a concept of the Zionist Movement 'which hitherto we have come across only in humorous journals or anti-Zionist organs . . .' (see 5 Z.C. Prot., p. 238). At that Congress Trietsch demanded the initiation of Jewish settlement in the Sinai Peninsula (ibid., pp. 359–60), but when Herzl conducted political negotiations on such settlement in 1902/03 (see n. 5 to No. 308), he did not bring Trietsch into the discussions and even accused him of favouring 'Klein-Kolonisation' (see Buber to Herzl, 12 May 1903, C.Z.A. HB 35, and also No. 366 and n. 3 there). For Trietsch's plans and the ensuing controversy see Oskar Rabinowicz, 'A Jewish Cyprus Project', New York c. 1962; Trietsch, 'Greater Palestine', in *Palästina*, I (1902), 3/4, pp. 154–259; 3 Z.C. Prot., pp. 232–3; 5 Z.C. Prot., pp. 236–9. For Herzl's attitude to settlement in territories adjoining Palestine, see Bein, *Theodore Herzl*, London 1957, pp. 412 ff.

The Society for the Technical Investigation of Palestine founded in Vienna,[76] and the activities of the official Palestine[77] committee, are sad examples of the earnestness of Zionist research work. It is similarly disagreeable to witness how research is left completely to private initiative, without the slightest official encouragement, as in the case of the Statistical Bureau[78] or the Society for the Investigation of Palestine.[79] Sometimes, as happened with El-Arish,[80] the A.C. suddenly turns against its own hitherto inflexible convictions and the equally rigid opinions of the Congress majority. It will deviate, in spite of itself, from the policy laid down at the Basle Congress and endorsed by the inertia of the majority. But it does this without prior discussion or explanation, so that inevitably astonishment is caused throughout the rank and file within the movement, and misgiving among serious people outside it. This does not mean that the acquisition of El-Arish, or even a survey of the region, would not be an extremely worthwhile undertaking.

In many other respects a responsible and practical approach is absent. But if official Zionism were to embark upon some noteworthy endeavour, it would not only benefit its own purposes; it would also gain the affiliation of new, responsible people, to produce a fundamental cure for the empty phrase-making of the existing organisation, and an increase in initiative. This is particularly true of the Russian organisation, which in this respect is dependent on the West.

The successes achieved by some private individuals, even of limited means, are evidence enough that the way outlined above is the only correct method of work. As we ourselves are engaged on these activities, we refrain from speaking about them in detail. Nevertheless we do not believe that you are unaware that through such institutions as the Statistical Bureau of the Palestine Committee,[78] the *Verlag* and University Bureau, etc., not only were Jewish and Zionist literature, art and science advanced and made more widely accessible, but also completely fresh, valuable circles

[76] This Society, the 'Verein für technische Studien in Palästina', had its preparatory committee meeting in Vienna on 11 Nov. 1900. Members of the committee attending the meeting included, among others, Herzl, Ozer Kokesch and Feiwel. It would appear that the Society did not carry out any actual work (see *Die Welt*, 16 Nov. 1900).

[77] Apparently refers to the Colonisation Committee of the Zionist Congress.

[78] The Jewish Statistical Association (previously the Jewish Statistical Bureau) (see Vol. I, n. 7 to No. 204).

[79] Refers to the Berlin Committee for Economic Research in Palestine (see n. 6 to No. 125).

[80] See n. 5 to No. 308, and cf. n. 75 above.

were brought closer to Zionism. Naturally, our activities are but a minute part of what might and in fact should be done; and further progress would be made if the people and activities concerned were not forced on to the defensive as if they were hostile and illegal. On the contrary, they need encouragement through a sign from those above them, and through the total mobilisation of our energy and means.

*   *   *

Much more could be said. We do not wish to tax your patience further. We have not only reported our own experience to you but also the results of much experience and observation on the part of others, as well as their judgment. One must be acquainted with both environments, Russian and West European, to reach the conclusions we have come to. We have had the opportunity to observe, live among, suffer and work with many levels of our people, from the drawing-rooms of Western Europe to the masses in the ghettoes. We have, moreover, experienced contact with all circles within Zionism, including its most estimable people. Particularly, we have come to know the youth as few others have.

Our reports, if at times unpalatable, do not represent a situation viewed through a pessimist's eye. Even less does their unpalatability reflect in our confidence or our desire to continue the work, and this applies equally to many of our friends. In fact the opposite is true. What we have set out here, and expressed with uninhibited candour to you as leader, originates only—please believe us—from a profound love for the cause and an urge to work for it with all our strength.

Perhaps we shall have succeeded in illuminating some points and gaining your sympathy for the outlook of the young Zionists. You are surely aware that it is precisely this youth, rejected by you, who belong among your most faithful and most eager supporters. They are everywhere on the alert in the vanguard of Zionism, even if they do not flood *Die Welt* with inflated items of news.

Possibly the clarification of these issues will have their impact upon the next Congress, and even earlier. Should this Congress produce the encouraging news on the territorial question[81] that is

[81] Orig.: 'Landfrage'. This term was then current to denote the complexity of problems involved in ensuring the requisite conditions for systematic Jewish settlement in any particular region—whether it be Palestine itself or one of the neighbouring countries (see, e.g., the address delivered by Trietsch at the Sixth Zionist Congress in Aug. 1903 on 'The Territorial Question in Zionism', 6 Z.C. Prot., pp. 37–45). The term is used here in the context of the negotiations for Jewish settlement in the El-Arish zone.

rumoured, then the leadership will have to see to it that no conflict develops between itself and the young and most active elements
of the movement. Misunderstanding will drive the youth into the
painful position of an opposition, to foreshadow much harm in the
future; but just a small amount of goodwill could convert it into
the finest working element.

Should the Congress not be able to indicate any progress in our
affairs, it would be an eventuality that the youth alone, with its
superiority of stamina and devotion, could sustain.

We realise that there is no dearth of gossip-mongers who make it
their business to spread dissension between the leadership and the
youth. It is hoped that this analysis will suffice to bring so pathetic
a form of sycophancy to a halt.

And if our interpretation has included some apparently sharp
censure against the leadership, we would implore you to ascribe it
neither to a passion for criticism nor to any personal motivation,
of which we know ourselves to be entirely free. We are keenly looking forward to the possibility of a united effort, and believe we have
offered a way towards it.

But if this proves impossible, the many who are with us will,
together with ourselves, remain absolutely undeterred in conducting our work in the future, despite the difficulties that have
hitherto assailed us.[82]

Dr. Ch. Weizmann

317. To Catherine Dorfman and Anne Koenigsberg, Zurich. *Geneva, (?)6 May 1903*[1]

Russian: Vcd. H.W.: W.A.

Dear Girls,

I am sending you a memorandum[2] with the condition that as
soon as you have read it you will hand it *personally* to Maria
Sokolow (Pension Plattenhof, Zürichbergstrasse). Then again, in
person, take it from her and send it back to me by registered post.
I cannot write another word as I am up to my eyes in work. Still

---

[82] For Herzl's reply to this memorandum, see n. 3 to No. 336.

317. [1] The date has been presumed from the statement re Bernstein-Kohan (cf.
No. 314) and the words 'I am sending you the memorandum': obviously referring
to the memorandum sent to Herzl on 6 May 1903 (No. 316), a copy of which W. had
promised to send Dorfman and Koenigsberg (see No. 314).
[2] See n. 1 above.

no news from K[ohan]-B[ernstein]. I telegraphed him for the third time.[3]

I hug you. Am sending 25 francs to Anya.[4]

318. To David Wolffsohn, Cologne. *Geneva, 6 May 1903*

German: T.W.: C.Z.A. W56.

Geneva, 6. 5. 03.
Rue Lombard 4.

Mr. D. Wolffsohn,
Cologne.   Registered.

Dear Fellow-Zionist,

In sending you the enclosed memorandum[1] we are adding a special request, and would be most obliged if you could find your way to fulfilling this.

As you will see from the memorandum, we have begun the issue of a publication[2] for propaganda activities. Some 8,000 roubles have been pledged in Warsaw and Lodz[3] for the purposes of our Bureau as well as for the publication, and the collection of this sum should by now have begun.

Owing to the terrible events in Kishinev, demanding material assistance from all circles within Russian Jewry,[4] we dare not at present engage on any collections, but must postpone doing so for another few weeks.

We would therefore like you to make us a loan of two to three thousand marks against this contribution and, unless we succeed in 'making' some money in Western Europe sooner, with a period of two to three months for repayment.

Although we have a few thousand francs for the Bureau on deposit in our account at the Jewish Colonial Trust, we do not wish to use these funds for the journal. When they were raised some time ago in Baku, etc.,[5] we had not as yet envisaged a journal and we desire to conform to the wishes of our donors.

---

[3] W.'s telegrams have not been found. Cf. No. 314 and n. 31 there.
[4] There is no signature.

318. [1] The report of the University Bureau (see n. 1 to No. 311).
[2] Refers to the preparations being made at that time for the publication of the periodical *Der Jude*.
[3] Cf. n. 4 to No. 301.
[4] See No. 310 and n. 4 there.
[5] See Vol. I, bridge-note after No. 317.

Most respectfully, and with regards from my friend Feiwel, who joins in this request,[6] as well as from myself,

Yours,
Ch. Weizmann

319. To Julius Moses, Mannheim. *Geneva, 6 May 1903*
German: Or. Copy. T.W.: W.A.

6. 5. 03.

Dr. Moses,
Mannheim.   Registered.

Dear Dr. [Moses],

May I take the liberty of sending you, both in my own name and that of my friend Feiwel, the enclosed report concerning our Bureau.[1] This should at the same time serve as a guide for the activities of your local committee, about which Feiwel spoke to you some time ago.[2]

We would also take this opportunity of making a special request to you, and would be most obliged if you could find your way to fulfilling it.

As you will see from the memorandum, we have begun the issue of a publication[3] for propaganda activities. Some 8,000 roubles have been pledged in Warsaw and Lodz[4] for the purposes of our Bureau as well as the publication, and the collection of this sum should by now have begun.

Owing to the terrible events in Kishinev, demanding material assistance[5] from all circles within Russian Jewry, we dare not at present engage on any collections, but must postpone doing so for another few weeks.

We would therefore like you to make us a loan of 1,000–2,000 marks against this contribution and, unless we succeed in 'making' some money in Western Europe sooner, with a period of two to three months for repayment.

---

[6] Wolffsohn's reply has not been found and it would seem that he did not comply with W.'s request (see No. 347).

319. [1] See n. 1 to No. 311.
[2] The establishment of a Jewish University Committee at Mannheim, under Moses's chairmanship, was decided upon during Feiwel's visit there in Feb. 1903 (see report of Jewish University Bureau, W.A. No. 30/5/0).
[3] See n. 2 to No. 318.
[4] See n. 4 to No. 301.
[5] See n. 4 to No. 310.

Although we have a few thousand francs for the Bureau on deposit in our account at the Jewish Colonial Trust, we do not wish to use these funds for the journal. When they were raised, some time ago in Baku,[6] etc., we had not as yet envisaged a journal and we desire to conform to the wishes of our donors.[7]

Most respectfully, and with Zion's greetings,

320. To Berthold Feiwel, Vienna.[1] *Geneva, 6 May 1903*

German: Or. Copy. T.W.: W.A.

Geneva, 6. 5. 03.

Dear Berthold,

Enclosed is a copy of the memorandum which is being sent to Herzl today.[2] The report on the University[3] will be fully distributed either today or at the latest tomorrow. There is still nothing from Kohan-Bernstein. I telegraphed yesterday but have as yet received no reply, and I find this most disturbing.[4]

Seidenman[5] of Warsaw sends notification of 500 roubles.[6] They must stop collections there, unfortunately, because everyone is now subscribing for Kishinev. Indescribable panic has seized all of Russian Jewry, and disturbances are expected everywhere. Should the reports from Russia be confirmed, I am planning to leave Geneva at once. So please prepare for such an eventuality. Try out some ways of getting money, Berthold.

With best wishes and warmest regards to you and Martin.

Ever yours,

P.S. Do write immediately as to how things are going with you and what you have done for our affairs.

---

[6] See Vol. I, bridge-note after No. 317.

[7] No reply from Moses has been found and it would seem that he did not comply with W.'s request (see No. 347).

320. [1] Feiwel was then in Vienna, or on his way there, after visiting his parents in Brno (see No. 329).

[2] See No. 316.

[3] See n. 1 to No. 311.

[4] W.'s telegram has not been found. Cf. No. 314 and n. 31 there.

[5] Simon Seidenman was erroneously named 'Seidman' in W.'s letters during this period.

[6] Seidenman's letter has not been found. He apparently informed W. that he would shortly be sending the University Bureau the sum of 500 roubles on account of the moneys pledged in Warsaw for the University (see n. 3 to No. 298). In the event only 200 roubles were transmitted, at the end of June (see n. 1 to No. 395, and also the balance-sheet of the University Bureau dated 15 July 1903, W.A.).

321. To Boris Greidenberg, Kharkov. *Geneva, 7 May 1903*

German: Or. Copy. T.W.: W.A.

7. 5. 03.

Dr. B. S. Greidenberg,
Kharkov.   Registered.

Dear Friend,

First of all I must ask you to forgive me for not writing till now. It is exactly 14 days since I arrived here. I don't want to make too much of it, but you will surely understand that I was incapable of work and exhausted from too much travel and excitement. On arrival I found a mass of urgent matters awaiting me. Without permitting myself a single day's rest, I threw myself into my work at the Bureau and the laboratory, and still have my hands full.

Our friend Feiwel and I have prepared the report[1] together. It is too long to be copied out by hand and so we decided to have it printed. I am sending you this report under separate cover. It is intended exclusively for yourself and the most intimate circle interested. I should be most happy to receive your comments and also trust, dear Doctor, that you will find the report enlightening in many respects. I would strongly request you to formulate such questions as may occur to you most carefully and we shall strive to reply with the same measure of exactitude. You may be assured that we are dealing with every recommendation and all advice with the utmost conscientiousness, and we trust that our co-workers and friends will consult with us as frequently as possible.

We respectfully direct your attention in particular to the elaboration of the programme.[2] I consider this to be the most essential task at present, and in this regard what you would have to say would be very much to the point, for you are fully conversant with the position of higher education among the Jews of Russia.[3] I would emphasize, as before, the need which has already become apparent to establish contact with Kiev and Odessa. Kharkov[4] can certainly assume leadership in this area. In the north the work will be done by our friends in Moscow.

Finally, may I, on behalf of our friends, extend a warm invitation

---

321. [1] Of the University Bureau (n. 1 to No. 311).

[2] For working out the Courses the proposed Jewish University would offer. Cf. No. 294 and n. 8 there.

[3] Refers to the situation produced by the *numerus clausus* in respect of Jewish students in higher educational establishments (see n. 6 to No. 316).

[4] It would seem that this had already been discussed by W. and Greidenberg in Kharkov in April (see n. 5 to No. 303).

to you to become a contributor to our journal. As you know, dear Doctor, a scientific discussion concerning the University project is to be ventilated in the journal. The participation of all friends of our project is, therefore, most desirable.

The first issue is ready for the printers, and promises to be very attractive.[5] We are however delaying publication because financially the undertaking is not yet completely secure. Needless to say, we would urgently request you to keep this point in mind as well.

Perhaps you might still contribute to the first number? You may write in any language you prefer; we shall attend to the German translation here.

Kind regards and best wishes.

Yours faithfully,

322. To Theodor Herzl, Vienna. *Geneva, 8 May 1903*

German: T.W.: C.Z.A. H VIII/915.

Geneva, 8. 5. 03.
Rue Lombard 4.

Dr. Theodor Herzl,
Vienna.

Dear Dr. [Herzl],

We are taking the liberty of sending you herewith our report[1] concerning the University project, previously mentioned.[2] We should be very happy to have your views on it.[3]

Most respectfully and with regards,

Dr. Ch. Weizmann

323. To Selig (Siegmund) Weicman, Warsaw. *Geneva, 8 May 1903*

German: Or. Copy. T.W.: W.A.

8. 5. 03.

Mr. Siegmund Weicman,
Warsaw.

Dear Friend,

The report on our Bureau's activities was completed only[1]

---

[5] For the contents of the first issue (never published) of the periodical *Der Jude*, see n. 6 to No. 311.

322. [1] See n. 1 to No. 311.
   [2] See No. 316.   [3] No reply from Herzl has been found.

323. [1] Typing error in the orig. 'es' instead of 'erst'.

today, and it has been sent to the people in Warsaw and Lodz.[2] This does not as yet represent all that I promised you and Gruenbaum,[3] because this statement, being of an intimate, informative character, is not suitable for propaganda purposes. Nevertheless, one does get a good overall view of the state of the project from it. I shall send you a further brief for propaganda throughout your local area,[4] but you must give me some time. You cannot imagine how much has had to be done here despite my state of fatigue, with which you are well acquainted.

I am aware that our cause will suffer somewhat because of the frightful events in Kishinev,[5] but may I ask you, dear friend, not to lose sight of the great objective. I know there is no need to go on about this, you will do all you can. Perhaps the time has already come for the Lodz visit. At all events let us hear from you soon.

With kindest regards,

Yours ever,

324. To Alfred Nossig, Berlin. *Geneva, 8 May 1903*

German: Or. Copy. T.W.: W.A.

8. 5. 03.

Dr. Alfred Nossig,[1]
Halensee.[2]

Dear Dr. [Nossig],

Today we posted several copies of our report concerning the University project on to you.[3] This statement is of a confidential nature, and I would ask you to deal with it accordingly.

Please excuse the delay, dear Doctor. I found such a mass of urgent work on arrival here, that it was impossible to prepare the report any earlier.

I would be most happy to hear from you shortly as to whether any steps have already been taken on behalf of our cause. May I

---

[2] See n. 1 to No. 311. The covering letters which doubtless accompanied the report have not been found, but it would seem that it was forwarded to, among others, the members of committees for the Jewish University in Warsaw and Lodz (see n. 2 to No. 297; n. 3 to No. 299). See also No. 344.

[3] It would appear that W. promised to send propaganda material when he visited Warsaw in March 1903.

[4] No such communication has been found.

[5] Cf. Nos. 318, 320.

324. [1] Nossig was a member of the Berlin Committee for the Jewish University (see n. 2 to No. 292).

[2] A district of Berlin.   [3] See n. 1 to No. 311.

ask you further to let us have your early comments on this document.

Doubtless Feiwel has by now sent you the article about the survey.[4]

In anticipation of your early reply, I remain, with regards,

Yours,

325. To Michael Kroll, Moscow. *Geneva, 8 May 1903*

German: Or. Copy. T.W.: W.A.

8. 5. 03.

Dr. M. B. Kroll,
Moscow.

Dear Friend,

As you see, my world tour is behind me now and I am already preparing for the next one. I have been back here exactly 14 days. You can imagine all the different tasks that awaited me. Many things had to be done urgently, and some of them are already completed.

A long report[1] which we have prepared concerning the University project has just come from the printers, and a copy is enclosed herewith. May I ask you, dear friend, only to give it or show it to the innermost circle of our friends. In a few days I shall send you another copy.

I should be very pleased to hear news from you regarding our affairs as soon as possible. Do you have any money?[2]

In sending my warmest regards to you and to all our friends, and in asking you to forgive this brevity caused by utter exhaustion,

I am,

Yours ever,

326. To Samuel Grusenberg, St. Petersburg. *Geneva, 9 May 1903*

German: Or. Copy. T.W.: W.A.

9. 5. 03.

Dr. S. Grusenberg,
Petersburg.

Dear Dr. [Grusenberg],

Some time ago we replied promptly to your enquiry, and on our

[4] Feiwel had undertaken to write an article summarizing the results of the student survey for *Jüdische Statistik*, of which Nossig was the editor (cf. n. 8 to No. 3; n. 2 to No. 335).

325. [1] See n. 1 to No. 311.   [2] I.e., for the University Bureau.

part put a number of questions to you. All our letters were sent 'registered', and we therefore assumed that you had received them.[1] Your reply is still not to hand and we are unable to explain the reason for your silence.

We would indeed be happy to continue the relationship we had established and look forward to hearing your views in this regard.

Enclosed is a synopsis of a report concerning our undertaking,[2] and we would ask you to publish it neither in part nor in its entirety. The report is intended *exclusively* for those people in our confidence; as for the Press, we feel obliged to hold back awhile.

May I at the same time enquire whether you would be prepared to accept some articles about the Fraction for publication in your esteemed periodical?[3]

Anticipating your early reply, I remain most respectfully, and with regards,[4]

Yours,

327. To Joseph Lurie, St. Petersburg. *Geneva, 9 May 1903*

German: Or. Copy. T.W.: W.A.

9. 5. 03

Dr. Joseph Lurie,
St. Petersburg.

Dear Friend,

Enclosed is our report on the University, which has just come out.[1] In our opinion nothing is to be [published] as yet; very soon we shall place an article at your disposal.[2]

Do please write me a few words on the question we discussed in Warsaw some time ago.[3] Is Motzkin still in Petersburg?

I would also request you to send me the correspondence that

---

326. [1] Only one previous letter from Grusenberg has been found (see No. 281), but it appears from No. 356 that in March 1903 W. also wrote him two letters from Berlin and Warsaw.

[2] See n. 1 to No. 311.

[3] Grusenberg was editor of the Russian-language Jewish weekly *Budushchnost'*. No article on the Democratic Fraction appeared in it.

[4] No reply has been found.

327. [1] See n. 1 to No. 311.

[2] Lurie was on the editorial board of the daily *Der Fraind* in St. Petersburg.

[3] While in Warsaw in Aug. 1902, W. had apparently spoken to Lurie about preparing a Hebrew translation of *Eine Jüdische Hochschule* (see Vol. I, n. 11 to No. 297).

you have received from Kishinev. Surely, for various reasons, you will not be able to use it all. Zangwill has asked us for material on Kishinev.[4] You can imagine that it is most important to make as many reliable reports as possible available to him. It is important to know which strata of the population were involved in the massacre and who were their unfortunate leaders.

Kind regards,

Yours ever,

328. To Joseph Pokrassa, Kharkov. *Geneva, 9 May 1903*

German: Or. Copy. T.W.: W.A.

9. 5. 03.

Mr. Joseph Pokrassa,
Kharkov.

Dear Friend,

I sent to Dr. Greidenberg yesterday, and to Levinson[1] today, a report on the University project which has just come off the press.[2] The report is a compilation of facts with which you are already familiar. I shall send a copy to you within the next day or two. The first issue of the periodical is now ready. It looks very promising, and is assured the participation of some very important European forces.[3] The editor of the *Neue Deutsche Rundschau*[4]—the best of German periodicals—has promised his constant collaboration and has already delivered an excellent contribution for the first issue.[5] Our cause is reaching ever wider circles and gathering new strength. Georg Brandes is also going to write for us.

The Kishinev calamity, however, has in its turn caused harm

---

[4] Zangwill was endeavouring to give as wide publicity as possible to the Kishinev pogrom in the British and American press, and he delivered an address on the subject in London on 17 May 1903. At the same time Feiwel was preparing a book on the pogrom (see Told [B. Feiwel], *Die Judenmassacres in Kischinew*, Berlin 1903).

328. [1] The banker G. S. Levinson. He and Greidenberg were joint chairmen of the Kharkov Committee for the Jewish University.
[2] W. informed Greidenberg about the dispatch of the report on 7 May (see No. 321); no letter to G. S. Levinson has been found. For the report, see n. 1 to No. 311.
[3] See n. 6 to No. 311.
[4] Oskar Bie (1864–1938), art historian and lecturer at the Berlin Polytechnic. Editor of the quarterly *Neue Deutsche Rundschau* (Berlin) from 1902. Bie was mentioned by Buber as one of the persons likely to show interest in the University project (see Buber to W., 6 Jan. 1903, W.A.).
[5] The subject of the article is unknown.

to our undertaking. Financial contributions from Lodz, etc.,[6] are of course difficult to collect now, and we have to bide our time. This delay is very painful and we must try and look after ourselves during this brief interval.

The people in Kharkov were certainly very much in favour of establishing a journal as a propaganda aid for our project.[7] Since we are giving prominence in it to the University question, the launching of a special publication for this purpose seems superfluous; but the people in Kharkov ought surely to support *Der Jude*. Please, dear friend, do write to me soon about all that is happening.

Warmest regards to you and all our friends.

I am,

Ever yours,

329. To Berthold Feiwel and Martin Buber, Vienna.

Geneva, 9 May 1903

German: Or. Copy. T.W.: W.A.

Geneva, 9. 5. 03.

Dear Berthold and Martin,

Today I sent a number of reports to you,[1] as registered printed matter. They have gone to other places also. You will surely have received my earlier letter by now,[2] as well as the memorandum.[3] The material for Wolffsohn and Moses went off the day before yesterday.[4] So far there has been no reply. I implore you, my friends, to look around for some money. It would be quite unfair to approach our Russian friends for money now.[5] I am convinced that something can also be done in Vienna, and it would be most desirable if you, dear Bert[hold], were to remain there an additional day for this purpose. The journal[6] must come out as soon as possible. This is important from every point of view. Later we shall have funds in plenty. It is a question now of short-term relief.

Let me hear from you at once.

Kindest regards,

Your

[6] Refers to the moneys promised in Lodz and Warsaw for the University Bureau (see n. 4 to No. 301).

[7] W. probably had discussions on the contemplated periodical when he was in Kharkov in April 1903 (see No. 303 and n. 5 there).

329. [1] See n. 2 to No. 311.   [2] See No. 320.
[3] See No. 316.   [4] See Nos. 318, 319.
[5] An allusion to the situation resulting from the Kishinev pogrom and the large fund-raising campaigns on behalf of the victims—cf. No. 320.
[6] The projected periodical *Der Jude*.

330. To Michael Kroll, Moscow. *Geneva, 9 May 1903*

German: Or. Copy. T.W.: W.A.

9. 5. 03.

Dr. M. B. Kroll,
Moscow.

Dear Friend,

Yesterday I sent you the report that has just come out on the University.[1] Today your letter arrived,[2] and I hasten to reply. Of course it is my intention to make my next trip to Moscow—most likely not before the late autumn since no-one is to be found in the city during the summer season. You will already have learned from the report of the success of my last journey.[3] What causes us most headaches now is the launching of the periodical. Although we have prospects of funds for this purpose,[4] fate, as I have already remarked, is playing a trick on us. We must now wait for two months at least until the pain subsides and people can think of something besides Kishinev.

If you have some money you might well place it at our disposal. Everything is ready for the press;[5] the only things missing are printer and paper.

Six weeks ago I had a large number of prospectuses sent to you from Berlin.[6] They do not seem to have reached you. This surprises me, for they were received in Kharkov and Warsaw without any problem.[7] Enclosed is a sample. I shall send a further consignment by registered post and trust you will really get it. . .

330. [1] See No. 325. For the report, see n. 1 to No. 311.

[2] Kroll to W., 20 April (3 May) 1903, W.A. Kroll stated that he might obtain a certain amount for the University Bureau, though only a fraction of what W. could raise if he were to visit Moscow (for cancellation of W.'s visit to Moscow, see No. 302 and n. 3 there; No. 303). Kroll wrote that it was difficult to obtain money for this purpose: 'Official Zionism, by the way, opposes the University; at all events, Tschlenow and his circle have definitely expressed themselves against a University outside Palestine.' Kroll also reported that the student survey in Moscow and Kazan had been concluded, but no information had been received from other cities. He added that members of the Democratic Fraction had not been active anywhere.

[3] W.'s trip to Russia in March–April 1903.

[4] Refers to the contributions for the Jewish University Bureau promised in Lodz and Warsaw (see n. 4 to No. 301).

[5] See n. 6 to No. 311.

[6] A prospectus relating to the proposed periodical *Der Jude* (see No. 292 and n. 8 there). Kroll wrote that he had not received the prospectus, although W. had informed him from Berlin of its dispatch.

[7] Prospectuses sent to Warsaw and Kharkov had not been delayed by the Russian censor.

Please write as often as you can. I am anxiously awaiting the pamphlet from Idelson.[8]

As ever yours,

331. To Simon (Shimshon) Rosenbaum, Minsk. *Geneva, 9 May 1903*

German: Or. Copy. T.W.: W.A.

9. 5. 03.

Attorney S. Rosenbaum,
Minsk.

Dear Friend,

Enclosed is a report on the state of the University project,[1] intended for you and the innermost circle of our friends.

I shall write the article as requested and send it to Belkovsky. It is a real pity that you did not send me the Minsk article.[2] You could have spared me a great deal of trouble; I have my hands full just now, and have not yet had time to rest up.

I sincerely implore you to write to me as to where our cause stands, if only in short headings. You can well imagine how important it is to be properly informed. I am counting on this.

With many kind regards and best wishes from Feiwel and myself to you and yours,

Ever your devoted

---

[8] A reference to the pamphlet in Russian *Zionism—First Lecture (Theoretical Basis)*, written by Idelson and published by Rothstein and Guinzburg in Saratov, 1903. In his letter of 20 April (3 May) 1903, Kroll had stated that he was sending the pamphlet to W.

331. [1] See n. 1 to No. 311.

[2] It seems that Rosenbaum had asked W. to write an article or memorandum on the Democratic Fraction for Gregory Belkovsky, the Zionist regional leader for the St. Petersburg area, in addition to the survey which W. had drawn up whilst in Minsk in April (the 'Minsk article' mentioned here, and see n. 3 to No. 306; n. 3 to No. 305). Glikin wrote to W. on 18 (31) May 1903 (W.A.): 'I have asked Rosenbaum for that "article". I wanted to send it to you, but he insisted that you must write another and send that to Belkovsky.' It is not known whether Belkovsky intended to publish W.'s article or give it to some individual or to functionaries in St. Petersburg. For Belkovsky's relations with the Russian Ministry of Interior, see his memoirs in the periodical *Hazioni Haklali*, 10 Jan. 1935, p. 8; and also Tulo Nussenblatt (ed.), *Zeitgenossen über Herzl*, Brno 1929, p. 24. It is also not known whether W. complied.

332. To Catherine Dorfman and Anne Koenigsberg,
Zurich. *Geneva, 10 May 1903*

Russian: Pcd. H.W.: W.A.

10/v. 03.

Dear Girls,

Now it's my turn to be astonished by your silence. I hope you received everything[1] from me. *Nu*?

Write often, and in great detail, about absolutely everything.

I have been very depressed lately. The news from *Golus*[2] affects me like poison, and is slowly but surely undermining my health. I want to scream and slash out, but haven't the strength.

Write at once.

I hug you.

Your Chaim, very worn out and exhausted.

333. To Catherine Dorfman and Anne Koenigsberg,
Zurich.[1] *Geneva, 13 May 1903*

Russian: H.W.: W.A.

Geneva, 13. v. 03.
Rue Lombard 4

Dear Girls,

You attacked me for my *Bericht*[2] most unjustly. It was intended for 'committee members'[3] exclusively, and only 50 copies were printed.

Now for your attitude, dear Katia, towards the project itself: let me counter this with my own attitude, motivated as it is by my feelings regarding the overall development of our cause, as set down in part in my letter to Herzl.[4]

332. [1] W. had written to Dorfman and Koenigsberg on 4 May 1903 and 6 (?) May 1903 (see Nos. 314, 317) and sent them the report of the University Bureau (see n. 1 to No. 311) as well as a copy of his communication to Herzl of 6 May 1903 (No. 316).

[2] Refers to reports on the position in Russia—see No. 320. In a letter to W. of 21 April (4 May) 1903, W.A., his brother Moses related that Kishinev had produced great tension among the Jews of Kiev and widespread panic fed by rumours that a pogrom was also to be waged there. Pokrassa reported similarly to W. in his letter of 22 April (5 May) 1903, W.A.

333. [1] The letter was in reply to one from Dorfman and Koenigsberg which has not been found.

[2] The report of the University Bureau (see n. 1 to No. 311).

[3] Members of the committees for a Jewish University. In fact, the report was also sent to non-members. [4] See No. 316.

I don't take the opinion of the Zionist Party in general very seriously[5]; first because it is vague, secondly because it is not representative, and thirdly because the major part *der führenden Elemente*[6] has no opinion of its own. However, the opinions of a few people who matter to me must be taken into consideration. I regard their views as a *Warnungszeichen*[7] keeping me on my guard. Let me assure you[8] once again that the more I work the more I realise that *I*, rather than 'those others', can take the very heart of our cause into my own hands. Certainly Posnansky cannot do so,[9] despite the fact that he has millions and is king in Lodz, nor even his son, who is an intelligent man.[10]

For various reasons I have not answered your question about the Congress; to begin with, I myself know nothing, and secondly . . . etc. Berthold is coming from Vienna on Saturday and I shall then know everything and shall write to you immediately afterwards.[11]

I shall certainly come to see you but I don't yet know just when. I shall try and come as quickly as possible, because I very much want to have a heart-to-heart talk with you, besides seeing you in your new *alma mater*.[12]

I am in an awful mood; can't bring myself to do anything. Judging by the letters I receive, the very air of that damned, terrible, barbaric land where our dear ones languish is filled with tears and lamentation.[13]

I cannot forget or ignore the situation even for a second. Everything here is repugnant to me—these gay, cheerful, smiling faces— I cannot even look at them. I crave for vengeance—terrible, bloodthirsty vengeance. . .

[5] Possibly an allusion to the opposition of many Zionists to the establishment of a University outside Palestine (see Vol. I, n. 4 to No. 320; n. 2 to No. 330 *supra*; n. 3 to No. 385).

[6] 'Of the leading elements.'   [7] 'Warning sign.'

[8] Both here and elsewhere there is no indication whether the style of address is singular or plural, i.e., whether Dorfman alone or Anne Koenigsberg, too, was intended.

[9] Apparently Dorfman had asked jocularly whether Dr. (Moritz) Posnansky, mentioned in the report of the University Bureau of May 1903 as a member of the Lodz Committee for the University, was the same Poznansky (non-Jewish) whom W. had described as the author of the memorandum on Zionism prepared for the Russian Ministry of Interior (see No. 316 and n. 11 there).

[10] Refers to Moritz Posnansky, son of Israel Klemens Posnansky (1833–1900), who for many years had been president of the Jewish community in Lodz. Both father and son were textile manufacturers in Lodz and noted philanthropists.

[11] The question concerning the Sixth Congress alluded to here is not known. W. wrote Dorfman a second time after Feiwel's arrival (see No. 336), but the question is not raised there.

[12] See n. 1 to No. 312.

[13] Cf. No. 320.

Not a word from K.-B. He was accused of ritual murder. For two whole days crowds stormed his house and demanded his life.[14] There is no end to the horrors.

Do write.

> I kiss you.
>
> Chaim.

334. To Stanislav Yarochinsky, Lodz. *Geneva, 14 May 1903*

German: Or. Copy. T.W.: W.A.

14. 5. 03.

Mr. Stanislav Yarochinsky,
Lodz.

Dear Sir,

Sincerest thanks for your kind letter of the 11th.[1] Although we are physically remote from the stricken area, we can nevertheless form a picture of the dreadful situation there, and every post brings alarming news. I can readily imagine how difficult it is to settle into one's work with tranquillity under such strain. For at least a brief period we have got to try and reconcile ourselves to the situation, unrelievedly black though it is.

But I feel in all sincerity that I must ask you to take whatever action is necessary the moment the opportunity arises.

I shall attend to the private matter separately; at present I still do not have the required information, and have written to Lyon[2] about it.

> Yours faithfully,

---

[14] Pokrassa informed W. on 22 April (5 May) 1903 (W.A.) that during the pogrom in Kishinev, Bernstein-Kohan and his family had been compelled to go into hiding for three days, after a blood-ritual libel had been spread about him. In his Memoirs, Bernstein-Kohan relates that a mob attack on his home during the night of the disturbances had been averted through the intervention of their Christian domestic servant, but there is no confirmation there for the statement made by Pokrassa—see *The Bernstein-Kohan Book* (in Hebrew), Tel-Aviv 1945–6, p. 128.

334. [1] Yarochinsky to W., 11 May 1903, W.A. Yarochinsky, who was a member of the committee for the University at Lodz, wrote that owing to the fund-raising campaign for the victims of the Kishinev pogrom, it was impossible to collect moneys for the University Bureau, but that this would be done after the emergency was over (evidently the contributions for the University that W. had been promised in Lodz—see No. 299 and n. 3 there).

[2] Yarochinsky had asked W. to obtain information about a chemist in Lyon who was about to be affianced to his niece (see his letter of 11 May 1903).

335. To Alfred Nossig, Berlin. *Geneva, 14 May 1903*

German: Or. Copy. T.W.: W.A.

14. 5. 03.

Dr. Alfred Nossig,
Halensee.[1]

Dear Dr. [Nossig],

Many thanks for your letter,[2] which was much appreciated. I telegraphed at once to Mr. Feiwel, but have just learned that he is going to Berlin.[3] I believe you will be seeing him there. I have also written to him to attend to the matter.[4]

Unfortunately, we are not at the moment in a position to fulfil your request and so carry out our promise. You must give us a little more time, dear Doctor. The mood in Russia is at present in such a state of ferment that pledges made to us cannot now be realised. I receive alarming news day by day, and everyone asks us to wait for the time when the panic will subside at least a little.[5]

I too have been depressed by all these happenings to a point where all desire to work is paralysed.

It would be as well to call a meeting of the Berlin committee as soon as possible. Buber writes that a committee may also have

---

335. [1] See n. 2 to No. 324.

[2] Nossig to W., 11 May 1903, W.A. Nossig wrote that he was about to approach 'the two professors of technology' (referring to Heinrich Rubens and Ludwig Grunmach, who had undertaken to draw up the plan for the Technical department of the Jewish University—see Nossig to W., 30 May 1903, W.A., and cf. No. 293 and n. 6 there). He wished to call the Berlin Committee for the Jewish University to its first meeting in order to discuss the organizational plan of the University and the prospects of establishing it in Berlin (cf. No. 293). Nossig stated that he had so far not received the article from Feiwel on the results of the student survey (see n. 4 to No. 324), and he asked for a payment on account of printing costs for the publication of *Jüdische Statistik*. Further, he proposed that the conclusions of the survey be published as a pamphlet by the Jewish Statistical Association of Berlin (in the event only a provisional summary appeared—see n. 9 to No. 396). Nossig asked for a loan of 500 roubles to finance the publicity of the Association, relying on W.'s verbal promise (this was in all likelihood discussed when W. visited Berlin in March 1903—cf. No. 292 and n. 2 there).

[3] The telegram to Feiwel has not been found. As to Feiwel's journey, see n. 4 to No. 311.

[4] The passage in the original is none too clear. The statement 'ich habe ihm auch geschrieben und die Angelegenheit erledigen' should apparently be 'ich habe ihm auch geschrieben und [ihn gebeten? veranlasst?] die Angelegenheit [zu] erledigen'. The letter to Feiwel mentioned here has not been found.

[5] For the reports received by W. from Warsaw and Lodz, see No. 320; n. 1 to No. 334. Pokrassa informed W. on 22 April (5 May) 1903 (W.A.) that owing to the campaign to raise funds on behalf of the Kishinev victims, it would be impossible to do anything in Kharkov for the Jewish University Bureau 'until the storm blows over'.

been formed in Vienna.[6] As yet I have no detailed information on this.

Rest assured, dear Doctor, that I shall do everything to redeem my promise. These unhappy events, so unforeseen, will I am sure serve to absolve me in your eyes.

Kindest regards,

Your

336. To Catherine Dorfman, Zurich. *Geneva, 18 May 1903*

Russian: Pcd. H.W.: W.A.

Geneva, 18/v 03.
Rue Lombard 4

My dear Katyusha,

Many thanks for your letter.[1] There is a great deal I ought to write to you about, but let me postpone this until tomorrow.[2] I did get a reply from Herzl.[3] Shall forward it on to you. Feiwel

[6] No letter written by Buber to W. in May 1903 has been found, and the extant correspondence provides no information about the constitution of the Vienna Committee.

336. [1] Not found.

[2] No further letter to Dorfman prior to 6 Sept. 1903 (see Vol. III) has been found.

[3] Herzl to W., 14 May 1903. The original letter has not been found, but a copy in W.'s handwriting is preserved in the Buber Archives (N.L.). Herzl's letter was in reply to the memorandum which W. sent him on 6 May 1903 (see No. 316); but Herzl devoted only a few words to the principal problems that W. had raised and dwelt mainly on a discussion of the attitude of the Democratic Fraction and its sympathizers towards the Zionist leadership generally and towards himself in particular, and his own attitude towards the Fraction. Herzl wrote, *inter alia*: 'The factual reports from Russia are unfortunately very gloomy, and our greater preoccupation here can only be to dispatch aid as speedily and as generously as possible. But I do not believe that the divisiveness that the conduct of the Fraction reveals can serve this common purpose. . . .' Proceeding, Herzl emphasized that 'the Smaller Actions Committee is not the unstable, shortsighted and narrow-minded body that is depicted in the controversies conducted, if not by the Fraction itself, then by friends whom the Fraction will find it difficult to repudiate . . . You know to what instances, to what newspapers and people my comment refers. I have always regarded the Fraction favourably, and for this many of the best Zionists have often reproached me . . . I am not oversensitive towards a reasonable opposition, neither do I want songs of praise sung to me. . . .' Herzl proceeded to express his displeasure at the recent behaviour of the Fraction, more particularly in connection with the Nordau–Ahad Ha'am affair (see ns. 10, 11 to No. 292), and at 'the alliances in which I see the Fraction appearing more and more'. Herzl promised to give most earnest consideration to the proposals made in W.'s memorandum, although most of them could only be discussed during the period of the Congress. He concluded: 'I regard you, Dr. Weizmann, as a person who has been temporarily misled, but nevertheless a useful force who will once more find his way back and proceed along the right road together with all of us. But I am becoming ever more strongly convinced that not all the gentlemen in your group are in this category, and I am ready for the time when, sooner or later, they will be lost to our movement.'

arrived.[4] Though I wasn't present at the site *des Leidens*,[5] it has been a long time since I was able to laugh, and if on occasion I do smile, *so lache ich Blut, oder Galgenhumor*.[6]

Listen, would it be possible to ask your sister[7] to tell us everything that took place, but everything . . .? Could she do this, I mean physically of course? If you think she can, please write to her. I will write on my part also and send you my letter to enclose with your own. But it would be better for you to send me your letter, then I would add mine and send them off to her. I shall probably see you very soon, as I have to go to Vienna.[8]

Kiss Anya for me.

With a warm kiss.
Chaim.

337. To Vera Khatzman, Geneva. *Munich, 24 May 1903*

Russian: Pcd. H.W.: W.A.

Munich,[1] 24. v. 03.

Dear Verochka,

Yesterday's meeting lasted until two in the morning and went off more than brilliantly. There was such an exalted mood, and the various Parties, including the Bund, responded so nobly—the like of which I never expected.[2]

A very, very large meeting is anticipated for tomorrow.[3] Today

[4] Feiwel had returned from a visit to Austro-Hungary and Germany (see n. 4 to No. 311).

[5] 'The suffering.' An allusion to the Kishinev pogrom.

[6] 'So I laugh blood, or with gallows-humour.'

[7] It is not known to which sister of Dorfman this refers.

[8] Concerning W.'s plan to go to Vienna to speak to Herzl, see Nos. 347, 391, and also 379. W. did not travel to Vienna after all, but apparently visited Zurich at the end of May (see No. 337).

337. [1] W. and Feiwel went to Munich to participate in protest meetings against the Kishinev rioting. W. apparently arrived on 23 May 1903 and Feiwel two days later (see Feiwel to Mayer, 21 May 1903, Eugen Mayer Papers, Jerusalem).

[2] The meeting of 23 May 1903 was apparently a student gathering. No further details of the proceedings are known.

[3] The meeting of 25 May 1903 was attended by about 600 people, and 400 marks was raised for the Kishinev victims. The principal speakers were Feiwel and W. W.'s speech is reported in a dispatch appearing in the *Jüdische Rundschau*: 'Adducing philosophical-ethical arguments, *Privatdozent* Dr. Weizmann proved that not only the elevated level of enlightenment among the masses, but also self-help and a spirit of solidarity among all Jews were an active and influential means against anti-semitic outbursts.' In his view, 'the emigration trend of Eastern European Jews must not be the object of philanthropic attention alone, but should be actively regulated through a healthy approach and in the Zionist spirit'. (See *Jüdische Rundschau*, 5 June 1903.)

I addressed a Zionist group in a closed session.[4] The Zionists who attended are a likeable crowd.

How are you, my dear girl? Do you miss me? It was hard having to leave you two days after your arrival,[5] but from now on we shan't part for a long time. Darling, send me a few lines to Zurich, c/o Manya Sokolow, Zürichbergstrasse, Plattenhof. I shall hear about you from Toldy, won't I?

Tender kisses to my dearest girl.

Chaimchik.

[ORIGINAL HAS POSTSCRIPT BY EUGEN MAYER]

338. To Eugen Mayer, Munich. *Geneva, 28 May 1903*

German: H.W.: Eugen Mayer Papers, Jerusalem.

Geneva, 28. v. 03.
Rue Lombard 4

Mr. Eugen Mayer,
Munich.

Dear Friend,

Many thanks for your kind letter,[1] as well as for the cuttings.[2] We have arrived safely and today are already hard at work.

As a consequence of what you write, a letter went off to Dr. Wolfskehl today.[3]

The only instruction we can give you is that for the time being you solicit the interest of scholars, artists, writers and financiers in our enterprise. Sufficient information for the initial steps is to be found in the brochures[4] and memorandum.[5] Should any questions or doubts arise, we can always discuss them.

---

[4] The reference is apparently to the local Zionist Society in Munich, as distinct from the student Zionist Societies. No details of W.'s address are available.

[5] V.K. had returned from a visit to her parents in Rostov.

338. [1] W. employed the formal mode of address at the beginning of this letter, but continued in the intimate form.

[2] Mayer to W., 27 May 1903, W.A. Mayer enclosed in his letter two press cuttings (not found) on the meeting in which W. and Feiwel took part (see n. 3 to No. 337). Mayer wrote that he and Karl Wolfskehl wished to establish a committee for the Jewish University in Munich and asked for instructions on the preparatory work, publicity, and functions of the committee.

[3] Feiwel to Wolfskehl, 29 May 1903, W.A. Feiwel explained the functions of the local committees for the University and suggested that Wolfskehl and Mayer endeavour to raise money for the proposed periodical *Der Jude.* As for Wolfskehl, see also No. 374.

[4] *Eine Jüdische Hochschule* (see Vol. I, n. 3 to No. 240).

[5] The report of the University Bureau of May 1903 (see n. 1 to No. 311).

It would be most useful to win over Prof. Graetz[6] of the Technical College.

We consider that now would be the right moment to work out the plan itself. We wish to come to the Congress with a concrete proposition, and are thinking of a scheme for a department of General Culture and Jewish Studies, and some kind of Technical department, perhaps Electro-Technology.

Prof. Graetz would be very suitable for this latter subject. He is, in fact, a physicist and electro-technologist.

Now the financial problem. We are going through a crisis at present because of Kishinev; we cannot raise funds for the Bureau anywhere and it would be most desirable if you could produce some money for us.

We may perhaps be able to repay this later, when money comes in from Lodz and Warsaw.[7]

Five copies of the memorandum are being sent to you today.

Warmest regards from Told as well as from

Your very devoted Chaim.

339. To Alfred Nossig, Berlin. *Geneva, 28 May 1903*

German: Or. Copy. T.W.: W.A.

28 May 1903.

Dr. Alfred Nossig,
Berlin.

Dear Dr. [Nossig],

We have not as yet had a reply to our last letter.[1] Mr. Trietsch has conveyed the views of the professors to us,[2] doubtless at your behest. But we would like to have more precise information on this. We consider it to be most essential that we come to the Congress with a concrete proposition. It would be best to work out a plan for some kind of Gen. Studies department connected with Jewish Studies, and also some kind of Technical department.

[6] Leo Graetz (see n. 2 to No. 53) was Professor of Physics at the University of Munich, not at the Technical College as W. had erroneously written.

[7] A reference to the moneys promised to Weizmann in Lodz and Warsaw (see n. 4 to No. 301); fund-raising had been deferred owing to the Kishinev pogrom.

339. [1] See No. 335.

[2] Evidently an allusion to members of the Berlin Committee for the University. It is possible that Trietsch spoke about this to Feiwel when the latter visited Berlin in mid-May.

Perhaps you, dear Doctor, would undertake, in association with such other forces as Franz Oppenheimer,[3] etc., to elaborate the project for the General Studies department. The time has also come to activate the Berlin Committee in some form. Would you, dear Doctor, be so kind as to write to us about this, by return if possible.

Most respectfully and with warm regards,

340. To Ch. Shpiro, Warsaw. *Geneva, 28 May 1903*

Russian: Or. Copy. H.W.: W.A.

28. v. 03.

Mr. Ch. Shpiro,[1]
Warsaw.

Dear Sir,

Our Bureau has made it a strict rule, *for the time being*, to publish as little as possible.[2] When our project has been concretely and finally worked out we shall give it wide publicity, but only then.

We have so far published *Eine Jüdische Hochschule*, a brochure which you are probably acquainted with, and recently we issued a report on what our office has done since it was established.[3] It would be desirable for extracts from these two publications to appear in Polish. This would, in our opinion, be quite adequate for the time being.

The results of our statistical investigations are soon being published.[4] Gruenbaum and Weicman[5] have all the information and you may get in touch with them for anything else you need.

With kind regards.

Dr. Ch. Weizmann.

[3] Franz Oppenheimer was a member of the Berlin Committee for a Jewish University. The committee was set up in March 1903 and undertook to arrange the drafting of an academic programme (see No. 294 and n. 8 there), but had not begun this by the time the present letter was written.

340. [1] Not identified.
[2] This was evidently written in answer to a letter from Shpiro that has not been found.
[3] See n. 1 to No. 311.
[4] See n. 4 to No. 324.
[5] Selig Weicman.

341. To Martin Buber, Vienna. *Geneva, 29 May 1903*

German: Or. Copy. T.W.: W.A.

29 May 1903.

Mr. Martin Buber,[1]
Vienna.

Dear Martin,

Motzkin's address is: Editorial Office, *Der Fraind*, Ekaterinsky–Kanal 71, Petersburg. Pokrassa: Office of Hoffman and Deuel, Meshchanskaya 17, Kharkov. I would only like to note that I have received news that Motzkin has resigned from the Fraction.[2] I do not know whether this is true. Yesterday the list of candidates[3] was sent to you. I spoke to Klausner about your collaboration in *Hashiloah*.[4] He is, naturally, gladly prepared to accept anything from you.

Money should be coming in this week, and we will then send you some immediately.[5]

With warmest regards,

Your

342. To Joseph Pokrassa,[1] Kharkov. *Geneva, 29 May 1903*

German: Or. Copy. T.W.: W.A.

29. [5]. 03.[2]

Dear Friend,

Your kind letter[3] arrived a few days ago. I was away,[4] however,

341. [1] It would appear that this letter was in reply to one from Buber which has not been found. But several of the matters it raised were dealt with also in a postcard that Buber sent to Feiwel and that W. probably also read (see ns. 3, 5 below). From No. 347 it seems that Buber had sent a number of letters and postcards to Feiwel at that time but did not write to W.

[2] Pokrassa wrote W. on 8 (21) May 1903 (W.A.) that he had learnt of Motzkin's withdrawal from the Democratic Fraction. No evidence for this report has been found, though in fact Motzkin did not participate in any subsequent Fraction activity.

[3] That is, Democratic Fraction candidates for the Sixth Zionist Congress. In a postcard to Feiwel (then in Geneva) dated 25 May 1903 (W.A.) Buber stated that according to a report he had received from Galicia, it was possible to secure from 12 to 20 seats for the Fraction there, and he asked that a list of candidates be sent immediately, especially of those who might not be elected elsewhere.

[4] Joseph Klausner had been editor of *Hashiloah* from the beginning of 1903.

[5] In a postcard to Feiwel dated 25 May 1903 Buber urgently asked for money for the periodical *Der Jude*.

342. [1] The name 'Pokrassa' appears on the original copy.

[2] The original was dated '29. 03', but was in reply to a letter from Pokrassa of 8 (21) May 1903 (see n. 3 below) and was obviously written on 29 May.

[3] Pokrassa to W., 8 (21) May 1903 (W.A.). Pokrassa wrote that there were no

[*Footnotes 3 and 4 continued on p. 345*]

and could not reply promptly. You can well imagine how it sickens me to start up this endless correspondence all over again. I really cannot understand why Dr. Greidenberg does not write now. He promised faithfully to keep up a correspondence on all matters.[5] Now a very unpleasant standstill has set in and I do not know how long it is going to last.

Der Jude still cannot appear, because a great deal of money is required for it. We counted upon Warsaw and Lodz, but no collection is possible in those places now—at least so they write.[6] Soon everyone will be going on holiday and then we shall have a long wait. If I had the physical ability to travel to Russia we could find some remedy there. Unfortunately I find it impossible to make another journey. I have no-one to take my place, and this is the saddest part of the entire business.

I did not know that Motzkin had resigned from the Fraction. But anything is possible.[7] At all events I am very concerned about the fate of the Fraction. It is attacked on all sides, by Ussishkin, [Rei]nes, Herzl, etc.[8]

On my return from Russia I wrote exhaustively to Dr. Herzl[9] to inform him about the situation in Russia as well as about the Fraction. In reply, I received the letter[10] which I am sending you[11] herewith. It is likely that a propaganda effort is to be instituted against the Fraction to prevent our members receiving any delegate mandates. I would ask you to ensure in good time that we appear

prospects of success for the University project in Kharkov owing to the inaction of the joint chairmen of the committee, Greidenberg and Levinson, and because of the Kishinev pogrom: 'Kishinev has ruined everything, the mood, our affairs, everything—completely.' Pokrassa promised to take action in support of the proposed periodical *Der Jude* and asked for several copies of the prospectus (see n. 8 to No. 292) and of the first issue.

[4] W. visited Munich—see No. 337 and n. 1 there.

[5] W. had conferred with Greidenberg when he visited Kharkov the previous month (see n. 5 to No. 303).

[6] Seidenman had already informed W. at the beginning of May that, owing to the Kishinev campaign, collection of the funds promised to W. in Warsaw for the Jewish University had had to be suspended (Seidenman's letter has not been found, but see No. 320). As for Lodz, see n. 1 to No. 334.

[7] See n. 2 to No. 341.

[8] Concerning Ussishkin's negative attitude to the Democratic Fraction, see Vol. I, n. 10 to No. 257, and also No. 346 below and n. 13 there. For the clash between *Mizrahi* and the Fraction, see Vol. I, n. 6 to No. 270; No. 316 above. For the enmity between *Mizrahi* and Democratic Fraction groups in Russia, see, *inter alia, From the East* (in Hebrew) Year II, No. 1: 'The Zionists supporting the covenant of culture have sallied forth to fight the *Mizrahi* strongly and have placed obstacles to hinder it on every side....' Concerning Herzl's view on the Fraction, see n. 3 to No. 336.

[9] See No. 316.

[10] See n. 3 to No. 336.

[11] The final paragraph employs the formal style of address.

in large numbers at the Congress. Likewise I would ask you not to lose sight of the University project completely.

Perhaps you will be so good as to let me know whether Dr. Bernstein-Kohan has already left for Kharkov.[12]

In anticipation of your early reply,

I remain,
Yours faithfully,

343. To Michael Kroll, Moscow. *Geneva, 29 May 1903*

German: Or. Copy. T.W.: W.A.

29. 3. 03.[1]

Dear Friend,

Yesterday I wrote to you[2] about the Fraction; today I wish to add that it seems most essential to prepare for the elections[3] as quickly and as thoroughly as possible. I believe I have already informed you that on my return from Russia we wrote an exhaustive memorandum to Dr. Herzl[4] in which we set the situation out in its entirety, both as regards Russia as well as the activities of the Fraction. We received a reply[5] which I enclose herewith.

As for the University, we are now in the middle of a crisis. The funds in Warsaw and Lodz cannot now be collected, because of Kishinev.[6] Therefore *Der Jude* still cannot be published. Some time ago you wrote that you have some money for the Bureau.[7] What about it? With a little money you can help us a great deal.

How is the statistical study getting on? We here are now completing the survey: it would therefore be excellent if we had your material.[8] Please send me a few lines about this.

Otherwise there is nothing new. It is being said that the Congress

---

[12] Bernstein-Kohan moved from Kishinev to Kharkov. He was among those responsible for instituting legal action against the culprits in the Kishinev pogrom, and had been warned that his life was in danger if he continued to live there. See *The Bernstein-Kohan Book* (in Hebrew), Tel-Aviv 1945–6, p. 135, and cf. n. 31 to No. 314.

343. [1] Erroneously dated 29 March, but the content indicates that the letter was written at a much later date and should be 29 May 1903; cf. No. 344 and n. 2 there.

[2] The plural should perhaps be inferred here, i.e. Kroll and Idelson; and cf. No. 347: '. . . This is the reason why I wrote to the people in Moscow.' No such letter has been found.

[3] For the Sixth Zionist Congress.   [4] See No. 316.

[5] See n. 3 to No. 336.

[6] See No. 320; n. 1 to No. 334.

[7] See n. 2 to No. 330.

[8] That is, the results of the student survey in Russia (cf. n. 2 to No. 330).

will go on for seven days this year and colonisation[9] will be a prominent topic.

I myself am not altogether well; I am utterly worn out, but there's no help for it—one must stay at one's post.[10]

344. To Samuel Goldflamm, Warsaw.[1] *Geneva, 30 May 1903*

German: Or. Copy. T.W.: W.A.

30. 3. 03.[2]

Dear Dr. [Goldflamm],

Some time ago I had the honour to send our report[3] to you as well as to other gentlemen of the Warsaw Committee.[4] I assume that all of you are in possession of the communication, and we would appreciate having your views on it at your earliest.

We now set great store upon publishing the University programme, at least in summary, as speedily as possible. The plan included our intention, as indicated in the report, to create a special organ that could deal with all the proposals embraced by the University project.

Furthermore, we made efforts to interest recognised experts in our cause and to charge them with the task of developing the scheme for a department of General Studies, and for a Technical department.[5]

Unfortunately, the tragic events of the last few weeks[6] have interfered with all normal calculations so that we in our turn must expect to encounter no little frustration and difficulty in our endeavours, either in the form of material obstacles or in a temporary waning of interest. We are equally vulnerable to both.

[9] It was assumed at this time that the plan for Jewish settlement in the Sinai Peninsula would be a focal point of discussion at the Sixth Zionist Congress (see n. 5 to No. 308). [10] The end of the letter is missing.

344. [1] The W.A. contain the copy of an identical letter to Greidenberg in Kharkov dated 30 May 1903. It would appear that it was addressed to Greidenberg in error and the letter was retyped with Goldflamm's address. See also n. 1 to No. 369.

[2] The letter was dated 30 March, but the content indicates that it was written at a later date. Undoubtedly this was 30 May 1903, the date of the identical letter in which Greidenberg's address was erroneously typed (see n. 1).

[3] See n. 1 to No. 311.

[4] See No. 323 and n. 2 there.

[5] On 28 May 1903 W. suggested to Nossig that he draft the plan for the department of General Studies 'in association with such other forces as Franz Oppenheimer, etc.' (see No. 339 and n. 3 there), and cf. also No. 362. As for the Technical department, see No. 293 and n. 6 there.

[6] The Kishinev pogrom (see n. 1 to No. 310).

Our approach to you, dear Doctor, is being made at this juncture with the earnest request that you do not deny us your energetic and positive support even during this somewhat trying period.

It is precisely now, as we embark upon the most difficult task, that no delay should be allowed to occur. I could add much more, but I believe, dear Doctor, that there is no need to labour the point in order to urge our common cause on your attention.

We shall await your kind reply with impatience.[7] You may be sure that we shall continue to carry forward the enterprise now launched with undiminished zeal, and in our view with success. Given the severe blows falling upon our people we feel constrained to maintain the difficult and responsible place assigned to us with even greater resolution, and to redouble our efforts.

With all good wishes, dear Doctor,

and most respectfully,

Dr. S. Goldflamm,
Warsaw.

345. To Selig (Siegmund) Weicman, Warsaw.[1] *Geneva, 30 May 1903*

German: Or. Copy. T.W.: W.A.

30 May 1903.

Dear Friend,

When I sent you our report some time ago,[2] I asked you to acquaint us with the progress of the University project in Warsaw.

I can well imagine why your reply has not yet arrived. I have no doubt that you would have written if you had something of substance to tell us.

You may argue that the spirit prevailing is such that nothing can be done. Although this may be true up to a point, we of all people nevertheless must not lose our heads just now, but mobilise all our energies and keep striving to build upon the ruins.

Dear friend, you will realise what effect reports of the tragic events[3] have had upon me in my present physical condition. We were as if paralysed, all of us. Now, however, it is precisely in our

---

[7] Goldflamm's reply has not been found.

345. [1] The words 'Weicman Warsaw' appear on the original copy in W.'s handwriting.

[2] See No. 323. For the report, see n. 1 to No. 311.

[3] The Kishinev pogrom (see n. 1 to No. 310).

work that we are seeking consolation and relief from pain. I am firmly of the view that you have similar thoughts, and you will therefore understand when I say: 'Do everything you can for the University!' Give the people no rest and don't let them hide behind facile talk. We can in no circumstance permit a standstill to develop now, lest an enterprise begun with so much effort be made to suffer. As I have written to Goldflamm, Minkovsky, Yarochinsky, and Silberstrom,[4] 'the pogrom must not be allowed to extend to the University'. There must always be a driving power to shake up the people. We are counting on you, and with justification.

Der Jude is ready for the printers,[5] and statistics are in preparation.[6] We are now going forward also with the scheme of the University programme itself; recognised experts[7] have been won over to do this. So you see, work has begun, but we dare not conceal the fact that a stoppage of means just now will result in irreparable damage. This is why I am so disturbed and in the mood to give you no rest either.

. . . .

At the same time I am calling your attention, and the attention of all our friends, to the fact that prior probably to this Congress a bitter struggle will be mounted against us from all sides, East and West. Herzl, Ussishkin, Reines, they are all mobilising against us.[8] We have to watch the situation regarding delegate mandates very carefully, so as not to be stuck away in the galleries. We are arranging everything we can from here, but this is still not enough. Use all your connections so as to get our candidates through.

Forgive me for writing so briefly, my friend. I have my hands so full that I can only concentrate on the most essential things.

Please give Seide[n]man my kindest regards.

As ever yours,

[4] For the letters to Goldflamm and Yarochinsky, see Nos. 334. 344. Letters to Minkovsky and Silberstrom have not been found.

[5] See n. 6 to No. 311.

[6] That is, summarizing the results of the student survey—see n. 4 to No. 324; n. 2 to No. 335.

[7] The Berlin Committee for the Jewish University had undertaken to draw up the academic programme, and Professors Rubens and Grunmach had promised to prepare the plan for the Technical department (see No. 293 and n. 6 there; No. 294 and n. 8 there). It is not known whether other academics had also promised to take part in formulating the programme, and cf. No. 344 and n. 5 there.

[8] See n. 8 to No. 342.

346. To Vladimir Tyomkin,[1] Elizavetgrad. *Geneva, 31 May 1903*

German: Or. Copy. T.W.: W.A.

31. 3. 03.[2]

Dear Friend,

For a long time now I have felt the need to have a full discussion with you[3] on several Party matters. Unfortunately, we had no time for this at our last meeting in Kharkov.[4]

On returning from my last journey I took pains, in a comprehensive memorandum composed by Feiwel and myself,[5] to enlighten Dr. Herzl with a description of the situation in Russia, and to some degree in Western Europe. We[6] sought in addition to make a few things clear to the leader about the Fraction. The paper is too long to send to you, but the reply[7] is enclosed herewith. As you see, Herzl now looks at everything from the point of view of Ahad Ha'am–Nordau.[8] I do not wish to dwell on this point, but one thing is clear to me from Herzl's general attitude—he will avail himself of this opportunity to remove some gentlemen disagreeable to him from the organisation.[9] Naturally, he will be happily sustained in this by the *Mizrahi*[10] and other faithful 'Zionists'. It seems to me that very diverse forces are getting together to deal the Fraction a political death-blow.[11] Who raised the hue and cry, whence the

---

346. [1] The name 'Tyomkin' appears in Stupnitzky's handwriting on the original copy.

[2] The letter was dated 30 March, but the content indicates that it was written at a later date, 31 May 1903: cf. No. 344 and n. 2 there.

[3] The style adopted is that of the intimate form.

[4] W. met Tyomkin in Kharkov on 8 April 1903 (see No. 303).

[5] See No. 316.

[6] The pronoun 'we' was erroneously omitted in the original.

[7] See n. 3 to No. 336.

[8] For the Ahad Ha'am–Nordau controversy, see ns. 10, 11 to No. 292, and see Herzl's references to this in his letter to W. of 14 May 1903 (n. 3 to No. 336). In a letter to Buber, Herzl wrote of his surprise at the attitude evinced by Buber and his colleagues towards the Ahad Ha'am–Nordau affair, 'since, as you know, I have so far regarded the opposition of the Fraction as an entirely healthy opposition, and not to be discouraged in any way whatever' (Herzl to Buber, 23 May 1903, C.Z.A. HB35). Herzl refused to collaborate in the contemplated periodical *Der Jude* owing to the attack by Buber, W., and Feiwel on Nordau—see n. 11 to No. 292 (Herzl to Buber, 14 May 1903, C.Z.A. HB35).

[9] Cf. Herzl's remarks at the end of his letter to W. of 14 May 1903 (see n. 3 to No. 336) concerning the members of the Democratic Fraction whom the movement was likely to lose.

[10] Cf. n. 8 to No. 342, and see the different formulation in No. 349: '. . . Naturally he will enjoy making use of the *Mizrahi* in this way.'

[11] The documents extant provide no confirmation for this surmise, and see also n. 15 to No. 349; n. 1 to No. 379.

source of such behaviour by the Party against the Fraction members, is not yet entirely clear to me. It appears to be partly connected with the information you gave me in Kharkov, and which I discussed in great detail later with Rosenbaum in Minsk.[12] It is very sad when Ussishkin permits himself these words: 'The Fraction and the *Poalei-Zion* will yet leave bloody traces on the history of the movement behind them.'[13] I need not tell you how unjustly and how hard such an accusation strikes at us. There is no need to stress that the Fraction is specifically the only group within Zionism constantly engaged in the very bitter and difficult struggle against Jewish opponents on the entire Russian front as well as here, and conducting successful activities within the ranks of the youth. If we see a rising generation of Zionists today, it is the Fraction that has mostly contributed to its education. Furthermore, most of the leading elements of the Fraction have been inside the movement since the beginning of Zionism, and have more than proved themselves by sheer Zionist conviction.

If, then, misunderstandings arise in certain quarters—and they can stem only from a lack of sufficient information concerning the Fraction in those quarters or through the effect of insinuations by a number of people penetrated, unfortunately, in Zionist periodicals[14]—it would be the direct and solemn obligation of those comrades speaking for Zionism in the places concerned to dispel them.[15] An utterance such as Ussishkin's, however, is likely to reinforce the grossly distorted view and cause mischief. These gentlemen, in stirring up a conflict against the Fraction and *Poalei-Zion*, are therefore making a grave mistake.

I am bringing this state of affairs to your attention because it

[12] An allusion to the alleged association between the Democratic Fraction and the Social Democratic movement, voiced in the memorandum on Zionism prepared for the Russian Ministry of Interior (see n. 18 to No. 316). W. apparently first learnt about the memorandum from Tyomkin when he visited Kharkov in April 1903 (see No. 303 and n. 9 there). There is also an allusion here to the negative attitude of Lopukhin, Director of the Police Department in the Ministry of Interior, towards the Democratic Fraction (see No. 364 and n. 1 there). For W.'s discussions with Rosenbaum on this matter, see n. 3 to No. 306. At this time the Fraction was being accused in some Jewish quarters in Russia of responsibility for the increased severity of the anti-Zionist measures adopted by the Russian Government (see, for example, *Hamelitz*, 26 Sept., 9 Oct. 1903, and see also Nos. 347, 357).

[13] The source of this quotation is unknown. Some months later Ussishkin categorically denied having made the remark or being capable of doing so (see Pokrassa to W., 8 (21) Nov. 1903, W.A.). In the light of what was said above in the letter (see n. 12), it is clear that what is here attributed to Ussishkin alludes to the apprehension lest the activity of the Democratic Fraction and *Poalei-Zion* incite the Russian authorities to initiate severe measures against them and perhaps against the Zionist movement generally.

[14] See No. 316 and n. 23 there.   [15] See n. 3 to No. 305.

appears dangerous to me. You know enough now and I need say no more. I have also written to Jacobson[16] in the same vein. You are the only ones whom I can turn to.

I would not like to burden dear Kohan-Bernstein with Party matters at this time.[17] My friend, do please write to me *immediately, fully, and honestly* on the position you take regarding these problems. And do all you can to clarify the situation. This heartfelt appeal to our many years of solidarity and friendship should be enough.

I fear that the fight is likely to start against us during the Congress elections, from various sides. The *Mizrahi* will exploit the situation to defeat our candidates. Feiwel, Buber, and I would like you to put us up as candidates in your region.[18] We could send you a further list of candidates, but I shall wait till I hear from you first.[19]

I shall write soon on University matters.[20]

With warmest regards,

Yours ever,

347. To Martin Buber, Vienna. *Geneva, 1 June 1903*

German: Or. Copy. T.W.: W.A.

1[1] June 1903.

Dear Martin,

I have read almost all your letters and postcards addressed to Berthold.[2] I am really sorry that everything has conspired to interfere with our activities. Nevertheless, I do not see things as darkly

---

[16] See No. 349. Although the date recorded on the letter is 2 June 1903, there is no doubt that this is the one referred to—both that letter and the present one are practically identical in text, and cf. also ibid.: 'I have written to Tyomkin in the same vein.' See also n. 2 ibid.

[17] Cf. n. 31 to No. 314; n. 14 to No. 333; n. 12 to No. 342.

[18] Tyomkin was Regional Leader for the Elizavetgrad area. See also Buber's letter to him of 3 July 1903 (C.Z.A. A157), in which Buber asked that he, Feiwel, Lilien and Trietsch be put up by Tyomkin as candidates in that region. Buber explained that they wished to join the group of Russian delegates at the Congress 'both because of personal sympathy and also so that we can discuss certain questions with the Russian delegates' (i.e. to enable them to take part in their meetings).

[19] W. was elected as a delegate to the Sixth Zionist Congress in Stavropol (Elizavetgrad region), Simferopol and Kerch (Simferopol region), which was headed by V. Jacobson); and also in Nikolayev. Buber was elected in Kharkov, Feiwel in Ursha and Orgayev (see C.Z.A. Z1/123).

[20] W. wrote to Tyomkin again on 26 June (see No. 388), but the affairs of the Jewish University are not mentioned in that letter.

347. [1] The orig. was typed 'L Juni' and was undoubtedly intended for 1 June.
[2] Only one postcard dated 25 May 1903 (W.A.) is extant.

as you do. True, we are momentarily in financial straits, but I hope it will not last more than ten days because we have initiated some counter-measures.[3] In the unlikely event that these arrangements should fail this time too, we shall withdraw part of the money lying in the bank in order to start the periodical.[4] Believe me, dear Martin, I am with you with all my heart and am leaving nothing untried for the thorough and conscientious handling of our affairs. The unexpected blows from which we have all suffered[5] are the only reasons for this crisis, and we shall overcome it.

Preparations for the Congress are in full swing here too. We wrote to all our key people in Russia and impressed upon them the need to gather their strength with all energy.[6] But I would not know where we could find a large number of Fraction candidates. I reckon on fifty at the most, and they would be quite sufficient in my opinion.

It is of great importance that the list being sent to you[7] should be put up for election in Galicia, if at all possible. We could not be so sure of these people's election in Russia, where an election campaign of the basest kind is not improbable. All that need happen would be for a few Russian A.C. members to spread the word that, in view of the attitude of the Russian government, Fraction members should not be elected;[8] this would spell defeat for all of us. This is a weapon against which we have no defence and is consequently extremely effective. All the omens seem to confirm my surmise. This is the reason why I wrote to the people in Moscow.[9] They will play their part there in strengthening our position somewhat. For the time being I have not replied to Herzl's letter.[10] Perhaps it would be useful to have a discussion with Herzl before the Congress. I would like your opinion on this.

Regarding the University, it is most essential to get something concrete done, or at least begun, prior to the Congress. What I have in mind is the programme for the departments of General Studies and Mathematics-Natural Sciences. You and Nossig, with

[3] Cf. No. 335 and n. 5 there. Concerning W.'s attempts to raise the necessary funds for the Bureau and publication of *Der Jude*, see Nos. 338, 343, 344, 345. Earlier, W. had approached Wolffsohn and Moses on this matter (see Nos. 318, 319), but it would appear that they did not reply.

[4] W. had written to Wolffsohn and Moses that he did not wish to use the funds of the Bureau deposited in the Jewish Colonial Trust for this purpose (see Nos. 318, 319). [5] The Kishinev pogrom—cf. No. 318.

[6] See Nos. 342, 343, 345, 346, and also No. 349, the date of which is given as 2 June 1903 but was perhaps written earlier.

[7] I.e., Democratic Fraction candidates—see No. 341 and n. 3 there.

[8] See No. 346, and ns. 12, 13 there.

[9] The reference is probably to the letter of 28 May 1903 mentioned in No. 343 (not found). [10] See n. 3 to No. 336.

the assistance of others, could undertake this task.[11] Please let me have your observations by return. The survey will also be completed before the Congress meets.[12] I am, further, very much in favour of publishing a comprehensive brochure beforehand and declaring our point of view in it regarding all questions facing the forthcoming Congress, while at the same time issuing a full report of our activities and plans.[13] But we would need an idea, roughly at least, of the Congress agenda. Have you any clues?[14]

Now calm yourself, Martin. We have nothing to lose—quite the contrary. Write at once.

As ever,

Yours,

348. To Stanislav Yarochinsky, Lodz. *Geneva, 2 June 1903*

German: Or. Copy. T.W.: W.A.

2 June 1903.

Dear Sir,

I hope you will forgive me for once again requesting your kind intercession with regard to the funds for the University Bureau which were promised in Lodz.[1] I would not make this request to you but for the difficulties we now find ourselves in owing to the events in Kishinev. We were unable to collect the moneys pledged for the work of our Bureau, and indeed in many instances are still unable to do so. Certainly not in south Russia,[2] for in the mood prevailing there we cannot bring up any subject that is not of burning urgency; nor elsewhere, because we do not wish to interfere with the relief campaigns in progress.

---

[11] Cf. No. 339.

[12] The reference is to the summarized results of the student survey—see n. 4 to No. 324.   [13] Cf. No. 362 and n. 6 there.

[14] The agenda for the Sixth Zionist Congress was drawn up at a meeting of the Smaller Actions Committee on 14 June 1903 (see C.Z.A. Z1/175).

348. [1] See No. 334 and n. 1 there.

[2] There is no knowledge of financial commitments given to W. in south Russia for the University Bureau apart from the amounts promised him in Baku and Rostov in the autumn of 1902 (see Vol. I, bridge-note after No. 317). By the summer of 1903 a payment of 2,508 roubles had been made on account of the approx. 4,500 roubles promised in Baku. The sum of 400 roubles was promised in Rostov and a somewhat larger amount—456 roubles—was received from that city (see balance-sheet of Jewish University Bureau, 15 July 1903, W.A.). Shriro of Baku also promised W., during their meeting at Lausanne in Jan. 1903, that he would make a contribution of 1,000 roubles for *Der Jude*, but it is not known whether the 900 roubles appearing in the balance-sheet for 15 July 1903 had in fact been paid to the University Bureau at the time the present letter was written (see No. 246 and n. 5 there).

As it happens we planned our principal activities specifically for this period before the onset of summer, and in such a way as to get through the two months of the *saison morte*[3] without interruption or standstill in our work. We had made our periodical ready for May 15th as regards copy and administration, by acquiring contributions from first-class writers and through announcements in the prospectus.[4] We also made our arrangements for future months.

You will have some idea of the embarrassment we shall experience both in the progress of our work and in our relations with collaborators if, through lack of funds, the appearance of the periodical will have to be postponed from week to week.

Since the periodical is by definition the sole medium of publicity for our undertaking among the circles important to us, the stoppage will also prove grievous to our propaganda effort.

It is on account of the great difficulty of our situation that we are prompted to request you, with all urgency, to recall your promise to engage actively on our behalf.

I would implore you particularly to approach the circle of people most immediately interested, with a view to their making their own contribution available to us now.

Given our present difficult situation we trust we may count on your urgent support, and would be grateful for an early reply.[5]

Most respectfully and with kindest regards.

Mr. Stanislav Yarochinsky,
Lodz.

349. To Victor Jacobson, Simferopol.[1] *Geneva, 2 June 1903*

German: Or. Copy. T.W.: W.A.

2 June 1903.[2]

Dear Friend,

For a long time now I have felt the need to have a full discussion with you on several Party matters.

---

[3] The term had been mistyped in orig.
[4] Relating to the projected first issue of *Der Jude*, see n. 6 to No. 311.
[5] Yarochinsky replied on 17 June 1903 (W.A.) that he was compelled to postpone activity for the University until the autumn because most of his friends were absent from Lodz and because they were all still disturbed by the Kishinev events.

349. [1] 'Dr. Jacobson, Simferopol' appears in W.'s handwriting on the original copy.
[2] The date was erased in the original and retyped over the erasure.

On returning from my last journey I took pains, in a comprehensive memorandum composed by Feiwel and myself, to enlighten Dr. Herzl with a description of the situation in Russia, and to some degree in Western Europe.[3] We also sought to make a few things clear to the leader about the Fraction. The paper is too long to send to you, but the reply[4] is enclosed herewith. As you see, Herzl now looks at everything from the point of view of Ahad Ha'am–Nordau.[5] I do not wish to dwell on this point, but one thing is clear to me from Herzl's general attitude—he will avail himself of this opportunity to remove some gentlemen disagreeable to him from the organisation.[6] Naturally he will enjoy making use of the *Mizrahi* in this way.[7] It seems to me that very diverse forces are getting together to deal the Fraction a political deathblow.[8] Who raised the hue and cry, whence the source of such behaviour by the Party against the Fraction members, is not entirely clear to me. It appears to be partly connected with the information given to me in Kharkov, and which I discussed in great detail later with Rosenbaum in Minsk.[9] It is very sad when Ussishkin permits himself these words: 'The Fraction and the *Poalei-Zion* will yet leave bloody traces on the history of the movement behind them.'[10] I need not tell you how hard and how unjustly such an accusation strikes at us. There is no need to stress that the Fraction is specifically the only group within Zionism constantly engaged in the very bitter and difficult struggle against Jewish opponents on the entire Russian front as well as here, and conducting successful activities within the ranks of the youth. If we see a rising generation of Zionists today, it is the Fraction that has mostly contributed to its education. Furthermore, most of the leading elements of the Fraction have been inside the movement since the beginning of Zionism, and have more than proved themselves by sheer Zionist conviction.

If, then, misunderstandings arise in certain quarters—and they can stem only from a lack of sufficient information concerning the Fraction in those quarters or through the effect of insinuations by a number of people perpetrated, unfortunately, in Zionist periodicals[11] —it would be the direct and solemn obligation of those comrades speaking for Zionism in the places[12] concerned to dispel them. An utterance such as Ussishkin's, however, is likely to reinforce the

---

[3] See No. 316.   [4] See n. 3 to No. 336.   [5] See n. 8 to No. 346.
[6] See n. 9 to the similar letter to Tyomkin, No. 346.
[7] Cf. n. 8 to No. 342 and see different formulation in No. 346: '. . . Naturally, he will be happily sustained in this by the *Mizrahi* and other faithful "Zionists".'
[8] See n. 11 to No. 346.   [9] See No. 346 and n. 12 there.
[10] See n. 13 to No. 346.   [11] See No. 316 and n. 23 there.

grossly distorted view and cause mischief. These gentlemen, in stirring up a conflict against the Fraction and *Poalei-Zion*, are therefore making a grave mistake.

I am bringing this state of affairs to your attention because it appears dangerous to me. You know enough now and I need say no more. I have written to Tyomkin[13] in the same vein. You are the only ones whom I can turn to.

I would not like to burden dear Kohan-Bernstein with Party matters at this time.[14]

My friend, do please write to me *immediately, fully, and honestly* on the position you take regarding these problems.[15] And do all you can to clarify the situation.

I fear that the fight is likely to start against us during the Congress elections, from various sides. The *Mizrahi* will exploit the situation to defeat our candidates.

I shall write soon on University matters.[16]

With warmest regards,

Yours,

350. To Samuel Shriro, Baku. *Geneva, 2 June 1903*

Russian: Or. Copy. H.W.: W.A.

2 June 03.[1]

Dear Friend,

Many thanks for keeping me in mind and for your frequent notes.[2]

---

[12] See n. 3 to No. 305.
[13] See No. 346.
[14] Cf. n. 31 to No. 314; n. 14 to No. 333; n. 12 to No. 342.
[15] In his reply of 5/18 May 1903 (W.A.), Jacobson wrote that he had always sympathized with the Democratic Fraction and its principles, but he recoiled from the negative attitude of its leaders towards a class of active Zionists which they condemned as 'a reactionary mass'. The Fraction had created nothing; its main strength was in criticism, and its existence was not felt at all in Russia. In Jacobson's view, there was no point in the Fraction's activities in Russia and they should be confined to Jewish students abroad. Jacobson added that he did not believe the Regional Leaders would 'persecute' the Fraction candidates for the Sixth Congress and did not think Herzl was scheming to liquidate the Fraction politically, although members of the Fraction in Simferopol had also made an allegation to this effect.
[16] No further letter to Jacobson has been found for the period prior to the Sixth Zionist Congress (Aug. 1903).

350. [1] In Latin characters in orig.
[2] Only one letter from Shriro during this period has been found— dated 11/24 May 1903 (W.A.), but this is not a reply to it. Shriro may have sent another by hand

With regard to Aberson, I too am reluctant to take the moral responsibility upon myself. He is at present in Berlin, not here. I wrote to him even before receiving your letter, though we quarrelled [----] when I tried to persuade him to come to his senses by making use of his stay in Berlin to collect the material and prepare it for publication.[3] Today [---- ---- ---- ---- ----].

If this has no effect, we shall have to give up the whole thing. As far as I know, he doesn't need money at the moment. If [---- ---- ---- ----] otherwise, I shall try and find some for him. I am worried that he might turn into a vagabond.

There is nothing new here. Mme. Shriro, Miss Lev[4] and Yashka[5] came to see us the day before yesterday and we have not had so pleasant a time in a long while; we all sat on the same bench and talked and talked. We spoke a great deal about you. My Verochka wants to be warmly remembered to you.

Obviously the money has not come from Lodz, my friend, because of Kishinev; consequently the present stagnation. Our correspondent in Lodz writes that we shall have to wait until things calm down a little.[6] If we could get just one-third of what there is lying in the offices at Lodz and Warsaw,[7] it would be enough. The problem is that the *saison morte* is approaching and soon everybody will be going away for the summer. This is why I have been writing you such plaintive letters.

Keep well, my friend.

Ever yours,
Chaim.

The Congress is on August 23 and [---- ---- ----].

through his brother Ilya, who visited Switzerland and brought Weizmann a sample of soap made from oil-waste sent by Shriro (see n. 11 to No. 96).

[3] Refers to the expansion of the text of a lecture which Aberson had delivered at the Zionist Youth Conference in Dec. 1901 on 'The Attitude of Zionism to Existing Trends in Judaism'. In *Trial and Error* (London 1949 edition, p. 89), Weizmann relates that he received a sum of money from Shriro for Aberson to enable him to complete the work. Aberson went to Paris to undertake research but never wrote the projected book. See also Vol. I, n. 1 to No. 225; No. 129 *supra*; No. 411.

[4] Leah Lev (?1885–1970). A student of chemistry in Geneva 1903–08, she married Samuel Itzkovitz in 1905. They settled in Palestine in 1910.

[5] Jacob Shriro (1890–1927), Samuel's son.   [6] See n. 1 to No. 334.

[7] The contributions to the University Bureau promised to W. in Lodz and Warsaw (see n. 4 to No. 301).

351. To Eugen Mayer, Munich. *Geneva, 3 June 1903*

German:[1] Pcd. H.W.: Eugen Mayer Papers, Jerusalem.

Geneva, 3. vi. 03
Rue Lombard 4

My dear Friend,

Why no news? Take pity on me and send the waistcoat.[2] By that I mean *the* waistcoat. The others are indecent.

Ever yours,
Chaim.

352. To Michael Kroll, Moscow. *Geneva, 3 June 1903*

German: Or. Copy. T.W.: W.A.

3 June 1903.

Dr. M. B. Kroll,
Moscow.

Dear Friend,

I am still without any reply from you to my various letters,[1] appeals and enquiries. It is more important than ever just now for us to work together in the closest co-operation so as to make preparations for the Congress. We ought by now to have a list of our candidates; we ought by now to know where in Russia we may count upon success. It will be of extreme importance that our Conference[2] this year prior to the Congress should be an all-embracing one. The question of colonisation, which will be in the forefront,[3] must be dealt with fundamentally. Revising the programme,[4] Party tactics, periodical—these roughly are the problems which should occupy our Conference.

351. [1] The postcard is written in German in Hebrew characters.
[2] W. had left his waistcoat in Munich at the end of May.

352. [1] See Nos. 325, 330. W. wrote Kroll two letters previously, at the end of May, of which only one (No. 343) has been found. The present letter was written before enough time had elapsed for him to receive replies to them.
[2] The Conference of the Democratic Fraction, also termed 'Zionist Youth Conference' and 'Youth Conference' in W.'s letters. As it transpired, the Conference did not take place (see No. 403) and there was instead a meeting of Democratic Fraction delegates to the Sixth Zionist Congress in Basle on 18 Aug. 1903 (see *Der Fraind*, 10/23 Aug. 1903).
[3] See n. 9 to No. 343.
[4] Programme of the Democratic Fraction formulated in June 1902 (see Vol. I, bridge-note following No. 298).

I would also like to have your opinion on Conference formalities: who, in your view, should participate. Please deal with this question most thoroughly, and let me have your immediate answer. I shall then provide full information from here to those of our comrades living in Western Europe. I shall also arrange the technical organisation of the Conference in its entirety. Either you or Idelson must undertake to speak on the revision of the programme; this also necessitates one or preferably both of you coming to the Congress. Similarly, Berger of Minsk must be asked to speak on his activities.[5] We shall probably have a scientific address on colonisation from Franz Oppenheimer,[6] with Buber and Feiwel on general cultural problems, and particulars about the University from myself. The question of tactics could be handled by Kohan-Bernstein and myself.[7]

Obviously, the programme as outlined here is not at all binding; we shall have to adjust ourselves carefully to the Congress agenda.[8] It is important, however, for preparations to commence now, and without a moment's delay. Location of the Conference—Basle, August 10th.[9]

I would at the same time call your urgent attention to the contents of my earlier letters, and stress the problem of money as well as the survey to you.[10]

Please write by return. Warmest regards,

Yours,

353. To Franz Oppenheimer, Wilmersdorf. *Geneva, 4 June 1903*

German: Or. Copy. T.W.: W.A.

4 June 1903.[1]

Dear Dr. [Oppenheimer],

You will doubtless recall your kind promise, made to Buber and myself in Berlin some time ago,[2] to deliver an address to the

---

[5] That is, in his capacity as head of the *Poalei-Zion* Centre in Minsk.
[6] See No. 353.   [7] Cf. No. 377 and n. 8 there.
[8] See n. 14 to No. 347.
[9] Subsequently the opening was fixed for 15 Aug.—see Nos. 357, 362.
[10] Cf. No. 343.

353. [1] Two almost identical copies of this letter to Oppenheimer are preserved in the W.A. One bears the date 3 June 1903, the other 4 June 1903. For some reason the first may not have been sent and was retyped the next day.

[2] Apparently Oppenheimer had given the undertaking when W. and Buber visited Berlin in March 1903 and he had agreed to join the Committee for the University (see Nos. 293, 294).

preliminary Conference of Young Zionists[3] taking place prior to the full Congress (August 23). Should you by chance have forgotten about your promise, I am taking the liberty herewith to remind you of it. What you should speak about is really quite clear: colonisation and its methods, with particular reference to Palestine and neighbouring countries.

You will then have an opportunity to speak before what will most certainly be an intelligent audience. It, on its part, will derive great benefit from the address and the discussion in preparation for the Congress. I would ask you most sincerely, in the name of my friends as well as myself, to reply affirmatively and to convey your decision to me as soon as possible.

With very cordial regards,

Yours faithfully,

Dr. Franz Oppenheimer,
Wilmersdorf.

354. To Hugo Schapiro, Dresden.[1] *Geneva, 4 June 1903*

German: Or. Copy. T.W.: W.A.

Geneva, 4 June 1903.

Dear Fellow-Zionist,

We thank you for your kind communication and are extremely happy that you have succeeded in forming a group in Dresden.[2]

You will doubtless understand that our affairs both here and in Russia cannot be described in just a few words. We are busily occupied, however, with preparations for the Congress, and we shall be sending you a circular shortly in which we shall express opinions on the main issues facing the movement.[3] You will obtain information concerning the University from the enclosed report,[4] which should be treated in confidence.

Unfortunately I find it impossible to come to Dresden, as I shall probably not be making any more propaganda tours before the

---

[3] See n. 2 to No. 352.

354. [1] The original copy has, in Stupnitzky's handwriting, 'Mr. Ch. Shapiro, Dresden', but it appears that the addressee was the student Hugo Schapiro of Dresden (see No. 199), whereas Stupnitzky may have been misled by the similarity of the name to that of Ch. Shpiro of Warsaw (see No. 340).

[2] Schapiro's letter has not been found. A Democratic Fraction group had apparently been formed in Dresden and invited W. to speak there.

[3] Cf. No. 362 and n. 6 there.

[4] See n. 1 to No. 311.

Congress. I came back from Russia not long ago, and have already been in Munich[5] since then. Mr. Aberson is now in Berlin but he might well be able to visit you. His address is: Aberson, care of I. Dubosarsky, Luisenplatz 7, Berlin.

I shall be pleased to hear from you from time to time about the progress of our cause in your locality.

With Zion's greetings,

Yours faithfully,

355. To Moses Glikin, Moscow.[1] *Geneva, 6 June 1903*

German: Or. Copy. T.W.: W.A.

6. 6. 03.

Dear Friend,

Your letter arrived today.[2] I am truly sorry that your stay in Moscow turned out to be so unpleasant.

I still do not know if I can manage to make it possible for you to come to the Congress, and by what means. Here we too are going through a critical period—funds for the Bureau are not coming in, for all concern is now centred on Kishinev, naturally; *Der Jude* cannot therefore appear as yet. You can well imagine how painful this situation is for us.

Furthermore, there is friction with the gentlemen from Vienna, foreshadowing unpleasant results.[3] They are fighting against the Fraction, with the intention of killing it off politically even before the Congress. I have written full details to our Moscow friends about this,[4] and trust they will do everything they can to secure at least a few delegate mandates for us. This is a matter of great importance, because everyone will take up the fight against us during the elections and their battle-cry is certain to come from Vienna.

---

[5] See No. 337 and n. 1 there.

355. [1] The original copy has, in Stupnitzky's handwriting, 'Mr. Glikin, Moscow'.

[2] Glikin to W., 18 (31) May 1903, W.A. Glikin wrote *inter alia* that he was not very happy in Moscow: there was no Zionist activity there, it was difficult for him to live in proximity with his religious father, and furthermore it was difficult to find employment in Moscow. He stated that he had written to Shriro concerning a post in Baku or Western Europe and asked W. to find temporary work for him in Germany or Switzerland so that he could take part in the Sixth Zionist Congress. Glikin told W. that Idelson would go to St. Petersburg on Fraction business—he wished to talk to the members there about the forthcoming Congress. See also n. 2 to No. 331.

[3] See n. 8 to No. 346 and also n. 3 to No. 366.

[4] W. wrote to Kroll about Democratic Fraction affairs on both 28 and 29 May 1903, but only the second letter has been found (see No. 343).

We are living in a state of war. My devout wish is that it will end peacefully.

I read in *Der Fraind* that Kohan-Bernstein, Jacobson and Bendersky have resigned their membership of the A.C. Do you possibly know why? Write at once.[5]

I am awaiting news from Shriro, perhaps something can be done with him.[6] At any rate, I shall endeavour to get your journey arranged.

Please write and tell me whether you hear anything from Motzkin. What is he doing in Petersburg? Tell Idelson he could write more often.

With kind regards,

Your

356. To Samuel Grusenberg, St. Petersburg. *Geneva, 6 June 1903*

German: Or. Copy. T.W.: W.A.

6 June 1903.

Dear Dr. [Grusenberg],

You will surely recall writing to us, of your own accord, on Feb. 20th, when you were good enough to volunteer your own and your esteemed paper's services for the University project. We were delighted with your letter and replied on Feb. 26th, at the same time sending you the printed material you had requested under separate cover.[1] Subsequently I wrote to you from Berlin requesting that you send your reply to Warsaw. Receiving no reply in Warsaw, I wrote you again from there.[2] Finally, on my

---

[5] The Regional Leaders Bernstein-Kohan, Jacobson, and Bendersky had tendered their resignations at the conference in Kiev of Russian Zionist Regional Leaders. This took place between 22–24 April 1903, Gregorian dates (see C.Z.A. Z1/380), and the report of their resignation appeared in *Der Fraind* of 15/28 May 1903. The reasons for the resignations are unclear. Rosenbaum wrote to W. in an undated letter —apparently either 10 or 11 June 1903 (W.A. No. 30/0/33): 'If K[ohan]-B[ernstein] and Jacobson leave the [Greater] Actions Committee, it is because there is no place now on the Actions Committee for people like us.' Pokrassa, who met Bernstein-Kohan in Kharkov, wrote that the latter had left the Actions Committee because he had been unable to work whilst in Kishinev (see n. 12 to No. 342), but now that he had moved to Kharkov he was ready to return and assume the leadership of a Region (see Pokrassa to W., 15/28 June 1903, W.A.). Bernstein-Kohan and Jacobson were re-elected to the Zionist Greater Actions Committee at the Sixth Zionist Congress (Aug. 1903).   [6] See n. 2.

356. [1] See No. 281 and n. 1 there.

[2] W. visited Berlin and Warsaw in March 1903. The letters referred to have not been found.

return from my journey on May 2nd[3] I wrote to you from this address. All my letters, with the exception of the ones from Russia, were sent 'registered', and it is to be assumed that they all reached you.

I am bound to interpret your relentless silence as signifying that you have completely changed your position regarding our cause. Although we have no desire to force our point of view upon everybody, nor the power to do so, we are nevertheless justified in requesting acknowledgement of our communications. It was, moreover, in your own best interest that you clarify your position to us: your present silence is in complete contradiction to your own letter, and must have a peculiar effect upon any disinterested person.

I would mention that we ourselves are accustomed to answering letters at all times, and to receiving replies to those that we write.

I find it necessary though painful to place all this on record. You may, for your part, make whatever use of this letter that you wish.[4]

Yours faithfully,

Dr. S. O. Grusenberg,
  Petersburg.

357. To Simon (Shimshon) Rosenbaum, Minsk. *Geneva, 6 June 1903*

German: Or. Copy. T.W.: W.A.

Geneva, 6 June 1903.

Dear Friend,

I have only indirectly been receiving news of you[1] and of the development of matters we discussed in Minsk[2] some time ago. I have also been informed that some of our Russian A.C. members are applying tactics in relation to this very question which, if my information is correct, are indescribable. These people seem inclined to exploit a situation against the Fraction which arose through pure misunderstanding and misjudgment in a certain quarter,[3] and in this way to conduct politics on narrow, partisan lines. I fear a calamity. In Vienna too they seem to be of the opinion

---

[3] Probably a mistaken reference to the letter of 9 May 1903 (see No. 326).

[4] No reply from Grusenberg has been found.

357. [1] Apparently a reference to Glikin's letter of 18 (31) May 1903, W.A. (see n. 2 to No. 331; No. 358).

  [2] See n. 3 to No. 305; n. 3 to No. 306.

  [3] See n. 12 to No. 346.

that it would be best to kill off the Fraction even in advance of the Congress, and I am convinced that their influence will already have been exerted upon the elections. Today I read in *Der Fraind* that Kohan-Bernstein, Jacobson and Bendersky have resigned from the A.C. I believe I can establish some connection between this sad fact and what is written above.[4] Dear friend, either you or Berger must enlighten me at once. It is vital for us here to be kept informed, or we shall obviously be defenceless. If you do not write, let Berger do so forthwith. I reiterate my point: we shall be paralysed in our Zionist activity unless a change is brought about.

The following is intended for Berger: he must come to the Congress; moreover, he must ensure that the *Poalei-Zion* delegate mandates are available to us. Residue that we are, we must remain solidly united.

I am calling a Conference for August 15th at which we shall make a final attempt to clarify the overall situation, and perhaps correct some errors.[5] I shall write in greater detail to Berger about this Conference.[6]

We are at the moment going through a crisis in the University campaign, brought about of course by the Kishinev events. Thus we cannot take steps towards publication of *Der Jude* because we have so far been unable to collect our funds.[7] I do hope that this problem will be favourably solved before the Congress. In view of all these developments, my spirits are unusually depressed. What a pity to have to undergo such an experience after long years of tireless effort, and after devoting almost all of one's time and best energies to the cause!

A copy of this letter is going to Berger.

With heart-felt greetings to you and all our friends, I am,

Ever yours,

Mr. S. Rosenbaum,
Minsk.

---

[4] Concerning the resignations, see n. 5 to No. 355. In his reply Rosenbaum wrote that, in his view, there was no basis for W.'s apprehensions (see n. 1 to No. 379).

[5] For the plan to convene a Conference of the Democratic Fraction see also No. 352.

[6] W.'s letter to Berger has not been found, but W. sent him a copy of the present letter and it may be assumed that there was a covering note (see also No. 392 and n. 2 there).

[7] The moneys promised to the University Bureau in Lodz and Warsaw (see n. 4 to No. 301).

358. To Nahum Sokolow, Warsaw. *Geneva, 7 June 1903*

German: Or. Copy. T.W.: W.A.

Geneva, 7 June 1903.

Very dear Friend,

I am very sad at not having received news from you for such a long time.[1] The little I know had to reach me in a roundabout way. Although I know that you are very busy, the tragic events of the last few weeks must also have affected your spirit—. Yet I am so eager to hear from you that despite everything I am asking you to write, however briefly. You have been in Kishinev, and in Odessa. You have experienced so much, I am anxious for a little information.[2]

We learned the really sensational news from *Der Fraind* today that Kohan-Bernstein, Jacobson and Bendersky have resigned from the A.C.[3] What is the *casus belli*?

I am looking forward to the forthcoming Congress with trepidation. In Vienna a spirit seems to prevail whereby whatever does not conform to the 'Viennese' concept of Zionism must be cast root and branch out of the Party. Everything is judged there from the point of view of the 'Ahad Ha'am–Nordau' business, and woe unto him who bears the mark of Cain in opposition to Nordau![4] A crusade has now been launched against the Fraction, and particularly against individual personalities within it, from many sides. Herzl, Ussishkin, the *Mizrahi*, all have got together to become the hangmen of the young, freedom-loving elements of the movement.[5] I have grounds for believing that the situation created by the events of which I spoke to you on my return trip is also to be used against us.[6] Instead of demonstrating solidarity in such circumstances, these people will, I fear, commit the irreparable error of not only failing to dispel the misunderstandings current in a certain quarter,

---

358. [1] Sokolow had helped in the fund-raising effort which W. conducted in Warsaw and Lodz in March 1903 (see No. 297, and also the University Bureau report of May 1903, W.A. 30/5/0). They met again in April (see hereunder and n. 9).

[2] Sokolow had attended a conference of lawyers in St. Petersburg which discussed the steps necessary to bring the instigators of the Kishinev pogrom to justice. He then visited Kishinev. See Ch. Shorer (editor), *The Kishinev Pogrom* (in Hebrew), Tel-Aviv 1963, p. 61. No information is available on Sokolow's visit to Odessa.

[3] See n. 5 to No. 355.

[4] See ns. 10, 11 to No. 292; n. 8 to No. 346.

[5] See also No. 342 and n. 8 there; No. 346 and ns. 9, 11 there.

[6] The reference is to the alleged association of the Democratic Fraction with the Social Democrats as imputed in the Russian Ministry of Interior's memorandum on Zionism (see n. 3 to No. 305, n. 18 to No. 316, n. 12 to No. 346). It appears that W. told Sokolow about this when he passed through Warsaw on his way back from Russia, about 20 April 1903.

but of deepening them by fighting the Fraction and possibly branding it as non-Zionist. Everything points to this, unfortunately, and I fear that the conflict between the three A.C. members and the other gentlemen has its roots in this lamentable fact.[7] I would be infinitely grateful to you if you were able and willing to give me some explanation. You can well understand that more than mere curiosity or partisanship prompts me to make this request—as you know, apart from Kohan-Bernstein I am the one most interested in this business.[8]

It is most distressing to be treated by the leadership in this way, when one is aware of having committed no other crime than to fulfil one's Zionist duty at all times, in all conscience and to the best of one's understanding.

As regards the University, we are now going through a crisis, and this was only to be expected in consequence of the Kishinev events. All interest is now centred exclusively on this one happening, and we are suffering morally and materially as a result. But I trust this stagnation will only be of a transient nature.

My own spirits are very low at the moment. Perhaps I see problems in a darker light than they really are. Would that I were wrong!

I do not want to put a thousand questions to you; you know how everything interests me. Interest is an understatement! In conclusion, I plead in all urgency: write[9] at once to

Your very devoted[10]

Mr. N. Sokolow,
Warsaw.

359. To Julius Becker, Berne. *Geneva, 8 June 1903*

German: Or. Copy. T.W.: W.A.

8 June 1903.

Dear Mr. Becker,

Thank you very much for sending me the manuscript, but we

[7] Cf. n. 5 to No. 355; n. 1 to No. 379.

[8] The activities of W. and Bernstein-Kohan were discussed in the Russian Ministry of Interior's memorandum on Zionism—see No. 316 and ns. 19, 20 there.

[9] Sokolow's reply never reached W. Sokolow later assumed that it had fallen into the hands of the Russian police authorities. In this letter Sokolow, *inter alia*, described his impressions of his visit to Kishinev (see Sokolow to W., 30 June 1903, W.A.).

[10] Several typewritten lines, apparently from Feiwel or Stupnitzky, were added to the original copy.

wish to point out that we consider neither the article nor its author
to be of sufficient importance to warrant your controversial stance
in our periodical.[1] We are familiar with the motives of Mr. Pinkus
in unleashing a diatribe against the Fraction.[2]

We would ask you to deal with the question detachedly, without
reference to Mr. Pinkus. Our journal is at your disposal for this
as well as for any other of your contributions.

Respectfully,

and with Zion's greetings,

Mr. Julius Becker,
Berne.

360. To B. Yoffe, Brussels. *Geneva, 8 June 1903*

German: Or. Copy. T.W.: W.A.

8 June 1903.

Dear Sir,

Many thanks for your kind letter and the information it contains.[1]
Also, I must express my thanks to you, belated as they are, for
sending us the material on the University of Brussels.[2]

I hope you will forgive me if I have not dealt with your much
appreciated letters in my usual prompt manner. I was away in
Russia on a long trip; then came the Kishinev events to side-track
all normal activities. I know I can count on your indulgence.

359. [1] See Becker to W., 7 June 1903, W.A. Becker sent W. an article for publication
in the projected *Der Jude* that he had written in reply to one entitled 'Organization
and Schism' by Pinkus that appeared in *Die Welt* of 10 April 1903. Pinkus had expressed opposition to the existence of inter-territorial factions in Zionism and especially
to the Democratic Fraction. He argued that opposition groups should confine their
activity within the framework of the Zionist Organizations in each country, as the
creation of comprehensive opposition networks brought about schism, breaches of
discipline, and disorder. In his letter to W., Becker emphasized that, although he
did not sympathize with the Fraction, he felt an obligation to take a stand against
the reactionary principles that Pinkus voiced. The manuscript of Becker's article
has not been found.
  [2] For the withdrawal of Pinkus from the Democratic Fraction see No. 258 and n. 1
there.

360. [1] The W.A. has a postcard written by Yoffe dated 5 May 1903 (No. 30/5/6, 6)
apparently in reply to the circular concerning the raising of funds for the Kishinev
victims distributed by the University Bureau (see n. 4 to No. 310). Yoffe undertook
to seek some support in Brussels, but pointed out that the city had only a few students
of Russian origin. It is not clear whether the reference here is to this postcard or to
a letter of later date that has not been found.
  [2] See Yoffe to W., 21 March 1903, W.A. The material arrived in March when W.
was in Russia.

It has been our wish for many years now to conduct an extensive propaganda tour through Belgium. I intend to campaign for Zionism there and then to work among Jewish intellectual circles especially for the University. I would be most obliged if you would give me your views on this matter. What do you consider the most suitable time for such a visit?[3]

Most respectfully and with kind regards, I remain,

Yours faithfully,

Mr. B. Yoffe,
Brussels.

361. To Sh. Margolin, Liège. *Geneva, 8 June 1903*

German: Or. Copy. T.W.: W.A.

8 June 1903.

Dear Sir,

Our sincere thanks for the prompt attention you have given to our circular, and for sending us the interesting newspaper cuttings.[1]

It has long been my intention to conduct a propaganda tour of Belgium and Holland. The cities I have principally in mind are Liège, Brussels and Antwerp. I would be most grateful to you if you would inform me whether, in your opinion, it would be worthwhile undertaking some lectures there on Zionism and on the University. I would, at the same time, endeavour to do some work in the University cause among local Jewish circles. It would be most convenient for me to leave here at the beginning of July, because until then I shall be busy at the University.[2]

In anticipation of your kind reply,

I am,

Yours faithfully,

Mr. Sh. Margolin,
Liège.

[3] In his reply of 23 June 1903 (W.A.), Yoffe wrote that, in his opinion, Zionist propaganda in Brussels would not be of great value as the majority of its Jewish inhabitants were assimilationists. On the other hand, the prospects of success were better in Antwerp. He added that a suitable time to conduct propaganda for the University was the beginning of the academic term.

361. [1] This apparently refers to the circular concerning fund-raising for the Kishinev victims which was distributed by the University Bureau (see n. 4 to No. 310). Margolin reported having sent 35 francs contributed by Jewish students, and he told of meetings concerning Kishinev organized in Brussels and Liège. He also enclosed press cuttings on the Liège meeting (see Margolin to W., 6 June 1903, W.A.).

[2] In his reply, dated 12 June 1903 (W.A.), Margolin expressed doubts as to the

[*Footnote 2 continued on p. 370*]

362. To Martin Buber, Vienna. *Geneva, 9 June 1903*

German: Or. Copy. T.W.: W.A.

9 June 1903.

Dear Martin,[1]

Yesterday we had a full discussion with Toldy regarding all the activities that ought to be initiated and carried out before the Congress. We also sought to effect a division of work which, if agreeable to you, can be very easily achieved.

UNIVERSITY. We consider it most necessary that you work out the plan for the department of General Studies as quickly as possible. It would be well for you to draw Ahad Ha'am, Neumark, Bernfeld, Nossig and Oppenheimer into this work, the first three for the purely Judaic disciplines, the others for the Jewish-social subjects. You are the one most suitable and capable for this undertaking, and with the help of the gentlemen named above the plan can be well prepared. We would like to have it printed before the Congress.

During the early days of next month I shall travel to Liège, Brussels, Antwerp and Amsterdam.[2] It is also possible that Berthold and I will go to Paris, since something can be achieved there for the University.[3] Berthold will also have the survey ready before the Congress.[4]

FRACTION AND CONGRESS. A Youth Conference[5] is to take place before the Congress (on August 15) with roughly the following agenda: 1) Revision of the Fraction programme. Speakers, Idelson —Aberson. 2) Organisation. Speakers, probably Kroll or Marek. 3) Zionism in practice. Speaker, Feiwel. 4) Colonisation. Speaker, Oppenheimer. 5) Cultural Problems. Speakers, Nossig, Buber and

prospects for propaganda on Zionism and the Jewish University among the student colonies in Liège and Brussels, as most students held Social Democratic and anti-nationalist views. Moreover, the timing would be wrong because of the university vacation. Margolin added that propaganda on behalf of the Jewish University idea among the communities of Antwerp and Brussels might achieve a certain success, and that the encouragement of local Zionists, to give their activities a 'truly Zionist trend', was most desirable.

362. [1] The original has a passage written in by Feiwel at the beginning, not reproduced here.

[2] See Nos. 360, 361. The tour did not take place.

[3] See also No. 375.

[4] Refers to an analysis of the results of the student survey (see n. 8 to No. 3). Feiwel had prepared an article giving a provisional summary for the volume *Jüdische Statistik* (see n. 9 to No. 396), and a conclusive summing-up was due to constitute a special publication (cf. n. 2 to No. 335, and see also No. 363: 'The booklet on the survey is being made ready').

[5] See n. 2 to No. 352.

Weizmann. The last two days of the Conference will be specially allocated to Congress problems.

I am awaiting your outline of the pamphlet due for publication before the Congress.[6] It will be expanded by Aberson, Eliashev and myself.

I am sending you the list of our candidates for the Congress as well as particulars of those localities in Russia where we can count upon Fraction mandates with certainty.[7]

DER JUDE. We hope to overcome the financial difficulties today, or at the latest by tomorrow,[8] and everything can then be set in motion. We shall then place the necessary funds at your disposal so that you too can have a free hand. Eliashev will then go to Palestine and he will therefore be able to give us a report on the school and university situation there.[9]

So you see, Martin, that if all goes smoothly we shall be very well equipped for the Congress and can hope to form a group. I shall undertake the organisation of the Youth Conference as well as the question of delegate mandates in Russia.

Will you please give me your opinion on these plans by return, and send me the promised information[10] together with the outline of the pamphlet.

With warm regards,

Your

Mr. Martin Buber,
  Vienna.

[6] The circular sent by W. to members of the Democratic Fraction on 17 June 1903 (W.A.) stated with regard to this pamphlet: 'We shall draft . . . here a sort of manifesto on the Fraction, in which we shall say all that is in our minds with respect to the aims and aspirations of the Fraction, its attitude on daily Zionist issues and questions of tactics. The pamphlet will also contain an appeal to Jewish youth.'

In a letter to W. dated 16 June 1903 (W.A.) Buber proposed a number of chapter headings, but the pamphlet was never produced.

[7] This list, as the one sent to Buber on 28 May 1903 (see No. 341), has not been found, but was apparently identical with the list of candidates and localities contained in the circular of 17 June 1903 (see n. 1 to No. 381).

[8] W. wrote the same day to Kroll and Idelson requesting them to procure finance necessary for the publication of the periodical *Der Jude* as a loan and to telegraph him on the matter (see No. 363).

[9] See also No. 363: '. . . We have decided to send our friend Dr. Eliashev to Palestine. His purpose will be to provide us, prior to the Congress, with a preliminary report on the education system in Palestine'; and see also n. 4 there. Eliashev's mission never took place.

[10] It is not clear what information this refers to.

363. To Abraham Idelson and Michael Kroll, Moscow.
Geneva, 9 June 1903

German: Or. Copy. T.W.: W.A. (First part of letter missing.)[1]

The booklet on the survey is being made ready; it too will come
out before the Congress.[2] We are urgently awaiting information
from you[3] in order to incorporate it.

Furthermore, in connection with the ultimate choice of a location for the University, we have decided to send our friend Dr.
Eliashev to Palestine.[4] His purpose will be to provide us, prior to
the Congress, with a preliminary report on the education system in
Palestine. This will also mark the completion of the first stage of
our preparations.

DER JUDE and FINANCE. This is the most painful point and I
would prefer to remain silent about it. At present we are in need
of two thousand roubles, as a matter of life and death; otherwise
all our activities will be paralysed. It would be a crime if all our
efforts were to come to a standstill now on account of a temporary
crisis. We do have adequate funds[5] but, as I have written on several
occasions to you, they cannot be collected because of Kishinev.
If I were in Russia now I could find the sum required. Now it is
up to us to find the money through a loan[6] and I request you to
telegraph information on this.[7]

FRANZ OPPENHEIMER'S MANDATE. He made his participation in
the Youth Conference, as well as in the Congress, conditional on
his being sent as a delegate.[8] It is most important that this valuable

363. [1] This appears to be the latter portion of the letter to Kroll and Idelson dated
9 June 1903 and mentioned in those to Pokrassa and Trietsch of 10 June 1903 (see
Nos. 364, 366). From Idelson's reply to the present letter, it would seem that the
earlier part dealt with the plan to summon a Conference of the Democratic Fraction
on the eve of the Sixth Zionist Congress (see Idelson to W., 2/15 June 1903, W.A.).

[2] See n. 4 to No. 362.

[3] I.e., the results of the survey in Russia (see n. 8 to No. 3).

[4] Concerning the opposing views on the policy to be adopted towards the location
of the University—in Palestine exclusively or the initial stage in Europe—see Vol. I,
n. 4 to No. 320; n. 12 to No. 83 *supra*; No. 149 and n. 1 there; n. 2 to No. 330.
Cf. also No. 376 and n. 3 there, n. 1 to No. 384; No. 385 and n. 3 there.

[5] Refers to the moneys promised W. in Lodz and Warsaw (see n. 4 to No. 301).

[6] The original copy had stated: 'You must now help with a sum of money in the
form of a loan,' and was amended by W. to read as given.

[7] No telegraphed reply from Kroll and Idelson has been found, but see n. 1 to
No. 384.

[8] See Oppenheimer to W., 6 June 1903, W.A. Oppenheimer wrote, in answer to
W.'s letter of 4 June 1903 (see No. 353), that he was prepared to address the Democratic Fraction Conference ('Youth Conference') were he to come to Basle, but in view
of the illness of his father-in-law he could undertake to come only if he were elected
a delegate to the Sixth Zionist Congress; and he did not know whether Herzl wished
him to be elected. (Oppenheimer at this time was in correspondence with Herzl over

force be committed to us through our securing a mandate for him. Moreover, I wrote to Oppenheimer[9] to the effect that he would undoubtedly be elected as a delegate and in this way kept him tied to the Fraction; if not, he is sure to be captured by officialdom. Since the colonisation question is the topic uppermost in everybody's mind,[10] an address by F. Oppenheimer is of the greatest importance to us. It must also be our primary concern that he is elected by one of our groups.

It goes without saying that the whole of this letter is of a confidential nature. I implore you, my good friends, to do all you can, and more, so as to take heed of my requests and proposals. Believe us, we on our side have been working tirelessly till now, straining all efforts; our lack of means and limited manpower notwithstanding, we are on the way to making significant advances. I am now in a state of extreme nervous tension because everything has reached the acute stage; but no matter how serious the crisis it must *à tout prix* be surmounted, otherwise . . . I do not wish even to express it.

Keep well. With warmest regards,

Very sincerely, your much burdened

Messrs. M. B. Kroll and A. Idelson,
Moscow.

364. To Joseph Pokrassa, Kharkov. *Geneva, 10 June 1903*

German: Or. Copy. T.W.: W.A.

10 June 1903.

Dear Friend,

Today I received your detailed letter[1] and find it most remarkable

---

settlement questions. Because Herzl was seeking to prevent him from linking up with opposition groups, Oppenheimer refused to accept a mandate from the opposition group in Berlin—see Herzl to Oppenheimer, 26 May 1903, C.Z.A. HIII a3; Schimmer to Buber, 27 July 1903, Buber Papers, N.L.).

[9] Weizmann wrote to Oppenheimer only on 11 June 1903 (see No. 368).

[10] See n. 9 to No. 343.

364. [1] Pokrassa to W., 21 May (3 June) 1903, W.A. Pokrassa wrote that the Democratic Fraction must continue to exist: 'It is essential that there should be within the Zionist Organization a group of people who feel themselves free, independent and strong so as to defend all that is enlightened in our cause.' This group should not constitute a political party, and its ranks should not be open to all. It should comprise the best elements in the Zionist Movement, '*Bnei Moshe* [see Vol. I, p. 18] without the mysticism'. The Fraction could have no existence unless reorganized on these

that people separated by such distance can think so much alike. Everything we engage upon here is directed towards giving the Fraction a definitive shape and keeping it free from the necessity for improvisation. We have put our position as clearly as possible to Herzl also; he is not, however, receptive to our arguments[2] in certain of its aspects. He has greater trust in his ignorant surroundings than in the words we have written with our life-blood! But we shall not allow ourselves to be weighed down. That Mr. Lopukhin takes a poor view of the Fraction has been known to me for a long time, and I have left nothing undone to clear up whatever doubts may exist on this;[3] I have also written about it to our friends in Minsk and Moscow.[4] The matter will also be dealt with at the next Conference,[5] and as you will understand, no effort will be neglected to make for its clarification.

I am enclosing herewith a copy of a letter sent yesterday to Moscow;[6] from it you will obtain a fair idea of how we are preparing ourselves for the Congress. The contents of the Moscow letter are to remain strictly confidential, however. We have learned that K[ohan]-Bernstein, Jacobson and Bendersky have all withdrawn from the Actions Committee.[7] For what reason?

I am writing to Greidenberg and Aleinikov[8] again; this must have some effect! I cannot describe how difficult I am finding work now. Everything is paralysed by the financial standstill but

foundations. Pokrassa reacted negatively to Herzl's letter of 14 May 1903 (see n. 3 to No. 336), of which W. sent him a copy, and especially against Herzl's identification with Nordau in his controversy with Ahad Ha'am (see n. 10 to No. 292). Pokrassa anticipated Herzl's launching a frontal attack on those not agreeing with him: 'He will bend, and is capable of destroying, anything standing in his way.' Pokrassa suggested that W. should explain to Herzl that he lacked a thorough understanding of the character of the Democratic Fraction, and should warn him that his stand in the Nordau–Ahad Ha'am controversy was liable to lose him the confidence of all the best elements in the movement. Further, Pokrassa stated that Lopukhin (Director of the Police Department of the Russian Ministry of Interior) had in a conversation with Bernstein-Kohan revealed a negative attitude towards the Democratic Fraction. But in Pokrassa's view this attitude was likely to improve if the Fraction were reorganized without the 'rag-tag and bobtail' introduced under Motzkin's influence. Pokrassa also declared that there was a prospect of securing a mandate in Kharkov for W. for the Sixth Congress.

[2] See letter to Herzl of 6 May 1903 (No. 316) and summary of Herzl's reply in n. 3 to No. 336.

[3] See n. 3 to No. 306; No. 331 and n. 2 there.

[4] See letter to Rosenbaum in Minsk of 6 June 1903 (No. 357). The matter is not mentioned in any known letters to Moscow, but W. may have written about it in his letter to Kroll of 28 May 1903 which has not been found (see No. 343 and n. 2 there) or in the earlier portion of the letter to Kroll and Idelson of 9 June 1903 (see No. 363 and n. 1 there).

[5] Apparently the contemplated Conference of the Democratic Fraction.

[6] See No. 363 and n. 1 there.   [7] See n. 5 to No. 355.

[8] See Nos. 365, 369.

nevertheless one must put up a good front and stay at one's post. Please convey my good wishes to our friends; do tell them, my friend, that they should not overlook the difficulties of the struggle we are waging; and the great tasks and obligations resting on just a few shoulders. Let them get into harness, just as we have done!

I shall be very happy to receive the mandate for Kharkov.[9] You know that I have always fulfilled my duty as delegate towards Kharkov[10] and shall now do so again.

I believe you will receive enlightenment on all points from the letter to Moscow.

Warmest regards,

from your devoted

Mr. J. Pokrassa,
Kharkov.

365. To Michael Aleinikov, Kharkov. *Geneva, 10 June 1903*

German: Or. Copy. T.W.: W.A.

10. 6. 03.

My dear Friend,

Now all that old letter-writing business begins again, for months have gone by and there has been no news from Kharkov regarding the state of our affairs. It seems that Dr. Greidenberg is in principle disinclined to reply to my letters. Today I am writing to him for the last time,[1] for the matter is beginning to become unpleasant. This is not what we are here for, to write letters without receiving replies. Really, I no longer know what to think of such conduct in general. However, I have no wish to continue in this vein; I am beset by too many bitter feelings. So much that is unpleasant and unjust has happened that one must be made of quite different stuff if one is to work calmly within the Zionist fold now. I wrote to

---

[9] See n. 1 *supra*. W. was not elected for Kharkov, as prior to the elections it was learned that he had already received a mandate for Nikolayev. It therefore became preferable to propose another member of the Fraction who had not been returned (see Pokrassa to W., 22 June/5 July 1903, W.A.).

[10] W. had been elected in Kharkov for the Fifth Zionist Congress (Dec. 1901) —see Pokrassa to W., 28 Nov. (11 Dec.) 1901, W.A.—and may also have received there one of his five mandates to the Russian Zionist Conference at Minsk (Sept. 1902)—see Vol. I, No. 304.

365. [1] See letter to Greidenberg of 11 June 1903 (No. 369).

Pokrassa about everything;[2] you have doubtless read the letters. You can reach some conclusions from them, but they represent not a tenth part of the heartache I could describe. Moreover, I have no wish to blame anyone; I know, and am becoming more and more convinced, that one can rely solely upon oneself, and upon one's own energies. When you reach exhaustion to the point of not being able to go on, you find yourself out in the cold without a tear being shed for you. We have worked very hard for the University to reach our present stage; but now, because the wretched funds are not coming in, everything must come to a halt. One can wear one's fingers out with writing and no-one considers it his duty even to reply.

If I turn to you on this occasion, it is not at all with the intention of asking for your further co-operation; I have done that often enough. I am now entitled to make this one demand: write me in all candour whether there is any further purpose in my approaching the gentlemen of Kharkov.[3] Their whole attitude is an absolute insult to the cause. I shall give Kharkov up with an easy heart for the time being, in the hope of better times to come. In this way we shall all save ourselves anguish. Furthermore, I have better things to do than write useless letters.

Please speak to friend Pokrassa on everything pertaining to Party matters.

With kind regards,

Yours ever,

Mr. M. Aleinikov,
   Kharkov.

366. To Davis Trietsch, Berlin. *Geneva, 10 June 1903*

German: Or. Copy. T.W.: W.A.

10 June 1903.

Dear Friend,

A copy of our letter to Moscow is enclosed[1] and from it you will

---

[2] See Nos. 328, 342, 364.

[3] In his reply dated 4/17 June 1903 (W.A.), Aleinikov wrote that, owing to the weakness of the Kharkov Jewish University Committee, no action could be expected from it, and in view of the Kishinev events and the large-scale fund-raising campaign for the victims, there was no possibility of getting money for the University Bureau. The only thing that could now be done was to publish the brochure *Eine Jüdische Hochschule* of which Vladimir Idelson had agreed to prepare a new Russian translation. (Cf. n. 3 to No. 270.)

366. [1] See No. 363 and n. 1 there.

see how we are getting ready for the Congress. If only we could surmount the financial crisis we would be able to look to the events ahead quite calmly. The unpleasant part, however, is that we are still without a definite answer from Baku,[2] and as a consequence everything is at a standstill.

We have so far done nothing with regard to Herzl.[3] We prefer to have our own affairs properly settled first, and then, if all goes well, we shall have a stronger basis to proceed.

Please write us on how matters stand with you.

With kind regards,

Yours,[4]

Mr. D. Trietsch,
Berlin.

367. To Alfred Nossig, Berlin. *Geneva, 10 June 1903*

German: Or. Copy. T.W.: W.A.

10 June 1903.

Dear Dr. [Nossig],

Further to our earlier letters[1] we would once more request you

[2] It appears that W. asked Shriro in Baku to support the publication of several books by the *Jüdischer Verlag* (of which Trietsch was director) and of the periodical *Der Jude*, which was to be published by the *Verlag*. It had apparently also been proposed to Shriro that he become a partner in the *Verlag* (see letters from Shriro, 11/24 May 1903; Buber, 27 June 1903; Trietsch, 12 June 1902, 10 July 1903—all in W.A.). Shriro had promised a contribution of 1,000 roubles for the publication of *Der Jude* as early as Feb. 1903, but it is not clear whether at the time the present letter was written the item 900 roubles in the Bureau balance-sheet for 15 July 1903 had already been paid (see No. 246 and n. 5 there).

[3] I.e. regarding Herzl's hostile attitude to the Democratic Fraction and its members (see n. 3 to No. 336; n. 8 to No. 346), and especially his threats to take public issue with Trietsch. Tension was rife at that time between Herzl and those associated with the *Jüdischer Verlag*, and there was a tendency in Vienna to regard the *Verlag* as a focal point of opposition to the Zionist leadership (see Herzl to Lilien, 11 May 1903, C.Z.A. HN3/48; Lilien to Herzl, 12 May 1903, C.Z.A. HVIII 511a). In a letter to Oppenheimer of 26 May 1903 (C.Z.A. HVIII a3), Herzl stated that it was rumoured that Trietsch was again actively advocating small-scale settlement ('Klein-Kolonisation') and was thereby endangering the solidarity of the movement (see also n. 74 to No. 316). Herzl added that he was obliged to condemn this firmly and perhaps even publicly. On 3 June 1903 Trietsch telegraphed Herzl asking him to refrain from any public measures until they had discussed the matter (see C.Z.A. Z1/345). It appears that Trietsch and Buber informed Feiwel and W. of the affair, and on 9 June 1903 Feiwel wrote Buber (W.A.): 'As regards Herzl, we have not done anything as yet. If some kind of act of solidarity in the Trietsch matter is required, we are ready for orders'; and see also Nos. 347, 391, concerning W.'s intention to meet with Herzl.

[4] Several typewritten lines had been added to the original copy, apparently by Feiwel, and have not been reproduced here.

367. [1] W. wrote to Nossig on 14 and 28 May 1903 (see Nos. 335, 339) and Nossig replied on 30 May (W.A.). Nossig dwelt on the reserved attitude of Profs. Rubens and Grunmach, who had undertaken to draft the plan for the Technical

to write us whether you would be willing to undertake the preparation of the programme for the department of General Studies.
We have written to Buber similarly, and we suggested that he communicate with Ahad Ha'am[2] who would be most suitable for the
specifically Jewish subjects. How is the Berlin Committee getting on ?

We are calling a Conference of the Fraction for August 15 with
this rough agenda:

1. Revision of the Fraction programme. Speakers: Idelson—
Aberson. 2. Organisation. Speaker: Kroll or Marek. 3. Zionism
in practice. Speaker: B. Feiwel. 4. Colonisation. Speaker: F. Oppenheimer. 5. Cultural problems. Speakers: Nossig? Buber and
Weizmann.

Would you, dear Doctor, undertake to deliver a lecture on cultural
problems ? Do you intend to come to Basle this year ?[3] It would
be most important that you did. You may perhaps receive a Russian
mandate.

In anticipation of your early reply, I am,

With many kind regards,

Your

Dr. Alfred Nossig,
  Berlin.

368. To Franz Oppenheimer, Wilmersdorf. *Geneva,*
 11 June 1903

German: Or. Copy. T.W.: W.A.

11 June 1903.

My very dear Dr. [Oppenheimer],

I am extremely grateful to you for your kind acceptance,[1] and
in this I am joined by the gratitude of my friends.

department of the Jewish University (see No. 293 and n. 6 there). Nossig also
announced his readiness to call a meeting of the Berlin Committee for the Jewish
University 'in order to determine, at least in its general lines, the (form of) organization
of the institution', and asked W. to explain how he envisaged the General department,
the plan of which W. had requested him to draw up (see No. 339). Although the present
letter is the earliest one found that was sent after the receipt of Nossig's letter of
30 May, it contains neither an acknowledgement of the latter communication nor a
reply to Nossig's queries. Consequently it may be assumed that W. answered Nossig
at the beginning of June and that this particular letter is not extant. The surmise finds
support in that W.'s letter to Nossig of 13 June 1903 (No. 375), reveals that Nossig
had not replied to previous letters, though we know of only one—the present communication—to which Nossig did not respond.

[2] See No. 362.   [3] For the Sixth Zionist Congress.

368. [1] Refers to Oppenheimer's agreement to address the Democratic Fraction
Conference conditional on his election as a delegate to the Sixth Zionist Congress
(see n. 8 to No. 363).

Since this acceptance is dependent only upon the receipt of a delegate's mandate, we may regard it as all the more definite; for one of our Russian-Zionist groups has already decided to appoint you as its delegate.[2]

Respectfully, I remain,

Yours very truly,

Dr. Franz Oppenheimer,
Wilmersdorf.

369. To Boris Greidenberg, Kharkov. *Geneva, 11 June 1903*

German: Or. Copy. T.W.: W.A.

11 June 1903.

Dear Dr. [Greidenberg],

Truthfully I find it embarrassing to approach you for the third time on matters relating to the University.[1] The cause of this embarrassment lies in the fact that my letters have until now remained unanswered. Needless to state, it was quite clear to me that the Kishinev events were bound to bring things to a halt. Nevertheless I did not consider it impossible that activities in the spirit of our very full discussion[2] would, at least in part, be continued; if not, there is always the danger of everything being shelved indefinitely.

You can well imagine, dear Doctor, how deeply painful it must be to see the ideal for which one has sacrificed time and effort fall into such disregard.

Some time ago we sent you our report,[3] and were entitled to expect your comments. Are we then to conclude from your silence that you attach no value to our further collaboration, either for the time being or in general? As much as I doubt it, and I *wish* to doubt it, I am forced to this conclusion by the facts.

[2] However, it would appear from W.'s letter to Kroll and Idelson of 9 June 1903 (No. 363) that Oppenheimer's election had still not been assured.

369. [1] This apparently refers to letters W. wrote Greidenberg after their meeting in Kharkov in April 1903, but only one previous letter of this period is extant (see No. 321). The W.A. has a copy of a letter dated 30 May 1903 on which Greidenberg's address was typed erroneously and was in reality intended for Goldflamm in Warsaw (see n. 1 to No. 344) and perhaps a letter was sent the same day to Greidenberg, though it has not come to light. For previous letters to Greidenberg, see Nos. 23, 278.

[2] See n. 5 to No. 303.

[3] The report of the University Bureau of May 1903 (see n. 1 to No. 311). W. informed Greidenberg of its dispatch on 7 May 1903 (see No. 321).

Even though nothing has happened, or could have happened, in Kharkov until this moment, a straightforward acknowledgement of the receipt of our letters would have adequately signified that we had no quarrel. Now, however, the relationship remains quite obscure!

I would ask you, dear Doctor, not to show resentment against my severity, and let me have the reply as I have requested.[4]

With most respectful greetings, I am,

Yours faithfully,

Dr. Greidenberg,
Kharkov.

370. To Eugen Mayer, Munich. *Geneva, 11 June 1903*

German: T.W./H.W.: Eugen Mayer Papers, Jerusalem.

Geneva, 11 June 1903.
Rue Lombard 4

Dear Friend,

When we were in Munich[1] we were told by Mr. Brief[2] and Dr. Kahn[3] that they might be in a position to secure a few of the German delegate mandates for the Fraction. Would you please write to us at once on how this matter stands: who, in your opinion, should submit their candidacy in Germany, and for which areas? It is essential that accord is reached in good time in this regard.

But you are so lax in your correspondence! I cannot be at all satisfied with the one card you sent to Berthold.[4] What form is your current University effort taking? Does the 'financier'[5] exist? He

---

[4] In his reply dated 9/22 June 1903 (W.A.), Greidenberg explained that, for various reasons, the Kharkov Committee for the Jewish University had not yet been convened, and he expressed doubts as to whether the University plan could be immediately accomplished. He wrote that his professional position (as Director of the District Hospital) made it difficult for him to be active for the project, and he hinted at an incident which, though it had ended well, made it necessary for him to be cautious in the future. He expressed the hope that a meeting would be held that month in order to discuss the Bureau's report as well as the work of the Committee (the meeting apparently did not take place).

370. [1] See No. 337 and n. 1 there.

[2] Paul Brief (1878–1939), a native of Odessa. He was then studying at the Polytechnic in Munich and was active in student Zionist circles there. A note in Feiwel's handwriting appears beside the name Brief on the original thus: 'Spoke (about this) with Brief.'

[3] Bernhard Kahn, then completing his studies at Munich.

[4] Not found.

[5] It is not known who is implied.

could do us a great deal of good were he so inclined. Pull yourself together and write me a detailed letter. How well we could work if only you would finally decide to make a journey in this direction! Please send me a few lines about that too. You see how inquisitive I am; you will be calming my raging curiosity.[6]

Warmest greetings,

from yours ever,

Chaim[7]

Mr. Eugen Mayer,
   Munich.

[8]For goodness sake send me the waistcoat! I need it so much!

371. **To Martin Buber, Vienna.** *Geneva, 12 June 1903*

German: Or. Copy. T.W.: W.A.

12 June 1903.

Dear Martin,

I have still not had a reply to my last two letters,[1] and I have got to have the outline of the pamphlet[2] without fail. I shall actually write it myself, but would not like to begin without your outline. Moreover, it is highly important to know whether you have communicated with Ahad Ha'am, etc., about working out the programme for the department of General Studies.

The financial crisis is far from over. We did manage to raise something to pay H[eymann][3] and cover current expenditure. Nevertheless we are still hopeful of reaching the point within the next few days that will make the appearance of the first issue possible. Everything else has been started and I feel that all is now proceeding on the right lines.

Why are you so lax in your correspondence? What's new in Vienna? Is anything known as yet about the Congress agenda?[4] Inform us immediately.

Hoping for your prompt reply,

I am your

Mr. Martin Buber,
   Vienna.

---

[6] No reply from Mayer has come to light.
[7] Feiwel's signature also appears on the original.
[8] Added in W.'s handwriting. See No. 351 and n. 2 there.

371. [1] See Nos. 347, 362.   [2] See No. 362 and n. 6 there.
   [3] Hans Gideon Heymann of Berlin apparently loaned Buber 250 marks for the projected periodical *Der Jude* and W. refunded half the amount to him (see letters from Buber: to W. and Feiwel, 12 June 1903; to W., 27 June 1903; to Feiwel, 1 July 1903—all in W.A.).   [4] See n. 14 to No. 347.

372. To Selig (Siegmund) Weicman and Simon Seidenman, Warsaw.[1] *Geneva, 12 June 1903*

German: Or. Copy. T.W.: W.A.

12 June 1903.

Dear Friend,

We were gratified to receive your card,[2] and in reply would urge you to employ all your energies now on the University's behalf. I had intended to telegraph Yarochinsky[3] and Dr. Goldflamm today, but thought better of it since not everything can be said in a telegram. The situation at present is as follows: we had planned for all our various activities—for example, publication of *Der Jude*, a journey embracing Liège, Brussels, Antwerp, Amsterdam[4] and Paris[5]—to take place in this period. The crisis that unexpectedly occurred has paralysed every initiative. As you know, during the dead season in a month's time nothing will get done. We must not touch the funds we have in the bank because they are meant for the running expenses of the Bureau. We were naturally depending on a portion of the money coming from Warsaw and Lodz. At this moment we are in absolute need of 1500–1800 roubles; without it I really do not know how we shall manage until the autumn. Our activities are being held up all along the line. You can well imagine how it pains me to see everything coming to a halt! This immediate situation must therefore be made urgently clear to Mr. Yarochinsky and Dr. Goldflamm; they will most certainly produce a solution.

Perhaps the money may be obtained, temporarily, in the form of a loan which can be easily and promptly repaid when the sums promised are collected. It is therefore most important to act as speedily as possible, and I request a brief telegram from you in reply to this letter.

I do hope you will do everything necessary to advance the cause.

372. [1] Although the letter was intended for both addressees, the salutation is in the singular. It is possible that two separate copies of the letter were sent.

[2] No postcard from either Weicman or Seidenman has been found, but there is a letter from Weicman dated 31 May 1903 (W.A.) stating that the collection of funds for the Kishinev victims was still in progress and consequently it was not feasible to begin raising the money promised for the University Bureau in Lodz and Warsaw (see n. 4 to No. 301). Weicman undertook to deal with the matter as soon as it became possible.

[3] The name Yarochinsky appears erroneously in the original. Yarochinsky was a member of the committee for the University in Lodz, and Goldflamm was a member in Warsaw.

[4] See Nos. 360, 361.

[5] See No. 375.

Both these gentlemen, who responded so enthusiastically to the University enterprise, are unlikely to leave it in the lurch now that deeds are called for.

I would again emphasise that you should notify me by telegram.[6] With all good wishes,

Your

Messrs.
Weicman & Seide[n]man,
    Warsaw.

373. To Nahum Sokolow, Warsaw. *Geneva, 12 June 1903*

German: Or. Copy. T.W.: W.A.

12 June 1903.

My very dear Friend,

I have not yet received a reply to my last letter and so must approach you again.[1] Briefly, the situation is as follows: shortage of money, insignificant in itself but for us of decisive importance, has brought all our activities to a standstill. The publication of our journal, visits to professors in Belgium,[2] and some other matters requiring attention unfailingly before the Congress convenes must be left undone because of approximately 1,500 roubles. We have no possibility of raising funds among our West European comrades here, where we are more likely to encounter obstruction rather than money. After various unsuccessful endeavours[3] we are left with no other choice but to address ourselves to you, much as we dislike troubling you. As you are aware, we have some 8,000 roubles outstanding in Lodz and Warsaw.[4] We wish to borrow 1,500 roubles from some source against this sum, naturally with our personal guarantee if necessary, and on your recommendation. Perhaps someone can still be found who will lend us this ridiculous amount without any ceremony.

---

[6] W. telegraphed Weicman on 19 June 1903 (telegram not found), and the latter replied the next day in a long letter (W.A.). He stated that Yarochinsky had refused to advance any money on the amounts promised to W. in Lodz, adding that he had also spoken to a member of the Warsaw Committee, Minkovsky, who had revealed indifference towards the University plan. Weicman further stated that little could be expected from the existing committee and he was thinking of setting up a new one.

373. [1] See No. 358 and n. 9 there.
    [2] To interest them in the project for a Jewish University. Cf. No. 360.
    [3] See Nos. 318, 319, 343, 345, 348, 363.
    [4] Cf. n. 4 to No. 301.

We would therefore request that you kindly make some effort on our behalf as soon as possible. We are staking everything on your intercession, in the conviction that you will help us.[5]

I have the honour to remain,

Very sincerely,

Your

Mr. N. Sokolow,
Warsaw.

374. To Saul Lurie, Darmstadt. *Geneva, 13 June 1903*

German: Or. Copy. T.W.: W.A.

13 June 1903.

Dear Saul,

The two brochures you requested are on their way to you under separate cover.[1] Some time ago we sent you our latest circular.[2] We would like you to deal with this as soon as possible.

Doctor Karl Wolfskehl, who takes a great interest in the University, is at present in Darmstadt.[3] He is a close acquaintance of Feiwel's, is a good Zionist, and comes from an influential Darmstadt family. It would be as well to solicit Professor Gundelfinger's[4] interest through him.

Why do we hear nothing from you? When are you coming to Switzerland? How is your work, and your health?

We are undergoing difficult times here, with a great deal of work and not a little worry. In material terms we have suffered much on account of Kishinev, and have a difficult crisis to surmount.

Warm regards from

Your

Mr. Saul Lurie,
Darmstadt.

[5] Sokolow telegraphed W. on 16 June 1903 (C.Z.A. A139/5), promising to try and raise an advance, but expressed doubt as to the prospects: 'Kishinev occupies everyone, including myself.'

374. [1] Refers apparently to *Eine Jüdische Hochschule*.
[2] Circular of 2 June 1903, W.A. The circular, which was evidently sent to correspondents of the Bureau in various university cities, explained the Bureau's plan for a survey among Jewish professors (cf. n. 9 to No. 13), and contained a request for appropriate names and addresses. It also asked for the recipient's views on the prospects of arousing the professors' interest in Jewish issues generally and the Jewish University project in particular.   [3] Cf. No. 338 and n. 2 there.
[4] See No. 193 and n. 3 there. In a postcard dated 18 June 1903 (W.A.), Lurie wrote that Gundelfinger had promised to approach Jewish professors in Germany in connection with the University project.

375. To Alfred Nossig, Berlin. *Geneva, 13 June 1903*

German: Or. Copy. T.W.: W.A.

13 June 1903.

Dear Dr. [Nossig],

I am surprised at not receiving a reply to my latest letters.[1] Meanwhile, a proposition has taken shape here which I would like to place before you. Paris has written us[2] that something could be done for the University there among professorial circles. In view of your own good connections there,[3] and provided you could arrange for leave of absence, we are asking whether you would visit Paris. This would also fit in very well with the journey I am about to undertake. In three weeks time I intend travelling to Brussels, Liège, Antwerp and Amsterdam;[4] perhaps we might then meet together in Paris.

We would be most obliged, dear Doctor, for your decision. We are anxiously awaiting your kind reply to our latest letter.

With warmest regards, I remain,

Yours faithfully,

Dr. Alfred Nossig,
Berlin.

376. To the 'Ivria' Society, Berne.[1] *Geneva, 14 June 1903*

Hebrew: Or. Copy. H.W.: W.A.

14/vi. 03.

To *Ivria*, Berne.[2]

Dear Friends,

In reply to your resolution sent us on 14th Sivan, [3]we have the

---

375. [1] This apparently refers to No. 367 and a previous letter, not found—cf. n. 1 to No. 367.

[2] It is not known to what letter this refers.

[3] Nossig had contacts with I.C.A. circles in Paris (see A. Nossig, *Die Bilanz des Zionismus*, Basle 1903, p. 26).

[4] See Nos. 360, 361.

376. [1] The letter is in Stupnitzky's handwriting. The copy is unsigned, but it may be assumed that W. signed the original.

[2] In Ger. in the orig. The rest of the letter is in Heb.

[3] '*Ivria*, General Society for Revival of the Hebrew Tongue' to Jewish University Bureau, 14 Sivan 5663 (9 June 1903), W.A. The letter was signed by Committee members J. L. Metmann-Kohan, B. Mossinson, and A. Robinson. They announced the decision of their society to take part in the creation of a 'Hebrew University'

honour to inform you that, equally with yourselves, we also retain our faith in the citadel of nationalism. Our intention is to create a Hebrew national institution in the fullest sense of the term, and there is absolutely no foundation for any of the rumours that are being spread. We have never waived any conditions and shall not do so in the future. The preparation of a material basis for this institution is our only task, and the conditions to which you have referred do not, for the present, come within the compass of our work. We on our part have already decided to investigate working conditions and methods in Palestine,[4] with the particular objective of becoming familiar with the laws of the country and the extent to which they facilitate the existence of institutions such as this. Furthermore, we are of the view that the first department to be established should be a general one connected with Jewish Studies; we have already entrusted a committee, located abroad, with the preparation of a programme for such a department. Among those who will be taking part in the preparatory work of the programme for Jewish Studies are Jewish scholars and writers like Ahad Ha'am, Dr. Neum[ark], and Dr. S. Bernfeld.[5]

We trust these details will be to your satisfaction.

With Zion's greetings,

on condition 'that it will be founded only in Palestine and that Hebrew will be its dominant language'. For this purpose it was necessary first of all to establish a Philosophical-Pedagogical department 'in which Jewish Studies in the broadest sense will occupy the most important place, because only such an institution is capable of creating the framework essential to the spiritual revival of our people in Palestine'. The society deemed it proper to specify these conditions because the brochure *Eine Jüdische Hochschule* seemed to indicate that the members of the Bureau were ready to forgo them (see Vol. I, n. 3 to No. 240), 'and there are already incessant rumours in our camp that you have already *expressly* given up the first demand' (i.e. locating the University in Palestine). In the society's view, the second demand (Hebrew as the language of instruction) was largely inter-connected with the first. The letter concluded with the hope 'that you will be able to remove all suspicion about this from our minds and the minds of our friends', whereupon the society would submit proposals as to the manner of its participation in the project. See also No. 398 and n. 3 there.

  [4] A reference to Eliashev's proposed mission to Palestine (see No. 363).

  [5] The special committee to draw up the plan for a department of General Studies was not established. W. asked Nossig and Buber themselves to undertake the drafting of the plan and to co-opt other people (see Nos. 339, 362); Nossig wrote W. on 30 May 1903 (W.A.) that he was ready to convene the Berlin Committee for a Jewish University 'in order to determine, at least in its general lines, the (form of) organization of the institution'.

377. To Jacob Bernstein-Kohan, Kharkov.[1] *Geneva,*
15 June 1903

German: Or. Copy. T.W.: W.A.

15 June 03.

My dear, good Friend,

I begin this letter with heavy heart. It is not easy to express in writing all one would wish to say after those brutal events.[2] I therefore feel compelled to leave fuller discussion of them till the next time we meet. We two have particular need to have certain matters clarified for us. I shall not remind you of the contents of my various letters—that would be too much. One thing I must establish at once: subsequent to our meeting in Vienna[3] I wrote to you time after time,[4] either on Party problems or on University matters, without ever receiving a single word in reply. This was, and remains, incomprehensible to me. I can think of only one possible explanation, that the whole of our correspondence was seized.

It was very painful for me, when I was in Pinsk some two months ago, to see one of your letters at Bregman's.[5] It said: 'Weizmann is asleep, and nothing is heard from him.' During all this time I have been the one to sleep the least; for the very contrary is true, *I* have never travelled so much as in these last ten months, and never had to work so hard. I am puzzled as to why you are so badly informed, and am eager for the explanation. It is so very regrettable when the closest friends among us lose contact with each other. How grievously our affairs suffer as a result! I beg of you, my dear friend, not to read the faintest reproach in this; I am very far from reproaching you. I only wanted to enlighten you, and to be enlightened. I cannot conceive of your holding something personal against me.

I now hear that you, Bendersky and Jacobson have all left the Actions Committee.[6] It would be of the utmost importance to us to know the true reasons for the conflict. We on our side are also treated in a very peculiar fashion by Vienna, and I am convinced that it is all connected.[7] I correspond regularly with Pokrassa,

---

377. [1] The name 'Bernstein-Kohan' appears on the original copy.

[2] The Kishinev pogrom.

[3] At the Annual Zionist Conference, Oct. 1902.

[4] See Nos. 51, 126. W. wrote another letter to Bernstein-Kohan after the Kishinev pogrom (see No. 310).

[5] Not found.

[6] See n. 5 to No. 355.

[7] Cf. n. 3 to No. 336; No. 346 and n. 8 there; Nos. 357, 358, 364; n. 3 to No. 366.

who has probably kept you informed to some degree. Nevertheless, it is now more essential than ever that we maintain the closest contact. I am now no longer able to say whether I shall still receive a delegate mandate for this Congress; other people are now required. Whatever may arise, we must be jointly prepared for eventualities.

I trust that this time you will keep me, and this warmly-made and fraternal request, very much in mind, so that you will let me have your views on the tactics that should be pursued at the forthcoming Congress.[8]

I have also written to Pokrassa[9] about our Conference and would refer you to my letter to him.

We are awaiting news from you with the greatest impatience. I [. . . . .] write on all these points.

With my most sincere regards and best wishes to you and yours, I remain,

As ever,

378. To Charles (Yeheskel) Wortsman, Basle. *Geneva, 15 June 1903*

German: Or. Copy. T.W.: W.A.

Geneva, 15 June 1903.
Rue Lombard 4.

Dear Fellow-Zionist,

I really do not know where you received the information that I wish to put myself forward as a candidate for Basle.[1] It would seem,

---

[8] W. suggested to Kroll on 3 June (see No. 352) that Bernstein-Kohan, together with himself, might possibly speak on party tactics at the Democratic Fraction Conference. But it appears that W. had not at that time suggested this to Bernstein-Kohan. In his reply of 29 June (12 July) 1903 (W.A.), the latter explained that he had not replied earlier because he had been busy with a propaganda campaign, which he had conducted in the spirit of the Democratic Fraction. However, he did not wish to belong 'to a non-existent Fraction' and consequently would not attend the Conference.

[9] W. wrote to Pokrassa on 10 June 1903 (see No. 364), enclosing a copy of his letter to Kroll and Idelson of 9 June 1903 (see No. 363), dwelling on the importance of Oppenheimer's participation in the Democratic Fraction Conference. The Conference was apparently also discussed in the latter portion, not found, of the same letter.

378. [1] In a letter to W. on 13 June 1903 (W.A.), Wortsman wrote that he had heard from Julius Meyer that W. wished to be proposed for election in Basle to the Sixth Zionist Congress, and expressed his surprise that W. had not previously revealed this intention. He had also heard that Pasmanik was angry with W. as a consequence. Wortsman explained that the Zionists in Basle were entitled to elect two delegates to the Congress; the election of Joel Weil (a member of the Greater Actions Committee) had been unanimously agreed, while the second candidate would probably be Sigmund Veit. Nevertheless they—Wortsman and Meyer—could have their own

indeed, to be some intrigue on the part of Dr. Pasmanik. I have told absolutely no-one that I want a mandate, and I intended least of all to submit myself for nomination in Basle or anywhere else in Switzerland. I hereby notify you, and our friend Meyer, that I have never spoken to Dr. Pasmanik and his comrades about the elections. On the other hand this gentleman came to Feiwel and informed him that he (Dr. Pasmanik) and Dr. Farbstein had *decided*, in the name of justice, to concede two Swiss mandates to the Fraction.[2] Everything else may be learnt from the enclosed copy of a letter that Feiwel proposes to write to Dr. Pasmanik.[3] This letter will go off at once if you write to the effect that he sent the information to Basle.

I do not know why the two gentlemen assume the role of masters of the situation. Obviously it would never have occurred to me to be a candidate in opposition to you or Meyer. However, if you think that Veit is being put up, and in the further event that neither you nor Meyer is offering himself for nomination, then I would certainly be a candidate for Basle. I would again emphasise: *only* with the agreement of both of you.[4] At the same time I wish to state that I have not even seen the famous Dr. Pasmanik for almost a month.

The Berne people have done very little for the Fraction. On my return from my journey I had to get all the machinery going.[5] You will learn about matters of significance from the letter sent to our friends in Moscow,[6] a copy of which is enclosed herewith. I would ask you to keep it confidential.

candidate returned as the Zionists of Russian origin would vote for him. Meyer was ineligible as he was not yet 24 years of age, and he, Wortsman, hesitated to put himself up because, if elected as a delegate of the Swiss Zionist Federation, he would be deprived by its statutes from taking part in the discussions of the Russian delegates. Further in the same letter Wortsman complained that he had not had a receipt for 10 francs he had sent to the Democratic Fraction Bureau in Berne (see n. 27 to No. 314), and asked whether the Fraction could publish his essay 'Zionism and the Worker' and whether it would be prepared to help him pay for a journey to England. Wortsman stated that he was about to sit for his doctoral examinations in chemistry and reminded W. of his promise to help him find a post (see No. 230 and n. 1 there).

[2] Pasmanik and Farbstein were members of the Central Committee of the Swiss Zionist Federation.

[3] The draft of Feiwel's letter has not been found. In his reply of 16 June 1903 (W.A.) Wortsman wrote that, in Meyer's absence, he was unable to say whether the rumour of W.'s candidature in Basle had originated with Pasmanik. He added his view that Feiwel's letter to Pasmanik was worded too sharply.

[4] In the event both Weil and Veit were elected in Basle, and Wortsman in London and Orgayev (see C.Z.A. Z1/123). W. did not apply for election in Basle.

[5] Cf. n. 27 to No. 314.

[6] Refers apparently to the letter to Kroll and Idelson of 9 June 1903 (see No. 363) of which the earlier part, probably dealing with Fraction affairs, is missing.

Also enclosed are two copies of our report about the University.[7]

Regarding the other questions touched upon in your letter, I am unable, at this moment, to give you a definite answer. So much is in a state of flux that it will be much easier to talk things over in about a month from now.

My warmest good wishes for your examination. Let us hope that everything will go well. Many kind regards to you and Meyer. I received the letters from the professors[8] some time ago, for which many thanks.

Sincerely,

Mr. Ch. Wortsman,
Basle.

379. To Simon (Shimshon) Rosenbaum, Minsk.
Geneva, 15 June 1903

German: Or. Copy. T.W.: W.A.

15 June 03.

Dear Friend,

I am very grateful for your letter,[1] which arrived today and was greatly appreciated. I shall look forward keenly to further communications from you.

If you consider it important for us to meet in Vienna, I am, naturally, prepared to come. It is hardly likely that we shall be

---

[7] See n. 1 to No. 311.

[8] Apparently letters from four Basle professors to Meyer relating to the University project. Meyer sent the letters to W. at the beginning of March (see Meyer to W., 2 March 1903, W.A.) and three of them are preserved in the W.A.: from F. Heman and Stephan Bauer of 17 Feb. 1903 and from Karl Joel of 22 Feb. 1903.

379. [1] Rosenbaum to W., undated (appr. 10 June 1903), W.A. No. 30/0, 33. Rosenbaum wrote that he was still unable to comply with W.'s request for information on the position in Russia (see Nos. 331, 357); important news was awaited—'I shall be going in the next few days in order to get information and to correct what is possible' (Rosenbaum was about to travel to St. Petersburg for the conference of Zionist leaders—see n. 4 to No. 402—and it is possible that while there he met the Minister of Interior, von Plehve—see M. Mishkinsky's article in the quarterly *Zion*, (in Hebrew), Vol. 25, issue No. III–IV, p. 249). Rosenbaum informed W. that he intended proceeding to Vienna with the information received and report on the situation and submit proposals, and he invited W. to go there too. He also wrote that, in his opinion, no one in the Actions Committee had, as W. suspected, plotted against the Democratic Fraction, and this was not the reason for the resignation of Bernstein-Kohan, Bendersky, and Jacobson from the Actions Committee (see No. 355 and n. 5 there; No. 357).

able to talk to Herzl, he is at present in such a mood as not to be receptive to reports and proposals coming from our side.[2]

May I ask you to induce Berger to reply to that point in my letter relating to preparations for the Congress.[3]

We are planning to call a Youth Conference[4] with roughly this agenda: 1. Revision of the Fraction Programme. Speakers: Idelson and Aberson. 2. Organisation. Speakers: probably Kroll or Marek. 3. Zionism in practice. Speaker: B. Feiwel. 4. Colonisation. Speaker: F. Oppenheimer. 5. Cultural Problems. Speakers: Nossig, Buber and Weizmann. The last two days are specially reserved for Congress problems.

With many kind regards, I am,

Your

Mr. S. Rosenbaum,
Minsk.

380. To Martin Buber, Vienna. *Geneva, 16 June 1903*

German: Or. Copy. T.W.: W.A.

16. 6. 03.

Dear Martin,

Your second telegram has just arrived.[1] You cannot imagine what difficult times we are experiencing here. The funds we anticipated receiving have not as yet arrived; demands are pouring in from all sides, and I really do not know what will result from it all. Activities are at a standstill, and I am unable to say whether the journeys can be undertaken as planned.[2]

Today I sent you 75 francs by telegraph, the last of the money I had. As soon as something comes in I shall send it to you. Have you been in touch with Nossig?[3] Do you know anything yet about the Congress?[4] Why are you all such lackadaisical correspondents?

[2] See n. 3 to No. 336; n. 8 to No. 346; n. 3 to No. 366.
[3] See W. to Rosenbaum, 6 June 1903 (No. 357), of which a copy was sent to Berger, and see also n. 6 there.   [4] See n. 2 to No. 352.

380. [1] Buber had telegraphed W. on 14 June 1903 (telegram not found) asking for money (see Buber to W., 14 June 1903, W.A.), and appears to have sent another telegram a day or two later. Buber, who was then in financial straits owing to a quarrel with his family, was owed money for literary fees and expenses he had incurred in connection with his editorial work for the projected periodical *Der Jude* (see Buber to W. and Feiwel, 16 June 1903; Buber to W., 22 June 1903, W.A.).

[2] W.'s contemplated visit to Belgium and Holland and that of W. and Nossig to France (see Nos. 360, 361, 375).

[3] Concerning the drafting of a plan for the department of General Studies of the Jewish University (see No. 362).

[4] I.e., the agenda of the Sixth Zionist Congress (see No. 347 and n. 14 there).

There is nothing new here, since we are totally dependent for our activities upon other people.

    Warm regards,

Yours ever,

381. To Saul Lurie, Darmstadt. *Geneva, 17 June 1903*

German: Or. Copy. T.W.: W.A.

17 June 1903.

Dear Friend,

    You will receive an approximate idea of the state of our affairs from the circular letter enclosed.[1] You will gather from it that we are for the moment experiencing a crisis that is the result of the Kishinev events. We believe, however, that this is merely a temporary situation and that we shall soon resume our activities.

    If you are in some way in a position to obtain the sum of 600 marks for us for two months, you would be making the appearance of the first two numbers of *Der Jude* possible prior to the Congress.

    Please let me know by telegram.

    You cannot imagine the difficulties we are at present contending with. If you were here for just one day you would experience something. There is so much to tell but I can only do so when next we meet.

    In the hope that you will gather a great deal from these few words,

I remain,

with many kind regards,

Your

P.S. Concerning Doctor Wolfskehl,[2] tomorrow![3]

Mr. Saul Lurie,
    Darmstadt.

---

381. [1] An unsigned circular to members of the Democratic Fraction dated 17 June 1903, W.A. This dealt with preparations for the Sixth Zionist Congress, and included a list of localities in Russia where there were prospects of electing Fraction candidates, as well as a list of 42 candidates (see also n. 2 to No. 389). It contained information on the proposed conference of the Fraction, the propaganda pamphlet which it was intended to issue prior to the Congress (see n. 7 to No. 362), and the preparatory activities of the Jewish University Bureau. The circular also advised of the intention to send an emissary to Palestine for the purpose of drawing up a report on the educational system there which would help to solve the problem of location for the University (cf. No. 363 and n. 4 there). Further, the circular dealt with the plan to publish the periodical *Der Jude* and the financial difficulties preventing its appearance.

[2] See No. 374. In a letter dated 16 June 1903 (W.A.), Lurie wrote that he did not know Wolfskehl but was willing to meet him.

[3] No further letter to Lurie prior to the one dated 24 June 1903 (see No. 385) has been found.

382. To Alfred Nossig, Berlin.[1] *Geneva, 18 June 1903*

German: Or. Copy. T.W.: W.A.

18 June 03.

Dear Dr. [Nossig],

Warmest thanks for your comprehensive letter,[2] from which we learn with pleasure that the Berlin Committee has assumed full responsibility in the matter. In accordance with your request I shall be sending you tomorrow all the programmes at present in our possession. I have ordered the other material and shall send them to you forthwith.

As for the plan of a General Studies department, I preferred Buber to work this out in detail and yesterday I telegraphed him accordingly.[3] I shall do my utmost to supply you with a plan for the Technical department by the 27th as well.

A visit to Paris seems most desirable to me. At present I can only be vague of course about the spirit prevailing there. I have been informed that within professorial circles an interest in questions of Jewish culture does in fact exist, and that well-known personalities may be won over to our undertaking. This is why I took the liberty to propose your going to Paris. I consider an investigation of the scene there to be worth the effort, even if the first visit does not yield substantial results.

You must also take the fact into account, dear Doctor, that hitherto we have hardly had a single reliable person in Paris.

382. [1] The words 'Dr. Alfred Nossig, Berlin' appear on the original copy in Stupnitzky's handwriting.

[2] Nossig to W., 15 June 1903, W.A. Nossig reported on discussions by the Berlin Committee for the Jewish University: Oppenheimer and Warburg could not take part in the meeting, but Warburg and Profs. Meyerhoffer and Landau showed considerable interest in the plan, whilst the agronomist Soskin was co-operating with the Committee. The members considered the existing plan of organization ('Proposed Plan for a Jewish University' which W. sent Herzl in May 1902—see Vol. I, n. 2 to No. 204) to be superficial and unrealistic, as the inclusion of courses in agriculture, architecture, and anatomy in its programme, in addition to the General and Technical departments, would be financially impracticable. The members were ready to draw up a new plan of organization, and Nossig asked W. to send him the syllabuses of a number of Polytechnics and Universities in time for the next meeting of the Committee on 27 June, and also to draft proposals for the programme of studies, technical organization, and staff of the University. Nossig also wrote that he was prepared to visit Paris if W. wrote him in greater detail on the possibilities of action there (see No. 375). Regarding a Conference of the Democratic Fraction, Nossig stated that it was necessary to create a united front of the entire opposition in the Zionist Movement so as to appear at the Congress as a unified party; and if 'terrorized' at the Congress, it should secede and establish a 'second Jewish national party'.

[3] The telegram has not been found, but see No. 362.

But this is too important a centre to be neglected for so long. Naturally, we shall gladly meet your travelling expenses.

I would plead with you to accept our proposal, and to be so good as to let us have your decision at once. In any event, I shall this very day order the expenses for the journey from the bank. We might very well meet in Paris in July.

[LETTER CONTINUED BY FEIWEL][4]

383. To Chaim Khissin, Berne; Julius Meyer and Charles (Yeheskel) Wortsman, Basle.[1] *Geneva, 21 June 1903*

German: Or. Copy. T.W.: W.A.

Strictly Confidential.   Geneva, 21 June 1903.

Dear Friend,

A caucus of delegates from Switzerland will take place next Sunday in Fribourg.[2] I have been elected to the caucus from Geneva,[3] but we are most interested in Feiwel and Aberson also being there. This wish stems from the disgraceful campaign that certain people have launched in the scandal-sheet called *Zionistische Korrespondenz*.[4] It contains attacks on us personally as well as on the institutions with which we are connected.[5]

---

[4] In completing the letter Feiwel rejected both in his own and W.'s name the proposal by Nossig to set up a united front of the opposition (see n. 2 above).

383. [1] The names of the addressees of identical letters were written on the original copy in Stupnitzky's handwriting.

[2] The Swiss Zionist Conference, which took place on 28 June 1903.

[3] W. was elected by the Student Zionist Society *Hashahar* of Geneva (see *Hamelitz*, 9/22 July 1903).

[4] The weekly *Zionistische Korrespondenz* was published in Berne by Pasmanik and Pinkus. Apparently only four issues appeared, between 19 June and 10 July 1903.

[5] An unsigned editorial in the first issue of *Zionistische Korrespondenz* of 19 June 1903 explained the policy of the journal. It stated, *inter alia*, that any tendency towards schism in the Zionist movement was to be avoided. The periodical would emphasize points of contact, combat symptoms of dissension within the ranks of the movement and oppose the creation of parties. Cultural and economic activities were the concern of individuals and should not occupy the organs of the movement. This issue also included an article by Pinkus, 'The Fractionalisation of the Zionists', in which the author endeavoured to prove that there was no justification for the existence of factions in the movement. It said that differences between the various trends were generally determined by countries of origin and consequently they found adequate expression through the organization of Zionists in territorial federations, whereas parties were likely to sabotage the policies of the leadership of the movement. A despatch appearing in the same issue contained a personal attack on W. It dealt with an appeal relating to the Kishinev pogrom and published by a group of Zionists

Unless an end is put to this intrigue at the meeting it will lead us, alas, to a calamitous situation even before the Congress. My own strength is not adequate to struggle against all those people; we must ensure that Aberson and Feiwel participate in the delegate caucus. A fervent plea to you and to our friends is, I believe, enough to guarantee your support in this matter. If you have any opportunity whatsoever to get the candidacy of one of these gentlemen through you will be rendering our common cause a service and at the same time performing an act of friendship. We therefore request you to telegraph us immediately on receipt of this letter.[6]

Trusting that you will accede to our request,

I remain,

Yours ever,

384. To Abraham Idelson and Michael Kroll, Moscow.

Geneva, 22 June 1903

German: Or. Copy. T.W.: W.A.

Geneva, 22 June 1903
Rue Lombard 4.

Dear Friends,

May I be allowed a fully detailed reply to your letters.[1] Of course,

in Lausanne that had aroused considerable indignation among Socialist students of Russian origin in Switzerland because it had stated that the proletariat, too, had been party to the pogrom; for this reason the appeal was even condemned by the Academic Zionist Society in Berne, most of whose members belonged to the Democratic Fraction. According to the despatch, the student J. M. Salkind had stated at a Zionist meeting that the appeal had been printed under W.'s auspices, but after the negative reaction became known W. withdrew in a cowardly manner and even refused to distribute the copies he had ordered (see also circular of Academic Zionist Society of 4 June 1903, Marmor Papers, Yivo, New York; *Hatzofe*, 27 May/9 June 1903). Apart from Salkind's charges, no information of W.'s involvement in this affair has been found. A reference to the report of the Jewish University Bureau of May 1903 (see n. 1 to No. 311) appearing in the same issue stated a public accounting of the income and expenditure of the Bureau was desirable.

⁶ Khissin replied on 22 June 1903 (W.A.) that the elections in Berne to the delegate Conference of Swiss Zionists had already been held. He added that fear of Pinkus was not justified, and that it was essential as far as possible to avoid settling private accounts at the Conference.

384. ¹ Kroll to W. 31 May (13 June) 1903; Idelson to W., 2/15 June 1903, W.A. After consulting members of the Democratic Fraction in Moscow and St. Petersburg (cf. n. 2 to No. 355), Kroll and Idelson suggested holding the Conference of the Fraction in Warsaw rather than Basle. Kroll explained that they feared the deliberations might assume a theoretical character if the Conference were held in Basle, where most of those taking part would be members from Western Europe. The Fraction members in Russia, being fully involved in Jewish life and its day-to-day problems, needed a practical plan, whereas those in the West, temporarily isolated from Jewish realities, were liable to complacent deliberation of abstract questions, and were

not everything can be expressed in the way one would wish within the limits of a letter, and you were correct in anticipating that I would find yours disappointing. Our friends here share this disappointment with me.

I can well understand that you attach great importance to the definite formulation of a practical programme of activities. I too have felt that this question must be solved as quickly and as effectively as possible. Your assertion that 'we in Russia really do not know what we are required to do' answers many of the questions that came to my mind as I read your letter. Before anything else, let me, however, ask you this: Do you believe that some kind of Conference in *Warsaw* will find the practical programme desirable for Fraction members?

I am convinced that this Conference will take the same course as all Russian Zionist conferences, with perhaps one difference— that of nuance. I will not be put off with the argument that I do not know the situation in Russia well enough. I maintain the contrary: there are few Zionists who are as well acquainted with our organization and its entire human resources as I am. On the basis of my experience, and on the basis of my knowledge of the

furthermore in a position to undertake literary and journalistic activity which corresponded with their environment and talents. Joint projects for members of the Fraction in Russia were lacking, and consequently a plan of action had to be evolved at the Conference. Kroll argued that the agenda proposed by W. bore an excessively theoretical character (W. sent Kroll suggestions for the Conference agenda on 3 June 1903—see No. 352); and it may be assumed that the first part of his letter to Kroll and Idelson of 9 June 1903 which has not been found (see No. 363 and n. 1 there) contained the agenda for the Conference sent the same day also to Buber (see No. 362). As regards the University project, Kroll stated that many members of the Fraction in Russia, particularly in St. Petersburg where they were apparently influenced by Motzkin, opposed a University outside Palestine. Motzkin had accused Buber, Feiwel, and W. of infringing Fraction discipline by disregarding the clause in its programme which prescribed that preparatory work should be undertaken towards the establishment of a University in *Palestine.* (See *Programm und Organisations-Statut der Demokratisch-Zionistischen Fraktion,* p. 16.) Kroll reported that, outside Moscow, the student survey in Russia had succeeded only in those places where it had not been conducted by the Fractionists, namely in Kazan and perhaps in Riga and Yureyev. No replies to the questionnaires had been received from St. Petersburg, Kiev, Warsaw, or Kharkov. As for the proposed periodical *Der Jude,* Kroll wrote that, in his opinion, few readers would be found in Russia and it was impossible to receive substantial financial support for it (cf. No. 363). Idelson wrote that so long as the Fraction constituted a faction in the Congress, it had no existence outside the Congress. Furthermore, he said, it had no great value as its practical programme differed little from the general Zionist programme, while in the cultural and economic field 'our success so far has not gone beyond verbiage and abortive committees, and even at the Congress we shall not progress any further, not because of outside interference but because we ourselves in our great erudition do not know how to fulfil concretely this or that objective in real life'. Idelson added that all speeches to be delivered at the Conference must deal with programmes of practical action.

situation in Russia in all its aspects, I claim that it is at present impossible to develop a planned programme of activities in the spirit of the Fraction. Your practical activities can, therefore, be carried out only within the framework of the general organisation. The major difficulty lies in the lack of human material and the absence of a desire for truly radical reform. As a consequence all activities are bound to take on the nature of repair work.

It is thus correct that at present the Fraction in Russia is without value outside the Congress and without justification as a *political party*. It must be converted into a league of freedom-loving Zionist elements and then, given energetic effort, it may master the situation.[2] You will have to make an attempt to enlist all the hitherto so-called friends of the Fraction into such a league: Kohan-Bernstein, Jacobson, Rosenbaum, Bendersky, Berger, with all the elements that are behind them. They could be united on the basis of such practical work as is feasible under the conditions obtaining in Russia. They could then encompass a large number of associations and perhaps combine ultimately into a federation. It should be understood that we visualise the formation of this federation only on the basis of practical work. It can never be a vehicle of a more profound Zionism. This will by no means be due to the inability of such a group to understand Zionism profoundly, but for the sole reason that, under existing conditions, they cannot relate practical deeds with a deep Zionist experience. They are condemned to peripheral and makeshift effort. But even this is highly necessary today and must be done if we do not wish to sink entirely into sleep. It is why I view your present intention of commencing with practical work as a healthy and worth-while principle; and not from the Fraction point of view but rather from a general Zionist standpoint, to be supported with all possible energy by those of us who live in Western Europe.

And now I come to our attitude towards the opinions expressed in the letter. What you characterise in your letter as 'theory and scholarship' is a vital activity. The fault we find with Zionism today is its complete superficiality and narrowness, as well as its utter helplessness in the face of questions which must and will arise. There is total ignorance of the problems encompassed by Zionism as an historical national movement; a stifling regime created by the personal party cult and the majority principle; a striving after petty, ephemeral successes in which the greater, universal aims of the movement become lost.

[2] In a letter to W. of 12 June 1903 (W.A.) Buber had proposed the establishment of 'Free Action Group' to replace the Democratic Fraction.

We, therefore, looked upon all the activities we initiated here as the type of preliminary effort which, though for the moment restricted, would subsequently pave the way to a change in the total concept and the total action. The central resources which we possess today, such as the *Verlag*[3] as a publishing organisation, the University Bureau as a cultural organisation, the Society for Statistics[4] and Palestine Committee[5] as a scientific and practical organisation, all these give us, even now, a certain capacity for critical and positive activity, exerting an essentially beneficial influence upon the concept and effort of Zionism in the round. We are provided with weapons against the absolute rule of the indolent, non-thinking, Congress majority, which is so formidable an obstacle.

This, however, is just a beginning and may be broadened into an entire system, as it should. Above all, if we are to exercise a liberating influence over Zionism to any substantial degree, we must concern ourselves with attracting and developing new human material. At the present we are still short of man-power at every move, and are lacking in the most rudimentary support. If we go on with our work of preparation and education towards a genuine Zionist reformation we shall sooner or later—certainly in Western Europe at least—be a hundred times more useful than if we were to adopt a so-called programme to rectify certain details relating to the democratic or cultural aspects of the overall organisation. For in the latter case we should not be able to effect a fundamental change of mood, which is really all that matters.

WARSAW CONFERENCE. Your proposals for a Conference in Warsaw strikes me, for many reasons, as inexpedient and unfeasible. In my opinion it is technically impossible to organise a Conference in Warsaw. Insofar as I know the local human material, we do not have a single person there who can accomplish so difficult a task in so short a time. Even if you were to gain ten additional people from Russia through this Conference, you would, on the other hand, lose other Russian members of the Fraction because of those who would find it impossible to give up enough time to visit both Warsaw and Basle.[6] I am not even talking about Western Europe; naturally no-one would come from there. For myself, it would be impossible to make a second journey to Russia after so brief a period, especially as I shall be going to Belgium and

---

[3] The *Jüdischer Verlag* of Berlin.

[4] The Jewish Statistical Association of Berlin (see Vol. I, n. 7 to No. 207).

[5] The Committee for Economic Research in Palestine (see n. 6 to No. 125).

[6] I.e., sufficient time to attend both the Conference of the Fraction in Warsaw and the Sixth Zionist Congress in Basle.

Holland.[7] Here, too, we have our hands full and must strain every effort in order to come to the Congress thoroughly prepared. And in view of the fact that a conflict between East and West has unfortunately been created, it follows that the participation of West Europeans in such a Conference would be indispensable. Otherwise we would never assume responsibility for decisions that may be taken in Warsaw.

I would like to add some personal factors, though I am hardly the one to involve our Zionist activities with personal problems. It has always been our aim to ensure the interests of the cause, and every active individual was gladly received. But for a number of years now a small group of people has been placed in a most invidious position. Buber, Feiwel and myself, for example, are compelled to contend here with a narrow-minded majority and with ill-treatment on the part of those in control. The outcome is that we are branded as theoreticians, unworldly dreamers, etc., by our Russian friends. Some people go so far as to regard our activities as nothing less than a breach of discipline—they are people who have not lifted a finger for years except to hinder or damage the achievements of others.[8] Some dare to charge us with a failure to understand the contemporary needs of Zionism. This would be tragic were it not so absurd.

You are very much mistaken if you think we have concentrated exclusively on literary activities. There is no field of Zionist endeavour, certainly in a much deeper and broader sense than is generally recognised, in which we have not played the most active part possible. We will permit no-one to deny us our consciousness of this, for it is our only source of satisfaction and joy. We do not wish to speak of certain machinations, however, clearly though we can discern them.

UNIVERSITY. I can also understand very well why the gentlemen of Petersburg are resisting us. Today it is the University, yesterday it was the *Verlag*,[9] tomorrow it may be something else. But this will in no wise interfere with our work. Things can never be worse, they can only improve. For the time being the University is our private endeavour. The Zionists have criticised us enough, with only a very few being helpful. From blocking our path in the early days with passive resistance they have gone on to demand the right to summon us before a tribunal—to such heights does their

---

[7] For W.'s plan to go to Belgium and Holland see Nos. 360, 361.

[8] The remarks are directed at Motzkin (see n. 1 *supra*).

[9] It is not clear to whom the remarks allude. As for the tension that prevailed between the *Jüdischer Verlag* and the Zionist leadership in Vienna, see n. 3 to No. 366 and also No. 391.

impudence ascend. Unless we were to take precautions in advance we could well predict the fate of the Jewish University in the forum of a Warsaw Conference if its future depended on the 'Petersburgers'. We are pleased to be able to state that the University idea is attracting ever wider and better circles. Though we are temporarily hampered by a financial crisis, we are not allowing ourselves to be overcome by it. If we had *Der Jude* by now we could achieve more. We are busily engaged in developing the project and will most likely be coming out with a serious proposition.[10]

SURVEY. I know that the survey has been carried out in Warsaw and Kiev. I cannot say anything definite regarding Kharkov. Send me whatever you have ready.

BASLE CONFERENCE. Having expressed absolute opposition to a Conference in Warsaw we wish to reiterate our proposal, advanced in previous letters, to hold a Conference in Basle. We suggest, however, that you present *your own* agenda. At the same time, we would note that we consider the lecture by Oppenheimer[11] to be of extreme importance, particularly before this Congress. But we have no wish in any circumstances to press our programme upon you, and would therefore drop the lectures we had planned. Please let us know immediately how to proceed. Time is short. Would you telegraph us whether it is to be Warsaw or Basle, and then send us the agenda in the post.

Forgive the somewhat sharp tone of my letter, friends. We have had so much to put up with lately that things become just too much. I trust you will understand my mood, as with all my old devotion and kind regards I remain,

Yours,

385. To Saul Lurie, Darmstadt.[1] *Geneva, 24 June 1903*

German: Or. Copy. T.W.: W.A.

24 June 03.

Dear Friend,

I am only today getting round to answering your letter[2] and

---

[10] See No. 382 and n. 2 there.
[11] See No. 353.

385. [1] 'S. Lurie, Darmstadt' appeared on the original copy in W.'s handwriting.

[2] Lurie to W., 19 [June] 1903 (orig. erroneously dated 19 May 1903), W.A. In answer to W.'s letter of 17 June 1903 and to the circular sent him (see No. 381 and n. 1 there), Lurie asked whether the Fraction was conducting propaganda in Russia, whether its candidates had any prospect of being elected to the Sixth Zionist Congress,

the questions it raises. You know my personal opinion regarding Palestine. I consider a University in Palestine to be totally impossible and wrong at present. The department of General Studies might perhaps be established there, but certainly not the Technical one. You are familiar, however, with the spirit now prevailing in the Zionist world and which is so formidable a consideration. If we do not so much as attempt to examine the Palestine question, we shall immediately have Zionist officialdom in a body on our necks.[3]

The Fraction is stirring in Russia; what the next Conference will look like can in no way be foretold. You will surely be able to participate in the Conference. We have also provided for sufficient delegate mandates to warrant the hope of getting all our candidates through. *Nothing* on the Fraction Conference is to be published for the present, as we still do not know the final agenda. We are in the throes of an exchange of correspondence with Moscow,[4] Motzkin has re-emerged,[5] and there are still some hard nuts to crack. Enclosed is a letter from Moscow, and our reply,[6] to enlighten you. Please return the former at once.

You cannot conceive what intrigues of the shabbiest kind are being conducted against us and all our activities from quite different quarters. Without a journal we are helpless, for the gentlemen may say whatever they please against us and we are totally unable to defend ourselves. Such loathsome acts are now being committed that one would readily withdraw in order to save one's self-respect. You may be glad you know nothing of this. We must have the journal, for the University will now be attacked from different sides; a great deal still lies ahead for us. Moreover, with a journal of prestige we could penetrate very valuable Jewish circles. Surely the present group of contributors confirms this assumption. We

and whether he could take part in the Fraction Conference. He also asked whether it was desirable to announce the convening of the Conference in the (Jewish) press in Russia. Lurie expressed support for the decision of the University Bureau to send a representative to Palestine to draw up a report on the teaching system there and to help solve the problem of the University's location—in his opinion it should be established in Berlin (cf. n. 6 to No. 386).

[3] See Vol. I, n. 4 to No. 320. The annual Zionist Conference (Oct. 1902) resolved to support the University project conditional on its establishment in Palestine. The Conference of Zionist Regional Leaders in Russia, held at Kiev from 22 to 24 April 1903 (Gregorian dates), decided by a majority vote to refrain from supporting propaganda for the University project if it was to be set up in Europe (see Proceedings of the Conference, C.Z.A. Z1/380). See also n. 2 to No. 330.

[4] See Nos. 325, 330, 343, 352, 363, 384.

[5] See n. 1 to No. 384.

[6] It appears that W. sent Lurie Kroll's letter of 31 May (13 June) 1903 and his reply dated 22 June 1903 (see No. 384 and n. 1 there).

need a loan of at least 1,000 roubles to lay its foundations.[7] In the autumn we[8] shall travel to Russia again and so collect the sums outstanding in Lodz and Warsaw.[9]

Yesterday we received a very friendly letter from Dr. Wolfskehl; he will be glad to make your acquaintance. Something can be done through [him]; we leave it entirely to your judgment. He is a friend of Gundelfinger.[10] Do not forget about finance. If I could talk to you you would understand why we are pressing for publication of the journal. We place great hope in your intercession.

With kindest regards,

Yours ever,

386. To Alfred Nossig, Berlin.[1] *Geneva, 24 June 1903*

German: Or. Copy. T.W.: W.A.

24 June 03.

Dear Dr. [Nossig],

Very many thanks for your kind communications.[2] You may rest assured that nothing will be revealed to the public from here.

---

[7] See No. 381 for W.'s request for a loan of 600 marks to enable publication of the first two issues of *Der Jude*. Lurie replied on 18 June 1903 (W.A. No. 30/6/18, 2) that he hoped to be able to raise a loan of 300 marks, even though he did not understand why the Bureau needed a periodical.

[8] Plural in the orig., although W. probably intended himself alone.

[9] The funds promised to W. in March 1903 (see n. 4 to No. 301).

[10] Cf. also No. 374. Wolfskehl's letter has not come to light, but it seems that he was replying to Feiwel's of 20 June 1903 (W.A.). Feiwel had asked Wolfskehl to get in touch with Lurie and Prof. Gundelfinger in order to co-ordinate action for the Jewish University Bureau with them.

386. [1] 'Dr. Nossig' appears on the original copy in W.'s handwriting.

[2] Nossig to W. and Feiwel, 22 June 1903, W.A. Nossig wrote that, now that W. had explained the purpose to him, he was prepared to visit Paris on 9 or 10 July (see No. 382 and n. 2 there). Asking that the matter be kept confidential, Nossig added that he, Trietsch, Soskin, and Lilien were systematically preparing for the Congress and intended to bring a comprehensive criticism of the policy of the Zionist Actions Committee there. They were of the opinion that the Fraction was incapable of forming a framework for the entire opposition, because it consisted mainly of young people and because of its inaction in the past; none the less, they believed the Fraction should appear at the Congress as a solid group. Although the rest of the opposition would reach an understanding with the Fraction, they must be ostensibly separate at the Congress and so create the impression of a spontaneous opposition. Nossig went on to state that some of Herzl's recent actions could not be ignored. As an example he gave the failure of *Die Welt* and other Zionist periodicals to mention the imminent appearance of *Jüdische Statistik*, of which Nossig was the editor (see n. 9 to No. 396), on the grounds that he, Nossig, had been wrongly suspected of writing an article directed against Herzl and Nordau (ref. to 'Jews of Yesterday', which appeared anonymously in the April 1903 issue of *Ost und West*).

We are also busy making our preparations for the Congress, and so together we shall be able to form an impressive group. We have sponsored your candidature in London, probably successfully. We shall also put you up in Russia.[3]

The unbridled campaign of 'the masters of creation' exceeds all limits. One encounters treachery at every step; the day of reckoning has got to come.

I shall keep you informed about everything relating to the Congress preparations and request you to do the same, so that we remain in constant touch.

*   *   *

UNIVERSITY.

I assume that you have already received the letters I sent from here on Monday morning.[4] Enclosed you will find my proposals for the Technical department.[5] Naturally, it is only a sketch. On the approval of the programme's general outlines the planning of the organisational details can begin. I believe that the first two courses, the ones which are preliminary as it were to the school for specialisation, can easily be instituted. Dr. Meyerhoffer is fully capable of making judgment regarding personnel and laboratories. I feel that chemistry and physics laboratories are all that would at present be required.

Professor Gundelfinger, (Ordinary Professor of Mathematics at the Technical College in Darmstadt) is very interested in our project. He is also very much in favour of Berlin, and will gladly cooperate.[6] He is a most important and influential man with an

[3] In his letter of 22 June 1903, Nossig asked W. to secure a delegate mandate to the Sixth Congress for him, and put him up for election in Galicia also. It appears that W. had asked Kalman Marmor, who visited Geneva in the second half of June, to try and secure the election of five Fraction delegates in London: Aberson, Buber, W., Nossig, and Feiwel. See Marmor to W., 23 July 1903 (W.A.); Delovitch to Marmor, 1 July 1903 (Marmor Papers, Yivo, New York). On 25 June 1903 W. asked Buber to look after Nossig's election in Galicia (see No. 387).

[4] Monday, 22 June. That same day W. seems to have sent Nossig, at the latter's request, syllabuses of study issued by various Universities (see No. 382 and n. 2 there), as well as a suggested syllabus for the departments of General and Jewish Studies of the Jewish University drawn up by Buber. Buber informed W. on 17 June 1903 (W.A.) that he was sending the syllabus to him and W. wrote Buber on 25 June 1903 that he had passed it on to Nossig (see No. 387). A draft of the syllabus, in Buber's handwriting, is in the W.A., No. 30/0, 57.

[5] See proposed syllabus of the Technical department of the Jewish University, 25 June 1903 (W.A.). W. suggested the introduction of a two-year course of preparatory studies. After this period students would go on to specialize in technical schools (for mechanical engineers, chemists, and electrical engineers) which would be set up under the aegis of the University.

[6] See Lurie to W., 18 June 1903 (W.A. No. 30/6/18, 3) and 19 [June] 1903 (W.A.). Lurie stated that Gundelfinger had promised to approach Jewish professors in

excellent technical education. I warmly recommend the Berlin Committee to draw him in immediately. We shall write to him if the Committee so desires. It would, however, be preferable if you did so directly from Berlin.

I am very curious about the meeting on Saturday.[7] Confidentially, the Party has started to intrigue against the University also.[8] We must consequently make sure that we have the plan prepared by qualified people as soon as possible and bring the professors into ever closer co-operation with us. *Il faut les engager*. We shall then be able to intensify our propaganda in the autumn when money will become available, and in this way the University will assist all our activities. Feiwel sends his best regards. He will write tomorrow.

Kindest regards,

Your

387. To Martin Buber, Vienna. *Geneva, 25 June 1903*

German: Or. Copy. T.W.: W.A.

25 June 03.

Dear Martin,

Today your telegram[1] arrived and I couldn't even bear to show it to Berthold. I do not know what to do, with all sources for the moment dried up. Intrigues are raging against us from every side; one cannot see how to defend oneself. This minute there isn't a penny in the till. But money should come in any day[2] and I will then send you some straightaway.

The plan of the Congress pamphlet[3] is, in my opinion, too long; we can use a portion of it. With so many worries and such anxiety we have not yet been able to get down to work. I have sent your

---

Germany concerning the University project and that in Gundelfinger's opinion the University should be located in Berlin where a large number of Jewish scientists lived.

[7] A meeting of the Berlin Committee for the University called for 27 June 1903 (see n. 2 to No. 382).

[8] The statement probably relates to those opposing the location of the University in Europe (see n. 1 to No. 384; No. 385 and n. 3 there).

387. [1] Not found. The telegram evidently repeated Buber's earlier request that W. send him some money (cf. No. 380 and n. 1 there).

[2] Apparently the money that Saul Lurie was trying to obtain for the University Bureau (see n. 7 to No. 385).

[3] See No. 362 and n. 6 there. In his letter of 16 June 1903 (W.A.), Buber suggested that the pamphlet should include an introduction on the Jewish national idea, a chapter on the history of Herzlian Zionism, and a chapter on the reforms necessary in Zionism.

scheme for the General department to Nossig in Berlin.[4] The people there wish to rough out an idea of such a department for themselves.

What about the delegate mandates? Can we absolutely depend on Galicia.[5] Nossig has to be put up as a candidate there without fail.[6] Write at once about this, for it is the most important matter at this moment.

I shall send you money as soon as we have some here.

Ever yours,

388. To Vladimir Tyomkin, Elizavetgrad. *Geneva,* *26 June 1903*

German: T.W.: C.Z.A. A157/2.

Geneva, 26 June 03.
Rue Lombard 4

Dear Friend,

I am still without a reply to my last letter.[1] I always believed, rightly I hope, that we should find you responsive. This is why your present silence touches me all the more painfully. The receipt of a letter should at least be acknowledged. I have nothing to add to my previous letters except to say that the situation is getting more and more acute: intrigues, lies, slanders[2]—in short, they are using every impossible weapon. Our 'friends' remain silent, however, and do not even reply to letters of the utmost seriousness.

Please write by return and say whether we may count upon your region carrying some of our candidates, namely: Buber, Feiwel, Nossig, Weizmann, Aberson.

I trust you will not leave me without an answer this time.[3]

Kindest regards from

Yours ever,

Mr. V. Tyomkin,
Elizavetgrad.

[4] See No. 386 and n. 4 there.
[5] Cf. No. 341 and n. 3 there.
[6] See n. 3 to No. 386.

388. [1] See No. 346.
[2] Cf. No. 383 and n. 5 there; see also n. 1 to No. 384 for Motzkin's grievances against W., Feiwel, and Buber.
[3] On 18 June (1 July) 1903 the secretary of the Elizavetgrad Zionist Region wrote to W. (W.A.) that Tyomkin would answer his letter on his return (from St. Petersburg), and stated that W. had been elected to the Sixth Congress for Nikolayev. No reply from Tyomkin has been found.

389. To Abraham Lichtenstein, Pinsk. *Geneva, 26 June 1903*

German: Or. Copy. T.W.: W.A.

Geneva, 26 June 03.
Rue Lombard 4.

Dear Abraham,

I have had great difficulty lately in writing a detailed letter to you. Never before have we had to make such efforts before a Congress. The noble 'guardians of Zion' have chosen their moment well to launch their dirty campaign, spreading every kind of false rumour and calumny.[1] Their activities are of international proportions. They have found support in the A.C. You would be shocked if I were to describe all their machinations. The bitterness is so great that I am filled with anxiety for this Congress. You will see how we are preparing ourselves for the Congress from our circular letter,[2] herewith enclosed.

Very much now depends on our mandates; we must make sure that we have a strong Congress group. We shall settle inner Fraction matters after the Congress this time,[3] and that will not be very easy either. But we must organise strong representation before the Congress. You, Bregman, Lieberman,[4] can all do a great deal for the cause in Pinsk and its environs. I need not elaborate to you, but the situation was never so desperately serious as now. One is universally betrayed, and so the faithful few have to strive all the harder. I implore you, therefore, to leave nothing undone in getting our candidates through. Get in touch with Berger without delay. We have written to him[5] also. The *Poalei-Zion* are closest to the

---

389. [1] The reference is apparently to Pinkus, Pasmanik, and their circle—see No. 383 and n. 5 there.

[2] Circular of 17 June 1903 (see n. 1 to No. 381). It appears from Lichtenstein's reply of 16/29 June 1903 (W.A.) that the circular sent to him contained additional names of Fraction candidates for the Sixth Zionist Congress which had been inserted in handwriting, but were not included in the original list in the circular. These additional names had all been proposed by Buber (see Buber to W. and Feiwel, 12 June 1903, W.A.).

[3] W. apparently did not regard the Conference of the Democratic Fraction due to convene prior to the Zionist Congress as a suitable forum for the settlement of 'inner Fraction matters', probably because of its public character. It may also be assumed that W. was already at that time considering cancelling the Conference, which in fact he did early in July (see No. 403).

[4] (Abraham) Joseph Bregman (1880–1946) was then a bank clerk in Pinsk, later a bank manager in Russia and Palestine. He was a Zionist leader in Pinsk and a member of the Democratic Fraction. For Meir Lieberman, see Vol. I, n. 2 to No. 315.

[5] See No. 357 and n. 6 there.

Fraction[6] even if they do not identify with it completely. We must do our work as quickly as possible.

Anticipating your immediate reply, I am,

Your

390. To Theodor Herzl, Vienna. *Geneva, 27 June 1903*

German: T.W.: C.Z.A. Z1/346.

Geneva, 27 June 1903.
Rue Lombard 4.

Dear Dr. [Herzl],

Would you kindly transfer to the Bureau the sum of 1,500 francs,[1] for the purpose of a propaganda tour in Belgium, Holland and some French cities,[2] as well as for current expenses of the Bureau.

Most respectfully and with Zion's greetings,

On behalf of the Bureau:

Dr. Chaim Weizmann

Dr. Theodor Herzl,
Vienna.

Registered.

391. To Theodor Herzl, Vienna. *Geneva, 27 June 1903*

German: H.W.: C.Z.A. Z1/346.

Geneva, 27. VI. 03.
Rue Lombard 4

Dear Dr. [Herzl],

I am availing myself of the opportunity[1] to return briefly to our exchange of letters;[2] there is a great deal to say, but for this a letter would be inadequate. I would merely like to draw your attention to the fact that in the meantime a wild campaign has been launched by a group of 'comrades'[3] against the *Verlag*,[4]

---

[6] For the positive attitude of the *Poalei-Zion* in Minsk to the Zionist youth movement and Democratic Fraction, see Vol. I, n. 6 to No. 139; n. 56 to No. 316 *supra*.

390. [1] Herzl was the trustee of the University Bureau funds deposited at the Jewish Colonial Trust (see n. 2 to No. 27).

[2] The reference is to W.'s proposed propaganda tour in Belgium and Holland (see Nos. 360, 361) and the imminent trip of W. and Nossig to Paris (No. 375). Nothing further is known of W.'s intention to visit any French cities beside Paris.

391. [1] The letter was probably sent together with No. 390.

[2] See No. 316; n. 3 to No. 336.

[3] Orig.: 'von gesinnungsgenösslicher Seite'.

[4] The inference is not clear, but see n. 3 to No. 366.

against the University Bureau, and yes, even against us personally.[5]
It is a calamity! Everywhere people are perpetrating slanders and
are lying in the name of Zionism! I am so agitated and indignant
at the tactics being employed against 'opponents' (?!) that I have
even been considering a journey to Vienna to tell you everything,
but everything.[6]

You may for the present feel embittered towards the Fraction,
or perhaps annoyed.[7] But I know that you would react with all
alacrity against this kind of assault upon the Fraction, because
you would never permit any dishonourable conduct within Zionism.

As to your opinion regarding confusion in the ranks of the
Fraction, this is based exclusively on false and *ill-intentioned*
information. I would be the first to pass severe judgment on the
conduct of the Fraction, but I know that we have always acted
bona fide and wished *only* to further our common cause.

Regarding the Ahad Ha'am matter,[8] I can only discuss this
personally, and will do so before the Congress.

It is regrettable that abuse has also been levelled against the
University, which is a new undertaking and absolutely neutral.
It has nothing to do with Party matters and for the time being is a
private concern.

I would be very happy if I could speak with you prior to the
Congress. I am willing to travel to Vienna at any time you indicate.
I could largely clarify the situation and perhaps remove some un-
pleasant misunderstandings.

I am going to Liège, Brussels, Antwerp, Amsterdam and Paris
from the 10th–12th on University business. Afterwards Feiwel
will be going to England.[9] I could therefore be in Vienna on the
6th [or] 7th, or any other place convenient to you.[10]

Most respectfully, and with Zion's greetings,

Yours very truly,

Dr. Ch. Weizmann

---

[5] See n. 5 to No. 383.

[6] Concerning W.'s offer to go to Vienna see No. 336 and n. 8 there; and cf. with
statement in No. 379.

[7] See n. 3 to No. 336; n. 8 to No. 346.

[8] The reference is to the Ahad Ha'am–Nordau affair (see No. 292 and ns. 10, 11
there, and also n. 8 to No. 346).

[9] In the event, W. went only to Paris in July; Feiwel did not go to England.

[10] No reply from Herzl has been found. W. did not go to Vienna.

392. To Isaac Berger, Minsk. *Geneva, 30 June 1903*

German: Or. Copy. T.W.: W.A.

Geneva, 30 June 03.

Mr. Isaac Berger,[1]
Minsk.

Dear Friend,

Today both your letter and the one from the *Poalei-Zion* Bureau[2] arrived. It goes without saying that I would consider submitting neither my own nor anyone else's candidature under the conditions offered. And may I state that I have regarded the *P.-Z.* as a more mature group than in reality it is. Even if it were true that the Fraction as such has achieved very little, the fact still remains that its members have worked a great deal. Furthermore, of all the Parties in Zionism, the Fraction is the only one containing members with whom the *P.-Z.* can associate.

At all events, those gentlemen in their Bureau have been over-hasty in singing their farewells to us. We have all been in the Zionist movement longer than these people, who only joined us yesterday but are now talking big. We have survived a number of crises, and will remain at our posts without lessons from such youngsters. Nothing gives them the right to write to me in so tactless a manner. They should wait until they have won their spurs in the movement. The rest will keep till we meet personally.[3] We shall be seeing each other in any case.[4]

With all my good wishes,

Your

---

392. [1] The letter is in the intimate form.

[2] Only the letter from the Bureau of the Minsk Centre of *Poalei-Zion*, signed by A. Rubenchik, I. Berger, A. Lapidus, and A. Grinhaus and undated, W.A. (No. 30/0, 52) has been found. It was sent in reply to W.'s letter (not found) of 6 June 1903 (see No. 357 and n. 6 there). Their letter from the *Poalei-Zion* Centre stated that in view of the inaction of the Democratic Fraction—which reflected on the standing even of the *Poalei-Zion* Bureau—it could not recommend *Poalei-Zion* groups to support the Fraction 'which either no longer exists or has already been compromised'. The Bureau would recommend individual candidates in the Congress elections, though without specifying their affiliation to the Fraction, if W. would personally guarantee that delegates receiving *Poalei-Zion* mandates would accept the following conditions: (a) They would only act in accordance with the instructions of *Poalei-Zion*; (b) they would take part in the caucuses of *Poalei-Zion* delegates, but voting rights would be accorded to members of *Poalei-Zion* societies only; (c) they would refrain in Congress from voting on all questions where their personal views and the decisions adopted by *Poalei-Zion* were not identical.

[3] In his reply of 24 June (7 July) 1903 (W.A.), Berger again explained that *Poalei-Zion* were unable to combine with the Fraction for electioneering purposes, as the

[*Footnotes 3 and 4 continued on p. 410*]

393. To Alfred Nossig, Berlin. *Geneva, 30 June 1903*

German: Or. Copy. T.W.: W.A.

30 June 1903.

Dear Dr. [Nossig],

In reply to your letter of the 28th,[1] which I deeply appreciate, I wish to state that as far as I know Buber went to see Prof. Meyerhoffer to ask him to join the Committee. It may well be that he did not find Prof. Meyerhoffer and had to do so in writing. Buber wrote to me to the effect that Meyerhoffer had joined. Perhaps he did this without the consent of Prof. Meyerhoffer because he was certain he would have it.[2]

---

latter did not exist as an active body and consequently they could not speak of solidarity of views. Nevertheless, Berger added, it was not to be assumed that differences of opinion would arise between the Fraction and *Poalei-Zion* in Congress debates, and even prior to receipt of W.'s letter the Bureau had submitted the names of candidates who were also Fraction members to *Poalei-Zion* groups. But their mandates would be revoked if they did not reach agreement with *Poalei-Zion* delegates at the Congress.

[4] At the Sixth Zionist Congress.

393. [1] Nossig to W. and Feiwel, 28 June 1903, W.A. Nossig reported on the second meeting of the Berlin Committee for the Jewish University held on 27 June 1903; most of its members held the view that the first step should be to establish a Science School (*Realgymnasium*) of two or three classes, to prepare Jewish boys from Eastern Jewry for higher studies and thus facilitate their admission into West European Universities. Committee members were generally in favour also of the creation of a *Technikum* (see n. 5 *infra*), and only if Universities continued to bar Jews should an actual Jewish University also be established. Meyerhoffer suggested setting up private laboratories were it proved that lack of laboratory space was the reason for non-admission of Jews from the East into the Universities. The Committee supported the creation of a 'Jewish Spiritual-National Academic Centre', but thought this could only be effectively attained in Palestine—and as Nossig had heard, the nationalist Jewish public in Russia also supported this viewpoint. As a first step in this direction it was suggested that a 'Free Jewish Academy' for teaching Jewish subjects in a scientific-secular spirit should be set up in Berlin. Warburg proposed that the University be established in Cairo if it were not practicable in Palestine. In Nossig's view the proposed plan would lack the aura of a University and there was also the danger that a preparatory establishment would serve only to accentuate the desperate situation in higher studies by increasing the number of applicants for the Universities. Nevertheless, Nossig supported the proposal to set up an institution of this kind because, after its inception, it would be easy to raise funds for the University and the German Government would gradually become accustomed to Jewish teaching institutions. Nossig suggested collating the results of the student survey as quickly as possible in order to ascertain whether a *Technikum* was in fact more necessary at this stage than a Polytechnic.

[2] In his letter of 28 June 1903 Nossig wrote that Prof. Meyerhoffer had told the meeting of the Berlin Committee for the Jewish University that he had not been invited to join the Committee and was astonished at the inclusion of his name in the list of members (W. had already announced Meyerhoffer's adherence to the Committee at the time of his visit to Berlin in March 1903—see Nos. 293, 294—and his name was

I consider the establishment of an Institute for preliminary studies to be very important; nevertheless, two or three classes seem too much to me. A course of one year and a half should suffice. This does not mean that graduates of this school will be admitted to the German Technical Colleges without further ado. Moreover, this school cannot be regarded by us as an end in itself. We must never lose sight of the larger goal, or we shall not be able to campaign for the lesser one either. What stirs enthusiasm for the project among Jews is the great vision of a national Jewish Institute, with precisely those positive values that will thereby be created for Judaism. Naturally, from this point of view it would be most preferable to establish the University in Palestine.

Since, however, a European-type University cannot materialise either in Palestine or the neighbouring countries at present, I believe that we can make a good beginning with that part of the project which on realisation will not evoke antagonism among national-Jewish elements.[3] If we bring the preliminary school and the courses for the first two years into operation, as indicated in my outline,[4] we shall have created something complete in itself which can nevertheless be transferred at any time. Substantial equipment is necessary only for the school in the specialisation stage.

For the following reasons the idea of a Technical College[5] does not appear practical to me: good Technical Colleges, such as those in Koethen, Mittweida and Winterthur, are very costly because they need exactly the same equipment as in a Polytechnic. Also they suffer from the disadvantage of not being Universities. The smaller Technical Colleges are not worth a great deal, and are hardly better than vocational schools.

Almost all foreign graduates of a Technical College continue their studies at a University. This is because people with local citizenship invariably have the opportunity of immediate technical employment, for these schools are always closely connected with local industry. Foreigners holding the diploma of a Technical College have difficulty in getting accepted. They are dependent upon positions outside Germany, and even then one does not get very far with such a diploma. Considering the fact that a good Technical College is very expensive anyway, costing substantially

mentioned as one of the Committee members in the report of the University Bureau of May 1903, W.A., 30/5/0). No letter of Buber's recording that Meyerhoffer had joined the Committee has been found.

[3] Cf. No. 385 and n. 3 there.

[4] See n. 5 to No. 386.

[5] In orig.: *Technikum*, i.e. a technical school at sub-academic level, as distinct from a *technische Hochschule* or *Polytechnikum*, which are at the academic level.

more than the University described in the outline,[6] and will even then not entirely answer the needs, I would propose that we reject the idea of establishing one. The private laboratories about which Prof. Meyerhoffer speaks could very well form part of our University. We must never overlook the aura of a University, otherwise we shall achieve nothing.

The Paris visit seems to me all the more necessary now.[7] We shall be able to meet there and discuss everything in person with each other. I can leave here as early as the 10th. In the event of a meeting still taking place before you leave for Paris, it would be as well to convey the content of this letter to the people concerned. Would you be able to refer to the existence of a Berlin Committee by the time you come to Paris?

Will you kindly have 100 reprints done of the article on Jewish students in the Year Book of Jewish Statistics[8] on behalf of the Bureau.

Please find enclosed the prospectus of the *Conservatoire national des Arts et Métiers*.[9] This kind of school, with certain changes and extensions, would be of enormous value to us, having in mind also future colonisation work.

Looking forward to hearing from you again, I remain,

With kindest regards,

Your

Dr. Alfred Nossig,
  Berlin.

394. To David Farbstein, Zurich. *Geneva, 1 July 1903*

German: Or. Copy. T.W.: W.A.

Geneva, 1st. July 03.
Rue Lombard 4

Dear Dr. [Farbstein],

It has come to my notice from various quarters that Mr. Lazar Felix Pinkus is spreading false rumours about my friend Feiwel

---

[6] See n. 5 to No. 386.

[7] Refers to the imminent journey of W. and Nossig to Paris (see No. 375, also No. 382 and n. 2 there).

[8] Refers to Feiwel's article in *Jüdische Statistik* analysing the results of the student survey (see n. 9 to No. 396).

[9] A Government establishment in Paris in which evening courses in technical subjects were given gratis. The Principal sent W. at his request various documents relating to the institute, including the schedule of courses taught there (see his letter of 25 June 1903 in W.A.).

and myself. Among other things he asserts that he wrote the brochure 'A Jewish University' and we published it in our name. This exceeds all conceivable limits.[1]

We request, dear Doctor, that you as a friend of the Party and as an attorney demand the appearance of Mr. Pinkus before you or before a Court of Arbitration, so that he might explain himself. We shall naturally meet all the costs involved.[2]

May we have your immediate reply.

With kind regards,

Yours very truly,

Dr. D. Farbstein, Attorney,
Zurich.

395. To the Jewish University Committee, Warsaw.

Geneva, 2 July 1903

German: Or. Copy. T.W.: W.A.

2 July 1903.

The Jewish University Committee,

For the attention of
Mr. August Minkovsky,
Warsaw.

Gentlemen,

We gratefully acknowledge receipt of 200 roubles[1] and we take note of your remarks, which are much appreciated.[2]

Our report mentions only those members of the Committee with whom we are in direct correspondence. Please be assured that this

---

394. [1] In a letter to the University Bureau of 5 July 1903 (W.A.), Pinkus wrote that he had not claimed to have written the monograph *Eine Jüdische Hochschule* (see Vol. I, n. 2 to No. 238), but had told a number of his friends that the first draft was his with some assistance from W., and that several passages had been transferred *in toto* from this draft to the brochure.

[2] It would appear from Pinkus's letter of 5 July 1903 that Farbstein had in fact approached him on this matter.

395. [1] See Minkovsky to W., 11 (24?) June 1903, W.A. On behalf of the Warsaw Committee for the University, Minkovsky sent W. 200 roubles for the Bureau's preparatory work (the amount had apparently been raised by Selig Weicman—see his letter of 20 June 1903, W.A.).

[2] In their letter of 23 June 1903—Gregorian date in the original (W.A.)—the members of the Warsaw Committee, Minkovsky, S. Goldflamm, B. Koral, and J. Muttermilch, stated that they continued to support the idea of a University but as they did not wish to invest the plan with political significance they suggested the removal of Hebrew headings from communications relating to the University. They further declared that, owing to the Kishinev pogrom and the summer vacation, they were compelled to adjourn any action until the autumn (see also ns. 2, 6 to No. 372).

is the sole reason, and is not intended as by-passing the other gentlemen of the Committee.[3]

We hope to be in a position shortly to submit a plan to you, prepared by experts, for the Jewish University.

Yours very sincerely,

In the name of the Bureau:

396. To Abraham Lichtenstein, Pinsk. *Geneva, 2 July 1903*

German: Or. Copy. T.W.: W.A.

2 July 1903.

Dear Abraham,[1]

I did not telegraph you because I expected nothing to come out of a talk with Gregory Lurie. On the other hand, you may show the circular to Reigrodsky[2] and Jacob Eliasberg;[3] though they must naturally promise to keep quiet about it. The entire election campaign has to be conducted with the greatest caution. According to

---

[3] The report of the University Bureau of May 1903 (W.A., No. 30/5/0) mentioned only Minkovsky and Goldflamm as members of the Warsaw Committee, but in the letter from the Committee members of 23 June 1903 Koral and Muttermilch were expressly included.

396. [1] This is in reply to Lichtenstein's letter, and its postscript by Joseph Bregman, of 16/29 June 1903 (W.A.). Lichtenstein, commenting on W.'s letter of 26 June 1903 (see No. 389) and the circular of 17 June 1903 (see n. 1 to No. 381; n. 2 to No. 389), wrote that he, Bregman, and Lieberman would assist the election campaign of Democratic Fraction candidates for the Sixth Zionist Congress, but in order to raise funds they needed to approach Jacob Reigrodsky, Jacob Eliasberg, and Gregory Lurie. Accordingly Lichtenstein asked W.'s authorization to show these persons the 17 June circular. At the same time he expressed doubt as to the advisability of applying to Lurie who, said Lichtenstein, had behaved disgracefully towards the Pinsk Zionists and they intended to defeat him in the Congress elections. He asked W. to telegraph the necessary instructions. Lichtenstein stated that the Fraction too was obliged to make a contribution towards the electioneering expenses; with adequate funds Bregman would be able to conduct propaganda in the Pinsk area and he himself in Courland. He pointed out that it had not been easy to conduct propaganda, as an unsympathetic attitude prevailed towards the Fraction in many places on account of its inaction. Further, Lichtenstein wanted to know the intended battle-slogan of the Fraction at the Congress—according to information that had reached them, cultural and economic questions would not be included in the Congress agenda (see n. 7 *infra*). He considered that the *Poalei-Zion* in Minsk could be relied upon and he would write to Isaac Berger, among others. He requested information on several of the Fraction candidates mentioned in the circular (see below).

[2] Jacob Reigrodsky, one of the earliest Zionists in Pinsk. He was later a manufacturer of chemical products in Kiev and Warsaw.

[3] Jacob Eliasberg (1881–1966), younger brother of Aaron Eliasberg. Born in Pinsk, he was then a student and active Zionist in Riga. Subsequently an industrialist in Moscow and Pinsk, he lived in Jerusalem from 1943.

our information great pressure will be at work in the elections, because the negotiations regarding El-Arish have ended in nothing and they fear a storm at the Congress.[4] Therefore, our battle-cry at this Congress must above all be a demand for clarity on the territorial question[5] and a scientific investigation of Palestine and the neighbouring countries. A stop has got to be put to the game of hide and seek once and for all. We shall also have to take action against the terrifying opportunism which has been so shamefully manifested by the leadership in affairs of colonisation.[6]

Questions such as raising the level[7] of the movement as a whole will be pushed to the background at this Congress because the main problem, the Bank[8] and National Fund and all that this involves, will have to be settled without fail. But whatever happens we must in no circumstances give the *Mizrahi* a chance to have the subject of raising levels shelved. It can be dealt with positively only if brought in under the heading of Statistics. Nossig has already published a very attractive Year Book,[9] giving us reason enough to make a demand of the Congress on behalf of the Statistical Society.

[4] In a circular dated 12 June 1903 (C.Z.A. Z1/212) the Smaller Actions Committee informed members of the Greater Actions Committee that negotiations regarding El-Arish had broken down (see n. 5 to No. 308). Although the circular was secret, the matter became widely known and Buber wrote W. and Feiwel that, in view of the failure, a storm was to be expected at the Sixth Zionist Congress and that instructions had been sent to Russia to rig the elections (see Buber to W., 27 June 1903; Buber to Feiwel, 1 July 1903, W.A.). It is likely that this rumour had its origin in a report that the Smaller Actions Committee had sent a list of candidates to various cities in Russia and asked that these be elected. At the Sixth Congress Charles Wortsman demanded that the mandates of those delegates recommended by the Actions Committee be rescinded (see *Der Fraind*, 6/19 Aug. 1903; 6 Z.C. Prot., p. 123).

[5] In orig.: 'Landfrage'. Concerning the connotation of this term see n. 81 to No. 316. From No. 413 it appears that W. had received a letter at about this time from David Farbstein suggesting the drafting of 'a programme for a group on the basis of the main principle: "Clarity in the Territorial Question" ', to which W. had replied in an affirmative spirit.

[6] 'K.-Affäire' (*sic*) in orig.—certainly an abbreviation for Kolonisations-Affäre, i.e. the El-Arish project (see n. 5 to No. 308). See also No. 316 and n. 81 there concerning W.'s contention that the Actions Committee had deviated from its declared policy in this matter.

[7] 'Die Fragen der Hebung' in orig. This refers to measures adopted for the improvement of the cultural, economic, and physical position of the Jewish people—the programme supported by the advocates of *Gegenwartsarbeit* in Zionism. The agenda of the Sixth Congress, which was fixed by the Smaller Actions Committee on 14 June 1903, did not include these questions.

[8] Jewish Colonial Trust.

[9] *Jüdische Statistik*, Berlin 1903. Edited by Alfred Nossig the book was published by the *Jüdischer Verlag* on behalf of the Jewish Statistical Association of Berlin. It was intended as the first in a series of annual publications but no others appeared, and comprised a bibliography and articles with *inter alia*, a provisional analysis by Feiwel of the results of the student survey conducted by the Jewish University Bureau.

I would propose that the election campaign be conducted not under the banner of the Fraction, but rather under that of the territorial question.

I cannot say anything about Gissin,[10] though I believe he is close to us. Zeitlin[11] is the well-known Jewish writer from Homel. Dr. Friedlaender, lecturer in Strasbourg, is the translator of Ahad Ha'am.[12] George Halpern is a student in Munich, and being a son of Halpern from Pinsk[13] he should not be a candidate in Pinsk. Saul Lurie, son of Idel Lurie, would make a very capable candidate. I wish to recommend particularly the candidature of Trietsch, Nossig, and Miss Ina Schimmer who is employed by the *Jüdischer Verlag*, all from Berlin, and Miss Shneerson, Rosa Grinblatt and Zvi Aberson. I would recommend Feiwel and Buber for Pinsk.

I received a letter from Berger in Minsk which laid down such conditions and was written in so presumptuous a tone that I promptly rejected it out of hand.[14] Please take notice of this. We shall gladly pay the expenses you incur in all this business.

I implore you, Abraham, to keep careful minutes, because they will show no mercy in stressing all the formalities relating to our delegates.[15] You will keep us constantly informed, of course, and we on our side will do the same for you. The youngsters[16] are not yet here.

Warmest regards to you and our friends,

Yours ever,

397. To Alfred Nossig, Berlin. *Geneva, 2 July 1903*

German: Or. Copy. T.W.: W.A.

2 July 03.

Dear Dr. [Nossig],

Following my previous letter[1] I would now ask how much

---

[10] In his letter of 16/29 June 1903 Lichtenstein asked whether W. would agree to the candidature of Boris Gissin in Mohilev.

[11] Hillel Zeitlin (1872–1943). Zeitlin and the others mentioned here were included in the list of Fraction candidates sent to Lichtenstein (see n. 1 *supra*).

[12] Israel Friedlaender's translations were published by the *Jüdischer Verlag* in 1904. See Ahad Ha'am, *Am Scheidewege, ausgewählte Essays, Übersetzung aus dem Hebräischen von Israel Friedlaender.*

[13] The industrialist Joseph Halpern, known for his extreme opposition to Zionism.

[14] See No. 392 and n. 2 there.

[15] That is, the Mandates Committee of the Sixth Congress would strictly investigate the propriety of the election of Democratic Fraction delegates.

[16] Refers to Moses Weizmann, W.'s brother, and their uncle Chaim Fialkov, who was approximately the same age as Ch. W. They were due in Switzerland for the Sixth Zionist Congress (see Lichtenstein's letter of 16/29 June 1903, W.A.).

397. [1] See No. 393.

money you will be needing for the visit to Paris.[2] Also, would you please inform us when you intend going.

We have secured plenty of delegate mandates.[3] All being well we shall have a fairly strong group.

Expecting to hear from you regarding the University plan,[4] and with kind regards,

I remain,
Most respectfully,
Your

Dr. Alfred Nossig,
Berlin.

398. To Ben-Zion Mossinson, Berne. *Geneva, 4 July 1903*

Hebrew: H.W.: C.Z.A. A45/10a.

Geneva, 4 July 1903[1]
8 Tammuz, 5663.[2]

Mr. Ben-Zion Mossinson, Berne.[3]

Dear Friend,

We the undersigned, directors of the University Bureau, have

[2] See No. 375; n. 2 to No. 386.

[3] For the Democratic Fraction and its sympathizers to the Sixth Zionist Congress—cf. n. 1 to No. 381.

[4] Refers to the deliberations of the Berlin Committee for the University (see No. 393 and n. 1 there).

398. [1] In the orig. Geneva is in German, as is the non-Hebrew date. The rest of the letter is in Hebrew.

[2] Thus in orig., but 4 July 1903 fell on 9 Tammuz 5663.

[3] This letter forms part of an agreement between the Jewish University Bureau and Mossinson concerning his participation in its work. It was reached after the exchange of correspondence between the Bureau and the *Ivria* Society in Berne (see No. 376 and n. 3 there). W. met Mossinson at the Swiss Zionist Conference (28 June 1903), and it appears that they came to a provisional agreement on that occasion. W. promised, *inter alia*, to meet Mossinson's expenses on behalf of the Bureau; on 30 June the Bureau sent him 15 francs 'as agreed with you at Fribourg' (see Stupnitzky to Mossinson, 30 June 1903, C.Z.A. A45/10). Mossinson came to Geneva at the beginning of July and the final agreement was concluded there. It seems that Mossinson made this conditional on the aims of the Bureau, and particularly its attitude on the question of location of the University, being clarified in writing, and it was agreed that this should be effected through an exchange of letters between him and the Bureau. Replying to the letter under notice, Mossinson declared that he subscribed to the Bureau's objectives and undertook to do his utmost in giving effect to the idea and in supporting the institutions connected with the Bureau, including the proposed periodical *Der Jude* and the *Jüdischer Verlag* publishing house. He promised to send

[*Footnote 3 continued on p. 418*]

the honour to inform you of our aims and purposes in the task we
have assumed. Our desire is to establish—if at all possible—a
Jewish University in Palestine. In the first instance we shall
endeavour particularly to inaugurate a department of Philology—
Pedagogy, so as to train teachers and school-principals for our
people. This department will be opened as soon as the necessary
means become available. We shall do all in our power to establish
the other departments in Palestine, but if this proves impossible we
shall begin by opening them elsewhere. However, we shall erect no
buildings, and make no attempt to remain abroad permanently, in
order to be able to transfer the institutions to Palestine at an appropriate moment. We would furthermore inform you that, should
there be a possibility of doing this in Palestine after the lapse of a
few years, then we would delay rather than hasten the opening of
the institutions outside the Land of Israel.

We look upon you as a member of our Bureau, and undertake to
send you all the letters and documents it issues, so that you will
be kept fully informed.

We trust that the matters agreed upon between us will be kept
in confidence by you.

Respectfully, and with Zion's greetings,

Dr. Chaim Weizmann.
S. I. Stupnitzky, Secretary.

399. To Regina Schimmer, Berlin. *Geneva, 5 July[1] 1903*

German: H.W.: C.Z.A. A110/29.

Dear Ina,

The cares of the past few months have prevented me from writing
to you. I did not wish to cause you fresh anxiety and this is why
my answer has been so long in coming.[2] I become more and more

an immediate circular to his friends in Russia (see n. 2 to No. 408) and to conduct
propaganda for the idea when he was there. It seems that Mossinson also undertook
to write to Ussishkin, with whom he was in close touch through his capacity as a
Zionist propagandist in Russia (see No. 405 and n. 4 there). Mossinson affirmed that
he would do nothing without the concurrence of the other members of the Bureau
(see Mossinson to the directors of the University Bureau, 4 July 1903, W.A.). The
present letter, as well as Mossinson's reply, is in the handwriting of Stupnitzky,
secretary of the University Bureau. See also Mossinson to Ussishkin, 11 Tammuz
5663 (6 July 1903), C.Z.A. A24/125.

399. [1] Date approximate. The letter was apparently written before W.'s departure for
Paris in mid July 1903, and see below: 'I urgently need his reply before the 12th.'
  [2] The W.A. have a letter from Schimmer to W. of 28 April 1903.

confused regarding Toldy; the subject is becoming immensely complicated and my intervention availed *nothing*. I shall try once again to settle the business before Congress, for otherwise I cannot imagine how he will be able to keep it up. His relations with Esther[3] are growing ever closer, but Manya[4] is convinced that Told belongs to her.[5] Old man Sokolow will exert his pressure and so the situation will become intolerable.

This is all I can say. I shall, however, attempt everything possible because Told really means well and he certainly has a noble character.

May I ask a favour, Ina dear? I requested Dr. Altschul to give me some names in Paris.[6] He is a fine person but lazy in his correspondence. Will you personally see to it, at once, that he replies by return? I urgently need his reply before the 12th.

Warm regards,

Your Chaim

400. To Ben-Zion Mossinson, Berne. *Geneva, 6 July 1903*

Russian: Pcd. H.W.: C.Z.A. A45/10a.

Geneva,
Rue Lombard 4
7. VII. 03.[1]

Dear Friend,

I have transferred 35 francs[2] to you through Becker. He will pay it to you in the course of the next few days. I shall send you the balance in a day or two. Please do the circular and write to Ussishkin.[3]

With friendly greetings,

Yours,

Ch. Weizmann.

---

[3] Esther Shneerson.
[4] Maria Sokolow.
[5] See also No. 309.
[6] The letter to Altschul has not been found.

400. [1] Thus in orig., but the Geneva postmark is 6 July 1903.

[2] W. promised to send Mossinson money to cover his working expenses at the University Bureau (see n. 1 to No. 398) and to loan 20 francs to the *Ivria* Society in Berne—see Mossinson to W., 11 Tammuz 5563 (6 July 1903), W.A. See also n. 4 to No. 421.

[3] See n. 3 to No. 398.

401. To Abraham Idelson, Moscow. *Geneva, 7 July 1903*

German: Or. Copy. T.W.: W.A.

Geneva, 7 July 1903.

Dear Friend,[1]

We wrote to Kroll in reply to your letters some time ago.[2] We declared ourselves at that time to be opposed to a Conference in Warsaw, and explained our position in detail. We still maintain this point of view, the only difference being that we shall not hold a Conference in Basle either.[3] First, because of the lack of time: it is already too late. Secondly, for the reasons which you expressed in part in your last letter.[4] We have indirectly learned that you are corresponding with Herzl;[5] it would be most desirable for us to be informed of the contents of the letters. In any case we are still awaiting your reply to our earlier letters.[6]

With kind regards,

Yours ever,

Mr. A. Idelson,
Moscow.

401. [1] The letter is in the intimate form.

  [2] See No. 384 and n. 1 there.

  [3] For the cancellation of the Democratic Fraction Conference see also No. 403.

  [4] Idelson to W., 17/30 June 1903 (W.A.). Idelson did not in fact mention the possibility of the Fraction Conference being cancelled in his letter, but expressed grave doubt as to the value of opposition activity within the Zionist Organization. He compared the movement, its leaders, and its meetings to 'a flock of sheep, not worth dealing with'. He did not expect anything to emerge from the Zionist Organization or the Congresses 'before all this collapses in ruins'. He went on: 'And we, the minority, in trying to thrust ourselves into this Organization are giving it a shadow of humanity, but only a shadow, for after all even we are doing nothing but quarrel with these fools . . . Let us not divert them from their acts. Let them collect money (after all, that's all they do) without culture and without a vestige of education . . .'

  [5] Glikin reported to W. on 30 June 1903—Gregorian date in orig. (W.A.), that, according to Tschlenow, Herzl had written to Idelson forbidding the Democratic Fraction people to continue their activities. No exchange of letters between Herzl and Idelson has been found.

  [6] W. sent Idelson in error a Hebrew letter intended for some person in Kharkov unknown (perhaps Vladimir Idelson) and apparently he also erroneously sent to Kharkov the letter of 22 June 1903 intended for Kroll and Idelson (No. 384) —see Idelson's letter of 17/30 June 1903 (W.A.).

402. To Moses Glikin, St. Petersburg.[1] *Geneva, 7 July 1903*

German: Or. Copy. T.W.: W.A.

Geneva, 7 July 1903.

Dear Glikin,

I shall do as you ask[2] and write to Ussishkin this very day.[3] I would like you, on your part, to keep me up to date, for you can understand how all aspects of our affairs interest me.[4]

Ask Dr. Lurie, in the name of Feiwel and myself, to accede to our request. We are placing full reliance in his promise and have made our arrangements accordingly.[5] Write at once. I have little faith that our Conference can still take place.[6]

Your

Mr. Glikin,
Petersburg.

403. To Davis Trietsch, Berlin. *Geneva, 7 July 1903*

German: Or. Copy. T.W.: W.A.

Geneva, 7th July 03.
Rue Lombard 4.

Dear Friend,

You will be surprised to see a letter from me for once. Incidentally,

---

402. [1] Glikin moved from Moscow to St. Petersburg in June and began working in the editorial offices of the daily newspaper *Der Fraind*.

[2] See Glikin to W., 30 June 1903 (Gregorian date in orig.) (W.A.). Glikin wrote that he wished for a post in the Anglo-Palestine Bank at Jaffa (established in July 1903 as a branch of the Jewish Colonial Trust), and asked W. to take the matter up with Ussishkin, then on a visit to Palestine, and Zalman Levontin, who had been appointed manager of the Bank.

[3] On 8 July 1903 W. asked Mossinson for Ussishkin's address in Palestine (see No. 405), but there is no record of any letter of his to Ussishkin at that time.

[4] Glikin's letter of 30 June 1903 (W.A.) stated that several Zionist leaders in Russia had met in St. Petersburg to discuss the dangers threatening the Zionist movement in Russia (see n. 5 to No. 414). These consultations were held from 29 June to 1 July 1903 (Gregorian dates).

[5] It is likely that Lurie complied with W.'s request of 9 May 1903 (see No. 327 and n. 4 there) to send him material on the pogrom at Kishinev. See also No. 403 for W.'s suggestion that an article on the pogrom be published in the first issue of *Der Jude*.

[6] Cf. No. 403.

you have no cause for complaint against Geneva, we have always kept you informed.[1]

MANDATES. You are mistaken in your assumption that Kohan-Bernstein could have helped us in any way, or even wished to. He replies to no letters. But this is not altogether his fault, for he still has no permanent address.[2] We have written to all those people in Russia who might be considered.[3] We hope to get most of the candidates through. It is not quite as easy as you think,[4] with all the pressures that are at work.[5]

FRACTION. We have abandoned the plan to summon a Conference of the Fraction. The atmosphere is not universally favourable; it will only lead to new frictions, of which we have had enough. Motzkin, by all appearances, has indulged in some intrigues in Russia and we shall once again have to bear the consequences.[6] Profound differences of opinion seem to have risen again between ourselves and the people in Russia concerning the nature and meaning of the Fraction.[7] Also, there are now police and political factors demanding the greatest caution.[8] We shall probably organise an advance study-session, limited in numbers, while in Basle; but our aim is to form a West European working body[9] with the Russian Fraction left to its own devices. It too will adjust to the conditions as they exist in the Party and so possibly accomplish something; but we refuse to bear responsibility for it any longer. A letter that has been despatched to Moscow[10] will enlighten you more exactly as to our thinking.

403. [1] Correspondence with Trietsch at this time was apparently dealt with by Feiwel, then in Geneva, and it may be assumed that the allusion here refers to a letter sent to Feiwel.

[2] Bernstein-Kohan moved from Kishinev to Kharkov after the pogrom in the former city (see n. 12 to No. 342), but according to a letter from Pokrassa to W., 15/28 June 1903 (W.A.), he was not as yet in Kharkov but would arrive there at the end of June (according to the Julian calendar). W. received no reply to his letters to Bernstein-Kohan during the period Dec. 1902–April 1903 (see Nos. 51, 126, 310) and Bernstein-Kohan replied to that of 15 June 1903 only on 12 July 1903 (see No. 377 and n. 8 there).

[3] See Nos. 342, 345, 346, 352, 355, 357, 388, 389, 396. It is likely that W. also sent the 17 June 1903 circular (see n. 1 to No. 381), containing the list of Fraction candidates, to a number of other people in Russia.

[4] For the problems of electioneering for Fraction candidates in Russia, see n. 2 to No. 392; n. 1 to No. 396.

[5] Cf. No. 396 and n. 4 there.

[6] See n. 1 to No. 384 for Motzkin's recriminations concerning breaches of party discipline by W., Feiwel, and Buber.

[7] See No. 384 and n. 1 there.

[8] See n. 3 to No. 305; No. 364 and n. 1 there, for the suspicious attitude of Russian Ministry of Interior circles towards the Democratic Fraction.

[9] See also No. 384 and n. 2 there.

[10] See No. 384.

JUDE. The eternal Jew[11], which has hitherto been only talk, must be made to appear soon. We wish to issue a trial number prior to the Congress, and so be enabled to work for the journal much more effectively at the Congress.[12] Please, Mr. Trietsch, do let me have your opinion on this subject *immediately*. The issue will have to contain a great deal on the University as well as on the other activities. It would be just as well to continue writing about Kishinev. But we must proceed very carefully, having regard to Russia. We might perhaps publish one number specially for Russia.

I am going to Paris for a few days with Nossig, and then if necessary to Brussels and Antwerp.

There is no other news. Spirits are below zero. What is new regarding El-Arish?[13] If nothing comes of it we shall have to transform ourselves into the ruling Party. Felix Pinkus, the human serpent,[14] is here. Probably he is turning Calvinist.

Warmest regards from

Yours ever,

Mr. D. Trietsch,
Berlin.

404. To Joseph Pokrassa, Kharkov. *Geneva, 7 July 1903*

German: Or. Copy. T.W.: W.A.

Geneva, 7 July 1903.

Dear Friend,

Your last letter[1] must have been composed when everything

---

[11] A pun in the orig.: 'der ewige Jude'.

[12] Pokrassa urged W. to publish the first issue of the periodical as soon as possible (see n. 1 to No. 404).

[13] See n. 5 to No. 308; No. 396 and n. 4 there.

[14] 'Der Schlangenmensch' in orig. For the conflict with Pinkus see No. 258 and n. 1 there; No. 383 and ns. 4, 5 there; No. 394 and n. 1 there.

404. [1] Pokrassa to W., 15/28 June 1903 (W.A.). Pokrassa levelled strong accusations of inaction against the Democratic Fraction, stating that this inaction would place the Fraction in an invidious position at the Sixth Congress. The achievements of W., Buber, and Feiwel could not be credited to the Fraction, Pokrassa argued, and the fatuous, empty circulars put out by the Fraction Centre in Moscow could not be taken seriously. In contrast, the *Mizrahi*, with its propaganda, its periodical (*Mi'Mizrah*), and the leaflets it circulated, went from strength to strength. Pokrassa rebuked W. for his complete absorption in the University project, contending that he was neglecting contact with the people and instead was bidding for the attention of 'the high and mighty' from whom no salvation would come. Pokrassa claimed that so long as the first issue of *Der Jude* did not appear, there was no prospect of obtaining financial support for the projected periodical. He added that W. and his associates would have to speak frankly to members of the Fraction, whose only strength lay in speechifying at the Sixth Congress. Finally, Pokrassa stated that there was

looked dark to you, and as a result you were even guilty of certain
mis-judgments. First of all, I should like to defend myself against
the accusation that during my propaganda tour I gave my attention
only to the most important people, so as to [win them over to the
University]. Till now, the purpose of my propaganda tours has
always been work for Zionism. If on this occasion I did in fact
work for the University also, nevertheless three of the four meetings
held in Kharkov were devoted to Zionist affairs, and were for the
mass of people, while only one was for the University;[2] and incidentally, that one was interrupted. This is exactly the way it
has been in the other cities.

With regard to *Der Jude* we cannot and will not learn anything
from other papers. Being so much greater in number than ourselves
the *Mizrahi*[3] will always find the means for publishing a scandal-
sheet. On the other hand, in our organisation we stand alone:
work and responsibility for what is done, or left undone, by our
groups fall on the shoulders of just three people.[4] We have, to
the best of our knowledge and conscience, carried out whatever
lay in our power to do. But when we turn to our closest friends for
support, we are answered by reproaches: 'Why did the Moscow
people write such poor circulars? Why does this person or that do
nothing? Why has nothing been published?'

To my certain knowledge we—I am speaking of Buber, Feiwel,
Nossig and myself—have been responsible for the following since
the Fifth Congress: the University endeavour in its entirety;
propaganda for both Zionism and the University with my two
extensive journeys to Russia,[5] Feiwel and Buber in Vienna, Brno,
Prague and Cracow;[6] Feiwel and myself in Munich twice, and in

apparently no mandate for the Congress available for W. in Kharkov (see also
No. 364 and ns. 1, 9 there).

[2] Five meetings in Kharkov at which W. spoke are known: three in Sept. 1901,
at one of which he dwelt, *inter alia*, on the University project (see Vol. I, No. 128),
and two in Oct. 1902, one of which was devoted to the University project (see Vol. I,
Nos. 318, 319). Nothing is known of the interruption mentioned here, but it may be
assumed to have occurred in Oct. 1902 at the meeting called to discuss the University
plan.

[3] The *Mizrahi* organization then had over 10,000 registered members (see n. 32
to No. 316). No systematic registration of Fraction members was apparently ever
made, but presumably their number never exceeded a few hundreds.

[4] This probably refers to Feiwel, Buber, and himself. Continuing, W. includes
Nossig among the few who bore the brunt of the work.

[5] Aug.–Oct. 1902 and March–April 1903.

[6] Feiwel visited Vienna, Brno, Budapest, Prague, and Berlin in May 1903 (see
Feiwel to Mayer, 20 May 1903, Eugen Mayer Papers, Jerusalem). Whilst in Vienna he
addressed a meeting of the 'Leo Pinsker' Student Zionist Society on the subject 'Before
the Zionist Congress' (see *Hatzofe*, 4/17 May 1903). Buber was then living in Vienna
and probably visited Cracow from there.

Mannheim, and Strasbourg;[7] Aberson, Feiwel and myself at all Swiss universities as well as those in Paris and Berlin.[8] Then there was all the work for the *Jüdischer Verlag*: publication of *Almanach* and *Rosenfeld*; the appearance last week of a splendid book on Kishinev; *Jewish Statistics* by Nossig, and *Junge Harfen*, a collection of young Jewish poets. *Künstler Buch* and two other works are shortly due to appear.[9]

We have also made all necessary preparations for *Der Jude*, and despite the obstacles will still publish one issue before the Congress. Four people, denied all support and who furthermore are compelled to struggle against constant obstruction, could have done no more because they also have to work for their livelihood. I am well aware that we have occasionally been remiss; but if you stood in our shoes for just a day or two you would understand the reasons for some errors. Of this we have no doubt: we have devoted the best of our time and effort to the cause. Under the conditions that have now arisen, however, we must say this, and it is our final word: we have had enough of dirty party politics; we have no desire to fritter our lives away struggling on behalf of a group that cannot and will not endure. We shall continue to stay at our posts so as to pursue with all energy the activities which we began.

[7] W. spoke at Munich in Feb. 1902 and May 1903, Feiwel in May 1903 (see Vol. I, n. 1 to No. 157; No. 337 *supra* and ns. 1–4 there). Feiwel visited Mannheim in Jan. 1903 (see Feiwel to W., 22 Jan. 1903, W.A.). W. was invited by Isaac Mamlock in May 1903 to address a meeting in Strasbourg on behalf of the Kishinev victims (see Mamlock to W., 15 May 1903, W.A.); he expected to fulfil the engagement in the second half of May, near the time of his visit to Munich (see n. 1 to No. 337), but there is no evidence that he did in fact do so—for W.'s intention to visit Strasbourg see Moses Weizmann to W., 16 (29) May 1903, W.A.

[8] For the visits of W. and Aberson to Lausanne and Berne at the beginning of 1903, see n. 5 to No. 251; No. 272 and n. 4 there; No. 280 and n. 1 there. Feiwel delivered an address in Berne at the beginning of Feb. 1903 (see *Hatzofe*, 27 Jan./ 9 Feb. 1903). Concerning the participation of Feiwel and Aberson in the debate with opponents of the University project held in Zurich in Feb. 1903, see No. 271 and n. 7 there. Aberson addressed the Jewish Students Society in Paris on the Democratic Fraction in April 1903 (see *L'Écho Sioniste* of 15 May 1903). W. visited Berlin on University matters in Aug. 1902, March 1903, and April 1903 (see Vol. I, Nos. 291–5; Nos. 292–4 *supra*, Nos. 307–8). Feiwel visited Berlin in March and May 1903 (see n. 1 to No. 292, and n. 6 *supra*).

[9] These titles relate to: *Jüdischer Almanach; Lieder des Ghetto*, by Morris Rosenfeld, translation from the Yiddish by Feiwel (see Vol. I, ns. 14, 15 to No. 238); *Die Judenmassacres in Kischinew*, by Feiwel (see n. 4 to No. 327 *supra*); *Jüdische Statistik* (see n. 9 to No. 396); *Junge Harfen* ('Young Harps'), an anthology of the work of contemporary Jewish poets, was edited by Feiwel and *Jüdische Künstler* ('Jewish Artists') by Buber, both being published in Berlin in 1903. The remaining two books mentioned were perhaps J. M. Judt's *Die Juden als Rasse* ('The Jews as a Race'), Berlin 1903, and a selection from the work of H. D. Nomberg, translated by Eliashev and Feiwel but never published. Both were announced by the *Jüdischer Verlag* in a list of future publications that appeared in *Junge Harfen*.

But from now on we assume no responsibility for others. From this point of view I am not concerned what happens to the Fraction.

It is also a matter of indifference to me how they treat us at the Congress. I am prepared for everything and will permit nothing to disturb me. It makes no difference to me moreover whether I am elected in Kharkov or not.

With kind regards from Feiwel and myself,

Your

Mr. Pokrassa,
  Kharkov.

405. To Ben-Zion Mossinson, Berne.[1] *Geneva, 8 July 1903*

Hebrew/Russian: H.W.: C.Z.A. A45/10a.

Geneva, 8 July.[2]

Comrade Ben-Zion Mossinson[3]

Dear Brother,

I am sending your letter to Ussishkin[4] back to you. I cannot send it to Mr. Ussishkin myself as I do not know his address. At the same time would you let me have Ussishkin's address in Palestine because I need it.[5]

Regarding the mimeograph, I have already written to Zurich so you will no doubt be receiving it soon,[6] as well as money. I have

405. [1] The orig. is in Hebrew except the passage below the signature, which is in Russian. It is in Stupnitzky's handwriting, with the exception of the salutation, the concluding 'Your affectionate friend Chaim Weizmann' and the postscript, all of which were written by W.

[2] Place and date in German in orig.

[3] This letter was in reply to Mossinson's communication of 11 Tammuz 5663 (6 July 1903), W.A. Mossinson enclosed a letter he had written Ussishkin and asked W. to amend it as necessary (see n. 4 *infra*). He also suggested that W. ask Ussishkin, then in Palestine, to inquire into the possibilities of establishing the University there.

[4] See Mossinson to Ussishkin, 11 Tammuz 5663 (6 July 1903) C.Z.A., A24/125. Mossinson informed Ussishkin that he had joined the University Bureau (see n. 1 to No. 398). He explained that the reaction by Jewish students of Russian origin to the pogrom in Kishinev had strengthened his conviction that a Jewish University was imperative: 'Things had reached the pass that our brothers and sisters would take an interest in the matter only if, God forbid, the Kishinev event would not harm the Russian Revolution' (see also n. 5 to No. 383). Mossinson asked Ussishkin, on W.'s behalf, to ascertain the possibility of setting up the University in Palestine.

[5] See No. 402 and ns. 2, 3 there.

[6] In his letter of 11 Tammuz 5663 (6 July 1903) Mossinson asked W. to write to Zurich 'and insist that they hasten to return the mimeograph to me, because until I get it I shall not be able . . . to prepare the circular letters' (concerning the proposed circular see n. 1 to No. 398).

sent part through our friend Mr. Becker,[7] and you will get the rest as soon as we receive the money they sent us from London.[8] As for the books of the *Jüdischer Verlag*, we shall send them to you as soon as we have the chance.[9] I do not possess these books just now. With regard to your proposal about Ussishkin,[10] we are in complete agreement with you and I shall also be writing to him one of these days,[5] but nevertheless may I request you to do as you said and write to him yourself.

Respectfully and with Zion's greetings,

Your affectionate friend,
Chaim Weizmann.

I like the letter to Ussishkin. It can go as it is.

406. To Alfred Nossig, Berlin.[1] *Geneva, 8 July 1903*

German: Or. Copy. T.W.: W.A.

8th. July 03.

Dear Dr. [Nossig],

Today we posted off 250 marks to you. We really could not send more in our present financial situation. On the other hand we shall be able to do rather better in the autumn.[2]

Would you please inform me by telegram of the date of your

---

[7] See No. 400 and n. 2 there.

[8] In a notice to the University Bureau of 2 July 1903 (W.A.), the Jewish Colonial Trust stated that, at Herzl's request, instructions had been given to remit the sum of 1,500 francs to the Bureau (see also No. 390).

[9] In his letter of 11 Tammuz 5663 (6 July 1903) Mossinson asked that the latest publications of the *Jüdischer Verlag* be sent to him (see n. 9 to No. 404) so that he might be active on its behalf in Berne.

[10] See n. 3 *supra*.

406. [1] The letter was in reply to Nossig's communication of 3 July 1903 (W.A.). Nossig wrote that he was in financial difficulties owing to the considerable expenditure he had incurred in producing *Jüdische Statistik*, published on behalf of the Jewish Statistical Association (see n. 9 to No. 396), and that the *Jüdischer Verlag* had not kept its promise to help raise the required funds. Consequently, Nossig announced, he could go to Paris only if W. sent him the sum necessary, 280–300 marks (concerning the intention to visit Paris see No. 375; n. 2 to No. 386). Nossig added that he proposed calling another meeting of the Berlin Jewish University Committee prior to his departure for Paris.

[2] Apparently a reference to the possibility of granting a loan to the Jewish Statistical Association (cf. n. 1 *supra*). Concerning W.'s promise to lend the Association 500 roubles see No. 335 and n. 2 there.

arrival in Paris, dear Doctor, and the hotel where you will be staying. Is there still to be a meeting of the Committee?

Till we meet again soon, with kind regards,

Your

Dr. Alfred Nossig,
  Berlin.

407. To the Jewish Colonial Trust, London. *Geneva, 10 July 1903*

German: Or. Copy. T.W.: W.A.

10 July 1903.

To the Jewish Colonial Trust,
London.

We acknowledge herewith receipt of 1,500 francs (fifteen hundred)[1] through Messrs. S. D. & E. Cohen in Paris.

Yours faithfully,

408. To Ben-Zion Mossinson, Berne. *Geneva, 10 July 1903*

German/Russian: T.W./H.W.: C.Z.A. A45/10a.

Geneva, 10 July 03.
Rue Lombard 4.

Dear Friend Mossinson,

Thank you for your prompt and efficient handling of our affairs. I find the circular[1] perfectly in order so far; I would just like to add these sentences for the sake of clarity:

'We hope to implement the project as follows: we shall seek to bring the Jewish department linked with General Studies to realisation in Palestine only. We anticipate no problems in this regard; on the other hand there seem at present to be many difficulties

---

407. [1] See n. 8 to No. 405.

408. [1] See Mossinson's stencilled circular, undated, C.Z.A., A45/16. The circular explains the need for the Jewish University, provides information on the activities planned by the Bureau at Geneva and requests financial support. The circular also includes the additional passage as W. asked, though in a slightly different formulation. Mossinson sent the circular to Zionist societies and a number of Zionist and non-Zionist friends in Russia (see Mossinson to W., 3 Ab 5663 (27 July 1903) W.A.).

in establishing the Technical department in Palestine. Should the establishment of such a department indeed prove impossible, we shall proceed with its temporary realisation abroad. We shall always be guided in this by the principle that the school should be constructed in *Golus* in such a manner that it would always be capable of transfer; its foundation can only be begun in Palestine. Naturally, we shall give all these problems our most earnest consideration.'

Tomorrow evening I am going to Paris, and next week I shall be in Berne. If you do not receive the mimeograph machine by today[2] it would be preferable for you to have the circulars hectographed. Please see that the letters are not too bulky, dear friend. Put them into envelopes of various colours and do not send them all by the same post.[3] Send them registered for the more important people.

With kindest regards,

> Your
> Ch. Weizmann

P.S.[4]

I have no National Fund stamps. I have paid their value.[5]

409. To Morris Rosenfeld, Yonkers. *Geneva, 10 July 1903*

Yiddish: Or. Copy. H.W.: W.A.

10. VII. 03.

Dear Sir,

Mr. Feiwel has informed us of your communication[1] to him concerning the University. We thank you cordially for all you have so far done for the cause. We regard it as a great honour, and we are very happy that you take such an interest in this important

---

[2] See No. 405 and n. 6 there.
[3] W. evidently feared confiscation of the circulars by the Russian censor.
[4] In Russian in W.'s handwriting.
[5] In his letter of 11 Tammuz 5663 (6 July 1903) (W.A.), Mossinson asked W. to affix a Jewish National Fund stamp on all letters sent to him. These stamps represented a voluntary contribution to the Fund—see No. 112 and n. 5 there.

409. [1] Not found.

and idealistic enterprise. It is a great pity that we [had] no news from you prior to the time your articles appeared.[2] We hope, however, to catch up on what we have missed.

From now on we [would like] you to [address] all your correspondence regarding the University to our 'Jewish University Bureau', and we can assure you of always receiving a prompt reply.

Furthermore, we wish only to repeat our request that you continue the propaganda effort you have begun in our interest. It would be excellent if you could write another article in the *Yiddishe Welt*. We are enclosing herewith our letter to the editor and this can serve as an introduction for your article.

With regard to the progress of our endeavour we are able to report some im[portant] and gratifying facts: we have managed to win over a large number of Jewish professors and scholars in Germany. In Berlin, for example, our committee includes such notable professors as Landau, the well-known [medical expert]; Prof. Warburg, who founded the settlements in Anatolia;[3] Dr. Alfred Nossig; national economist Franz Oppenheimer; Meyerhoffer, the Prof. of [Chemistry] at Berlin University, and others.

This committee is now engaged in preparing a plan [----] the University,[4] and we hope to publish it after the Congress. Meanwhile, the Bureau has concluded an important and interesting *enquête* on the position of Jewish students in which the [----] for the importance of a [Jewish] University emerge. Our Jewish intelligentsia are finding it increasingly difficult to pursue their studies and must therefore assimilate among strangers. Economic and cultural needs grow ever greater.

The vast majority of students have expressed their sympathies for the plan.[5] We shall still publish the statistical findings in

[2] Refers to articles by Rosenfeld on the Jewish University project—see his 'A Jewish University', published in *Die Yiddishe Welt/The Jewish World* of 8 Jan. 1903. Rosenfeld expressed enthusiastic support for the plan, about which he had learned from the brochure *Eine Jüdische Hochschule*. Possibly he was also the author of an unsigned article, 'Propaganda for a Jewish University', in *Die Yiddishe Welt* of 2 July 1903. This dealt with the work of the Jewish University Bureau in Geneva, particularly W.'s efforts on behalf of the project, and was apparently based on information taken from the report of the Bureau published in May 1903 (see n. 1 to No. 311).

[3] Three agricultural settlements for Jewish refugees from Rumania were established in Anatolia during 1900–1 at the initiative of Otto Warburg, who hoped that some 100,000 Jews could be settled in agriculture there (see Warburg, Jüdische Ackerbau–Kolonien in Anatolien, *Palästina* i, 2 (1902), pp. 66–71).

[4] See n. 2 to No. 382; n. 1 to No. 393.

[5] Feiwel's article on the survey in *Jüdische Statistik*, p. 253: 'More than one-half of those canvassed declared that they favoured the plan to establish a Jewish University.'

advance of the Congress,[6] and this will constitute the first research ever to be completed on the situation of our youth.

Also prior to the Congress we [shall be] seeking the interest of Jewish scholars and well-known personalities in Paris and Brussels.

Broadly speaking, the plan now being scientifically prepared in all its details by the experts[7] is as follows: to inaugurate the department of General and Jewish Studies in Palestine, and the Technical department in Western Europe. We shall therefore investigate the possibilities for an establishment in Palestine[8] immediately after the Congress. As for the Technical department in Europe, we hope to initiate this as soon as possible after receiving the recommendations of the Berlin Committee.[9] When a beginning has been made with at least one department, the task will proceed much more smoothly. Ultimately our plan is of course to combine both parts in Palestine, giving them an authentically Jewish basis.

Following on the Congress we hope to launch a major propaganda effort in England, and later in America. [We] have also got to have [our own] periodical through which to interest West European Jews in Jewish cultural problems and the University. This journal will appear monthly, and we have already won over the best Jewish writers for it.[10]

We require money for all these purposes: a commission for Palestine; [----] of the Bureau; the journal; travelling. These are all very expensive items. We have already [---- ---- found in Russia].[11] But the destruction of Kishinev did a great deal of harm to our project. As you are aware, little can be done among the [Jews] of Western Europe. We have therefore been long considering [----] knocking on the gates of America. It is probable that one or both of [us], Feiwel and Weizmann, will later visit America. But in the meantime [---- ----] we must do the work and money is urgently required. We could produce positive results with from five to seven thousand dollars. Some of this may be found at the Congress, but we are not very hopeful. One finds the minimum of sympathy

---

[6] I.e., a final summing-up of the results of the student survey (see n. 4 to No. 362).

[7] Probably refers to the discussions of the Berlin Committee.

[8] Eliashev was due to investigate this matter prior to the Congress, but his visit to Palestine did not take place (see No. 362 and n. 9 there).

[9] In fact most members of the Committee held the view that only a *Realgymnasium*, and not a technical school or department, should be set up in the first stage— see n. 1 to No. 393.

[10] For writers who had contributed to the first issue of *Der Jude*, or had promised to do so, see n. 6 to No. 311. L. Jellinek agreed to edit the bibliographical section of the periodical—see Buber to Feiwel, undated (? 7 June 1903), W.A. No. 31/0, 5.

[11] Probably the money promised W. in Lodz and Warsaw (see n. 4 to No. 301) but not collected owing to the fund-raising campaigns on behalf of the Kishinev victims.

for cultural purposes there, and so we place our greatest hope in America.

We believe that sympathetic articles and other publicity on your part, together with our own personal propaganda efforts, would help. You yourself write that you can do great things. You may perhaps be able to establish contacts for yourself and for us with writers of note, and with scholars and good [Jews] in general in [America]. We are as yet unfamiliar with the situation there, though you of course know yourself what needs [to be done] there.

We would be most grateful if, in your reply, you let us know how one can conduct propaganda also among the non-Russian Jews of America, what else is possible there, and the methods, etc., to be employed. It is a pity you cannot come to the Congress, but during the period October–November we hope to make it possible for you to come to Europe.

Feiwel and Buber will be in touch with literary circles in Vienna, Berlin, Frankfurt, Cracow and Lemberg to arrange a lecture tour, for which we hope not only to cover the expenses but even to make a small profit.

We very much look forward to your speedy reply.[12]

Most respectfully, and with kind regards.

Berthold Feiwel   Dr. Chaim Weizmann

410. To Vera Khatzman, Hilterfingen. *Paris, 13 July 1903*

Russian: Pcd. H.W.: W.A.

13. VII. 03, Hôtel Bergère.

Dear Verochka,

I start my canvassing today—tramping from 'Jew to Jew'.[1]

---

[12] Replying to this letter and one from Feiwel not found, Rosenfeld wrote Feiwel on 26 July 1903 (W.A.) that he intended publishing more articles on the Jewish University, and generally to do his utmost to bring it to the attention of the Jewish public in the United States. He hoped to interest his friend Seligman (Edwin Seligman, Professor of Political Economy and Finance at Columbia University) in the project. Rosenfeld asserted that money was obtainable in the U.S.A. for this purpose, but caution was necessary because 'one false step can spoil everything'. Rosenfeld expressed doubt as to W.'s suggestion that he undertake a lecture tour in Europe. Rosenfeld feared his earnings would be inadequate to support him during such a tour.

410. [1] W. and Nossig met representatives of the *Alliance Israélite Universelle* and Jewish Colonization Association in Paris, and requested their assistance in setting

I shall leave for Geneva tomorrow evening, I think. Nossig and I have thrashed everything out very thoroughly, and now I hope that 'things' will take a turn for the better. I am very glad that you have settled in nicely; I shall come to you very soon.[2]

I wrote to your relative[3] and shall go to see him as soon as I hear from him.

I kiss you lovingly.

Your Chaim

Regards to all.

411. To Vera Khatzman,[1] Hilterfingen. *Geneva, 15 July 1903*

Russian: Pcd. H.W.: W.A.

Geneva, 15. VII. 03.
Rue Lombard, 4

Dear Children,

I arrived from Paris today. Tomorrow I leave for Zurich and will see you on Friday.

up the University as well as a Jewish secondary school (concerning the plan for the secondary school see No. 393 and n. 1 there). In a second draft, in Hebrew, of the brochure *Eine Jüdische Hochschule* and titled *A Hebrew University* (see n. 4 to No. 420) it was stated that W. and Nossig had succeeded in 'interesting [the *Alliance*] in the idea and it has promised to study the matter and give it maximum support. The leaders of the Association (I.C.A.) also promised to support the institution . . .' It appears, however, that these discussions dealt mainly with assistance in setting up the secondary school (see Warburg to *Jüdischer Verlag*, 15 July [1903], W.A.; Nossig to W., 17 July 1903, W.A.). It is not clear whom W. met in Paris; on 28 July 1903 he wrote Mossinson: 'I saw a large number of professors there' (see No. 414), and it is most likely that he also met the Chief Rabbi of France, Zadoc Kahn, who was Honorary President of the *Alliance Israélite Universelle* and a member of the I.C.A. Council (see Nossig to W., 8 July 1903, W.A.). After W. returned to Switzerland, Nossig met Sonnenfeld, one of the I.C.A. directors, who evinced his readiness to help establish the secondary school. Nossig also tried unsuccessfully to enlist the interest of the archaeologist and historian Salomon Reinach, Vice-President of the Central Committee of the *Alliance Israélite Universelle* and a member of the I.C.A. Council (see Nossig to W., 17 July 1903, 16 July 1902, W.A.). See also No. 420.

[2] In addition to V.K., those staying at Hilterfingen, the resort on Lake Thun in the Bernese Oberland, at that time included Moses Weizmann (W.'s brother), Chaim Fialkov (W.'s uncle), Maria, Henrik, and Florian Sokolow (children of Nahum S.) and Anna (Nyusya) Ratnovskaya.

[3] Refers to Solomon (Monia) Fluxman, brother of V.K.'s mother, who was then living in Paris. W.'s letter to him has not been found.

411. [1] The postcard was sent to V.K. but was addressed, in part, also to W.'s other friends and relatives then on holiday at Hilterfingen (see n. 2 to No. 410).

Verchik, don't fret. Everything will be all right when I come back. I am bringing the little machines[2] with me.

I kiss you lovingly,

Chaim

No Aberson and no book![3]

412. To Kalman Marmor, Unterseen.[1] *Hilterfingen,* *20 July 1903*

Yiddish: Pcd. H.W.: Marmor Papers, Yivo Archives, New York.

20. VII. 03.

Dear Marmor,

Stupnitzky has forwarded your postcard[2] on to me and it filled me with amazement and pain. I do not wish to write too much about it; as we are neighbours would you kindly visit me here. Feiwel will also be here. I think it is not more than an hour's journey by steamer. I await your reply.

Adieu, your Chaim Weizmann

Hilterfingen (also Oberhofen) care of Miss Karlen[3]

413. To Kalman Marmor, Unterseen. *Hilterfingen,* *25 July 1903*

Yiddish: H.W.: Marmor Papers, Yivo Archives, New York.

Hilterfingen, 25. VII. 03.

Dear friend Marmor,

I received your letter yesterday afternoon[1] and in reply wish to

---

[2] Reference obscure.

[3] Refers to the edited version of Aberson's address to the Zionist Youth Conference in Dec. 1901 on 'The Attitude of Zionism to Existing Trends in Jewry'. See also Vol. I, n. 1 to No. 225; No. 129 *supra*; No. 350 and n. 3 there.

412. [1] Marmor, who was then living in London, came to Switzerland in June 1903 for convalescence and in order to take part in the Sixth Zionist Congress scheduled to be held in Basle in August. He was in Geneva in the second half of June (see n. 3 to No. 386; No. 413 and ns. 5, 24 there).

[2] The postcard has not been found. Doubtless it contained criticism of W. in the spirit of Marmor's letter of 23 July 1903 (see n. 1 to No. 413).

[3] The address is in Latin characters in the original.

413. [1] Marmor to W., 23 July 1903 (W.A.). Marmor wrote, *inter alia*, that he opposed

tell you the plain truth, whereby I hope to dispel your doubts and destroy the false opinions that you are nurturing.

In the first place, I am very grateful for your candour; it is such a rare quality among our Zionists and I am always glad to find someone who will tell me even unpleasant things to my face. One gentle introduction, dear Mr. Marmor: you only know me a little and I can produce nothing except my goodwill and good intentions, as well as my Zionist past, in my defence. I have been in our movement for some ten to twelve years, and so far as I am aware I have never been of that large mass which pursues petty glories or petty means,[2] nor tawdry laurels or ephemeral success. I am prepared to swim against the tide and do battle with the will of the majority in the search for truth, because it is my conviction that any false note creeping into the movement is mortally dangerous, causing it to degenerate and die. I have never wavered[3] in this vital principle and never shall! . . . I never chased after praise from *Hamelitz* nor after a seat on the Actions Committee. You know very well how *Hamelitz* and similar journals have made my life bitter;[4] you know very well that I wrote to our leader with the blood of my very weak heart.[5] You have yourself ascertained

the Democratic Fraction because it did not have a homogeneous character, but he was ready to go along with its most active leaders and had even sought to secure their election in London as delegates to the Sixth Zionist Congress (see n. 3 to No. 386). He expressed his astonishment that efforts on behalf of Fraction candidates in England had not won the support of W. or his colleagues; that they had not repudiated allegations of their having been a party to a declaration (relating to Kishinev) by anti-nationalist students in Berne (see n. 36 *infra*), and that they had not declared that their tactics were based on an issue of principle rather than against Herzl personally, and that furthermore they did not support Ahad Ha'am against Nordau. (The *Shivat-Zion* Society in London refused to vote for the Fraction candidates proposed to it in view of a rumour that the Fraction intended demonstrating at Congress against the Zionist leadership and Nordau—see Delovitch to Marmor, 1 July 1903, Marmor Papers, Yivo, New York. Concerning the Ahad Ha'am–Nordau controversy, see ns. 10, 11 to No. 292.) Marmor spoke of his surprise at the news that W. had received a neutral mandate in Leeds (see below). He had lately heard from (Jacob) Rabinovich that W. had become 'neutral social-politically', a sympathizer with the *Mizrahi* and an enemy of the Democratic Fraction (see further and n. 27 *infra*). 'In consequence,' he went on, 'I had been waiting patiently to see you a member of the Actions Committee, Director of the Jewish Colonial Trust . . . elected with the support of speeches by Avinovitzky and ardent articles in the *Express* (cf. n. 34 *infra*) and *Hamelitz*.' Marmor noted that his fears had been strengthened by the reported cancellation of the Fraction Conference (see No. 403), but, he added, he hoped to obtain explanations from W. that would persuade him that his negative impression was baseless.

[2] In orig.: ‏קליינע מיטטעלן און קליינע טיטעלן‎.
[3] The words 'I have never wavered' were added above the line.
[4] Concerning articles in *Hamelitz* hostile to W. and his group, see Vol. I, No. 137 and n. 3 there; n. 1 to No. 140; n. 6 to No. 156.
[5] W. had apparently shown Marmor a copy of his memorandum to Herzl dated 6 May 1903 (No. 316) when Marmor visited Geneva in the latter half of June 1903.

how ruthlessly people fought against me, and against the causes for which I spent myself. It has necessitated travelling from townlet to townlet, city to city, sometimes being stuck in railway coaches among strangers, many of them hostile, for three to four months of the year.

Should you not be aware of this, permit me to stress that I have been devoting almost all of my strength and effort[6] exclusively to the movement for some three to four years now. No day goes by without my working for at least six hours for Zionism, in addition to the interminable propaganda tours,[7] in addition to contending with 'comrades' and opponents. And in all these activities I would always declare my position clearly and without equivocation, stating frankly whatever was in my heart.

I cannot fully understand how you have come to your doubts, but for the sake of the truth[8] I shall do all I can to explain things to you.

1) FRACTION. You know very well, and it seems that I made it clear to you in our discussion, that the present state of the Fraction is unsatisfactory. Being one of the sources of all evil,[9] and one of those who helped to build and establish the Fraction, I would be the first to say that it cannot and ought not continue to exist in its present form. Why? Because to date the Fraction has hardly achieved even one of the objectives it took upon itself; because it has not as yet properly defined its programme;[10] because the theoretical work which it was to have accomplished still remains but a figment of the theoreticians' imagination; because in the field of propaganda and organisation it has not achieved a twentieth part of what it could have achieved; in brief, because most of the 'activists' in the Fraction were asleep when they should have been in the vanguard.

A few people did actually work, but only as 'individuals'. And they were the ones to carry the responsibility for a failure to work on the part of the others. As a consequence, the small band of workers encountered enmity both within the ranks of the faithless

---

[6] Hebr. in orig.: ‏ראשית כחי וראשית אוני‏: cf. Genesis 49:3.

[7] The reference is to W.'s propaganda tours in Russia in the summers of 1901 and 1902 as well as to his numerous visits to university cities in Switzerland and Germany (see ns. 7, 8 to No. 404).

[8] Hebr. in orig.: ‏בשם האמת‏.

[9] ‏אבות הטומאה‏ in orig.

[10] The Democratic Fraction programme was framed by the Programme Committee in June 1902 (see Vol. I, bridge-note following No. 298), but W. proposed that it be re-examined, and he included the issue in the agenda of the cancelled Fraction Conference (see Nos. 352, 362). Buber also demanded that the programme be revised (see Buber to W. and Feiwel, 12 June 1903, W.A.).

Fraction members as well as among the other Zionist groups. The Fraction existed only in the maligning speeches of our dear 'comrades', and in the mind of the Actions Committee as it waged warfare against us. Feiwel, Buber and a few others together with myself had always to be in the front line. There is no organisation and we are responsible for the stupidity of others, none of whom gives us any support. Kohan-Bernstein cries that the Fraction does nothing.[11] Pokrassa in Kharkov, the gentlemen in Moscow, Rostov, etc., all of them cry that the Fraction does nothing.[12] Yet when I say to them: 'For goodness sake, children,[13] you too are Fraction members, where is your activity, what positive results can you claim ?' I receive no answer. On the other hand, we can demonstrate that all that has been done till now—University, statistics, *Jüdischer Verlag*, the periodical *Palästina*,[14] propaganda in Russia and abroad—was time and again undertaken by individuals whose number can be counted on the fingers of one hand.

Believe me, friend Marmor, I am not unaware that all was not done perfectly. I realise that we are open to criticism, but we have the right to say this: 'We have invested our sincerest intentions, the major part of our time and our best efforts, into what we have achieved'. Had there been more people there would have been more work with more positive result. Now, what did the small group gain from all this ? Nothing except beatings and abuse costing me three years of my life; but support—never! So what of the future ? All of us, and I am speaking in the name of our small group to which Nossig, Kohan-Bernstein and some others must be added, have reached the conclusion that a change must take place and order effected. A closely-knit, *active group* must be constituted, perhaps in the pattern of a Progressive League[15] as Kohan-Bernstein had proposed at the Youth Conference.[16] But for this we must be

---

[11] See No. 377 and n. 8 there. In an undated letter apparently written in the first half of July, Rothstein stated that Bernstein-Kohan 'reviled the Fraction everywhere' and that he had inveighed against it in a speech delivered in Rostov.

[12] For charges of inaction against the Fraction by Pokrassa in Kharkov and Idelson in Moscow, see n. 1 to No. 404; n. 1 to No. 384. As regards Rostov, W. may be alluding to Rothstein's report on 30 June (13 July) 1903 (W.A.) of anti-Fraction speeches heard at a Zionist meeting in Rostov, and of the failure of Fraction candidates to be returned at the elections to the Sixth Zionist Congress held there. And see also n. 11 *supra*.

[13] In orig.: גוואלד קינדער.

[14] For the Jewish Statistical Association of Berlin, see Vol. I, n. 7 to No. 204; for the *Jüdischer Verlag*, see Vol. I, n. 14 to No. 238; for the periodical *Palästina*, see n. 3 to No. 5 *supra*.

[15] Concerning the plan to establish an 'Action Group' or 'Working Group', see also No. 384 and n. 2 there.

[16] At the Zionist Youth Conference (Dec. 1901) J. Bernstein-Kohan had proposed

certain that we have the people, and are not operating in a vacuum. We dare not fail again. I believe we can constitute such working groups in the sense in which I spoke to you in Geneva[17] some time ago. A gathering of the 'Fraction' where we tell one another that nothing has been done would be pouring oil on the flames, to give delight to the 'Guardians of Israel'.[18] Consequently we active ones do not want such a gathering, and our view is shared by the Moscow members of the Fraction.[19] I know that there is fertile soil for a good, healthy movement in England and Russia, and long before your arrival in Geneva I was preparing to throw up everything that I have or do not have in Geneva, and go to America and England with a view to settling[20] in one of those countries for a few years.[21] Prior to the Congress we shall have a small gathering at which we shall discuss our tactics; after that our plans will depend upon the quality of the people available—this much, I think, is clear!

I now come to the subject of a social-political group, and to what has been said by Mr. Rabinovich,[22] among others. You are aware of our strained [relations] with Dr. Pasmanik,[23] of the deep personal bitterness, etc. As you yourself know, because I asked you to be the mediator,[24] it is my fervent desire to put an end to the public washing of dirty linen. Wherever we can we ought to work hand-in-hand, and for the rest let each proceed along his separate course. At the delegates' Conference in Fribourg[25] I had an open and honest exchange of views with Pasmanik in the presence of Dr. Farbstein. Subsequently I received a letter from Dr. Farbstein in which he proposed that a plan be prepared with a view to

the formation of a youth organization to assume specific Zionist tasks without engaging in politics (see Protocol in W.A., Dec. 1901 box).

[17] In June 1903.

[18] Hebr.: שומרי ישראל—here used ironically.The reference is apparently to Pinkus, Pasmanik and their group (cf. statement on 'guardians of Zion' in No. 389 and see No. 383 and n. 5 there).

[19] In fact differences existed between W. and Kroll and Idelson of the Democratic Fraction Centre in Moscow over the question of a Fraction Conference (see No. 384 and n. 1 there). On 7 July W. informed Idelson that he had decided against it 'for the reasons which you expressed in part in your last letter', but in effect Idelson had not suggested cancelling the Conference (see No. 401 and n. 4 there) nor has any letter from Idelson or Kroll been found in which their consent to this step was given afterwards.   [20] 'Settling'—Hebr. in orig.

[21] See Vol. I, No. 260.   [22] Jacob Rabinovich (see n. 1 *supra*).

[23] Concerning Pasmanik's opposition to the Zionist Youth Conference in 1901, see Vol. I, No. 134 and n. 5 there. In the summer of 1901 Pasmanik was one of the editors of the weekly *Zionistische Korrespondenz*, which published sharp attacks on the Fraction generally and W. in particular (see n. 5 to No. 383).

[24] This was probably discussed during Marmor's visit to Geneva in the second half of June 1903.

[25] The Swiss Zionist Conference on 28 June 1903.

organising a group whose primary intention would be to 'seek clarity on the territorial question' and to ensure that a clear colonisation policy would be laid down at this Congress: in short, the most important point in Zionism.[26] All sensible Zionists, irrespective of Party, are united on this. I replied verbally to Farbstein, in Dr. Pasmanik's presence, to the effect that I would be prepared, and in this I believe all our political friends would concur, to try and introduce clarity into the central issue of Zionism! I can say nothing about a social-political group until I know what it would involve. At all events, I have always emphasised that I cannot share the materialist outlook of Dr. Pasm[anik] and Dr. Farbstein. In a discussion on the Fraction with Pasmanik when Rabinovich was present I said exactly what I am now writing to you, and I said further that we would try and form serious, active groups. Regarding the *Mizrahi* I said that I was not concerned with them in any way, provided they did not seek to foist their image on the movement. This is my attitude and we shall continue speaking on these lines.[27]

In the course of our meeting in Geneva I referred to the question of culture, and voiced the opinion to you that the Congress must be principally concerned with a solution to the colonisation problem. Anything that might be accomplished in the cultural field will be buried in talk and argument. I did not discuss the Nordau–Ahad Ha'am affair[28] at all. You know the views of my friends and myself on this: we are opposed to Ahad Ha'am because he is not a political Zionist, but we consider Nordau's conduct reprehensible.

[26] Farbstein's letter has not been found. Cf. letter to Lichtenstein of 2 July (No. 396), in which W. said: 'Our battle-cry at this Congress must above all be a demand for clarity on the territorial question. . . .'

[27] Nothing more is known of W.'s contacts with Pasmanik and Farbstein in the summer of 1903. There had already been talk the previous winter of setting up a group which would place a solution to the question of settlement in Palestine at the forefront of its demands (see No. 176 and n. 2 there; concerning the slogan 'clarity on the territorial question' see also n. 81 to No. 316). The substance of the 'social-political' tendency which Pasmanik and Farbstein wished to attribute to the group may be gauged from 'The Social Politics of Zionism', an article which Pasmanik published in *Zionistische Korrespondenz* of 26 June 1903. This stated that Zionism must aspire to a normalization of the economic life and social structure of the Jewish people, the achievement of which could only occur within a cohesive Jewish community established in Palestine and its environs. From this it is evident that Pasmanik regarded a solution to the settlement problem as a prior condition to the attainment of the social aims of Zionism. Similar views were expressed by Farbstein in an article which he published in *Die Welt* of Dec. 1901 (issues of 20 Dec. 1901 and 27 Dec. 1901). As for the 'materialistic outlook' of Pasmanik and Farbstein, see for example the draft of Pasmanik's article 'Culture and Zionism' (1901) in C.Z.A. A186/2, and also Farbstein's article mentioned above.

[28] See ns. 10, 11 to No. 292 concerning the controversy stirred by Nordau's reaction to Ahad Ha'am's criticism of Herzl's *Altneuland*.

We are similarly opposed to *Altneuland,* but we will not raise the issue at the Congress. However, if others attack us we shall defend ourselves. We consider it important to react in this way, because the prestige of the Congress is valuable to us all, for it stands above everything.

I believe I have clarified everything to the best of my knowledge and in all conscience. I have not changed a single word of anything we discussed at that time.

Some final observations: we shall be seeing each other to talk things over personally, but I ask you now to understand my mood exactly. I know that nothing came of El-Arish,[29] but I see how they fight us and I have reached the conclusion that the leaders are taking the wrong path. I would like to cry out with all my heart: 'This is not the way!'[30] I am convinced that all those with their eyes open and who are neither blind fanatics nor claque-Zionists with their 'hear, hears'[31] at the spurious gatherings in London, will join their voices to mine. I feel that we are descending into the slime, heaven protect us,[32] with everything in jeopardy.

Ever since I learned, some two weeks ago, that absolutely nothing came of El-Arish, my mind has refused to rest with wondering how to prepare for the Congress, and by what means.[33] I see how our small group commands insufficient strength to defend itself against all attacks, so that the bitter thought frequently comes to my mind—and it poisons my life—that everything recorded in my Zionist past will have to be erased. It is a painful experience for us, after so many years of effort, to become enveloped in so desperate a mood. Naturally we shall go on searching, ever searching, for people, and strive to establish relationships. I hope all goes well.

As for the campaign of defamation launched by the gentlemen of the *Express,*[34] you may believe me when I say that I have never

---

[29] For the negotiations for Jewish settlement in the El-Arish region, see n. 5 to No. 308; n. 4 to No. 396.   [30] לא זה הדרך—Hebr. in orig.

[31] English in orig. In his letter of 23 July 1903, Marmor said of the English Zionist leaders Joseph Cowen and Leopold Greenberg: 'They are incapable of organizing even ten people and consequently they display their bravery towards the common people, who do not understand their English language but merely shout "hear, hear", or applaud at every pause.'   [32] אל תפתח פה לשטן in orig.

[33] See No. 396 and n. 4 there.

[34] In his letter of 23 July 1903, Marmor stated that the English Zionist Federation and the weekly newspaper *Yiddisher Express* were bitterly opposed to the election of the Democratic Fraction candidates in England (see n. 3 to No. 386 and also n. 37 *infra*). See the article 'To the Sixth Congress' in the *Yiddisher Express* of 1 July 1903, wherein the author warned Zionist Societies in England against electing candidates of the Democratic Fraction to the Sixth Congress and claimed that the Fraction 'aimed at destroying Herzl's authority'. The article further stated that it had to

read the paper. I consider one of my strong points to be that I do not read the so-called Press, heaven help us![35] I do know, however, that the people in Berne have replied. I think they sent their answer off a long time ago. Honestly, I had much more important things to do than pay attention to such nonsense and filth.[36]

Please do not spread my personal remarks around. Zionism will always be sacred to us, but in my view Zionism as it is lived today is but a profanation of the idea. Write when you are coming. Feiwel is likely to be here on Monday. Things are not at their best with me, but nothing can be done about it.

The London Federation will only court disgrace by its decision.[37] Oh yes, about the mandate from Leeds. A gentleman named Fried offered it to me and he informed me that this society is neither Fraction nor *Mizrahi*, but is composed of ordinary Zionists.[38] I said that naturally I was able to accept a neutral mandate and I proposed Nossig. I have the moral right to accept it not so much because the mandate is *neutral*, but because it does *not belong to the opposition*, and furthermore the gentleman who wrote to *me* knew very well who I was.[39]

Now, take care of yourself and keep well.

Your Chaim Weizmann

be established that any delegate 'aiding the Fraction in its condemnation of Nordau' would be regarded as committing a betrayal of the Zionist movement. See also n. 1 *supra*. [35] Hebr. in orig.: רחמנא יצילנו.

[36] An allusion to the meeting on 5 and 6 May 1903 of the Russian student colony in Berne (largely Jewish) held in protest against the Kishinev pogrom—see n. 1 *supra*. The meeting refused to carry Chaim Khissin's motion that moneys collected for the victims be transmitted through the Russian Jewish newspaper *Voskhod*, nor would it endorse A. M. Borukhov's motion that the meeting express 'its feeling of solidarity with those of our brethren who grieve over the Kishinev event as a national disaster'. The text of the declaration adopted by the meeting is not known, but a *Hamelitz* dispatch of 6/19 June 1903 spoke of 'the decision of the "Russian colony" in Berne to contribute towards the welfare of the people plundered in Kishinev, though not as "Jews" but as "people" '. See also *Hatzofe* of 4/17 May 1903. In an article signed 'Yizrael' (Eliezer Leizerovich), which appeared in the *Yiddisher Express* of 8 July 1903, reference was made to this meeting with an implication that members of the Fraction supported the resolution as adopted. Marmor sent this article to W. together with his letter of 23 July 1903.

[37] In his 23 July 1903 letter, Marmor wrote that after W., Feiwel, and Aberson had been nominated in London for the Sixth Congress (see n. 3 to No. 386), the English Zionist Federation decided not to approve the candidacy of 'foreign' delegates (i.e., non-residents of Great Britain or the British Empire—see also the circular of the E.Z.F. of 15 July 1903, W.A.). In spite of the Federation's decision, all three were elected on 19 July 1903 by the 'Herzl–Nordau' Society in London—see letter from the Society of 21 July 1903, W.A.

[38] See L. Fried (Secretary of the Zionist Society in Leeds) to W., 3 July 1903, W.A.

[39] In his reply of 3 Ab (27 July 1903), Marmor said: 'I am once more convinced that your conscience is clear and that all your actions have been inspired by a noble desire for truth and justice.'

414.　To　Ben-Zion　Mossinson,　Berne.　*Hilterfingen,*
28 July 1903

Russian: H.W.: C.Z.A. A45/10a.

Hilterfingen, 28. VII. 03.

Friend Mossinson,

I have not written to you because there was nothing special to write about. Besides, I was so very tired that I wanted at least two weeks rest after the terrible days I have recently been living through.[1]

Nossig and I sounded out the situation in Paris. There are possibilities,[2] and we shall have to return this autumn. But we must first decide upon our tactics vis-a-vis I.C.A. and the *Alliance,* both of whom are sure to support us. I met a large number of professors in Paris, and they were all very sympathetic.

Zionism generally is *schwach.*[3] El-Arish *came to nothing.*[4] It all fell through. We are facing a ban in Russia.[5]

The information given in *Novosti* is *for the present untrue.*[6] The

414. [1] In the letter to W. of 3 Ab (27 July 1903), W.A., Mossinson complained that he was receiving no information from the University Bureau and that W. and Feiwel had not visited him as promised.

[2] See No. 410 and n. 1 there.

[3] The Yiddish term ('debilitated') in Cyrillic script in orig.

[4] See n. 4 to No. 396.

[5] Rumours were already circulating in June 1903 of the imminent proscription of Zionism in Russia—see, e.g., Belkovsky to Kokesch, 22 (?) June 1903, C.Z.A., Z1/231; Sokolow to W., 30 June 1903, W.A.; and see also n. 4 to No. 402. Indeed, early in July the Russian Ministry of Interior ordered the heads of district and local authorities to impose far-reaching restrictions on Zionist activity, although these could not be construed as a complete ban on Zionism, as Zionist circles had feared. In a secret circular dated 24 June (7 July) 1903, signed by von Plehve and Lopukhin, 'Governors, Mayors and chiefs of police' were ordered to forbid Zionist propaganda 'in public places and meetings which have a public character', and also to prohibit the activity of Zionist organizations 'in so far as these assume an open public form'. Similarly forbidden were Zionist fund-raising campaigns not authorized by the Government and the sale of shares and securities by the Jewish Colonial Trust. The circular also stated that it was necessary 'to maintain supervision' over Jewish cultural institutions conducted by Zionists and that 'Jewish schools . . . under Zionist direction must not assume the character of institutions favouring the segregation of Russian Jewry'. The circular explained that the Russian Government had no reason to oppose Zionist activity so long as its principal purpose was to encourage emigration to Palestine, but of late this activity had been directed 'to the development and consolidation of the Jewish national idea'. This tendency was hostile to the assimilation of the Jews and contradicted the 'foundations of the Russian national concept', and consequently could not be tolerated. (See original text of circular in C.Z.A., Z3/866.) In the event the new restrictions were only partially imposed.

[6] In his 3 Ab (27 July 1903) letter to W., Mossinson wrote that 'the ban on Zionism' had been published in *Hamelitz,* and he feared lest it would also affect the work of the University Bureau. *Hamelitz* of 10/23 July 1903 had quoted a report in the St. Petersburg daily paper *Novosti* to the effect that an order had been received in

affair is being investigated at the moment, and is so far unresolved.
I shall be in Berne soon.

I feel worse than rotten.

Your Chaim.

415. To Nahum Sokolow, Warsaw. *Hilterfingen, 31 July 1903*

German: H.W.: C.Z.A. A18/13/9.

Geneva, Rue Lombard 4
At present in Hilterfingen (Bernese Oberland), 31. VII. 03.

Dear Friend,

Please excuse my not writing for so long. It was very difficult
for me. I did not wish to confront you saddened in spirit, or perhaps
weighed down by gloomy introspection. I was waiting for 'better
times'. Now the times are calmer again, and more clear—so you
see I am writing again.

First of all, please accept my heartiest congratulations on the
success of your plan.[1] I cherish the hope that you will complete this
great task splendidly, for it will constitute your life's work; that
you will bring vitality to our language, of which you are the master,
and widen its horizons; and that you will do the same for our
scholarship. Manya, Henya, Flor,[2] all of whom are staying in this
house with me, have told me everything, and I am pleased beyond
words.

We are busily preparing for the Congress. We are still not sure
about our tactics—there has been so much ground for bitter complaint. This is not merely the dissatisfaction of an 'opposition',
as some people seek to represent it. We are deeply convinced that
unless we rise to the occasion at this Congress with responsible
actions, our cause will go under. If I had to make really positive
proposals, they would concentrate on these main issues of our
movement:

1) Territorial question.[3] Diplomacy is not a subject for debate,

Ekaterinoslav from the Minister of Interior 'forbidding Zionist meetings and the
collection of money for the Zionists'. It appears that W. still knew nothing at that
time of the instructions issued by the Russian Ministry of Interior (see n. 5 *supra*)
and believed that the report was untrue; cf. No. 417 and n. 6 there.

415. [1] Sokolow's plan to publish a Universal Encyclopaedia in Hebrew and about
which he had addressed the Fifth Zionist Congress (see 5 Z.C. Prot., pp. 421–2).
In mid July 1903 Sokolow stated that he had been promised the requisite finance
and he had begun to implement the project (see *Hatzefirah*, 3/16 July 1903). However,
the Encyclopaedia never saw the light.

[2] I.e., the Sokolow children Maria, Henrik, and Florian.

[3] See n. 81 to No. 316.

but it would be very desirable if some light were shed on this subject. No more would be required than for Herzl to talk with a few trustworthy, serious persons elected by the Congress. A more important question in my eyes, however, is the investigation of Palestine and the neighbouring countries. This should have served by now as the vital sinew of our movement but it has been completely neglected by us. It is utterly disgraceful that nothing at all has been done by Zionists in this direction. A responsible committee must be appointed and supplied with a budget—only then[4] would it be able to do its work effectively.[5]

2) Cultural questions. Jewish statistics, Jewish library in Jerusalem,[6] the establishment of several publishing houses.

3) Propaganda. The disgusting swindle of philanthropic Zionism (Hungary–Nordau!)[7] must be eradicated.[8] The entire propaganda effort needs to be carried out with appropriate earnestness, with new people drawn in. An end must be put to all the phrase-mongering and transparent theatricals, and in their place let us have the truth unadulterated. I have so much more to say but will leave it for when we meet again.

Manya tells me that you wish to bring me into the work for the E[ncyclopaedia].[9] I do not have to tell you that I am for it with all my heart and will be happy to place my scientific knowledge to the service of the cause. I am most grateful to you, and assure you that I am ready to work with the utmost conscientiousness. It would make me extraordinarily happy to use my specialist knowledge in a Jewish endeavour, if only once. I consider myself qualified (oh!) to collaborate; I have a sufficient knowledge of Hebrew to check a

[4] The words 'nur dann' (only then) added above the line.

[5] Colonization Committees had already been nominated at previous Congresses but they had not been given the requisite means and consequently undertook no substantial activities (see statement by Soskin at Sixth Congress—6 Z.C. Prot., p. 271). Late in July or early Aug. 1903, Pasmanik and Nossig proposed to the Smaller Actions Committee that a permanent Palestine Survey Committee be set up in Berlin with an adequate budget (see minutes of proceedings of Smaller Actions Committee on 8 Aug. 1903, C.Z.A., Z1/175; *Der Fraind*, 7/20 Aug. 1903; Nossig to W., 26 July 1903, W.A.).

[6] Refers to the National Library in Jerusalem founded by Joseph Hazanowitz (known as the Jewish National and Hebrew University Library from 1925). At that time the Library received limited financial support from the Zionist Organization, but its means were insufficient to cover even its modest needs and this deficiency retarded its development (see, e.g., *Der Fraind* of 27 June/10 July 1903).

[7] See No. 316 and n. 67 there.

[8] Hebr. in orig.: לֹא יִזָּכֵר וְלֹא יִפָּקֵד—'Let it be neither remembered nor numbered'.

[9] In a letter dated 29 July 1903 (W.A.), evidently not received by the time W. wrote the present letter, Sokolow stated that work had begun on the Encyclopaedia project (see n. 1 *supra*) and invited the co-operation of W., Feiwel, and Eliashev.

translation thoroughly. Naturally, I shall be able to write *only* in German, but I would always be prepared to check the Hebrew translation as well. I can most assuredly undertake *Chemistry, Physics* and *Mineralogy*. All branches of Chemistry (such as Technology, etc.), of course; Physics and Mineralogy only the general outlines (principal laws, classifications, etc.).

Again, many, many thanks and kindest regards from yours ever,

Chaim

416. To Vera Khatzman, Hilterfingen. *Lucerne, 3 August 1903*[1]

Russian: Pcd. H.W.: W.A.

Dear Verochka,

I stayed here overnight and am now leaving for Weggis. This evening I shall be in Winterthur and tomorrow evening in Geneva. Don't grieve, dear girls, live in friendship. It upsets me to see you all sulking.[2]

I kiss you all affectionately.

Chaim.

417. To Vera Khatzman and Moses Weizmann, Hilterfingen. *Winterthur, 4 August 1903*

Russian: Pcd. H.W.: W.A.

Winterthur, 4/VIII 03.

Dear Verochka,

I am now leaving for Biel. I learned all I needed to know and examined everything carefully; the director gave me a great deal of information. It was all very useful. Actually, the visit to Biel is now no longer necessary, but I shall go there just the same.[1]

Jacobson and I talked all day yesterday and reached agreement on almost everything.[2] This evening I shall be in Lausanne and

416. [1] Date and place as given on postmark.

[2] For those staying with V.K. at Hilterfingen, see n. 2 to No. 410. The allusion here is obscure.

417. [1] W. visited the technical schools in Winterthur and Biel apparently to obtain information that would assist him in the planning of the Jewish University (see also No. 418).

[2] Victor Jacobson arrived in Switzerland at the end of July and remained until after the Sixth Zionist Congress. It appears from a later letter that he met Weizmann and Feiwel at Weggis and that they discussed ways to unify the Zionist opposition (see Jacobson to W., 22 Oct. (4 Nov.) 1903, W.A.). At this meeting W. presumably put forward his plan for the establishment of 'a league of freedom-loving Zionist

tonight in Geneva. I shall probably telegraph from Lausanne. Don't fret, dear ones, and don't miss me.

I kiss you lovingly,

Chaim

Moisseychik,

Mandelstamm is either in Interlaken or Beatenberg. Write to him *poste-restante*, Interlaken. But you can also get his address from the *Fremdenliste*.[3] Petka's trial is on 25th August. (It is a trial by jury behind closed doors.)[4] Mironov and Karabachevsky are defending.[5] I met Belkovsky yesterday. Politically, the Zionist position is serious but not hopeless.[6]

I kiss you and Chaim.[7]

Chaim.

Regards to Nyusya.

418. To Vera Khatzman, Hilterfingen. *Biel, 4 August 1903*

Russian: Pcd. H.W.: W.A.

Biel, 4. VIII. 03.

Dear Verochka,

I looked over the school here; it looks nice but is not as good as

elements', mentioned in his letter to Kroll and Idelson of 22 June (No. 384). No further details have come to light concerning these discussions and their outcome.

[3] 'Aliens list', i.e. the register of foreign visitors.

[4] Peter (Pinhas) Dashevsky (1884–1934) attempted on 17 June 1903 to assassinate Pavel Krushevan, editor of the anti-semitic journals *Bessarabietz* (Kishinev) and *Znamia* (St. Petersburg), for his role in the agitation preceding the Kishinev pogrom. Dashevsky was sentenced to five years' imprisonment but released in 1906. Prior to his arrest he had been a student at the Kiev Polytechnic and a member of the *Kadimah* and 'Young Israel' Student Zionist Societies. He had been friendly with Moses and Samuel Weizmann and at Passover 1902 was a guest at the Weizmann home in Pinsk. See H. Weizmann-Lichtenstein, *In the Shadow of Our Roof* (in Hebrew), Tel-Aviv 1947–48, pp. 142–50; Ch. Shorer (ed.) *The Kishinev Pogrom* (in Hebrew), Tel-Aviv 1963, p. 126.

[5] In fact Dashevsky had only one defence attorney in the Court of First Instance— M. G. Mironov. N. Karabachevsky was an attorney in the suit for damages instituted by the Kishinev victims.

[6] Before arriving in Switzerland, Gregory Belkovsky visited Herzl and reported on the position of Zionism in Russia and on the conference of Zionist leaders held in St. Petersburg (see n. 4 to No. 402). He also tried unsuccessfully to persuade Herzl not to travel to St. Petersburg for a meeting with the Russian Minister of Interior, von Plehve (see *Hamelitz*, 21 Jan./3 Feb. 1904, and also Belkovsky's Memoirs in T. Nussenblatt (ed.) *Zeitgenossen über Herzl*, Brno 1929, p. 24. For Herzl's visit to St. Petersburg, see Bein, *Theodore Herzl*, London 1957, pp. 447 ff.). It appears that W. learned for the first time from either Belkovsky or Jacobson that new restrictions had in fact been imposed on Zionist activity (see No. 414 and ns. 5, 6 there).

[7] Chaim Fialkov.

the one in Winterthur.[1] I telephoned Nossig, and he will meet me in Lausanne.[2] I shall then know whether I am to remain in Gen[eva] tomorrow or leave for home[3] as soon as I get there.

I shall telegraph you tomorrow.

Regards to all.

I kiss you,

Your Chaim.

419. To Max Hickel, Brno.[1] *Geneva, 5 August 1903*

German: Or. Copy. T.W.: W.A.

Geneva, 5 August 1903.

Dear Fellow-Zionist,

Forgive me for not replying to your letter,[2] which I very much appreciate, until today. I have been away for a prolonged trip and my correspondence only reached me during the past few days.[3]

Thank you very much for your invitation to contribute to your journal.[4] I have no doubt that you would accept an article however independent. I feel I must state, however, that what I have to say cannot be expressed within the limits of a newspaper article. Moreover, I am so fully engaged with a large variety of matters that I cannot allow myself even the briefest holiday.

However, I shall be at your disposal at some date in the future. Most respectfully, and with sincerest Zion's greetings,

420. To Davis Trietsch and Regina Schimmer, Berlin.[1]
Geneva, 5 August 1903

German: Or. Copy. T.W.: W.A.

5 August 03.

Dear Friends,

You were wondering at my whereabouts.[2] It would have been

418. [1] See n. 1 to No. 417.

[2] Nossig was then staying in Morges near Lausanne (see his letter to W. of 30 July 1903, W.A.). [3] Refers to Hilterfingen.

419. [1] 'Mr. Hickl, Brünn' appears on the original copy in Stupnitzky's handwriting.

[2] Not found.

[3] W. was absent from Geneva from 16 July to 4 Aug. 1903.

[4] Hickel was editor of the *Jüdische Volksstimme* published in Brno.

420. [1] The copy is marked 'D. Trietsch, Berlin' in W.'s handwriting, but from its salutation and content the letter was evidently intended also for Schimmer.

[2] Schimmer wrote to W. on 26 July 1903 (W.A.): 'Where actually are you now? Really, it is bad that no one knows even where you are.'

difficult to give you an address, because I have been travelling constantly. I think that I shall now be able to sit still until the Congress and make some preparations for it. We have established connections in Paris with the 'I.C.A.' and the '*Alliance*', organisations upon whose support we shall certainly be able to count.[3] I am now writing a second brochure about the University and expect to be able to send it to the printers as early as next week.[4]

As far as we can tell, we shall have at least 75 delegates of our own at the Congress.[5] We may count upon the full support of the Russian members of the Actions Committee.[6] Those in authority are going to be absolutely surprised when they see the opposition at this Congress. Let us hope it will be both a thorough and objective Congress. We all want to be in Basle by the 16th, and to open our Bureau there.[7] The balance-sheet of the Bureau is enclosed.[8] When are you coming? What did you accomplish in England?[9]

I am off again on my travels immediately. Warmest regards

from your

My address until the 15th: *Pension* Karlen, Hilterfingen (Bernese Oberland).

---

[3] See No. 410 and n. 1 there.

[4] The reference is to a Hebrew brochure, 'A Hebrew University', which never appeared in print. The W.A. has a draft in Stupnitzky's hand with W.'s marginal comments. The draft explains the need for a Jewish University and reports on progress already made. It states that the directors of the University Bureau had reached the conclusion that the institution should be established in Palestine and embrace departments for General and Jewish Studies. A secondary school or technical college would be founded in Europe to prepare youngsters for admission to the University (see also ns. 1, 5 to No. 393).   [5] I.e. Democratic Fraction delegates.

[6] The remark was apparently based on W.'s discussions with Jacobson of 3 Aug. 1903 (see No. 417). For Regional Leaders sympathetic to the Democratic Fraction, see No. 384.

[7] I.e. a branch of the Jewish University Bureau was to be opened at Basle for the duration of the Sixth Zionist Congress (see *Hamelitz*, 6/19 Aug. 1903) ; the Bureau was perhaps intended also to deal with Democratic Fraction affairs.

[8] See balance-sheet of the University Bureau of 15 July 1903, W.A. A summary was published in *Die Welt*, 14 Aug. 1903.

[9] Trietsch had been in London to enlist the interest of the Colonial Office in possible Jewish settlement in Cyprus, and to establish business connections for the *Jüdischer Verlag* (see Schimmer to W., 26 July 1903, W.A.).

421. To Ben-Zion Mossinson, Berne. *Hilterfingen, 11 August 1903*

Russian: H.W.: C.Z.A. A45/10a.

Hilterfingen, 11. VIII. 03.

Dear Friend,

I had to remain in Lausanne and Geneva two days longer than I had anticipated. I really don't know where Mr. Metmann-Kohan got the idea that I was lecturing on the *Hochschule*.[1] He may have talked to me about it in Fribourg,[2] but I will *not* lecture there. Thus everything remains in accordance with our conversation here.

Nor do I understand your question about '*Klarheit*'.[3] Everything seems very clear to me. I talked to Becker and he promised to send the money at once. I shall make him send it today.[4]

In view of conditions in Russia all our plans, intentions and desires will of course be completely changed now. Everything will have to be done differently, assuming there will be something left to be done[5] . . .

On Monday[6] I shall be in Basle.

Yours,

Ch. Weizmann.

---

421. [1] Relates to an address to a gathering of Hebrew-speaking persons convened in Basle on 18 Aug. 1903 by the *Ivria* Society of Berne in order to set up a Union of Hebrew Language Societies. Despite W.'s refusal to speak there, the agenda included an address by Weizmann on 'The Hebrew University' (see *Hatzofe*, 13/26 July 1903, 31 July/13 Aug. 1903).

[2] During the Swiss Zionist Conference on 28 June 1903.

[3] 'Clarity'. Doubtless the question was contained in Mossinson's letter, which has not been found.

[4] W. informed Mossinson on 6 July (see No. 400) that he had sent him 35 francs with Julius Becker (to meet expenses of the Jewish University Bureau). Two days later W. again wrote (see No. 405) that he had sent the money with Becker and would send more. It appears that W. nevertheless enclosed another 35 francs with that letter; for in a letter dated 'Thursday, 13 Tammuz', in apparent error for 'Thursday, 14 Tammuz'—9 July 1903 (W.A.), Mossinson wrote: 'This morning I received your letter together with thirty-five francs.' Subsequently Mossinson informed W. 'I have not received from Becker one centime of the thirty-five francs about which you wrote me . . . and nothing remains of the thirty-five francs which you sent me' (see letter from Mossinson dated 'Wednesday, 4 Menahem Ab' though apparently 'Wednesday, 5 Ab'—29 July 1903, W.A.).

[5] An allusion to the ban on Zionist propaganda in Russia (see n. 5 to No. 414; n. 6 to No. 417). On 3 Ab (27 July 1903), Mossinson wrote W. (W.A.): 'It seems to me that the ban on Zionism . . . will cause great harm to the University project in Russia also . . . I am afraid that my circular letter will not bring in the substantial material aid which I expected' (concerning the circular, see n. 1 to No. 408).

[6] Monday, 17 Aug. 1903. The following day, 18 Aug. 1903, a meeting of Democratic Fraction delegates to the Sixth Congress was due to be held (see *Hamelitz*, 5/18 Aug. 1903).

422. To Kalman Marmor, Basle[1]. *Hilterfingen, 13 August 1903*

German: H.W.: Marmor Papers, Yivo Archives, New York.

13/VIII. 03.
Hilterfingen

Dear friend Marmor,

What about the mandate for Nossig?[2] So far no news at all. Why did the people not reply? Has the protest against the Federation been forwarded?[3]

On Monday[4] I shall be in Basle.

Your Ch. Weizmann

423. To Menahem Ussishkin, Haifa. *Basle, c. 20 August 1903*[1]

German: T. C.Z.A.: A24/125.

IN PRINCIPLE FAVOUR ESTABLISHING UNIVERSITY IN PALESTINE COMING IF NECESSARY[2] ZION'S GREETINGS WEIZMANN

422. [1] No address appears on the original, but it is known that Marmor arrived in Basle on 13 Aug. 1903 (see *Hatzefirah*, 3/16 Aug. 1903).

[2] Nossig was one of the Democratic Fraction candidates proposed to the *Shivat-Zion* Society in London but not elected (see n. 1 to No. 413). However, Nossig ultimately was elected in London.

[3] Wortsman proposed that the 'Herzl–Nordau', *Maaravi*, and *Degel-Zion* Societies should lodge protests to the Mandates (Credentials) Committee of the Sixth Zionist Congress (against the decision of the English Zionist Federation to disallow candidates not resident in the United Kingdom or British Empire—see n. 37 to No. 413). W. supported this proposal (see Wortsman to Posniak, 5 Aug. 1903, Marmor Papers, Yivo Archives, New York).   [4] Cf. n. 6 to No. 421.

423. [1] The telegram was received in Haifa on 25 Aug. 1903, but its date of despatch cannot be precisely determined, for delays of about a week were not infrequent in delivering telegrams from Europe in Palestine at that time. W. apparently arrived in Basle on 17 Aug. 1903 (see No. 421 and n. 6 there), and the Sixth Zionist Congress opened there on 23 Aug. 1903. The telegram was a further step in W.'s efforts to obtain Ussishkin's support for the University project and to utilize the latter's visit to Palestine to explore the possibility of setting up the institution there. As early as July, Mossinson, with W.'s consent, had approached Ussishkin on this matter (see No. 405 and ns. 3, 4 there), and in his reply, sent from Jaffa, Ussishkin wrote: 'I am ready to work heart and soul for the founding of the University here and I shall oppose its establishment elsewhere with all my strength.' He added that the conference of Hebrew teachers in Palestine, then about to be held, would deal with the issue (see Ussishkin to Mossinson, 24 Tammuz (19 July 1903), C.Z.A., A45/10). In his address to this conference, which opened in Zichron-Yaakov on 27 Aug. 1903, Ussishkin dwelt on the University plan. He emphasized his opposition to the establishment of the University in Europe and proposed that a Polytechnic be set up in Palestine, as its graduates could obtain a livelihood more easily than graduates of a University devoted to the Humanities. He thought the *Alliance Israélite Universelle* might render the project financial support, but he expressed doubt as to the possibility of immediate implementation of the plan (see *Hamelitz*, 5/18 Nov. 1903).

[2] Some misspellings occur in the orig.

BIOGRAPHICAL INDEX

ALEINIKOV, MICHAEL (1880–1938). B. Smolensk. While law student in Kharkov active in Zionist circles there. Joined D.F., was its delegate to VI Z.C.,1903,and worked for Jewish University project. Practised law in Kharkov for a time, subsequently settling in Odessa as legal adviser to Baku petroleum concerns and engaging in Zionist propaganda activities there. Participated in Russian Zionist Conferences at Helsingfors (1906) and The Hague (1907). Delegate VII, VIII, XI, XIII Z.C., 1905, 1907, 1913, 1923. In 1913 he moved to St. Petersburg. There, besides his industrial and commercial pursuits, was on Russian Zionist Central Committee until leaving Russia. Following February Revolution, 1917, directed Department of Jewish Political Affairs of Russian Zionist Central Committee and was member Political Bureau of Jewish Deputies to Duma. Published Zionist periodical *Raszviet* ('Dawn') which reappeared in July 1917. In 1919 at Paris Peace Conference representing Russian Zionist Central Committee and one of representatives of National Jewish Council. Elected G.A.C. July 1920. For some years member Committee of Jewish Delegations in Paris. In 1926 emigrated to Palestine, settling in Haifa and devoting himself to public activity. From 1931 member Council of Hadar-Hacarmel, the first exclusively Jewish quarter of Haifa, and was its chairman from 1932 until his death.

ALTSCHUL, MICHAEL (1866–1931). B. Novogrodek, White Russia. Chemist. Editor scientific publications in Germany. Worked 1893–1915 in Prof. Raoul Pictet's gas liquefaction company, and subsequently engaged in business in Berlin.

BECKER, JULIUS (1881–1945). B. Waldenburg, Silesia. Journalist. Studied at Breslau and Berne and among founders of Student Zionist Societies in these cities. Doctorate from University of Berne 1906. Appointed secretary of the Berlin Department of Central Zionist Office 1907. Employed by Ullstein

Publishing House 1908–33, mainly working on *Die Vossische Zeitung*. From 1908 editor of German Z.O. publication *Jüdische Rundschau*. Aug.–Dec. 1913 edited *Die Welt*, organ of W.Z.O., having been on Central Committee German Z.O. from 1910. Sent to Constantinople in 1917 as agent for Ullstein's and on behalf of Z.O. Transferred to Geneva 1919 as representative of Ullstein News Service and League of Nations correspondent of *Die Vossische Zeitung*. Thereafter an active member of Swiss Z.O., on its Central Committee and its Geneva leader. In 1933 invited by Chinese Government to set up a modern Press Service there. Represented Jewish Agency at League of Nations 1934–5. Delegate VIII, IX, X, XI, XV, XX Z.C., 1907, 1909, 1911, 1913, 1927, 1937. Emigrated to New York 1941.

BERLIGNE, ELIYAHU MEIR (1866–1959). B. Mogilev. Prominent communal figure in Palestine. After law studies in Moscow went into business in Tsaritsyn (Stalingrad, Volgograd), where he joined Zionist Committee. Delegate V, VI Z.C., 1901, 1903, and Russian Zionist Conference, Minsk, 1902. Member D.F. In 1907 emigrated to Palestine where among founders two years earlier of Atid manufacturing concern. Pioneer settler in Tel Aviv 1909 and chairman of its Municipal Committee 1917–19. Member, Jewish Community Delegation to Peace Conference, 1919. On Executive of Jewish National Council (*Va'ad Leumi*) throughout its existence (1920–48), occupying various posts: Treasurer, member of its Education Committee, Board chairman of Otzar-Hayishuv Bank (1926), representative of National Council on Actions Committee. On supervisory committee of *Geulah* Society 1922–35, chairman of Board of Governors of Haifa Technion from 1941, on Board of Supervisors of Herzlia Gymnasium. Signatory to Declaration of Independence on proclamation of statehood and a General Zionist representative on Council of Provisional Government of Israel.

BERNFELD, SIMON (1860–1940). B. Stanislav, Galicia. Rabbi and historian. Following studies at University of Berlin and *Hochschule für die Wissenschaft des Judentums* in Berlin, awarded Doctorate and ordained in 1885. Chief Rabbi of Sephardic Jewish communities in Belgrade 1885–94, then returned to Berlin where he remained until his death. While occupying no specific post in Berlin, he engaged in research and literary activities, much of which was in Hebrew.

BIENENSTOCK, MAX JACOB MEIR (1881–1923). Pseudonyms: Stock, Ginz, Kaveret. B. Tarnow, Galicia. Author and educationalist. Joined *Hatehiya* Zionist Society while at high school. Founder and chairman, Zionist Academic Society *Bar-Kochba* in Tarnow, 1902, and librarian and secretary Zionist Academic Society *Przedswit* ('Before Dawn') while student in Cracow, 1902–4. Participated in conferences of Austrian Z.O., 1905, 1906. Teacher, Royal Gymnasium in Wadowice, 1904–7, obtained Doctorate Cracow University 1908 and passed teaching examinations 1909. Instructor at Royal Gymnasium in Stryy from 1909. In Vienna from outbreak of War till 1916, afterwards devoting himself to public activities. With annexation of Eastern Galicia to Ukrainian Republic, he was among architects of Jewish autonomy, with membership of local Council, and subsequently Central National Jewish Council member responsible for educational network. On Polish absorption of Galicia, appointed instructor at Jewish Gymnasium in Lvov 1919, and following year its Principal. He was among founders of Zionist Labour Party,

Hitahdut, and was its delegate XII Z.C. (1921). Elected to Polish Senate 1922 as a Nationalist Jewish representative. He published various works on German literature and pedagogy, and was author many articles on politics.

BIENSTOCK, BERTHOLD (1861–1940). B. Krotoszyn, district of Poznan. Physician and bacteriologist. Graduated in Breslau 1888 and subsequently practised as ear, nose, and throat specialist in Mulhouse, where he also engaged in scientific research. In 1900 he discovered the microbe *bacillus potrificus Bienstock*. Author various scientific works. Delegate V, VII Z.C., 1901, 1905.

BLAU, JULIUS (1861–1939). B. Pleschen, district of Poznan. Prominent in Jewish community of Frankfurt-on-Main, and its president from 1903 until his death. Active in many Jewish organizations, among them I.C.A. Executive Committee.

CHAPIRA, BERNARD ELEAZAR DOV (1880–1967). Pseudonym: Eldash Hagelili. B. Safad. Semitic scholar, teacher, and journalist. Early in century, when he was already contributing to Hebrew Press, studied Semitic languages in Paris and was Hebrew teacher at People's Academy established by Zionists. On editorial staff of *L'Écho Sioniste*, organ of French Zionists. Supported Jewish University project. After First World War lecturer in Semitic languages at *École des Hautes Études* in Paris. Librarian at *Bibliothèque Nationale* and *Alliance Israélite Universelle*. Settled in Jerusalem in 1947 and published booklets and articles on linguistic and biblical research.

ELIAS, ALFRED (1866–1940). Physician in Mulhouse and active in Regional Zionist Bureau in Alsace-Lorraine. Delegate III–VII Z.C., 1899–1905. Actively engaged in K.H. from its inauguration. Member, from 1906, of Central Committee of German Z.O.

FIALKOV, CHAIM (?1874–1920). B. Serniky, White Russia. Uncle of W. (his father's brother). Educationalist. Studied at Hebrew Teachers Seminary, Vilna. In 1897 taught at Hebrew School in Nikolayev, where active in Zionism and among founders of reformed *heder* (religious elementary school). Delegate VI Z.C., 1903. From 1905 he was in St. Petersburg as supervisor of the schools within the Pale that belonged to Society for Promotion of Culture among the Jews of Russia, serving as its representative on Committee for Popular Education advising Education Ministry of Kerensky regime. He was influential in raising standards of Hebrew schools and contributed to pedagogic monthlies *The Hebrew School* and *The Harbinger of Hebrew Enlightenment*.

FRIEDLAENDER, ISRAEL (1876–1920). B. Kovel, Ukraine. M. Lilian Ruth Bentwich. Orientalist and American Jewish leader prominent in Conservative religious movement. Studied at Rabbinical Seminary and University, Berlin. Obtained Doctorate in 1901 at University of Strasbourg and in 1902 appointed lecturer in Department of Semitic Languages there. Professor at Jewish Theological Seminary, New York, 1903. Favoured establishment of Centre in Palestine for advancement of Jewish ethical ideals together with continued survival of Judaism in Diaspora. Executive member of Federation of American Zionists (since 1918: Zionist Organization of America) 1905–6, 1907–11, 1917–20, and chairman of its Education Committee 1906–7. Delegate III–VII,

X Z.C., 1899–1905, 1911, and first president Young Judea, Zionist youth movement founded 1908. Chairman, Board of Trustees of Bureau of Jewish Education when this was established in New York in 1910. Literary critic and translator, he was author of works on linguistics, Islam, and Judaism. Killed by bandits while on mission for Amer. Joint Distribution Committee in Ukraine.

FRIEDLAND, Ben-Zion (Benya) (?1880–1919). Early in century member of *Kadimah* and Young Israel Student Zionist Societies in Kiev. Delegate VI Z.C., 1903. A leader of Zionist Socialist group *Vozrozhdenye* ('Renaissance') of which main centre was in Kiev. Briefly on Central Committee of Zionist Socialist Workers Party (Territorialist), and subsequently prominent in Jewish Socialist Workers Party (Autonomist, Sejmist).

GINIS, Samuel (1867–1932). B. Kishinev. Chemical engineer. Among founders of H.Z. in Kishinev and Odessa. Towards end of century settled in Baku, becoming manager of Rothschild oil refinery and petroleum works. On Baku Zionist Committee and founder Hebrew Gymnasium there. With 1917 Revolution he was appointed commercial consultant for petroleum to Soviet Government in Constantinople and London. Settled in Palestine 1928.

GINZBURG (Hermoni), Aaron (1882–1960). B. Swieciany, Lithuania. Journalist. Attended Mikveh Israel School, Palestine, from 1898, later teaching at Gederah. Engaged in Zionist and journalistic activities from 1902, while student in Switzerland and Nancy. Correspondent of *Hatzofe* at VI Z.C., 1903, and of *Hazman* at VII Z.C., 1905. Assisted Nahum Sokolow in editing *Ha'olam* 1907–8, then edited *Hamevasser* in Constantinople 1910. Following First World War he managed Hebrew Cultural Centre in Berlin, subsequently going to France where he contributed to French and Hebrew papers. Returned to Palestine 1934 and engaged in literary work. During latter part of his life employed in Knesset archives.

GLUSKIN, Wolf (Ze'ev) (1859–1949). B. Slutsk, White Russia. A founder (1906) of Palestine Vintners Association, which he headed until 1923. Among leaders of H.Z. Society and *Bnei-Moshe* in Warsaw, where he lived from 1880. Delegate II, III, V, VII Z.C., 1898, 1899, 1901, 1905. Prominently associated with establishment in Warsaw of *Ahiasaf* Publishing House, 1893, and newspaper *Hatzofe*, 1903. He helped form *Menuhah-Venahlah* Society that founded Rehovot (1890), and Warsaw branch of *Geulah* Society (1904), to acquire land in Palestine. As a founder of Carmel-Mizrahi Co., he engaged in marketing Palestinian wines in Europe, 1896–1906, then settled in Rishon-LeZion. During First World War was in Alexandria, where active in relief of Palestine exiles and war-victims, and in formation of Zion Mule Corps, returning to Palestine in 1918 as a financial adviser to the Zionist Commission. From 1924 lived in Tel Aviv, where he headed office of *Geulah* Society from 1926, and served as its president 1935–46. Board chairman of Kupat-Am Bank 1936. He helped establish cultural institutions in Tel Aviv. Hon. citizen Rishon-LeZion 1937, Tel Aviv 1939.

GOLDE, Paul (?–1925). B. Plotsk, Poland, of well-to-do family active in public affairs and tending toward assimilation. Settled in Wloclawek early in century, occupying prominent position in public life. Prior to First World War member of Jewish Community Council. Published weekly newspaper in Polish, headed credit and savings bank and philanthropic institutions. After War became manager of Bank of Commerce and Industry in Wloclawek and president of its Municipal Council from 1919 until his death. Briefly supported Zionism and was delegate V, VI Z.C., 1901, 1903.

GOLDFLAMM, SAMUEL (1852–1932). B. Warsaw. Neurologist. Notable figure active in public affairs. On Warsaw Committee for Jewish University 1903. After First World War among founders of Friends of Hebrew University, participating at opening, Jerusalem 1925. In 1929 elected a non-Zionist representative to Jewish Agency Council, subsequently to its Administrative Committee. On Directorate K.H. Member, Warsaw Jewish Community Council and prominent in various Jewish organizations in Poland concerned with public health.

GOTTHEIL, RICHARD JAMES HORATIO (1862–1936). B. Manchester. Linguist and Orientalist. A founder and first president (1898–1904) of Federation of American Zionists, and on its Executive 1908–9. Emigrated 1873 to U.S.A. with his father, Rabbi Gustav Gottheil, himself a pioneer Zionist. Following studies at American and European universities and the *Hochschule für die Wissenschaft des Judentums* in Berlin, obtained Doctorate at Leipzig in 1886 and was appointed lecturer in Assyriology and Rabbinical Literature at Columbia. Professor and head of Department of Semitic Languages at Columbia 1892. Headed Oriental Department of New York Public Library 1896. In 1922, together with Stephen Wise, he established Jewish Institute of Religion, serving on its Board of Trustees. Member of various scientific societies and author of books and articles in his own field of scholarship as well as on contemporary affairs. Delegate II, III, IV, VI, X, XV Z.C., 1898, 1899, 1900, 1903, 1911, 1927. Member G.A.C. 1898–1905, 1907–11. His wife, Emma (they married 1891), among founders of Hadassah and delegate to several Z.C.s.

GRUENBAUM, ISAAC (1879–1970). B. Warsaw. Lawyer and journalist. A leading figure in Polish Jewry and Zionist movement. While student in Warsaw member of Student Zionist Society *Kadimah*, and prominent in *Hatehiya*, a radical youth organization. Connected with D.F. 1902–3. From 1905 secretary to Nahum Sokolow, then Zionist representative in Poland, participating all Z.C.s from Seventh (1905). Editor and contributor Zionist publications in Hebrew, Yiddish, Polish, and Russian, among them the weekly *Glos Zydowski* ('Jewish Voice'), of which editor 1906–7. Participated in Russian Jewish Press Convention and third Russian Zionist Conference, Helsingfors (1906), where he was among formulators of 'Helsingfors Programme' committing Russian Z.O. in struggle for civic and national rights of Russian Jewry. Edited *Ha'olam* (Vilna), Hebrew organ of Z.O., 1908–10, and *Dos Yiddishe Folk*, 1914. During First World War he joined editorial staff in Petrograd of *Raszviet* and *Evreiskaya Zhizn*, simultaneously editing *Petrograder Tageblatt*. At seventh Russian Zionist Conference in Petrograd (1917) he championed recognition of Yiddish as the Jewish language of Diaspora and secularization of the Jewish community. Returned to Warsaw 1918 and appointed general secretary Zionist Central Committee in Poland. Edited *Dos Yiddishe Folk* again and *Hatzefirah*. Elected Actions Committee 1921. Chairman Provisional National Jewish

Council in Poland, member of Sejm 1919–32 and chairman of its Jewish group. Established National Minority bloc in Sejm 1922. Member of Warsaw City Council 1924. During this period a consistent opponent of the Zionist leadership, contesting expansion of Jewish Agency. He established *Al-Hamishmar* ('On Guard') group and edited its publication *Zionistishe Bletter*. Following victory of *Et-Livnot* ('Time to Build') group in 1925, he resigned from Polish Zionist Central Committee. Chairman J.N.F. in Poland 1930–2. Elected to Jewish Agency Executive and emigrated to Palestine 1933. Held these offices in Agency: Head of Labour Department 1933–48; Head of Immigration Department 1933–5; Head of Mossad Bialik 1935–48; Treasurer 1949–50; Investigating Judge 1950–1. In Second World War engaged in Istanbul in establishing contact with Jews in Occupied Europe. Among Jewish leaders detained in Latrun 1946. Minister of Interior in Provisional Government of Israel. Campaigned, with own independent party list, for separation of religion and state in first Knesset elections, but failed to be elected.

GRUSENBERG, SAMUEL (1854–1909). Pseudonym: Letopisets. B. Kherson district, Ukraine. Physician and journalist. Studied at St. Petersburg University and Military Medical Academy. From 1884 to 1899 on editorial staff, and sometime acting-editor, Jewish periodical *Voskhod* ('Sunrise'), responsible for foreign news. Influenced paper's moderately assimilationist policy opposing emigration from Russia and calls for national renaissance in Palestine. Editor-publisher 1899–1904, Jewish weekly *Budushchnost'* ('Future') that allocated extensive space to Zionism. Later abandoned journalistic and Jewish activities, returning to medicine. Frequent contributor to medical journals, writing also in Hebrew.

HAAS, JACOB DE (1872–1937). B. London. Journalist and Zionist leader. Active H.Z. Associate-editor Anglo-Zionist organ *Jewish World* 1892–1900. Among founders of English Zionist Federation in 1898, close associate of Herzl and devotee of 'political' Zionism. Delegate first six Z.C.s, 1897–1903, XVI, XVII, 1929, 1931. On G.A.C. 1898–9, 1901–5. At Herzl's request, settled in United States 1902 to help organize American Zionism. Secretary, 1902–5, of Federation of American Zionists and editor of its official organ *The Maccabean*. On Executive, Federation of American Zionists 1905–7, but withdrew to become owner-editor Boston *Jewish Advocate* 1908–18. Helped form American Jewish Congress and one of its representatives at Peace Conference 1919. His return to Zionist movement began in 1916, when appointed secretary of Provisional Zionist Executive Committee in America, and he was executive secretary of Zionist Organization of America 1918–21. Withdrew from Z.O. in 1921 together with Brandeis group, concentrating instead on economic development of Palestine through Palestine Development League. Again on Executive of Zionist Organization of America 1930–4. A General Zionist with views similar to Vladimir Jabotinsky's, he joined Revisionist movement in 1935 and was among founders of New Zionist Organization.

HALPERN, GEORGE GAD (GODYA) (1878–1962). B. Pinsk. Economist. Studied in Vienna, Berlin, and Munich, obtaining Doctorate 1903. Chairman Zionist Society in Munich and among organizers of Jewish Student Union there. Member D.F. and assisted Jewish University project. Delegate all

Z.C.s from Seventh (1905), and from 1906 member Central Committee German Z.O. On G.A.C. 1911–13, when also in management of large petroleum concern in Vienna and Lvov. After First World War worked in Zionist financial institutions. At London Zionist Conference (1920) re-elected G.A.C. and to Finance Committee, and at XII Z.C. (1921) to Financial and Economic Council. From 1921 to 1928 in London as member, Board of Directors of J.C.T. (1922–8 its Managing Director). Among founders, and a Director, K.H. Left London 1928 to engage in marine insurance in Hamburg. Emigrated to Palestine 1933, when he joined Board of Directors of J.N.F. and Palestine Development Company. Among founders in 1934 of Migdal Insurance Company, and for over a decade its chairman. A Board member of Palestine Electric Corporation for many years and its chairman 1954–6. Hon. chairman Bank Leumi.

HEYMANN, Hans Gideon (1882–1918). B. Berlin. M. daughter of Johann Kremenetzky (q.v.). Banker and industrialist. Joined Zionist movement while student in Munich. Chairman, Berlin Zionist Association 1911–14. From 1910 responsible for financial affairs of German Zionist Central Committee. Delegate VII, VIII, X, XI Z.C., 1905, 1907, 1911, 1913. On G.A.C. from 1913. As 'practical' Zionist, worked actively for economic projects in Palestine, and from 1909 he was a Director of Palestine Development Company.

IDELSON, Vladimir Robert (1881–1954). B. Rostov-on-Don. Lawyer. While student in Kharkov joined Student Zionist Society *Kadimah*, and Committee for a Jewish University. D.F. delegate to VI Z.C., 1903. Member J.N.F. Committee in Berlin, where he obtained Doctorate. Law practice in Russia from 1906. On Board of Directors Anglo-Russian Bank 1914–17 and Committee-member Russian Association of Banks. Consultant to Russian Ministry of Finance 1917. Moving to London in 1918 he worked as expert in Russian and International Law. Called to Bar 1926 and became British subject 1930. On Law Advisory Committee of British Council. Publications on Banking, Insurance, and International Law. Worked to advance Anglo-Israel scientific co-operation and for higher education in Israel.

JOCHELMAN, David S. (1868–1941). B. Postavy, Lithuania. Chairman of Zionist Academic Society and D.F. in Berne, where he obtained Doctorate. Enthusiastic supporter of East Africa project. Delegate VII Z.C., 1905, and among founders that year of Jewish Territorial Organization (I.T.O.). Head of I.T.O. Emigration Department and for some years editor of its publication *Wohin?* From 1913 lived in England, where managed insurance and transport companies dealing with Russia. In 1917 elected to Board of Deputies of British Jews and Executive of Russo-British Chamber of Commerce. Among founders of Jewish War Victims Fund and Jewish War Prisoners Fund (chairman of latter). Driving force behind 'Russian Committee for Matters of Military Service' established 1917 for welfare of Jewish servicemen and their families. Organized mass protests against pogroms in Russia and Poland 1918–19. Chairman, 1920, of Federation of Ukrainian Jews (later incorporated in Federation of Jewish Relief Organizations of Great Britain). Also chairman after First World War of Palestine Workers Fund, and active in O.R.T.

KAHN, Bernhard (1876–1955). B. Oskarshamn, Sweden. Jewish emigration expert. Studied at Fulda, Wuerzburg, and Munich, obtaining Doctorate.

Committee-member Zionist Society in Munich while student there (1899–1903). Delegate VI, VII Z.C., 1903, 1905. Secretary, 1904–21, of *Hilfsverein der Deutschen Juden* in Berlin and director of Central Bureau for Jewish Emigration. From 1921 with American Joint Distribution Committee in administrative capacity, and director of its European office 1924–38. Non-Zionist representative on Jewish Agency Executive 1931–3. In 1939 moved to New York where hon. chairman Joint European Executive Council. On Executive of K.H. and other bodies engaged in economic development of Palestine, including Palestine Economic Corporation. Active in range of social and economic institutions, Jewish and general.

KANN, JACOBUS HENRICUS (1872–1944). B. The Hague. Banker. At I Z.C., 1897, and among initiators of J.C.T. A founder Dutch Z.O. Friend and co-worker of David Wolffsohn, of whose estate he was Executor. On G.A.C. 1901–5. Very active in administration of Z.O. during Wolffsohn's presidency, on S.A.C. 1905–11 and delegate all Z.C.s from 1905 to 1913. He was mainly concerned with finance, and was on Board of Directors J.C.T. 1904–22, frequently its vice-chairman. Dedicated to 'political' Zionism, and sustained activities following Wolffsohn's withdrawal from leadership 1911, retaining association with J.C.T. and resuming membership G.A.C. till 1921. During First World War on J.N.F. Executive in The Hague and member of political committee established there in 1917. Hon. Dutch Consul in Palestine, where immigrated 1923. Returning to Holland after some years, deported to Theresienstadt 1942 where he died.

KELLNER, LEON (1859–1928). Pseudonym: Leo Raphaels. B. Tarnow, Galicia. Author, educationalist and specialist in English literature. Close friend and early supporter Herzl, and was his Literary Executor. Obtained Doctorate in Vienna, after which he taught at *Realgymnasium*, Troppau, 1891–4. Lecturer till 1900, and professor till 1904, University of Vienna. Contributor literary subjects to *Neue Freie Presse* and joined Herzl on appearance of *Judenstaat* in 1896. Delegate IV, IX, X Z.C., 1900, 1909, 1911. Contributed, mostly pseudonymously, to *Die Welt* throughout periodical's existence, and served briefly as its editor. Professor at Czernowitz 1904–14 and a Zionist member of Bukovina Legislative Assembly. Returned 1914 to Vienna, and was professor at Polytechnic there. Austrian Presidential Adviser on British affairs. His literary work included an edition of Herzl's Zionist writings in 1910, and in 1922 he published Herzl's diaries and a biography of the leader.

KOHN, JULIAN (1861–1932). B. Warsaw. Lawyer. In his youth took part in H.Z. movement but subsequently withdrew. Founded *Wiedza* ('Knowledge') Society, which had assimilationist connections. Member of Jewish Community Council and other public bodies.

KREMENETZKY, JOHANN (JONAH, JOHANAN) (1850–1934). Also known as JOHANN MEYER. B. Odessa. Engineer and industrialist. One of earliest followers and among closest associates of Herzl, and first head of J.N.F. Educated in Berlin and Paris, he settled in Vienna 1880 and won wide reputation as electrical engineer, with many inventions patented. In 1899 established electric lamp factory, then among world's largest, in Vienna. Delegate III–VII Z.C.s, 1899–1905, IX Z.C. 1909, with membership S.A.C. 1897–8, 1901–5, and of G.A.C. 1905–20. A Trustee of Herzl's estate. He helped to found J.N.F. at V Z.C. 1901, and was actively associated with this body till 1921, having been its director until 1907, when J.N.F. headquarters transferred from Vienna to Cologne. Contributed funds and expertise for industrial development of Palestine, and financed W.'s first visit there 1907. Established Silicat brick-works in Palestine 1920 and on his final visit there, 1932, was made hon. citizen of Tel Aviv.

KRINSKY (later LEVITE), SALOMEA (LUNIA). B. 1884 Warsaw. Active in Zionist student circles while at Berne University 1903–7. M. Dr. Leon Levite, prominent Polish Zionist, 1909. Polish correspondent of *Berliner Tageblatt*, 1910–14. Was active in Z.O. and W.I.Z.O. (of which she was among founders) in Poland. Emigrated to Palestine 1940.

KROLL, MICHAEL MOSES (?– ?). B. 1880s. Neuropathologist active in public affairs. Member, *Kadimah* Zionist Society in Moscow. Attended second Russian Zionist Conference in Minsk 1902. Among leaders Moscow D.F. Bureau 1902–4, and active in Jewish University project. Subsequently member Jewish Socialist Workers Party (Autonomist). In First World War active in O.R.T. and Society for Promotion of Culture among Jews of Russia. Lecturer at Moscow University in twenties, later Dean of Medical School, University of Minsk. Joined Communist Party. Professor of Neurology, Moscow Health Institute, during thirties, and died in early forties.

LEVONTIN, ZALMAN DAVID (1856–1940). B. Orsha, White Russia. Member H.Z. in Kremenchug and Odessa, emigrating to Palestine 1882, where among founders Rishon-LeZion and chairman of its village council. Returned to Russia 1883 and was manager Bank of Commerce in Minsk. Delegate H.Z. conference in Kattowitz 1884. Specialized in problems of colonization and development in Palestine, publishing many articles in this field. In 1901 invited by Herzl to manage J.C.T., and attended V Z.C. that year. In Palestine again 1903, he organized Anglo-Palestine Bank in Jaffa and was its manager until 1924. Played major role in country's settlement and development efforts, insisting these be based on economic rather than philanthropic considerations, and among originators of co-operative credit. In 1909 among first Tel Aviv settlers, and as manager Anglo-Palestine Bank greatly helped in its development. During First World War in Alexandria, where he established branch Anglo-Palestine Bank to help Palestinian exiles, participating also in committees for their welfare. Among initiators of Jewish Legion. A financial adviser to Zionist Commission 1918. Opposed establishment of Jewish National Council (*Va'ad Leumi*) as usurping functions of Zionist institutions. Following his retirement from Anglo-Palestine Bank in 1924 he continued public activities. Made hon. citizen Tel Aviv 1936.

LOEWY, JULIUS (1881–1953). B. Lostice, Moravia. Journalist. Studied in Vienna and Prague, contributing also to newspapers in these cities. Zionist from early youth, member D.F. and assisted Jewish University project. After some years Zionist activity in Bohemia and Austria, became, 1910–11, one of editors *Die Welt*, then official Z.O. weekly being published in Cologne. Later editor *Selbstwehr*, Prague Zionist publication. From 1919 to 1927 edited *Wiener Morgenzeitung* and from 1928 *Die Stimme*, both of them Zionist newspapers in Vienna. In approximately 1936 he emigrated to Palestine where he contributed to Labour daily *Davar*.

LOPUKHIN, ALEXEI ALEXANDROVICH (1864–1928). After graduation Moscow University, employed in various legal institutions. Headed Police Department in Russian Ministry of Interior 1902–5. In 1906, during trial in St. Petersburg following 1905 Revolution, he sent two letters to Oscar Grusenberg, lawyer for the defence, in which he exposed the role of the government and its institutions in organizing the anti-Jewish pogroms. Exiled to Siberia 1909 for revealing the treachery of the Tzarist double agent Azev during 1905 Revolution, but pardoned 1911. From 1913 he was assistant manager of Moscow branch of St. Petersburg International Bank of Commerce.

LUBZHINSKY (later LUBIN), MOSES FREDERICK (1871–1932). B. Motele, White Russia. Brother of Chaim Lubzhinsky, W.'s brother-in-law. Studied Pinsk Technical High School, emigrating 1887 to United States. Employed as engraver in New York. In later nineties learned metal etching in Germany and founded first U.S. metal etching factory, Chicago, 1905. Friend of W. from student days in Pinsk and was W.'s host during his visits to United States. He was president Etching Company of America.

LVOVITCH, DAVID (1882–1950). Also known as DAVA and DAVIDOVICH. B. Lugansk (Voroshilovgrad), Ukraine. Studied engineering at Munich Polytechnic, where joined Student Zionist Society *Kadimah*. Delegate VII Z.C., 1905. On returning to Russia he was among most active members of Socialist Zionist Party (Territorialist). He concentrated on drawing up a programme for the world-wide emigration of Jews from Eastern Europe linked to a co-operative economic system. During First World War he was engaged in United States on a scheme for Jewish immigration there subsequent to hostilities. After Feb. 1917 Revolution he returned to Russia, where he organized Jewish Farmers Council. He represented this body at first convention of Russian farmers in Petrograd, and was elected to Constituent Assembly. In Poland from 1919 as a leading official of O.R.T., and transferred to Berlin as member its Executive in 1923, and to Paris in 1933. Joint chairman with Aron Singalowsky of O.R.T. Executive from 1945, undertaking several missions to U.S.A., where he helped negotiate collaboration between O.R.T. and Amer. Joint Distribution Committee. He initiated O.R.T. operations in Palestine.

MAMLOCK, ISIDORE ISAAC. B. 1877 Podwitz, East Prussia. Chemist and pharmacist. Studied Rostock and Strasbourg (where research student), joining Zionist movement while at University. He was active in Regional Zionist office in Strasbourg. On completing studies 1904 became pharmacist in Berlin, and 1908 emigrated to Palestine as representative *Hilfsverein der Deutschen Juden*, but returned Berlin shortly after. Emigrated to Palestine again 1920, engaging pharmacy Petah-Tikva, Jaffa, and Tel Aviv, and prominent in efforts for Jewish–Arab understanding. Delegate VI, VIII, IX Z.C., 1903, 1907, 1909.

MAREK, PESAH PETER (1862–1920). B. Shadov (Seduva), Lithuania. Yiddish and Russian author and scholar. As law student in Moscow among founders *Bnei-Zion* Society there 1884. Later joined Z.O., attended Russian Zionist Conference, Minsk 1902, where elected deputy member of its Cultural Committee. Among leaders Moscow D.F. Bureau, and its delegate VI Z.C., 1903. A book-keeper, he was devoted to literary research, publishing works in field of Jewish studies.

MARMOR, KALMAN ZEVI (1876–1956). B. Meiszagola, near Vilna. Left-wing Yiddish journalist and author. Joined illegal Jewish Socialist movement while youth in Vilna. Student in Berne and Fribourg 1899–1902. Member Student Zionist Society *Kadimah*, Berne, and among founders of *Ihud Ivri*, for development of Hebrew language. Delegate V Z.C. (and Zionist Youth Conference preceding it), 1901, VI, VII, VIII Z.C., 1903, 1905, 1907. Although not D.F. member he supported its demand for educational work among Jewish masses. Taught chemistry London 1902, establishing radical nationalist group *Maaravi* there and editing its publication *Der Kotel Maaravi*. Among organizers *Poalei-Zion* London late 1903, and editor of its publication *Die Yiddishe Fraiheit*. Moved to United States and established and edited (1906–7) *Poalei-Zion* periodical *Der Yiddisher Kempfer*. Among founders of World Union of *Poalei-Zion* 1907, then visited Palestine for extended stay. Active educational and cultural affairs of Jewish Labour movement through Workmen's Circle, New York and Chicago. Resigned *Poalei-Zion* 1916 to join American Labour Alliance. Editorial work for Yiddish Socialist papers *Die Welt* and *Vorwaerts* 1917–19. In 1920 joined Workers (Jewish Communist) Party, editing its publication *Neien Welt Emes*, which he converted in 1922 into daily *Fraiheit*. On establishment International Workers Order appointed to its cultural committee, becoming editor its publication *Der Funk* and secretary of its schools. In Kiev 1933–6 at invitation of Institute for Jewish Cultural Research, and subsequently director of *Arbeiter Universitet*, New York. Spent last years in Los Angeles.

MARMOREK, ALEXANDER (1865–1923). B. Mielnica, Galicia. Brother of Oskar Marmorek (q.v.). Gynaecologist and bacteriologist. Close associate of Herzl. Studied medicine in Vienna, where obtained Doctorate 1889. In practice in Vienna till 1894, then entered Pasteur Institute, Paris, where appointed a laboratory director. In 1896 he discovered and produced streptococcus serum against puerperal fever, and an anti-tuberculosis vaccine in 1903. Légion d'Honneur 1900. An Austrian subject, he served in Austrian Army Medical Service during First World War, returning Paris 1920 to concentrate on typhus research. Among founders of Student Zionist Society *Kadimah* in Vienna, and was in Zionist leadership of France, where helped establish *L'Écho Sioniste*. One of Herzl's main supporters in controversy over East Africa project, later joining David Wolffsohn and Max Nordau in leading 'political' Zionists. Delegate II–X Z.C., 1898–1911. Member G.A.C. 1898–1905, 1907–21, S.A.C. 1905–7. After 'practical' Zionists assumed Z.O. leadership in 1911, and following Nordau's withdrawal, he remained chief spokesman for 'political' Zionism. After First World War he continued his advocacy of political maximalism in opposition to policy of W. and Zionist Executive. Ceased Zionist activities during his last years.

MARMOREK, OSKAR (1863–1909). B. Skala, Galicia. Brother of Alexander Marmorek (q.v.). Architect, and friend of Herzl. Member Student Zionist Society *Kadimah*, Vienna, he won a reputation as contributor to professional journals in Austria, France, and Germany, and was awarded the title 'Imperial Architect'. Helped Herzl establish Z.O. in 1897, delegate I–VIII Z.C., 1897–1907. Managed financial affairs of Zionist Bureau in Vienna and of *Die Welt*, of which among founders and part-editor. Member S.A.C. 1898–1905, and on El-Arish Mission 1903. After Herzl died he remained in movement and was member G.A.C. 1905–7.

MAYER, Eugen (1882–1967). B. Zweibruecken, Saarland. M. Hebe, daughter Herbert Bentwich. Lawyer and journalist. A student Zionist leader while at University in Munich 1900–4, and worked for Jewish University project in 1903. Employed in I.C.A. administration in Paris 1910–14, and was legal adviser to Jewish community in Frankfurt-on-Main 1919–33. Settled in Jerusalem 1933. Economic and literary editor *Palestine Post* (later *Jerusalem Post*) 1943–57.

METMANN-KOHAN, Judah Leib (1869–1939). Also known as MATMON-KOHAN. B. Ukraine. Educationalist and among founders of Herzlia Gymnasium, Tel Aviv. Ordained rabbi at Mir *Yeshiva*. Began teaching in Bialystok 1890, and in 1891 he established Hebrew school in Kalarash, Bessarabia. While science student in Odessa from 1897 he taught in Hebrew school, and established Hebrew kindergarten there, besides founding Student Societies *Sefat-Zion* and *Tsva-Hatehiya* whose members trained themselves for educational work in Palestine. Later he studied education, Semitic languages, and science in Berne, obtaining Doctorate 1904. Spent a year in Paris as student and among founders *Ivria* Society there and in Berne. Delegate VI Z.C., 1903, and one of *Zionei Zion* opposing East Africa project. Emigrated to Palestine in 1904 to become a school Principal in Rishon-LeZion. In 1905 he founded, and was Principal during first year of, Jaffa Hebrew Gymnasium (subsequently Herzlia Gymnasium), with 17 students. Was a director till 1910, continuing teaching there until 1936. Active in organizations devoted to entrenchment of Hebrew language. He was among founders of Tel Aviv in 1909. With inauguration of Hebrew Gymnasium in Jerusalem he was its provisional Principal. During First World War had sole responsibility for Herzlia Gymnasium, and with evacuation of Jews from Jaffa (1917), he transferred it to Shefeya, then until war's end to Haifa. Among founders of Ramat-Gan, where he established the High School and became its Principal. Active in *Poalei-Zion* and *Le'ahdut-Haavoda*. Delegate first Jewish Elected Assembly (*Asefat Hanivharim*) 1920. Active in Tel Aviv Workers Council and Tel Aviv branch of Teachers Union. In latter years joined Federation of General Zionists. Author, principally of textbooks.

MEYER, Julius (1881–1918). B. Freiburg, Germany. Merchant. Lived larger part of his life in Basle. Contributor on Zionist affairs to *Basler National Zeitung* and *Basler Nachrichten*. Settled in Paris 1911.

MINKOVSKY, August (1849–1942). B. Minsk. Jewish public figure in Warsaw. Studied at a Minsk *yeshiva*, but self-educated in secular subjects. In seventies of last century was works supervisor railway construction in Rybinsk and Nizhni Novgorod. Later was a broker on St. Petersburg stock exchange. Founded a bank in Warsaw 1893, and active in Jewish and general public affairs there. Joined Committee for Jewish University project in 1903. For some time after First World War member of Warsaw Municipal Council. On Nazi occupation Poland died in Otwock ghetto.

MONTEFIORE, Claude Joseph Goldsmid (1858–1938). B. London. Scholar, philanthropist, and Anglo-Jewish communal leader. Studied at Oxford and *Hochschule für die Wissenschaft des Judentums* in Berlin, then engaged in Jewish and general educational activities in London. In 1888 he established, and was one of editors, *Jewish Quarterly Review*. Among founders and first president of Jewish Religious Union, organization of Liberal Judaism in Britain, 1902. President London Liberal Jewish Synagogue from 1910, and World Union for Progressive Judaism from 1926. President Anglo-Jewish Association, one of the two central organizations of British Jewry, 1895–1921, with simultaneous co-chairmanship Conjoint Committee for Foreign Affairs concerned with rights of Jews overseas. Member I.C.A. Council 1896–1921. Against Zionism from its beginnings, on the grounds that Judaism was a religion only and its uniqueness lay in its universality, he opposed Balfour Declaration 1917 and was among founders of League of British Jews.

MONTEFIORE, GEORGES LEVI (1832–1906). B. London. Grew up in Belgium. Engineer and industrialist. Liberal Party Senator 1882–1901. Founder Montefiore Electro-Technical Institute, Liège, later incorporated in University there. He endowed many scholarships for students from Russia and Rumania.

MOSES, JULIUS JACOB (1869–1945). B. Altdorf (Pfalz), Germany. Physician engaged in psychotherapy and public health research. Practised from 1896 in Mannheim, where he directed psychotherapy centre for retarded children. Lecturer from 1918, and from 1929 professor, Mannheim Business College. Joined Z.O. on its foundation, chairman Mannheim Jewish community and Zionist Society, delegate IV, V, VI, VII, IX Z.C., 1900, 1901, 1903, 1905, 1909. Supported D.F. and was chairman Mannheim Committee for Jewish University project. Member G.A.C. 1903–5. On German Zionist Central Committee from 1910. In 1934 emigrated to Palestine, where active in public health work. He published extensively in his own field of research.

MOSSINSON, BEN-ZION (1878–1942). B. Andreyevka, Ukraine. Among pioneers Hebrew education in Palestine. While teaching in Berdyansk joined Young Israel Society. Protagonist of Hebrew language and participated H.Z. conferences. At Zionist Youth Conference preceding V Z.C., 1901. Studied 1902–7 in Berne, obtaining Doctorate. Sometime chairman Zionist Academic Society in Berne, and actively opposed East Africa project. Prominent in *Ivria* Society and member of Jewish University Bureau. Undertook many propaganda tours in Russia, Western Europe, and America. Delegate all Z.C.s 1903–39. With transfer central office *Ivria* from Berlin to Jaffa, emigrated (1907) to Palestine as its secretary, simultaneously teaching Bible and Jewish history in Jaffa at Hebrew (later Herzlia) Gymnasium and joining its Directorate. He was its Principal 1910–11, 1912–15, and 1919–40. Among founders Tel Aviv, but banished from Palestine by Turkish authorities 1915 and went to United States for four years as Zionist emissary. Delegate first Jewish Elected Assembly (*Asefat Hanivharim*), and executive member Jewish National Council (*Va'ad Leumi*) 1925–9. From 1925 on Actions Committee. Appointed director Department of Education in National Council 1939. Prominent in Federation of General Zionists, he was chairman of Teachers Association and published works on education, the Hebrew language, and Bible teaching.

NEUMARK, DAVID (1866–1924). B. Szczerzec, Galicia. Historian of Jewish philosophy. An early Galician Zionist, he was delegate I, II Z.C., 1897, 1898. From 1887 to 1892 studied at Lvov, then at University of Berlin and *Hochschule für die Wissenschaft des Judentums* there. Obtained Doctorate 1896, ordained 1897. Rabbi of Rakovnik (Rakonitz) in Bohemia 1898–1904. Served 1904–7 in Berlin as editor of section on Jewish Philosophy and Talmud of projected Hebrew Encyclopedia *Otzar-Hayahadut*. Professor of Philosophy at Hebrew Union College, Cincinnati, from 1908. He published many works, some of them in Hebrew.

OPPENHEIMER, FRANZ (1864–1943). B. Berlin. Sociologist and economist. Originally a medical practitioner in Berlin, he abandoned medicine in 1895 for the social sciences and journalism. Edited *Welt am Montag* 1897–9. Obtained Doctorate 1909 and that year appointed lecturer (*Privat-Docent*) in economics at Berlin University. Professor of Economics at Frankfurt 1919–29. Left Germany 1938, arriving United States via Japan 1940, settling in Los Angeles. He described his theory of Liberal Socialism, first outlined in his *Die Siedlungsgenossenschaft*, published 1896, as 'the third way between Capitalism and Communism'. Ascribing the shortcomings of industrial Capitalism to agrarian Capitalism, he advanced as the solution co-operative settlement on free soil. Drawn into Zionism in 1903 by Herzl, he addressed VI Z.C. on his ideas as applied to Palestine, and was nominated, with Selig Soskin and Otto Warburg (q.v.), to the Commission for Investigation of Palestine. Delegate also VII, IX, X, XI, Z.C., 1905, 1909–13. Under his direction Merhavia co-operative settlement established 1911. Opposing principle that all Zionist members should emigrate to Palestine, he withdrew from movement following German Zionist Convention, Leipzig 1914. In First World War he founded and was active force in German-Jewish Committee for the liberation of Russian Jews, later known as *Komité für den Osten*, that collaborated with German Foreign Ministry on behalf of Jews in German-occupied territories. On establishment of enlarged Jewish Agency for Palestine, 1929, he was reconciled to Zionist movement. Published many works on his socio-economic theories.

PHILIPPSON, MARTIN EMANUEL (1846–1916). B. Magdeburg. Historian. Lecturer, University of Bonn, from 1871, and from 1878 professor at Brussels, where for a time in 1890 University Rector. Settling in Berlin, he devoted himself to Jewish community affairs. On Directorate of *Hochschule für die Wissenschaft des Judentums* 1896–1904, 1913–16. Chairman German-Israelite Union of Communities 1896–1912. Initiator and first president Association of German Jews (*Verband der Deutschen Juden*) 1904. A moving spirit behind foundation, 1902, of Society for Advancement of Jewish Studies (*Gesellschaft zur Förderung der Wissenschaft des Judentums*). Directed organization for study Jewish history and literature (*Verband der Vereine für Jüdische Geschichte und Literatur in Deutschland*).

PINSKI, DAVID (1872–1959). B. Mogilev. Socialist writer, pioneer of modern Yiddish literature. Associated with H.Z. from early youth, he founded, together with Reuben Brainin, *Bnei-Zion* Society in Vitebsk 1890. Began publishing in Yiddish while a student in Vienna 1891–4, and later under auspices of Bund, of which he was a sometime member. His works were the first in Yiddish to have proletarian emphasis. Collaborated with J. L. Peretz in *Yom Tov Blettlech* (Warsaw), marking new era in Yiddish Letters. After three years in Berlin, emigrated to United States 1899 where he engaged in journalism and was among founders American *Poalei-Zion* 1905, serving on its Central Committee from 1914. Appointed editor *Poalei-Zion* weekly *Der*

Yiddisher Kempfer 1917–20, then in 1920 *Die Zeit*, a daily. For many years president Jewish National Workers Alliance of America. Emigrated to Palestine 1949 to become hon. president Yiddish Writers Union.

PLEHVE, VYACHESLAV KONSTANTINOVICH (1846–1904). B. Lithuania. Lawyer, Russian Minister of Interior. In service of Russian Department of Justice from 1867, first as assistant to State Attorney in Warsaw, then as State Attorney in St. Petersburg. Appointed Chief of Police Department in Russian Ministry of Interior 1881, and in 1884 Assistant Minister of Interior with membership of Imperial Council and title of State Secretary. Minister of Interior 1902. Implemented Russification programme of Western Provinces, thereby arousing animosity of Lithuanians, Poles, and Finns. During his tenure Kishinev pogrom took place (1903), and in same year he had meeting with Herzl. Assassinated July 1904 by a member of Revolutionary Socialist Party (S.R.).

POKRASSA, JOSEPH (?–? 1926). B. sixties of last century. Head book-keeper of Hoffman and Deuel pharmaceutical company. Early this century he was secretary Central Committee Kharkov Zionist Societies, a member *Bnei-Zion* in Kharkov, *Kadimah* Student Zionist Society, D.F. and Committee for Jewish University project. Delegate V, VII Z.C., 1901, 1905, and Russian Zionist Conference preceding V Z.C. Delegate Russian Zionist Conference, Petrograd May 1917. Following Revolution he remained in Kharkov and was active in *Tarbut*, an organization concerned with establishing Zionist Hebrew educational and cultural institutions in Russia and Poland.

POZNANSKY, SAMUEL ABRAHAM (1864–1921). B. Lubraniec, Poland. Rabbi, scholar, and educationalist. Rabbi at Central Synagogue in Warsaw from 1897. Delegate I Z.C., 1897. An active Zionist, he participated in Hebrew educational programmes of *Tarbut* in Poland. In 1918 he initiated Committee in support of Hebrew University that later became Society of Friends of Hebrew University in Jerusalem. Appointed Warsaw Chief Rabbi just before he died. He published many works of research in Talmud and Jewish sects.

REINES, ISAAC JACOB (1839–1915). B. Karlin, White Russia. Rabbi, founder of *Mizrahi* movement. After occupying pulpits from 1867 in Shukyan and Swieciany, appointed Rabbi of Lida (Vilna district) 1885, remaining till his death. Initiated changes in Talmud study and urged broadening of *Yeshiva* curricula with inclusion secular studies. Attracted to H.Z. movement from its beginnings, but arrested on journey to its Conference in Kattowitz 1884. Delegate IV, V, VI, VII, X, XI Z.C., 1900, 1901, 1903, 1905, 1911, 1913. Following V Z.C. he reacted to establishment of D.F. (whose aims included educational activities) by forming *Mizrahi* in effort to range Orthodox Jewry and Z.O. together. Summoned first *Mizrahi* Conference in Vilna 1902, and led movement throughout his life. In 1905 established his modern *Yeshiva*, with Zionist emphasis, in Lida. Supported 'political' Zionism. Author many works of Talmudic scholarship and Zionist thought.

ROSENFELD, MORRIS MOSES JACOB (1862–1923). B. near Suwalki, Poland. Noted American Yiddish poet. Itinerant tailor travelling between Poland, United States, and England till 1886, when he finally settled in New York as garment worker. His first collection of poems, *Die Gloke* ('The Bell'), published

1888. His poetry voiced the Jewish worker's suffering, was adopted by the masses and sung to well-known folk melodies. Much of it was translated into other languages. Delegate IV Z.C., 1900, his national poems appeared in collection *Zum Firten Zionisten Kongress*. He contributed to Yiddish newspapers in United States.

SAPIR, JOSEPH (1869–1935). B. Kishinev. Gynaecologist. Settled in Odessa after completing studies, and on its H.Z. Committee till this ceased existence in 1915. In 1897 joined Z.O., becoming chairman Odessa Central Committee of Zionist Societies and Zionist Regional Leader. Delegate V–XI Z.C., 1901–13, and XIII Z.C., 1923. On G.A.C. 1905–11. Following Kishinev pogrom, 1903, among organizers Jewish self-defence in Odessa. Active in *Zionei-Zion* (opponents of East Africa project). Founded *Die Zionistishe Kopeke Bibliothek*, publishing Zionist propaganda in Russian and Yiddish, and helped establish the *Kadimah* publishing house. Editor, 1906, Zionist weekly *Kadimah* and subsequently weekly *Evreiskaya Mysl* ('Jewish Thought'). Following First World War service as Russian army doctor, he returned Odessa to become chairman J.N.F. and last president Z.O. in South Russia. Organized relief of Jewish emigrants passing through Odessa, the self-defence force during civil war, and the smuggling out of *Halutzim* (Palestinian pioneers). In 1922 he escaped to Kishinev, then in Rumania, where headed K.H. and established *Die Zionistishe Folks Bibliothek*. Emigrated to Palestine 1925 and directed Department of Gynaecology at Bikur-Holim hospital, Jerusalem. A painter and sculptor, he also published several books.

SCHACHTEL, HUGO HILLEL (1876–1949). B. Sulmierschüz, district of Posen. Dentist and Zionist writer. Student in Breslau, where he settled 1897, organizing Zionist Society there of which he was chairman for many years. Founder-editor *Der Zionist*, a monthly, and from 1901 on Central Committee of Organization of German Zionists. Delegate Z.C.s from IV (1900) to XV (1927). Helped Jewish University project 1902–3. A 'practical' Zionist, he was actively engaged J.N.F., establishing its bureau in Breslau and other Silesian cities, and conducting propaganda cn its behalf. He published tracts on Zionism and the Zionist Congresses. Prominent in Breslau communal affairs, he was president of *Bnei-Brith* there, member of *Hilfsverein der Deutschen Juden* and of presidium of Breslau Rabbinical Seminary. Settled in Haifa 1932, establishing *Bnei-Brith* lodge there. Active in Association of German Immigrants in Palestine.

SCHAUER, RUDOLF (1869–1930). B. Mainz. Expert in International Law. Among founders, Organization of German Zionists. Chairman Zionist Society in Mainz and a leading advocate of Zionism in South and West Germany. Participated in early Z.C.s but ceased his movement activities after Herzl's death. Lived, mostly in poverty, in Paris (from 1905), Berlin (early twenties), and finally Geneva.

SEIDENMAN, SIMON (SOLOMON) (1878–1948). B. Lublin. Lawyer. After his studies in Warsaw, 1901–7, became a leading member of the Legal Association there. For many years chief Counsel to Warsaw Jewish community and ultimately a member of its executive. Counsel to Warsaw Merchants Association. Elected to first Warsaw Municipal Council 1916, and in 1937 he was elected to Polish Sejm. A devoted Zionist from student days, he was particularly active as publicist. *Inter alia*, he edited, with Isaac Gruenbaum (q.v.) and Appolinary Hartglas, *Glos Zydowski* ('Jewish Voice'), the first Zionist periodical in Polish. Member D.F. and delegate Fourth Russian Zionist Conference at The Hague (1907). After First World War on Central Committee Polish Z.O., delegate XIII, XIV Z.C., 1923, 1925. A leader of *Et-Livnot* ('Time to Build') group. Chairman J.N.F. in Poland 1925–9. Escaped Poland on outbreak Second World War, reaching Palestine in 1940. Settling in Jerusalem, he was chairman of committee aiding refugees from Poland.

SILBERSTROM, MOSES (?1860–1928). Physician in Lodz, and faithful adherent of Herzl. Delegate II, III, VI, XII Z.C., 1898, 1899, 1903, 1921. He was dedicated to fostering national Jewish education in Poland, and in his latter years was active on Lodz Committee of Friends of Hebrew University.

SOKOLOW, FLORIAN EPHRAIM (1887–1967). B. Warsaw, son of Nahum Sokolow, brother of Henrik and Maria (q.v.). Journalist. Studied at Universities in Russia, Berlin, and Paris. Edited various periodicals in Poland. Emigrated to England 1932 and became correspondent of *Gazeta Polska*, contributing also to Press in Britain, United States, and various East European countries. During Second World War he was a Polish commentator for British Broadcasting Corporation.

SOKOLOW, HENRIK ISAAC HIRSCH (HENYO, HENYA) (1883–1929). B. Warsaw, son of Nahum Sokolow, brother of Florian and Maria (q.v.). M. Helena Krinsky. Electrical engineer. While student in Warsaw arrested and banished by the authorities, continuing studies in Germany. He finally settled in Berlin.

SOKOLOW (later MENDELSON; HEYMAN), MARIA (?1880–1969). Daughter of Nahum Sokolow, sister of Florian and Henrik (q.v.). Attended I Z.C., 1897, as young journalist accompanying her father. Studied in Switzerland early in century. Associated with D.F., delegate VI Z.C., 1903. Later employed in I.C.A. Bureau in Warsaw and on newspaper belonging to her first husband, Stanislav Mendelson. On his death 1913, she married Dr. Stephen Heyman. During First World War employed in secretariat of Zionist administration in Berlin, and subsequently lived in England and Italy.

STEIN, LUDWIG (1859–1930). Pseudonyms: Eduard Volmer, Diplomaticus. B. Erdoebenye, Hungary. Philosopher, rabbi, and journalist. Studied at Berlin University from 1876 and at Rabbinical Seminary there, where ordained. Preacher in Berlin 1881–3, and among founders Society for Jewish History and Literature. Lectured in history of philosophy at University and Polytechnic in Zurich from 1886, professor 1888–90. Professor of Philosophy at Berne University 1891–1910. President International Institute of Sociology 1909–11. Lecturer Humboldt Academy in Berlin 1911–24. Author many works, among them volume of Memoirs, correspondent several newspapers and active in international diplomacy, particularly after War. Founder-editor *Archiv für Geschichte der Philosophie* 1887–1929 and *Nord und Süd* 1912–29. Although not a Zionist, he was friend of Herzl and Nordau and sought to help Zionist movement through his extensive connections. Visited Palestine 1885 and returned pessimistic about its colonization potential. Later revised his views and during twenties joined Committee for Palestine in Germany.

WARBURG, Otto (1859–1938). B. Hamburg. Botanist. Obtained Doctorate 1883. Published works of botanical research. During nineties he was active in organizing German societies for overseas colonization. Joined *Kolonial Wirtschaftliches Komité* 1896, edited periodical *Tropenpflanzen* 1897–1922. Professor at University of Berlin from 1898. From 1894 member of *Ezra*, the H.Z. Society in Berlin. Joined Z.O. 1897, paid his first visit Palestine, Anatolia, and Cyprus 1900 and developed his ideas for settlement in Palestine, subsequently devoting himself to this subject. At VI Z.C., 1903, chairman of East Africa Committee. Was chairman also of Committee for Investigation of Palestine, which from 1904 published monthly *Altneuland*. There he advanced pleas for scientific research and vocational training as basis for Zionist work to lead to independent economy in Palestine. He helped develop such economic instruments as the Syndicate for Industry. Member S.A.C. from 1905, its chairman 1911–20, and virtually Z.O. president. Leading spokesman for 'practical' Zionism, he established Palestine Bureau in 1907, Palestine Land Development Company in 1908 (of which he was head throughout his life), and among founders of Bezalel School of arts and crafts and Olive Tree Fund, as well as Agricultural Experimental Station in Atlit. Engaged in various economic enterprises in Palestine. During First World War he was strongly preoccupied with influencing German Foreign Ministry to protect Jews in the Ottoman Empire. On W.'s election to Z.O. presidency he remained on G.A.C. Settling in Palestine, he founded Agricultural Institute in 1922, and became head Hebrew University Institute of Palestine Natural History in 1925. On Board of Directors J.N.F. 1907–25, chairman 1933–5. Returned to Berlin owing to wife's illness.

WEICMAN, Selig (Siegmund) (1873–1943). B. Wyszogrod, Poland. M. Fruma, W.'s sister, 1908. Zionist leader in Warsaw and Palestine. On completion of studies at Warsaw School of Commerce, employed as book-keeper in Lodz and later manager of a business house in Warsaw. Active in *Kadimah* and *Hatehiya* Societies. Member D.F., delegate VI Z.C., 1903, and opposed East Africa project. Book-keeper for Atid factory in Haifa on emigration there 1908, and engaged in community activities. With failure of Atid company he returned with his family to Warsaw. The family went back to Palestine in 1913, but he was caught in Warsaw by War, and remained to engage in public and Zionist affairs. He organized youth movement that evolved as *Hashomer-Hatzair*, was chairman of *Maccabi* and for a period secretary of Polish Zionist Central Committee. After War resumed life in Palestine as book-keeper successively for Zionist Commission, Hebrew University, Phoenix Society, Haganah Command, and Jewish Palestine Exploration Society. His communal activities were widespread.

WEIZMANN (later Law), Minna (?1888–1925). B. Motele, White Russia. Sister of W. Studied medicine at Zurich and Berlin. Emigrated to Palestine 1914 and worked as physician in Jerusalem. M., 1921, A. N. Law, a government official in Jaffa and later Deputy District Commissioner, Haifa district.

WERNER, Siegmund (1867–1928). B. Vienna. Physician, dentist, and journalist. Among founders of Vienna Jewish student fraternity *Gamala*. One of Herzl's closest friends and followers, he joined the Zionist Organization on its creation. Editor of *Die Welt*, organ of Z.O., 1897–9, 1903–5. Chairman 1902 of Committee (later Association) for Jewish Statistics in Vienna. After

Herzl died he settled in Iglau (Jihlava), Moravia, where he practised dentistry and remained active in the Zionist cause.

WOLFSKEHL, KARL (1869–1948). B. Darmstadt. Scholar, poet, and art critic. Studied linguistics, comparative mythology, and history of religion at Giessen, Leipzig, and Berlin, obtaining Doctorate. Joined Stefan George Circle (of *littérateurs*) 1893. His home in Munich, where he lived from 1898, became well-known literary salon. Contributor to *Blätter für die Kunst* 1892–1919, and *Jahrbücher für die Geistige Bewegung* 1910–12. Besides his poetry, translated the classics into German. From 1920 he held senior post in management of *Münchener Ruprecht Presse*. Left Germany for Switzerland and Italy in 1933, and emigrated to Auckland, New Zealand, in 1938, where he died. An early Zionist, he remained in close touch with others, including Martin Buber and Eugen Mayer (q.v.). During his last years he was connected with the Jerusalem publishers Schocken.

WORTSMAN, CHARLES (YEHESKEL) (1878–1938). Pseudonyms: Ben-Adam, Ba'al-Dimyonot, Ish-Emet. B. Zhvanets, Ukraine. Left-wing journalist. While chemistry student Basle (where graduated 1903) was chairman *Zion* Society of East European Zionists. Among founders Academic Zionist Society in Berne. Contributed, *inter alia*, to *Hayoetz* (Bucharest) and *Der Yud* (Warsaw–Cracow). Delegate first six Z.C.s 1897–1903. Member D.F. Moved to London 1904, founding radical Zionist periodical *Die Yiddishe Zukunft* there, and transferring it that same year to Warsaw. Emigrated United States 1907, where he was active in *Poalei-Zion* movement. Engaged in Jewish journalism and revived *Die Yiddishe Zukunft*. On staff Amer. Joint Distribution Committee 1920–1, with missions to Europe and Palestine, and sometime employee K.H. in New York.

YAROCHINSKY, STANISLAV (?1852–?). B. Lodz. Son of Sigmund Yarochinsky, textile manufacturer and philanthropist. Manager Goldfeder Bank in Lodz. With his brother, continued their father's philanthropic and public service activities after Sigmund's death in 1909, particularly the Yarochinsky Vocational School that he had founded. Member Warsaw Committee for Jewish University project 1903. Died in Lodz sometime between World Wars.

YELSKY, ISRAEL (1865–1927). B. Slonim, White Russia. Rabbi, graduate Jewish Theological Seminary in Breslau, he obtained Doctorate at University there. Preacher at Modern Synagogue in Lodz from 1891. Among first supporters of Herzl in Poland. Member G.A.C. 1898–1905 and Zionist Regional Leader for Lodz district. Supported East Africa project, and was sole delegate absent from Kharkov Conference to consider scheme in October 1903. From 1905 lived in Germany, and on outbreak First World War in Geneva.

ZANGWILL, ISRAEL (1864–1926). B. London. Novelist, playwright, and public figure. Began writing while young teacher at Jews Free School in London slums. His *Children of the Ghetto* gained him international acclaim and appeared in several languages. Many other works followed, among best known *The King of Schnorrers*, and the play *The Melting Pot*, dealing with immigration to America. Edited satirical weekly *Ariel*, pseudonymous contributor to many periodicals, translated medieval poet Ibn Gabirol and sacred Hebrew texts. Herzl's first London contact, he joined Z.O. and was delegate first seven Z.C.s 1897–1905. Among leading protagonists East Africa project and following its defeat at VII Z.C. he withdrew from Z.O. to found Jewish Territorial Organization (I.T.O.) which survived until 1925 with aim of securing Jewish homeland in any suitable part of world. Toward end First World War he became partially reconciled Z.O., but opposed British policy in Palestine and disagreed with Zionist Executive. He never returned to Z.O. He also wrote general works, including trilogy of pacifist plays.

ZEITLIN, Moses (1872–1907). B. Voronezh. Engineer, economist, and journalist. After studies Cracow Polytechnic he worked in Baku and contributed to South Russian newspapers. In his youth close to revolutionary circles, but following IV Z.C. (1900) became active Zionist in Baku. Supported effort for Jewish University in 1902. Delegate V, VII Z.C., 1901, 1905. Moved to St. Petersburg 1906 for editorial work Zionist periodicals and to study economics. Died in railway accident on his way to The Hague as delegate VIII Z.C. (1907).

INDEX

Bold-type page numbers indicate the place giving the most detailed information, as regards both individuals and associations or institutions. Cross-references to Volume I are given where appropriate.